Religion and the American Civil War

RELIGION

AND THE

AMERICAN CIVIL WAR

Edited by
Randall M. Miller
Harry S. Stout
Charles Reagan Wilson

with Afterword by James M. McPherson

New York   Oxford
OXFORD UNIVERSITY PRESS
1998

Oxford University Press

Oxford   New York

Athens   Auckland   Bangkok   Bogotá   Buenos Aires   Calcutta
Cape Town   Chennai   Dar es Salaam   Delhi   Florence   Hong Kong   Istanbul
Karachi   Kuala Lumpur   Madrid   Melbourne   Mexico City   Mumbai
Nairobi   Paris   São Paolo   Singapore   Taipei   Tokyo   Toronto   Warsaw

and associated companies in
Berlin   Ibadan

Library of Congress Cataloging-in-Publication Data
Religion and the American Civil War / edited by Randall M. Miller,
Harry S. Stout, Charles Reagan Wilson.
p. cm.
Essays presented at a symposium held at the Louisville
Presbyterian Theological Seminary, Oct. 1994.
Includes bibliographical references.
ISBN 0-19-512128-7 (cloth); ISBN 0-19-512129-5 (pbk.)
1. United States—History—Civil War, 1861–1865—Religious
aspects—Congresses. I. Miller, Randall M.   II. Stout, Harry S.
III. Wilson, Charles Reagan.
E468.9.R46 1998
973.7′78—dc21 97-47510

The poem on page 27 is reprinted by permission of the publishers and the
Trustees of Amherst College from *The Poems of Emily Dickenson*,
Thomas H. Johnson, ed., Cambridge, Mass.: The Belknap Press of
Harvard University Press, copyright © 1951, 1955, 1979, 1983 by the
President and Fellows of Harvard College.

3 5 7 9 8 6 4 2

Printed in the United States of America
on acid-free paper

Preface

From the days of the Civil War and after, Americans have wrestled with the religious significance and effects of their "ordeal by fire." Many, in their American conceit, gave the war cosmic meaning, as Lincoln had done at Gettysburg. However they might have disagreed on the sanctity of their own cause and God's favor, countless preachers and politicians, among others, echoed the belief that the war not only touched and tapped America's soul but also pointed the way to the salvation of republican order and society everywhere. Historians, too, have noted the pervasiveness of religious language and symbols among soldiers and civilians and the ways Americans invoked religion to drum up support for their side in the war and to justify their actions during and after it. Yet, for all the recognition of religion's centrality in and to the war, surprisingly few scholars have undertaken extended, extensive studies of the subject. The need for such work led John M. Mulder, president of the Louisville Presbyterian Theological Seminary and a noted historian in his own right, for one, to ask what might be said about religion and the Civil War. As it turned out, plenty.

This book began with conversations among Mulder's colleagues at the Seminary and in the historical profession over two years. Those conversations soon bloomed into a major symposium on religion and the Civil War, co-sponsored by the Louisville Institute of the Louisville Presbyterian Theological Seminary and the Center for the Study of Southern Culture at the University of Mississippi, and funded by the Pew Charitable Trusts, thanks in large part to Joel Carpenter, who had participated in the early discussions on the need for such a symposium. The symposium was held at the Seminary in October 1994 and brought together many of the leading scholars of American religious history and the Civil War era, all of them charged only with the call to provide an original work on some aspect of the conference theme. The conversations there proved to be open and wide-ranging. The success of the symposium in turn spawned the book.

The Louisville site was fitting. The Seminary had played a pivotal role in reunifying the northern and southern "branches" of the Presbyterian church in

1983, after more than a century of sectional division caused by differences over theology and social conscience, especially the issue of slavery. Louisville itself was both "northern" and "southern" in its institutions, interests, and identity. Louisville thus symbolized the gathering together and intellectual fellowship the conference hoped to achieve—reinforced by the convergence of students of religion, history, African-American studies, women's studies, and other disciplines.

The lengthy gestation period from conception to publication of this book owed to the vastness, variety, and complexity of the subject. Recasting papers into publishable essays responsive to the many astute comments from discussants, participants at the conference, and readers also took time. This book was not rushed to print. The commentators at the symposium and the readers at Oxford University Press would not have it so. Certainly, the book benefited much from the insightful commentary provided by John Boles, Dwight Hopkins, James Moorhead, George Rable, the late Armstead Robinson, and Anne C. Rose at the conference and from the anonymous readers at the press. So, too, the valuable questions and observations from the many participants who gathered in Louisville for four days in 1994 added immeasurably to both the general conversation on religion and war and the content and character of this book.

No consensus emerged among authors and others regarding the specific ways to approach the subject or even on how religion defined the war and the age. But all those involved in the symposium and the book came to appreciate anew how central matters of religion, broadly defined as a system of belief and a culture, were to definitions of slavery, society, polity, and so much more in nineteenth-century America. Participants also came to understand how slavery, politics, and war affected religious beliefs and church structures. They realized that too much might be made of religion and cautioned readers that the sacred and the profane did not always converge in Americans' minds and actions. War brought many men and women closer to their God, but it also shattered the belief of others. What the authors did agree on was the need to sustain the conversation begun in Louisville. Thus came this book.

The essays gathered herein stand at various stages of maturity. Several essays provide syntheses of larger works already underway, while others offer initial forays (invitations, really) into subjects as yet little explored. To broaden the intellectual range of inquiry, the editors invited submissions from outside the original symposium circle, with an eye to gaining fresh perspectives from younger historians and established scholars outside the historical profession. Several such essays are included in this book. Two subjects that the editors commissioned did not become fully realized essays for this book, and one conference participant chose not to revise for publication at all. As a consequence, some subjects needful of attention are not fully represented herein. Rather than wait to try to fill in a canvas already crowded and large, the editors followed the urgings of readers and conference participants to publish the revised, finished essays now. This book, after all, makes no claim to being comprehensive. Its purpose is principally to inspire and inform a wider and deeper examination of the connections among religion, war, and society—to begin a discussion rather than settle it.

In the end, this book represents a collective effort, the product of many hands. Foremost among those who made the book possible are several persons whose names do not appear anywhere on the title page or table of contents. Daryl Hart of the Institute for the Study of American Evangelicalism at Wheaton College played a vital role in conceptualizing the conference. John M. Mulder translated ideas into action by mobilizing the resources and reputation of Louisville Seminary to sponsor, arrange, and manage the major conference from which this book grew. At the Seminary, James W. Lewis, Director of the Louisville Institute, ground out the daily details and headed the team of advisors who gave life to the symposium idea. Charles Brockwell, Director of Graduate Studies at Louisville Seminary, coordinated all the arrangements for the conference in Louisville. An advisory board—led by Lewis and Mulder and including the editors of this book and Daryl Hart—drafted the proposal for funding, enlisted scholars to present at the meeting, and tracked the progress of all the proceedings. The Pew Charitable Trusts generously underwrote the conference and the editing process. More than just money, the Pew Charitable Trusts, through the presence of Joel Carpenter at the conference, encouraged other scholars to invest in the ideas advanced there. The Seminary and the Pew Trusts wanted the conversations to continue with as wide, diverse, and varied a participation as possible.

With the conference completed, the command center shifted southward to Oxford, Mississippi. There the editors mixed visits to William Faulkner's Rowan Oak and local barbecue and catfish eateries with several days' review of essays and rethinking of the book's organization and themes. At the University of Mississippi, Charles Reagan Wilson took hold of the basic correspondence and other managerial duties to keep the project going. Bill Ferris and Ann Abadie, director and associate director of the Center for the Study of Southern Culture, provided encouragement and support throughout the project, and Susan Glisson and Mary Annie Brown typed and phoned and provided other essential assistance. In the true ecumenical and interregional spirit that governed the conference and the book, Saint Joseph's University, in Philadelphia, provided additional support. There, and at the libraries of Haverford College, the Historical Society of Pennsylvania, the Library Company of Philadelphia, and the University of Pennsylvania, Randall M. Miller was able to check references and do other background editorial work thanks to the assistance of the many librarians and historians who answered queries, opened resources, and became downright interested in the book. At Saint Joseph's University, Stephanie McKeller deserves special kudos for her friendly and efficient handling of a host of administrative tasks. Stretching into New England, the editorial work profited from Harry Stout's wise counsel and good offices at Yale University.

To all, we say thank-you and hope that the ideas in this book, and the work that emanates from it, will repay many times the confidence and investment so many people and institutions have given this project.

Contents

Contributors

KURT O. BERENDS earned his doctorate at Oxford University and has taught at Calvin College. He is currently completing a book on the uses of the Bible by southern evangelicals during the Civil War era.

DREW GILPIN FAUST is Annenberg Professor of History at the University of Pennsylvania. She is the author of numerous studies, including *A Sacred Circle: The Dilemma of the Intellectual in the Old South, 1840–1860* (1977), *James Henry Hammond and the Old South: A Design for Mastery* (1982), *The Creation of Confederate Nationalism* (1988), and most recently, *Mothers of Invention: Women of the Slaveholding South in the American Civil War* (1996).

ELIZABETH FOX-GENOVESE is Elenore Raoul Professor of the Humanities at Emory University. Among her many books are *Within the Plantation Household: Black and White Women in the Old South* (1988) and *Feminism without Illusions: A Critique of the Individual* (1991). She also has written many articles examining religion among slaveholders and women, as well as a classic essay on Scarlett O'Hara as a modern woman.

GEORGE M. FREDRICKSON is Edgar E. Robinson Professor of History at Stanford University. Among his books are *The Inner Civil War: Northern Intellectuals and the Crisis of the Union* (1965), *The Black Image in the White Mind: The Debate on Afro-American Character and Destiny, 1817–1914* (1971), *White Supremacy: A Study in American and South African History* (1981), and *Black Liberation: A Comparative History of Black Ideologies in the United States and South Africa* (1995).

EUGENE D. GENOVESE is Distinguished Scholar-in-Residence at University Center in Georgia. Beginning with *The Political Economy of Slavery* (1965), his studies have explored the worldview of the antebellum South, including *The World the Slaveholders Made* (1969), *Roll, Jordan, Roll: The World the Slaves*

Made (1974), and *The Slaveholders' Dilemma: Freedom and Progress in Southern Conservative Thought, 1820–1860* (1993).

CHRISTOPHER GRASSO earned his doctorate at Yale University and is now Associate Professor of History at St. Olaf College in Northfield, Minnesota. His book, *A Speaking Aristocracy: Transforming Public Discourse in Eighteenth-Century Connecticut*, will be published in 1999.

PAUL HARVEY is Assistant Professor of History at the University of Colorado at Colorado Springs. He received his doctorate in American history from the University of California at Berkeley and in 1997 published his book, *Redeeming the South: Religious Cultures and Racial Identities among Southern Baptists, 1865–1925.*

SAMUEL S. HILL is Professor Emeritus of Religion at the University of Florida. He is the author or editor of *Southern Churches in Crisis* (1966), *The South and the North in American Religion* (1980), *The Encyclopedia of Religion in the South* (1984), and most recently, *One Name but Several Faces* (1996).

RANDALL M. MILLER is Professor of History at Saint Joseph's University. He has written or edited numerous books on ethnic history, religion, and the South, including *"Dear Master": Letters of a Slave Family* (1978, rev. ed. 1990), *Catholics in the Old South: Essays on Church and Culture* (1983), and *Dictionary of Afro-American Slavery* (1988, rev. ed. 1997).

REID MITCHELL teaches history at the University of Maryland, Baltimore County. A native of Georgia, he earned his doctorate in American history at the University of California at Berkeley. He wrote *Civil War Soldiers: Their Expectations and Their Experiences* (1988), *The Vacant Chair: The Northern Soldier Leaves Home* (1993), and *All on a Mardi Gras Day: Episodes in the History of New Orleans Carnival* (1995).

MARK A. NOLL is McManis Professor of Christian Thought at Wheaton College in Illinois. He has written or edited several books, including *Princeton and the Republic, 1768–1822* (1989), *Religion and American Politics: From the Colonial Period to the 1980s* (1989), and *The Scandal of the Evangelical Mind* (1994).

PHILLIP SHAW PALUDAN is Professor of History at the University of Kansas and the author of *A Covenant with Death: The Constitution, Law, and Equality in the Civil War Era* (1975), *Victims: A True Story of the Civil War* (1981), *"A People's Contest": The Union and the Civil War, 1861–1865* (1988), and most recently, *The Presidency of Abraham Lincoln* (1994).

HARRY S. STOUT is the Jonathan Edwards Professor of American Religious History and Master of Berkeley College at Yale University. He has written extensively on religion in colonial America, including *The New England Soul:*

Preaching and Religious Culture in Colonial New England (1986), *The Divine Dramatist: George Whitfield and the Rise of Modern Evangelicalism* (1991), and *Benjamin Franklin, Jonathan Edwards and the Representation of American Culture* (edited with Barbara B. Oberg, 1993).

DANIEL W. STOWELL is an editor with the Lincoln Legal Papers in Springfield, Illinois. He is the author of *Rebuilding Zion: The Religious Reconstruction of the South, 1863–1877* (1998).

CHARLES REAGAN WILSON is Professor of History and Southern Studies at the University of Mississippi. He is the author of *Baptized in Blood: The Religion of the Lost Cause, 1865–1920* (1980) and *Judgment and Grace in Dixie: Southern Faiths from Faulkner to Elvis* (1995). He edited *Religion in the South* (1985) and the *Encyclopedia of Southern Culture* (with Bill Ferris, 1989).

BERTRAM WYATT-BROWN is Richard J. Milbauer Professor of History at the University of Florida. He is the author of, among other works, *Lewis Tappan and the Evangelical War against Slavery* (1969, 1997), *Southern Honor: Ethics and Behavior in the Old South* (1982), *Yankee Saints and Southern Sinners* (1985), and *The House of Percy: Honor, Melancholy, and Imagination in a Southern Family* (1994).

Religion and the American Civil War

Introduction

The essays in this collection originated at a conference on Religion and the Civil War held at Louisville Presbyterian Theological Seminary in October 1994. The question before the participants can be simply stated: What, if anything, did religion have to do with the Civil War?

In organizing the conference, we recognized that, like the social history of the Civil War, the religious history of the war has yet to be written. To be sure, a few books treat interesting corners of the total subject (for example, studies of religious ideology by James Silver on the Confederacy and James Moorhead on the North), and excellent monographs detail religious aspects of the conflict leading up to the war, as well as religious features of the war itself (revivals in the military camps, the religion of Stonewall Jackson, the role of the Sanitary and Christian Commissions, the services of chaplains). And several scholars have attempted to find the soul of Lincoln and to link it to American civil religion. Regarding the war, recent work by Drew Gilpin Faust and Eugene D. Genovese is particularly noteworthy in highlighting religious concerns of, respectively, southern women and southern slaveholders (themes that they develop further in this volume). Yet the sort of sustained, productive attention that has been paid to religion in the colonial period, the Revolutionary era, and the modern age is simply not present for the Civil War. Despite the uncontested and unrivaled centrality of the Civil War in American history, despite its importance for both the history of the South and the history of African Americans, and despite its nearly mythic place in the popular mind (as seen in the massive continuing interest in Abraham Lincoln and Robert E. Lee, as well as the huge popularity of the Ken Burns PBS series), surprisingly little attention has been devoted to the war as a religious experience and event. Historian Maris Vinovskis's prescient question—"Have social historians lost the Civil War?"—applies with equal, and perhaps more urgent, force to historians of religion.

There are, undoubtedly, many reasons for this surprising lacunae, but our concern was less with understanding the silence than breaking it. Our approach took us to many corners of the war as each contributor to this book was asked to explore religion's role from his or her own scholarly perspective. Whatever the vantage point, we asked what of religion can be found in this location? Was it at the center of popular perceptions of the Civil War or on the periphery? Did it lead the armies and home front, or simply follow? What, in the most general sense, did religion have to do with the Civil War?

In understanding this subject, we realized that ours was but the initial probe. A subject of vast proportions had been unveiled, and we could only offer glimpses. Like William Faulkner's imaginary Yoknapatawpha County, we had discovered a world that had been but dimly perceived. The answer to our guiding questions, though preliminary, was irrefutably clear: Religion, understood in its broadest context as a culture and community of faith, was found everywhere the war was found—in the armies and the hospitals; on the farms and plantations and in the households; in the minds and souls of men and women, white and black. In short, wherever our contributors chose to look, the findings were substantial. God was truly alive and very much at the center of this nation's defining moment.

Beyond the specific religious themes addressed in individual essays, it is now clear how, in fundamental respects, religion stood at the center of the American Civil War experience. Politicians on both sides of the conflict invoked God to justify their actions, soldiers and their families prayed for God's blessing, religious-based organizations mobilized relief and urged reform, and the slaves reaching for freedom praised God for their day of Jubilee. Throughout the struggle Americans spoke in religious metaphors because, save for constitutional rhetoric, that was the only language that had common meaning for them. They already had fought one war for national liberation as a "sacred cause." And in 1861 they would fight another. Americans believed that God was on the side of those who were right with Him. And both North and South, slave and free, knew with certainty whose side that was. More than from the hammer blows of Grant and Sherman, more than from the ironclads and rifled muskets, victory went, Americans believed, to those whom God had chosen. Midway through the war, some southern clergymen began to preach sermons calling for a new religious revival to cleanse the South of its failures to get right with God by treating the slaves humanely, while at the same time some northern ministers urged the Union to convert a war for a political objective into one for a moral one. African Americans had claimed such a moral cause as their own from the start, and knew that one day God would deliver them from their oppressors. Religious revivals swept through both the northern and southern armies during the war. If the American Revolution created "a more perfect union," the Civil War forged "one nation, under God," dedicated, as Lincoln reminded people at Gettysburg, to "a new birth of freedom." Defining that freedom became a religious and moral test for Americans thereafter.

The United States was the world's most Christian nation in 1861 and became even more so by the end of the war. In the late 1830s Alexis de Tocqueville had remarked on the pervasive influence of religion on American private and public life, and swelled by revivals during the 1830s and again during the 1850s, membership in churches rose dramatically. Organized religion provided the spine of an otherwise "invertebrate America" (to use Allan Nevins's term). Bible, tract, home missionary, and Sunday school societies, along with hundreds of religious newspapers, provided common reading materials that reached across a vast continent as religious leaders tried to create a Christian American empire. Advice books and magazines, even popular fiction, purveyed religious themes. Basic reading in common schools rested on the Bible and primers, especially McGuffey's readers, with an unabashed Protestant message of Christian morality.

Religious values drove reform throughout the antebellum period, as reformers, with Bibles in hand, fought such evils as strong drink and prostitution. Politics itself often divided along religious lines—immigrant Catholic Democrats versus nativist Protestant Whigs on such issues as the use of the Protestant Bible in public schools or the role of government in promoting moral and social reform. Manifest Destiny rested on the premise that God ordained American expansion, as, indeed, much of the political oratory of antebellum America (and after) spoke of Americans as an anointed people. The Puritans' "city upon a hill" had become the American "redeemer nation." And by casting the slavery issue in moral terms of good and evil, Americans made it nonnegotiable. One of the principal reasons for the intensity of northern and southern differences over slavery was the conviction each side had that its peculiar society best embodied republican, Christian virtue and that the other threatened both republican liberty and Christian order. In the end, neither side dared yield, for to do so would invite not only political defeat but, surely, also God's wrath. When war came, both sides blessed the sword with the Cross and marched out as Christian armies. And in victory and defeat, each side looked to God for meaning.

Clearly no single volume of essays can make up for a century of neglect. But the present collection does, in our view, represent a platform of depth, dimension, and diversity upon which subsequent studies might build. In the lead essay, Phillip Shaw Paludan explores the religious dynamics of the war from a variety of perspectives embracing many interests in American society. By weaving economic, political, and literary themes with religious issues, Paludan reveals many of the complexities that are examined in greater detail by the more narrowly focused essays that follow. At its heart, these complexities centered on the issue of how God was to be understood in relationship to His chosen people. Abraham Lincoln, Harriet Beecher Stowe, Henry Ward Beecher, for the North, and Robert E. Lee, Thomas "Stonewall" Jackson, Bishop George Foster Pierce, for the South—each had his or her answers. So, too, Paludan writes, did the freed slaves. With emancipation, African Americans were free to recreate their own religious life and to understand God's relationship to them in their own way. All, in their own ways, were self-consciously a "chosen people" going on to war. And all marched onward dying to make men holy and, they thought in various ways, to make them free.

In grouping the essays into a coherent body, we discovered a curious reversal from the mostly military-based scholarship on the Civil War. The essays in this collection largely concentrate their attention outside the armies and focus instead on civilian populations caught up in the horror of total war. When taken as a whole, they fall rather neatly, if unevenly, into three general categories: ideas, people, and places. The subject of religion and civil war also invites comparisons to other civil wars—a subject essayed by Charles Reagan Wilson in this book. While none of these categories and subjects is treated definitively, they do suggest lines for further research. The afterword by James M. McPherson helps point the way.

Ideas

Historians have long debated the role of ideas in the American sectional crisis of the mid-nineteenth century, but Union commander Ulysses S. Grant had no doubt that soldiers as well as intellectuals knew what the war was about, insisting afterwards that "our armies were composed of men who were able to read, men who knew what they were fighting for." James M. McPherson recently has noted that the same could be said for the Confederate soldiers. The ideology of soldiers and civilians, of both northerners and southerners, reflected the inheritance of American traditions of political liberty and religious freedom. People in the warring regions nonetheless had differing interpretations of influential republican and Protestant belief systems.

Americans at war in the nineteenth century drew from the legacy of the American Revolution, the common war effort of an earlier generation. Many northerners saw the Constitution establishing the federal government as the embodiment of a republican experiment in government. A free labor ideology viewed republican freedom as rooted in unfettered economic opportunity that would release the energies of an independent, self-reliant producer class. Free labor was the ideological foundation for a virtuous citizenry that should play a responsible role in protecting republican government. Many southerners, on the other hand, saw the best protection of republican freedoms lying in the preservation of a well-ordered, hierarchical society. The slave society rested on patriarchal and paternalistic values that would ensure the rights of free white men within a stable, secure social order with a place for everyone. Sometimes the concern for freedom nurtured, though, an alternate southern libertarian tradition championed especially by plain whites in nonplantation areas.

Religion was intertwined with these concerns for political and economic liberty. Protestantism had been the religious buttress of most colonies, with churches from the Reformed tradition proving especially influential in shaping moral notions that would become part of the belief system of early America. Evangelicalism appeared in the early nineteenth century as the dominant faith for most Americans, and its moral passion would significantly affect the sectional debate. An important thrust of much of northern Protestantism was an emphasis on individual salvation that also demanded individual responsibility for the social order. The early Puritan idea of a covenanted society between a human community and the Almighty survived in American thought as the basis for a continuing concern of religious people for establishing a righteous world. Some northern ministers saw this as a need for radical reformism, as with abolitionists who wanted to root out the evil of slavery altogether, but conservative Protestants preached the necessity of preserving a social order in which moral evils could be gradually addressed. The southern church, on the other hand, expressed a single-minded interest in personal salvation that worked against concern for the broader social order. Influential southern Presbyterians, for example, often cited that denomination's doctrine of the spirituality of the church to justify noninvolvement in politics and social reform. While undoubtedly significant, the doctrine did not prevent southern divines from vigorously participating in the proslavery debate that gave religious sanction to southern society.

In any event, religion joined with republicanism to interpret events in the United States as part of a divine plan. The actors in the drama of the Civil War were working out, in their own minds, the meaning of God's destiny for the American people. Each side saw itself as guardian of the nation's heritage of liberty. Theological ideas became tied with cultural issues, legitimating the causes of both North and South but pointing to theology's role in the cultural context of mid-nineteenth-century America.

As Mark A. Noll demonstrates in "The Bible and Slavery," the Scriptures rested at the center of the American religious imagination in the early nineteenth century. One hundred fifty years of experience had led to a distinctive American approach to the Bible, which became implicated in the sectional crisis and "created a theological crisis of the first order." Reformed churches had been especially significant in encouraging belief in the possibility of a literal reading of the texts, and Noll remarks upon the central role of Reformed ministers and theologians in the events of wartime. He sees the underlying issue not as one of exegesis so much as "cultural hermeneutics." The American way of interpreting the Scriptures emerged in an increasingly democratized society, an expression of the growing faith in the ability of ordinary people to manage their own religious lives. The Bible became the national book open to all to read and understand.

By the time of the Civil War, though, this belief in commonsense interpretation of the Bible had led to profound disagreement over what exactly the Scriptures meant on the crucial issue of slavery. Churches North and South disagreed, shattering a consensus based on common assumptions about reading and interpreting the Bible. African Americans, Catholics, Lutherans, and northern border-state Reformed churches offered alternative modes of understanding the Scriptures, but none of them had the cultural authority to challenge effectively the dominant American way of theology grounded in literalistic Scriptures. Noll's final judgment is that Americans' racial views would not allow them to favor alternative views of interpreting Scripture. They confused commonsense intuitions of racial inferiority with commonsense ways of interpreting the Bible.

Eugene D. Genovese, in "Religion in the Collapse of the American Union," looks at ideas in the context of social relations. The social relations of the slave society permitted Christian orthodoxy and a conservative interpretation of the Constitution to flourish, whereas the social relations of capitalism undermined those interpretations. Systematic thought and group sensibility reflected the divisions of northern and southern worldviews, as much as political institutions and perhaps more profoundly for limiting reconciliation between the sections.

The Presbyterian church was a crucial denomination in championing religious ideologies that pervaded the sectional crisis. Orthodoxy remained a powerful influence in the antebellum North, but the liberalism of Unitarianism and Universalism threatened to undermine it. Southern Presbyterians were a vital force for orthodoxy. Whether in the Old School or New School factions, they espoused traditional theologies strongly rooted in Calvinism. In the end, it was a general Christian traditionalism, though, and not specifically Calvinism, that gave coherence to southern theology. Genovese concludes that southern theorists, whether theologians, social philosophers, or political thinkers, saw religious orthodoxy as part of one organic system with traditional social values and conservative republicanism.

The southern ministers in Bertram Wyatt-Brown's "Church, Honor, and Secession" are more ambivalent about the southern cause than those of Genovese. The latter have a clear-eyed bead on the dangers of an encroaching northern worldview rooted in an alien social system. According to Wyatt-Brown, however, southern clerics hesitated during the secession crisis to commit themselves to a complete rupture from the nation. Although not hostile to the idea of national independence for the South, the preachers did not rush to promote radical change. They found themselves unable to embrace slavery without doubts, and a war for slavery thus created troubled minds. These were temperamentally conservative religious folk, and deep disturbances to the social order were bound to give pause. The ethic of honor coexisted with the religious, not only in the South in general but also in clergymen themselves, and that ethic worked in the crisis of 1860–1861 to make them question, at least for a while, the disloyalty of abandoning the Union. As the political situation evolved, the ministers adapted and came to embrace the Confederacy, but not without a painful period of assessment as the crisis came to a head.

Northern ministers also had complex reactions to the war, which George M. Fredrickson explores in "The Coming of the Lord: The Northern Protestant Clergy and the Civil War Crisis." The wartime events enabled northern clerics to play a larger role in defining broad cultural meanings associated with America. As the moral dimensions of slavery became preeminent, preachers took center stage. This development occurred at the same time as Protestant ministers were trying to enhance their status and authority as a professional group. They competed with lawyers before the war for preeminence as guardians of republican virtues associated with the nation, but wartime demands bolstered the ministerial efforts, providing new opportunities for "political preaching" that would extend Protestant influence over the body politic.

Most northern ministers rejected the immediate abolitionism that became prominent, though not preeminent, in the 1840s. Instead, they preferred to witness for a gradual social reformism that was in line with their postmillennial dreams of earthly progress. But the Kansas-Nebraska Act in 1854 was a wake-up call that energized moderate Protestant clerics to the dangers presented by a newly aggressive "Slave Power." After this, ministers were increasingly active in working for a more clearly recognized role of religion in the national ideology. Efforts began in this period to amend the Constitution to recognize overtly the Protestant predominance in American life. Although these attempts failed, clergymen had blurred traditional lines separating church and state. As Fredrickson notes, clerical activism in the Civil War era concealed "quasi-theocratic ambitions." Political preaching gave the northern war effort a religious sanction and made a powerful patriotic force. At the same time, the ministers furthered their professional reputations. The moral decline of the postwar years shocked northern ministers all the more because they had invested their status and authority in endorsing the political activities of the Republican party. Fredrickson sees the later Social Gospel movement as a continuation of the social-political role of northern ministers begun during the Civil War.

By examining the Confederate religious military press, Kurt O. Berends takes a different approach to understanding the relationship between religious ideas and the Civil War. The first religious military paper did not begin until 1863, but the press played a dynamic role in evangelizing soldiers, articulating war aims, and building morale. The image of the Christian had feminine overtones to southern men at the beginning of the Civil War, but the religious military press fostered a new image of the good soldier who was also a manly Christian. The belief in Providence gave the Christian soldier the confidence to face any battle or foe without flinching, exhibiting courage that other warriors could admire. The ritual of baptism had special meanings when performed among soldiers, and, Berends argues, gave soldiers an intense identity that helped motivate them to proselytize after the war. The most popular message the military press delivered emphasized the immediacy of death and the hope for eternity that Protestant Christianity offered, but it also promised triumph over temptation, a fellowship of believers, and a reconciliation of honor and faith.

The editors of the religious military press early identified the Confederacy as holy, blurring the distinctions between secular and sacred and nurturing a southern civil religious patriotism. They identified the Confederacy as protector of civil liberties and constitutional political rights, but they went further and saw religious liberty itself at stake in the conflict, portraying the Confederacy as defender of that heritage. The press faced its greatest challenge in explaining deaths, disablement of soldiers, and battle defeats, but editors looked for hope in even the darkest news. They saw defeats as simply "Divine rebukes" to the southern failure to live up to the highest standards. The wartime situation came to affect the Christian message, as the editors insisted that soldiers and home-front civilians had to respond directly to the hope of salvation. Arminian influences appeared among all writers for the press, even those from religious traditions not identified with it.

Paul Harvey, in " 'Yankee Faith' and Southern Redemption: White Southern Baptist Ministers, 1850–1890," traces the contributions of Southern Baptist ministers to a definition of religion as part of the South's public culture. In so doing, he suggests that southern ministerial concerns about their place in public life and their ability to translate God's plan for southerners did not begin or end with the war. Before the war, southern clergymen participated fully in the proslavery argument. Harvey charts the development of Baptists into a self-conscious cultural establishment in the early nineteenth century, but also explores an antimission folk movement that dominated much of the old Southwest and represented an alternative Baptist culture. Harvey identifies contributions of Southern Baptists to the war effort and sees the Civil War revolutionizing southern religious life, reshaping the relationship of the ministry to public life. After a withdrawal from public affairs immediately after the war, the clergy was energized by opposition to Reconstruction and again engaged in "political preaching," especially proclaiming a political ideology of white supremacy through the late nineteenth century and beyond.

By the late nineteenth century, ministers with the Southern Baptist Convention controlled much of the religious life of their region. They had grown in numbers after the war, and despite the individual poverty of many congregations, by sheer numbers they had consolidated a hegemonic position within the South. A growing racial consensus among whites North and South allowed southern whites to manage their own race relations, and Southern Baptists participated fully in mythologizing the Lost Cause and southern white resistance to Reconstruction. Southern Baptist ministers were now leading cultural figures throughout the South.

The death of one southern soldier proved to be especially significant in considering religion's role in the Civil War. In "Stonewall Jackson and the Providence of God," Daniel W. Stowell argues that southern Christians interpreted Jackson's death by a stray bullet from one of his own soldiers as a message from God, an example of "extraordinary providences." Ministers at the beginning of the war had portrayed military victories as God's blessings, so reverses then became Divine chastisements. Southerners were perplexed by Jackson's death. Some ministers saw it as punishment for southern sins, including the idolization of Jackson himself. Sermons at the time of Jackson's death in 1863 sharpened theological understandings of the war and God's role in it that would be applied again after Appomattox. In 1863 and again in 1865, southern Christians tried to intuit God's larger plans for them, but ultimately they embraced the assurance that at least God would not abandon them. Defeat did not mean Divine disapproval but rather God's judgment for southern shortcomings, preparing the region's people for future achievements.

Abraham Lincoln, in contemplating the imminent victory of the Union, was not so sure about God's plans for victor or vanquished. As Ronald C. White Jr. shows in "Lincoln's Sermon on the Mount: The Second Inaugural," Lincoln used the occasion of his second inaugural in 1865 to preach "malice toward none" rather than terrible swift swords. He noted the irony of how both northern and southern soldiers read from the same Bible and prayed to the same God and how the "prayers of both could not be answered, [and] that of neither has been answered fully." The speech, which Lincoln regarded as his best and which Frederick Douglass thought was "more like a sermon than a state paper," was brief but profound, a meditation on God's acting in history and America's place in that history. By examining Lincoln's rhetoric, White shows how Lincoln was caught up with the larger meaning of the war and resigned to the mysterious reality that "the Almighty has his own purposes." As he spoke about slavery and God, Lincoln moved from passive to active voice and reminded Americans that slavery came by human action and so it must end that way, as must "charity for all" and the call to "finish the work" and "bind up the nation's wounds." But, in the end, writes White, Lincoln abandoned himself, and the nation, to God, "whose ways were not always known but were always just."

Although no consensus about the war's meaning emerged from the four-year ordeal by fire, the force of religious ideas in shaping the ways northerners and southerners thought about slavery, defined sectional interest, and went to war could not be ignored. By giving such subjects moral meaning, the ministers and politicians also converted them to moral imperatives and hardened positions. Few public figures were so willing as Lincoln to confess that God had His own purposes that humans could not wholly divine. The conviction that God was on one's own side provided the certainty that drove the northerners and southerners apart. The war tested that certainty, as it also forced northerners and southerners to rethink their relationship with God and knowledge of His plan.

People

The experience of lay women and men, of "the people," in responding to calls to act honorably in defense of "nation" both reflected and affected their definition of religion in fundamental ways. The war pushed lay people increasingly into an active religiosity, as it also encouraged introspection on God's plan and humanity's place and even fed doubts about God's favor and one's own faith. With ministers away, church services disrupted, and the social order unraveling, especially in the South, lay people assumed more direct control over their spiritual lives. Perhaps at no other time did the people become the priesthood as during the war.

Scriptural language, the basic grammar and vocabulary for thought and expression among many Americans, was suffused with an emphasis on discipline and discipleship. Those themes laced the private correspondence and public admonitions of northerners and southerners during the war. Preachers thundered invocations for people to do their duty by God and government, but the people defined what and to whom they would direct such obligation. The ambiguity many of the ministers felt about the war aims and the conduct of the war by their government vitiated some of the clergy's claims to authority over the religious meaning and responsibility of the war. But the exigencies of war more than anything else drove people to their own readings of God's will. Women running the farms and plantations, slaves fleeing bondage, and men marching off to fight—all drew on religious images and ideas to bring order to their new circumstances and condition. The rhetoric of family and faith informed the various ways different people at home and in arms defined and met their public responsibilities.

Women played vital roles in defining religious and public duty during the war. As Elizabeth Fox-Genovese argues in her study of "Days of Judgment, Days of Wrath: The Civil War and the Religious Imagination of Women Writers," such widely read women writers as Harriet Beecher Stowe, Elizabeth Cady Stanton, Louisa May Alcott, and Augusta Jane Evans subscribed to common concerns about women's need to honor biblical teaching on women's "special nature and responsibilities." Family and faith were fused together in thinking about women's charge, irrespective of region. But such writers also revealed how much definitions of women's place mirrored regional cultures. In the South, for example, where paternalism held sway more fully than in the North, women did not control religious instruction in the home.

Before the war, northeastern Protestant women used cultural assumptions of their own supposed innate moral superiority to men as a way to enter public discussion on virtue and duty, and in the case of Stanton even to insist on a place on the dais to argue for social reform and against slavery. The war invigorated their sense of the righteousness of their faith and the need for women's moral stewardship amid rapid social, cultural, and economic change. Protestant northeastern women moved to reform the world. The war, however, also hastened the end of the New England village life from which many such women writers came and on which they built their images of a proper social order.

For southern women, the war brought on a crisis of faith. The end of slavery, so long defended as right in Scripture, and the defeats of southern battalions called into question the southerners' antebellum conceit that God was on their side. More directly, the loss of men and property thrust women into the world. During and after the war southern women found new purpose as moral beings by engaging in relief, rebuilding, and reform. Suffering confirmed their faith in God's will and in themselves. It also pointed southern women toward "the social and religious path" already taken by their northern counterparts.

Drew Gilpin Faust, in her essay, " 'Without Pilot or Compass': Elite Women and Religion in the Civil War South," further examines the changes in self-perception and religious duty wrought by war. Protestants (North and South, white and black) shared a common evangelical outlook, but they differed in their understanding of power and social relationships in a Christian society. Condition, color, class—so many factors affected perspectives on God, society, politics. Slaveowning women, for example, found comfort and meaning in a paternalistic worldview that emphasized their submission to a merciful God and honor-bound men who would protect them and uphold morality. Such thinking offered little to black slave women. Then came the war.

The war demanded more of southern elite women's God and men than either could give them. With men away, or dead, and with defeat and deprivation everywhere, older assumptions of female passivity no longer made sense. The war pushed southern white women into leadership roles, as religious practice moved from the "more public and male to a more private and female sphere." The church and public square still mattered for worship, fellowship, and rallying support, but the home increasingly became the principal locus of religious practice and authority. Among elite southern women, the feminization of religion occurred in the parlors more than in the pews. The emphasis shifted from preacher-inspired conversion to home-centered piety and discipline.

Elite southern women did not confine their influence to the home. They reached into the public sphere once ruled by men alone, writing letters to newspapers and government officials urging fast days and public prayer. The women further insisted that their men get right with God, not only to save their souls and to stay God's wrath but also to ensure a "blessed reunion" of loved ones "in the great hereafter." Writing public and private letters was not the same as smashing windows and demanding bread, as lower-class and immigrant women rioters did in Richmond in 1863, but it did mark a dramatic step beyond what had been the prescribed bounds of women's "place" before the war.

The hard lessons of war also altered conceptions of God. The elite southern women left to fend for themselves saw God less as "the benevolent, all-loving and forgiving father" known to them in antebellum days and more as a "severe, vengeful, wrathful God of the Old Testament . . . willing to demand rather than committed to relieve the suffering of his subjects." Women responded with resignation, anger, and then action. When men and God failed to protect them and brought defeat, elite southern women had no choice but to become both "pilot and compass" in a changed social, economic, and political order.

If southern white women reluctantly assumed new burdens and authority in church and society, southern blacks seized the moment of war to free themselves and their churches. Blacks moved from biracial or secret religious settings of slavery days to public proclamations of independent faith in black churches at war's end. The war redrew the religious map of the South, as it also shifted the geographical center of gravity of pre-existing black denominations from North to South. In the South, the war spurred black self-separation from white-run churches that left most white denominations without any significant black presence and led most blacks to church membership in their own churches by 1867. In matters of faith, more than anywhere else, blacks achieved freedom to put belief into action.

The war opened the South to missionary efforts by both white and black northern churches. The disruption of regular church services and the erosion of planter power further made African Americans look to new arrangements for worship. Most important in pulling blacks out of southern white churches and into black ones was the slaves' and ex-slaves' almost universal desire for autonomy. That need contributed to the southern blacks' overwhelming preference for independent black Baptist congregations over hierarchical church organizations when African Americans could choose where and with whom to worship after the war.

The effect was more than ecclesiastical. Autonomy also meant responsibility. Black churches invested in education and moral discipline so that blacks might know as well as feel their God and respect His teachings. By being accountable for their own religious lives, churched blacks became responsible public persons. Black churches built the institutional infrastructure that made possible an ordered life. The black churches provided the seedbed for an African-American community consciousness that grew into political as well as educational, cultural, and reform interests.

In that regard, southern blacks' self-separation into their own churches was not just a flight from whites. Far from it. By organizing and running their own churches, blacks could engage whites as free people. In the South, especially, one became a member of the larger society by being part of a particular community. Church membership counted heavily by the end of the nineteenth century in identifying someone as having a place, as being a somebody. However much race and poverty kept blacks down, their churches lifted them up. Organized religion gave blacks the self-respect slavery had denied them.

Catholics and immigrants also wanted respect. As Randall M. Miller argues in his essay, "Catholic Religion, Irish Ethnicity, and the Civil War," the war promised a way for the Catholic church to beat back nativism and bigotry by showing that Catholics would serve their country. In the North the church rallied to the flag. It also sought to use the war to invigorate Catholic faith among and through the soldiers, whose noble deeds and Christian character would provide models of discipline back home.

The demands of war soon exhausted the church's resources. There were not enough priests to serve as chaplains and not enough religious literature to instruct and inspire soldiers. The chaplains improvised, while necessity dictated that Catholic soldiers assume primary responsibilities for their own devotional lives and moral discipline. Lay initiative increased in the camps, even as the church sought to impose religious uniformity and increase clerical authority in the parishes.

Irish Catholics especially felt the brunt of public disfavor about a foreign faith and foreigners in a Protestant land. They, too, saw the war as a chance to answer their critics. Irish politicians traded on national and religious identity to form Irish Catholic Union regiments. But Irish Catholics' loyalties to the Union were conditional. Having joined the ranks after appeals to their self-interest and identity as Irishmen, they felt little obligation to fight for a cause that increasingly threatened both their interest and their identity. Reminded of the Republicans' ties to nativism and disgusted with the Lincoln administration's move toward black emancipation, many Irish Catholic soldiers felt betrayed. Heavy losses of Irish soldiers at the front and many hardships at home caused the women to call their men back. After 1863, only pay and bounties justified Irish enrollments in Union ranks. Poor Irish immigrants fleeing starvation in the old country and often ignorant of their Catholic duties signed on. By war's end the Irish soldier in the Union army was, in fact, very unlike the ideal earlier praised by recruiters and churchmen.

Memories of Irish Catholic involvement in the war painted a different picture. The organized Irish Catholic effort to remember the war in story and statue emphasized the soldier's fidelity to faith, flag, and family. The priest became the embodiment of Catholic commitment to the cause. Irish Catholics, the church's patriotic boosters proclaimed, were Christian soldiers.

After the war, in the mythology of the Lost Cause, southerners also used "memory" to write history. With Protestant clergy in the lead, the southern memory of the war showed that theirs had been a noble cause fought by Christian men. As Reid Mitchell argues in his essay, "Christian Soldiers?: Perfecting the Confederacy," postwar southern memorialists made much of revivals in the Confederate ranks during the war to contrast the supposed Christian fervor of southerners with the impersonal, machine-like Yankees, who won by overwhelming numbers rather than righteous purpose or character. God might chastise southerners for sins by visiting defeat on them, but the Union military victory in no way meant that God had forsaken the South. God showed His favor by bestowing spiritual gifts on the South. So said the southern apologists. Thus, in the mythology of the Lost Cause, the southerners became like the Israelites of the Old Testament. They remained God's people, who would enter the promised land if they kept His commandments and covenants, among which was fealty to their noble cause.

Historians often echoed such themes. Indeed, the image of the Confederate Christian soldier became a stock figure in historical literature. A closer examination of the sources for such imagery reveals that the story of widespread Confederate conversions was largely the product of two influential books— William W. Bennett's *A Narrative of the Great Revival Which Prevailed in the Southern Armies During the Late Civil War* (1876) and J. William Jones's *Christ in the Camp* (1887)—rather than from the soldiers themselves. The myth of the Confederate Christian soldier also was part of the late-nineteenth-century effort by Protestant clergy to promote muscular Christianity. Images of virile chaplains and manly Christian soldiers promised to strengthen Christianity's appeal to young men at a time when much organized Protestant religion seemed "feminine." Only recently, opines Mitchell, have historians begun to separate the myths from their sources and appreciate the extent to which Confederate apologists won the war by casting Confederates, embodied in the almost saintlike Robert E. Lee, as morally superior to the "bumming" Yankees who ravaged the land without conscience. Only recently have historians begun to recognize that religious activity among Union soldiers seems to have been as strong as among Confederates. And only recently have historians considered non-Protestant and black soldiers in their assessment of religion in the ranks.

Whether revivals actually worked to bind faith and flag together in the soldiers' mind, as the postwar southern apologists assumed, is also not so clear. Revival sermons sometimes linked patriotism and piety, but soldiers likely responded more to "old time religion" than to veiled appeals for the Confederate cause. The soldiers, Mitchell concludes, sought comfort and reassurance rather than confirmation of the Confederacy's divine ordination.

The people's actions did not necessarily follow the words and demands of the preachers, politicians, and postwar memorialists. The people met God on their, and His, terms. Personal spiritual, psychological, and social needs informed politics and the public religious culture. By viewing the lay people— soldiers and civilians alike—as active agents in the process whereby private religious beliefs and public religious expression interacted and informed one another, a more complicated, variegated religious experience emerges from the war.

Places

Throughout the war, the attitudes and behavior of the men in arms derived from and responded to the character of the communities from which they came, and vice versa. Those attitudes and behavior were constantly in flux. God was a mighty bulwark, to be sure, but how and when one found strength and comfort in religion varied according to person (man or woman, black or white, northerner or southerner), faith, circumstance, among many factors. But place counted much, too, in defining how people approached, saw, experienced, and remembered the war. By looking closely, with almost microscopic analysis, at particular communities or congregations at war, it becomes possible to examine large questions in local contexts and to give abstract issues names and faces.

In their essay, "Civil War, Religion, and Communications: The Case of Richmond," Harry S. Stout and Christopher Grasso explore the effect of war on the Confederate capital. During the war, Richmond functioned as the political center of the Confederacy and as an important manufacturing city, and through Jefferson Davis's calls for fast days and through the religious press and ministerial preachments, it also became a "spiritual" source for an incipient Confederate nationalism. It also became a gathering point for many different interests and people from across the South and, as such, a microcosm of the Confederacy. The "new" wartime Richmond in some ways collided with the "old" Richmond community, which had its own history and identity before war brought so much change and so many strangers. Rather than one Richmond, Stout and Grasso discovered layers of community(ies) and interests in one place.

For years, the cry "On to Richmond" had animated northern politicians and generals. But, ask Stout and Grasso, what about the leaders and citizens of Richmond? How did they experience the war and, more specifically, what religious meanings did they take from it? The answer, as it unfurled year by year, defies any simple category of monolithic presence. True believers in God and the Confederacy abounded along with deep skeptics and cynics. Meanings shifted as the war shifted, sometimes in diametrically opposed and conflicted directions. But always religion was there, front and center, both in the citizens' consciousness and in their leaders' pronouncements. If, as some scholars have argued, a cause-numbing guilt and sense of sin defeated the Confederacy in the end, such guilt and sin, Stout and Grasso conclude, could not be found in wartime Richmond.

In his essay, "Religion and the Results of the Civil War," Samuel S. Hill studies two communities: the Wesley Methodists of western New York State and the Yearly Meeting of the North Carolina Friends. Hill's concern is less with religion's role during the war itself than on the war's longer term effects on religion after the cessation of hostilities. His findings point to the ways two disparate communities found common cause in the horrors of civil war. Despite the distances between them, the "zealots" from New York had social and religious intercourse with the "radicals in a heartland of slaves and hotbed of support for slavery." In both cases, Hill argues, "denominational dynamics changed, as a direct consequence of the war, in ways that no one could have predicted or foreseen."

The war revealed that no one religious culture, no one religious experience stood for all, even as it also showed how in particular cases common bonds of Christian purpose might extend across sectional and denominational lines and become stronger when (and perhaps because) political ties broke. The war also showed how much religion mattered in people's efforts to make sense of a world coming apart and to put their lives and communities back together after the war. In all of this, they expected to find their ways of survival and renewal charted by God.

Comparisons

The American experience with civil war invites comparisons with other civil wars in the Christian world. Charles Reagan Wilson, in "Religion and the American Civil War in Comparative Perspective," examines the similarities and differences among the English Civil War of the 1640s, the American Civil War of the 1860s, and the Spanish Civil War of the 1930s. He concludes that all had constitutional aspects, with the very future of certain organized religions at stake in England and Spain but not in the United States. Neither combatant in the American Civil War threatened the security of the dominant northern or southern Protestantism, nor was the fundamental constitutional arrangement of voluntary religious affiliation ever endangered. In addition, the functions of religious groups and leaders in the three civil wars were similar. They dealt with the human tragedies of war, legitimated the ideologies of both sides, and promoted moral reformation. Finally, religion's overall role in the three conflicts was to promote nationalism. It sharpened national consciousness and imbued the nations with providential support. Wilson sees the American Civil War as particularly significant in developing deep religious nationalism, embodied in a civil religion.

Nationalism was indeed a compelling force in the mid-nineteenth century, and Americans felt its impact. It helped motivate northerners to rally around the Union and southerners to justify their independence. Religion provided a powerful supportive passion that reinforced that of nationalism. Uncompromising abolitionists and impassioned southern fire-eaters drew on theological arguments and moral imperatives to buttress their arguments for dramatic changes. But moderate and conservative religious leaders also shaped the sectional debate. In the end, ideological disagreements were crucial in defining the sectional positions that drove northerners and southerners to war and helped sustain them during the conflict to fight for their ideas to the end of a total war.

In 1867, the good ladies of Columbus, Mississippi, laid flowers and said prayers over the graves of Union and Confederate soldiers buried in the local cemetery. In so doing, they not only paid their respects to fallen heroes and lost loved ones but also inspired other women and men to public gestures of sectional reconciliation. More than that, they demonstrated anew what the war had taught them—namely, that private religious beliefs demanded public expression, that women as well as men bore responsibility both for their personal and their region's redemption, and that religious sensibilities promised a way to unite Christian people divided by regional loyalties.

The last lesson was not so clear or fully realized after the war. Bloody-shirt sermons bellowed in the North, and Lost Cause pageantry paraded in the South. But preachers and politicians did not always speak for the folk. The war had demonstrated that much. Indeed, the power of lay religious feeling and action to shape the political culture and direct social behavior had been an important element during the war in the way and why people fought.

So, too, the need to get on with one's life, while burying the dead with honor, echoed the reality of a war that had rended families and even strained relations between those in uniform and those at home. The women in Columbus, after all, turned from their graveside vigil to more pressing matters of rebuilding homes and farms shattered by invasion, emancipation, and defeat. They prayed for their own relief and renewal in body and spirit as much as for the souls of those interred before them.

But no one could bury the war, especially one that had become invested with so much religious meaning. That scholars are only just now digging up the many ways religion defined and directed the war should not diminish the significance of religion's fundamental place in that war and, at least for the generation that lived through and after it, in defining self and society. In fact, as the essays in this book suggest, rather than being peripheral to the story of the Civil War, as much historical writing about the war would have it, religion cut to the marrow of Americans' identity and interests. Religious language and imagery were not just words and abstractions. People used them to survive and interpret the war and to build new lives after the war. Therein lies one of the principal "truths" about religion and the Civil War and one of the principal roads worth taking in thinking about the meaning of the war—then and now.

I

OVERVIEW

1

Religion and the American Civil War

PHILLIP SHAW PALUDAN

This volume gathers experts on many aspects of the very large subject of religion and the American Civil War. What I will provide comes from being a generalist, and every generalist is at the mercy of specialists. Yet in our best moments, generalists and specialists both recognize that they benefit from the perspective of the other, that understanding of the past proceeds through conversation far more than through the victory of one perspective over another. To that extent we are all at each other's mercy, each dependent on the other so that the conversation can endure. I offer as my contribution to the conversation a story about what happened to Christianity, and essentially Protestant Christianity, in the Civil War era. While telling that story, I will pose some questions that I find intriguing about the era that may be worth considering both here and in the future.[1]

The story of religion in the Civil War era takes place in the context of a larger story. That is the story of the transition of the United States from an agrarian society into a market-driven and more industrialized society, which linked together the lives and fortunes of strangers miles away from each other who began to experience events and trends that were increasingly beyond their control. And while many people benefited from the growth in wealth that this economic change brought, there came also in its wake protest from both North and South that the nation was losing its soul in the search for wealth. In these years, perhaps not coincidentally, membership in churches grew in America from one person in fifteen to one in seven. At a time when the median age of the population of the nation was 19.4, that is a very big number.[2]

Economic change inspired religious questions because, from the beginning, Americans had defined this nation in religious terms. As early as 1630, on eve of sailing to the New World, Puritan divine John Cotton preached from II Samuel 7:10: "Moreover I will appoint a place for my people Israel, and I will plant them, that they may dwell in a place of their own and move no more." Things had changed little in linking God's purposes with those of the nation by the time the war began. On the eve of civil war, Francis Vinton told Trinity Church in New York of his vision of the United States: "The people of these United States, under the Federal Constitution, are ONE NA-TION organic, corporate, divinely established, subject to government, and bound in conscience to obedience. Disloyalty to the Constitution is therefore impiety toward God." And as war raged, Methodist Bishop Matthew Simpson summarized the view: "If the world is to be raised to its proper place, I would say it with all reverence, God cannot do without America."[3]

Since the nation was God's nation, corruption of it was a cosmic catastrophe. And as the secession crisis grew, each section pointed fingers at the other as the most corrupt, most dangerous to God's plan, and hence made the division in the nation all the more serious. Both sides to the struggle insisted that they were being attacked by the corruptions that spread from economic and social changes. And since it was slavery that divided the sections, both sides found themselves talking about slavery. Northern critics believed that slavery epitomized the corruption of market-driven morals. William Seward explained the rise of the "Slave Power" by talking of corruption, of the "demoralized virtue" of the nation. Another Republican said that the Kansas-Nebraska Act had been possible only because "a gross materialism, the success of trade, the progress of gain, an external expediency is preferred to the lofty ideal aspirations and spiritual truth" that the nation's founders had followed. The most persuasive antislavery writing of the age said that at the core of slavery's power, over the North and South, was that it treated people as commodities—children sold from their mothers, fathers sold from their wives and children. Uncle Tom's awful fate arose because, as in the original subtitle of Harriet Beecher Stowe's book, Tom was "The man who was a thing."[4]

Slavery's defenders had markets and the corruptions of mammon also on their mind. One of slavery's strongest defenses was that it treated people as parts of interdependent Christian communities where the responsibility of white people made their power that of parents not masters. George Fitzhugh liked to quote Lawrence Stern's epigram: "Whosoever says 'I am thy servant' robs me of the power of master.'" But the North was a world where so-called economic equality hid in base hypocrisy the self-centered idolatry of the race for wealth. In fact, free society denied God's admonition to love one another by atomizing it into a race of each against all. But slavery was blessed by the Bible, had existed throughout human history (a sure sign of God's approval), and established a sacred duty upon masters to be as benevolent toward their slaves as God was toward mankind. Slavery thus created an organic Christian commonwealth, which an increasingly materialistic selfish North hypocritically challenged. Christian slaveowners could point in fact to the amelioration of slavery by their faith. Even Mrs. Stowe seemed to concede that point. When she wanted to show slavery at its most horrible on Simon Legree's plantation, she made it a place where Legree, not Jesus, ruled.

While these critiques were aimed outside at the contending sections, they also targeted failures within each section. Proslavery advocates were asking that the South live up to the ideals they were defending against the abolitionist critiques. They were trying to create a unity and a purpose within the system that would shape a Christian Republic. Abolitionists and other critics of northern society were also attacking the corruptions of their section. Abolitionists called even northern churches corrupt; and attackers of slavery like Stowe knew that slavery was protected by northern corruption manifested in a world where men were kept from doing justice by the rewards and power of the legal, political, and especially the economic systems.[5]

When war came, it seemed to promise at first to solve the internal corruptions of both societies and to provide God's judgment on the other. The South would be defeated, the North would be defeated, and that would be God's judgment on the false path the enemy had chosen. Meanwhile, by devoting themselves to values such as self-sacrifice and protecting the virtuous republic, individuals within the society would direct it toward God's purposes, not man's. Both sides, therefore, predicted a victory for God's nation and believed that they would themselves become more godly while securing that victory. In both cases, the spiritual would triumph over the material world, and by inference the dangers and the anxieties spawned by an industrial-market–driven world would be controlled.[6]

But that was before they discovered that victory required the strength and vitality of the very economies they had challenged and criticized. That was before they learned that God was on the side of the strongest battalions, and that those battalions were generated and empowered by the materials and wealth and even the values of that industrializing society.

In the North, the realization undercut the prophetic challenges to the society of the prewar years. Religious leaders of the North, who had divided on many questions of faith and practice, now began to gather under the same banner. Both conservatives and reformers joined forces.

The northern conservatives had been defending the status quo in several respects. Even while deploring excessive materialism and individualism in the North, ministers like Henry Ward Beecher and Horace Bushnell had essentially defended an economic system and did so in religious imagery. Bushnell's metaphors rang with acceptance of the prewar economy. God "invested" in mankind and did so confidently, "like a banker whose fund is in." And religion could only prosper among prosperous people. "Give me as a minister of God's truth, a money loving prosperous and diligent hearer." Beecher argued that wealthy people by their success provided examples to poorer people to achieve. These ministers agreed that the nation might purify itself in the war, but their sense of purification emphasized that the suffering of the war would simply awaken northerners to the recognition that the state ultimately served God while preserving order. These ministers joined the huge chorus of northern defenders of the Union who insisted that the secession crisis and then the firing on Fort Sumter were a crisis in law and order. They differed from more secular people only in highlighting God's place at the top of that order.[7]

But abolitionist reformers also began to join the chorus that saving the union was a divine purpose. Once they had acted as prophets excoriating the state for enforcing legal protections of slavery; now they moved toward seeing the government at war with the forces of slavery. And when emancipation became a war aim, as it did throughout 1862, more and more abolitionists supported the state much more than they criticized it. They continued to push Lincoln in the name of divine ideals toward emancipation, but as they moved, they inexorably, and I believe legitimately, lost or at least severely weakened their ability to cry "Woe unto thee oh Israel."[8]

Thus, an almost fully united North joined the fight against the sins of the South. There was, of course, still criticism of the age of shoddy and the growth of wartime fortunes, but the Republican-led government was moving clearly Zionward.

Soldiers and civilian relief agencies marched and sang as Christian soldiers to war. The hymns of the age are martial Christianity at its most militant. "Stand up, stand up for Jesus, ye soldiers of the cross," the Presbyterian hymn proclaimed. But this refrain was bested by the hugely popular "Battle Hymn of the Republic," which, despite its title, says nothing about a republic and a great deal about the coming of the Lord.[9]

On both sides, the intertwining of God and State was almost complete. It could be seen north and south as Lincoln and Davis both proclaimed days of fasting and/or thanksgiving in the name of God as the war progressed. Both men believed that God might be appeased, or at least that the public might be strengthened by such religious devotions. Davis even converted to Anglicanism in 1862.

Religion was in the armies, as well, that marched to those rhythms. "Soldiers are Christians if anyone is," Sherman said, and many soldiers, as Drew Faust, Gardiner Shattuck, Reid Mitchell, and others have shown, took religion very seriously and found greater strength to fight. As Union soldier John Copley put it, peace would come when "we as a nation and as individuals acknowledge [God's punishment] and repent our sins as a nation and as individuals . . . and turn to God and respect his laws."[10]

Religion was ubiquitous wherever the armies fought and camped. There were constant religious meetings and camp revivals. Every regiment had its chaplain. In addition, civilian preachers and groups spread the Gospel to the large captive audiences of young men. The extent of religiosity is hard to determine, but it was by no means small. Revivals swept both armies, with the Confederates especially involved after defeats. But the Union armies also kept the faith. The Army of the Potomac built sixty-nine chapels in 1864. Soldiers at least attended services in good numbers. Wilber Fisk, from Vermont, serving with the Army of the Potomac in March 1864, described meetings every night of two hundred men at a time, which was all the tent could hold, and that many had to leave because no seats were available. Still, Fisk did not attribute the size of the gatherings to faith alone. Some simply found the meetings a welcome change from camp monotony; it was fun to gather and sing and talk and listen. In addition, the meetings were a novelty after the heavy marching and fighting that they had seen. And yet there was a hard-core faith as well as social diversion forged here. In addition to the services, Fisk reported Bible study groups where tracts and papers on religious themes were freely circulated. "A good work is begun here," Fisk said, "one which every Christian will rejoice to see prosper."[11]

Sherman's army on the march through Georgia saw themselves and were portrayed in the popular literature of the time as Christian soldiers "marching as to war." One of my favorite stories tells of the time when, on the march through Georgia, one of the regimental bands began to play the hymn known as "Old One Hundred." Band after band throughout the army picked up the hymn and the soldiers joined in until five thousand voices could be heard singing "Praise God from whom all blessing flow." Then they quieted down, broke camp, and proceeded through central Georgia to gather some of those blessings. But Sherman reflected the views of Americans north and south in saying "Christian army I've got—noble fellows—God will take care of them— war improves character." And generals as well as privates were known and admired for their religious faith. O. O. Howard was recognized as the "Christian soldier" and Bishop Leonidas Polk in the South had a similar reputation. Stonewall Jackson was practically obsessed by God's purposes in the war, as well as alert to the impact of that image on his society. "I have been but the unworthy instrument whom it pleased God to use in accomplishing His purposes," Jackson announced frequently. Such men were not alone.[12]

The religious quality of the war on the northern side was exemplified in the two major relief organizations that the war created. While the leadership of the Sanitary Commission presented itself as tough minded and anything but sensitive to Christian compassion, the vast majority of commissioners and agents were as religious as the Christian Commission, which sent Bibles and tracts by the hundreds of thousands to soldiers of both armies and prayed with and for the soldiers that they met and served in the field. In the Confederacy, private churches and local committees performed similar duties.[13]

The fact that so many of the agents in both commissions and among the southern faithful were women alerts us to a facet of the war that deserves more attention than it has had. Indeed, the war seems to have changed the very nature of the Christianity that women were involved in. The prewar period had seen a feminine Christianity growing in power that emphasized sentiment as somehow a solution to the problems of slavery.[14] While hundreds of women did move through public spaces, circulating petitions for emancipation, the most powerful voice against the sin of slavery trapped women in a sentimental nonsolution. Harriet Beecher Stowe's *Uncle Tom's Cabin* took as its heroes Little Eva and Uncle Tom, both of whom are profoundly feminine in how they react to the slavery around them. Their deaths make everyone weep at the evils of the institution. But neither of them acts positively against it. In fact, their deaths do not free a single slave. Note that after Eva dies, Tom gets sent to Simon Legree's plantation, where he refuses to fight back as he is whipped to death. While Stowe does admonish the women of the North to take some public steps to help slaves and blacks, the solution she highlights and italicizes is to "feel right." It is a self-indulgent solution that suggests that because you have wept and felt bad about slavery, you have helped the slaves. The book is almost the epitome of a publicly disempowered, frail female Christianity.[15]

But the war changed things dramatically. There were still feminine values to speak and write about, but women took dramatic steps off the pedestal. Thomas Wentworth Higginson, in the midst of the war, contrasted what he termed the "negative" feminine religious virtues of patience, meekness, and resignation with the positive religious impulses that made his men zealous, energetic, and daring. The war certainly emphasized men's acts and motivations as the imperative sources of national survival, but now women proclaimed and embraced them as well. Nothing illustrates this transition better than the move from the character of Uncle Tom to the ideals of John Brown and Nat Turner.[16]

When war came, even Harriet Beecher Stowe said farewell to Uncle Tom. Writing in the *Atlantic Monthly* in January 1865, Stowe spoke not of Tom's meekness, nor of the need to end slavery by feeling right or weeping in the parlor, but of a God whose purposes were fulfilled in "The prophetic vision of Nat Turner, who saw the leaves drop blood and the land darkened. . . . The work of justice which he predicted is being executed to the uttermost." And Stowe's world was no longer that of imagination and fantasy. It was now one of concrete evils and problems. She was especially concerned about the poverty and want that widows and young girls suffered when the soldiers, their fathers and husbands, died. It was not time to weep; it was time to act. "Will anyone sit pining away in inert grief, when two streets off are the midnight dance houses where girls of twelve, thirteen, and fourteen are being lured away into the way of swift destruction? How many of these are daughters of soldiers who have given their hearts blood for us and our liberties?" Now active Christianity was the undiluted message, and turning the other cheek had been replaced by recognizing that God acted through the Nat Turners of the world, not just in fiction, as her work *Dred* suggested, but in bloody and desperate reality. God's "strange work of judgement and justice [was] consummated . . . through a thousand battles and ten thousands of precious deaths." There was no Eva or even Tom turning another cheek to Legree's brutality. Violence was God's, not Legree's, instrument.[17]

At the same time, the war provided an expanded vocation for women: they could use what their age saw as their maternal virtues to move into active Christianity in an environment of high public purpose and at a time of physical danger. They became angels of mercy when the wounds of battle were unmistakable. Their role as nurses would soon be exchanged for that of Yankee schoolmarms who, like so many others of the time, "did Christianity" instead of simply "believing Christianity." This combination of feminine maternal virtues in an activity—war—that was the essence of manhood was symbolized in the frequent use of the name "Mother" to describe the women organizing charity and relief efforts, such as "Mother" Mary Anne Bykerdyke, who marched with Sherman's army. Christian nurturing was part of Christian war making, as the war may have united a religious image that had been divided by gender before the war. The Christian soldiers were now both male and female.[18]

But while this united front of men and women of almost every Christian faith swelled the chorus of those who saw God in a Union uniform, there were other, more subtle and thoughtful responses. The need and the capacity for judgment and prophesy remained.

There still was a quiet but fierce challenge that came out of Amherst and spoke of, if not to, this age. Emily Dickinson wondered if heaven even cared, if Christian comforting was possible. After Antietam, she wrote:

> At least—to pray—is left—is left—
> Oh Jesus—in the Air
> I know not which thy chamber is—
> I'm knocking—everywhere—
> Thou settest Earthquake in the South—
> And Maelstrom, in the Sea—
> Say, Jesus Christ of Nazareth—
> Hath thou no Arm for Me?

In one of her letters she was a bit more clear, but as usual never too clear: "The see[th]ing pain one can't relieve makes a demon of one. If angels have heart beneath their silver jackets, I think such things could make them weep, but Heaven is so cold! It will never look kind to me that God, who causes all, denies such little wishes. It could not hurt His glory, unless were a lonesome kind. I 'most conclude it is."[19]

War raised complex questions about what it meant to be a disciple of the prince of peace. A quick and simple answer might have been to read the Sixth Commandment literally: "Thou shalt not kill." But the question was not an easy one—fight or turn the other cheek? And there was the more complex matter of the "third party beneficiary." If men of peace did nothing, then slaves remained in bondage. The complexities of that situation led most Quakers to see an inner light, which helped them find ways to support and often to fight on the Union side.[20]

People in the North who insisted on northern purity and knew that God wore blue were also learning that the war had more than triumph in store. The early war gained the approval of churchmen and women almost everywhere. But that approval echoed a time when people thought of short wars. After Bull Run, it was quickly and brutally evident that God was not going to let them off so easy. The war produced a painful purging. Young men died so that the nation could be redeemed, and so that the sins of the slaveowners might be expiated. Mrs. Stowe caught the point in talking about the deaths of defenders and opponents of slavery: "Our sons must die, their sons must die. We give ours freely; they die to redeem the very brothers that slay them; they give their blood in expiation of this great sin, . . . for which God in this great day of judgment is making inquisition in blood."[21]

And Horace Bushnell, for all his sympathy with the underlying values of the industrializing economy, still explored deeply the religious meaning of the war in his 1866 work *The Vicarious Sacrifice*. Bushnell wondered if the war might be good, in Sydney Ahlstrom's words, in the same way that Good Friday was good—it was a "Vicarious Sacrifice" by which innocent soldiers suffered to redeem others. Bushnell developed a new vision of what the sacrifice of the crucifixion meant, one that differed from Stowe's and from traditional ideas. Older views held that Jesus' act did something *for* mankind: it purified humankind because an innocent son of God had died. Bushnell argued that, more important, the crucifixion did something *to* mankind by showing that all human beings have a capacity to sacrifice for others. The death of Christ, for Bushnell, was not a single, unique event that for all time appeased "an angry God offended by human sin." That is, it did not require only a sinless Christ to make such a sacrifice. Because each person has "the same ethical nature as God," all might make a similar sacrifice for others. The purpose of the crucifixion of Jesus was "to beget in human character the same kind of sacrifice that is found, or revealed in Christ." Jesus was not an innocent son sent by his Father to die. Jesus was rather simply obeying God's law of love and right.[22]

For Bushnell, as well as for other theologians of the day—Philip Shaff, Orestes Brownson, and Henry Bellows come to mind—this sacrifice had national meaning. It would create a whole, integrated nation alert to its position in the world as God's nation, freed from selfish individualism, no longer self-centered and unconnected in its sovereign localism, but rather a coherent, mature united nation aware of its responsibility and its nature—a nation made aware of the importance of that responsibility through the blood that had redeemed the nation. "These United States," Bushnell said after the war, "having dissolved the intractable matter of so many infallible theories and bones of contention in the dreadful menstruum of their blood are to settle into a fixed unity and finally into a nearly homogeneous life."[23]

There was also more complexity and subtlety in the ways that some ministers considered the emancipation question. Abolitionist immediatists might simply damn slaveowners as evil, but that was too easy for men like Charles Hodge of Princeton Theological Seminary. Hodge argued that one could believe slavery was an institutional evil and still wonder if making war on the families and communities of the South was a Christian solution, a Christlike thing to do. Slavery was mentioned in the Bible; it was tolerated by the laws of the land; it involved decent Christians who were hardly free to leave their way of life to escape it. There were many sins in the land, but that did not mean that making war on the sinners was justified.

And yet men like Hodge gradually accepted emancipation as justified. They came to believe that God, by prolonging the war, was revealing His purpose that slavery be destroyed. They began to believe that ending slavery through war, while not a moral goal for decent Christians, might be a legitimate *means* to reach the larger end. An abiding bloody war seemed to signal that God wanted more, that He was bringing the destruction of slavery onto the agenda.[24]

Implicit in this belief was a complex idea about the relationship between God and the United States that Abraham Lincoln embodied. The temptation in dealing with Lincoln is simply to focus on and analyze the substance and style of the Second Inaugural Address. But I believe Lincoln embodied the three goals that the prophet Micah says are necessary for someone to do what God requires: "Do justly, and to love mercy and to walk humbly with thy God" (Micah 6:8). The last of these is the most important for understanding Lincoln and the importance of his religious ideas in the Union war effort.

It is worth noting that, while Lincoln spoke of the nation as the last best hope of earth for popular government, he seldom if ever indicated that he knew what the purposes of the nation were. He spoke of the people of the United States as an "almost chosen people." When told that God was on the Union's side, he replied that his hope went the other way, that the Union might be on God's side. In the Second Inaugural, Lincoln said that "the almighty has His purposes," but he emphasized that those purposes might not be those of human beings. At Gettysburg, he spoke of defending government of, by, and for the people, so that the nation could realize not a certainty but a proposition.[25]

These doubts about God's purposes had an obvious political meaning and value. It kept Lincoln from being the impassioned fundamentalist for a particular faith. It made him profoundly tolerant and accepting of the opinions of others, in religion and politics. His favorite saying was, "I believe in short statutes of limitation in politics." But this attitude did not mean that he had no ideals or principles. It meant that others had to be respected for their beliefs. There is a contrast that might be explored here, with Jefferson Davis's single-minded certainty, which hindered internal reconciliations in the South: Was the problem Davis's faith or the widespread religious idea in the South that only one view of faith was possible?

Still, Lincoln's fatalism did not lead to inertia regarding ideals. Clearly he didn't find acceptable Deep South views about disunion. And he didn't tolerate much bargaining about slavery either, when push came to shove. Not knowing what God's ultimate purpose was didn't mean that people resigned themselves to whatever fate might bring. In the Second Inaugural, Lincoln spoke not only of malice toward none, a posture that could arise from and inspire resignation and passivity, but also of firmness in the right as God gave people to see the right. And he insisted that the nation go forth to bind not only the wounds of war but also the wounds of slavery. Lincoln believed that overcoming the lash as well as the sword was the duty of the nation. He believed that men had the duty to fulfill God's purposes as they could best understand them.

But Lincoln's humility, as well as his beliefs, advanced him toward those purposes. The self-righteousness of the abolitionists, which motivated them and their supporters to do justice and love mercy for the slaves, also alienated large segments of the population whose very support they needed. By avoiding that self-righteousness and walking humbly but firmly, Lincoln kept together an imperative coalition that worked to free the slaves. Doing justly and loving mercy depended, in a constitutional democracy, on walking humbly with God. Reinhold Niebuhr has argued that the practical Christian statesman cultivates his uncertainty about God's will. Lincoln was his example.[26]

But Lincoln's religious ideas were not focused only on emancipation. They arose in the context of his commitment to constitutional democracy itself. Sidney Mead has argued that the processes of democratic government were vital to Lincoln and to the nation because they were the means whereby people could work out and understand God's plans for the nation. Since God did not provide a clear blueprint of His purposes for America, the open debate among diverse views offered Americans the only way to discover and understand what God's providence was. Lincoln and other northerners thus opposed secession and the attack on Fort Sumter because those two acts threatened to destroy the constitutional processes whereby God's purposes for them and their future were to be unfolded. It is thus easily understood why Lincoln used biblical language and metaphors at Gettysburg to show how the war would preserve a government of, by, and for the people—a government that would test the *proposition* that all men are created equal.[27]

By the end of the war, there was little dissent among the faithful in the North. The Methodists especially were leading the ranks; "Methodism *is* loyalty," the secretary of war announced. The other northern faiths were in the regiment, too. The Union seemed clearly to be God's nation blessed with victory, and the preachers who had endorsed northern economic values, even while deploring their excesses, generally saw a Union that God had blessed and had endorsed by bringing that victory. There were a few ministers who acted as prophets, reminding Americans of how far from God's perfection human nations still were. But the link between God and Union victory was almost complete. When it came time to choose who ought to speak for the North, at ceremonies in Fort Sumter in April 1865 again raising the nation's flag, Lincoln selected the nation's most prominent minister, Henry Ward Beecher. The choice seemed just right.

But religion also served more mundane purposes than to link God and country. The 620,000 dead young men were not just soldiers of the cross. They were someone's son, husband, father, and lover. And the people of the war era needed comfort, not just reassurance of their purity.

A major purpose that religion served in the war was not just to justify the killing but also to provide the comfort that 620,000 deaths required. Ideas of heaven were changed by this war, from a rather distant and strange place to a home to which the boys could return. Before the war, books on heaven were few in number and not concrete in meaning and description. Heaven was a vague place where people would somehow be with God. Perhaps people had been happy with that view because of their previous experiences with death. The dominant cultural practice for the hour of death at the time seems to have been a ritual played out at home, in which the dying person understood his condition and his loved ones were with him to observe his attitude upon dying. The ideal scene mirrored Little Eva's deathbed drama in which she accepted her fate and happily went to join God.[28]

But after the war people began to demand a more detailed view of heaven, a situation which may have arisen because few families witnessed the death of all the young men on the battlefields and in the hospitals. Close to 25,000 Union soldiers and a similar number of Confederates, in fact, died unknown. No one witnessed their deaths, no one knew whether the heaven they saw at the moment of death was joyful or not. So after the war, there was a huge outpouring of books on heaven. Before the war, fewer than one book a year on the subject was published in the United States. In the ten years following the war, almost a hundred (94) such books appeared. These books described in graphic detail what heaven looked like. And predictably, heaven looked just like home. The beloved was not dead; he was just in the other room. Funeral parlors even became funeral "homes." The young men who had died, away from family and their communities, had come home.

Confederates shared these experiences. God was on their side, affirming what they had been saying before the war. Ministers probably played the most important role in keeping the faith in the Confederate cause. They not only defended a way of life free of the corruptions of the North but also used the same arguments that northerners used for fighting a just war. Defensive wars were just, Thomas Aquinas had said. As in the North, southern ministers spoke of having to fight to defend themselves. But they also put on their great seal the words *Deo Vindice*. Shortly afterward, the Union used "In God We Trust" for the first time (good Yankees that they were) on its money. Through fast days and in the ongoing rhetoric of newspapers and from the pulpits, Confederates heard about their divine mission. They were the city on the hill that the Puritans, now gone astray in Yankeedom, had proclaimed. "A pure Christianity is wrapped up in this revolution," one minister announced, and he heard thousands of "Amens" throughout the Confederacy.[29]

These affirmations also set a context for judgment: Was the Confederacy living up to what God required of His people? That question unleashed other questions and raised many options. Since people seldom do live up to what God requires, and since the losses that the South was sustaining hardly indicated God's pleasure, there were lots of ideas to challenge. Some said that too much democracy or not enough godliness was the problem. Political reaction might save them. Dixie's prewar democratic movement was seen by southern leaders as a step away from divine authority. And Confederate constitutional conventions reflected a similar conservative mood. Like Union leaders, Confederate speakers and writers deplored the greed that war unleashed. Speculators were clearly seeking their own gain rather than the unity necessary to sustain a godly republic. God might judge southerners harshly for that, but still the society deplored such selfishness as personal, not systemic.[30] (The thought does occur that when southerners saw themselves sinning in the same way Yankees sinned, they lost some of their faith in the war.)

There is argument among historians about the extent to which southern concern over God's will and the extensive defeats in battle undercut the will to fight. Many cite Josiah Gorgas in late 1864; "What have we done that the Almighty should scourge us with such a war. . . . Is the cause really hopeless?"

Others rebut by saying that religion brought southerners together and kept them there even when the South was driven down. The truth is probably in both arguments. As in every intellectual issue worth considering, the crucial question is one of degree. Were southerners guilty about slavery and so ready to see God against them? One way to deal with this question is to make a distinction between the institution of slavery and the practice of it.[31]

Few southerners saw much contradiction in slavery as an institution. They believed that slavery identified them as a society more Christian than their foes. Indeed, the proslavery ideology seems to have been enlivened by war, as the press and pulpit continued to insist that slavery was a Christian institution at its heart. The Christianity of the slaves was a guarantor of the benignness of the institution. Furthermore, the shared suffering of blacks and whites allegedly brought them into Christian harmony. A famous and wonderfully popular painting of the day, "The Burial of Latané," shows mistress and slave united in their grief, praying for the hero who has fallen in defense of their shared cause. The war thus validated the institution that lay at the foundation of the South.

But if the institution of slavery itself was good in God's eyes, the practice came under increased scrutiny. As the war increased the influence of ministers, it also broadcast more widely their discussion of slavery in practice, even practices before the war. As the suffering from the war grew, some wondered if God was not punishing southerners for failing to live up to the ideal of Christianity that slavery could exemplify. Bishop George Foster Pierce raised that question before the Georgia legislature when he asked for amelioration of slavery's harsher practices. "If the institution of slavery cannot be maintained except at the expense of the black man's immortal interests," Pierce said, "in the name of Heaven I say *let it perish.*"[32]

And yet this rhetoric could have little impact in war and seems to have been almost forgotten in peace. Take the case of Methodist minister John Caldwell of central Georgia. He joined in the prewar view that supported slavery and yet urged that its practice conform more to Christian ideals by allowing marriages, ending the sale of families, and securing humane treatment and religious instruction for the bondsmen. He attacked the North as the war began for being "despotic . . . wicked . . . enemies of the human race." But as the war ended, Caldwell thought that the South had lost because it had not practiced slavery in a Christian way: "If our practice had been conformed to the law of God he would not have suffered the institution to be overthrown."[33]

But in the summer of 1865, when Caldwell gave the first of two sermons on this theme, half the congregation walked out before he was finished. Bishop Pierce removed Caldwell from his church, and Caldwell had to turn to the ranking military officer in the area to keep him in that church. Caldwell did not stay long in the old Confederacy. He resigned from his church and moved north.

What explains this changed view of slavery, from Pierce in war to Pierce in peace? Drew Faust says that before the war there was too much pressure from northern attacks to allow slavery to be changed. But surely there were even greater pressures in the war, as Union forces marched south. After the war, surely there was less need for unity in all things southern. It is true that following the war northern challenges to southern institutions remained potent. But surely a nation at peace provided a better climate for an admission that even Christian slaveowners had failed to practice what they preached.

Charles Reagan Wilson's study of the religion of the Lost Cause suggests what may have happened to the postwar Caldwell, and even to the wartime Pierce. In their effort to establish the righteousness of the Lost Cause and to build a South united against the ongoing threat of hypocritical and secularizing Yankeedom, many influential southern ministers forgot the challenges to slavery in practice. They focused their attention on the Lost Cause, which was sanctified and praised as the defining element of white southern life. Since that Lost Cause was inextricably tied to slavery, the South could never take a first, basic step that might lead to some reconciliation between the races. Southerners could not admit their guilt—not for being slaveowners, but even for failing to practice the institution in a Christian way. And since the Lost Cause symbolized the central religious myth of the time, it anointed not just a status quo but also a status pre quo—a world of the past that the future celebrated. Little reform was possible when the most Christian of acts was to try to live up to the standards of a slave society in the name and memory of the pure white soldiers who had died. The white southerner's conviction was that "his regional values and cultural symbols were holy." Thus he lost the possibility of prophecy too. Since southern society represented the holy, there was nothing to reform. Indeed, at its most repugnant, the Lost Cause religion helped spawn the Ku Klux Klan, which fought most possibilities of social change, let alone reform.[34]

The white South celebrated the rituals and faith of the Lost Cause, avoiding social reform—indeed, challenging it as a Yankee secular corruption of the City of God, even as northern Christianity became social gospel. The white South became, in a religious sense, what it believed about Christianity, rather than what it did to carry it out. It thus weakened prophecy and extolled uniformity, preserving economic, political, social, as well as religious, orthodoxy. This may be another way of saying that the prewar and wartime battle over God continued. The white South claimed, as the repository of virtue and godliness, the right to judge the nation, while it lost the capacity to judge itself. Black ministers would later have much to say about that—they would reestablish prophecy in the southern faith—but their time had not yet come.[35]

Meanwhile, in the black community, a very different story was being told. The war gave freed slaves the chance to create their own churches. They had heard enough white preachers extolling the virtues of slavery. They had seen enough hypocrisy about turning the other cheek, from men and women who smote that cheek systematically to enforce slavery. They wanted their own religious life. Besides, their practices of religion differed—when they felt the spirit, they shouted and sang. White services were less likely to make much noise at all, let alone a joyful noise. In freedom, blacks were free to create their own religious life and to deal with God in their own ways.[36]

Southern whites turned away from helping blacks, turned away from being the Christian patriarchs of the prewar years, whose purity was seen in their caring for "their" people. They worshipped a Lost Cause in which they had been pure in that way before and during the war. With eyes cast over their shoulders, they could avoid any responsibility for acting pure after the war. Perhaps the fact that blacks no longer sustained the myth also accounts for white behavior.

So blacks took steps to establish their own place in the united and more free nation, trying to make their religion more respectable. They moved away from ring shouts and brush arbor meetings, and even in some instances away from camp meetings. Their music was domesticated to include larger and costly instruments like pianos and organs, and they began to sing songs from Ira Sankey and Dwight Moody's collection, *Sacred Songs and Solos with Standard Hymns.* As Walter Pitts says, "The antebellum Negro spiritual, while still sung in the AfroBaptist ritual was pushed aside as a stigma reminding blacks of their recent condition of servitude." With the failure of Reconstruction, blacks sang fewer white hymns, and under the leadership of Charles Albert Tindley, they developed a combination of blues and Sankey songs. Shortly after 1900 black Baptists were singing songs like "I'll Overcome Someday," "We'll Understand it Better By and By," and "The Storm is Passing Over." And some African singing styles endured, while ring shouting may have been revived— it certainly endured into the twentieth century. The primitive quality of much of that practice inspired W.E.B. Du Bois to criticize it. It seems that more careful study of the hymns and practices of the faith during Reconstruction would explain the short- and long-term impact of war on the black religious experience.[37]

At the same time in the North, active Christianity made sense in a world in which northern armies had given Yankees the power to do what they wanted. They turned toward reconstructing the South with an early form of social gospel that built on military success and the ability of religious-minded soldiers, nurses, and commissioners to free slaves and provide comfort to soldiers and freed families.[38]

Yet the social gospel crusade of Reconstruction soon faded. Southern hostility, which wrapped itself in Lost Cause religiosity and proclaimed its own interpretation of God's message, surely helped defeat the northern effort. But other factors, born in the war itself, may also offer an explanation for the northern retreat. For example, the evidence in James Moorhead's *American Apocalypse* suggests that the linkage of God's purposes with secular goals may have undercut Reconstruction even as it inspired it.

The religious values of the war echoed on. Lincoln's assassination was seen as the final sacrifice for the North to learn that sacrifice was necessary for purity. Reconstruction crusaders kept their religious rhetoric and spoke of having to redeem a defeated South, to teach it the Christian faith that war had proved triumphant. But it is striking that Reconstruction reformers integrated their earthly crusade so fully with their spiritual ideals that they came to define their religious successes by secular measures. Thus when blacks proved too slow in accepting the white values that the victorious North had fought for, or when they had their own agendas, or when they needed more protection from obstinently unrepentant southerners, white Reconstruction crusaders lost their faith and retreated. They were unwilling to use the prophecy of the prewar years to attack the racist society of the postwar era as passionately as they had been to flay the prewar slave society.

On the other hand, although it gradually gave up protecting freed men and women, the postwar North at least did not abandon the idea that, as Harvey Cox says, Jesus wanted people to *do* Christianity and not just believe it. The Social Gospel reformers migrated to the northern cities and tackled the problems of laborers and their families. The moral equivalent of war had an outlet in the ideals of groups like the Woman's Christian Temperance Union and Edward Bellamy's Nationalist movement, which Mary Aston Livermore called "practical Christianity." Washington Gladden and Walter Rauschenbusch would later expand the practice. Christian soldiers were still marching.[39]

But historians have not recognized the connections. For example, Susan Curtis's fine book on the Social Gospel makes no reference to the Civil War. Sydney Ahlstrom also ignores the connection, as do other books on Social Gospel figures. But the Civil War has a significance that I believe cries out for study. Curtis, for example, links the rise of the Social Gospel with Victorian ideas of masculinity. She speaks of fathers who went away on business, or who died when their sons were very young. These fathers left future Social Gospel leaders like Walter Rauschenbusch to be raised by their mothers. Interestingly, Social Gospel thinkers emphasized not a distant god but a more nurturing, more human divinity. And they adopted values of nurture and self-sacrifice to modify or in some cases reject the extreme individualism of their fathers.[40]

I would like to know if the 2 or 3 million absent fathers and the hundreds of thousands of dead fathers might not have added to the potential congregations ready to believe and follow the Social Gospel message. They, too, had lost fathers and had been raised by mothers who taught nurturing and caring. Furthermore, as mentioned before, women of the war years showed that nurturing could be a public as well as a domestic value. Horace Bushnell, in his book *Christian Nurture* (1861), had suggested that path. The war years brought that vision into the public sphere and endorsed it in the name of nation saving and slave freeing. Now hundreds of thousands of children abandoned by their fathers (children don't often care why daddy's gone to war; they just know he has left them) turned to the ways of their mothers and took Christianity out of the home to save the world. Did the Social Gospel movement arise from these family losses as well as the gains of the Civil War?[41]

With all the hopes and dreams and beliefs and justifications, all the expectations that God's providence would purge corruption, would teach the significance of religious values, what is striking is how little of these were realized. The South had lost, of course, and it could assert its values only in its part of the country. Since those values celebrated a Lost Cause, they were not particularly vital for changing the world in God's image. The Christian soldiers of the North had triumphed, and the Christian nation they envisioned might, though not fully realized, at least be adopted as a standard. That may have been true in some places. The Social Gospel movement suggested that the vision still had some power. But by late in the century, the Christian crusade was losing its Civil War fire and some people began to challenge the idea that God had lent His banner to "killer angels."

When Oliver Wendell Holmes Jr. wrote of "The Soldier's Faith," he was not singing "Onward Christian Soldiers." Holmes's vision was existential, and God was gone from that faith. "The faith is true and adorable," Holmes wrote, "which leads a soldier to throw away his life in obedience to a blindly accepted duty, in a cause which he little understands, in a plan of campaign of which he has no notion, under tactics of which he does not see the use."[42]

When Mark Twain linked religion and war, he was bitter at the hypocrisy of standing up for Jesus while condoning the slaughter of thousands. His "The War Prayer" asserts that when people pray for victory in war, they utter the following thoughts:

> O Lord Our God, help us to tear [enemy] soldiers to bloody shreds with our shells; help us to cover their smiling fields with the pale forms of their patriot dead; help us to drown the thunder of the guns with the shrieks of their wounded writhing in pain; help us to lay waste their humble homes with a hurricane of fire; help us to wring the hearts of their unoffending widows with unavailing grief; help us to turn them out roofless with their little children to wander unfriended the wastes of their desolated land in rags and hunger and thirst. . . . We ask it in the spirit of love, of him who is the Source of Love, and who is the ever-faithful refuge and friend of all that are sore beset and seek His aid with humble and contrite hearts.

Reid Mitchell has pointed out the irony, at least, of comparing Jesus to a soldier since the fundamental duty of the soldier is to kill, not to suffer. The "Battle Hymn of the Republic" might read, Mitchell says, "as He killed to make men holy let us kill to make men free."[43]

Twain, of course, spoke as a cynical southerner in the early twentieth century, dubious about the value of any war he had lived through. And Holmes, always the skeptic and with three war wounds to educate him about crusades, was poorly positioned to see the hand of God in the great slaughter. But millions of Americans on both sides had died to make men holy, even though they fought over God's views on making men free. After the war, that sweeping and impassioned religiosity was probably gone. What might explain that—God's providence? Or man's?

As is probably obvious from this overview, there is a great deal to study, to think about, and to explore concerning religion and the American Civil War. Can the theological ideas that the conflict developed provide an agenda for examining the social and cultural experiences? Did the complex theology of Bushnell and Lincoln provide excuses not to realize the ideals of emancipation? If all have sinned and fallen short of the glory, might not white southerners deserve forgiveness as fellow sinners? If the true purposes of religion are salvation and piety, rather than trying to improve the world that God made, might it not be best to abandon crusades against the evils that God has often used to chastise sinners? And perhaps the fact that both sides read the same Bible and prayed to the same God meant that reunion would be facilitated when people could emphasize Lincoln's prayer for "malice toward none," and forget his advocacy of "firmness in the right."

I would also like to understand better the relationship between belief in God's inscrutability and the bloody cost of war. When Lincoln and others wondered if God's purposes were knowable, was that an emotionally imperative intellectual maneuver? To see 620,000 dead and recognize the limited victories of Reconstruction, to link these to the knowable purposes of God and be able to say, "So that's what God wanted," is to acknowledge something not easily thinkable about God. Better to save Him by making Him inscrutable.

But beyond such irreverent speculation, I would like to know what happened to serious discussions of God. As the proponents of a social gospel increasingly emphasized Jesus, and paid less attention to God the awesome father or creator of the universe, was that God's punishment for killing all those young men?[44] A god inscrutable enough to kill children in the hundreds of thousands might have dealt Himself out of a few rounds of human history. Can an agenda for dealing with this question be drawn from visions of God in the Jewish community after the Holocaust? So many questions and so far only a few good answers. The contributors to this volume have provided many of those answers in the past. Their essays here expand and illuminate the issues even more.

Notes

1. I acknowledge the invaluable assistance of Brian Dirck, Ph.D. candidate in History at the University of Kansas.

2. Phillip Shaw Paludan, *"A People's Contest": The Union and Civil War, 1861–1865* (New York, 1988), chap. 1.

3. Sidney Mead, "Abraham Lincoln's 'Last Best Hope of Earth': The American Dream of Destiny and Democracy," *Church History* 23 (March 1954): 8; Francis Vinton, *The Christian Idea of Civil Government* (New York, 1861); Simpson quoted in Peter J. Parish, "The Instrument of Providence: Slavery, Civil War and the American Churches," *Studies in Church History* 20 (1987): 294. I am deeply indebted to Parish's work for setting a direction for this paper. See also James E. Kirby, "Matthew Simpson and the Mission of America, *Church History* 36 (September 1967): 299–307.

4. Paludan, *"A People's Contest,"* xviii; "The Kansas Question," *Putnam's Magazine* 6 (October 1855): 431–433; Roy P. Basler, ed., *Collected Works of Abraham Lincoln* (New Brunswick, NJ, 1954): vol. 1: 108–115; vol. 2: 318, 403–404.

5. George Fitzhugh, *Sociology for the South* (Richmond, 1854), 243–244; Drew Gilpin Faust, *A Sacred Circle: The Dilemma of the Intellectual in the Old South, 1840–1860* (Baltimore, 1977), 45–49, 64–67, 121–122; Eugene D. Genovese and Elizabeth Fox-Genovese, "The Social Thought of Antebellum Southern Theologians," in *Looking South: Chapters in the Story of an American Region*, eds. Winfred B. Moore and Joseph Tripp (New York, 1989), 31–40.

6. George M. Fredrickson, *The Inner Civil War: Northern Intellectuals and the Crisis of the Union* (New York, 1965), chap. 4–5; James W. Silver, *Confederate Morale*

and Church Propaganda (Tuscaloosa, 1957); Haskell Monroe, "Southern Presbyterians and the Secession Crisis," *Civil War History* 6 (December 1960): 357–360; Sydney Ahlstrom, *A Religious History of the American People* (New Haven, 1972), chap. 40–41; Drew Gilpin Faust, *The Creation of Confederate Nationalism: Ideology and Identity in the Civil War South* (Baton Rouge, 1988), 22–40.

7. William McLoughlin, *The Meaning of Henry Ward Beecher* (New York, 1970), 142–151; Barbara Cross, *Horace Bushnell: Minister to a Changing America* (Chicago, 1958), 44–48; Paludan, *"A People's Contest,"* chap. 14; James Moorhead, *American Apocalypse: Yankee Protestants and the Civil War* (New Haven, 1978), 38–41; Phillip Shaw Paludan, "The American Civil War Considered as a Crisis in Law and Order," *American Historical Review* 77 (October 1972): 1013–1034.

8. James McPherson, *The Struggle for Equality: Abolitionists and the Negro in the Civil War and Reconstruction* (Princeton, 1964).

9. Laura Richards and Maud Howe Elliott, *Julia Ward Howe, 1819–1910* (Boston, 1916), I: 188–189; Julia Ward Howe, *Reminiscences, 1819–1899* (Boston, 1899), 273–276.

10. Reid Mitchell, *The Vacant Chair: The Northern Soldier Leaves Home* (New York, 1993), 118–119; Drew Gilpin Faust, "Christian Soldiers: The Meaning of Revivalism in the Confederate Army," *Journal of Southern History* 53 (February 1987): 63–90; Faust, *Confederate Nationalism*; Paludan, "Civil War as Crisis in Law and Order," 1013–1034; P.C. Headley, *Life and Military Career of Major General William T. Sherman* (New York, 1865), 174, 364.

11. Gardiner Shattuck, *A Shield and Hiding Place: The Religious Life of the Civil War Armies* (Macon, GA, 1987); Wilbur Fisk, *Hard Marching Every Day: The Civil War Letters of Private Wilbur Fisk*, eds. Emil and Ruth Rosenblatt (Lawrence, KS, 1992), 200–201;

12. Charles Royster, *The Destructive War: William Tecumseh Sherman, Stonewall Jackson, and the Americans* (New York, 1991), 69–71, 213–214; Albert Kirwan, ed., *The Confederacy* (New York, 1959), 80–81; Paludan, *"A People's Contest,"* 351.

13. Fredrickson, *Inner Civil War*, 98–112; Jeanie Attie, "Warwork and the Crisis of Domesticity in the North," in *Divided Houses: Gender and the Civil War*, eds. Catherine Clinton and Nina Silber (New York, 1992), 247–259. Fredrickson undervalues, I believe, the religiosity of the Sanitary Commission.

14. Ann Douglas, *The Feminization of American Culture* (New York, 1977).

15. I follow James Baldwin, "Everybody's Protest Novel," *Partisan Review* 16 (1949): 578–585. His critique of the book, in my opinion, withstands the defenses of *Uncle Tom's Cabin* in recent years. Criticism of Baldwin's view is most effective in Jane Tompkins, *Sentimental Designs: The Cultural Work of American Fiction, 1790–1860* (New York, 1985). See also Eric Sundquist, ed. *New Essays on Uncle Tom's Cabin* (Cambridge, 1986).

16. Higginson, as quoted in *The Real War Will Never Get in the Books: Selections from Writers During the Civil War*, ed. Louis P. Masur (New York, 1993), 194.

17. "The Chimney Corner," *Atlantic Monthly* 15 (January 1865): 109–115.

18. See Paludan, *"A People's Contest,"* 354–355.

19. Dickinson poem from Thomas H. Johnson, ed., *The Poems of Emily Dickinson* (Cambridge, MA, 1955), 385; letter quoted in Shira Wolosky, *Emily Dickinson: A Voice of War* (New Haven, CT, 1984), 44.

20. Peter Brock, *Radical Pacifists in Antebellum America* (Princeton, 1968); Brock, *Pacifism in the United States: From the Colonial Era to the First World War* (Princeton, 1968), 717–723; Edward Needles Wright, *Conscientious Objectors in the Civil War* (Philadelphia, 1931); Paludan, *"A People's Contest,"* 351–362.

21. Quoted in Masur, ed., *The Real War*, 245.

22. Horace Bushnell, *The Vicarious Sacrifice, Grounded in Principles of Universal Obligation* (New York, 1866); Robert Edwards, *Of Singular Genius, Of Singular Grace: A Biography of Horace Bushnell* (Cleveland, 1992), 246–248; Ahlstrom, *Religious History*, 685–686.

23. See William Clebsch, "Christian Interpretations of the Civil War," *Church History* 30 (June 1961): 212–222; Edwards, *Of Singular Genius*, 233; Fredrickson, *Inner Civil War*, 130–150.

24. Parish, "Instrument of Providence," 297–298, 309–310.

25. Lincoln's religious ideas have been studied in William J. Wolfe, *The Religion of Abraham Lincoln* (New York, 1963); David Hein, "Lincoln's Theology and Political Ethics," in *Essays on Lincoln's Faith and Politics*, ed. Kenneth Thompson (Lathan, MD, 1983), 105–156; Glen Thurow, *Abraham Lincoln and the American Political Religion* (Albany, 1976); Reinhold Niebuhr, "The Religion of Abraham Lincoln," in *Lincoln and the Gettysburg Address*, ed. Allan Nevins (Urbana, 1964); Sidney Mead, "Abraham Lincoln's 'Last Best Hope of Earth,'" 3–16; Richard Current, *The Lincoln Nobody Knows* (New York, 1958), chap. 3; David Hein, "Lincoln's Faith," in *The Historian's Lincoln*, ed. Gabor Boritt (Urbana, 1988). The argument advanced here is implicit in my *The Presidency of Abraham Lincoln* (Lawrence, KS, 1994) and explicit in Paludan, *"A People's Contest,"* 369–374.

26. Richard Fox, *Reinhold Niebuhr: A Biography* (New York, 1985), 277.

27. Mead, "Abraham Lincoln's 'Last Best Hope of Earth,'" 3–16.

28. I follow here my more extended discussion in *"A People's Contest,"* 364–370. See also Mitchell, *The Vacant Chair*, chap. 8.

29. Faust, *Creation of Confederate Nationalism*, chap. 2; Fredrickson, *Inner Civil War*, 139.

30. I follow Faust, *Creation of Confederate Nationalism*, in the above paragraphs.

31. Richard Beringer, Herman Hattaway, and Archer Jones, *Why the South Lost the Civil War* (Athens, GA, 1986), 351ff.

32. Faust, *Creation of Confederate Nationalism*, 81.

33. Daniel Stowell, " 'We Have Sinned and God Has Smitten Us!' John H. Caldwell and the Religious Meaning of Confederate Defeat," *Georgia Historical Quarterly* 78 (Spring 1994): 1–38.

34. Charles Reagan Wilson, *Baptized in Blood: The Religion of the Lost Cause* (Athens, GA, 1980), 5–9, 104–106 and passim.

35. Ibid., 8–10.

36. Leon Litwack, *Been in the Storm So Long: The Aftermath of Slavery* (New York, 1979), 465–467; Eric Foner, *Reconstruction: America's Unfinished Revolution, 1863–1877* (New York, 1988), 88–99; Clarence Walker, *A Rock in a Weary Land: The African Methodist Episcopal Church during the Civil War and Reconstruction* (Baton Rouge, 1982).

37. Walter Pitts, *Old Ship of Zion: AfroBaptist Ritual* (New York, 1993), 82–83; W. E. B. Du Bois, *The Souls of Black Folk*, in *Writings of W. E. B. DuBois*, Library of America edition (New York, 1986), 483–505.

38. Joe M. Richardson, *Christian Reconstruction: The American Missionary Association and Southern Blacks, 1861–1890* (Athens, GA, 1986).

39. Paludan, *"A People's Contest,"* 387–388.

40. Susan Curtis, *A Consuming Faith: The Social Gospel and Modern American Culture* (Baltimore, 1991); see her notes on pp. 279ff; and Ahlstrom, *Religious History*, 785–804.

41. See William Tuttle, *"Daddy's Gone to War": The Second World War in the Lives of America's Children* (New York, 1993), chap. 3 and passim, for the relationship between female-led households and attitudes of children.

42. Oliver Wendell Holmes Jr., "The Soldier's Faith," (1895) in *The Mind and Faith of Justice Holmes: His Speeches, Essays, Letters and Judicial Opinions*, ed. Max Lerner (Garden City, NY, 1943), 20.

43. Mitchell, *Vacant Chair*, 147; Mark Twain, "The War Prayer," in *The Portable Mark Twain*, ed. Bernard DeVoto (New York, 1946), 579–583.

44. For the change of emphasis from God to Jesus, see Susan Curtis, "The Son of Man and God the Father: The Social Gospel and Victorian Masculinity," in *Meanings for Manhood: Constructions of Masculinity in Victorian America*, ed. Mark C. Carnes and Clyde Griffen (Chicago, 1990), 67–78.

II

IDEAS

2

The Bible and Slavery

MARK A. NOLL

A brief observation in Abraham Lincoln's Second Inaugural Address highlighted the greatest theological conundrum of the Civil War. Both North and South, he said, "read the same Bible." The profundity of this statement was twofold. Most obviously, both North and South read the Bible, almost universally in the Authorized Version. More important for a theological understanding of the Civil War, both read the Bible *in the same way*.[1]

The problem of the Bible and slavery was always an exegetical problem, but never only an exegetical problem. If the Bible was God's revealed word to humanity, then it was the duty of Christians to heed carefully every aspect of that revelation. If the Bible tolerated, or actually sanctioned, slavery, then it was incumbent upon believers to hear and obey. The logic was inescapable. By 1861, the application of that logic had created a theological crisis of the first order. Despite widespread distaste for slavery and a good deal of antislavery activity from some quarters, more and more Americans had come to believe that—at least in some senses and with respect to some purposes—the Bible did sanction slavery. If, however, the preponderant view concluded that the Bible allowed or upheld slavery, anything but unanimity existed about how to act upon that conclusion. The immediate crisis was created by the fact that four sizable and vocal constituencies offered conflicting answers to the problem. From a modern perspective, it is clear that a theological crisis was also created by the appearance that only four responses were possible for the problem.

The first option was to admit that the Bible sanctioned slavery and, therefore, to abandon the Bible, at least in anything like its traditional shape, in order to attack slavery. This option was by far the least popular, but it enjoyed widespread publicity since it was defended by radical abolitionists of great notoriety like William Lloyd Garrison and Gerrit Smith.

The response that most directly contradicted this first position was to conclude that, since the Bible sanctioned slavery in passages like Genesis 14:

14, Leviticus 25:44ff., or I Corinthians 7:21ff., <u>faithful Christians should</u> accept the legitimacy of slavery as it existed in the United States out of <u>loyalty to the Bible's supreme divine authority.</u> This was the stance of most southern theologians and a large number of their northern colleagues as well, however they might differ on the practical questions left in the wake of this conclusion—whether slavery should be supported as a positive good, reformed to bring it in conformity with broader ethical standards, or opposed through a casuistry of expediency.

A third, and the most complicated, response was held by some abolitionists and moderate emancipationists. They conceded that, <u>while the Bible did indeed sanction a form of slavery, careful attention to the text of Scripture itself would show that the simple presence of slavery in the Bible was not a necessary justification for slavery as it existed in the United States.</u> Countless variations of this argument appeared in the generation before the war, but for two reasons they were not as common as a more direct way of evading the letter of Scriptures—this argument required a movement from the words of the Bible to theories about how the Bible should be applied to modern life, and it often seemed indistinguishable from the next response.

That fourth response, also promoted by the less radical abolitionists and some moderate emancipationists, was to <u>distinguish between the letter of the Bible (which might be construed to allow slavery) and the spirit of the Bible (which everywhere worked against the institution).</u> The way in which the third position could shade over into the fourth is illustrated by the career of Albert Barnes, prominent New School Presbyterian. His *Inquiry into the Scriptural Views of Slavery* (1846), after careful work on the definition of slavery, concentrated on Old and New Testament texts that mention slavery. Barnes argued that the realities about which those texts spoke did not correspond to the realities of nineteenth-century American society.[2] Thirteen years later, however, Barnes had come to the conclusion that, in Bruce Mullin's summary, "a clear distinction had to be drawn between the historical facts Scripture attested to, and the moral principles it taught, only the latter [being] normative and binding."[3]

All who wished to use the Bible for arguing in any way against slavery—whether by denying that the letter of the Bible should prevail over its spirit, or by denying that what the Bible seemed to teach it did not really teach, or by denying that what the Bible in fact taught did not fully justify the system of American slavery—faced a double burden of staggering dimensions. On the one hand, they had to execute the delicate intellectual task of showing that straightforward, proslavery conclusions did not adequately exegete the biblical texts. On the other hand, they also were compelled to perform a religious highwire act by demonstrating why arguments against slavery should not be regarded as infidel attacks on the authority of the Bible itself. In assessing the nature of biblical arguments on all sides, it is essential to remember that the overwhelming public attitude toward the Bible in the antebellum United States—even by those who in private neither read or heeded it[4]—was one of reverential, implicit deference.

By the start of the war, the issue had become acute, as indicated by the collection of fast sermons published in early 1861, which gathered together addresses from both South and North.[5] From the record of these sermons, it is evident that proslavery advocates had largely succeeded in winning the Bible, when taken in its traditional sense.

The South's leading theologian, James Henley Thornwell, could treat the matter as a foregone conclusion: "that the relation betwixt the slave and his master is not inconsistent with the word of God, we have long since settled. ... We cherish the institution not from avarice, but from principle."[6] When theologians did bend to rehearse the exegesis supporting slavery, that exegesis came from *northerners* whose fear of the religious havoc wrecked by Bible-scorning abolitionists was far greater than their worry about the social damage caused by inappropriate application of a biblically sanctioned slavery.[7]

Against such onslaughts, antislave biblicists continued to struggle. Their most typical stance, however, entailed the very attitudes toward the Bible that the conservatives, for distinctly religious reasons, feared. Henry Ward Beecher of Brooklyn's Plymouth Congregational Church was the featured representative of this position. In place of the straightforward exegesis of the proslavery defenders or the subtle hermeneutics of those who would finesse the slavery in the Bible, Beecher blustered:

> When the Bible is opened that all the fiends of hell may, as in a covered passage, walk through it to do mischief on the earth, I say, blessed be infidels!
> ... [W]here a man takes the Bible and lays it in the path over which men are attempting to walk from Calvary up to the gate of heaven—I declare that I will do by the Bible what Christ did by the temple: I will take a whip of cords, and I will drive out of it every man that buys and sells men, women, and children; and if I cannot do that, I will let the Bible go, as God let the temple go, to the desolating armies of its adversaries. ... I should like no better amusement than to answer the sermons of men who attempt to establish the right of slavery out of the Bible. It would be simple butchery![8]

The most telling indication of the weakness of Beecher's own position is that, although he said it would be an easy thing to refute the proslavery biblical arguments, he did not adduce even a single text to that end.

Here, then, was the situation with the Bible and slavery on the eve of the war, and here it stood throughout the war. In theological terms, the four early responses to the proslavery consensus could be reduced to a forced dichotomy—either orthodoxy and slavery, or heresy and antislavery.

In fact, there were always far more than four possible responses to the dilemma posed by the biblical record on slavery. That there seemed to be only four positions testifies to the fact that the issue of the Bible and slavery was more than an exegetical question, that it was always a question of who had the power to interpret the Bible as "America's book" and who (though perhaps reading and heeding the Bible in the United States) had no voice in determining what an "American Bible" should look like. The issue from first to last was one of cultural hermeneutics as well as biblical exegesis.

The hermeneutical situation was formed by two realities: (1) the argument over the Bible and slavery took place in a society where traditions of biblical interpretation as well as a tradition of confidence in the Bible were deeply rooted in American experience; (2) the argument over the Bible and slavery also took place in a society where convictions about racial difference—related only casually, if at all, to traditional confidence in Scripture—affected biblical interpretation at every level.

In 1857, a visitor from Britain, James Stirling, published a record of his journeys in the South, where he described the American biblical situation more clearly than any American of the period. Stirling praised the logical capabilities of southern defenders of slavery like George Fitzhugh and Albert Taylor Bledsoe, but, as an opponent of slavery himself, he was convinced that "the common sense and moral sentiments of mankind" would soon destroy the institution. Stirling was especially impressed with the skill of the proslavery apologists at "metaphysics," by which he meant also their skill as biblical exegetes. His description of that skill, however, provides a key for beginning to unpack the hermeneutical from the exegetical issues involved:

> A large portion of Bledsoe's book is devoted to the Scriptural argument in favour of slavery; and here, I must confess that, as against his opponents, the orthodox Abolitionists, he is perfectly triumphant. . . . [A consideration of the patriarchs, the Mosaic law, and the New Testament] are irresistable proofs that the institution was recognized by the founders both of Judaism and Christianity. How those who adhere to a literal interpretation of the Bible, and consider every direction contained in its pages as applicable at all times to all men, are to reconcile these facts with modern anti-slavery notions, it is, thank goodness, no business of mine to find out.[9]

As Stirling described the matter, however, it was not just the Bible, but "a literal interpretation of the Bible" and a belief that "every direction contained in its pages [is] applicable at all times to all men" that won the palm for proslavery in exegetical battles with its foes.

If Stirling could see so clearly that there was a particular hermeneutic implicated in the defense of slavery, even if he was not particularly interested in exploring the possible relevance of other hermeneutics to the problem, why did Americans not also see it that way? If it was not merely the Bible but a particular way of reading the Bible that provided the rationale for the institution, how could proslavery champions rest so confidently on their laurels? Why did northerners uneasy about slavery flail in so many directions—professing a willingness to give up Scripture if it could not be employed against slavery, attacking abolitionists as infidels for undermining Scripture, squirming diligently to show that the Bible did not in fact approve the sort of slavery present in the South, or shouting louder and louder to draw attention away from exegetical questions?

The reason almost no American could articulate a distinction between the Bible and the Bible-as-read-in-America was precisely that Americans shared so implicitly the hermeneutic that Stirling identified. The reason they held it so implicitly was precisely that this hermeneutic—compounded of a distinctly

Reformed approach to the scope of biblical authority ("every direction contained in its pages as applicable at all times to all men") and a distinctly American intuition that privileged commonsense readings of scriptural texts ("a literal interpretation of the Bible")—had functioned as the vehicle through which the Bible was unleashed in the creation of American civilization. Opponents contending to the death for the future of the United States were in no position to examine, with critical detachment, the assumptions that had made the fate of the United States worth contending for. Of those assumptions one of the most pervasively powerful was that the people had the right to read all of the Bible for themselves.

A hermeneutic compounded of Reformed theological instincts and commonsense literalism had been emerging in America for two and a half centuries before 1860. On the Reformed side, this hermeneutic was descended from New England Puritans and mid-state Presbyterians, and beyond them from Scottish, English, Dutch, South German, and Swiss forms of the Protestant Reformation often labeled "Calvinist." Reformed approaches to Scripture have loomed so large in standard accounts of American religious history that it is easy to forget that they were neither the first nor the only orthodox Protestant ways of appropriating the Bible. Reformed approaches followed at least three principles that distinguished Calvinists from two other sixteenth-century forms of orthodox Protestantism, Lutheranism and the high-church Anglicanism represented by Richard Hooker.

Although a full range of internal differences divided "Calvinists" from each other, they were united in holding the following beliefs about the Bible: (1) *Scriptura sola* (the Bible was an authority set over against all other religious authorities); (2) the "regulative principle" (English Puritans developed this concept out of general Reformed leanings; it held that believers are required to do what the Bible commands and are equally required not to do those things about which the Bible is silent); and (3) the Third Use of the Law (the moral teaching of Scripture existed not only to show an individual's need of salvation but also to provide a blueprint for how the Christian, in grateful obedience to God, should live out one's entire life).

The hermeneutic inspired by Reformed milieux revered the Bible as the supreme guide to life and inculcated a suspicion that all other authorities beside biblical chapter and verse were not just secondary but also dangerous—in other words, all of the Bible, and only the Bible, for all of life. It is necessary to repeat, however, that this approach to Scripture was neither the first nor the only orthodox Protestant approach to Scripture.

The Reformed hermeneutic became dominant in America because varieties of Reformed Protestantism were the dominant American churches. The hermeneutic fueled the most intensely religious colonial settlements, energized early American higher education, and midwifed the revival tradition that began in the mid-eighteenth century. It also contributed a full share to the spirit of the American Revolution and to the creation of early American nationalism. It defined as well the approach to Scripture that drove the great voluntary movements in the two generations before the Civil War.

To illustrate the public weight of Reformed voices in public during the Civil War, crude measures are useful. When, in April 1863, a convention of southern ministers appealed to their fellow Christians in the world, ninety-four of the ninety-six signers came from Baptist, Methodist, Episcopal, Presbyterian, and Disciples churches, all branches of English-speaking Reformed Protestantism.[10] In David Chesebrough's two compendious books on northern sermons during the war, well over 90 percent of the texts he studies came from the same ecclesiastical family.[11] A Reformed approach to the Bible had divided into many American variations, but it also defined the theological instincts with which most theologians at the time of the war read, inwardly marked, and outwardly applied the Scriptures.

At least two full generations before the Civil War, however, the prevailing American hermeneutic had come to embody, along with Reformed predispositions, what Stirling called "a literal interpretation of the Bible." This literalism owed more to American historical circumstances than to the Reformed regulative principle, for the first great Reformed theologians (Calvin, Heinrich Bullinger, Peter Martyr, many English and American Puritans) had practiced a theological rather than a literal approach to Scripture. The point of intersection between traditional Reformed hermeneutics and American popular religion was antitraditionalism, long ingrained in the former and promoted vigorously by the latter in the wake of the American Revolution.

The engine that drove Reformed approaches to Scripture into uncharted American territory was social transformation. The revolution in American society from hereditary, deferential hierarchy to democratic, ideological antihierarchy—a revolution described brilliantly by Robert Wiebe, Nathan Hatch, and Gordon Wood[12]—created a distinctly American form of biblicism.

In the early years of the United States, Scripture became the national book *par excellence*. Confidence in the ability of ordinary people to understand it fueled the formation of many new sects and was one of the main engines in the revitalization and expansion of Protestantism in the early republic.[13] Broad familiarity with its contents characterized both ordinary people and elites.[14]

Up to and through the Civil War, publishing and distribution of the Bible dwarfed all other American enterprises relating to books.[15] During the war itself, the American Bible Society distributed more than 3 million Bibles or New Testaments to combatants; something like 300,000 Bibles passed from northern publishers into the South (despite a ban on trade between the sections); and Moses Hoge of Richmond by himself braved the Union blockade to smuggle 10,000 Bibles, 50,000 New Testaments, and 250,000 portions of Psalms and Gospels from England back to the South.[16]

Throughout the period, the written Scriptures created an irrefutable warrant for common people to manage their own religious, and often social, lives. In this appropriation the American hermeneutic was critical. As Nathan Hatch has put the matter: "It proclaimed a new ground of certainty for a generation distressed that it could no longer hear the voice of God above the din of sectarian confusion. This approach to Scripture also dared common people to open the Bible and think for themselves. It even challenged them to limit religious discussion to the language of the Bible. Finally, this approach freed people from staid ecclesiastical traditions, thus befuddling the respectable clergy."[17]

It is significant that American Protestants almost never tried to defend their interpretive practices toward the Bible through a direct appeal to Scripture. Rather, the Reformed, literal hermeneutic grew from the special circumstances of American life as much as from simple confidence in the Bible itself. But even if literal biblicism was not rooted directly in a literal use of Scripture, it was nonetheless the norm in and through the Civil War.

The hermeneutical crisis of the Civil War—the crisis arising from the full deployment for more than two generations of a common set of Reformed and American assumptions about how to read, interpret, and apply the Scriptures—was a crisis on two levels. The obvious crisis that bore directly on the fate of the nation was that "simple" reading of the Bible yielded violently incommensurate understandings of Scripture with no means, short of warfare, to adjudicate the differences. The less obvious crisis was more directly theological; it concerned the fate of biblical authority itself.

A Clash of Interpretations

Because of the way Reformed and literal interpretations of the Bible had empowered ordinary people and their leaders to create a Christian civilization, that hermeneutic enjoyed immense implicit authority. A manifest difficulty by the late 1850s, however, was that this wonderfully energizing use of Scripture had created multiple, conflicting Christian civilizations. Several cultures, purporting to read the Bible the same way, were at each others' throats. The Bible sanctioned slavery and by implication the society in which it existed. The Bible allowed for slavery but also pronounced judgment on societies where the slave–master relation was abused. The spirit of the Bible condemned slavery and so demonstrated the moral inferiority of any society where slavery existed.

If at our late date we might conclude that, within the interpretative framework of the period, proslavery won the exegetical battle, no Bible-believing abolitionist would admit it. Moreover, many moderates who felt that the Bible tolerated slavery were rapidly and easily converted to some form of abolitionism once war itself was declared and a chorus of influential voices—including President Lincoln and Protestants from other lands[18]—convinced them that the survival of the Union depended upon the ending of slavery.[19]

The Reformed, literal hermeneutic had helped build a biblical civilization—in fact, multiple biblical civilizations. But the hermeneutic itself could not reconcile the divergent interpretations it had produced.

The shape of that dominant hermeneutic was no better illustrated than in a sermon on the eve of conflict by the North's best-known minister. In his fast-day address of January 4, 1861, Henry Ward Beecher gave classic expression to the deeply ingrained belief that the Bible, if simply left alone, would interpret itself. Most of the great themes that had created the American hermeneutic went into his paean to the liberating power of the Scriptures. His words were thick with the vocabulary of republicanism, fear of Roman Catholicism, pride in American exceptionalism, and confidence in the common sense of ordinary people. It was a remarkable statement:

> Now what has been the history of the Book but this: that wherever you have had an untrammeled Bible, you have had an untrammeled people; and that wherever you have had a trammeled Bible, you have had a trammeled people? Where you have had a Bible that the priests interpreted, you have had a king: where you have had a Bible that the common people interpreted; where the family has been the church; where father and mother have been God's or- dained priests; where they have read its pages freely from beginning to end without gloss or commentary, without the church to tell them how, but with the illumination of God's Spirit in their hearts; where the Bible has been in the household, and read without hindrancy by parents and children together— there you have had an indomitable yeomanry, a state that would not have a tyrant on the throne, a government that would not have a slave or a serf in the field. Wherever the Bible has been allowed to be free; wherever it has been knocked out of the king's hand, and out of the priest's hand, it has carried light like the morning sun, rising over hill and vale, round and round the world; and it will do it again![20]

Beecher's rhetoric was intense, but as usual he had things all screwed up. Nowhere in the world as of January 4, 1861, was the Bible freer and more open to the public than in the United States of America, nowhere did less authority from tyrants, prelates, or priests constrict the meanings that ordinary men and women took from the Bible, and nowhere in the world did more pious believers hold (often with considerable unease) that the Holy Scriptures sanctioned the institution of slavery.

Beecher's confidence in the ability of ordinary people to interpret the Bible correctly, if only they were left to themselves, was misplaced. Yet that confi- dence, so deeply ingrained in the relatively short history of the United States, helped start the Civil War, and it was one of the reasons the war became a moral crusade for both sides.

Theological Crisis

The division over the meaning of the Bible that contributed to the national crisis also signaled a theological crisis of the first order. This crisis, which was less obvious than the overt military struggle, centered on the question of the "American Bible" itself. Despite the fact that the United States was one of the most ostensibly Christian societies on the face of the earth, the Civil War's division of the country's ardent Bible believers called into question the ade- quacy of the Bible as an omnicompetent, infallible authority for life now and forever, at least as that adequacy had been formulated by Protestants since the Reformation.

For the history of theology, the issue was whether the war offered con- clusive demonstration of the Roman Catholic assertion, dating back to the

Reformation, that to give the Bible to everyone was to take it away from everyone.[21]

The Civil War presented American theologians a golden opportunity for showing how one might retain an authoritative Bible in a republican, individualistic polity. Given the violently tragic results of the Reformed, literal hermeneutic being played out in the battlefields of the war, it would seem that all serious Protestants would have been striving to save, not only the nation (Union or Confederate) but also the Bible itself.

As it happens, sectional controversy and the war did lead to the articulation—or at least the anticipation—of several alternatives to the Reformed, literal hermeneutic. One alternative, explored well in books by George Fredrickson and Anne Rose, was simply to abandon, usually by default rather than by direct attack, the Bible in any traditional sense.[22]

The best-known alternative was the move from the Bible's letter to its spirit that abolitionists like Jonathan Blanchard, Albert Barnes, Henry Ward Beecher, and Gerrit Smith practiced, with varying degrees of deference to traditional views on Scripture. This move led directly or indirectly to the theological liberalism of the last third of the twentieth century.

Reasoning that led to liberal theological conclusions was prominent in the United States from the 1840s and became even more so in the decades after the war.[23] But it was never the only alternative to the Reformed, literal hermeneutic. The prominence of liberal reasoning, however, made it extraordinarily difficult for orthodox alternatives. These alternatives faced the task of supplanting an approach to Scripture that, by contributing to the Christianization of the nation, had become part of the national myth. But especially on the application of the Bible to slavery, they also bore the burden of demonstrating that efforts to relativize individual texts seeming to affirm slavery did not at the same time subvert biblical authority itself.

At least three barriers made that a daunting challenge. Attacks against the liberal move to the Bible's spirit made it difficult for alternatives to Reformed literalism even to gain a hearing. Similarly, the pattern of eighteenth-century precedents was imposing. In the British world with which American theologians were most familiar, the standard account held that, when Protestants retreated from literal views of Scripture, their only alternatives were "Church-authority, the Spirit [i.e., enthusiasm], or Reason"[24]—all destinations that orthodox Americans considered abhorrent.

The third barrier was the highest. With relentless pressure, skillful defenders of slavery insisted that any attack on a literalist construction of biblical slavery was an attack on the Bible itself. A clear example of this strategy appeared in James Henley Thornwell's fast day sermon of November 21, 1860, when Thornwell took special pains to denounce the idea that Africans constituted a species distinct from Caucasians. When Thornwell denied that this heresy of multiple human origins originated in the South, this larger purpose was manifest: "it is as idle to charge the responsibility of the doctrine about the diversity of species upon slaveholders, as to load them with the guilt of questioning the geological accuracy of Moses." He then drove home the polemical dagger. Heretical teachings questioning the Bible's account of a common human origin, as well as heretical teachings questioning the Bible's account of the age of the earth, indicated clearly the kind of teaching that questioned the depiction of slavery in both Old and New Testaments. Heresies concerning Adam and Eve as well as on the geological record "are assaults of infidel science upon the records of our faith, and both have found their warmest advocates among the opponents of slavery."[25] To audiences predisposed toward biblical literalism, Thornwell's reasoning was persuasive. To propose for whatever reason that the Bible did not sanction slavery was to attack not just slavery but the Bible as well.

Powerful as this reasoning was in the United States, its limits are suggested by the fact that it had virtually no influence outside the country, even among those who shared the conservative theology of proslavery defenders. This fact begins to suggest why the American debate over the Bible did not affect the general history of Christian theology. A preliminary survey of Protestant writings on the American Civil War from England, Scotland, and Canada has turned up almost no support for Thornwell's biblical reasoning on slavery, although the same sources reveal considerable antagonism to the North and much political sympathy for the South.[26] Even among Thornwell's fellow-Presbyterians abroad, some of whom held to a form of the regulative principle as rigorous as Thornwell's, there was only contempt for efforts to defend southern slavery on the basis of the Bible.

The limitations of Thornwell's reasoning were seen most clearly in the Free Church of Canada (a Presbyterian denomination formed in sympathy with the Free Church of Scotland). Canadian Free Presbyterians were wary of American New School Presbyterians because (with objections that Thornwell shared) the New School seemed weak on "the extent of the atonement, and the imputation of guilt and righteousness in the Adamic and Christian covenants." But these conservative Presbyterians in Canada, who hewed so closely to the high view of Scripture in their ancestral confessions, also felt that the American Old School Presbyterians were far too equivocal in their toleration of the institution.[27] Thornwell, the Presbyterian exegete, made sense in Canada, but not Thornwell, the exegetical defender of slavery.

Other foreign Presbyterians evinced little of the northern moderates' fear of looking like antibiblical infidels for questioning the legitimacy of slavery. Yet these foreign Presbyterians were also evangelical biblicists who, while sharing Thornwell's theological tradition, repudiated the racial, social, and economic contexts upon which the force of Thornwell's hermeneutic depended.

Only in an environment where the principles of the American hermeneutic prevailed could Thornwell be regarded as a supernal, rather than simply a formidable, theologian.[28] The limited appeal of Thornwell's biblical arguments to foreigners does not, however, alter the fact of their power in the United States. Those who in the United States attempted to show how one might be both orthodox on Scripture and yet not a practitioner of literalist exegesis had to address the same audiences that Thornwell addressed and also speak out of the same universe of meaning from which he spoke.[29]

If it was difficult in mid-nineteenth century America to gain purchase for orthodox alternatives to American literalism, at least four such alternatives nevertheless existed. All proved ineffective, and so exerted little influence on the unfolding crises—both political and theological. But each articulated a hermeneutic that, while at odds with American Reformed literalism, still pre-served the authority of the Bible and an orthodox faith. As such, these alter-native hermeneutics also opened the possibility (even among conservatives who had no wish to exercise the possibility) of using an orthodox, authoritative Bible against, rather than for, slavery.

The most radical orthodox alternative to Reformed literalism was offered by the least noticed theological voices of the day, the voices of African Amer-icans; the most offensive to Protestant sensibilities came from representatives of the most numerous Christian institution in the world, the Roman Catholic Church; the most innocuous arose from Lutheran and German Reformed high-church Protestants; and the most plausible was the work of northern and border-state Presbyterian intellectuals caught between asserting and compro-mising the literalistic hermeneutical principles of their American evangelical confreres.

African Americans

African-American Christians were as likely to be champions of the Bible only and of biblical literalism as their white contemporaries. Thus, Daniel Payne, leading bishop of the African Methodist Episcopal Church, gave way to no white man in proclaiming the sole sufficiency of Scripture. For his part, Fred-erick Douglass resembled Horace Bushnell in believing that the United States was a chosen nation and that republican language provided the best way of expressing the nation's privileged status under God.[30]

Similarities to white counterparts notwithstanding, African Americans did not replicate Reformed literalist exegesis. The reasons were as weighty as those shaping African-American religion in general. For Christians who had regu-larly been discouraged from efforts to read the Bible, who sustained expressive forms of African ritual practice, and who developed in the Spiritual an indig-enous narrative theology, habits of mind could not fit easily into the categories of Enlightenment, republican, nationalistic (and white) exegesis.[31]

Rather, the hermeneutical practice of African Americans featured the Bi-ble as a source of prophecy, magic, conjuring, and dreams; the Bible as a dramatic, narrative book; and the Bible as a book of grand, controlling themes.

In the first instance, as Theophus Smith has recently documented, African-American believers retained in their Christian usage features of pro-phetic religion and formulary magic that adapted the written text to African traditions.[32] It thus posed no difficulty for Daniel Payne, who promoted the Bible as ardently as the strictest Old School Presbyterian, to be guided by dreams at strategic moments in his life.[33]

Alternatively, blacks put the Bible to use dramaturgically. Frederick Doug-lass more than once gave full vent to his frustration about religious reasoning in defense of slavery. In October 1860, he wrote that "The Northern people have but a faint conception of the intensity with which Southern religion clings to the fleshless skeleton of a theological system. The belief in certain dogmas, through whose web there runs now a thread of truth, and then a thread of absurdity in most inexplicable confusion, has usurped, in the gospel of the South, the place of justice, mercy, and purity." Douglass's means of refuting this error, however, was not counter-exegesis, but a story recounting how a pious slaveholding mistress unmercifully beat a nine-month-old slave child for a trivial offense.[34]

Finally, African Americans regularly approached the Bible as a source of grand themes rather than for instruction in experiential particulars (that is, in traditional Protestant categories, more like the Lutherans than the Reformed). So it was that use of the Bible was dominated by thematic texts like Psalm 68:31, which Albert Raboteau has called "without doubt the most quoted verse in black religious history" ("Princes shall come out of Egypt and Ethiopia shall stretch out her hands unto God");[35] or Acts 17:26 (God "made of one blood all nations of men for to dwell on the face of the earth"), which Timothy Smith found repeatedly in black religious writing.[36]

Again, Frederick Douglass illustrates the nature of this alternative biblicism. Much more than most white exegetes, he was an apocalyptic, millennial thinker in the mold of Nat Turner or John Brown.[37] When Douglass reviewed G. W. Brownlow's use of the Bible to defend slavery, his response was twofold. First he ridiculed the performance by saying that Brownlow merely "culled out and grouped together sundry passages of Scripture, which, by wresting them from their relations, would seem to countenance slavery." But then he sought to overwhelm Brownlow's exegesis by evoking an absurdity: When Brownlow "sees this noble, Christian missionary institution [of slavery], with all its Christ-like appliances of whips, chains, gags, thumbscrews, cat-o'-nine tails, fetters, and bloodhounds, assailed, he almost stands astonished and appalled by the awful depths of Abolition wickedness!"[38]

In sum, African-American appropriation of Scripture featured (alongside literalist Reformed patterns) narrative, talismanic, and perhaps African ways of appropriating a sacred text. These approaches, though they provided great resilience to African-American believers, left the ground of rational exegetical argument to the Reformed literalism that defended slavery. Even if African Americans had not been socially marginalized, the fact that this pattern of Bible reading diverged from the American norm doomed their biblicism, however orthodox, to irrelevance.

Roman Catholics

Though the numbers of Roman Catholics in the United States were rising rapidly by the 1860s, they still stood far from the center of American public influence.[39] Yet if any Protestant had been able to pay attention, the Catholic church possessed two different alternatives to the standard Reformed, literal hermeneutic. First, but important more for the twentieth century than the nineteenth, was the effort of John Henry Newman in Britain to show how a traditional doctrine of Roman Catholic permanence could accommodate organic change over time. Newman's *Essay on the Development of Christian Doctrine* was a difficult work when it was published in 1845, but it did find American readers (and opponents). Its contention for the possibility of change as a form of development might have offered a few American theologians a hint of parallel procedures for Protestants if they had not read the work simply as Roman Catholic propaganda.[40]

Far more common, however, was a Catholic appeal to authority as a way of overcoming Protestant divisiveness. In many cases, to be sure, Catholic responses to the war resembled Protestant in simply following the dictates of regional convention.[41] But they also could pose a challenge to received American opinion. The subject of Catholic reaction to the Civil War has begun to receive the serious study it deserves,[42] but (to my knowledge) Catholic alternatives have never informed more general studies on the theological meaning of the conflict.

During the war several Catholics made a more far-reaching claim with direct relevance to the use of Scripture. The fighting, in this view, arose not from some grand clash of Right against Wrong, but from Protestant principles like private judgment, antiauthoritarianism, and the private interpretation of Scripture. Catholic commentors like Orestes Brownson put such arguments with considerable skill. In April 1865, the *New York Tablet* made the charge bombastically: "Protestantism is essentially rebellious; . . . its origin is the spirit of secession and revolt, . . . its history is but a chronicle of insurrection, and . . . , in short, sedition and mutiny are but fruits of the Lutheran leaven spreading under the special names of Liberty and Independence into all the ramifications of political, social and domestic life."[43]

The argument was made with greatest skill, however, in a discerning foreign discussion of the American situation. The essay came from Rome in a Jesuit periodical published in January 1861. Its discussion might well have been intended also as a comment on tumultuous forces then at work in Italian politics. The author in *Civiltà Cattolica* expressed considerable sympathy for the United States in its time of trial. But he also highlighted the Protestant character of the United States as a prime factor in explaining the breakdown of political, moral, and social unity:

> Here is where we found the true cause of their great mistake. Here is the principle that is dissolving a great union. Among the many elements of strength and endurance it possesses, one element is missing—religious unity. It is therefore impossible to have a reconciliation, because they are divided on a moral question, and moral questions are fundamentally grounded in religious dogma.
>
> Some states are for slavery and some states are against it. Since none dare define slavery as either good or unrighteous, simply because it is profitable or unprofitable for that one, both parties use biblical arguments to

defend their rights. But supposing that these rights were assured by an *authority* respected by both parties. Then the Bible could come into the conflict not as a play-thing, but as in a contest of truth against falsehood. Would not such an authority perhaps have an almost invincible strength over the two parties, so that one would surrender or that both would be reconciled to each other? But in the states dogmas are very free, as are also moral principles, and everything in these spheres is mere probability. Their independence makes it impossible to find a solution to their quarrel, both because they lack a central religious authority and because they lack moral honesty, which is itself a consequence of not having a central religious authority.[44]

The Roman Jesuit had made a serious point about the need, in the American environment, for a force above democratic competition. But it was a point no American Protestant was willing to hear, even if *Civiltà Cattolica* was distributed fairly widely in the states, and some American Catholics made arguments of a similar sort. Intrinsic value notwithstanding, Roman Catholicism was too thoroughly "the Other" in the myth of a godly, Protestant America to edge into the public conversation. Whatever the American Civil War may have shown about the desirability of a magisterial interpretation of Scripture, most Americans were hardly in position to consider Rome as the source of that authority.

Churchly Protestants

Immigrant Lutherans and the high-church Mercersburg movement among the German Reformed offered another orthodox alternative to the literal Reformed understanding of Scripture. Both Lutherans and the Mercersburg theologians employed approaches to Scripture that, while orthodox, deviated from the dominant American hermeneutic. These "church Protestants" tended to approach the Bible as an organic whole. Following Martin Luther, Lutherans stressed the exercise of Law and Gospel in the Bible, thus asking how a passage illuminated the standing of the reader before God in sin or grace, instead of seeking immediately to discover its ethical implications for the believer. Early polemics with Calvinists over the meaning of the Lord's Supper, and later skirmishing with Anabaptists and Baptists on the question of who should be baptized and at what stage of life, had given the Lutherans—who, to be sure, could cite literal chapter and verse when it suited their needs—a habit of defending their distinctive views of the real presence of Christ in the Lord's Supper and baptismal regeneration for infants as much from the general meaning of the whole Bible as from the dictate of any one text.

In America, the foundations for articulating such a hermeneutic had been laid early and well. Henry Melchior Mühlenberg (1711–1787), patriarch of Lutheranism in North America, eventually became skilled in the use of English, but he did not Americanize his approach to Scripture or Lutheran traditions. Mühlenberg's successor as the leading American Lutheran, J.H.C. Helmuth, spoke out even more sharply than his predecessor about the need to retain Lutheran hermeneutics as well as Lutheran doctrine in the American sea of democratic individualism. In 1793, he registered a Lutheran protest to what, even at that time, was becoming the characteristic American approach to the Bible:

> It is altogether harmful when someone reads his whims and fantasies into this holy book. When such ones explain spiritual things according to their own imaginations and dig into the great mysteries where God has not made them known, where God has chosen rather to communicate events that really took place. This is to make a weathervane out of Scripture and so turn it in every direction of the imagination, pointing to the East with this one and with others who knows where.[45]

However shrewd Helmuth's observations were, few Lutherans in the decades before the next major European migrations maintained his critique of the American hermeneutic.

For their part, the Mercersburg theologians emerged as sharp critics of American revivalistic individualism and as critics of what they called "Puritanism" (or woodenly literal) approaches to biblical doctrine.[46] In a series of works that both set out his differences with American Protestant individualism and expressed his own blend of sixteenth-century Protestant confessionalism with nineteenth-century mediating romanticism, J. W. Nevin defended what he felt he had learned from the German Reformed Heidelberg Catechism about the Christ-centered nature of Bible religion, the union of believers and Christ in the church, and the centrality of the sacraments (interpreted organically rather than mechanically) for the Christian. After Philip Schaff, fresh from study with Germany's conservative mediating theologians, joined Nevin in Pennsylvania, Mercersburg featured a respect for history and church traditions (including the Roman Catholic) otherwise unusual in American Protestantism.[47]

The result was a theology that, at least in principle, offered a churchly, sacramental, Christ-centered alternative to literal Reformed exegesis. On the eve of the sectional struggle, an author in the *Mercersburg Review* explained how "synodical church authority" differed from both the Roman Catholic concentration of authority in a single person and the opposite mistake of American individualistic Protestantism "which makes this power culminate in the people." On the basis of the theological foundation established by Nevin and Schaff, the author claimed that the synod, or corporate mind of a Protestant church, "is the final judge of error in doctrine, and error in conduct."[48]

With both the Lutherans and the German Reformed, therefore, there existed an approach to the Bible and the exercise of Christian authority at odds with the axioms that prevailed so widely in American Protestantism. As the events of mid-century unrolled, however, this alternative remained hidden away in German-language enclaves or proved far less distinctive in the particular cases of slavery and sectional conflict than the background theories might have suggested. Mercersburg theologians turned out to reason just like their Protestant fellows when it came to specific issues—that is, they reasoned from Scripture and intuition rather than from the deliverances of a synod.[49] The presence in the abstract of a theological alternative to the Reformed literal exegesis was no guarantee that this hermeneutic could actually function in the face of pressing circumstances.

The distinctive Lutheran approach to Scripture also remained virtually mute in public discussion. A process of Americanization encouraged Lutheran leaders like Samuel Schmucker of Gettysburg and John Bachman of South Carolina to soften Lutheran distinctiveness in order to assist the broader Protestant purposes of evangelization and Christianization. Such moves left Lutherans without a distinctly Lutheran contribution. Schmucker, for example, was a strong backer of the Evangelical Alliance, a strong defender of temperance, and an advocate for sabbath observance; his vigorous antislavery stance was of a piece with these American positions.[50] Bachman's defense of slavery was southern rather than Lutheran.[51] Not until after the war did an articulate "old Lutheran" voice emerge. Its articulation in combination with the swelling tides of German and Scandinavian immigrants eventually restored a distinctly Lutheran theology, but also removed it almost entirely from meaningful dialogue with American public life.[52] In sum, the churchly Protestant alternative to literal Reformed exegesis delivered far less at the time of the Civil War than the internal shape and the distinguished heritage of the positions made possible.

Conservative Reformed

The orthodox alternative to literal Reformed biblicism with the best chance of securing a hearing during the Civil War era was the confessional Reformed biblicism practiced by Old School Presbyterians of the border and northern states. Old School Presbyterians—by exploiting the literal Reformed hermeneutic—provided the South with its strongest biblical arguments for slavery. Northern conservative Presbyterians were, by the very principles that constructed their faith, in the best position in the North to show how orthodox employment of Scripture could escape the conclusions that Thornwell and his allies defended.

If the Reformed impulse was always imperiled by its own success as well as by degeneration into mere pietism, mere dogmatism, or mere morality, it also displayed remarkable powers of renewal. Even as the American Civil War unfolded, both phases of the cycle could be observed in Europe. In Scotland, the break-up of the established Kirk in 1843 and the subsequent failure of either Kirk or Free Church to reestablish moral hegemony was leading to the decline of a powerful Reformed civilization.[53] At the same time, however, in the Netherlands the piety of a folk revival was drawing into its ranks some leaders of great intellectual energy—like a young minister, Abraham Kuyper, who was being converted from Enlightenment rationalism to Reformed pietism in the little village of Beesd at the very time that the great armies of North and South were facing off against each other in the United States.[54] Soon that mix of piety, intellect, and worldly wisdom would blossom into a renaissance of Reformed cultural influence in Holland.

In America, similar Reformed energy, in several guises, had contributed to the christianization of the nation in the decades after the Revolution. In the South, the defense of slavery so coopted this energy, however, as to leave Reformed leaders the servants of culture rather than its arbiters.[55] In the northern and border states, while the temptation to subordinate theology to the zeitgeist was nearly as strong, enough space remained for theologians to shape their environment even as they were shaped by it.

If there had been in America at the time of the Civil War what there had been in Calvin's Geneva, seventeenth-century New England, the Scotland of Thomas Chalmers, or the Netherlands of Abraham Kuyper—that is, a pious, doctrinally rigorous and culturally encompassing vision—it would have come from the conservative Presbyterians. If it had been possible to rescue the Reformed hermeneutic from proslavery, they would have been the ones to do it. If it had been possible to be spurred by the agonies of the war to general theological breakthrough, they would have been the ones to carry it out.

It did not happen.

It did not happen among Congregationalists because the most able defenders of the conservative positions—like Moses Stuart of Andover Seminary—were gone by the time of the war, and their successors had mostly embarked on the path of dividing historic Reformed understandings of Scripture into a letter that could be held lightly and a spirit that remained. It did not happen among New School Presbyterians—like the extraordinarily capable Henry Boynton Smith of New York's Union Seminary—for a more complicated set of reasons. For the sake of exerting influence on the mass of Americans who trusted a literal Bible, Smith was too quick to concede "the sinfulness of the slave system," and in his major writings on the war he was drawn off too easily from the question of the Bible and slavery in order to demonstrate for Americans and especially the British, "the pestilent heresy of *secession*."[56]

Conservative Presbyterians who felt the force of the proslavery biblical argument but who yet retained a desire to shape culture in Christian ways offered the best chance for articulating an orthodox hermeneutic that could escape the proslavery defense championed by their Southern Presbyterian contemporaries. The two most likely candidates for this role were Robert Breckinridge (1800–1871) of Kentucky and Charles Hodge (1797–1878) of Princeton.

Both Breckinridge and Hodge felt the force of proslavery arguments, yet both resisted the hermeneutical logic of the South. Breckinridge did so by attempting to define slavery, not in the abstract, but as it existed concretely in the slave states. He did this most effectively as early as 1833, and, despite a gradually weakening position, he maintained something of his early edge on the question.[57]

Hodge moved in a different direction. In a series of learned works, he conceded the biblical grounding for slavery as an institution, but argued that a proper understanding of Scripture, as well as a right judgment on American circumstances, should move toward the amelioration of slavery and then its effacement.[58]

Unfortunately for Hodge's later reputation, his attack on the biblical exegesis of abolitionists has been remembered more clearly than his defense of gradual emancipation. His attack on the abolitionists and his defense of obeying the fugitive slave laws were so effective that two of his earliest essays on the subjects were incorporated in the compendium, *Cotton Is King*, published on the eve of the Civil War.[59] What the editor of this work abridged out of the reprinting, however, was Hodge's predictions about the course of slavery in the South:

> The South, therefore, has to choose between emancipation by the silent and holy influence of the gospel, securing the elevation of the slaves to the stature and character of freemen, or to abide the issue of a long continued conflict against the laws of God. That the issue will be disastrous there can be no doubt. . . . If the South deliberately keep these millions in this state of degradation, they must prepare themselves for the natural consequences, whatever they may be.[60]

The shape of argument was similar for both Breckinridge and Hodge. Both conceded that the Bible sanctioned "slavery," but Breckinridge denied that what the South practiced was biblical slavery, while Hodge felt that the Bible hedged the practice of a legitimate slavery with so many ameliorations that the practice must end when those ameliorations were pursued to their logical "gospel" conclusion.

The specifically hermeneutical stance adopted by both was a tacit abandonment of biblical literalism. Both took for granted that the Bible must be an interpreted book, and that the meaning of its words must be conditioned by other realities—with Breckinridge, shifting social conditions over time, with Hodge the fuller context of the Scriptures themselves. Both retained the Reformed conviction that the Bible provided norms for all of life, but both insisted that these norms be interpreted with respect to the entire message of the Bible, new social conditions, or both.

There existed, therefore, at least the potential of an orthodox Reformed hermeneutic at work as an alternative to literal, Reformed biblicism. Along with hermeneutics from churchly Protestants, Roman Catholics, and African Americans, these stances preserved historic orthodoxy but set out principles for interpreting the Bible that rescued it from the grip of American proslavery.

In the event, none of these hermeneutics worked. None influenced in a substantial way theological reasoning on or during the Civil War. In addition, none was able to compete after the war with the growing strength of the liberalism that had been spurred by separating the letter from the spirit, or with the revamped biblical literalism that by the end of the nineteenth century had reconfigured itself in dispensational, Holiness, pentecostal, and southern conservative forms of populist Protestantism.

The alternative orthodox hermeneutics failed for several reasons. In the first instance, the groups that proposed them were culturally marginal. The Catholic hermeneutic was beyond the pale because Catholicism was beyond the pale. Lutherans and German Reformed mediating theologians were not sufficiently American. African-American hermeneutics shared much with dominant American patterns, but blacks appropriated the American hermeneutic in ways that violated, or were irrelevant to, the white consensus on how to read the Bible. The Reformed alternative to literalism was not marginal, but it could not overcome its greatest potential strength—its very similarity to the dominant hermeneutic. The difficulty was both structural and personal.

Conservative Reformed thinkers struggled to decide whether slavery was an evil in itself (*malum in se*) or a permissible institution that might engender evil if it were not regulated correctly.[61] The importance of the *malum in se* argument was linked to the hermeneutical issue. There seemed to be only one practical course, if one concluded that the Bible did not regard slavery as a *malum in se*. Because of the populist regulative principle in which it was necessary to find a command in the Bible to carry out an action, Bible-believing emancipationists felt they had to find slavery a *malum in se* in Scripture in order to campaign against it.

Hodge and Breckinridge were prevented by the stultifying influence of the regulative principle (and especially in its southern variation as "the spirituality of the church") from asking what general principles should be sought in a polity controlled not by a Semitic tribe warring against other tribes nor dominated by Romans bent on ruling the world but in a state where both Constitution and legislation were influenced by eighteen centuries of Christian development and where some of the legislators were themselves Christians. Hodge and Breckinridge seemed to realize implicitly that when conditions in which words were spoken changed, so did the implications of the words. But unlike their contemporary John Henry Newman, they were never able to justify that implicit sense.

In the end, personal factors also made it impossible to make Newman's case in Presbyterian dress. Breckinridge lacked the mental agility to make his case. As the struggle intensified, so too did his flight to the merely rhetorical and to a simple filiopietism of nation.[62] For his part, Hodge was hamstrung by a constitutional conservatism that left him more troubled by the abolitionist threat to biblical truth than slavery's threat to biblical holiness.[63]

Race

The main reason, however, that alternative hermeneutics failed, as well as the main reason for the conceptual confusion on Scripture in the division between North and South, was race. The Bible and race was not the same question as the Bible and slavery, although only African Americans perceived this reality clearly. With the others it was virtually impossible for Americans to recognize that these issues were not the same, precisely because of the intuitive biblical literalism that prevailed among the country's dominant Protestant bodies. Only a biblical exegesis informed by the self-confidence of moral intuitions on race could have been blind to the fact that a biblical defense of slavery and of a slave system restricted to African Americans were two different matters. What David Brion Davis has written about the economic situation, however, was just as true for the theological situation: "In the United States . . . the problem of slavery . . . had become fatally intertwined with the problem of race. Race had become the favored idiom for interpreting the social effects of enslavement and emancipation and for concealing the economy's parasitic dependence on an immensely profitable labor system."[64]

Some African Americans, like Frederick Douglass, were certainly able to see the problem. In March 1861, he wrote that "nobody at the North, we think, would defend Slavery, even from the Bible, but for this color distinction. . . . Color makes all the difference in the application of our American Christianity. . . . The same Book which is full of the Gospel of Liberty to one race, is crowded with arguments in justification of the slavery of another. Those who shout and rejoice over the progress of Liberty in Italy, would mob down, pray and preach down Liberty at home as an unholy and hateful thing."[65]

One southern intellectual, at the far end of the ideological spectrum from Frederick Douglass, saw things the same way. In works from 1854 (*Sociology for the South or, The Failure of Free Society*) and 1857 (*Cannibals All! or, Slaves Without Masters*), George Fitzhugh of Virginia included full discussion of biblical arguments for slavery. In contrast to Douglass, he thought an open-and-shut case existed for slavery in Scripture. But with Douglass, he thought the Bible was color-blind. In 1857, Fitzhugh concluded, "if white slavery [i.e., as well as black slavery] be morally wrong . . . , the Bible cannot be true."[66] Fitzhugh, however, made just as scant an impact on the general discussion as did Douglass.

Although debate over exegetical questions had indeed advanced by the time of the war, that advance did not affect prevailing intuitions about race. Belief that the Curse of Canaan from Genesis 9:25ff applied to blacks in mid-nineteenth-century America still flourished among the people at large, but was largely passé among intellectual elites. Occasional theologians like Philip Schaff or Rabbi Raphal might be willing to speculate on the relevance of the passage to the modern situation of American slaves.[67] But most elite theologians had long since dismissed that kind of application in favor of a reading that saw the prophecy fulfilled when the children of Israel conquered the Promised Land.[68]

The problem with race and the Bible was far more profound than the interpretation of any one text. It was a problem exacerbated by the intuitive character of the reigning American hermeneutic. This hermeneutic merged two positions: (1) The Bible was a plain book whose meanings could be reliably ascertained through the exercise of an ordinary person's intelligence; moreover, the primary reason for trusting the Bible's assertions was an intuitive sense, sealed by the Holy Spirit, that the Bible was true; (2) The same intelligence that through ordinary means and intuitions could trust the Bible as true also gained much additional truth about the world through intuitive processes that were held to be the deliverances of universal common sense.[69]

In American discussion of the Bible and slavery, the two positions became one. The precise problem was the indiscriminate mingling of truths delivered by plain, universal, intuitive common sense. Exegetes merged their conclusions from the Bible (derived through intuitive literalism) with their conclusions from commonsense intuitions that blacks were an inferior people fit by nature for what Philip Schaff called the "wholesome discipline of slavery."[70]

On slavery, exegetes stood for a commonsense reading of the Bible.

On race, exegetes forsook the Bible and relied on common sense.

Exegetes were unable to tell the difference between commonsense reading of the Bible and other commonsense intuitions because of the dominant Protestant rejection of self-conscious traditions, procedures, and arguments, even if these mediating constructs were drawn from Scripture. Intuitive judgments on American slavery were, therefore, sanctified by the culture's intuitive biblicism and literally *colored* by the culture's intuitive racism.

Confusion existed between commonsense biblicism and commonsense racism in almost every one of the period's significant writings on the subject. Lay southern intellectuals, for example, were pleased to repeat the biblical arguments of theologians in defense of slavery, but when they pinpointed Africans as the proper subjects of biblically sanctioned slavery, they were as likely to cite Herodotus, Josephus, or other ancient historians as the Scriptures.[71]

As for the theologians, I single out conservative Reformed leaders, since their reasoning was the most rigorous and the most self-consciously orthodox on Scripture. Among these theological luminaries, Charles Hodge was the most profound theological reasoner on both slavery and the traumas of the war. His publications on slavery, from a first major essay in 1835, tried consistently to differentiate between biblical reasoning on the institution of slavery and on the dignity owed to all people under God. During the war, he was the one major theologian to ponder the way in which multiple cause-and-effect relationships seemed to be at work in American moral, military, social, and religious life.[72]

But even this great theologian—who was so careful to base his every conclusion on the warrant of Scripture as discovered through an intellectually rigorous, morally sensitive study of the whole Bible—blithely incorporated racial assumptions into the exegetical process as if they carried the same weight as his conclusions from Scripture. To cite examples only from his first major essay on the subject, Hodge insisted that, whatever authorities radical abolitionists or proslavery defenders might enlist, he would "recognize no authoritative rule of truth and duty but the word of God. . . . It is our object . . . not to discuss the subject of slavery upon abstract principles, but to ascertain the scriptural rule of judgment and conduct in relation to it." But as soon as Hodge left the arena of what could be deduced from Scripture and entered into a discussion of the American situation, other warrants than simply the Bible immediately leaped to the fore. So it was, for example, that the hereditary "organization of society" was enough to justify making "the free colored man" at birth "a disfranchised outcast' "; it was a truth "on all hands admitted" that blacks "could not, consistently with the public welfare, be entrusted with the exercise of political power"; and it was "the *acknowledged* [my italics] right of the State to govern them [blacks, slave or free] by laws in the formation of which they have no voice."[73] Not once did recognition dawn that, in letting these self-evident intuitions of white American society function as warrants, Hodge deviated from his stated intention to restrict reasoning to the Bible alone.

Charles Hodge was a consequential theologian and thoroughly convinced that the life of the Christian must be normed by the Bible and the Bible alone. But so pervasive was the instinct of racism, even in his guileless soul, that he could not see how thoroughly he intertwined conclusions about what the Bible taught and opinions about the nature of African Americans that arose from no text of Scripture. The Bible was a lot clearer on slavery than on the enslavement of one race only, but Hodge could not tell the difference.

If Hodge, the most perceptive Old School Presbyterian in the North, could not tell the difference, it is little wonder that the distinction between slavery and the enslavement of African Americans was completely lost on his southern counterparts.

Shortly after the conclusion of the war, failure to note the difference between reasoning from the Bible on slavery and from cultural instincts on race was illustrated with great force by Robert L. Dabney, a once-generous theologian of painstaking morality and winning qualities whom the defeat of the South turned into an acidic jeremiah. When, immediately after the war, Presbyterians in the upper South proposed to ordain African Americans as clergymen, Dabney opposed the proposal with a spontaneous speech that both he and observers later called the greatest rhetorical performance in a long life studded with magnificent oratory.[74] When Dabney, who as an advocate of "the spirituality of the church" held to the regulative principle even more strongly than Hodge, rose to speak in the Synod of Virginia on November 9, 1867, the Bible went right out the window. The first half of his speech offered only intuitive tribal sentiment, especially on the spectre of black-white intermarriage. This spectre was not, as Dabney described it, a "blind, passionate prejudice of caste, but [came from] the righteous, rational *instinct* of pious minds." Only after this appeal to intuition did Dabney then turn to lame arguments from the Bible, but here he reasoned very much as the abolitionists whose arguments he so abominated had reasoned on the question of slavery—that the tendency, spirit, or precedents of the Bible spoke against such ordination in a white church.[75] In this instance the vaunted doctrine of "the spirituality of the church"—which held that a church should follow the Bible and the Bible only—was demonstrated by one of its most ardent exponents to be a thoroughly unreliable guide to exegesis.

Another of the most telling examples of race crowding out exegesis came in one of the most important pronouncements of the South's most respected theological leader, James Henley Thornwell. In May 1861, Thornwell was asked to draft a defense of secession and the southern way of life for the new Southern Presbyterian Church, then meeting in its first general assembly.

When he came to defend slavery by the Bible, Thornwell began with the ritualistic, but no less vital, profession that he would reason only from Scripture: "let it be distinctly borne in mind that the only rule of judgment is the written word of God. . . . [The church] is founded . . . upon express *revelation*. Her creed is an authoritative testimony of God, and not a speculation. . . ." Thornwell then offered an abridged version of the standard biblical defense of slavery.

When, in the course of his discussion, however, he began to talk about slavery in the South, he made—without noticing it at all—the critical discursive shift from talking about "slavery" as legitimated in Scripture to blacks as the sole objects of American slavery. There is only the hint of a beat with the beginning of a new paragraph to mark the shift from "slavery" to "Africans," but that hint is immediately muffled as Thornwell lays on the white noise of Providence to obscure the transition:

> We feel that the souls of our slaves are a solemn trust, and we shall strive to present them faultless and complete before the presence of God.
>
> Indeed, as we contemplate their condition in the Southern States, and contrast it with that of their fathers before them, and that of their brethren in the present day in their native land, we cannot but accept it as a gracious Providence that they have been brought in such numbers to our shores, and redeemed from the bondage of barbarism and sin.

Then in what would have been an obvious departure from the profession to reason from the Bible alone—had not the American hermeneutic absorbed so thoroughly the principles of intuitive moral reasoning—Thornwell defended southern practice by the intuitions of moral philosophy. In this line of argument, Thornwell continued to assume—rather than argue for, or adduce Scripture to demonstrate the propriety of—mixing categories by saying "slaves" when he meant "African slaves."

Eventually Thornwell's reliance on the intuitive deliverances of moral philosophy was blatant. His justification for treating Africans as the lowest class of human beings (as well as the assumption that humans could be divided into classes by race) sounded pious, but arose entirely from intuition: "The truth is, the education of the human race for liberty and virtue, is a vast Providential scheme, and God assigns to every man, by a wise and holy decree, the precise place he is to occupy in the great moral school of humanity. The scholars are distributed into classes, according to their competency and progress. For God is in history." As a warrant for such conclusions, Thornwell relied on an authority having nothing to do with the Bible. It was intuition alone that capped his argument on slavery: "That test is an inward necessity of thought, which, in all minds at the proper stage of maturity, is absolutely universal. Whatever is universal is natural. We are willing that slavery should be tried by this standard." Finally, at the end of his appeal to intuition, Thornwell drifted back from Africans to slavery: "the overwhelming majority of mankind have approved it."[76]

The confusion in Thornwell's thought is further suggested by one of his most courageous pronouncements. Before the dignitaries of Columbia at the South Carolina state fast day on November 21, 1860, Thornwell urged his hearers to apply the Golden Rule in the treatment of their slaves: "Here we render to our slaves what, if we were in their circumstances, we should think it right and just in them to render to us."[77] Given the way in which race influenced the American interpretation of the Bible, it is certain that Thornwell meant—"if we were black and the slaves were white"—and most emphatically did not mean—"if the black children of Daniel Payne would one day come to own the white children of J. H. Thornwell."

One can imagine counter-factually that those who felt the Bible sanctioned slavery in general could have mounted arguments from the Bible to justify the enslavement of Africans, and only Africans, in particular. But since there are no arguments in the Bible of the latter kind, a hidden hand had to function in the exegetical process if the Bible were to justify the racial slavery that existed in the United States—and if faith in America's Bible-only literalism were to be preserved. That hidden hand was the widespread, deeply ingrained, thoroughly American—though hardly biblical—conviction that among the peoples of the earth only Africans were uniquely set apart for chattel bondage.

The question of the Bible and slavery in the era of the Civil War was never a simple question. The issue involved the American expression of a Reformed literal hermeneutic, the failure of hermeneutical alternatives to gain cultural authority, and the exercise of deeply entrenched intuitive racism, as well as the presence of Scripture as an authoritative religious book and slavery as an inherited social-economic relationship. The North—forced to fight on unfriendly terrain that it had helped to create—lost the exegetical war. The South certainly lost the shooting war. But constructive orthodox theology was the major loser when American believers allowed bullets instead of hermeneutical self-consciousness to determine what the Bible said about slavery. For the history of theology in America, the great tragedy of the Civil War is that the most persuasive theologians were the Rev. Drs. William Tecumseh Sherman and Ulysses S. Grant.

Notes

1. The stimulating essays of Eugene D. Genovese and Elizabeth Fox-Genovese have opened up this subject in a truly remarkable way, especially Genovese, *"Slavery Ordained of God": The Southern Slaveholders' View of Biblical History and Modern Politics,* 24th Annual Fortenbaugh Memorial Lecture, Gettysburg College, 1985; Genovese and Fox-Genovese, "The Religious Ideals of Southern Slave Society," *Georgia Historical Quarterly* 70 (Spring 1986): 4–5, 13–14; Fox-Genovese and Genovese, "The Divine Sanction of Social Order: Religious Foundations of the Southern Slaveholders' World View," *Journal of the American Academy of Religion* 55 (Summer 1987): 211–233; and Genovese, *The Slaveholders' Dilemma: Freedom and Progress in Southern Conservative Thought, 1820–1860* (Columbia, SC, 1992). Two fine essays helped convince me to take seriously the integrity of proslavery use of Scripture: Jack P. Maddex Jr., " 'The Southern Apostasy' Revisited: The Significance of Proslavery Christianity," *Marxist Perspectives* 7 (1979): 132–141; and Gaines M. Foster, "Guilt Over Slavery: A Historiographical Analysis," *Journal of Southern History* 56 (1989): 665–694. From a full literature on the question of the Bible and slavery in the era of the Civil War, I have been especially helped by Caroline L. Shanks, "The Biblical Anti-Slavery Argument of the Decade, 1830–1840," *Journal of Negro History* 16 (1931): 132–157; Timothy L. Smith, *Revivalism and Social Reform: American Protestantism on the Eve of the Civil War* (New York, 1957), 178–224; Perry Miller, *The Life of the Mind in America from the Revolution to the Civil*

War (New York, 1965), 93–94; Lewis M. Purifoy, "The Southern Methodist Church and the Proslavery Argument," *Journal of Southern History* 32 (August 1966): 325–341; David Brion Davis, *The Problem of Slavery in the Age of Revolution, 1770–1823* (Ithaca, NY, 1975), 531–556; Drew Gilpin Faust, "Evangelicalism and the Meaning of the Proslavery Argument: The Reverend Thornton Stringfellow of Virginia," *Virginia Magazine of History and Biography* 85 (January 1977): 3–17; James H. Moorhead, *American Apocalypse: Yankee Protestants and the Civil War, 1860–1869* (New Haven, CT, 1978); Robert Bruce Mullin, "Biblical Critics and the Battle Over Slavery," *Journal of Presbyterian History* 61 (Summer 1983): 210–226; Ron Bartour, "American Views on 'Biblical Slavery': 1835–1865, A Comparative Study," *Slavery and Abolition* 4 (May 1983): 41–55; John R. McKivigan, *The War Against Proslavery Religion: Abolitionism and the Northern Churches, 1830–1865* (Ithaca, NY, 1984); and Larry E. Tise, *Proslavery: A History of the Defense of Slavery in America, 1701–1840* (Athens, GA, 1987). For a historian who, like myself, regards the Bible as divine revelation in a traditional sense of that term, but who also feels that Scripture was abused in defending American slavery, the danger of historical partiality when treating this subject is great. I trust that the arguments developed here, though they serve that combination of convictions, will be sufficiently attentive to what actually took place to merit attention from those who do not share my views.

2. Albert Barnes, *An Inquiry into the Scriptural Views of Slavery* (Philadelphia, 1846).

3. Mullin, "Biblical Critics and the Battle Over Slavery," 226n42; on Albert Barnes, *Inquiries and Suggestions in Regard to the Foundation of Faith in the Word of God* (Philadelphia, 1859), especially 44–53.

4. For a discussion of the large evangelical factor in every election from 1840 through 1860, see Richard J. Carwardine, *Evangelicals and Politics in Antebellum America* (New Haven, CT, 1993).

5. *Fast Day Sermons: or the Pulpit on the State of the Country* (New York, 1861).

6. Thornwell, "Our National Sins," in ibid., 44.

7. See the sermons by Henry J. Van Dyke and Rabbi M. J. Raphall, in ibid.

8. Beecher, "Peace, Be Still," in ibid., 286, 287, 289.

9. James Stirling, *Letters from the Slave States* (London, 1857), 117, 118, 120. I was alerted to Stirling's observations by Genovese, *Slavery Ordained of God*, 30n58.

10. *An Address to Christians Throughout the World, by a Convention of Ministers, Assembled at Richmond, Virginia, April, 1863* (Philadelphia, 1863), 17–20.

11. David B. Chesebrough, *God Ordained this War: Sermons on the Sectional Crisis, 1830–1865* (Columbia, SC, 1991), 297–349 (where identifications of ministers are incomplete); Chesebrough, *"No Sorrow Like Our Sorrow": Northern Protestant Ministers and the Assassination of Lincoln* (Kent, OH, 1994), xvi, 149–192 (where denominational identification is nearly complete).

12. Robert H. Wiebe, *The Opening of American Society from the Adoption of the Constitution to the Eve of Disunion* (New York, 1984); Nathan O. Hatch, *The Democratization of American Christianity* (New Haven, CT, 1989); Gordon S. Wood, *The Radicalism of the American Revolution* (New York, 1992).

13. See on the rise of "Christians" and "Disciples," Richard T. Hughes and C. Leonard Allen, *Illusions of Innocence: Protestant Primitivism in America, 1630–1875* (Chicago, 1988), 102–132; and, on the general phenomenon, Hatch, *Democratization of American Christianity*.

14. Works in which this familiarity is particularly well illustrated or defined are Lewis O. Saum, *The Popular Mood of Pre-Civil War America* (Westport, CT, 1980);

Carwardine, *Evangelicals and Politics*; and Genovese and Fox-Genovese, "Religious Ideals of Southern Slave Society," 9–14. Reference to the use of Scripture between the Revolution and the Civil War in the testimonials of presidents and other social leaders, by Bible societies, in the naming of children and places, and in public iconography is found in Mark A. Noll, "The Image of the United States as a Biblical Nation, 1776–1865," in *The Bible in American Culture*, eds. Nathan O. Hatch and Mark A. Noll (New York, 1982), 40–41, 52–53.

15. Margaret T. Hills, *The English Bible in America* (New York, 1962), 1–266; Peter J. Wosh, *Bibles, Benevolence and Emerging Bureaucracy: The Persistence of the American Bible Society* (Ithaca, NY, 1994).

16. Hills, *English Bible in America*, 255; Philip Schaff, *Der Bürgerkrieg und das christliche Leben in Nord-Amerika* (Berlin, 1866), 31, 50; and W. Harrison Daniel, "Bible Publication and Procurement in the Confederacy," *Journal of Southern History* 24 (1958): 191–201.

17. Hatch, *Democratization of American Christianity*, 182–183.

18. A preliminary survey of Protestant periodicals from England, Scotland, and Canada reveals that these foreign Protestants often spoke out energetically against both slavery and the North, but also that the American debate over the use of Scripture had almost no resonance outside the United States.

19. Once the war began, northern moderates and conservatives were often driven to abolitionism by the extreme southern defense of slavery as a biblical institution. The case of Charles Hodge is instructive. Southern Presbyterians opined at their General Assembly in 1864 that, "We hesitate not to affirm that it is the peculiar mission of the Southern Church to conserve the institution of slavery, and to make it a blessing both to master and to slave." Hodge's reaction showed how far the war had moved him on the question of slavery: "It is enough to humble the whole Christian world to hear our Presbyterian brethren in the South declaring that the great mission of the Southern church was to conserve the system of slavery. Since the death of Christ no such dogma stains the record of an ecclesiastical body." Hodge, "President Lincoln," *Princeton Review* 37 (July 1865): 439. The Southern Assembly is quoted (and Hodge at length refuted) in John Adger, "Northern and Southern Views of the Province of the Church," *Southern Presbyterian Review* 16 (March 1865): 389.

20. Beecher, "Peace, Be Still," in *Fast Day Sermons*, 289.

21. One of the earliest Catholic polemics against Protestant Bible–only thinking made this argument in classic form, Robert Bellarmine, *Disputationes de Controversiis Christianae Fidei* (1586–1593).

22. This response is well canvased in many of the individuals studied in George M. Fredrickson, *The Inner Civil War: Northern Intellectuals and the Crisis of the Union* (New York, 1965); and Anne C. Rose, *Victorian America and the Civil War* (New York, 1992).

23. See the early pages of William R. Hutchison, *The Modernist Impulse in American Protestantism* (Cambridge, MA, 1976).

24. Mark Pattison, "Tendencies of Religious Thought in England, 1688–1750," in *Essays and Reviews* (London, 1860), 328. The presence of Pattison's historical essay in this work ensured that it would be widely read, since the book's modernist proposals (Pattison's piece is much less radical) and the notoriety it had gained in England meant that it was widely reviewed in the states as well.

25. Thornwell, "Our National Sins," in *Fast Day Sermons*, 50.

26. Journals sampled include those from Canadian and Scottish Presbyterians, as well as English Anglicans; supporting this conclusion are several essays by W. Harrison

Daniel, including "The Reaction of British Methodism to the Civil War and Recon-struction in America," *Methodist History* 16 (1977): 3–20; "The Response of the Church of England to the Civil War and Reconstruction in America," *Historical Magazine of the Protestant Episcopal Church* 47 (1978): 57–72; and "English Presbyterians, Slavery and the American Crisis of the 1860s," *Journal of Presbyterian History* 58 (1980): 50–62.

27. Richard W. Vaudry, *The Free Church in Victorian Canada, 1844–1861* (Water-loo, Ontario, 1989), 78–79, with quotations from Free Church minutes.

28. On Henry Van Dyke's veneration of Thornwell, see Moorhead, *American Apoc-alypse*, 128n122. The lack of foreign sympathy for his biblical reasoning speaks against the notion that Thornwell was "arguably, second to none [among theologians] in the United States"—Fox-Genovese and Genovese, "The Divine Sanction of Social Order," 217. On the question of preeminence, a comparison with Charles Hodge is instructive. To an uncomfortably large degree, Thornwell's reputation rested on the accidents of American social development as those accidents had constructed a singular hermeneu-tical framework, rather than on his insights concerning the *depositum fidei* itself. No African American ever said of Thornwell what Bishop Daniel Payne said of Hodge, that he was "the greatest theologian which America has yet produced" (Payne, *Recol-lections*, 248). Few if any foreigners came to South Carolina to study with Thornwell, but by the 1860s scores had arrived at Princeton from Ireland, Scotland, and Canada to study with Hodge; Peter Wallace and Mark Noll, "The Students of Princeton Sem-inary, 1812–1929: A Research Note," *American Presbyterians* 72 (Fall 1994): 203–215.

29. Apart from Thornwell's own report in 1860 that some of his essays had been reprinted to approval in the *British and Foreign Evangelical Review* (Benjamin Morgan Palmer, *The Life and Letters of James Henley Thornwell* [Richmond, VA, 1875], 454), I am not aware of attempts to trace the appeal of Thornwell's exegesis outside the United States in the substantial body of solid scholarship that now exists on him—including Morton H. Smith, *Studies in Southern Presbyterian Theology* (Philipsburg, NJ, 1962), 121–182; James Oscar Farmer Jr., *The Metaphysical Confederacy: James Henley Thornwell and the Synthesis of Southern Values* (Macon, GA, 1986); Luder G. Whitlock Jr., "James Henley Thornwell," in *Southern Reformed Theology*, ed. David F. Wells (Grand Rapids, 1989), 61–74; John H. Leith, "James Henley Thornwell and the Shaping of the Refomed Tradition in the South," in *Probing the Reformed Tradition*, eds. Elsie Anne McKee and Brian G. Armstrong (Louisville, 1989), 424–447; and William W. Freehling, "James Henley Thornwell's Mysterious Antislavery Moment," *Journal of Southern History* 57 (August 1991): 383–406.

30. David W. Blight, *Frederick Douglass' Civil War: Keeping Faith in Jubilee* (Baton Rouge, 1989), 111–113.

31. On the importance of Scripture for African-American Christians, I have found the following to be of great use: James Weldon Johnson, ed., *The Book of American Negro Spirituals* (New York, 1925), 20–21; William H. Pipes, *Say Amen, Brother! Old-Time Negro Preaching: A Study in American Frustration* (Westport, CT, 1951); Law-rence W. Levine, *Black Culture and Black Consciousness: Afro-American Folk Thought From Slavery to Freedom* (New York, 1977), 3–189; Albert J. Raboteau, *Slave Religion: The "Invisible Institution" in the Antebellum South* (New York, 1978), 239–43; Vincent L. Wimbush, "The Bible and African Americans: An Outline of an Interpretive History," in *Stony the Road We Trod: African American Biblical Interpretation*, ed. Cain Hope Felder (Minneapolis, 1991); Timothy E. Fulop, " 'The Future Golden Day of the Race': Millennialism and Black Americans in the Nadir, 1877–1901," *Harvard Theological Review* 84 (1991): 75–99; Janet Duitsman Cornelius, *When I Can Read My Title Clear: Literacy, Slavery and Religion in the Antebellum South* (Columbia, SC, 1992);

and the sources employed in the discussion of African-American use of Scripture in Noll, "The Image of the United States as a Biblical Nation," 48–51, including Eugene D. Genovese, *Roll, Jordan, Roll: The World the Slaves Made* (New York, 1976 [orig. 1974]), 159–284; Timothy L. Smith, "Slavery and Theology: The Emergence of Black Christian Consciousness in Nineteenth-Century America," *Church History* 46 (December 1972): 497–512; Donald G. Mathews, *Religion in the Old South* (Chicago, 1977), 185–236; Paul D. Escott, *Slavery Remembered: A Record of Twentieth-Century Slave Narratives* (Chapel Hill, 1979), 114; Charles V. Hamilton, *The Black Preacher in America* (New York, 1972), 38–39; E. Franklin Frazier, *The Negro Church in America*, with C. Eric Lincoln, *The Black Church Since Frazier* (New York, 1974; orig. 1963), 17–18; Henry H. Mitchell, *Black Preaching* (Philadelphia, 1970), 113; Dena J. Epstein, *Sinful Tunes and Spirituals: Black Folk Music to the Civil War* (Urbana, IL, 1977), 217–237; and Monroe Fordham, *Major Themes in Northern Black Religious Thought, 1800–1860* (Hicksville, NY, 1975), 111–137.

32. Theophus S. Smith, *Conjuring Culture: Biblical Formations of Black Americans* (New York, 1994).

33. Payne, *Recollections*, 16, 34, 85.

34. Douglass, "Slaveholding Religion," *Douglass' Monthly*, October 1860, 340.

35. Raboteau, quoted in Fulop, "Future Golden Day of the Race," 85.

36. Smith, "Slavery and Theology," 504.

37. Blight, *Frederick Douglass' Civil War*, 8, 101–103, 120–121.

38. Douglass, "Ought American Slavery to be Perpetuated?" *Douglass' Monthly*, Jan. 1859, 5.

39. On numbers of Roman Catholics during the mid-nineteenth century, see Roger Finke and Rodney Stark, *The Churching of America* (New Brunswick, NJ, 1992), 110–15.

40. For an exposition of Newman's argument and also of how Newman considered it to be a conservative argument, see Owen Chadwick, *From Bossuet to Newman*, 2nd ed. (Cambridge, 1987), 139–163.

41. For an example of such a conventional view, see "Martin John Spalding's 'Dissertation on the American Civil War' [April or May 1863]," ed. David Spalding, C.F.X., *Catholic Historical Review* 52 (April 1966): 66–85.

42. Helpful contributions include Anthony B. Lalli, S.X., and Thomas H. O'Connor, "Roman Views on the American Civil War," *Catholic Historical Review* 40 (April 1971): 21–41 (to which I owe a reference to the essay from *Civiltà Cattolica* quoted below); Walter G. Sharrow, "John Hughes and a Catholic Response to Slavery in Antebellum America," *Journal of Negro History* 57 (July 1972): 254–269; Walter G. Sharrow, "Northern Catholic Intellectuals and the Coming of the Civil War," *New-York Historical Society Quarterly* 58 (1974): 35–56; Judith Conrad Wimmer, "American Catholic Interpretations of the Civil War," Ph.D. dissertation, Drew University, 1980; and James Hennesey, S.J., *American Catholics* (New York, 1981), 143–157. An important recent book for the background to the Civil War is Jenny Franchot, *Roads to Rome: The Antebellum Protestant Encounter with Catholicism* (Berkeley, 1994).

43. April 1, 1865, as quoted in Wimmer, "American Catholic Interpretations," 285n15.

44. "La Disunione negli stati uniti," *Civiltà Cattolica* 4 (23 January 1861): 317–318. I am grateful to Maria Walford for the translation of this passage.

45. J.H.C. Helmuth, *Betrachtung der Evangelischen Lehre von der Heiligen Schrift und Taufe; samt einigen Gedanken von den gegenwärtigen Zeiten* (Germantown, PA, 1793), 67. I owe reference to this work to A. G. Roeber's unpublished essay, "J.H.C.

Helmuth and the Dilemma of American Lutheran Theological Education, 1773–1826."

46. A good summary of that criticism is found in E. Brooks Holifield, "Mercersburg, Princeton, and the South: The Sacramental Controversy in the Nineteenth Century," *Journal of Presbyterian History* 54 (Summer 1976): 238–257.

47. For a sampling of works by Nevin and Schaff, see *The Mercersburg Theology*, ed. James Hastings Nichols (New York, 1966).

48. Henry Harbaugh (Lancaster, PA), "Synodical Church Authority," *Mercersburg Review* 12 (Jan. 1860), 130, 129.

49. For example, Philip Schaff, "Slavery and the Bible," *Mercersburg Review* 13 (April 1861): 288–317; Schaff, *Der Bürgerkrieg*; and J. W. Nevin, "The Nation's Second Birth" [4th of July address], *German Reformed Messenger* 30 (no 47; July 26, 1865), 1.

50. Paul P. Kuenning, *The Rise and Fall of American Lutheran Pietism* (Macon, GA, 1988).

51. Robert M. Calhoon, "Lutheranism and Early Southern Culture," in *"A Truly Efficient School of Theology": The Lutheran Theological Seminary in Historical Context, 1830–1980*, eds. H. George Anderson and Robert M. Calhoon (Columbia, SC, 1981), 17–18; and E. Brooks Holifield, *The Gentlemen Theologians: American Theology in Southern Culture, 1795–1860* (Durham, 1978), 163, 165. For an overview of Lutheran accommodations to the views of their various regions, see Robert Fortenbaugh, "American Lutheran Synods and Slavery, 1830–60," *Journal of Religion* 13 (January 1933): 72–92.

52. A representative sample of that conservative work is found in Theodore G Tappert, *Lutheran Confessional Theology in America, 1840–1880* (New York, 1972). For an assessment of the surprisingly scant Lutheran impact on American public life, see Mark A. Noll, "Ethnic, American, or Lutheran? Dilemmas for a Historic Confession in the New World," *Lutheran Theological Seminary Review* (Winter 1991): 17–38.

53. For a well-rounded, recent discussion, see Stewart J. Brown and Michael Fry, *Scotland in the Age of the Disruption* (Edinburgh, 1993).

54. James D. Bratt, ed., *Abraham Kuyper: A Centennial Reader* (Grand Rapids, 1998), 55–61.

55. James Farmer's study of J. H. Thornwell shows how habitually even this strong theologian followed the path that Farmer describes in these words: "when theology clashes with the dominant ideology of a culture, theology is revised" (*Metaphysical Confederacy*, 201; and for examples of this phenomenon, 205, 216, 230, 264, 279, 281).

56. Henry Boynton Smith, "The Presbyterian General Assemblies," *American Theological Review* 4 (July 1862): 553; Smith, "The Moral Aspects of the Present Struggle," *American Theological Review* 3 (October 1861): 729; cf. also Smith, "British Sympathy with America," *American Theological Review* 4 (July 1862): 487–544.

57. Robert Breckinridge, "Hints on Colonization and Abolition; with reference to the black race," *Biblical Repertory and Princeton Review* 5 (July 1833): 281–305.

58. Charles Hodge, "Slavery," *Princeton Review* 7 (1835), reprinted in Hodge's *Essays and Reviews* (New York, 1857), 573–611; "West India Emancipation," *Princeton Review* 10 (October 1838): 602–644; "Abolitionism," *Princeton Review* 16 (October 1844): 545–581; "Emancipation," *Princeton Review* 21 (October 1849): 582–607.

59. Hodge, "The Fugitive Slave Law" (from "Civil Government," *Princeton Review* [1851]) and "The Bible Argument on Slavery" (from "Slavery," *Princeton Review* [1835]), in *Cotton Is King, and Pro-slavery Arguments*, ed. E. N. Elliott (Augusta, GA, 1860), 810–840, 841–877.

60. Hodge, "Slavery," in *Essays and Reviews*, 510.

61. For an outstanding discussion of the *malum in se* problem, see Mullin, "Biblical Critics and the Battle Over Slavery."

62. Breckinridge's sermon on the national fast day, January 4, 1861, is all rhetoric with no exegesis ("The Union to Be Preserved," in *Fast Day Sermons*). On Breckinridge's difficulties in maintaining his early position—against intense Kentucky opposition and his own deep fear of racial "amalgamation"—see James C. Klotter, *The Breckinridges of Kentucky, 1760–1981* (Lexington, KY, 1986), 51–81, especially 71.

63. See William S. Barker, "The Social Views of Charles Hodge (1797–1878): A Study in 19th-Century Calvinism and Conservatism," *Presbyterion: Covenant Seminary Review* 1 (Spring 1975): 1–22; and John W. Stewart, *Mediating the Center: Charles Hodge on American Science, Language, Literature, and Politics*, Studies in Reformed Theology and History, vol. 3, no. 1 (Princeton, 1995), 71–87.

64. David Brion Davis, "Reconsidering the Colonization Movement: Leonard Bacon and the Problem of Evil," *Intellectual History Newsletter* 14 (1992): 4.

65. Frederick Douglass, "The Pro-Slavery Mob and the Pro-Slavery Ministry," *Douglass' Monthly*, March 1861, 417–418.

66. George Fitzhugh, *Cannibals All!*, ed. C. Vann Woodward (Cambridge, 1960), 200; for a good discussion of Fitzhugh and the Bible, see John Ashworth, *Slavery, Capitalism, and Politics in the Antebellum Republic, Vol. 1: Commerce and Compromise, 1820–1850* (New York, 1995), 210–215, 236–237.

67. Philip Schaff, "Slavery and the Bible," *Mercersburg Review* 13 (April 1861): 289–291.

68. On the fate of the curse of Canaan arguments, see David Brion Davis, *Slavery and Human Progress* (New York, 1984), 21–22, 36, 39, 42–43, 83, 86–87. For a sharp statement of the problem, as I am construing it here, see Winthrop Jordan, *White Over Black: American Attitudes Toward the Negro, 1550–1812* (Chapel Hill, 1968), 18: "the question becomes why a tale which logically implied slavery but absolutely nothing about skin color should have become an autonomous and popular explanation of the Negro's blackness."

69. Elite versions of this commonsense instinct are well explored in the extensive literature on the rise and dominance of Scottish philosophy in post-Revolutionary America. Populist versions are well described in Hatch, *Democratization of American Christianity*; and Hughes and Allen, *Illusions of Innocence*.

70. Schaff, "Slavery and the Bible," 292.

71. Eugene Genovese, reporting on the work of T. R. R. Cobb, in *Slavery Ordained of God*, 13.

72. Hodge, "President Lincoln," *Princeton Review* 37 (July 1865): 435–436. Hodge's meditation for Princeton Seminary students on the Sunday after Lincoln's assassination is also noteworthy, in comparison with other similar efforts, for not mentioning Lincoln or the nation (at least in notes for the meditation), but also by reminding students that God saves through suffering. Transcript of notes courtesy of William Harris, Archivist, Princeton Theological Seminary. On many efforts that same day to spell out the meaning of providence for the nation, see Chesebrough, *No Sorrow Like Our Sorrow*.

73. Hodge, "Slavery" (1835), as reprinted in Hodge, *Essays and Reviews*, 479, 480, 500, 502–503, 503, 511.

74. Thomas Cary Johnson, *The Life and Letters of Robert Lewis Dabney* (Edinburgh, 1977; orig. 1903), 319–321.

75. R. L. Dabney, "Ecclesiastical Equality of Negroes," in Dabney's *Discussions: Evangelical and Theological* (London, 1967; orig. 1890), 2: 199–217, with quotation 207.

76. Thornwell, "A Southern Address to Christendom," in *American Christianity: An Historical Interpretation with Representative Documents*, eds. H. Shelton Smith, Robert T. Handy, and Lefferts A. Loetscher (New York, 1963), 2: 205–210.

77. Thornwell, "Our National Sins," in *Fast Day Sermons*, 52.

3

Religion in the Collapse of the American Union

EUGENE D. GENOVESE

I can fight your battles so long as you make the constitution your fortress," Governor William L. Marcy of New York wrote John C. Calhoun. "But if you go to the Bible or make it a question of ethics, you must not expect me or any respectable member of the free states to be with you." Marcy did not understand that the scriptural defense of slavery provided the moral foundation of the slaveholders' worldview. And as for the southern slaveholders, so for their opponents. "As I view the contest," an antislavery farmer wrote Abraham Lincoln, "it is no less than a contest for the advancement of the kingdom of Heaven or the kingdom of Satan."[1]

The abolitionists had long denounced slavery as a sin, and the Free Soil party declared slavery "a sin against God and a crime against man, which no human enactment nor usage can make right." Leonard Bacon cried out that if slavery is not wrong, nothing is wrong. Bacon appealed to the spirit of the Bible. Ferdinand Jacobs of Charleston replied that the Word expresses the Holy Spirit: "If the scriptures do not justify slavery, I know not what they do justify. If we err in maintaining this relation, I know not when we are right— truth then has parted her usual moorings and floated off into an ocean of uncertainty."[2]

As both sides well understood, the designation "sin" was decisive. "Moral evil" would not do, for both antislavery and proslavery men could speak of slavery as a moral evil and yet mean radically different things. Antislavery men equated the two terms. Although proslavery men occasionally also did so, they usually distinguished between them, assigning the moral evil of slavery to the category of all human institutions necessitated by original sin. To declare slavery a sin meant to reject all proposals for gradual emancipation, to say nothing of amelioration, for it condemned every slaveholder as a wanton sinner. It was a call to holy war.[3]

North and South shared a common Protestant Christianity, but beneath the surface a chasm was widening.[4] Slavery lay at the heart of the matter, and not only or even primarily because of the race question, for the social relations of slavery provided the soil on which cultural tendencies and attendant world-views could flourish in a manner that set the South on a course of separate national development. Southern theology—and constitutional theory—did not grow out of the social relations of slavery: empirical evidence shreds any such reductionism. Rather, the social relations of capitalism were dissolving the ground on which Christian orthodoxy and a conservative interpretation of the Constitution could be sustained, whereas the social relations of slavery were permitting them to flourish.

North and South shared language, religion, the common law, the heritage of the Revolution, political institutions, and the Union itself as myth, symbol, and ideal.[5] We should nonetheless be warned against easy generalizations by the strong cultural ties that bound the thirteen colonies to the Mother Country, as well as by the experience of such peoples as the Germans and Austrians or the Egyptians and Syrians.[6] Peoples often cohere into a nation only by fighting against a common enemy in a war that crystallizes disparate elements of sep-arate nationality. When such wars end in defeat, we all too easily assume that the rebels must not have constituted a nation after all.[7]

Two errors beckon us. We may grossly overestimate the cultural separation of North and South before 1861 and thereby impart an inevitability to the emergence of a southern nationality; or we may grossly underestimate that cultural separation and thereby implausibly reduce secession to a political blun-der or to a narrow struggle over discrete political and economic interests. On balance, however, southerners and northerners were emerging as separate peo-ples who nonetheless shared so much that they looked like a single people to foreign visitors and to many among themselves.

Americans were a religious people. Not only did they attend church but they also sought divine sanction for their social and political views. At the least, the country's most socially and politically influential leaders were either committed Christians themselves or demonstrated that they knew their polit-ically decisive constituents to be so. Both abolitionists and slaveholders ap-pealed to Scripture. Larry Tise has reported that almost half of all the pros-lavery tracts in the United States were written by ministers.[8] Roughly the same could probably be said for the antislavery tracts, and most of the antislavery and proslavery tracts by secular writers invoked scriptural argument.

Few doubt that religious conviction deeply influenced the political course of the North. Certainly, Abraham Lincoln did not doubt it, as the religious rhetoric in his political speeches proves. In contrast, many contemporary north-erners and subsequent historians have doubted that the South was a deeply religious society. It remains commonplace to assume that no honest Christian could be a slaveholder, much less regard slavery as a divinely sanctioned insti-tution. Yet southerners, high and low, were committed believers. Statistics on church membership prove little for either the South or the North. As late as 1861, in the South, as in the North, no more than 10 to 20 percent of the white population belonged to a church. But evidence abounds that many of the most pious men and women refused to join a church for a wide variety of reasons: an unwillingness to commit themselves to a particular theology; a deep sense of unworthiness in their Christian professions; an inability to submit fully to the stern demands of church discipline; the lack of a preferred denominational church in their vicinity; and more. These people nonetheless went to preaching on Sunday and often during the week, sometimes attending two or three services in a day; they often commented on the texts and sermons in their diaries and family correspondence; they certainly read their Bible; and they prayed at home as well as in church.[9]

Northerners and southerners agreed that the abolitionists were accomplishing one great feat: step by step, in the face of resistance by conservatives and moderates, they were convincing northern public opinion that, however much slavery might be tolerated for practical reasons, it was sinful. In contrast, the Reverend John Adger of South Carolina wrote in 1858 that southerners had overcome doubts about slavery, thanks to a "calm and quiet" review of Scripture. He lauded the unity of the southern churches in defense of slavery: "There is no earthly power that can overcome a whole people when animated by such convictions!" Albert Barnes, the abolitionist warrior, made the point in another way with special reference to the North: "*No influence out of the Church* could sustain slavery an hour, if it were not sustained in it."[10] The South would have been internally rent if the southern preachers had not convinced their people that slavery was ordained of God, scripturally sanctioned as part of the divine order.[11]

The influence of the churches proceeded in tandem with the extension of education. The North was astonishing the world by its rapid generation of a solidly educated population. The South, in apparent contrast, had only a feeble public educational system until after the war. Yet southerners were also being educated to an extent remarkable in that day, achieving a literacy rate of well over 80 percent. Increasingly, the yeomen as well as the slaveholders emerged as educated and capable of reading the Bible and following the controversies. Farmers and all but the poorest folks learned to read, write, and do arithmetic at home, in Sabbath schools, in old field schools and academies. The more affluent and even some of the less so attended academies and the rapidly mushrooming colleges in which they received a good classical education. The rest learned enough to qualify them as a politically knowledgeable public. Proportionately, more white southerners than northerners were attending college in 1860, and many of the southern colleges had excellent faculties and strong curricula. In both North and South the ministers presided over the educational system, but secularization was advancing markedly only in the North. In the South, religious guidance of the schools remained virtually unchallenged.[12]

"Moral Philosophy," the one generally required course in both northern and southern colleges, grounded a comprehensive social science in Christian doctrine. The churches, acting in concert and suppressing denominational differences, supervised the education of southern youth and trained the leaders of society. Political economy and political science, as well as the natural sciences, were taught within the framework of a Christian worldview, buttressed by the widely accepted philosophy of Scottish Realism. Yet, despite a common starting point, northern and southern schools parted company on the implications and ramifications of the Christian doctrine they assumed they were espousing in tandem.

The North and South generated alternate hegemonic worldviews, which, like all hegemonic worldviews, left a great deal of room for deep theological, political, and other dissent on secondary issues. The social relations of free labor and slavery, and their attendant ideological principles, go a long way toward explaining the growing political rift, manifested not merely in institutions but also in sensibility and systematic thought. As shorthand, I shall here focus on the Presbyterian church, although numerically it lagged well behind the Methodist and Baptist churches in both sections, for the Presbyterians exercised disproportionate influence over the educational system and set an ideological line closely adhered to by the Methodists, Baptists, Episcopalians, and others.

Consider especially the related trends in formal theology and popular sensibility. Christian orthodoxy, whether in Calvinist or Arminian form, remained strong in the North as well as in the South, but with an impressive difference. In the North, the orthodox were fighting a rear-guard action against a rising tide of theological and ecclesiastical liberalism. The powerful influence of Unitarianism and Universalism in New England and beyond has been well studied and amply documented.[13] Even such self-proclaimed bastions of orthodoxy as Andover and Yale looked anything but orthodox to southerners. Southern divines like James Henley Thornwell, the South's greatest theologian, saw them in a shame-faced retreat to heterodoxy. Among ordinary people in the North, religious orthodoxy remained strong but was nonetheless in retreat before mounting challenges. In contrast, only scattered and feeble challenges confronted orthodoxy in the South.

Increasingly, orthodox northerners, but not southerners, were fighting heterodoxy by making dangerous concessions to it.[14] The concessions concerned original sin, human depravity, the very nature of sin, and the shift in emphasis from an Old Testament "jealous" God of wrath to a Christology that emphasized love and forgiveness in a manner that southerners found irresponsibly one-sided.[15] And it also concerned a literal reading of the Bible as against an appeal to its spirit. Nowhere were these dichotomies absolute; everywhere, serious Christians struggled to avoid *culs de sac*. But the divergence in tendency and emphasis ran deep and wide.

Sad to say, the proslavery divines, relying on the Word, forged a strong case for the scriptural sanction of slavery, or "slavery in the abstract"—that is, slavery as the natural and proper condition of all labor, rather than for racial slavery. Indeed, their argument for the scriptural sanction of a racial slavery based on Noah's curse was so feeble that Thornwell, among others, ignored it. The southern divines pressed their opponents hard to show a single passage in the Bible that condemned slavery as sinful. Few of the antislavery divines wholly abandoned their effort to prove the Bible to be antislavery, but they never did make a good job of it. Before long, any number of them, from the abolitionist Albert Barnes to the moderately antislavery Francis Wayland, were saying that if it could be shown that the Bible sanctioned slavery, it would mean that the Bible was the Devil's book, not God's.[16] Among the southern faithful, that argument was tantamount to a declaration of infidelity. By the 1850s, the southern divines were denouncing their northern co-religionists as "baptized infidels" who no longer had faith in the Bible as the revealed Word of God. Meanwhile, the abolitionists were denouncing southerners, as well as conservative northerners, as "so-called Christians," taking for granted that real Christians could neither be slaveholders nor fail to see that slavery was inherently sinful.[17]

In accounting for the shift of the southern churches from their early opposition to slavery to a willingness to tolerate it and finally to its celebration, historians invoke a wide variety of political and sociological explanations, most of which contain an element of truth: the gentrification of the churches and their direct complicity with slave property, a growing reign of terror against antislavery ministers, and the necessity of the churches to accommodate slavery in order to get the slaveholders' permission to preach to the slaves and thereby save their immortal souls. But the early antislavery positions of the churches ran into immediate opposition, which forced a series of intense debates over Scripture. Once confronted by the assertion that slavery was inherently sinful, the divines went scurrying back to the Bible. In the event, they forged a strong proslavery case, which they carried onto the hustings as well as into the schools and theological seminaries. Their case, buttressed by impressive biblical and historical scholarship, readily accounts for the ease with which slaveholders and yeomen alike accepted slavery as divinely ordained.[18]

The division of the churches along sectional lines on the slavery issue had a subtext. The Presbyterian split of 1837 into Old School and New School sent shock waves through the United States. William Lloyd Garrison, among many, saw the beginning of the end of the Union, interpreting the split as at bottom over slavery. The place of the slavery question in the split has remained a source of controversy, for the church ostensibly divided not over slavery but over questions of theology and church governance, which probably would have arisen if slavery had not existed. But the northern synods accused of heterodoxy were hotbeds of antislavery, and the southern churches finally moved to support their expulsion in large part as a way of getting rid of a political nuisance. Old School and New School emerged with roughly equal strength in the North, whereas the South became an Old School bastion.

Many of the New School churches retreated from Calvinist orthodoxy and tolerated, when they did not promote, abandonment of longstanding commitments to the doctrines of predestination, original sin, human depravity, and much else. Meanwhile, the Old School, especially as represented in the great Presbyterian intellectual centers of Princeton, New Jersey, and Columbia, South Carolina, held the line for the Westminister Confession and for as strict a Calvinism as could practicably be sustained.[19] The slavery question increasingly rent the northern wings of the churches of both the Old and New

Schools, but the southern wings of both churches adhered to a proslavery position, or, more accurately, to the view that slavery, being scripturally sanctioned, was a civil matter in which the church had no right to interfere. Until the eve of the Civil War, the Old School, North and South, agreed that slavery was not a sin (*malum in se*), whereas the New School in the North attracted increasing numbers of those who condemned slavery as sinful and therefore as incompatible with Christian fellowship.

With a smattering of exceptions, the southern New School churches remained as theologically orthodox as the Old School. The decision of some southern churches to go with the New School in 1837 flowed from ecclesiastical concerns—that is, they regarded the expulsions as a violation of the church constitution. In effect, they were defending the traditional southern constitutional principle of strict construction as applied to the constitution of their own church. The position of the southern New School churches, translated into secular politics, was worthy of Calhoun. Yet the Presbyterian church in the South, New and Old Schools alike, remained both theologically orthodox and proslavery, while the church in the North was becoming a battlefield between theological orthodoxy and liberalism, with the liberals steadily gaining ground.

The Presbyterian split of 1837 was a shot across the bow. The direct and heavy fire came in 1844 and 1845, with the formal split in the Methodist and Baptist churches over slavery. Political leaders of all stripes, including Calhoun and Clay, echoed Garrison's outcry of 1837, albeit in a different spirit. They asked in dismay how much longer northerners and southerners could be expected to share the same political union when they could no longer worship together in the same Christian churches. We need not belabor the familiar story of the Methodist split, which came over the refusal to permit a slaveholder to serve as bishop.[20] At the decisive National Conference of 1844, the antislavery forces insisted that slavery was sinful and therefore precisely the issue. They did not explain how the church could refuse to have slaveholding bishops on grounds of sin and yet make no move to defrock slaveholding ministers or expel communicants, for that matter.[21] But probably everyone knew that exclusion would be expanded in due time. The southerners and their northern allies doggedly took ecclesiastical—that is, constitutional—ground and tried not to get drawn into a debate over slavery itself. They insisted that since the Bible did not declare slavery sinful, the church had no right to do so.

Notwithstanding the politically prudent decision to fight on the narrowest and most formal line possible, the southerners could not resist hinting at the slavery question. William A. Smith of Virginia, who led the southern contingent on the floor, stayed close to the constitutional issue, but the fiery George Foster Pierce of Georgia warned that the refusal to consecrate a slaveholder would spell the end of traditional Methodism in the North. Pierce insisted that the virtual expulsion of proslavery southerners would leave the northern churches defenseless against the onslaught of theological and ecclesiastical liberalism, which threatened to flood them with infidelity, secularism, and political radicalism. Pierce spoke for the leaders of every large denomination in the South when he argued that the churches had to be embedded in a Christian society sustained by some form of slavery.[22]

One after another, the southern divines insisted that their struggle against the abolitionists and free-soilers was nothing less than a struggle between Christ and anti-Christ. Here Thornwell spoke for all denominations in 1850: "The parties in this conflict are not merely Abolitionists and Slaveholders; they are Atheists, Socialists, Communists, Red Republicans, Jacobins on the one side, and the friends of order and regulated freedom on the other. In one word, the world is the battle ground, Christianity and Atheism the combatants, and the progress of humanity the stake."[23]

Thornwell blended theology and ecclesiology with natural science, moral philosophy, and the social and political sciences, as did the leading divines of his own and the other churches. Thornwell had plenty of company when he defended slavery as a labor system appropriate to all races—as a God-ordained relation necessary for the stability of a Christian social order. And he had plenty of company when he boldly attacked the free-labor system as inhumane, unstable, and destined to burn itself out in revolutionary conflagration. On these issues he was even joined by Parson Clapp, the Unitarian pastor in New Orleans who was theologically an extreme liberal.[24]

No less than the northern divines, the southern admired Scottish Realism and brought philosophy to the support of theology by stressing the natural order of the world. And as students of classical political economy, they concluded from Ricardian and Malthusian theory that the capitalist countries were sailing into a social catastrophe, with the laboring classes immiserated and driven toward social revolution. The solution, they argued, lay in some form of "Christian slavery," which would unite the interests of capital and labor by making men responsible for the welfare of those dependent upon them. This view flowed not from Calvinism but from a general Christian orthodoxy, as orthodoxy was understood in the South even by Arminian theologians. Calvinists and Arminians differed sharply in their respective interpretations of the fall of man, but their differences did not affect this issue. Thornwell's Calvinism did, however, give a special form to his insistence that Presbyterian doctrine blended especially well with American constitutionalism, as interpreted by Calhoun and the southern state-rights school. For in orthodox Calvinism, the sin of Adam was made to fall on the entire human race since Adam was its federal representative, and therefore, in good republican fashion, the entire human race bore responsibility for his sin.[25]

The Arminians had their own variations on these themes, but Arminians and liberal Calvinists all began and ended in the same place. They began with a strict interpretation of the Bible and with a strong notion of sin and human depravity; they moved through a firm commitment to social and political hierarchy as God ordained; and they ended with a ringing defense of slavery as the natural and proper condition of all labor.[26] Along the way, they denounced egalitarianism and radical democracy on principle and preached a conservative republicanism that frankly recognized hierarchy in all human affairs. Almost in unison, they cried out with Frederick Ross that the Holy Ghost had not sanctified the philosophy of Thomas Jefferson.[27] Southern theorists, secular and clerical alike, regarded religious orthodoxy, traditional social values, and conservative republicanism as of a piece. They insisted that society in the North and in Western Europe was unraveling in the wake of the spread of infidelity and heresy. And they found the social root in the free-labor system itself, which everywhere promoted a marketplace mentality incompatible with spiritual values. The end, they argued, could only be anarchy, followed either by military despotism or a return to some form of organic slave society.

Thus, the southerners broke decisively with their more conservative northern brethren, who also were fighting for religious orthodoxy at Princeton and within the principal denominations and who were also expressing alarm at the spread of an egocentrism that was perverting the meaning of Christian individualism and poisoning social life. Southerners acknowledged that many good Christians in the North were fighting against religious heresy, political radicalism, and moral and social disintegration. But they correctly insisted that the northern conservatives who defended the constitutional rights of slaveholders were themselves overwhelmingly antislavery, supporting the free-labor system and deploring slavery as a social, economic, and political evil, even if not a sin per se.[28] Northern conservatives could not see that it was precisely the South's slave institutions that provided a firm basis for a Christian social order. The southern divines argued that northern conservatives were undermining their own good work by helping to destroy the slaveholding social system that encouraged and supported the Christian life. Worse, they were supporting a system of social relations that made the marketplace the determinant of human affairs. They were therefore condemning themselves to defeat in their effort to reverse the deterioration of northern society and were supporting a war against the one social system that offered the thing most needful.

The southern divines ended by counterposing a theologically based worldview to that of the northern conservatives. During the war they threw themselves into the Confederate cause with as much fervor as many of their old northern conservative allies threw themselves into the Union cause. Either openly commit yourself to Christ, northern and southern divines alike warned their people, or prepare to face the wrath of God. In the North, the bolder divines preached that, if the people did not meet their holy obligation to destroy slavery once and for all, God would punish the United States by permitting the infidel secessionists to succeed. And the boldest courageously campaigned against racial discrimination as well. In the South, the leading divines opened a campaign to reform the slave codes drastically. They demanded that cruel masters be sternly punished, that the slaves be taught to read the Bible, that slave families be protected at law. They demanded, in short, that southern slavery be brought up to the highest standards of the Abramic household and the teachings of Christ. And they warned that, unless the great reformation occurred, God might well use the infidel Yankees to punish His chosen southern people, much as He had used heathens to punish His chosen Israelites of old when He found them wanting.[29]

The free market, especially the market in labor power, with its radical individualism and rejection of all forms of slavery, provided the northern counterpart to the Abramic household envisioned by proslavery southerners. Soon enough, the Confederacy did in fact face the wrath of God, or at least the wrath of the Yankees, but we may wonder if Thornwell, Palmer, Pierce, and the other southerners who pushed for an official Christian Confederacy did not have the last grim laugh. For they had warned that if the Union, based on free labor, the marketplace, and radical democracy, prevailed, the ground would be cut from under the churches—that, inexorably, political and social democracy would generate overwhelming pressures for ecclesiastical democracy and, through it, for theological liberalism and eventual unbelief. Southerners insisted that the dissolution of the family, the collapse of social order, and the repudiation of any concept of legitimate authority must inexorably proceed in step with the eclipse of Christian orthodoxy, which could be sustained only by organic social relations. We may breathe a sigh of relief at the defeat of their proslavery cause. But from the vantage point of our own day, can we, in all honesty, pretend that they had not in fact read the signs of the times?[30]

Whether viewed as root or manifestation, religious doctrine and sensibility rent the Union, as becomes clear through an examination of the fierce struggle over the constitutional doctrine of the Higher Law. According to the classic formulation of William H. Seward, God-ordained natural law overrode any sanction for slavery that might be found in the Constitution or the laws of man. The Founding Fathers themselves, following Locke, offered resistance to tyranny as an obligation to natural law and a duty to God. Man has property in himself but not sole property. He belongs to his Maker and, therefore, has no right to alienate that which he does not wholly possess or to surrender himself completely to the arbitrary will of any being other than God. If this doctrine applied to colonial Americans who were rebelling against a metaphorical "slavery," surely it applied to those for whom slavery was concrete.

Hardly a politician or periodical in the South failed to condemn the Higher Law doctrine as enunciated by Seward and the antislavery divines, and, in consequence, a misunderstanding has arisen, which attributes to southern thought a positivistic defense of man-made law as beyond appeal. A moment's reflection should scotch such an idea, for the southerners spoke as Christians and, as such, could not repudiate Higher Law doctrine without exposing themselves as hypocritical or, worse, stupid. They did no such thing.

Secular as well religious theorists could not rule Higher Law doctrine out of court, for any action, however much sanctioned by the Constitution, the laws, or a democratic consensus, could violate the injunction to render unto God the things that are God's. Southerners condemned the specifics of antislavery Higher Law doctrine rather than the underlying principle. They challenged their opponents to ground the specifics of their appeal to Higher Law in Scripture—to demonstrate that the Bible actually condemned slavery as sinful. And this, despite mighty gyrations, the opponents of slavery could not do, except to the satisfaction of those prepared to advance their private version of the Holy Spirit as self-evident truth. In response, supporters of slavery accused their opponents of deserting the Word for an appeal to individual conscience divorced from divine command.

Conservative northern divines leveled a similar attack on the abolitionists and their allies. Led by Moses Stuart of Andover, they rallied to Daniel Webster's Seventh of March Speech in 1850 and denounced what they perceived as a perversion of the right of private judgment. Throughout the North, disputes over the proper interpretation of Higher Law doctrine marked the fierce debates over the Compromise of 1850.[31] In principle, no southern Christian could object to the formulation in Theodore Parker's sermon on conscience: "The laws of matter depend for their execution only on the infinite will of God, and so cannot be violated. The laws of man depend for their execution also on the finite will of man, and so may be broken." Every southern divine said essentially the same thing. Robert L. Dabney spoke for all when he said of an immoral law: "How shall a free conscience act? I answer, it asserts the higher law by refusing to be an accessory to the sin."[32]

For the defenders of slavery, the appeal to a Higher Law to condemn slavery constituted not an appeal to the Bible but to an individual conscience that not only stood above the Constitution but also the revealed Word of God. The theologically orthodox Reverend Ferdinand Jacobs of Charleston explained, "Ours is not a Union held together by the energy of a central power. . . . Constitutional provisions, knowing no 'higher law,' by an upright and honest and religious people, should be held inviolate." The theologically liberal Reverend James Worley Miles, also of Charleston, here took similar ground. Addressing the graduating class of the College of Charleston in 1852, he launched into an attack on utilitarian and materialistic theories of morals and counterpoised absolute standards derived from God: "It is not necessary to prove here, what has become an axiom of jurisprudence, that no precept, enforced even by a legal authority, can make that Right which the Natural Law condemns as wrong."[33] Secular writers, no less than clerical, accepted Higher Law doctrine, repudiating only its perversion.[34]

The southern defense of a biblically sanctioned individual freedom and of limits on governmental power corresponded to the Jeffersonian tradition and the slaveholders' jealousy of their prerogatives, but it did not solve the most difficult problems. The various arguments over constitutional theory, interstate comity, and the proper nature of republican government had a common denominator in their insistence upon the legitimacy of property in man or, as most southerners would have it, in property in man's labor and services.[35] Behind the endless constitutional argumentation lay a powerful historical defense of a particular theory of property. Accordingly, the growing anger that thundered from the southern bench over violations of comity, and from the politicians over the territorial and other questions, should have been expected. Northerners saw then, as many historians see now, only a tedious repetition of self-serving arguments—little more than hair splitting and logic chopping— but the southerners had good grounds for accusing their adversaries of bad faith. In southern eyes, abolitionists and free-soilers were reducing Higher Law to nothing more than personal opinion.

In North and South, the scriptural and constitutional arguments were of a piece. Together as well as separately, they exposed the centrality of slavery to the sectional quarrel and to the radical split in national consciousness, for they identified southern slavery as a system of social relations and not merely a congeries of economic and social interests. The ablest northern writers—for example, George Cheever in biblical exegesis and Harriet Beecher Stowe in didactic fiction—emphasized the essential sinfulness and immorality of slavery as a system that perverted the best of its practitioners.[36]

Southerners rejected the argument at its root, insisting that slavery conformed to the Word of God and that, therefore, so did the Constitution of the United States, which, while itself not God's Word, was designed to be consistent with it. The doctrine of strict construction began with Scripture and ended with the constitutional structure of the republic. Far from being an abstraction or a matter of arid theorizing, it lay at the core of the slaveholders' determination to establish a separate nation-state, however much they erred in trying to divorce it from slavery in their polemics and subsequent historical justifications. Despite much puffery, rationalization of special interests, and demagogy, the northern and southern divines who preached holy war knew what they were about. As that northern farmer wrote Lincoln, the war pit the Kingdom of God against the Kingdom of Satan. But tragically, honest Christians could not agree on which was which, for they assumed that, as Christians, northerners and southerners shared the same moral values, derived from a commonly held Christian doctrine. They were wrong. For in fact, they disagreed on the essentials of Christian doctrine and morality, and, in consequence, they held incompatible visions of the social relations necessary to sustain Christianity in a sinful world.

Notes

1. Quoted in the Introduction to Robert Johannsen, ed., *The Lincoln-Douglas Debates of 1858* (New York, 1965), 9; Marcy quoted in John Niven, *John C. Calhoun and the Price of Union: A Biography* (Baton Rouge, 1988), 202.

2. For Calhoun's concern with the religious argument, see Charles M. Wiltse, *John C. Calhoun: Sectionalist* (Indianapolis, 1944), 169–170; John R. McKivigan, *The War Against Proslavery Religion: Abolitionism and the Northern Churches, 1830–1865* (Ithaca, NY, 1984), 150 (quoting Free Soil party platform of 1852); Bacon quoted in Louis Filler, *The Crusade against Slavery, 1830–1860* (New York, 1960), 195; Ferdinand Jacobs, *The Committing of Our Cause to God* (Charleston, 1850), 20. Bacon's words became famous when Lincoln invoked them without attribution.

3. For the limited purposes of this paper, I shall have to bypass the black religious experience, which had considerable impact on the larger story but bore lightly on the questions here at issue. The black experience contains a striking paradox that has not yet found its historian. The religion of the slaves, which proved central to their struggle for survival, contained much that was theologically orthodox while it also embraced concepts, partly of African derivation, that were more compatible with theological liberalism. But the antislavery preaching and writing of the black abolitionists largely, if not entirely, flowed from theologically liberal, not to say radical, premises on the relation of the Word to the Holy Spirit. Unfortunately, so far as I can tell, black abolitionists, as readily as white, simply assumed everything they had to prove and therefore made no special contribution to the clarification of the issues under discussion here, notwithstanding their formidable contributions on other matters.

4. A consideration of cultural divergence would have to include concepts of the family and much else. Conservative and church-going northerners and southerners fretted over the palpable decline in "family values," which, however, was largely a problem in the North. But northerners and southerners had radically different notions of "family," which for the former designated kinship and for the latter meant an extended household that included servants and laborers. See Elizabeth Fox-Genovese, *Within the Plantation Household: Black and White Women of the Old South* (Chapel Hill, 1988), chap. 1; Eugene D. Genovese, " 'Our Family, White and Black': Family and Household in the Southern Slaveholders' World View," in *In Joy and in Sorrow: Women, Family, and Marriage in the Victorian South*, ed. Carol Bleser (New York, 1991), chap. 5.

5. See David Potter, *The South and the Sectional Conflict* (Baton Rouge, 1968), esp. chap. 3. For recent studies that illuminate the development of southern nationalism, see Drew Gilpin Faust, *The Creation of Confederate Nationalism: Ideology and Identity in the Civil War South* (Baton Rouge, 1988); Mitchell Snay, *Gospel of Disunion: Religion and Separatism in the Antebellum South* (New York, 1993).

6. Arabs have long vehemently asserted the existence of an "Arab Nation" but could not even sustain the merger of Egypt and Syria in the 1950s. Today, Syria is at sword's point with Iraq while the Pan-Arab Ba'ath Party rules both.

7. This has been the fate of those who lost their war to establish the independent republic of Biafra in Nigeria in the 1960s, whereas we now recognize the independent nationality of the Eritreans, who defeated the Ethiopians.

8. Larry E. Tise, *Proslavery: A History of the Defense of Slavery in America, 1701–1840* (Athens, GA, 1988), xiii.

9. For an elaboration, see Eugene D. Genovese and Elizabeth Fox-Genovese, "The Religious Ideals of Southern Slave Society," *Georgia Historical Quarterly* 70 (1986): 1–16.

10. John B. Adger, "The Revival of the Slave Trade," *Southern Presbyterian Review* 9 (April 1858): 102–103; Barnes quoted in Harriet Beecher Stowe, *The Key to Uncle Tom's Cabin* (Washington, 1968 [1853]), 219.

11. Southerners taunted abolitionists by saying that if the Bible could be proved to be antislavery, they would repent in sackcloth and ashes and dispense with it immediately. See, for examples, Thornton Stringfellow, "The Bible Argument: Or, Slavery in the Light of Divine Revelation," in *Cotton Is King and Pro-Slavery Arguments*, ed. E. N. Elliott (New York, 1969 [1860]), 459–521; E. J. Pringle, *Slavery in the Southern States by a Carolinian* (Cambridge, 1852), 44; William A. Smith, *Lectures on the Philosophy and Practice of Slavery* (Nashville, 1856), 13, 34–35; James Henley Thornwell, "Sermon on National Sins," in Thornwell, *The Collected Writings of James Henley Thornwell*, 4 vols. (Carlisle, PA, 1986), 4:539; also "Relation of the Church to Slavery" and "The Christian Doctrine of Slavery," 4: 381–397, 398–436; Linton Stephens to Alexander H. Stephens, June 29, 1860, in James D. Waddell, *Biographical Sketch of Linton Stephens Containing a Selection of His Letters, Speeches, State Papers, Etc.* (Atlanta, 1877), 224.

12. For an elaboration, see Eugene D. Genovese, "Higher Education in the Defense of Slave Society," in *The Southern Front: History and Politics in the Cultural War* (Columbia, MO, 1995), chap. 8.

13. See especially Daniel Walker Howe, *The Unitarian Conscience: Harvard Moral Philosophy, 1805–1861*. All studies of religious thought in the North demonstrate a retreat from Trinitarianism or at least a tendency to reinterpret the Trinity in a manner that revealed more and more concessions to the Unitarian viewpoint.

14. Predestinarianism was not the principal issue between northern and southern churches. On that issue, Timothy L. Smith, in his controversial study of religion and

reform in antebellum America, was right to claim a broad victory for Arminianism all over America; *Revivalism and Social Reform: American Protestantism on the Eve of the Civil War* (Baltimore, 1980).

15. See, for example, H. Shelton Smith, *Changing Conceptions of Original Sin: A Study in American Theology since 1750* (New York, 1955); and *Southern Presbyterian Review* for the 1850s, which contains attacks on the tendency to separate benevolence from justice.

16. Lewis Perry, *Radical Abolitionism: Anarchy and the Government of God in Antislavery Thought* (Ithaca, NY, 1973), 49, 122; Ronald G. Walters, *The Antislavery Appeal: American Abolitionism after 1830* (Baltimore, 1976), 42.

17. The abolitionists bitterly denounced not only the slaveholders but also all clergymen, northern and southern, who refused to condemn slavery as sinful. See Louis Filler, *Crusade against Slavery*, 77; Walters, *Antislavery Appeal*, 41; Perry, *Radical Abolitionism*, passim; William S. McFeely, *Frederick Douglas* (New York, 1991), 102, 124. Harriet Beecher Stowe devoted the first chapter of Part Four of *Key to Uncle Tom's Cabin* to quotations from proslavery southern divines, bolstering the charge that the churches were the bulwark of slavery. For southern responses, see William Sumner Jenkins, *Pro-Slavery Thought in the Old South* (Gloucester, 1960), chap. 5.

18. For an elaboration, see Eugene D. Genovese, *"Slavery Ordained of God": The Southern Slaveholders' View of Biblical History and Modern Politics* (Gettysburg, PA, Fortenbaugh Memorial Lecture, Gettysburg College, 1985). The construction of an antislavery theology remains a possibility, but the abolitionists failed to do it.

19. Many of the New School leaders insisted upon their own Calvinist orthodoxy, none more vehemently than Lyman Beecher. Yet the more closely one reads his defense, the clearer his heterodoxy becomes. See Lyman Beecher, *Autobiography*, ed. Charles Beecher, 2 vols. (New York, 1871), I, 165, 242; II, chap. 18. See also Vincent Harding's evaluation in *A Certain Magnificence: Lyman Beecher and the Transformation of American Protestantism, 1775–1863* (Brooklyn Co., 1991). George Marsden has argued strongly for the essential orthodoxy of the New School in the North in the 1850s, but he acknowledges the toleration of heterodoxy and, implicitly at least, the stretching of the notion of orthodoxy; *The Evangelical Mind and the New School Experience: A Case Study of Thought and Theology in Nineteenth-Century America* (New Haven, CT, 1970).

20. The essentials of the Methodist split apply to the Baptist split as well.

21. C. C. Goen asserts that historians have largely ignored the impact of the split in the churches on the course of national politics. It would be more accurate to say that they have indeed noted and discussed the question at length, but they have had great difficulty in justifying the course taken by the abolitionists, either theologically or constitutionally. Goen himself assumes the validity of the antislavery case while he laments the split. In the end, he in effect laments the unwillingness of the southerners to strike their colors whether they found themselves out-argued or not; C. C. Goen, *Broken Churches, Broken Nation: Denominational Schisms in the Coming of the American Civil War* (Macon, GA, 1985).

22. For an elaboration, see Eugene D. Genovese and Elizabeth Fox-Genovese, "The Social Thought of Antebellum Southern Theologians," in *Looking South: Chapters in the Story of an American Region*, eds. Winfred B. Moore Jr. and Joseph F. Tripp (New York, 1989), chap. 3; and Elizabeth Fox-Genovese and Eugene D. Genovese, "The Divine Sanction of Social Order: Religious Foundations of the Southern Slaveholders' World View," *Journal of the American Academy of Religion* 55 (1987): 211–233.

23. Thornwell, "The Christian Doctrine of Slavery," *Collected Writings*, 4: 405–406. Thornwell's reputation among non-Presbyterians could hardly have stood higher. See,

for example, James Oscar Farmer Jr., *The Metaphysical Confederacy: James Henley Thorn-well and the Synthesis of Southern Values* (Macon, GA, 1986), 64.

24. Thornwell's theological and scientific defense of slavery in the abstract was paralleled by such Presbyterians as Benjamin Morgan Palmer, Robert L. Dabney, John Adger, John L. Girardeau, and George Armstrong; such Methodists as William A. Smith, George Foster Pierce, William G. Brownlow, and R. H. Rivers; and such Baptists as John L. Dagg, Thornton Stringfellow, and J. R. Graves. See Thornwell, "Sermon on National Sins," in *Collected Writings of James Henley Thornwell*, 4: 541. For a Methodist version, see W. A. Smith, *Lectures on the Philosophy and Practice of Slavery* (Nashville, 1856), 11–12.

25. Thornwell, *Collected Writings*, 1:445–488, 544–546; 2:18–19, 297. See also Charles Hodge, *Systematic Theology*, 3 vols. (Grand Rapids, 1993; reprint), esp. 2:197; John L. Girardeau, *The Will in Its Theological Relations* (Columbia, 1891), 330–332; and for a more recent statement, see Loraine Boettner, *The Reformed Doctrine of Predestination* (Philipsburg, n.d.; reprint of 1932 ed.), 75–80.

26. On the relation of the defense of slavery to the religious foundations of the social order, see especially E. Brooks Holifield, *The Gentlemen Theologians: American Theology in Southern Culture, 1795–1860* (Durham, 1979); Anne C. Loveland, *Southern Evangelicals and the Social Order, 1800–1860* (Baton Rouge, 1980); and Jack P. Maddex Jr., "Proslavery Millennialism: Social Eschatology in Antebellum Southern Calvinism," *American Quarterly* 31 (1979): 46–68; Jack P. Maddex, " 'The Southern Apostasy' Revisited: The Significance of Proslavery Christianity," *Marxist Perspectives* 7 (1979): 132–141. On the intellectual currents in the northern and southern churches, see Theodore Dwight Bozeman, *Protestants in an Age of Science: The Baconian Ideal and Antebellum American Religious Thought* (Chapel Hill, 1977); and Theodore Dwight Bozeman, "Science, Nature, and Society: A New Approach to James Henley Thornwell," *Journal of Presbyterian History* 50 (1972): 307–325.

27. Frederick A. Ross, *Slavery Ordained of God* (New York: 1969 [1857]), 97.

28. Charles Hodge, who staunchly opposed the notion that the Bible condemned slavery as sinful, nevertheless opposed slavery on other grounds and even voted Republican. See Charles Hodge, "The Fugitive Slave Law" and "The Bible Argument on Slavery, in Elliott, ed., *Cotton Is King*, 809–840, 841–877. See also Alexander A. Hodge, *The Life of Charles Hodge* (New York, 1969 [1881]).

29. The pioneering discussion is Bell Irwin Wiley, "The Movement to Humanize the Institution of Slavery During the Confederacy," *Emory University Quarterly* 5 (1949): 207–220. For a contemporary statement, see Calvin H. Wiley, *Scriptural Views of National Trial* (Greensboro, NC, 1863).

30. See especially the superb treatment of the manner in which the war destroyed the conservatives of both North and South, in Lewis P. Simpson, *Mind and the American Civil War: A Meditation on Lost Causes* (Baton Rouge, 1989). On the responsibility of the churches to the rise of unbelief, see James Turner, *Without God, Without Creed: The Origin of Unbelief in America* (Baltimore, 1985).

31. Victor B. Howard, *Conscience and Slavery: The Evangelistic Calvinist Domestic Missions, 1837–1861* (Kent, OH, 1990), 95, 98.

32. Theodore Parker, "The Function of Conscience," in *"God Ordained This War": Sermons on the Sectional Crisis*, ed. David Chesebrough (Columbia, SC, 1991), 37. Robert L. Dabney, "Civic Ethics," in *Discussions: Evangelical and Theological*, 3 vols. (Carlisle, PA, 1967), III, 115; Dabney, *Systematic Theology* (Carlisle, PA), 72, 118–119, 137, 139, 299, 560; also, Thornwell, *Collected Writings*, 1:358, 366; 3:92–94, 129–134; 4:35, 401; 444–446; 530–531; John L. Dagg, *Manual of Theology: A Treatise on Christian Doctrine and a*

Treatise on Church Order, 2 vols. in one (New York, 1980 [1857–1858]), 1:16–17, 40, 157, 161; George Howe, "Secondary and Collateral Influences of the Sacred Scriptures," *Southern Presbyterian Review* 7 (1853), 52–60.

33. Jacobs, *The Committing of Our Cause to God*, 3; James Worley Miles, *The Ground of Morals* (Charleston, SC, 1852), 19.

34. See, e.g., Richmond *Daily Dispatch*, December 14, 1853, in *A Documentary History of Education in the South Before 1860*, ed. Edgar W. Knight, 5 vols. (Chapel Hill, 1949–1953), 5:291; see also "The Doctrine of the 'Higher Law': Mr. Seward's Speech," *Southern Literary Messenger* 17 (1851); Jesse T. Carpenter, *The South as a Conscious Minority, 1798–1861* (New York, 1930), 160; Henry Cleveland, *Alexander H. Stephens in Public and Private, with Letters and Speeches, Before, During, and Since the War* (Philadelphia, 1866), 649; Alexander H. Stephens, *A Constitutional View of the Late War between the States; Its Causes, Character, Conduct and Results.* Presented in a Series of Colloquia at Liberty Hall, 2 vols. (Millwood, NJ, 1960 [1868, 1870]), 1:626.

35. For an elaboration of the property question, see Elizabeth Fox-Genovese and Eugene D. Genovese, *Fruits of Merchant Capital: Slavery and Bourgeois Property in the Rise and Expansion of Capitalism* (New York, 1983), chap. 12.

36. George B. Cheever, *God against Slavery: And the Freedom and Duty of the Pulpit to Rebuke It as a Sin against God* (Cincinnati, 1857); Stowe, *Key to Uncle Tom's Cabin*, and the novel itself.

4

Church, Honor, and Secession

BERTRAM WYATT-BROWN

nger and frustration were the root emotions that drove southerners to secede, a visceral response to a collective sense of humiliation. Years of transatlantic criticism of slaveholding and growing northern indifference to southern interests had been a constant source of vexation. Contrary to some historical opinion, white southerners were alarmed not simply because they feared what Abraham Lincoln and the Republicans might do once in power. Parties were soon swept in and out of office, prudent men advised. Have patience; conservatism would yet return. Much more disturbing was the very election of an antislavery president. Southern politicians and editors had long threatened that such a political victory would mean national dissolution, but slave-state grievances and claims to political parity were contemptuously swept aside by northern balloting. It was bad enough to be insulted, but to have all warnings ignored was the final blow to southern pride.[1]

Given the intensity of the humiliation, how can one explain why prominent churchmen of the region were so slow to join the political outcry for secession, particularly in the months leading to the election showdown? After all, the churches had been the first national institutions to split apart, setting an example for officeholders to follow some fifteen years later.[2] Moreover, nearly all recent scholars agree that religion exercised enormous power in the cultural and even the political life of the United States, in the slave states no less than in the free ones. In the South, as Sydney Ahlstrom observed, the clergy rightfully claimed to be "the official custodians of the popular conscience."[3] Richard Carwardine likewise argues that evangelical clergy and laity, North and South, placed themselves in the thick of antebellum political discourse by forming a "special-interest" bloc. That term is, however, misleading when it comes to the sectional crisis of 1860–1861. The slave-state clerical voice was ambivalent. Far from endorsing slavery's positive goodness, clerics sounded various themes on the subject. None was hostile, but few called it holy. Most clerics would rather have left the topic alone if they could have done so. C. C. Goen observes that those who glorified slavery as biblically sanctioned revealed an inconsistency by simultaneously claiming that "it was strictly a civil institution beyond their concern." Perhaps by justifying slavery as a moral good, they could then claim to place the matter solely in the hands of civil government. Yet if such a strategy saved the southern clergy from gross contradiction, they still had to conform in every respect to the dictates of the state as well as society, a loss of ecclesiastical and moral independence that few divines probably even dared to notice. Even so, Methodists, who generally deplored a mingling of religion and politics, seldom applauded slavery as such and even boasted of their reticence on sectional controversies.[4]

Clergymen, of course, were citizens and held private opinions about politics that they knowingly suppressed in the pulpit. What concerns us are not informal pronouncements or private convictions but instead the public expression of clerical favor or disfavor on the regional decision of 1860–1861. If, as Larry E. Tise suggests, over 60 percent of proslavery ministers with college degrees were northern trained and many northern bred, a cautious approach about secession was understandable. In a famous essay, "The Travail of Slavery," Charles Grier Sellers Jr. argued that slaveholding conservatives faced what he called "a paralysis of will." Inner conflicts, even a sense of guilt, engendered that response on the eve of war. Their confusion, Sellers contended, permitted the dominance of the Fire-Eaters. Sellers's interpretation, however, carries the matter too far. Guilt over bondage was very rare, apart from occasional death-bed contrition.[5] Nonetheless, great reluctance to promote radical political change did characterize the southern clergy in 1860 and 1861.

Three major factors accounted for clerical foot-dragging as the political crisis grew increasingly ominous.[6] First, even though wedded to the practical exigencies of slaveholding, sophisticated church leaders recognized that they could not win polemical battles by upholding all the realities of slavery that abolitionist and antislavery critics constantly denounced. Second, they entertained a Whiggish and temperamental reluctance to disrupt the status quo. Finally, many of them held that regional honor required loyalty to the old Union with its compromises that neither endorsed nor repudiated human bondage. As a result, between Abraham Lincoln's election and the firing on Fort Sumter, the southern clergy followed but seldom led the movement toward disunion. Some did so with heavy hearts and with premonitions of death and defeat. Even those who embraced the new rebel order and sang the praises of slavery did so with a note of desperation. Being realists and conservatives, however, they lauded the new status quo with a vigor and dedication less based on Christian feeling than upon the regional concept of honor.

With regard to a modulated rather than strident defense of slavery, some churchmen, chiefly in urban centers, were very much aware that the proslavery cause had its limitations. As Drew Faust has noted, most were "less troubled about *whether* slavery was right than precisely *why* it was right and how its justice could best be demonstrated."[7] But justifications not only had to satisfy

Christian slaveholders at home but southern sympathizers beyond the borders. In that process, churchmen could not entirely forget their denominations' antislavery past, however tentative had been former criticism of bondage. Methodists were particularly embarrassed by early church pronouncements against the system. As a result, the latter-day followers of antislavery John Wesley themselves seldom meddled with the issue at all from their pulpits, except, as one journal put it, "to enforce the scriptural duties which grow out of the relation of master and servant." The same reversal occurred in the Baptist church. Likewise, Presbyterians in 1818 declared at their General Assembly that slavery had to be condemned as "a gross violation of the most precious and sacred rights of human nature," a condition "utterly inconsistent with the law of God."[8] As late as 1861, the Rev. James Henley Thornwell of South Carolina argued that the church had neither the right to require slave ownership "as a duty" nor "to condemn it as a sin." Slavery, he had also explained in 1850, "is a part of the curse which sin has introduced into the world, and stands in the same general relations to Christianity as poverty, sickness, disease or death. . . . It is not absolutely a good—a blessing—" but rather "a natural evil which God has visited upon society." He did not argue, on this occasion at least, that slavery was an immutable and divine institution, blessed by God but rather a circumstance with forlorn consequences—unless one were to welcome rather than simply endure with fortitude the visitations of illness and the other scourges in God's Providence that he mentioned. Admittedly, Thornwell's logic did not signify an abrupt conversion to immediate abolition, but his words did imply that "good and evil," as he continued, "are relative terms, and what may be good for one man may be evil for another." The point is not that Thornwell had abandoned the southern cause; rather, he had hedged any endorsement of slavery as a spotless instrument of God's design. According to Beth Barton Schweiger, "few Virginia pastors believed that the presence of slavery in their society made it a righteous one. . . . If they argued that slavery was closer to the Biblical ideal of social organization than the Northern system, they saw signs everywhere that all was not well." Balance, prudence, sober objectivity—these were the watchwords of the proslavery argument—for the clear purpose, declared George Frederick Holmes, of winning over those outside the South who "wished for argument instead of abuse."[9] Such an approach left room for more circumspection and even uncertainty about the issue, as churchmen saw it, than we have assumed.

By and large, the southern clergy joined Thornwell in considering slavery a condition of life like death and taxes—not to be celebrated but to be borne stoically and practiced humanely. Professor Nathaniel Beverley Tucker of William and Mary might exclaim to southern slaveholders, "You have been chosen as the instrument in the hands of God, for accomplishing the great purpose of his benevolence." That kind of boasting, however, would make the thoughtful preacher wince. A solemn message of slavery as concomitant of all-too-human sin was perhaps theologically preferable—but not very inspirational, especially when compared with the Manichaean simplicity and self-confidence of abolitionist immediatism.

Clerical defenders of slavery knew that few outside the South were shaken by their plodding justifications, despite alleged biblical foundations for southern precedent. In most northern churches, the spirit rather than the letter of the Old and New Dispensations served as answer to the literal analogies that proslavery clergy drew between Mosaic servitude and African-American bondage. Like the Rev. Nehemiah Adams and a few other proslavery preachers in the North, Henry J. Van Dyke of Brooklyn, New York, reiterated the long-familiar arguments for a scriptural system in the South. While avoiding a strictly abolitionist rejoinder, a Professor Tayler Lewis, however, responded in rational style in the New York *World*: "the difference . . . between what was called servitude in the days of the patriarchs and slavery *as it exists* in the modern states of Mississippi and Texas, is so immense that no fair comparison can be made between them." Slavery in Middle Eastern antiquity was domestic, noncommercial, and nonracial, a total "absence of that feeling of caste, which is the curse of American slavery." No patriarch in Israel "ever *sold*, or thought of selling, for money, the humblest of his dependent vassals." Mercenary slavery was, by its soulless nature, brutal and self-serving, Lewis continued. "Have we been constantly improving it by giving it more of the social and less of the mercenary; more of the humanizing and less of the dehumanizing character; more of the fraternal and less of the caste aspect? Then may we quote the patriarchs—if not to the honor, at least not the shame of our Christianity." The dignity of man—a God-given sense of personality—could be achieved under bondage in which its subjects were by law and custom debased. With allusion to recent opinions from the bench of Thomas Ruffin of North Carolina, Lewis argued, "To be *owned* is degrading; to be *property*, and nothing more, is dehumanizing." These were sentiments, framed in Christian terms, that were not easily refuted by reference to a dry-as-dust scriptural literalism. As Lewis concluded, perhaps southern Christians themselves felt that slavery induced in them "a hidden trouble of conscience" or "an obscure feeling, not allowed to come out in distinct thought, but which tells them there is, somewhere, something wrong about it." Even if he had not accurately read the southern mind, Lewis struck a chord that even the most diffident northerner was learning to appreciate.[10]

Part of the southern clergy's polemical hesitancy might well have stemmed from the numerical weakness of the slave-state church system. Powerful men—meaning most politicians—paid lip service to the Kingdom of Christ on Earth, but by and large most were absorbed in more worldly excitements than the pious emotions of the revival. In addition, there were over twice as many clergymen in New York than in all thirteen slave states put together, and the same number as preached in all the South served the single state of Pennsylvania. To put it another way, in the North, out of 187 inhabitants 1 was a minister, and in the South, the ratio was 1 to 329.[11]

Still more damaging to clerical self-esteem was the knowledge of how extensive and deep antislavery sentiment seemed to be growing throughout Christendom year by year. The skeptical reception of the proslavery argument in the greater world bears analogy with that of white South Africa in recent times. Southern apologists, lay or clerical, had to face the fact that few listened to their self-justifications unless to refute them. The theoretical and scriptural arguments for black bondage seemed the work, scoffed Horace Greeley of the New York *Tribune*, of some "very curious maggots." They had overcome "the torpid stagnation" of their "planter brains" to bore the world with diatribes promoting slavery. Such views might be anticipated from a journalistic champion of the Republican party, but southern defenders of slavery did not find anywhere an attentive and receptive audience in the North or in Victorian Great Britain, which at the time was the moral and cultural arbiter of Western life.[12]

Unluckily for the conservative cause in those days, no spokesman as popular as Rush Limbaugh or Jerry Falwell rallied the Christian Right to defend slavery in all its facets. An exception, it might seem, was George Fitzhugh's visit to Yale College in 1855. There he proposed his special vision of the beauties of enslavement not for blacks alone but as an institution suitable to deal with labor conditions the world over. After his presentation, the listeners, Fitzhugh wrote his friend George Frederick Holmes, fell to "thinking and talking . . . Professor Silliman and many of the leading citizens paid me great attention." Academics are always intrigued with outrageous propositions, but the fun can last only so long. Fitzhugh might as well have offered himself as an exhibit for P. T. Barnum's collection of curiosities. In fact, most of the proslavery literature that northerners were likely to read came to them in the form of printed colloquies, such as the reply of James Henry Hammond, former Governor of South Carolina, to Thomas Clarkson, the venerable English antislavery leader, or that between the Rev. Francis Wayland of Brown University and Richard Fuller, Baptist leader of South Carolina. A work like E. N. Elliot's *Cotton Is King* surely found few buyers north of the Potomac.[13] Thomas Smyth, Presbyterian divine of South Carolina, sounded hurt to the quick when he declared that conservative northern divines like Presbyterian Charles Hodge "profess to have lost confidence in our morality."[14]

Even southerners did not read or comment on intellectual and theological productions with much interest. As contemporary southern humorist Roy Blount Jr. recently observed, "It is easier to enter into the kingdom of Heaven through the eye of an onion ring than it is to sell a book in the South."[15] After writing a major defense of slavery, the Rev. James Thornwell complained to a friend that he had found "hardly a notice of it in any of the papers."[16] The gloomy academician George Frederick Holmes, as Drew Faust points out, mourned that proslavery prophets, who, like himself, were ordained by God to warn a sinful world, had to expect nothing but "disbelief, dishonor, outrage, contempt, persecution." "I have long seen that you were not 'honored in your own country,'" James Henry Hammond commiserated with William Gilmore Simms.[17] To some degree, clergymen felt the same sort of disrespect against which the secular leaders of intellect in the South murmured. When the boom of cannon announced the beginning of war, Holmes, embittered by debts and an unheeding, anti-intellectual southern populace, echoed a sentiment that some of the Whiggish clergy may also have privately uttered. The horrors of war, the professor moaned, were God's punishment for the southern people's "misplaced ambition . . . greed, rapacity, drinking, gambling, [and] dissipation."[18]

To be sure, the abolitionists had similarly difficult problems getting their message before an impervious public more preoccupied with mundane things than with church debates over slaveholding. Most northern Christians mistrusted and resented the antislavery reformers in their midst. Nonetheless, church moderates and conservatives in the North heeded at least part of the abolitionist message and refused to embrace mindlessly an unadulterated proslavery doctrine. Particularly after the passage of the Fugitive Slave Law in 1850 and the Free Soil struggle over the spoils of the Mexican War, what they chiefly sought was noncomplicity with slavery. No slave catching, no support for bondage in the territories were the negatives of an antislavery position, as it were, but they were highly ominous signs of northern opposition to the institution. For any Yankee to defend the southern racial order would mean a repudiation of free-labor capitalism along with the notion of steady progress toward personal liberty and Christian fulfillment, as Yankee churchmen understood it. Reflecting an almost universal northern complacency on the topic, Horace Bushnell pointed out, "Why should I be contriving the abolition of slavery when the Almighty Himself has a silent campaign of inevitable doom against it, marching on the awful census tramp of South and North to push it away forever."[19]

Exasperated by similar signs of Yankee condescension and self-righteousness, James Henley Thornwell of South Carolina pointed out that for years northern friends of the plantation South had not been playing fair. At best they treated the slaveholding region as if it were fit only for Christian charity. Thornwell complained that these so-called clerical allies continue to "pity the South as caught in the folds of a serpent, which is gradually squeezing out her life." What good was there in having such conservative supporters? When defending slaveholders from the abolitionist charge of sinful man-stealing, these Yankee brethren were ready with "so many distinctions" between slavery in the abstract and slavery in the concreteness of southern laws and plantation practices that such a "defence would hardly avail to save us, if there were any power competent to hang and quarter us," Thornwell protested.[20] By the late 1850s, northern material and demographic power had grown so great, as Bushnell had observed, that southern opinion made little or no intellectual difference. How galling it must have been to such productive theologians and thinkers as Thornwell to realize their own irrelevance in the world beyond the slave regime. "The North is the thinking power—the soul of the Government," he wrote in the *Southern Presbyterian Review*. "The life of the Government is Northern—not Southern. The North becomes the United States, and the South a subject province."[21]

Thornwell's sense of frustration was based on actual and not imagined slights. Another New Englander, Leonard Bacon of Connecticut, for instance, in 1854 charitably exonerated southern proslavery ministers from loving slavery for the sake of "filthy lucre" but instead claimed their views had been perverted because they feared denunciation and even assassination if they professed the former antislavery credo of their denominations. Outside Bacon and Bushnell's New England, parts of the country that should have been staunchly favorable to the South did not rally to the proslavery cause. For instance, at Princeton, a major seat of northern clerical conservatism, Charles Hodge and other Old School Presbyterians had gradually swung away from their southern allies. Stately in appearance, sophisticated in manner, and affiliated with several leading families of the mid-Atlantic states, Hodge exercised great influence if only because he had trained over 2,000 clergymen, North and South, at the Princeton Seminary. Moreover, his *Biblical Repertory and Princeton Review* was one of the most prestigious church publications in the country. Outspoken in his opposition to the abolitionists, Hodge appealed to Yankee isolationism. "We do not expect to abolish despotism in Russia, by getting up indignation meetings in New York."[22] In like manner, Hodge continued, northerners had neither the right nor the need to hurl epithets at slaveholders and expect them to repent. Yet even this arch conservative limited his defense of his southern brethren in Christ. As early as 1836, Hodge had observed in a widely disseminated essay that from a Christian perspective the power of masters was strictly circumscribed. The slave "can be used only as a rational, moral and immortal creature can, according to divine law." Moreover, he implied that a genuinely thorough movement to Christianize the South would provide "a peaceable and speedy extinction of slavery." Such a thought hardly seemed agreeable to slave-state clergymen. They were inclined to think evangelization would mean improved slaveholding, not its swift disappearance. Such argumentation forced the southern church leaders to tailor their own defenses in a similar fashion, an effort that took much of the spice and energy out of the enterprise.

Thus, Thornwell, Richard Fuller, Thomas Smyth, and others agreed with Hodge that, in practice, masters ought not to exercise unlimited power over bondsmen but should confine themselves to exploitation of their labor and recognize only a right of slave proprietorship. Following the example that Hodge and other northern conservatives were setting, the southern churchmen preached that God was enjoining masters "to provide for the intellectual and moral education of the slave."[23] Moreover, marital and parental rights were to be respected, meaning that families ought never to be broken up. Once again, southern clergy heeded their northern conservative allies and proposed at church conventions and assemblies instruction in literacy and other ameliorations for slaves. They had little choice. To ignore northern conservatives on these matters might snap crucial fraternal links. After all, even the *Saturday Evening Gazette*, a reactionary publication of New England, observed that "it needs no ghost from the grave to tell us that slavery is a great social and economical evil, and that every patriot and every Christian should be glad to see it removed."[24] To be sure, complete isolation from the rest of Christendom might inspire a martyr complex useful at home, but that state of affairs would shrink the moral and even political force of the proslavery argument beyond recovery. As a result, the southern clergy had to show gratitude and even admit slavery's shortcomings that ought to be corrected. These endeavors could only be half-hearted, however, because neither the politicians nor the planters were about to surrender a slaveholder's untrammeled authority, least of all through the intervention of government. The southern clergy might convert thousands of slaves through their earnest mission enterprise, but they could hardly boast of success in the state legislatures. For all the talk of an evangelical "special-interest" agenda, to borrow Carwardine's phrase, their lobbying, timid and sporadic, had produced not a single law that protected slave families, encouraged manumissions, or authorized even the most rudimentary forms of slave education. They felt much more at home complaining of tavern licensing, gambling, and other legal matters that posed little or no sectional peril. No wonder the clergy feared disunion: the prospect of still greater isolation from their northern church allies was scarcely welcome.

Yet the policy of cooperation with sympathizers outside the South presented difficulties as well. Although the point might be conveniently overlooked, northern conservative church fathers refused to sanctify slavery as an eternal condition appropriate solely to black-skinned descendants of Adam. Charles Hodge, for instance, carried his logic to a point that few southern clergy dared to applaud. "Any laws inconsistent with these principles are unscriptural and unjust, and ought to be immediately abrogated." If Christian command were followed, Hodge continued, "the gradual elevation of the slaves to all the rights of free citizens" would proceed. "The feudal serf first became a tenant, then a proprietor invested with political power. This is the natural progress of political society, and it should be allowed freely to expand itself, or it will work its own destruction."[25]

Throughout the northern states, most clergymen took a line similar to Hodge's. They failed to insist that slaveholding was inherently sinful, much to the relief of their Christian colleagues in the slave states. Yet they did object to what Charles Hodge criticized as "the slave system" of the South.[26] Southerners could take satisfaction that a general attack on the heretical position of the abolitionists accompanied these criticisms. Nevertheless, southern slavery was still stigmatized as cruel and ungodly in practice—and this assessment came from the South's most loyal clerical allies in the North. The pronouncements that northern conservatives made about slavery comforted the southern leaders but hobbled any bolder defense of the institution—a more radical position that would inevitably have placed them at the forefront of secession.

The second factor restricting southern clerical fervor for disunion was their relationship to the national and regional polity. Southern churchmen had always been much more circumspect about politics from the pulpit than their radical northern opponents. The antebellum southern clergy tiptoed around most controversial public issues. The *Southern Christian Advocate*, a Methodist paper, worried that the "preacher politician" would neglect the saving of souls, "say hard, and unkind, and uncharitable things" about adversaries, and rush after "worldly honor," a vice more "absorbing than avarice."[27] Even pulpit denunciations of duels were couched in terms of honor—true honor being defined as obedience to God and "false honor" a cowardly fear of disrepute.[28]

Adversarial by temperament, southern politicians were largely drawn from military and lawyerly ranks, but clergymen destined for city and town parishes were more likely to have quite pacific temperaments. For that reason, there was always a public suspicion that clergymen were too often effete and pusillanimous. More slaveholders failed to join a church than the number that did. Men outside the evangelical orbit thought them more comfortable in the parlor drinking tea with the ladies than attending political rallies or watching musterground parades. In fact, as Donald Mathews points out, sixty-five women filled the pews for every thirty-five men in the congregation, even though "men outnumbered women in the general population (51.5 : 48.5)."[29]

From the 1820s forward, moral reform in the North had largely emanated from politically minded clergy and lay evangelicals. Their approach was far from being sophisticated but instead divided the world between Good and Evil in the starkest terms imaginable. They did so perhaps because of a hidden uncertainty. As a friend of William Ellery Channing of Boston Unitarianism observed, they felt "less confident of being amongst the elect" because they had forsaken Calvinism and adopted doctrines of free will the better to serve their own salvation and their missionary purposes.[30] The first issue to arouse their concern had been federal desecration of the Sabbath. One remedy, they urged, was to close down the U.S. Postal Service one day a week. With some success the Democratic party under Andrew Jackson stigmatized the movement as a fanatical effort of a "Christian party in politics" that endangered the republic. Such leaders of the Sabbatarian cause as the merchants Lewis and Arthur Tappan and Amos Phelps, however, then took up a new and much more politically troublesome crusade—the struggle against American slaveholding,—applying the customary evangelical principles of Manichaean light and darkness.[31] The southern clergy had reacted in horror to such mingling of moral and partisan matters. The New York abolitionists' Postal Campaign, summer 1835, opened their eyes to the dangers ahead.[32] As a northern clerical sympathizer later wrote Virginia Presbyterian Moses Hoge, "the fierce demon of religious fanaticism breathes out threatening and slaughter."[33] Yet the southern clergy's response to abolitionism was certainly mild if compared with the hot words that southern politicians customarily adopted.

Defending their slaveholding parishioners from the antislavery calumny of "men-stealing" sin could be carried out in the context of a pure and holy churchmanship even if it was hard to reach anyone outside the South save their northern clerical friends. Clamor for changing allegiance from one government to another, however, was quite another matter. This sentiment was particularly true for Old School Presbyterians in the South. As James O. Farmer has noted, of all southern church fathers, they were the most likely to hold Whiggish convictions.[34] In 1859, Thornwell, leader of South Carolina Presbyterians, invoked the longstanding sanction against clerical politicking to back his Unionist sentiments. The church, he preached, was a "spiritual body, clothed only with spiritual powers," so that "intermeddling" with politics would be "foreign" to the church's "office and derogatory to its dignity."[35] Likewise, Unionist Robert L. Dabney, an influential Virginia Presbyterian, had long maintained that ministers ought never to plunge into partisanship when acting "ministerially, publicly, or any way representatively of God's people as such." They risked squandering their "moral power" as "peacemakers and mediators." The people of the South, Dabney continued, were already "abundantly touchy" and needed no clergymen to prod them along the road to disunion. "There were plenty of politicians to make the fire burn hot enough, without my help to blow it," Dabney concluded.[36] One might suspect that since the church and the political party system sought to reach the same audience, rivalry for public attention induced clergymen to keep the distinctions between church activity and political partisanship as separate as possible.

The third element inhibiting southern clerical support for secession concerned the ambivalent role that the ethic and rhetoric of honor played in southern life and discourse. Clergymen were unlikely to rattle sabers and glorify the chivalry in the manner of William Faulkner's Gail Hightower. So long as the political situation remained fluid and no northern coercive action had been taken, the body of gentleman theologians was content with the status quo. To them it seemed, in fact, a sectional disgrace to turn against the martial ardor that had produced the Revolution, the victory of New Orleans in 1815, and the triumph over the Catholic Mexicans. Yet the church had also to confront the warlike character of southern whites. They scarcely could encourage secession with clear Christian consciences while the nation was still at peace and the existing order remained politically challenged. After reporting on local reaction to the secession crisis in January 1861, for instance, John Cowper Granbery, a young preacher of Charlottesville, Virginia, informed his fiancée: "I will check myself abruptly and violently so as not to pursue the path of political discussion which everybody travels these days. What have women and preachers to do with succession [sic] and war?"[37]

The minister meant that he and members of the gentler sex had loftier duties. They not only had to fight "sin"—that is, those basic faults to which all mankind was subject—they also had to confront a system of rigid and sacralized customs that stressed masculinity over effeminacy and other formulations that separated what we might call Christian dominion from antique but still virulent male privilege. With regard to the age-old patriarchy to which the southern father, brother, and husband were dedicated, biblical sanctification of tradition served the churchmen and the men of honor alike. Yet the aim for moral improvement was bound to require clergymen to stress the need for humility, penitence, and other signs of godly behavior in the face of human pride, hallmark of honor. They were aware that conceit, fear of shame, and hope for public acclaim affected all men, but most especially those used to the obedience of slaves and all other dependents. "It is a characteristic of our people that they are . . . vainglorious, to a degree that makes them ridiculous. They love to boast, and they love to sacrifice to their own drag and to burn incense in their own net," intoned James Thornwell. For that reason, along with his steadfast dedication to Whiggery, Thornwell long opposed secession. In 1850, he wrote a friend, "The prospect of disunion is one which I cannot contemplate without absolute horror." The consequent war, he foresaw, would be "the bloodiest, most ferocious, and cruel in the annals of history." Ten years later, he steadfastly maintained that withdrawing from the Union would bring "defeat, and disaster, insecurity to slavery, oppression to ourselves, ruin to the State." In the opinion of Presbyterian Robert Dabney of Virginia, South Carolina "is as great a pest as the abolitionists." If he could have his way, Dabney proposed, the federal government "might whip her to their heart's content, so they would only do it by sea and not pester us."[38]

Fear of political change and a mistrust of what might be called the Hotspur mentality led other divines to deplore secessionism as well. Despite Lincoln's election in November 1860, James Otey, Episcopal bishop of Tennessee, for instance, thought principles of honor and patriotism demanded continued loyalty to the Union. Otey called South Carolina's preparations for separation "infamous. There is not a redeeming trait about the movement to save it from the just and deep condemnation of Posterity." Otey was dismayed enough to hope that President James Buchanan would be impeached for not having "throttled nullification" in the spirit of Otey's Tennessee compatriot, Andrew Jackson. In a subsequent appraisal, Otey, like some northern politicians and reformers, expressed the view that for at least twenty-five years a party of unmanly and subterranean conspirators had sought a pretext for southern separation. Like Thornwell, he predicted that the unplanned outcome of secession would be a "speedy inevitable extinction [of slavery], as certainly as the sun's rays fall upon the Earth."[39] The reason for slavery's demise, he shrewdly continued, was that the South would no longer have the moral support that a government with over 30 million people provided. If fugitive slaves were not likely to be returned in every case by a Lincoln government, the South had no chance of getting them back after separation. To think otherwise, he exclaimed, was "simply preposterous." The free states "will make no such treaty stipulations and we shall not have the color of law or pretext to demand them." Just look at the secessionists, Otey advised. They claim that "*they can whip all creation*—Cotton will make them 'princes and rulers in all lands'! Depend upon it, this is the pride that goes before a fall. . . . The day of vengeance I verily believe is near at hand."[40] Otey issued a pastoral letter in which he cautioned his Tennessee clergy to present themselves as men of "moderation" and " 'study to be quiet, and to mind their own business.' "[41] The fire-eater sensibility had no attractions for him but instead seemed a foolish as well as dishonorable, treacherous policy.

To be sure, Otey and other Whiggish clergy, particularly in the border states, scarcely spoke for all clergymen and pious laity. His version of honor was not universally accepted, even in clerical ranks. In fact, his fellow bishop, the Rt. Rev. Francis H. Rutledge of Florida, came out boldly for secession, backing his convictions with a five-hundred-dollar donation to the state legislature, payable upon news that an ordinance of secession had been passed. Originally from South Carolina, Rutledge "had himself already seceded with his native state, and in advance of Florida." Edmund Ruffin of Virginia, then in Florida, rejoiced in the bishop's decisiveness. An irascible fire-eater, Ruffin seldom had a good word for anyone, but on his visit to stir Florida to disunion he found that he "was very much pleased with the venerable old minister, & with his ardent & active patriotic sentiments."[42]

Although many of the state politicians and militia leaders were Episcopalians with equally strong disunionist opinions, Bishop Rutledge, who was also rector of St. John's Church, Tallahassee, did not win over former Whig governor Richard Keith Call and founder of St. John's. Call worked tirelessly against Florida's departure. When a fire-eater exulted over the state's secessionist decision in Call's presence, the Unionist retorted, "Yes, you have opened the gates of Hell."[43]

Rutledge was by no means the only ecclesiastical figure to sport his disunionist colors openly. The honor of being the first clerical authority to propose disunion in 1860 went to the editor of the *Southern Presbyterian*, published in Columbia, South Carolina, capital of disunionism.[44] As early as the Nullification Crisis of the early 1830s, the Rev. Thomas Goulding at the Presbyterian Theological Seminary in Columbus, South Carolina, had announced that "Disunion would be, in national politics, to prefer weakness to strength—degradation to honorable rank." Likewise during the same episode, Richard P. Cater linked South Carolina's pride to exemplary Christian fervor and urged his congregation to "prefer the stillness and silence of the grave, to the heart chilling clangour [*sic*] of the chains of slavery."[45] In the 1830s, these clerical hotheads were the noisy exceptions of their day, but the ranks of clerical disunionists did not grow by very alarming numbers, even as late as 1859. Southern clergy did grow ever more weary of northern Christians who seemed to be straying into a godless wilderness to chase after "Mormonism, Millerism, Comeoutism, Universalism, or with an Americanized edition of German Rationalism." By and large, however, both press and pulpit throughout the South were reluctant to advocate so violent and wrenching a policy.

As the crisis over the election of Lincoln developed, the mood gradually shifted, yet it did so against a firm resistance to change, particularly in the upper South. The *Central Presbyterian*, published in Richmond, warned in the September before Lincoln's election that secession would inevitably bring on "a horrible civil war." Also in the upper South, the Rev. Robert Breckinridge of the Presbyterian church tirelessly spoke out for the Union. He lambasted the secessionists by warning his fellow Kentuckians, "If we desire to perish, all we have to do is to leap into this vortex of disunion." Like Bishop Otey of Tennessee, he thought the seceding slave states would destroy God's glorious plans for a united nation. Slavery was much better protected within the Union than it would be in a separate country. "So long as the union of the States survives," he preached, "the constitutional guaranty and the Federal power, which have proved adequate for more than seventy years, are that much added to whatever other force States or sections may possess to protect their rights."[46] His widely disseminated views helped immeasurably to keep the border states within the Union.

In the lower South, however, Breckinridge's onetime friend Benjamin M. Palmer, a Presbyterian minister in New Orleans, adopted the secession cause, making rhetorical use of southern adherence to the ancient ethic. The clergyman argued that fanaticism had sundered the Union by electing a purely sectional candidate. As a result, southern statesmen were forming a government "to uphold and perpetuate what they cannot resign without dishonor and palpable ruin."[47] Palmer insisted that the southern white people's "providential trust" required them "*to conserve and to perpetuate the institution of slavery as now existing.*" His widely distributed sermon had as much impact for secession in the lower South as Breckinridge's for Unionism in the border states. Yet even this fire-eating divine conceded that the relationship of master and slave was scarcely all that the church could hope for. "Still less," he admitted, "are we required dogmatically, to affirm that it will subsist through all time." Residual loyalty to the policy of a circumscribed defense of slavery induced him to express such sentiments.

Palmer, however, provided the basis for the dramatic turn that soon overwhelmed the Whiggish clergy, even outside the lower South. He challenged Unionists like Breckinridge of Kentucky, who contended that the federal executive was not the servant of the sovereign states but their master. "Had the Constitution been regarded as a compact whose bonds were mutual honor and good faith," Palmer concluded, "the apprehension of a rupture would have been the surest guaranty of its observance." The northerners' "numerical majority" encouraged their aggression and imperialist ambitions, whereas a loose bond of states would have upheld "every consideration of honor and interest."[48] Such sentiments as these led the clergy of the lower South into the secessionist ranks as their states left the Union in the early months of 1861. In the upper South, Otey, Bishop William Meade of Virginia, and other Unionists remained loyal, but only until the firing on Fort Sumter in April. Soon thereafter most of them were echoing the demands for manhood and honor that once had been most closely identified with the disunionists of the 1850s.

The character of that discourse was well exemplified in the rhetoric of Jefferson Davis. At a state convention in 1851, the future Confederate president exclaimed that Mississippi's "honor was the first consideration" before the citizens in the face of northern perfidy; "her flag was hoisted to the mast and he for one" pledged to "cut away the halyards, and there let it float." The state's honor, Davis proclaimed, "was his honor." He called upon brave men to "transmit to their descendants the same heritage which had been given to themselves," Davis chanted in the customary discourse. Such expressions, which resounded through the length and breadth of the region, were bound to affect the clergy. They belonged to communities where the language of honor flourished; they could not escape its dictates. The idiom had long served as "the lingua franca" of southern sectionalism.[49]

The clergy easily adjusted to the style because the rubrics of honor were part of the Hebraic and Christian traditions. Codification of the ethic could be located in Scripture itself. Middle Eastern cultures, then and now, have been partly based upon rigid rules of honor and heightened fears of disgrace and humiliation. In Holy Scripture, the worship of God was conceptualized in terms of that code. The prophets' jeremiads denounced the wayward Israelites for the dishonoring offense of impugning the blamelessness of God. They took from God due honor and glory—two interconnected modes of praise rendered in the one Hebrew word *kabod*. Even the commandment, "love thy neighbor as thyself," meant, according to Rabbinic tradition, to hold others— their properties and families—in honor as you would have them respect you, your relations, and your possessions. Southern Protestants had no difficulty adopting such an approach.[50]

In sum, the Old Testament rendering of honor endured among southern-ers accustomed to face-to-face, small-scale, family-oriented usages that bore analogy with the pastoral society that produced the Holy Word.[51] As a result, biblical injunction seemed to supply the southern clerical fire-eater and later rebel with ample self-justifications. In March 1863, Rabbi M. J. Michelbacher informed the congregation of the German Hebrew Synagogue in Richmond: *"Thou dost call upon the people of the South in the words Thou gavest to Nehemiah: 'Fight for your brethren, your sons, and your daughters, your wives and your houses.'"*[52] The *Central Presbyterian* proudly boasted in May 1861, "Virginia's gallant sons . . . have sprung forward to the defense of their insulted Mother; assured that they are contending for the most sacred rights, and for the dearest interests for which patriot soldiers ever drew the sword."[53]

If biblical quotation did not fill the space reserved for honorable sentiment, the Confederate preacher could always turn to traditional sensibilities about manhood and glory. Warning that shame, the polar opposite of honor, was even a greater threat than death itself, a Presbyterian paper in 1862 preached that *"Defeat will be the death to us,* and worse than death it *will be* INFAMY."[54] Even the antipolitical Methodists took up the cry. The Georgia Methodist Conference in 1863 declared that giving up the fight would be "a disgrace to our manhood, a surrender of principles, a sin against our dependents and chil-dren."[55] In advocating secession in his impassioned address in New Orleans, November 1860, Benjamin Palmer pledged that "Not till the last man has fallen behind the last rampart" shall the South yield its noble standard. If the new Confederacy were supinely to abandon the cause, she would transmit a shame-ful "curse as an heir-loom to posterity."[56] Likewise, Thomas Smyth of South Carolina urged a martial boldness to protect "the undefiled purity and honor of our wives and daughters; unpillaged property; unravaged fields, uninjured harvests; uncontaminated servants; all—every thing that is sacred to honor and to happiness" were "involved in this contest."[57] Samuel Henderson, an Alabama Baptist editor, similarly argued that his state "owes it to her own honor . . . to secede from the Union."[58]

In other words, the Whig clerical elements made up for past doubts re-garding disunion with a zeal typical of the recent convert. As James H. Moor-head has noted, "The almost joyous abandon with which the churches had thrown themselves into the business of war was in part an escape from am-biguities that had become too burdensome to sustain."[59] He was referring to the northern churches, but the point was equally valid for the southern ones. In clerical opinion, such sentiments advantageously united all white southerners behind a single aim rather than perpetuating the divisions of political parties.

Ministers generally believed that petty partisanship had no place in the Christian scheme. At the outset of the war, southern evangelicals had high hopes for a widespread spirit of cooperation behind Jefferson Davis and his colleagues in Richmond, a dream soon to vanish.[60]

In this southern discourse, honor to God and honor to self were closely bound together. As a result, it was possible for church-goers to reconcile the traditional ethic and evangelical belief. For instance, Sarah Dorsey, a wealthy plantation mistress of Louisiana, presented Confederate General Leonidas L. Polk, prewar Episcopal bishop of Louisiana, a battle flag upon which she had emblazoned the "Labarum"—that is, the Cross of Constantine. "We are fighting the Battle of the Cross against the Modern Barbarians who would rob a Christian people of Country, Liberty, and Life," she wrote him. As Dorsey's words suggest, romantic heroism and Christian zeal were congenially united.[61]

The abrupt transition to Confederate allegiance freed the new clerical loyalists from former deference to northern conservative church opinion. In 1861, southern Old School Presbyterians were horrified when such longstanding friends as Gardiner Spring of New York City backed resolutions at the General Assembly firmly supporting the Union. Yet such expressions of Union fealty freed the rebel clergy from further national ties.[62] Later in the same year, Lewis Harvie pronounced, "We are hereafter to meet this question of slavery in a totally different spirit from that which controlled us" before. We must "become slavery propagandists."[63] The new freedom came at a price for some. Thomas Smyth of Charleston in 1863 sounded almost desperate when he proposed that God had decreed what amounted to a "divine right of slaveholding." Perhaps the ghost of the beheaded Charles I had risen to give a blessing to the new order. Smyth asked rhetorically, "what if God, by a positive divine enactment, ordained that throughout the history of the world, slavery should exist as a form of organized labor among certain races of man?" In his judgment, the North would be cursed forever for waging "a war of extermination against slavery." Yankee defiance was nothing short of blasphemy—a "rebellion against the Lord God omnipotent, who ruleth." The clergyman made these observations under the heading, "the divine right of secession."[64]

Even for churchmen less impassioned than Thomas Smyth, a sense arose that the issues of slavery and antislavery were happily no longer relevant. Lincoln's Proclamation to begin military operations against the rebel states freed them from the perplexing question of whether slavery was right or wrong. As a Virginia ecclesiastical biographer put it, "Henceforth, in the minds of her sober, Christian men, it was not a question of slavery, of secession, or of Union. It was a question of self-defence, self-government, and constitutional liberty." Warfare simplified decision making; emotions could take the place of rational thought.[65]

Such strongly Unionist clergy as Bishop Otey and Thornwell, however, continued to doubt a bright future. They had had little trouble swearing fidelity to the new government. Prudence, fear of lost reputation, and dread of dwindling congregations—and above all their loyalty to rebel kindred and neighbors—had shoved them into the secessionist parade. Thornwell, for instance, echoed the language of his honor-conscious compatriots in South Carolina when he concluded in late 1860, "a free people can never consent to their own degradation."[66] Nonetheless, a note of sadness and expectation of ruin crept into his public utterances in favor of Confederate rule. In a fast-day sermon on the eve of South Carolinian secession, Thornwell thundered, "We can make every pass a Thermopoylae, every street a Salamis, and every plain a Marathon. If we are overrun, we can at least die."[67] In the language of honor, his tone was meant to be grimly determined, but it sounded almost suicidal. Rather than pray for victory, Thornwell made the disunion enterprise seem all too problematic when he declared, "leaning upon the arm of everlasting strength, we shall achieve a name, whether we succeed or fall . . . posterity will not willingly let die." He ended the sermon on a depressing note by predicting that the state of South Carolina was bound to "suffer" and was doubtless "destined to fall." He repeated the word *suffer* four times within the closing paragraph, to drive home the upcoming perils about which Carolinian secessionists were so dismissive.[68] Even after South Carolina had seceded and hopes were running high for other states to join the movement, Thornwell had to observe that most men of his acquaintance could only pronounce "the word DISUNION, with sadness of heart."[69]

If ambiguity and pessimism were evident in southern churchmen's reaction to disunion, matters did not wholly improve in the war itself. The rebel government did not take very seriously the need for clergymen on the field of battle. Confederate army regulations never mentioned the role, duties, or even presence of chaplains in the ranks. Demonstrating their own indifference to religion—despite presidential appeals for fast days—Jefferson Davis and others in high places thought paid chaplaincies a misallocation of scarce resources. Separation of church and state was carried to an extreme that could not have helped army esprit de corps in the long run. Eventually, the Confederate Congress grudgingly provided chaplains with a private's level of wage and rank. As a result, few clergymen took up the labor for long; even the pious Stonewall Jackson could supply but half of his regiments with chaplains. In the entire military establishment, only fifty ministers served through the duration.[70]

No wonder clerical morale during the war was not much better than that of the civilian population as a whole. Manfully, pastors, preaching to dwindling flocks, denounced the federals, abolitionists, and "black Republicans" and swore that God was simply testing His chosen people before lavishing future glory and victories upon them.[71] Yet sustaining a buoyant outlook was not easy when churches were being turned into hospitals and military headquarters and the Yankee enemy was burning or vandalizing those that fell into their hands. As morale—and church alms—fell ever lower, James Thornwell tried to inspire his congregation's patriotic spirit, but even he alluded to the probability of defeat in set battles. He urged a continuation of the fighting in the form of "guerrilla" warfare—to what godly purpose he failed to say.[72] Likewise, in her letter to Leonidas Polk, Sarah Dorsey phrased her Confederate convictions in unrecognized pessimism. "Never defeated, annihilated, never conquered," she boasted, but then ended on this note: "When the land is conquered it will be time for us to die." Dorsey did not say *if* the land is conquered but "when" that tragedy occurred, death would be welcome.[73] Unhappily, these Whiggish Christians proved better prophets than they would have ever wished to be. Like Bishop-General Polk himself, Dorsey's "Labarum" and the cause for which it stood were destined to fall in the dust.

Notes

1. See Bertram Wyatt-Brown, *Yankee Saints and Southern Sinners* (Baton Rouge, 1985), 183–213.

2. Donald G. Mathews, *Slavery and Methodism: A Chapter in American Morality, 1780–1845* (Princeton, 1965); Robert M. Calhoon, *Evangelicals and Conservatives in the Early South, 1740–1861* (Columbia, SC, 1988); C. C. Goen, *Broken Churches, Broken Nation: Denominational Schisms and the Coming of the Civil War* (Macon, GA: 1985); John McKivigan, *The War Against Proslavery Religion: Abolitionism and the Northern Churches, 1830–1865* (Ithaca, NY, 1984).

3. Sydney Ahlstrom, *Religious History of the American People* (New Haven, 1972), 672.

4. Goen, *Broken Churches, Broken Nation*, 169.

5. See Larry E. Tise, *Proslavery: A History of the Defense of Slavery in America, 1701–1840* (Athens, GA, 1987), 143; Charles Grier Sellers Jr., "The Travail of Slavery," in *The Southerner as American*, ed. Charles Grier Sellers (Chapel Hill, 1960), 40–71. For an elegant review of this aspect of the proslavery debate in historiography, see Gaines M. Foster, "Guilt over Slavery: A Historiographical Analysis," *Journal of Southern History* 56 (November 1990): 665–694. See also Orlando Patterson, *Slavery as Social Death: A Comparative Study* (Cambridge, 1982), 262–296, on the meaning or lack of meaning of southern manumissions.

6. Cf. C. C. Goen, "Broken Churches, Broken Nation: Regional Religion and North-South Alienation in Antebellum America," *Church History* 52 (March 1983): 21–35. Goen argues that "southern church leaders could easily think of themselves as the first line of defense for the South and its way of life (22)." Perhaps so, but on the whole politicians were much more eager to engage the issue than they were.

7. Drew Gilpin Faust, "Introduction: The Proslavery Argument in History," in *The Ideology of Slavery: Proslavery Thought in the Antebellum South, 1830–1860*, ed. Drew Gilpin Faust (Baton Rouge, 1981), 5–6.

8. Review of N. Scarritt, *Position of the M. E. Church, South, on the Subject of Slavery* in *Quarterly Review of the M. E. C.—South* 13 (January 1859): 134–135; Lewis M. Purifoy, "The Southern Methodist Church and the Proslavery Argument," *Journal of Southern History* 32 (August 1966): 325–341; James David Essig, "A Very Wintry Season: Virginia Baptists and Slavery, 1785–1797," *Virginia Magazine of History and Biography* 88 (April 1980): 181; Presbyterian General Assembly quoted in McKivigan, *War Against Proslavery Religion*, 26.

9. James Henley Thornwell, quoted in Goen, *Broken Churches, Broken Nation*, 165; second quotation, Thornwell, *The Rights and Duties of the Master: A Sermon Preached at the Dedication of a Church, Erected in Charleston, S.C. for the Benefit and Instruction of the Coloured Population* (Charleston, SC, 1850), 31, 32. See also Beth Barton Schweiger, "The Transformation of Southern Religion: Clergy and Congregations in Virginia, 1830–1895," Ph.D. dissertation, University of Virginia, 1994, 182. George F. Holmes quoted in Faust, "Introduction," 10.

10. Tucker quoted in Faust, "Introduction," 13; Prof. Tayler Lewis, "Patriarchal and Jewish Servitude No Argument for American Slavery: Published in 'The World' in Reply to the Preceding Sermon of Rev. Henry J. Van Dyke," in *Fast-Day Sermons, or The Pulpit on the State of the Country* (New York, 1861), 181–183.

11. Figures derived by Andrew Frank of the University of Florida from the Eighth U.S. Census, 1860. New York clergy numbered 49,597, Pennsylvania 19,208, and in the states of Alabama, Arkansas, Florida, Georgia, Kentucky, Louisiana, Maryland, Mississippi, North Carolina, South Carolina, Tennessee, Texas, and Virginia, a total of 19,803. See also James Oscar Farmer Jr. *The Metaphysical Confederacy: James Henley Thornwell and the Synthesis of Southern Values* (Macon, GA, 1986), 12. One must remember, however, that part-time ministries were more common in the southern and other rural and western states than in the more urbanized North. Nevertheless, the sectional divergences are notable.

12. See New York *Tribune* quoted in Bertram Wyatt-Brown, "Proslavery and Antislavery Intellectuals: Class Concepts and Polemical Struggle," in *Antislavery Reconsidered: New Perspectives on the Abolitionists*, eds. Lewis Perry and Michael Fellman (Baton Rouge, 1979), 310.

13. George Fitzhugh to George Frederick Holmes, March 27, 1855, in George Frederick Holmes copybook, Duke University Library; James Henry Hammond, *Gov. Hammond's Letters on Southern Slavery: Addressed to Thomas Clarkson, the English Abolitionist* (Charleston, SC, 1845); Richard Fuller and Francis Wayland, *Domestic Slavery Considered as a Scriptural Institution: In a Correspondence Between the Rev. Richard Fuller, of Beaufort, S.C., and the Rev. Francis Wayland, of Providence, R.I.*, rev. ed. (New York, 1845); E. N. Elliott, ed., *Cotton Is King, and Pro-Slavery Arguments: Comprising the Writings of Hammond, Harper, Christy, Stringfellow, Hodge, Bledsoe, and Cartwright* (Augusta, GA, 1860).

14. Rev. Thomas Smyth, D.D., "The War against the South Vindicated," *Southern Presbyterian Review* 15 (April 1863): 481, see also 497, 499.

15. Roy Blount Jr., poster from Atlantic Monthly Press/Little Brown, and Company, available at the Southeast Booksellers' Association meeting, Kissimmee, FL, September 28, 1994.

16. James Henley Thornwell to Matthew Williams, August 26, 1850, in Benjamin Morgan Palmer, *Life and Letters of James Henley Thornwell, D.D., LL.D.* (Richmond, VA, 1875), 344.

17. Holmes and Hammond, quoted in Drew Gilpin Faust, *A Sacred Circle: The Dilemma of the Intellectual in the Old South, 1840–1860* (Baltimore, 1977), 48.

18. Faust, *Sacred Circle*, 140.

19. Bushnell, quoted in James H. Moorhead, *American Apocalypse: Yankee Protestants and the Civil War, 1860–1869* (New Haven, CT, 1978), 93; McKivigan, *The War Against Proslavery Religion*, 154.

20. J. H. Thornwell, *The State of the Country: An Article Republished from the Southern Presbyterian Review* (Columbia, SC, 1861): 21–22.

21. Thornwell, *The State of the Country: An Article Republished from the Southern Presbyterian Review*, 22.

22. Bacon, quoted in Jack P. Maddex Jr., " 'The Southern Apostasy' Revisited: The Significance of Proslavery Christianity," *Marxist Perspectives* 2 (Fall 1979): 133; Charles Hodge, "The Bible Argument on Slavery," in Elliott, ed., *Cotton is King*, 843.

23. Alexander Archibald Hodge, *The Life of Charles Hodge, D.D. LL.D.* (1881; New York, 1969), 335–336; *Princeton Review* article quoted in Moorhead, *American Apocalypse*, 89.

24. From the Boston *Courier*, in David Christy, *Pulpit Politics; Or, Ecclesiastical Legislation on Slavery in Its Disturbing Influences on the American Union* (1862; New York, 1969), 613.

25. Quoted in Hodge, *Charles Hodge*, 334–335. See Goen, *Broken Churches, Broken Nation*, 146–147.

26. Hodge, *Charles Hodge*, 333; Lewis G. Vander Velde, *The Presbyterian Churches and the Federal Union, 1861–1869* (Cambridge, MA, 1932), 34–36.

27. *Southern Christian Advocate*, quoted in Anne C. Loveland, *Southern Evangelicals and the Social Order, 1800–1860* (Baton Rouge, 1980), 117.

28. Loveland, *Southern Evangelicals and the Social Order*, 181.

29. Bertram Wyatt-Brown, *Southern Honor: Ethics and Behavior in the Old South* (New York, 1982), 410; Wyatt-Brown, "Religion and the 'Civilizing Process,'" in the Early American South, 1600–1860," in *Religion and American Politics: From the Colonial Period to the 1980s*, ed. Mark A. Noll (New York, 1990), 172–198; Donald G. Mathews, *Religion in the Old South* (Chicago, 1977), 47 (quotation), 245. See also Suzanne Lebsock, *The Free Women of Petersburg: Status and Culture in a Southern Town, 1784–1860* (New York, 1984), 226–227.

30. Quoted in Bertram Wyatt-Brown, *Lewis Tappan and the Evangelical War against Slavery* (Cleveland, 1969), 60.

31. George M. Marsden, *The Evangelical Mind and the New School Presbyterian Experience: A Case Study of Thought and Theology in Nineteenth-Century America* (New Haven, 1970), 26–27.

32. Bertram Wyatt-Brown, "The Abolitionists' Postal Campaign of 1835," *Journal of Negro History* 50 (October 1965): 227–238.

33. Peyton H. Hoge, *Moses Drury Hoge: Life and Letters* (Richmond, VA, 1899), 143.

34. Farmer, *The Metaphysical Confederacy*, 245.

35. James H. Thornwell, quoted in "The Princeton Review on the State of the Country and of the Church," *Biblical Repertory and Princeton Review* 37 (October 1865): 645.

36. Dabney, quoted in Hoge, *Moses Drury Hoge*, 139. Virginia Episcopalians reacted in a similar fashion. See Leonard I. Sweet, "The Reaction of the Protestant Episcopal Church in Virginia to the Secession Crisis: October, 1859 to May, 1861," *Historical Magazine of the Protestant Episcopal Church* 4 (June 1972): 137–151.

37. Granbery, quoted in Schweiger, "Transformation of Southern Religion," 204–205.

38. James Henley Thornwell to Rev. Dr. Hooper, March 8, 1850, in Palmer, *Life and Letters of Thornwell*, 477–478; James Henley Thornwell, "Our National Sins: A Sermon Preached in the Presbyterian Church, Columbia, S.C. on the Day of the State Fast, Nov. 21, 1860," in *Fast-Day Sermons*, 44. Also Thornwell, quoted in Margaret Burr DesChamps, "Union or Division? South Atlantic Presbyterians and Southern Nationalism, 1820–1861," *Journal of Southern History* 20 (November 1954): 494. Dabney, quoted in W. Harrison Daniel, "Southern Presbyterians in the Confederacy," *North Carolina Historical Review* 44 (Summer 1967): 234.

39. James H. Otey to Edward Calohill Burks, November 23, 1860, in James E. Walmsley, ed., "Documents: The Change of Secession Sentiment in Virginia in 1861 [Part II: Letters of James H. Otey to E. C. Burks]," *American Historical Review* 31 (October 1925): 98–99.

40. James H. Otey to Edward Calohill Burks, November 23, 1860, in Walmsley, ed., "Documents: The Change of Secession Sentiment in Virginia in 1861," 98–100.

41. Joseph Blount Cheshire, *The Church in the Confederate States* (New York, 1912), 11.

42. Joseph D. Cushman, *A Goodly Heritage: The Episcopal Church in Florida, 1821–1892* (Gainesville, FL, 1965), 42–44; entry for January 4, 1861, William Kauffman Scarborough, ed., *The Diary of Edmund Ruffin: Toward Independence October, 1856–April, 1861*, 3 vols. (Baton Rouge, 1972), 1: 524.

43. Quoted in Cushman, *The Goodly Heritage*, 45.

44. See Daniel, "Presbyterians in the Confederacy," 232; *Central Presbyterian*, quoted in Loveland, *Southern Evangelicals and the Social Order*, 259–260.

45. Goulding and Cater, quoted in Mitchell Snay, "Gospel of Disunion: Religion and the Rise of Southern Separatism, 1830–1861," Ph.D. dissertation, Brandeis University, 1984, 14 and 19.

46. *Central Presbyterian*, quoted in Daniel, "Southern Presbyterians in the Confederacy," 231; Breckinridge, quoted in James C. Klotter, *The Breckinridges of Kentucky, 1760–1981* (Lexington, 1986), 80; second quotation, Robert J. Breckinridge, "The Union to Be Preserved: A Discourse Delivered at Lexington, Ky., on the Day of the National Fast, Jan. 4, 1861," in *Fast-Day Sermons*, 112.

47. Benjamin M. Palmer, "Slavery a Divine Trust, Duty of the South to Preserve and Perpetuate It: A Sermon Preached in the First Presbyterian Church of New Orleans, La., Nov. 29, 1860," in *Fast-Day Sermons*, 77.

48. Palmer, quoted in *Quarterly Review of the Methodist Episcopal Church—South* 13 (July 1861): 460–461.

49. Jefferson Davis, "Speech at Fayette," July 11, 1851, in Lynda Lasswell Crist, ed., *The Papers of Jefferson Davis: 1849–1851* (Baton Rouge, 1983), 4: 209, 213; Christopher Olsen, "Community, Honor, and Secession in the Deep South: Mississippi's Political Culture, 1840s–1861," Ph.D. dissertation, University of Florida, 1996, chap. 2, 1; Wyatt-Brown, *Yankee Saints and Southern Sinners*, 183–213.

50. Everett W. Huffard, "Biblical Word Study KABOD: 'Honor,'" *The Exegete* 3 (October 1983): 1–5, esp. 3; Johannes Pederson, *Israel, Its Life and Culture I–II* (London, 1926).

51. Paul Friedrich, "Sanity and the Myth of Honor: The Problem of Achilles," *Ethos* 5 (Fall 1977): 285.

52. Quoted by James W. Silver, "The Confederate Preacher Goes to War," *North Carolina Historical Review* 33 (October 1956): 503.

53. Quoted in Goen, *Broken Churches, Broken Nation*, 173.

54. Quoted in Silver, "The Confederate Preacher Goes to War," 506.

55. Quoted in Willard E. Wight, "The Churches and the Confederate Cause," *Civil War History* 6 (December 1960): 368.

56. Palmer, "Slavery a Divine Trust," 77, 79.

57. Smyth, "The War against the South Vindicated," 513.

58. Jon G. Appleton, "Samuel Henderson: Southern Minister, Editor, and Crusader, 1853–1866," M.A. thesis, Auburn University, 1968, 8.

59. Moorhead, *American Apocalypse*, 82.

60. See Schweiger, "Transformation of Southern Religion," chap. 7.

61. Sarah A. Dorsey to Leonidas L. Polk, February 20, 1862, Leonidas L. Polk Papers, Jessie Ball DuPont Memorial Library, University of the South, Sewanee, TN.

62. J. Treadwell Davis, "The Presbyterians and the Sectional Conflict," *Southern Quarterly* 8 (January 1970): 124–125.

63. Harvie, quoted in Drew Gilpin Faust, *The Creation of Confederate Nationalism: Ideology and Identity in the Civil War South* (Baton Rouge, 1988), 61; see also ibid., 61–62.

64. Smyth, "The War of the South Vindicated," 497–498; see also J. William Flinn, ed., *Complete Works of Thomas Smyth*, 10 vols. (Columbia, SC., 1908–12), 7: 724–725.

65. Anonymous to Moses D. Hoge, April 16, 1861, in Hoge, *Moses Drury Hoge*, 145.

66. James H. Otey to Edward Calohill Burks, July 17, 1861, in Walmsley, ed., "Documents: The Change of Secession Sentiment in Virginia in 1861," 100; Thornwell, quoted in David B. Chesebrough, *"God Ordained This War:" Sermons on the Sectional Crisis, 1830–1865* (Columbia, SC, 1991), 196.

67. Quoted in Silver, "The Confederate Preacher Goes to War," 504.

68. James Henley Thornwell, "Our National Sins: A Sermon Preached in the Presbyterian Church, Columbia, S.C. on the Day of the State Fast, Nov. 21, 1860," in *Fast-Day Sermons*, 56.

69. Thornwell, *The State of the Country: An Article Republished from the Southern Presbyterian Review*, 24. See also Mary Jones to the Hon. Charles C. Jones, January 3, 1861, in Robert Manson Myers, ed., *The Children of Pride: A True Story of Georgia and the Civil War* (New Haven, CT, 1972), 641; and Haskell Monroe, "Southern Presbyterians and the Secession Crisis," *Civil War History* 6 (December 1960): 353.

70. Schweiger, "Transformation of Southern Religion," 219–220.

71. See Daniel, "Presbyterians in the Confederacy," 236–255.

72. James Henley Thornwell, "Our Danger and Our Duty," in Palmer, *Life and Letters of Thornwell*, Appendix II, 586.

73. Sarah A. Dorsey to Leonidas L. Polk, February 20, 1862, Leonidas L. Polk Papers.

5

The Coming of the Lord

The Northern Protestant Clergy and the Civil War Crisis

GEORGE M. FREDRICKSON

On April 14, 1865, a large crowd of Union partisans gathered in the harbor of Charleston, South Carolina, to celebrate the return of the American flag to its prewar position atop the battlements of Fort Sumter. The featured speaker at this most important and richly symbolic of northern victory ceremonies was the Rev. Henry Ward Beecher, pastor of the Plymouth Church in Brooklyn, New York. The choice of Beecher to be the orator of the day was a recognition of his personal services to the Union cause and those of the profession to which he belonged—the clergy of the principal northern Protestant denominations.[1]

The proper role of Protestant ministers and their churches in American public life has been a contentious issue since the founding of the republic. The generally accepted principle of separation of church and state has been interpreted in one way by those who (following the secular libertarian tradition of Thomas Jefferson) have viewed religious fervor as a potential danger to freedom of thought that requires a high wall of separation to protect government from sectarian influences, and in another by those who have made a distinction between the establishment of a national church, which was admittedly unconstitutional and unAmerican, and governmental endorsement of the common beliefs and values of the major Protestant denominations. Those advocating an offical recognition of mainstream Protestantism as America's faith have generally tried to give the sanction of law and public authority to cultural practices and moral standards that were not shared by religious (or nonreligious) minorities.

During the Jacksonian period, between the 1820s and the 1840s, the high-wall separationists, entrenched in the Democratic party, had the upper hand, at least in national political affairs (as reflected, for example, in the failure of efforts to force the federal government to cease transporting the mail on the sabbath). But the conflict over slavery and the Union in the 1850s and 1860s gave the clergy and the churches a new opening for the extension of an ecumenical Protestant influence into the affairs of state. "Political preaching," including open partisanship on the political choices before the country, became acceptable to a majority of church-going northerners, and a campaign was launched to give interdenominational Protestantism quasi-official recognition as the national religion. But the United States did not come out of the Civil War as the kind of quasi-theocratic Christian nation envisioned by some of the clergy. The paradoxical result of the wartime politicization of religion was that the clergy and the churches lost some of their earlier capacity to perform what Cornel West has described as the "prophetic" role of religion—criticizing and judging the secular order in the light of a higher morality than can be found in the marketplace or the corridors of power.[2]

To understand the clergy's role in the crisis, it is necessary to combine the insights of social and intellectual history, or, more specifically, to look at mid- to late-nineteenth-century Protestant ministers as members of a profession that was seeking to protect or enhance its status and authority and also as participants in the debate on the meaning of America that the sectional controversy and the Civil War had inspired. The two aspects have been studied separately by historians, but no one has made a systematic effort to combine them.

Works on the history of the professions highlight the responses to new conditions of an occupational group that had undergone a major institutional transformation between the late colonial period and the middle of the nineteenth century. The colonial minister, especially in New England, had been likely to spend all or most of his career serving a single church that was often virtually coterminous with a town or community. His associations and orientations were likely to be almost exclusively local, but his authority within his parish, which came more from his "office" than from his personal popularity, was likely to extend to public affairs as well as to matters of faith. By the mid-nineteenth century, a radical change had occurred. Clergymen changed pulpits and localities much more frequently and were more dependent on persuasion and lay approval for success. Congregations found it easier to dispose of ministers they did not like, and charismatic clergymen had less difficulty changing pulpits in the pursuit of larger congregations and higher salaries. These new career patterns tended to transform the Protestant ministry from a hieratic elite into a species of democratic leaders. Indeed, as Laurence Moore has recently pointed out, the parallel with the contemporaneous shift of political leadership from officeholding by local gentry to government by professional party politicians is striking. Denominations became somewhat like parties in their need to proselytize in competition with other denominations, and ministers often resembled politicians seeking electoral victory when they conducted revivalistic campaigns to increase church membership.[3]

One result of this situation was that ministers, like politicians, had to avoid offending or antagonizing the people they were trying to influence. It was dangerous in both cases to run too far ahead of public sentiment. The colonial minister speaking from his high pulpit and secure in his "office" had more freedom than his clerical descendants to render judgments that might be displeasing to influential members of his congregation. It would seem to follow, therefore, that "political preaching" in the mid-nineteenth century would normally conform to the preexisting political attitudes of congregations rather than clashing with them. Recognizing the extent to which ministers had to tailor their views to conform with those of their parishioners can serve as a useful check on interpretations that adopt a thoroughly "from-the-top-down" view of religious opinion on public issues, making it appear that ministers were completely autonomous agents rather than democratic leaders who were responsive to the views of their followers.

But one should not go to the opposite extreme and make ministers nothing but mouthpieces for lay opinion. Many were, in fact, unhappy with their dependence on congregational approbation and hankered for independent authority. To some extent, they could find it in the new clerical roles opened up by the growth of organized revivalism and benevolence in the early nineteenth century. As itinerant evangelists, missionaries, agents of moral reform societies, and denominational officials, they could exercise their own judgment to a considerable extent. They also could write books or articles for religious periodicals that were read mostly by other ministers rather than by the laity. Ministers customarily criticized politicians precisely because they had no higher view of things than what they could easily sell to the voters. Their own self-image as men of God meant they were supposed to be expounding the truths they had derived from Scripture and their own religious experiences rather than merely representing popular views. In this respect, they resembled lawyers and judges rather than elected politicians. Both the legal profession and the clergy had ambitions for professional authority that conflicted with the democratic populism of the Jacksonian era. But they had conflicting prescriptions for curbing the democratic excesses of the age. For lawyers, a rational appreciation of legal precedents and procedures was the key to republican order and community. For the clergy, it was religious sentiment and moral conviction, aroused and channeled by trained and certified religious specialists, that offered salvation from corruption and anarchy.[4]

The clerical and legal professions were therefore in competition for the role of guardians or guarantors of the values that sustained the republic. The lawyers had a great advantage in that they could claim expertise in interpreting the Constitution and were in a position to provide much of the nation's political leadership. (There was no barrier to a mixing of law and politics, as there often was in the case of religion and politics.) But, as Robert Ferguson has suggested, the rise of the slavery controversy and the apparent inability of lawyers and lawyer-politicians to resolve it provided the clergy with an opportunity to exert a broader kind of social and political leadership. When public questions were defined as moral issues rather than matters of legality or practical politics, the authority of ministers was enhanced because they were recognized as having special competence in ethical questions.[5]

The political preaching of the 1850s and 1860s was a break with the pattern of clerical activity that developed between the 1820s and the 1840s. The first response of ministers to the separation of church and state—a process that was completed when Congregational churches of Connecticut and Massachusetts lost the last vestiges of state support and sponsorship in the late 1820s and early 1830s—was to embrace the revivalism and organized benevolence of the Second Great Awakening. Previously established churches now learned to compete for membership with denominations, like the Methodists and Baptists, that had never known or sought government sponsorship and financial support. Recognizing that persuasion and not coercion was now the key to denominational success, Congregationalists and Presbyterians emulated some of the revivalistic methods pioneered by the Methodists and Baptists. As a result, the mainstream of American Protestantism became aggressively evangelical. Only non-Calvinist ritualistic churches like the Episcopalians and the Lutherans resisted the new methods.[6]

The ministers of the evangelical denominations were remarkably successful in increasing church membership and inculcating ascetic moral values in a large segment of the northern population. As social historians have shown, the new emphasis on personal piety and abstemious behavior, and the establishment of moral reform societies, served the needs of important elements in their congregations, especially women seeking an expanded role for the values associated with the cult of domesticity, business owners concerned with a disciplined workforce, and, more generally, an emerging middle class hoping to bring order and virtue to cities and towns emerging out of frontier conditions or disrupted by the economic and social conditions associated with the rise of a national market economy.[7]

Such achievements required relatively little coercive action by governments and were principally devoted to improving "civil society" through voluntaristic means. But churchmen and other observers hailed the growth of evangelical Protestantism for its indirect but indispensable contribution to American public life. Ministers in the 1830s and 1840s were supposed to avoid direct involvement in partisan politics, but this did not prevent them from viewing their work as essential to the success of the republic. In 1833, Alexis de Tocqueville had described America's disestablished religion with its nonpartisan ministers as "the foremost of the political institutions of the country" because it inculcated the virtues essential to republican government.[8] The Rev. Robert Baird, in his massive tome of 1843, *Religion in America*, made the case from within the evangelical establishment for religious voluntarism as the salvation of the American polity.

> The government and the church are mutual friends; neither is the slave of the other. The church simply asks for protection of the rights of conscience, and this she receives in the amplest manner. And what does the state receive in turn? It receives the immense moral influence of the Church—of the preaching of the Gospel, at so many thousands and tens of thousands of points, all over the land—of the Sabbath School—of the Bible class, and all the other influences of Christianity. It is in these that the laws find their surest basis, and their most effective sanction. It is just because of these in-

fluences—the Sabbath, the Church, the Bible—that a vast country of more than twenty-seven millions of people can be governed, and is governed, without the bayonet, and the cannon.[9]

Baird's ideology, which might be called evangelical republicanism, sanctioned democratic government but only in a qualified and provisional way. If the virtue deemed essential to the preservation of a republic depended on popular adherence to evangelical Christianity, what happened if a majority refused to act in accordance with its precepts? It would seem to follow that republican government would cease to be possible and that the populace would have to be governed by the bayonet and the cannon. When they discussed politics and politicians, ministers of the Jacksonian period often called attention to the dangers of the kind of democracy that drew its inspiration from the secular theorizing of the Enlightenment. According to them, the kind of government that draws its inspiration exclusively from a belief in natural rights, government by consent, and popular sovereignty degenerates rapidly into anarchy. It is not surprising that ministers were uneasy about the tendency of Jacksonians to defer to a popular will that was assumed to be naturally virtuous and therefore not in need of religious guidance and correction. The public opposition to ministerial partisanship made it difficult for them to give open support to the Whigs, and, in any case, the opposition party was little better than the Democrats when it came to pandering to unregenerate elements in an electorate based on universal manhood suffrage. But up to the time of the sectional crisis and the Civil War, most of the articulate evangelical clergy persisted in believing that the growing "conservative" influence of religion would protect the political and constitutional system against the excesses of democratic radicalism and obviate the need for an authoritarian state to repress vice, crime, and disorder.[10]

The rise of abolitionism in the 1830s brought the slavery issue to national attention and posed a difficult challenge for the northern clergy. The abolitionist claim that slavery could not be tolerated for another instant because it was a sin in the eyes of God was a radical application of the call for national purification made by the revivalists and moral reformers of the Second Great Awakening. But for the most part, the ministers of the mainstream denominations did not embrace the radical antislavery cause. Many of them recognized that slavery was an evil, but, unlike the sins that they had preached against—drinking, sexual immorality, sabbath breaking—it was an institution that had woven itself into the very fabric of the nation and could not easily be rooted out by moral suasion or constitutional action. They feared that vituperative attacks on slaveholders and efforts to deny them the fellowship of northern Christians would promote violence and disunion rather than furthering the cause of evangelical republicanism. Doubts also existed as to whether the slaves were ready, or capable, of being free men and women. Since evangelical republicanism required a citizenry made virtuous by the right kind of religious nurture and experience, it was assumed that slaves required the prolonged and sustained attention of missionaries before they could be entrusted with self-government. Some ministers, influenced by the racial ideologies of the time, even questioned whether blacks had the same God-given capacity as whites to perform the duties of democratic citizenship. Clergymen concerned about slavery and the elevation of the Negro race were likely to support the colonization movement even after abolitionists had repudiated it. Not wanting to risk the disunion and anarchy that forceful northern action against slavery might arouse, the ministers of the 1830s and 1840s, with a few conspicuous exceptions, rejected the abolitionist demand for immediate emancipation, and counseled Christians to be patient until such time as Divine Providence willed that the evil of slavery would pass away.[11]

Reliance on the workings of Providence to bring an end to slavery was consistent with the postmillennialism that dominated antebellum Protestant thought. The belief that a religious revival and the resulting improvement in human faith and morals would eventually usher in a thousand years of peace and justice antecedent to the Second Coming of Christ was an impetus to the promotion of progressive reforms, as historians have frequently pointed out. At the height of the Second Great Awakening in the 1830s, some evangelicals had expected the millennium to arrive within a few years. But by the 1840s such expectations had cooled, and postmillennialism was turning into a theological analogue of the broader middle-class ideology of gradual moral and material progress. Ministers often condemned the idolatry involved in secular celebrations of American perfectibility and economic or territorial growth, but rather than rejecting the ideal of national and universal progress, they sought to spiritualize it and bring it under the discipline of evangelical Christianity.[12] As the model for the redemption of America shifted from sudden conversions at revival meetings to the gradual process that the Rev. Horace Bushnell called "Christian nurture," it seemed clearer than ever that the abolitionist tactic of calling slavery a sin and demanding immediate emancipation risked endangering the slow and delicate process of elevating slaveholders and slaves to the point where emancipation would be feasible. The unwillingness of most northern churchmen to denounce all slaveowners as sinners, even after denominational schisms over the issue of slaveholding by bishops, clergymen, or missionaries, revealed that postmillennialism was not necessarily an impetus to radicalism. Only the minority that believed the millennium was so close at hand that Christians should act as if had already arrived were spurred to radical abolitionism. The majority of the northern Protestant clergy recognized that there could be no American millennium until slavery was abolished, but believed that this great reform would come about in God's good time and as the by-product of a general improvement in faith and morals.[13]

The Rev. Jesse T. Peck, prominent Methodist and quasi-official historian of antebellum evangelical Christianity, looked back from the vantage point of 1868 on the prewar clergy's generally cautious attitude on the slavery question and attempted to justify it. Like Robert Baird, Peck saw the religious revival as a conservative force rather than an invitation to radical reformism. "A revival of religion is a revival of national life," he wrote. "As far as it extends, the tendency to insubordination is broken; the very propensities which give all governments their most serious problems are reduced to control and finally eradicated." It followed that the northern clergy, while anticipating the eventual demise of slavery, tolerated the institution before the 1850s out of devotion to their "great dominant ideal of unity." "We thought and felt," Peck recalled, "that everything must bow to the one great sentiment of cofraternity." The abolitionists were rightly opposed by the bulk of the religious community because of their "un-Christian temper, and a disposition to prompt and summary justice not in harmony with the laws and plans of God." Antislavery agitation was "honestly discouraged by a very strong conservatism in the Church and Nation. It seemed likely to sweep away the very foundations of public order, and result in the wildest anarchy." According to Baird, whose memories were accurate, the mainstream evangelical movement had managed to combine a postmillennialist faith in the "plans of God" with a powerful commitment to "public order" and a fervent opposition to the kind of radical agitation that threatened to plunge the nation into "the wildest anarchy."[14]

What, then, are we to make of the apparent antislavery militancy of so many prominent northern clergymen during the crisis of the 1850s? Peck attributed the impulse behind the transition from clerical reticence on the slavery issue to militant defense of "free soil" to the fact "slavery reached out its arm to grasp more power and dominate more millions."[15] Some of the most conspicuous of these outspoken political preachers, the prominent Congregationalist and Presbyterian ministers typified by the Rev. Henry Ward Beecher, characterized themselves as "independent moderates." They opposed the Fugitive Slave Act and the Kansas-Nebraska Act as the products of an aggressive "slave power conspiracy" that violated the traditional understandings that were the basis of sectional accommodation. Like other "free-soilers" and supporters of the new Republican party, they opposed the expansion of slavery, but were willing to tolerate for the time being its continued existence in the slave states. Hence they held themselves aloof from the abolitionist movement with its commitment to immediate emancipation, leaving the end of slavery itself to the future operation of Divine Providence.[16]

A radical minority of the clergy found the Republican free-soil position increasingly inadequate as the sectional conflict intensified in the late 1850s and moved closer to the abolitionists. The Church Anti-Slavery Society, formed in 1859 under the leadership of the Congregationalist ministers George and Henry Cheever, was radical enough to earn the qualified endorsement of William Lloyd Garrison's American Anti-Slavery Society.[17] But most of the large number of evangelical ministers who preached on the issue of slavery's future operated within the safe confines of a developing sectional consensus that was anti-southern and fearful of a "slave power conspiracy" without being pro-emancipation and pro-black. Their sectionalist preaching became overtly political and frequently violated the old taboo against supporting political parties and candidates from the pulpit. What made such behavior acceptable to their congregations was the fact that the ministers in many of the northern churches were in step with their parishioners, who did not really have to be told to vote Republican.

Even those northern clergymen who normally took ultra-conservative stands on social and political issues could be aroused to militancy by the Kansas-Nebraska Act, which they viewed as an aggressive effort on the part of the South to repudiate a compromise on the spheres of slavery and freedom that was as much a part of the legal basis of American nationality as the Constitution itself. Thus, the Rev. Francis Wayland, a leading Baptist minister and educator, denounced the Kansas-Nebraska Act as "revolutionary," using much the same terminology that he had earlier used to condemn Dorr's rebellion in Rhode Island. The Bible, Wayland affirmed, made it clear that rebellion against constituted authority was a sin, and to his way of thinking repudiation of contractual agreements was a form of rebellion. Extending slavery, he argued, would tend to "dissolve the government itself, for when the essential element of a compact is reversed, every contracting party is released from its obligations in respect to it."[18] When Wayland and others like him appealed to "higher law," they were not referring to the right of the individual conscience to disobey immoral laws but to an organic basis of national unity that transcended a mere act of Congress. The Kansas-Nebraska sermon of the Rev. Ezra Stiles Gannett of Boston, one of the many Unitarian ministers whose social and political views jibed with those of clergymen of more theologically conservative denominations, contained a rejection of emancipation as impractical and a demand that the Constitution be venerated as the law of the land, because "order is the first condition of a safe and prosperous community," but nevertheless charged that southern efforts to extend slavery into the federal territories were calling the value of the Union into question.[19]

Ministers had a special stake in the outcome of the struggle over the future of the western territories. The South, many felt, was threatening the institutions of the North by resisting their natural westward expansion. All the traditional hopes for missionary activities in the West, all the expectations that the frontier could be saved from "barbarism" by the community pattern of New England with its towns, churches, and schoolhouses, came into play in the controversy over Kansas. What was new was the willingness to resort to force and the decline of a belief that the moral and spiritual influence of Christianity could by itself bring order out of American chaos. The great outburst of political preaching and clerical manifestos that began with the response to the Kansas-Nebraska Act and soon became support for the free-state settlers who were battling with proslavery forces in Kansas signified a reorientation of a large segment of the northern clergy on the question of their relationship to the state and public life. It was no longer sufficient to inculcate virtue and respect for law as general principle. When controversial public questions were thought to involve profound moral issues, the clergy felt obligated to take a stand. Along with this growth of outspokenness and partisanship, there was also a turning away from the original evangelical belief that peaceable persuasion was the Christian means of preparing the way for the Kingdom of God on earth. "Bleeding Kansas" seemed to show that the Slave Power understood only force, and that ministers might properly raise money to arm northern emigrants. The growing acceptance of coercive means in conflict with the forces of evil was not limited to the slavery controversy. With the passage of the Maine Law in 1851, the church-inspired temperance movement turned from persuasion to legislation in the ongoing war against demon rum. The sympathy of recent historians for the side that clergymen espoused in the debate over the expansion of slavery may have obscured the extent to which the clerical activism of the Civil War era concealed quasi-theocratic ambitions and threatened the Jeffersonian view of the relationship between church and state. The full dimensions of this threat would become apparent during the war itself.

The outbreak of the war for the Union found the clergy of the principal Protestant denominations unified and fervent in its support for the northern cause. A historian of the Pennsylvania clergy found that "the ministers of the gospel probably rallied more completely to the support of the government than any large, influential class."[20] The Cincinnati clergy, according to another local study, "transferred the war into a moral venture, a blending of Christian and national loyalty and a condemnation of the enemy and his way of life as subversive of government, civilization, and religion. The unity of the diverse ministry in wartime was exhilarating."[21] Individual denominations made official pronouncements on the crisis that expressed the same depth and unanimity of clerical commitment to the Union. A Presbyterian synod compared the southern rebellion to Satan's revolt against the throne of God, Methodist conferences featured emotional flag-raisings and the taking of loyalty oaths, and ministers of various faiths acted in effect as a recruiting agency for the Union army, unabashedly employing revivalistic methods to bring forth a flood of volunteers.[22] Ministers in several denominations lost their remaining inhibitions about the propriety of political preaching, and sermons with "loyalty" for their theme were widely reprinted so that those beyond the preacher's voice might become aware of their God-given duty. As propagandists for the Union, ministers succeeded in giving the war a religious sanction and thus played a vital role in maintaining northern morale and determination during the long struggle. It seems likely, in fact, that the Protestant pulpit was the single most important source of northern patriotic exhortation. As spiritual leaders of a crusade for the Union, the clergy enhanced its professional status, attaining a position of public respect that was probably greater than at any other time in the history of the United States. But a reading of wartime sermons shows that ministers were not simply bending with the wind and telling their patriotic congregations what they wanted to hear. They had an agenda of their own deriving from the evangelical republican traditon.

Early in the war, many ministers continued to resist the call for emancipation. In September 1861, the Rev. Ichabod Simmons of Simsbury, Connecticut, advised his Methodist congregation that "the war is not being conducted for the purpose of liberating the Southern slaves; it is the government saving itself." Lack of an antislavery policy should not concern them, for Providence would deal with slavery in due time.[23] When emancipation became imminent, however, the bulk of the clergy hailed it as God's way of purging the nation of the sin of slavery. Providence had acted more quickly and dramatically than had been anticipated, but it was not for human beings to question God's right to act in unexpected ways. In 1863, the Rev. Gilbert Haven, who before the war had been one of the most prominent abolitionists among the Methodist clergy, explained how the majority of his fellow ministers had come to support freeing the slaves. The main obstacle before 1861 had been their reverence for the Union and a belief that abolitionist agitation was destroying it. Now, however, it was clear that "abolitionism meant union and only under its banner could the nation be preserved."[24]

That the churches during the war at last became "active antislavery agencies" did not therefore mean that they had come to embrace the abolitionist view that slavery violated a "higher law" than the Constitution. Emancipation was now justified, many sermons pointed out, because slavery had made war on the Constitution. Anti-southern passions generated by the war and a new application of the law-and-order conservatism that had earlier engendered hostility to abolitionism were more conspicuous in clerical advocacy of wartime emancipation than humanitarian revulsion at human bondage.[25] Sympathy for the black victims of "the peculiar institution" and forthright condemnations of racial inequality as the essence of slavery's sinfulness were not the dominant themes in this emancipationist discourse. Some prominent northern clergymen even contributed to the Malthusian or proto-Darwinist racism that permitted white supremacists to support emancipation on the expectation that it would lead to a struggle for existence between the races that would end only with the elimination of the exotic African stock from the American population.[26]

Many clergymen celebrated the war as a means of purging the nation of sins or vices that seemed to them more fundamental than tolerating southern slavery. The Rev. J. M. Sturtevant, a leading Congregationalist and president of Illinois College, addressed the alumni of Yale College in July 1861 on "The Lessons of Our National Conflict" and specified four vices that might be cured by "the lessons of adversity." They were "*a morbid philanthropy; an ostentatious and costly self-indulgence; a lack of loyal admiration and reverence for a strong and energetic government; and a disposition in our notions of national policy to substitute the will of majorities, instead of justice, and the will of God.*" Arguing that the war had discredited the antebellum humanitarian movement, he pointed specifically to pacifism and opposition to capital punishment as examples of the kind of "morbid philanthropy" that was being purged. Turning to luxury and the pursuit of pleasure, he zeroed in on the favorite object of jeremiads since the seventeenth century and rejoiced that the sufferings of war would serve as a "corrective of these vicious tendencies." Antebellum Americans, he charged, had also lost their reverence for strong government and had grown so contemptuous of all forms of authority that they were in danger of becoming "incapable of virtue." Fortunately, however, the war "will furnish the very discipline we need." Sturtevant may have been unusually ferocious in his celebration of the salutary power of blood and sacrifice, but many other ministers echoed these themes in only slightly softer tones.[27]

The sectional crisis and the war had not changed the fundamental goals of evangelical republicanism, but it *had* discredited the voluntaristic means that had been relied upon before the 1850s to create and maintain a virtuous citizenry. A conspicuous lack of virtue in southern secessionists and in the substantial portion of the northern population that was sympathetic to the South in the fifties and lukewarm about the war effort thereafter made necessary a new and unprecedented recourse to coercion. If the unity, order, morality, and homogeneity deemed essential to a Christian republic could not be accomplished by persuasion, ministers were now quite ready to unsheathe the sword. The justification was readily found in the New Testament. According to Romans 13:1, 4 "the powers that be are ordained of God," and it is a duty of Christians to obey them, for the ruler who bears the sword is "the minister of God, a revenger to *execute* wrath upon him that doeth evil." Applying this text to the current crisis, ministers charged the South with a sinful rebellion against constituted authority, not so much because Lincoln had been democratically elected as because the established government of the United States, whatever its origin and precise character, was divinely ordained. According to the Rev. Joseph T. Duryea of the Collegiate Dutch Reformed Church of New York, preaching in 1863, the doctrine that "government is ordained of God, sanctioned and entrusted with power by him" meant that Americans in the North as well as the South needed to be coerced into virtue by a strong state, for "the law must be enforced by power until the people are trained to obey from principle."[28] Horace Bushnell, Congregationalist minister and a prominent theologian, proclaimed in 1864 that "the magistrate is sovereign over the people, not they over him, having even a divine right to bind their conscience by his rule."[29] The biblical justification of "the divine right" of rulers to compel the obedience of their subjects became the single most popular text of the war sermons that have come down to us in printed form. Sermons on the sin of rebellion or revolution outnumbered those on the sin of slavery. Everywhere in the North "unconditional loyalty" to the state was preached as a Christian imperative.[30]

Prewar sermons that touched on political theory also had been known to invoke Romans 13 and use it to condemn the kind of republicanism that was based on such notions as natural rights, government by compact, and the right to rebel against those who ruled without the "consent of the governed." But the antebellum context had muted the antidemocratic authoritarianism of such pronouncements. Admonitions to obey "the powers that be" were then directed at the citizens of a peaceful and unified republic and, as a practical matter, meant enjoining citizens to obey the laws that had been passed by their representatives. In the war years, the unqualified preaching of this doctrine had broader implications. The positive predilection for repressive government that now emerged was based on a belief that the war itself was the result of a breakdown of authority stemming in large part from the prevalence among the people of "atheistic" theories of popular government that invited insubordination and an excess of democracy. The absolute denial of the right of revolution that was often implicit and sometimes explicit in these sermons echoed strangely in a nation with a revolutionary past. One of the few dissenters from the dominant mode of political preaching—F. C. Ewer, Episcopal Rector of Christ Church in New York—complained in 1864 that there was "something radically wrong in the sweeping, arbitrary meaning, which divines nowadays draw out of [Romans:13]." The prevailing interpretation, he pointed out, would deny legitimacy to all the revolutionary movements of history, including the Protestant Reformation and the American Revolution.[31]

The new exaltation of power and authority as antidotes to democracy run amok was vividly expressed in the wartime sermons and addresses of those prominent Congregationalist ministers who stood in the front ranks of the political preachers. According to J. M. Sturtevant in 1861, the "want of reverence for a strong government was producing disastrous effects on the whole national character. The element of reverence for a rightful authority was slipping out of the national mind. Our young men were beginning to feel that all authority is despotism, all government tyranny, and all obedience servility. Just in proportion as such views prevail among any people, they become incapable of anything that is truly great and noble in character." Fortunately, he concluded, the discipline of war was providing the necessary corrective.[32] In a notable series of war sermons and writings, Horace Bushnell called on his fellow citizens to reject the notion that loyalty to a republican government was conditional upon its responsiveness to the will of the people and its protection of natural rights. "Popular government," no less than monarchical or aristocratic polities, had a claim on the unconditional allegiance of its citizen-subjects. Any state, including the American, was "a grand providential order," not a contractual relationship produced by the rational choices of human beings and deriving legitimacy from its respect for natural rights and "popular sovereignty." The war was demonstrating that the un-Christian political doctrines espoused by some of the Founding Fathers had bred secession, anarchy, and revolution.[33] In his own peculiarly graphic way, Henry Ward Beecher made a similarly sweeping claim for "the divine right" of rulers in a time of popular resistance to authority. "Large portions of this country," he reported in 1862, "cannot be governed by anything but a monarchy now, and there is danger that such will be the case with the entire nation, unless there is a change. . . . Whenever from any cause large portions of any community become barbarous, they necessitate monarchies, and the prevailing governments must either grow strong or fail entirely."[34]

The authoritarian rhetoric of the war years did not, of course, mean that clergymen were actually bent on establishing a monarchy or a dictatorship to replace the government of, by, and for the people that Abraham Lincon had extolled at Gettysburg. The Constitution being defended against secessionists established a republican government, and ministers were in fact giving the sanction of their faith to the representative institutions that were mandated in the great national charter. But the philosophy of the Declaration of Independence was clearly under attack, and few ministers would have shared Lincoln's view that the spirit of the Declaration informed the Constitution.[35] What they, in fact, stood for was a conservative republicanism that, especially in times of crisis, would give the preservation of order a higher priority than democratic procedures and the rights of individuals. In manifesting such attitudes, they were justifying in a bold and sweeping fashion some of the extraordinary actions taken by the Lincoln administration on the narrower grounds of practical necessity. In doing so, they revealed some of the ways in which Protestantism could reinforce the persistent "law-and-order" tradition of American conservatism—the tendency to call on the strong arm of government to curb the apparent disorderliness and immorality of outgroups, minorities, and dissenters. The fact that the rebellious minority of the 1860s happened to be defending slavery has inhibited subsequent generations of liberal historians from appreciating the depths of clerical conservatism. So long as that conservatism remained primarily cultural and voluntaristic, relying mainly on persuasion to influence public values and behavior—as it did through most of the antebellum period—democratic republicans had no cause for complaint. But the wartime glorification of coercive government as the agent of God had ominous implications, if not for the basic structures of democratic government, at least for the separation of church and state that secular democrats believed was essential to American freedom.

The most dramatic war-inspired assault on the high-wall conception of church-state relations that had predominated in the antebellum period was the campaign to amend the Constitution to acknowledge the authority of God and Christ and in effect establish a nonsectarian Protestantism as the national religion. In 1864, representatives of eleven Protestant denominations established the National Reform Association to push for an amendment to the preamble of the Constitution in which "We the people" would acknowledge "Almighty God as the source of all authority and power in civil government, the Lord Jesus Christ as the Ruler among nations, his revealed will as the supreme law of the land, in order to constitute a Christian government. . . ." The movement gained the official support of several churches, including the Methodists and the two principal Presbyterian bodies. The amendment was advocated from pulpits all over the North and gained substantial popular support. Agitation on its behalf continued long after the war, and it did not become a dead issue until the turn of the century.[36]

If the "Sovereignty of God" amendment failed of adoption, there were nevertheless subtle ways in which the relation between church and state was altered as a result of religious influences on the Union government. During the war, "In God We Trust" was first engraved on coins, and the Protestant religious feast of Thanksgiving was made a national holiday. Before 1861, recognition of the Christian God was virtually absent from the official discourse and defining texts or slogans of the American Republic. Wartime Christian nationalism failed to knock down the wall between church and state, but it lowered it to an extent that might have made Jefferson turn over in his grave.[37]

Another indication of the clerical retreat from religious voluntarism was a tendency to acknowledge that the gospel enterprise itself might require the strength of government and its willingness to wield the sword. Barnas Sears, Baptist minister and president of Brown University, maintained in 1863 that the very success of the American evangelical movement required an unconditional Union victory. Inverting the prewar doctrine that evangelical persuasion was a substitute for the bayonet as an enforcer of national unity, Sears contended that northern Christians could not tolerate a division of the Union, for the loss of the South would reduce "their power and facilities for doing good" by restricting their "theatre of action." "The tide of Christian benevolence rising in the East and setting westward ought to meet no barriers this side of the Mexican line and the Pacific coast."[38] It now appeared that persuasion had no chance unless unity was maintained by force of arms. Some of the ecclesiastical implications of this doctrine became apparent when northern Methodist and Baptist ministers allowed themselves to be installed by the military as pastors of unwilling southern congregations with absent or "disloyal" ministers. Both during and immediately after the war, northern churches took advantage of the processes of military Reconstruction whenever possible. They did this on the assumption that the South was a "barbarous" region beyond the reach of mere persuasion.[39]

As they engaged in strenuous wartime activity, whether as patriotic preachers, missionaries to the South, Army chaplains, or volunteers ministering to the troops under the auspices of the Christian Commission, the men of the cloth acquired a heady new sense of themselves as redeemers of the republic. What they failed to perceive was that their new role actually undermined their search for professional autonomy and cultural authority. By acting as direct agents of a political cause that they had sanctified in their sermons, they tended to blur the distinctions between the sacred and the profane, between religion and patriotism, between Christian ideals and the realities of northern society, and between the war for the Union and the Christian mission to convert the world. One clergyman writing in 1865 described the role of religion in a way that left no doubt about its instrumental role as servant of the state: "Patriotism demands that the sanctions of our holy religion be given to [the government's] combat for humanity, freedom, unity, and stable peace; and the vigorous arms of its soldiery must not be palsied, their earnest hearts must not be chilled with doubts as to the righteousness of their vocation."[40]

As the war drew to a close, Protestant leaders summed up its results and proclaimed the triumph of Christian nationalism. The *Christian Herald and Presbyterian Recorder* of Cincinnati reported in April 1865 that "the Christian sentiment of the country" had "grown to be the controlling element in the war."[41] In July, after the dust of battle had settled, Professor Charles Hodge of Princeton's Old School Presbyterian seminary concluded that never before "has there been such a religious spirit manifested by the people of this land. . . . Never before have there been such frequent, open, devout recognition of the authority of God as the ruler of nations, and of Jesus Christ, his son, as the Saviour of the world by our public men. . . ."[42] Five months later, the Rev. C. B. Boynton, chaplain of the House of Representatives, described to members of Congress gathered for a Thanksgiving service the momentous changes that had taken place. "Before the war," he asserted, "the United States as a political organism had no definite religious character or purpose." Now, however, the nation was under the sway of a "religious sentiment," and was officially committed to the "propagation and defense" of "an aggressive American Christianity." "The American nation," he told his audience of elected politicians, "occupies a position never held by any people before. It stands the representative and champion of a true *Christian* democracy in church and state. ... We stand on the threshold of this new era the mightiest Christian nation on earth ... mighty through the teaching of war ... with a national life strong enough to control a continent, and which will brook no dictation from a foreign power."[43]

Boynton's sermon reveals some of the ways in which the war had transformed the outlook of the northern clergy. Prewar Protestant spokesmen had entertained the hope and expectation that the spirit of reformed Christianity would eventually pervade all aspects of national life and provide a basis for order, harmony, and public virtue. But, recognizing a gulf between the ideal and the actual, they had maintained a degree of critical distance from the realities of politics, government, and business. One group that ministers had frequently condemned as relatively impervious to Christian influence were politicians and office-holders. Boynton's description of the United States as a full-fledged Christian polity, like Hodge's paeans to the religious faith of public men, showed how the crisis had reduced the capacity of the clergy to make critical or prophetic judgments on the conduct of public life. Patriotic euphoria had lessened their distrust of the nation's secular leadership and had led many of them to idealize the dominant political party and involve themselves directly in its internal affairs.[44] A belief that the Republicans were the party of God made an important segment of the clergy unprepared to resist the decline in public morality that characterized the Grant era.

Equally revealing was Boynton's straightforward identification of the future growth of evangelical Christianity with the physical power and imperial destiny of the United States. Prewar ministers had affirmed an American mission to convert the world to Christian civilization, but as means to this end they had normally prescribed the power of an American example and the growth of a mission enterprise based on peaceful persuasion. In the years that followed the war, many ministers were more willing to sanctify the advancement of "Christian civilization" through the use of force and to view the nation's imperial ambitions and the missionary enterprise of the churches as conjoined or interdependent projects. A transcendent God who might have his quarrels with the American Republic was being replaced by an immanent deity who expressed himself directly through the power and prestige of the nation.[45]

The effect of the Civil War crisis on the relationship of Protestant clergy to the American Republic can therefore be viewed in two ways that may seem contradictory but were in fact compatible. On the one hand, the national government seemed to be giving more support and recognition to Protestantism as the majority religion of the American people. But the other side of the coin was that religion itself was in danger of becoming completely identified with the secular interests of the nation and thus losing its critical autonomy. It is clear in retrospect that the secularizing of American Protestantism was a more fundamental process than the spiritualizing of American patriotism. As the religious historian Sidney Mead describes the effect of the war, "Christianity and Americanism" tended to merge and the result was a strengthening of the ties of religion to the "powers that be" rather than an increase in the independent authority of religious perspectives on national life.[46] Clerical endorsement of Gatling guns in the labor strife of the 1870s and what Henry May called Protestantism's "massive almost unbroken front in defense of social status quo" in that turbulent postwar decade surely owed something to the wartime sanctification of the "powers that be."[47]

Immediately after the war, however, the northern clergy and the churches for which they spoke did for a time lend some vital support to the efforts of congressional Republicans to guarantee civil and political rights to the recently freed African Americans of the South. They also sent missionaries to the freed people and established a number of schools and colleges designed to inculcate the values of Christian citizenship in those released from bondage. The attitude of ministers toward Reconstruction has not been thoroughly studied, but it appears that the moderate antislavery tradition that inspired most of these efforts provided an inadequate defense against the upsurge of southern racism that challenged and eventually overthrew Radical Reconstruction. The disorder and corruption popularly associated with the Reconstruction governments eventually led many of the clergy, along with other northerners, to conclude that the experiment with nonracial citizenship had been misguided or premature. Consequently, the clergy as a whole failed to resist the North's "retreat from Reconstruction," and some of them actively supported it.[48]

If we take a longer view, however, and look ahead to the 1880s and 1890s, it is clear that one strain of wartime Christian nationalism helped to lay the foundations for a renewal among the clergy of critical perspectives on American society and politics. Religious liberalism, the dominant theological tendency of the Gilded Age, could and often did lead to an uncritical celebration of economic and social progress under the "invisible hand" of laissez-faire capitalism. As James Moorhead has pointed out, the logic of war-inspired glorification of the state and the organic view of society that often lay behind it might have led to clerical advocacy of intervention into economic life in order to make the marketplace—with its frequently berated tendency to foster materialism and selfishness—more responsive to altruistic Christian values. But during the immediate postwar years it rarely did so.[49]

By the 1880s and 1890s, however, some ministers were applying such ideas to the class conflict and industrial strife that had replaced the controversy over slavery and race as the central problem being confronted by American reformers. The Social Gospel movement was, to a greater extent than has been generally appreciated, a conscious revival of the political preaching and religious activism of the war period, as well as a new application of the Christian statism of that era. The Rev. Elisha Mulford, the Episcopal rector who summed up the new reverence for organic nationalism that the war had inspired, in his influential book *The Nation* published in 1870, also argued for the subordination of property rights to the organic will of the whole people as expressed through the government. Mulford in effect sanctioned a form of Christian socialism, and his work was a major inspiration for the Social Gospel movement's attack on unrestrained capitalism as a violation of the ethics of the New Testament.[50]

But those who applied Mulford's ideas in the 1880s were often not clergymen themselves. Many were young men of Christian upbringing and convictions who had once entertained thoughts of going into the ministry, or even studied for it, but had instead pursued careers as academic economists and social scientists.[51] The importance of the "ethical economists" in developing the ideology of the Social Gospel (and, of course, influencing some ministers to embrace its principles) suggests that the rise of the clergy to professional ascendancy as the primary custodians of the North's public values in the 1850s and 1860s had been a temporary phenomenon. The war also had encouraged scientific professionalism, and in the postwar battle for intellectual authority to guide the public on social and political issues, those who could claim the imprimatur of science for their judgments had an advantage over those who sought to influence educated opinion from a supernaturalist perspective. Ministers still commanded respect when they promoted religion as a guide to private life, but to be persuasively applied to political, social, and economic questions, Christian principles seemed to require a scaffolding of professionally certified social-scientific knowledge. The loss of public influence and status for the ministry of the mainstream northern Protestant denominations was attributable in part to the split within Protestantism itself between the liberal descendants of the postmillennialist evangelical leaders of the prewar era, who for the most part purveyed undemanding doctrine to self-satisfied middle-class denominations, and the premillennialist fundamentalists who made emotional appeals in the revivalist tradition to lower-middle-class and working-class Protestants but condemned as futile most human efforts to achieve the Kingdom of God on earth. The dream of a Christian state, guided if not ruled by the Protestant clergy, which had seemed so close to realization in 1865, appeared by the 1890s to be more remote than ever.[52]

Notes

1. Clifford E. Clark Jr., *Henry Ward Beecher: Spokesman for a Middle-Class America* (Urbana, IL, 1978), 165–166.

2. See Cornel West, *Prophetic Fragments* (Grand Rapids, 1988). For a good survey of recent writings on "Church State Issues in the Period of the Civil War," see the essay by William F. Deverell in *Church and State in America: A Bibliographical Guide: The Civil War to the Present Day*, ed. John F. Wilson (New York, 1987), 1–32. The most thorough and authoritative study of the response of northern Protestantism to the Civil War is James H. Moorhead, *American Apocalypse: Yankee Protestants and the Civil War, 1860–1869* (New Haven, CT, 1978).

3. See Daniel Calhoun, *Professional Lives in America: Structure and Aspirations, 1750–1850* (Cambridge, MA, 1965), 88–177; Donald Scott, *From Office to Profession: The New England Ministry, 1750–1850* (Philadelphia, 1978); and Laurence Moore, *Selling God: American Religion in the Marketplace of Culture* (New York, 1994), 66–89.

4. For an earlier effort of mine to describe the rival "conservatisms" of lawyers and

ministers, see "The Search for Order and Community," in *The Public and Private Lincoln: Contemporary Perspectives*, eds. Cullom Davis et al. (Carbondale, IL, 1979), 86–98.

5. See Robert A. Ferguson, *Law and Letters in American Culture* (Cambridge, MA, 1984), 18, 234–235, 313–314.

6. For a perceptive exposition of this process, see Sidney Mead, *The Lively Experiment: The Shaping of Christianity in America* (New York, 1963). See also William McLoughlin Jr., *Modern Revivalism: From Charles Grandison Finney to Billy Graham* (New York, 1959).

7. See, especially, Paul E. Johnson, *A Shopkeeper's Millennium: Society and Revivals in Rochester, New York* (New York, 1978); and Mary Ryan, *Cradle of the Middle Class: The Family in Oneida County, New York, 1790–1864* (Cambridge, MA, 1981).

8. Alexis de Tocqueville, *Democracy in America*, ed. Phillips Bradley (New York, 1956), 1: 314–318.

9. Robert Baird, *Religion in America* (New York, 1843/1856), 664–665.

10. On antebellum clerical conservatism, see Charles Cole, *The Social Ideas of the Northern Evangelists* (New York, 1954), especially 138–157; John R. Bodo, *The Protestant Clergy and Social Issues, 1812–1848* (Princeton, 1954), especially 51–54; and Perry Miller, *The Life of the Mind in America: From the Revolution to the Civil War* (New York, 1965), chap. 2, *passim*. A recent study of the political and social thought of antebellum Protestantism reassesses the dissent of religious leaders from prevailing ideologies by calling attention to their tendency to criticize capitalist acquisitiveness and liberal individualism. This more positive evaluation does not, I think, refute the conclusions of Cole, Bodo, and Miller that churchmen were ideologically conservative. It does suggest, however, that their "conservatism" was not a simple matter of defending the status quo against radical change. It raised fundamental questions about the liberal-democratic values that validated the antebellum status quo, and might even be described as a form of "traditionalist" or "pre-modern" thought. See Mark Y. Hanley, *Beyond a Christian Commonwealth: The Protestant Quarrel with the American Republic* (Chapel Hill, 1994).

11. For a good account of how antebellum northern churches responded to the slavery issue, see John R. McKivigan, *The War Against Proslavery Religion: Abolitionism and the Northern Churches, 1830–1865* (Ithaca, NY, 1984).

12. See Hanley, *Beyond a Christian Commonwealth*.

13. For a general discussion of millennialism in nineteenth-century Protestant thought, see James H. Moorhead, "Between Progress and the Apocalypse: A Reassessment of Millennialism in American Religious Thought, 1800–1880," *Journal of American History* 71 (December 1984): 524–542. On the radical type of millennialism that could lead to radical abolitionism, see Lewis Perry, *Radical Abolitionism: Anarchy and the Government of God in Antislavery Thought* (Ithaca, NY, 1973).

14. Jesse T. Peck, *The History of the Great Republic* (New York, 1868), 560, 570, 574.

15. Ibid., 576.

16. Clark, *Beecher*, 97–98, and *passim*.

17. McKivigan, *War Against Proslavery Religion*, 137–141.

18. *Dr. Wayland on the Moral and Religious Aspects of the Nebraska Bill*, 15, cited in Cole, *Social Ideas*, 216.

19. Ezra Stiles Garnett, *The Relation of the North to Slavery: A Discourse Preached in the Federal Street Meeting House in Boston, June 11, 1854* (Boston, 1854), 12, 17, 20–21.

20. George D. Harmon, "The Pennsylvania Clergy and the Civil War," *Lehigh University Publications* 14 (July 1940): 15.

21. Samuel Haber, *The Quest for Authority and Honor in the American Professions* (Chicago, 1991), 175–176.

22. Lewis G. Vander Velde, *The Presbyterian Churches and the Federal Union, 1861–1869* (Cambridge, MA, 1932), 50–64, *passim*; and William W. Sweet, *The Methodist Episcopal Church and the Civil War* (Cincinnati, 1912), 73–77, *passim*.

23. Ichabod Simmons, *Our Duty in the Crisis: A Discourse Delivered on the Occasion of Our National Fast, September 26, 1961, M.E. Church, Simsbury* (Hartford, 1861), 20.

24. Gilbert Haven, *National Sermons* (Boston, 1869), 383. On the shift in Methodist opinion, see also Donald G. Jones, *The Sectional Crisis and Northern Methodism: A Study in Piety, Political Ethics and Civil Religion* (Metuchen, NJ, 1979), 83–89.

25. See McKivigan, *War Against Proslavery Religion*, 193–201. A good example of the kind of sermon that justified the war as a defense of divinely ordained authority and characterized emancipation as an unexpected act of God rather than of human benevolent intentions is David Magee, D.D., *Discourse Delivered in the Second Presbyterian Church, Elizabeth, N.J.* (New York, 1863).

26. George M. Fredrickson, *The Black Image in the White Mind: The Debate on Afro-American Character and Destiny, 1817–1914* (Middletown, CT, 1987), 155–159.

27. J. M. Sturtevant, "The Lessons of Our National Conflict," *The New Englander* 19 (October, 1861): 894–912.

28. Joseph T. Duryea, *Civil Liberty: A Sermon Preached on August 6, 1863* (New York, 1863).

29. Horace Bushnell, "Popular Government by Divine Right," sermon of November 24, 1864, in *Building Eras in Religion* (New York, 1881), 309.

30. Moorhead, *American Apocalypse*, 129–146; Jones, *Northern Methodism*, 80–82, 215–219. Some examples of sermons using this doctrine to repudiate secular republicanism and make loyalty to the government a religious obligation—in addition to those cited elsewhere—are John F. Bigelow, *The Hand of God in History: A Discourse Delivered in the Baptist Church, Keeseville, N.Y., July 7, 1861* (Burlington, VT, 1861); Joseph Parris Thompson, *The Test Hour of Popular Liberty, and Republican Government* (New Haven, CT, 1862); J. R. W. Sloane, *Three Pillars of the Republic* (New York, 1862); Thomas Laurie, *Government is of God, A Sermon Preached in Dedham and West Roxbury, May 12, 1861* (Boston, 1861); Sermon by the Rev. Mr. Weston in *Sermons by the Rev. Mr. Weston and the Rev. Byron Sutherland in the House of Representatives, April 28, 1861* (Washington, 1861); Horace Bushnell, *Reverses Needed: A Discourse Delivered on the Sunday after the Disaster at Bull Run* (Hartford, 1861); William Barrows, *Our Government and Our Religion and Their Harmony: A Discourse Delivered in Old South Church, Reading, Mass., March 2, 1862* (Boston, 1862); and Henry W. Bellows, *Unconditional Loyalty* (New York, 1863).

31. F. C. Ewer, *A Rector's Reply to Sundry Demands and Requests for a Political Sermon* (New York, 1864), 10, 11.

32. Sturtevant, "Lessons of Our National Conflict," 895–896.

33. Quoted in George M. Fredrickson, *The Inner Civil War: Northern Intellectuals and the Crisis of the Union* (Urbana, IL, 1993), 137–141.

34. Beecher, Sermon of November 22, 1862, in *Patriotic Addresses*, 386.

35. See Gary Wills, *Lincoln at Gettysburg: The Words That Remade America* (New York, 1992).

36. Moorhead, *American Apocalypse*, 141–142; Philip Schaff, "Separation of Church and State," *Papers of the American Historical Association*, II; no. 4 (New York, 1888), 38–39; Anson Stokes, *Church and State in the United States* (New York, 1950), 2: 234;

Henry F. May, *The Protestant Churches and Industrial America* (New York, 1949), 91.

37. According to the entry on Thanksgiving Day in the 1972 edition of the *Encyclopaedia Britannica*, "President Lincoln proclaimed a national harvest festival on Nov. 26, 1863. From that time on, Thanksgiving Day has been an annual holiday in the United States, proclaimed yearly by the president and the governor of each state." (Vol. 21, p. 941). In his 1864 sermon, "Popular Government by Divine Right," Horace Bushnell noted the appearance of "In God We Trust" on coins and maintained that this was the first time the federal government had officially acknowledged the existence of God. (See Fredrickson, *The Inner Civil War*, 139.)

38. Barnas Sears, "The Moral and Religious Value of our National Union, *Bibliotheca Sacra* 20 (January 1863): 147–151.

39. For an exposition of clerical beliefs about the "barbarism" of the South and its need to be ruled by the sword, see Chester F. Dunham, *The Attitude of the Northern Clergy toward the South, 1860–1865* (Toledo, 1942), *passim*. For an account of the cooperation between the missionaries of one denomination and the military rulers of the South, see Ralph E. Morrow, *Northern Methodism and Reconstruction* (East Lansing, MI, 1956).

40. Joseph Horner, "Christianity and the War Power," *Methodist Quarterly Review* 60 (April 1865): 185. See also Moorhead, *American Apocalypse*, 126–128.

41. Quoted in Dunham, *Northern Clergy*, 207.

42. Charles Hodge, "President Lincoln," *Biblical Repository and Princeton Review* 37 (July 1865): 443.

43. C. B. Boynton, *Discourse, National Thanksgiving Services, House of Representatives, December 7, 1865* (Washington, DC, 1865), 12–13.

44. Jones, in *Northern Methodism*, details the entanglement of organized Methodism in wartime Republican politics, including the pursuit of patronage (40–50). Other mainstream denominations became similarly involved in party affairs.

45. This late-nineteenth-century merger of Protestantism and American nationalism is described in John Edwin Smylie, "Protestant Clergymen and American Destiny," *Harvard Theological Review* 56 (October 1963): 297–311. But Smylie fails to indicate precisely how and why the Civil War crisis had strengthened this tendency. The classic statement of this evangelical imperialism is the Rev. Josiah Strong's *Our Country* (New York, 1886), chap. 14.

46. Mead, *The Lively Experiment*, chap. 7.

47. May, *The Protestant Churches and Industrial America*, 91.

48. See McKivigan, *War Against Proslavery Religion*, 196–199; James M. McPherson, *The Antislavery Legacy: From Reconstruction to the NAACP* (Princeton, NJ, 1975), 143–160, 224–243; and Jones, *Northern Methodism*, 251–263, 297.

49. Moorhead, *American Apocalypse*, 161–163.

50. Elisha Mulford, *The Nation: The Foundation of Civil Order and Political Life in the United States* (Boston, 1870). I have pursued the connection between Civil War Christian nationalism and the Social Gospel in an unpublished paper, "Intellectuals and the Labor Question in Late Nineteenth-Century America," which was presented at the 1986 convention of the American Historical Association and is in my possession.

51. See Dorothy Ross, "Socialism and American Liberalism: American Social Thought in the 1880s," *Perspectives in American History* 11 (1978): 15–18, and Mary O. Furner, *Advocacy and Objectivity* (Lexington, KY, 1975), 51.

52. On the rise of social science to a position of intellectual authority, see especially Thomas Haskell, *The Emergence of Professional Social Science* (Urbana, IL, 1977), and

Furner, *Advocacy and Objectivity*. For information on the internal situations of the clerical and academic professions in the late nineteenth century, see Haber, *Authority and Honor*, 240–293. Mainstream religious liberalism is treated in William R. Hutchison, *The Modernist Impulse in American Protestantism* (Cambridge, MA, 1976). On the rise of fundamentalism, see George Marsden, *Fundamentalism and American Culture* (New York, 1980).

6

"Wholesome Reading Purifies and Elevates the Man"

The Religious Military Press in the Confederacy

KURT O. BERENDS

Throughout the second half of the Civil War, the religious military press (henceforth referred to as (RMP) sought to provide beneficial reading for the Confederate army. "Wholesome reading purifies and elevates the man," wrote the Rev. John Leyland, editor of *The Soldier's Visitor.* "It inspires him with better thoughts and impulses, it encourages him to that which is good, it restrains him from evil." Leyland and other editors defined purity as more than just conformity to the evangelical lifestyle. Purity, for the editors of the RMP, suggested a certain type of soldier. Although the religious character of the soldiers was important for these preachers turned editors, their message contained civil and social implications as well. The pure soldier was the disciplined soldier, attentive to duty and always hopeful of the cause. Of course, for soldiers to be truly pure they must first be saved from their sins. According to the RMP, the large revivals that spread throughout the army created a Christian army—an "elevated" army. Naturally a Christian army fought for an elevated cause—God's cause. The Civil War, according to the editors, was a war not just for political independence but also for religious freedom. Within the RMP, editors created and explained a framework of beliefs—a worldview—that sustained an unvanquished optimism for southern independence. Until the very end, editors professed hope of Confederate victory. Since the Confederacy lost, the optimism and bravado may seem misplaced as if editors had held onto a cause long lost. This interpretation has driven some historians, but it is mistaken; for the writers of the RMP, such optimism was the logical conclusion to their whole message. The message of the RMP was that Christianity embodied the same values that would bring southern victory. The ideal soldier was a Christian soldier. He modeled commitment to the Confederate cause and the cause of Christ. By probing the values and beliefs in the religious military press, one catches a glimpse of a dynamic and interpenetrating relationship between religion and culture during the Civil War. Together, these newspapers acted as a significant voice that clamored to be heard during the Civil War. They also provide a window on the interplay of culture and religion within the Confederacy and the postwar South.[1]

While not the only religious voice uttered in the South, the RMP was nonetheless one of the most widespread and significant. Impetus for these publications came from the ever-growing churches throughout the region. Religious publishing—especially the religious weekly—had been a thriving and rapidly expanding ministry in the antebellum South. When the war started, publishers naturally enough addressed the troops as well. But being civilian, the focus of these weeklies commonly was on civilian concerns. When the war continued longer than anyone had anticipated, the churches began publishing the RMP especially for soldiers. By 1863, there were five papers: *The Soldier's Friend* (Baptist; Atlanta); *Army and Navy Messenger* (Evangelical Tract Society; Petersburg, Virginia); *The Soldiers' Visitor* (Committee of Publication, Presbyterian Church in the Confederate States; Richmond, Virginia); *The Soldier's Paper* (Soldier's Tract Association, Methodist Episcopal Church, South; Richmond, Virginia); and *Army and Navy Herald* (Soldier's Tract Association, Methodist Episcopal Church, South; Macon, Georgia). The *Army and Navy Messenger for the Trans-Mississippi Department* (Evangelical Tract Society; Shreveport, Louisiana), a paper for the western front, issued its first number on September 15, 1864.[2] Between January 10, 1863, and May 15, 1865, the army received a steady print diet of evangelistic sermons, explanations of the Confederate cause, and stories glorifying the Christian soldier who exemplified commitment to the cause. The RMP also sought to build morale among the troops and to encourage discipline and attention to duty in order to be the best soldier, a Christian soldier.

There are several reasons the churches waited until 1863 to issue the first religious military paper. Initially, the churches continued with their missionary endeavors in civilian centers. They intensified their efforts to reach the army only after experiencing failure at home. Other factors also influenced the 1863 starting date. Many people, both North and South, assumed the war would be brief. At the outbreak of war, most southern denominations already published religious weeklies and for a time editors thought their circulation among the troops would suffice. It was a number of months before the reality of an extended conflict settled into southern minds. When it became apparent that this war might last for years, and that armies were a permanent institution, churches began to refocus their efforts. One of the earliest tasks was to create a southern counterpart to the New York–based American Tract Society, the largest publisher of religious materials in antebellum America. The result was the Evangelical Tract Society. First conceived in July of 1861, it took a number of months to raise funds and begin publishing the *Army and Navy Messenger* (henceforth referred to as *Messenger*). The *Messenger* was joined by other papers after the rapidly spreading revivals in the army in the fall of 1862. Encouraged by news of a great work in the field, ministers sought to fan the flames with other periodicals designed especially for soldiers. On January 10, 1863, in Atlanta, Baptist Adolphus Spalding Worrell printed the first issue of *The Soldier's Friend*. It marked the start of a widespread push to put religious newspapers into the hands of fighting men.[3]

The effort to reach the army with the Christian message through newsprint was remarkable. Publishers had to deal with the demands and uncertainties brought on by war. Rapid inflation, shortages, distribution breakdowns, and interruptions by battles created momentous challenges. The ability of the publishers to maintain, and in some cases even expand, their operations testifies to the importance—at least in the minds of the publishers and those who contributed to the work—of the RMP.[4] In light of these challenges, nearly every issue contained pleas for financial assistance, which came in varying amounts from a wide variety of sources. A good portion of the money came from within the military. Robert E. Lee, one of the first to respond to the call for money, contributed $100 to the Evangelical Tract Society for distribution of the *Messenger*. General J. H. Cooke donated $1,000, the largest single gift from a member of the armed forces. Most gifts ranged from $5 to $50. Typically, someone in a regiment, in response to a printed financial request, took up a collection and sent it in. The Methodist *Army and Navy (Herald)* sent "collecting agents" throughout the countryside and into the camps to solicit funds. Several papers also sought partial funding through the sale of advertising space. The majority of money, however, came from concerned citizens interested in the mission of the papers. *The Soldier's Friend,* a Baptist product, solicited contributions through Georgia Baptist weeklies. All papers except for the *Mississippi Messenger* offered a limited number of subscriptions to readers outside the military. As the war continued, financial challenges increased. Runaway inflation combined with shortages of food and other basic necessities to create severe financial obstacles for the publishers. Contributions could not keep up with inflation. Still, the churches found ways to continue publishing their message. All raised their subscription rates during the course of the conflict. Advertising rates in the *Herald* doubled several times. *The Soldier's Paper* rescinded its offer of subscriptions to civilians in order to meet the demands of the army. Even nonmonetary gifts like "waste cotton" became useful for publishing the papers.[5]

The war also engendered problems with distribution and production. The consistent failure of copies of the *Messenger* to reach troops located in the trans-Mississippi region—caused in part by the destruction of rail lines—led to the publication of the *Army and Navy Messenger for the Trans-Mississippi Department* (henceforth referred to as *Mississippi Messenger*). Twice, the Evangelical Tract Society halted printing of the *Messenger* because of difficulties brought on by the conflict. Yet not all production and distribution problems could be blamed on Yankees. Postmasters were often accused of tossing aside bulky packages of religious materials, and traders allegedly stole papers to use as packing materials. Throughout the war, editors did everything they could to counteract such problems. Editors requested soldiers and chaplains immediately to post changes of address, and many papers gave explicit instructions for obtaining a subscription.[6]

Despite such difficulties, the religious military press continued publications throughout the war. In fact, the religious military press represented some of the largest publishing ventures ever undertaken in the South. The largest civilian denominational papers printed between 3,000 and 5,000 copies weekly or bimonthly. In comparison, the Atlanta-based *Soldier's Friend* distributed 10,000 copies per week. The Soldier's Tract Association claimed to deliver 20,000 copies of *The Soldier's Paper* semimonthly, while the Evangelical Tract Society issued 10,000 copies of the *Army and Navy Messenger* semimonthly. Even the smallest RMP, *The Soldier's Visitor,* published by the Presbyterian church, issued forth at a rate of 8,000 copies per month. Only a few secular papers in the largest southern cities exceeded these numbers during the war.[7] Both the large print runs and the unyielding efforts by editors to publish in difficult times reflect the importance they placed on their message.

"The Simplest Way to Convert a Nation Is to Convert Its Army"

All papers claimed to set aside denominational differences and focus their efforts on converting the men in the army. In the early stages of publication, Philip Slaughter, editor for the *Messenger,* reminded his readers. "Our messenger, in its sphere applies . . . but one test in religion, and that is loyalty to the banner of the cross." Over a year and a half later, the *Messenger,* under the editorial guidance of W. B. Wellons, confidently proclaimed the same theme, "Remember, we are not laboring to promote the interests of any party or sect, but simply to lead men to Christ, to make them disciples of the Saviour." A. S. Worrell, writing for *The Soldier's Friend,* advanced a comparable purpose. The paper's chief objective, he wrote, "is to prepare them, if possible, for the greatest of emergencies, *death.* The enterprise, therefore, has claims, at once, on the Philanthropist, *Patriot* and *Christian.*" Likewise, in the first issue of the latecomer *Mississippi Messenger,* editor William B. Norris noted, "Our object in this enterprise is the welfare of our soldiers." Articles should aim "to bring our friends in the army, that knowledge, which maketh wise unto salvation." Editors shared a nonsectarian outlook throughout the war.[8]

The RMP functioned as one printed voice in the evangelical mission to the army. The revivals, already well under way by the time the religious military press issued its first number, received excellent publicity and support within the pages of the RMP. In return, the newspapers' message of evangelism to the army was further aided by the soldiers' encounters with revivals in the camps. Thus, while the RMP was not the only agent for the mission to the army—chaplains, missionaries, and colporteurs[9] performed central tasks in preaching sermons and distributing tracts, Bibles, and other religious materials—it did play an important role in sustaining and expanding the work of revivals. More important, it also played a central role in defining the significance of the revivals to the troops who participated in them. The importance of the revivals is not found in the number of troops converted, although revival participants and historians alike have indicated the revivals' success by measuring the number of soldiers converted. Even the RMP attempted this task. In December 1864, W. B. Wellons of the *Messenger* wrote, "It is estimated that no less than *one hundred and forty-thousand* soldiers in the Confederate army have been converted during the progress of the war, and it is farther [sic] estimated that fully one-third of the soldiers now in the field are praying men and member of some one of the different religious denominations." Yet focusing on revival conversions understates the revivals' prominence. Rather, the fact that the revivals gained extensive coverage in the RMP is significant. The military revivals became a major cultural event.[10]

The location, duration, and timing of revivals varied throughout the war. Some took place in the aftermath of defeats on the battlefield. Others occurred after victories. Some reports indicate small revivals directly before combat. Many of the extended revivals appear to have happened during the winter months when soldiers were camped in one location for lengthy periods of time. Although ministers noted religion's influence "gradually increased" among the soldiers during the fall of 1861, the following autumn marked the beginning of large revivals, which would characterize much of the Confederate military experience for the remainder of the war. Beginning with their very first issue, editors of the religious military papers labored to spread information on the expanding fires of military revival. "These tokens of Divine presence and power, should not go unheralded and unsung; they should not exist merely as traditions when the war is over," wrote William Norris for the *Mississippi Messenger*. Rather, "the religious history of our armies during this war would be a work of as striking interest, as the history of the war itself." Soldiers, chaplains, and colporteurs enthusiastically provided the much sought after news. Nearly every issue carried letters from men in the field reporting religious events in the army. Communiqués recited a litany of statistics: 76 joined the church in Marmaduke's Brigade, 400 men in Longstreet's Corp openly sought Christ, while "50 to 100 join the church daily" in the Army of Tennessee.[11] Editors duly reminded readers of the RMP of the significance of revival news. The steady flow of conversions revealed the mighty hand of God in their midst.

Beyond fanning the flames of revivals in the camp, published accounts of revivals served another equally important function. To the writers of the RMP, revivals validated their confidence in the success of the Confederate cause. Their logic dictated that the more conversions the army experienced, the closer final triumph loomed on the horizon. "The fact that God has been pleased to bless our armies with a wide-spread revival of religion, is a most cheering one," penned one Presbyterian writer, "not only as regards the precious spiritual fruits which are gathered, but as to the assurance it inspires of the ultimate triumph of our cause." In the context of war, individual salvation led to corporate salvation. Of course, few editors expected the whole army to convert. But if enough repented, success would follow. *The Soldier's Visitor* expressed this opinion in an article entitled, "Shall We Succeed?" The author's hope rested in the belief that God "saves communities and nations 'for the elect's sake.'" For these men, the expanding revivals offered substance to southerners' prayers for God to "make our army a holy instrument in thy hands, to punish insolent tyrants who are now endeavoring to subjugate our people . . . and to take from us all that in thy goodness, thou hast given us." Would God abandon true believers? The men of arms were not only "soldiers for their country," but "soldiers of the cross of Christ." "Surely, for their numbers," exhorted one writer for the trans-Mississippi paper, "they will be invincible, and add fresh laurels to their wreaths of victory."[12]

Confidence in final triumph did not rest solely upon the assumption that God would remain faithful to his warring children; it also embodied the evangelical conviction that conversion changed a person both inside and out. Translated into the milieu of war, the best soldier was a Christian soldier. The influence of religion brought forth the "heroic spirit in man." At the start of the war, evangelicals battled the notion that Christians were poor soldiers. This belief found its roots in southern notions of honor and manliness, as well as the perception of Christianity as feminine, gentle, and pure. In part, the clergy's portrayal of Christian women fostered this belief. Sermons, tracts, and articles depicted Christian women as gentle, soothing, pure, virtuous, and sensitive. Such attitudes and descriptions, along with the female-dominated church population in the antebellum South, seemingly confirmed the belief that the church was a woman's place.[13]

Editors counteracted this feminine image of Christianity with essays that faithfully portrayed the Christian as the superior soldier. From history, both distant and recent, authors found examples. "A man need not be any less a Christian because he is a soldier, nor any less a soldier because he is a Christian. Havelock, Vickars, Jackson and Lee . . . unite in their own persons both of these characters beautifully." Another tack exemplified by Bishop William Atkinson, decried the dominant "law of honor" that allowed men to judge their own conduct differently from women's. "It is not God's standard," noted Atkinson, that permits men "to do many things with impunity which are forbidden to women as unpardonable sins." Most articles, however, accentuated the exceptional conduct of Christian soldiers in the present conflict. "War is a great revolutionizer," began one article in *Soldier's Visitor*. "The old time idea that a good Christian cannot make a good soldier, has been thoroughly exploded. . . . It has been proved, that other things being equal,—the better Christian, the better soldier." Of course, the Christian soldier had two distinct advantages over the unbeliever. He had no fear of death, and he understood his obligation to duty. With his eternal destiny secure, the soldier of the cross could boldly and confidently face the enemy, for the most important battle was already won.[14]

The size and fervor of the revivals, and the impact they had on the character of the soldier, led more than one writer to speculate on the impact of the Confederate army in a postwar world. Baptist editor Adolphus S. Worrell called for schools to train the wounded to read and write, with the hope that these new converts would "fill the pulpits of the land." Others dreamed of more comprehensive goals. *"The simplest way to convert a nation is to convert its army,"* concluded Reverend Stiles. "Fire all the strong young men of a great people with the spirit of Christianity, and now disband them and send them home to make all the laws, fill all the offices, control all the families, and inspirit all the churches of the land—and what . . . could prevent that whole nation from being carried over bodily to the Lord's side?" Commenting on the role of Providence in history, another author envisioned even greater implications in the spring of 1865: "We have in trust the commercial, social, political, and moral welfare of the world." According to the worldview articulated within the RMP, the success of the revivals confirmed Divine favor. The new nation's act of rebellion contained profound implications for both home and abroad.[15]

The Confederacy's war against the Union also held significant implications for the gospel message itself. Editors, in their efforts to be sensitive to the needs of the soldier, began shaping their gospel presentations in response to the events at hand. As historian Anne Loveland notes, effective revival preaching in the antebellum South "had less to do with the doctrines that were presented and more to do with the way they were presented. . . . They stressed practical rather than doctrinal preaching." Nevertheless, in their appeal to the heart, editors did not forgo addressing the mind. Writers offered a message that both offered hope and made sense in the experience of war. The basic content of these numerous appeals for conversions was consistent from paper to paper. People were sinners and needed the Saviour. Every edition confronted the soldier with this, his greatest need. Some essays sketched a simple, straightforward, evangelistic appeal. Sermons like "The Blood of Atonement" printed various Scripture verses under headings of Redemption, Forgiveness of Sins, Justification, and Eternal Life. Other features, "You Are In Danger," and "Eternal Punishment," warned readers of an eternity in hell unless they turned to God. During the war, editors set aside doctrinal disputes over baptism and forms of church government. Instead of the characteristic denominational fracases of the antebellum period, all papers reported favorably on the efforts of others to convert the men in the army. Yet this unified purpose did not mean all papers sounded alike. There were distinct differences in the tone of papers. The Presbyterian *Soldier's Visitor* did not read like the Baptist *Soldier's Friend* or the Methodist *Army and Navy Herald*.[16]

Writers, while proclaiming the same core message of salvation, employed different paradigms. The use of family and peer relationships was a standard method. Stories and letters, many fabricated but also some genuine, implored the soldier to turn to God. Pleas from a fictitious "affectionate father," "affectionate brother," "sister," or fellow "soldier" frequently contained the rudimentary gospel message. Letters from soldiers, like the one from Samuel T. Preston, similarly challenged readers to turn their lives over to God. Chaplains often recounted deathbed conversions of soldiers in their efforts to cajole the readers to seek Christ. Numerous parables reiterate these relational themes.

The Soldier's Visitor printed the story of a little boy with a heavy burden who was too stubborn to accept help from a kind old man. The child, symbolic of both the many young soldiers in the war and also the feelings of vulnerability brought on by war, stood in stark contrast to a gracious, helpful, all-powerful God who stood ready to lift the child's load of guilt.[17]

Another common example used for presenting the gospel culled illustrations from army life. W. B. Wellons wrote of his conversation with a soldier wounded during the siege of Atlanta and the gospel lesson that the soldier learned from the experience. Feature stories memorialized Civil War heroes like Jackson, Polk, and Lieutenant Colonel Thornton. These brief tributes urged the reader to emulate the example of these great men by following Christ. Editors eagerly drew from the lives and experiences of the common soldier in demonstrating the power of the Christian message. On January 1, 1864, *The Messenger* offered the first installment of a three-part series on the life of private Randolph Fairfax. What made Fairfax's life worth writing about? His Christian commitment. For twenty-three columns—the largest article in any issue of the RMP—Fairfax's life story stood as a testimony to the power of the gospel. His morality and his attention to duty combined to make him an excellent soldier. The story proved so popular that the Evangelical Tract Society eventually reprinted it as a gospel tract for the soldiers. Past military heroes offered additional models. Popular examples included George Washington, Napoleon, and British General Sir Henry Havelock.[18]

Writers for the RMP also offered the military men a variety of reasons why they should accept the gospel. Almost all of the writers contextualized their message of salvation according to perceived needs of the soldiers brought on by the crisis of war. One popular appeal emphasized the promise of peace and happiness to all who responded to the gospel message. Soldiers could find peace, both amid the uncertainties of war and for eternity, by trusting in Christ. Furthermore, they would obtain happiness despite being surrounded by the horrors of war. "There is no metaphysical mummery about it," penned one writer for the *Mississippi Messenger*. "If you come to [Christ], it will cheer your soul, it will gladden your eye. It will warm you with the glow of life that angels feel." In the article "The Gospel Effects of Religion," readers discovered that becoming a Christian "will brighten the most gloomy scene, smooth the most ragged path, and cheer the most despairing mind . . . . It will give hope to the heart, health to the face . . . . It will make life pleasant, labor sweet, and death triumphant." Editors regularly described their meetings with these happy soldiers both in the army camps and in the streets of cities like Richmond. One such encounter recorded in the Presbyterian *Soldier's Visitor* told of an unusually cheerful soldier whose "countenance fairly glowed." In fact, "he was the happiest looking soldier we have seen since the war commenced." The call to follow Christ soon followed, "Reader, do you not wish to be thus happy?"[19]

Yet the promise of happiness presented only one of many compelling reasons to accept the Christian message. In the worldview of southern evangelicalism, both blessings and curses, whether for the individual or a nation, came from the hand of God. For all Christians, God's Providence might not always be understood, especially as it related to the death of outstanding Christian soldiers. But the belief in Providence offered peace of mind because One greater than mankind was in charge. Writers carefully weaved the theme of God's providential care for the soldiers into their written sermons and stories. Often addressed to the wounded or ill, these essays asked readers to consider the "good fortune" of their position. Surely, the very fact that they were only wounded or ill displayed God's loving providential care for them. "It is time to think of *God's mercy in delivering you* . . . . You cannot think that it was by chance that the ball which struck you, or the sword or lance which wounded you, did not enter some vital part, and cause your death." A similar message also confronted the healthy soldier. "Many, very many of your friends and comrades have fallen. Some seemingly stronger and healthier than yourself have sickened and died." This blessing, the writer continued, should lead to reflection, reflection on the "message of mercy [that] comes to you . . . and invites you to draw nigh to God."[20]

The most popular proselytizing message, though, emphasized the immediacy of death. Long a staple of evangelistic sermons, the tremendous loss of life in the Civil War added new meaning to this omen. Printed sermons with titles like "A Voice of Warning," and "Time is Short" recounted deathbed experiences of unrepentant sinners. Each sermon ended with a warning and a call to respond to the gospel. William Norris urged his readers, "Stop, reflect. You may be killed in the next skirmish or battle. How would you appear before the Judge?" Essays reminded readers that "Friend after friend drops into the tomb, warning us that the time is short to prepare our souls for that tribunal to which *we* may be summoned next." Letters from chaplains also often spoke about the brevity of life in times of war. One chaplain remarked how it was always on his mind that when he preached to the soldiers "it might be the last time that many of them would ever hear the sound of the gospel, and it made him feel more and more the importance of preaching the plain and simple gospel all the time."[21]

The warning of imminent death inevitably became the reality of death in some gospel treatises. Yet even in stories of death, writers conjured up ample reason for the fighting men to accept the gift of salvation. The *Herald* reprinted the incident of a young private who fell on the battlefield of Sharpsburg. In the heat of battle regimental lines disappeared and soldiers found themselves fighting next to strangers. "None who knew him, saw him when he was struck; no familiar voice spoke a word of sympathy or cheer; no kind hand was extended to aid him; but, with a shout, the living mass of men around him, all strangers, rushed past him in a charge, and he was left to die alone—*no, not alone, for God was with him.*" Soldiers confronted their own mortality every day: in the passion of battle, in the depressing atmosphere of the military hospitals, in the sermons of chaplains, and in the pages of the religious military press. To some extent, because of the ubiquitous character of death in war and out of psychological necessity, the soldiers ignored the humanity of those who died.[22] Nevertheless, death did force many a soldier to consider the fleeting nature of life and listen carefully to the claims of the RMP about life, death, and eternity.

If the reality of death offered a forceful rationale for soldiers to consider the gospel message, it also compelled the men who proclaimed this message to consider their words more carefully. Although all ministers understood their proclamations to rest firmly within the scope of orthodox Christianity, for those within the Reformed tradition subtle changes were under way. Traditional Reformed proclamations of the gospel portrayed people as waiting upon God for the gift of salvation. It was God's exclusive initiative that brought about conversion. The Spirit prompted a person's conviction of sin, which ultimately occasioned despair of one's ability to gain salvation. Again, through the Spirit's prompting, an awareness of faith emerged and despair turned to joy. In the early editions, several of these newspapers carried autobiographical accounts of soldiers who patiently and fervently sought the Lord. One private wrote, "For nearly four years I have been seeking peace, and only heard my Saviour on the 3d of this month speak these glad words: 'Thy sins are forgiven.'" But as the war progressed, similar stories of conversion diminished. More and more sermons, letters, and stories of conversion emphasized men responding to God, or choosing God *now*. Simply being a penitent seeker might no longer be good enough. As the editors of the RMP suggested, soldiers actually might die in tomorrow's battle. They had to respond to God's call today. In a language suggestive of strong Arminian influences, chaplains were advised not to force "religious conversation" upon soldiers who lacked interest, but to "gently lead them into it, and gain a silent and gradual influence, rather than attempt to storm their citadel of errors and prejudices." If, as the war persisted, chaplains and missionaries to the army did not gain conversions, they failed, one editor noted, because of their "lack of knowledge of human nature, and the best means of gaining access to the hearts of the men in the ranks." Editors regularly but carefully confronted soldiers with their responsibility to make a decision for God.[23]

The success of the revivals begs further explanation. The most obvious reasons for the success of the evangelistic message have to do with the nature of war and the message contextualized to the needs of soldiers. The promise that death was not the end, when death often appeared imminent and final, offered security to soldiers, Yet to claim that the promise of eternal life makes evangelical Christianity predominantly an "otherworldly" religion is to do injustice to the whole of the message. Soldiers, daily faced with the horrors of war, did find that the promises of peace and happiness offered hope when in many ways hope seemed all too distant. Numerous letters, diaries, and autobiographies of evangelicals give testimony to the emotional satisfaction gained in the conversion experience and Christian life. Moreover, the Christian message of salvation held significant implications for the soldiers here on earth that they themselves found attractive. Writing to the *Mississipi Messenger*, one soldier remarked, "Perhaps I cannot inspire a generous ardor in those around me; but at least I will make sure of one." By conforming to the discipline inherent in the message of evangelical Christianity, many soldiers gained feelings of satisfaction. Likewise, the promise of victory over temptation, the sense of community provided by fellow Christians, and the fusion of the Christian soldier with the theme of honor, all appealed to soldiers in their present situation.[24]

The dearth of women in the army is also significant in explaining why the men responded in such large numbers to the message of the gospel. For the first time, chaplains and missionaries held captive the audience they so often sought in vain in the antebellum years. Negative prewar associations of femininity and Christianity lacked substance in an all-male environment. Heroic actions of Christian soldiers further shattered stereotypes of a feminine Christianity. Soldiers both heard and experienced—through the actions of "Christian soldiers"—a manly brand of Christianity. The impact of this masculinization of the setting and Christian message is evident in more than just the large numbers of men who responded to the gospel message. On more than one occasion, the *Mississippi Messenger* noted the unusual success of the "Baptist brethren" in their revival work. Immersion, much more than sprinkling, is an act with masculine overtones. Sprinkling, and its close identification with pedobaptism, is a ritual that holds inherent nurturing, feminine symbols. Many practitioners of infant baptism, especially those of a Reformed orientation like the Presbyterian church, emphasize the role of God in the ritual. They stress infants—or adult converts—being brought into the family of God, in the Church, by God. Their use of the term *sacrament* to describe baptism further points to the divine nature of baptism. Baptists, on the other hand, tend to underscore the role of human response in baptism. Immersion is a volitional decision each believer makes. Baptists' use of the word *ordinance* to describe baptism underscores the fact that converts chose to identify with Christ's death, burial, and resurrection by entering the waters of baptism. The soldier who entered the "waters of baptism" engaged in a highly visible act in front of his peers—and sometimes in front of the enemy. John William Jones, in his history of the wartime revivals, described baptismal services that took place in rivers dividing the two hostile forces. Although on occasion "several men were wounded while the ordinance was being administered," for the most part the rite attracted respectful observers from both sides. At one baptism, Jones recalled "about five thousand soldiers, from the general to the private, lined the banks." Another chronicler of the army revivals, William Bennett, also wrote of the symbolic power of baptismal ceremonies, describing how an "entire regiment with which the converts were connected turned out to witness the ceremony."[25]

The power of the ritual of immersion and the success Baptists experienced leading revivals during the war are, perhaps, suggestive of the denominational configuration in the postwar South. The rapid Baptist gains in the second half of the nineteenth century—as opposed to Methodist and Presbyterian decline during that same period—has been well documented. Several historians have touched upon the role Confederate veterans performed in the expansion of religion in the aftermath of defeat, especially as revivalists, ministers, Christian educators, and propagandists of the Lost Cause. If it is true that the ritual of baptism by immersion created an identity that appealed to men in the army, and large numbers of these men played an important role in the expansion of religious sentiments after the war, it may help explain the rapid growth of Baptist churches after the war.[26]

A masculine identity resonated in the RMP's gospel presentations, which captivated the troops and shattered traditional images of a feminine Christianity. If the threat of death reshaped the traditional understanding of humanity's role in the process of salvation, the message in the RMP also transformed the soldiers' understanding of the war. The possibility of being both a superior soldier and a superior Christian seemingly became a reality for many men. As the war dragged on, this Christian identity readily fused with the mission proclaimed by the editors. Revivals and the RMP offered dual testimony that the Confederate army fought a battle with both immediate and eternal implications. Yet the rhetoric that created this unity of identity and mission came not just from the RMP's gospel presentations but also in their descriptions and explanations of the cause.

"We Are Fighting Not Only for Our Country But Our God"

If enlisting men in the army of Christ was, as the editors claimed, the most important cause, support for the Confederate cause followed close behind. Philip Slaughter reminded the readers of the *Messenger* that all articles had "but one test to politics, and that is loyalty to the Confederate flag." At first, the RMP clearly differentiated between the cause for God and the cause for the South. But as time went on, it became increasingly difficult to tell the two apart. Everyone, everywhere described the war as "just," "holy," and "righteous." This vocabulary, although significant, was not the only result of the fusion of the two messages. More important, editors and preachers, in their tracts and sermons, pointed to a special relationship with God for the Confederacy. This relationship rested on the Christian character editors claimed for the Confederacy. All of the writers found ample Divine sanction for the Confederate cause in the pages of the Bible. Comparisons made between the armies, peoples, and churches in the North and South further supported their conviction that their cause was just. Calling men to support the Confederate cause, then, sounded remarkably like calling men to follow Christ. Their language blurred distinctions between Christianity and civic liberty until at times the two became interchangeable.[27]

The ease with which the rhetoric of the cause shifted from civil to religious liberty belied much of southern antebellum churches' view on politics. Before the war, the doctrine of the "spirituality of the church" forbade any hint of political posturing from the realm of the church. Only two years before the war broke out southern Presbyterian divine James Henley Thornwell firmly insisted, "The church is exclusively a *spiritual* organization, and possesses only *spiritual* power." Yet southern divines' claims of separate spheres for church and state did not match actual practice. In the antebellum South, temperance reform found a home among many Baptists and Methodists. And although these politically tinged efforts never gained the popular support accorded northern efforts, their numbers were not insignificant. Perhaps the "spirituality of the church" is best understood as a Presbyterian ideal rather than a southern church mandate. Of course, all professed intentions of keeping church and politics separate quickly ended with the election of Lincoln. Professor Harry Stout locates the occasion for this remarkable turnabout in the "Confederate jeremiad" proclaimed in the public fast. With the barrier between church and state broken down, it was not long before ministers sacralized the cause of the Confederacy. By defining the new nation as Christian, editors were able to convey a sacred status upon the war effort. Although some ministers used the word *covenant* to convey this sacred status, the RMP's editors never made this direct claim. Instead, they found parallels in history, and especially in Israel's experience, that both justified and explained their cause.[28]

Despite the churches' Christianizing of the cause from the start of the war, the editors' earliest explanations of the cause in the RMP focused primarily on the question of civil liberties. The Confederate nation was the true heir and protector of the liberties garnered in 1776. In the very first issue of *The Soldier's Friend,* Worrell announced, "We are fighting for the right to govern ourselves." Likewise, the editor for the Methodists' *The Soldier's Paper* defined the struggle as one for "peace and independence." *The Soldier's Visitor,* prepared by the Presbyterian Committee of Publication, based its very first arguments upon principles found within the Declaration of Independence. And in a similar vein, the Evangelical Tract Society's *Army and Navy Messenger* argued, "Our purpose is (if we properly appreciate the precious legacy to posterity of the founders of the constitutional liberty . . .) faithfully to maintain and to preserve inviolate the chartered liberties of the people, and the sovereign rights, privileges and franchises reserved in the Constitution of the States and the compact of alliance between them." This language of civil liberties and constitutional heritage did not completely disappear when speaking of the Confederate cause, but by the latter half of 1864 the editors merged it with a second rhetoric of freedom, religious freedom. At times in conjunction with this rhetoric of civic liberty, more often in its place, the editors of the RMP articulated a defense of freedom of religion, a defense of orthodoxy, as central to the Confederate effort.[29]

If appropriating the mantle of 1776 was important to the editors of the RMP, a second heritage proved to be of much greater significance. "It is not often," began C. C. Gillespie, "in the history of the world that such great criseses *[sic]*, involving the very fundamental elements of truth, conscience, and manhood, are allowed by Divine Providence to occur. . . . Such was the position of the Hebrew nation in the midst of the Gentile world; such was the position of the martyr church of Christ. . . . Such is our position now." God had bestowed this heritage upon the new nation. It entailed the fundamentals of God's design for the world. In the *Messenger,* one writer revealed the combined civil and religious vocabularies in his explanation of "what they fought for": "They fight not for conquest, for plunder, or for fame, nor is it from a feeling of hatred to their opponents. . . . They fight for a sacred principle—for the right of self-government, for the protection of their homes, their families and their altars." Two columns later, W. B. Wellons, the newly installed editor of the *Messenger,* celebrated the paper's return to print to "cheer them on in the struggle for civil and religious liberty—for the right of self-government, and the privilege of worshipping God according to the dictates of the conscience and the teachings of His word." Writing for the trans-Mississippi army, William Norris offered an even more forceful statement concerning the divine nature of the war, "This war is on our part, a war for our Religion. . . . The import of these instructive sentences has not been enough studied by our people for them to see how much this war has put our religious interests in peril." Six months later, Norris's *Mississippi Messenger* reiterated the same truth. "The character of the war is, with us, essentially and necessarily religious. . . . In its simplest form, the war with us [is] for freedom of conscience—freedom to interpret the Bible and worship God according to the dictates of our own consciences."[30] The war for freedom in the Confederacy was more than just a military contest for civil liberties, the editors argued. It was a war for religion, a war against infidels, a war by God's chosen nation for God's plan for the universe.

According to the editors, fundamental differences existed between the North and the South. Many of these incongruous attributes substantiated Confederate claims of a Christian republic. Writers found primary differences in the contrasting characters of the two peoples, and especially their armies. Countless articles described the evils of the federal army. They murdered, raped, and robbed indiscriminately throughout the South. They were immoral, profane, and Sabbath breakers. However, it was not simply the sins of the army, or the fact that the Yankees trusted in their military strength, that differentiated them from their southern counterparts. The fundamental difference lay in whom they did not trust—God. This failure to trust God explained such vile behavior. Southern soldiers should not be "amazed at the savage barbarities they [Yankees] perpetrate. . . . These things are not an accident. . . . These things are a revelation of the inmost nature; a natural and true expression of the consistent character of the people who are now striving to conquer us." Northern efforts, *The Soldier's Friend* charged, "blasphemously invade the prerogatives of God. . . . They war against Sabbath and sanctuaries—against God and man."[31]

The RMP located the blame for this failure in the federal army with the Union churches. The northern church, more than any other person or institution, stood responsible for the evil character of the army of invaders. Yankee Christianity was politicized Christianity. What else, asked one writer, could be expected from the Union army in light of the "prostitution of the Northern pulpit" to the war effort. Editors loved to quote Yankee sources that supported this contention. *The Soldier's Paper* repeated an essay from the *New York Journal of Commerce* that decried the "total prostration of some churches and some of the clergy to the war spirit." Another essay noted, "One of the largest denominations in the North . . . at their last General Conference reported *not a single conversion* among their troops." This, the author continued, stood in marked contrast to the "religious prosperity of the South," The *Mississippi Messenger* printed a piece entitled, "Massachusetts, and a War for Religion." In it, the columnist traced a history of religious abuse in that northern state. Beginning with Roger Williams and continuing all the way through the recent burning of the convent at Charlestown, the author described the horrendous persecution of religious freedom in Massachusetts. Even "their persecution of the great and good Jonathan Edwards is a matter of history." Only the Presbyterian press sounded slightly more conciliatory in their assessment of northern religion. Yet it quickly confirmed the superiority of southern churches "We cannot join in the prevailing wholesale denunciation of all professing Christians at the North. . . . Many of these disapprove of war, and long and pray for peace. . . . But after making the most liberal allowance for these classes, it is our firm conviction . . . that the type of piety in the Southern churches is simpler and purer than at the North; and as to the relative purity of doctrine, there can be no question."[32] The perceived doctrinal and spiritual purity of southern churches shaped the RMP's view of the Confederate nation. It also allowed editors to find a place for their Christian republic in God's plan for the ages.

The Rev. Whiteford Smith summarized God's agenda for the new nation. Southern activities stood "in conformity with the apostolic injunction, the Confederate States withdrew from a political association with just such persons as St. Paul denounced." The problem, according to Smith, began long before, at the time of the American Revolution: *"E pluribus unum,"* one from many. The original Union stood in direct opposition to the "order of God." Smith found biblical precedent for his analysis in the book of Genesis. There, God prevented humanity from joining together at the tower of Babel by confusing the tongues of men. Today, Smith observed, he obstructs us through war. "It is not hard," he continued, "to discover in the history of our present struggle the special interposition of Divine Providence, to prevent a reconstruction of our former Union. . . . It has now been demonstrated that we are two peoples, essentially and forever separate." Other writers joined Smith in finding God's hand at work in both the cause and outcome of the war. They, too, found plentiful testimony in the world around them declaring the differences of two nations. "This is the ordering of God's Providence," declared the *Mississippi Messenger,* "which forbids the permanent union of heterogeneous nations." Fundamental differences separated North and South: dissimilar climate and institutional, mental, and moral characteristics all demonstrated the need for secession.[33] These features confirmed the southern nation's autonomous relationship with the Father.

The shift in the language of the cause from a defense based on civil liberties and freedom to one founded upon religious liberties and biblical analogies should not be surprising. Nor should it be construed as a shift away from rational discourse to a more absurd or unreasonable form of speech. Although the language of religion tugged more fully at the emotions of people, it did not represent an abandonment of logic by those who voiced the message. As Confederate defeats became more frequent, the language needed to validate the tremendous losses and still inspire hope evolved. The rhetoric of religion sacralized the cause. It firmly planted the source of war in the providential plan of God and placed ultimate hope for victory in Him. "We are fighting not only for our country but our God. This identity inspires our hope and establishes our confidence. It has become for us a holy war, and each fearful and bloody battle an act of awful and solemn worship." Such impassioned speech did not deny humanity's role in the war, but reflected its importance. As one writer summarized, "the blood of martyrs was the seed of the Church, the blood of our heroes is the seed of liberty."[34] Their rhetoric acknowledged One greater than all human efforts combined. It recognized a God who—according to their reading of the Bible—demanded obedience, and blessed those who complied.

"Let Us Look to Ourselves and to God Especially for Our Deliverance"

The religious military press evangelized the troops, defined the nature of the war in which the soldiers fought, and sought finally to build troop morale. As the *Mississippi Messenger* reminded the soldiers, the paper tried to "animate their zeal, quicken their courage, revive their fortitude, and stimulate their hopes." These themes were important according to the paper because, "When engaged in a struggle for the cause of God and Humanity, much depends upon the morale of the troops." From the editors' vantage point, nothing undercut war efforts more quickly than a despondent army. Reaffirming the prestige of departed comrades, offering hope to the disabled, and interpreting defeat became essential elements of this task. Drawing upon both the Bible and Confederate history to illustrate their beliefs, editors offered an explanation of defeat designed to inspire hope as well as action. These explanations rested heavily upon the special relationship the Confederacy enjoyed with God and the guarantee of victory it brought. Exhortations to individual piety also dominated the pages of the RMP. If converting the army was the first task, the need to purify the army followed close behind. Within this "rhetorical world" of southern evangelicalism and the Civil War, one writer exclaimed, "every revival of religion in your midst . . . is a signal, bloodless victory over the enemy of our country."[35] The same could be said for every repentant act. Editors never questioned the faithfulness of God, only the response of humanity. At first, they located sin in the army. As time went on, it became apparent that much of the problem resided back home among civilians. Whether the problem was in the camp or at home, both claimed the same solution: people must repent of their sins and do their duty. The success of the new nation depended on such individual acts.

The religious military press took advantage of the psychological trauma experienced by soldiers' daily encounters with death to proclaim a gospel message of peace, happiness, and hope. It also sought to comfort the comrades of the departed. If death itself frightened the fighting men, the ignoble treatment of the dead equally alarmed them. Soldiers believed a man willing to lay down his life for his country deserved both the recognition of his country and a proper burial from his country. In the pressures of war, this proper treatment of the dead rarely occurred, even by one's own army. Writers for the religious military press could not rectify the ignoble burials many soldiers received, but they could recognize the dead for what they were—heroes, martyrs, and patriots. Numerous poems sought to remind the living comrades of the memory of the dead. Stories recounted the valiant deaths of individual soldiers. And all who died, whether from wounds or illness, died heroes of the cause and wore a "martyr's crown." *The Soldier's Paper* typified this effort with a regular column called "Our Departed Heroes." Beneath a brief two-stanza poem that ennobled the death of the brave, editors printed eulogies of common soldiers written by their comrades-in-arms. These tributes gloried in the departed's bravery and Christian faith.[36]

Physical disablement represented another emotional and physical reality of the war that demanded attention. Partly a result of advancing weapon design—especially rifling—and partly a result of the standard medical practice of amputation, the Civil War left thousands of men physically handicapped. By 1864, the Confederate nation operated 154 major hospitals to deal with the wounded. The RMP strove to mitigate the emotional and physical needs resulting from illness and injury in a variety of ways. Papers printed "Soldiers' Guides," listing the location of the wounded and ill for the benefit of family and friends. Numerous articles referred to the brave, heroic action of the wounded. Crutches, one author told the disabled soldier, served as "a public advertisement of his devotion to his country and the cause of liberty." Still, for these men, the majority of whom were accustomed to farming the land for a living, the postwar future appeared exceedingly bleak. One solution frequently proposed in the RMP involved educating the disabled for the purpose of developing teachers and pastors. Illiteracy, estimated to be 15–20 percent in the southern army, made the proposal all the more challenging. To rectify this problem, editors encouraged chaplains and educated soldiers to form classes, both in hospitals and camps, in order to teach the illiterate soldiers how to read and write. These cheering proclamations in the RMP demanded corresponding activity by the chaplains, missionaries, and colporteurs in the field, otherwise the words of encouragement would have been meaningless. Many chaplains responded. Their activities convinced many soldiers that the churches did care. It buoyed their hopes of a brighter future.[37]

Addressing the psychological needs brought on by death and disability concerned editors of the RMP, but confronting and explaining reports of defeat demanded even greater vigilance. Every paper carried battle updates. Surprisingly, the majority of these accounts sounded optimistic. Even in seemingly catastrophic losses such as the surrender of Vicksburg, the fall of Atlanta, and the retreat from Gettysburg, editors found signs of hope. Implicit in many stories of battle losses stood the conviction of a special relationship between the Christian Confederacy and God. A defeat then, as much as a victory, served as proof that ultimate victory would come at last. Military updates often listed news of a battle with estimates of the casualties sustained by both sides. The majority of reports indicated federal losses that greatly exceeded Confederate casualties. According to the *Messenger,* the enemy's loss in the Mississippi campaign totaled around 96,000; Confederate losses, 6,000–7,000. A summary of battles near Murfreesboro, Tennessee, claimed twice as many federal losses as Confederates. In the *Herald,* one writer triumphantly described how forty-two men repulsed an army of 12,000 at Sabine Pass. A later article in the *Herald* described Johnston's March 19 attack of Sherman at Bentonville, North Carolina. The sketch trumpeted news of 5,000 Yankee casualties compared with a Confederate loss of "not more than 500." These initial news reports, as well as updates of ongoing battles, virtually always proclaimed Confederate victory. "Atlanta is now in our possession. We have no doubt of its accuracy," reported the *Mississippi Messenger* on October 27, 1864. Seven weeks earlier Sherman had wired Lincoln that Atlanta had been "fairly won." Many of these statistical summaries and updates, though not all, were exaggerated. Instead of the 2:1 casualty ratio claimed for Murfreesboro, federals losses amounted to roughly 12,906 while Confederate totals reached 11,739. Similar claims for Johnston's success at Bentonville also proved false. Instead of the 5,000 Yankees lost, there were only abut 1,500, while the Confederate toll mounted to over 2,600 killed, wounded, and captured.[38]

Distorted battle updates were accompanied by pretentious editorials claiming imminent victory. On March 16, 1865, less than a month before Lee's surrender, William Norris declared, "It is quite probable that within the next three months the war shall be either closed, or its character entirely changed." To most observers the message rang true. From all appearances the Confederacy had lost the war long ago. Yet Norris wrote of Confederate victory, not defeat. "Grant, Thomas and Smith have been whipped so often that we need not take them into the calculation. In South Carolina, Sherman is confronted by an equal force with all the natural advantage on our side. Let Sherman be destroyed, and the supremacy of the Confederacy is established." "Truly," Norris continued, "there is no reason for despondency, just the reverse. . . . 'The Confederacy controls the whole situation.' "[39]

The hope that southern armies would conquer overwhelming odds found their parallel in biblical accounts of Israelites overpowering numerically superior forces time and again. These Bible stories served multiple functions. First, they provided popular reading for the soldiers. More important, they imparted hope to embattled men that God would once again reach into history and protect His children from the mighty enemy. Tales like Moses' and Joshua's victory over the Amalekites, and Gideon's triumph over the Midianites, portrayed God as the author of victory on behalf of His obedient children. With only three hundred men to assist him, Gideon slew an army of thousands. A greatly outnumbered Confederate army could expect similar Divine intervention. Finally, these narratives offered a powerful weapon for the Confederate arsenal— prayer, "What we have to do is to give ourselves to *prayer,* 'to go up to the top of the hill,' as did Moses, and there entreat the Lord if peradventure he will hear," proclaimed an essay in the *Messenger.* Of course, God did listen. During heavy federal shelling of Petersburg, the *Messenger* reported only "four white persons . . . and fifteen colored persons" died. "The number of casualties seem almost incredibly small," declared the paper. But a simple explanation sufficed, "A daily prayer meeting of all the different denominations has been kept up. . . . In answer to prayer we have been delivered." Time and again editors expounded on the integral relationship between prayer and success. Many papers printed prayers for soldiers to repeat; prayers for the sick, the wounded, the needs of the country, and the government all found their way into the RMP. In language reminiscent of the Psalms, "A Prayer Against the Enemy" called upon God to deliver his people in a time of trouble. One author found a clear correlation between Stonewall Jackson's success on the battlefield and his prayer life. Writers ensured the readers did not miss the parallels between Israel and the Confederacy. In the annals of history, both nations served Divine purposes.[40]

Bible stories and prayer, however, could not entirely combat the reality of defeats. The passage of time often revealed initial reports to be grossly inaccurate. Claims of victory at Gettysburg and Atlanta collapsed as information continued to pour in. Still, optimism prevailed. Writing after the fall of Atlanta, William Norris declared, "It is already ascertained that there was no disaster. . . . Gen. Hood never believed that he could hold Atlanta permanently. His great object was to hold it as long as he could, and to make the possession of it by the enemy cost him as much as possible. This object has been fully attained." *The Soldier's Paper* commended the southern valor while mourning the fall of Vicksburg; "they were triumphant over the foe to the last, and only fell before the terrors of starvation. The enemy knew that their prowess had not gained the victory." Writers routinely described losses as "temporary." The *Mississippi Messenger* revealed, "The loss of our great cities is probable. This occurred in the Revolutionary war, and occurs in most wars; but if the heart of the people is right, never determines the result." Six weeks later, Richmond succumbed to federal forces. Papers took the news in stride. "The taking of Richmond will have no more effect upon the final result of the war than the taking of Philadelphia, (the Capital of the Colonies) in 1777," declared the *Herald*. "While our armies are still in a state of organization and in good spirits, we have no cause for discouragement."[41] Even when discussing seemingly disastrous setbacks, editors maintained an optimistic outlook.

Underlying this positive assessment of a bright Confederate future in the face of military defeats stood an assumption of eventual triumph. Although all papers expressed supreme confidence in the "rightness" of the cause, only one, *The Soldier's Friend*, with its emblem "Fight the Lord's Battle," refused to correlate that with success. In the article "For What Shall We Pray?," Worrell noted, "In our patriotic ardor, we rarely add, *'thy will be done.'* Indeed, who among us would be willing for God's will to be done, in relation to our national destiny, provided it should be His will for us to be subjugated? . . . Our future to us is all dark—the will of God on this subject has not been revealed to us— we should, therefore, do all we can to make our destiny what we think it ought to be, and daily and hourly commit the result to God." One week later, Worrell expressed similar sentiments: "It is heralded in most of our papers, proclaimed from the pulpit, and generally endorsed by the people, that *'because we are in the right we will succeed.*' " Acknowledging that the cause was right, Worrell denied it guaranteed success. Instead, he asked, "Would any true Southern man believe that our cause is wrong, even if we should be subjugated? I think not. It would not shake my faith in the justice of our cause, if the Yankees should entirely overrun and subdue the South."[42] Worrell stood alone in expressing such beliefs. A few other writers made passing references about a person's inability to know the mind of God, then quickly and boldly reaffirmed their belief in the eventual triumph of the South. The rest of the editors found crowning evidence for the Confederacy's future success in the Christian identity of the nation. Because writers assumed the eventual achievement of the cause, they explained each defeat on its own terms, a sort of micro-analysis of what happened. It appears never to have occurred to the writers that a succession of defeats could lead to total defeat. Rather, contributors for the RMP wrote optimistically of individual defeats precisely because they were just that, individual defeats. No matter how strategically significant the loss of Vicksburg, Atlanta, or Richmond might be, writers understood them as singular rather than symptomatic events.

Military defeats, the editors argued, while temporary, contained vital lessons for the army. The lessons focused on the collective righteousness of the new nation. The Confederacy's Christian status, according to the editors, guaranteed God's interest in the success of the cause. Defeats revealed God's chastening and purifying hand in preparing His people for this mantle. Looking back after a summer of setbacks, *The Soldier's Visitor* better understood southern defeats. "Disasters will sometimes occur in spite of all that skill and bravery can do. There are uncertainties and contingencies which no human foresight can anticipate or provide for." A proper knowledge of God's way, the Presbyterian paper continued, explained everything. "What, then, if occasional disasters are allotted to us?—What if Vicksburg and Port Hudson after having bid defiance to the most formidable forces by water and land, were at last compelled by starvation to succumb? ... Shall we therefore be disheartened? Never! ... Reverses in war as well as individual life, often prove blessings. Unvarying success would tend to ... lead to forgetfulness of God as our strength and helper. ... Let all, therefore, cheer up." Like the wounded who were reminded their misfortunes were "indispensable badges" of sonship, so, too, the editors called the nation to remember, "God chastens those he loves." The *Messenger* encouraged its readers to peruse the book of Job from time to time with this reminder: "The general scope of its moral is that the troubles and afflictions of the good man are designed as tests of his virtue, out of which he will, at last, triumphantly emerge with increased happiness." Time and again, writers depicted battlefield failures as a testimony of God's love for His new nation. "The fact that he chastens severely is not evidence that he does not pity and love, and will not at length deliver." Defeats, as Divine rebukes, performed a purpose in the overall scheme of things. It was essential that the new nation stand pure before God. One analyst, reviewing the carnage of three years of war, reaffirmed the blessings of war. "The war will pay for its cost in blood by the elevation of character which it must bestow." Union victories both served as a national cleansing and opened the door for introspection. It also prompted soldiers to engage in one of their most important duties, repentance.[43]

What better place than the Bible to find lessons on repentance. The editor for the *Herald* cited *The Soldier's Pocket Bible* to substantiate his claim. This special edition of the Bible contained single sentences followed by a selection of verses meant to render clear the lesson. Passages like Deuteronomy 24:25, Joshua 7:10–11, and Jeremiah 40:2–3 supported the assertion. "For the iniquities of God's People, they are sometimes delivered into the hands of their enemies." In a similar fashion, Lamentations 3:40 and Joshua 7:13 called people to repentance; "Therefore, both Soldiers and all God's people upon such occasions must search out their sins." For a more lengthy argument, editors printed the entire chapters. Deuteronomy 28, reprinted in the *Messenger*, recounts Israel's renewal of its covenant with God. The first fourteen verses recite a litany of blessings God will provide for Israel if they keep this law. Verse fifteen begins a series of warnings and punishments God will bring upon the nation if it should turn its back on Him. Here, the *Messenger* found clear lessons for this new nation: turn from sin, honor God, and all will be well.[44]

In the first months of publication, numerous articles in the RMP expressed concern over the debilitating influence of camp life on the character of soldiers. Removed from "the salutary influences of home, of female society, and of the privileges of religion," most churches believed men's souls to be in grave danger. Hundreds of articles, short stories, sermons, tracts, and letters warned the soldiers about the evils of camp life. Four sins in particular came to be singled out for special attention: drunkenness, swearing, Sabbath breaking, and gambling. Throughout the war, writers cautioned soldiers about succumbing to these four sins. Stories warned of comrades who fell victim to the bottle and sacrificed their loved ones at home. Distilleries, according to one article, consumed enough grain to supply the needs of all destitute families. Gambling, writers charged, destroyed families. Sabbath breaking was equally grievous; it denied God what was rightfully His. Profanity mocked the God upon whom all hope rested. Only through repentance would the army gain favor with God.[45]

The concern for sin in the army was ever apparent, but the editors also believed that the tremendous revivals in the army had a positive and expanding moral impact on camp life. The revivals offered "a stand point amid the smoke and blood and disruption of the times from which the earnest minded Christian may look toward the future with hope." The Presbyterian *Soldier's Visitor* expressed gratitude that "it has pleased God, to arrest in a large measure this desolating tide. The army ... has become to a large extent pervaded by a wholesome and powerful religious influence.... The circumstances, at first deemed so unfavorable to their moral and spiritual welfare, have been turned to be a source of the richest blessings." Reports from chaplains on the noticeable curtailment of gambling and swearing seemingly substantiated such opinions. Frequent deprecating comparisons with Yankee soldiers further solidified their belief in the expanding morality of the southern army. As the war persisted, southern fighting men's moral behavior was reported on the rise.[46]

But such analysis of the growing morality of the troops posed a dilemma. Defeats had been linked to sin. As camp evils declined, expectations for victory rose. When the expanding revivals failed to reverse the patterns of defeat, editors were forced to relocate the source of sin from within the army to the civilian population. Compared to the many sins editors found in the army, the sins of the civilian population were few: extortion and speculation. From the start of the war, attacks on the sin of extortion filled the pages of both the secular and religious presses. Popular literature, sermons, and legislative initiatives joined in the condemnation. The genesis for this overwhelming public concern with extortion lay in the rapid economic expansion and rapidly climbing cotton prices of the 1850s. At the beginning of publication, the RMP joined in the attack of this most important of civilian sins, though editors still located the primary cause of defeat within the army itself. By September 1863, with revivals dominating the news coming out of the camps, the search for the source of defeat slowly began to shift in the RMP. Both soldier and editor perceived sins greater than those in the army as undercutting the Confederate cause. Rumors of speculation traveled quickly through the army. A letter from a soldier to *The Soldier's Visitor* decried the sins of "extortion and speculation" at home. The ensuing issue followed up on that theme; "But for the demoralized condition of our home-staying population, but for their speculation, extortion, avarice, and mammon worship,—we should feel entire confidence that we were now in a fair way to reach the longed for goal of our hopes." In March 1864, one writer declared, "The talent, the energy, patriotism—and now, it should seem, the piety of the country is, for the most part, to be found in the army." As the war continued and supplies for the army dwindled, few seemed inclined to disagree. People who engaged in the extortion were labeled enemies to both God and country. A few verbal assaults focused on ethnic groups—the Jews and Dutch, or "a few ambitious avaricious and timid men." The majority of condemnations, though, applied to the civilian population as a whole.[47]

The history of the newly formed Confederate nation shed further light on the connection between sin and defeat. On February 23, 1865, chaplain R. F. Bunting surveyed the history of the war up to that point in time. Assuring his audience that "the Lord has as much to do *now* with the affairs of men, as when the glory of His presence filled the tabernacle . . . or when He conversed with Abraham," Bunting proceeded to analyze the previous three years of Confederate successes and failures. Each victory arose from prayerful supplication. Yet "foolish boasting," claiming that "this Confederacy [is] the work of *our own* hands," showed how quickly people forgot their entire dependence must rest in their Creator. For three columns, Bunting carefully summarized the role of Divine Providence in the war. Every public fast was followed by a victory. Sadly though, the months after each victory revealed a nation not yet prepared for brilliant success." Noting President Davis's most recent call for a day of fasting and prayer, Bunting charged his readers to be faithful in their vows to God. God is offering the South a "glorious birthright." It was ready to be claimed. If faithful, "*He will again draw near* and give us deliverance from our present perils, crowning our arms with glorious victory."[48]

In condemning sin, whether in the camp or on the home front, editors clearly located the responsibility for change in the individual. Almost every article that condemned evil offered a solution—repentance. "Our fate is in a great measure in our own hands," Philip Slaughter reminded his audience. "We are free agents.—God has laid before us the path of duty, and not only told us to walk in it, but has offered us all the help we need to keep from straying." Article after article sounded out this familiar theme. The army and the people must determine to do their "whole duty." Only through virtue would the people ensure God's blessing "on a cause so clearly righteous in its origin." Final responsibility for success rested upon the people. The Christian character the editors claimed for the nation demanded a righteous life from the people. In calling the army and civilians to that life, the editors called them to victory.[49]

Conclusion

The southern churches' largest voice to the army, the religious military press, argued that the Christian message had immediate implications for the conflict at hand. Christians made the best soldiers precisely because they were attentive to all of their obligations. Each soldier had a responsibility toward duty, both military and moral. In the worldview espoused by editors, proclaiming God as the source of all blessings and afflictions did not preclude proper human response; it demanded it. Defeats were "acceptable" because they were understandable. Explanations for defeat provided a means of converting setbacks into triumphs. Christianizing the cause broadened individual responsibility to include both the secular and spiritual realms. Revivals, then, were as significant as military victories. Both assured the writers for the RMP that God sanctioned this war for freedom and promised victory. The revivals were the "first fruits" of the war. "What stronger evidence can we have that he favors the war which we wage, not for conquest or plunder, but for those dear and cherished rights which his own hand hath given us?"[50]

The fact that the Confederacy lost the war does not mean the churches failed to adequately support the war effort, as some historians have suggested. This viewpoint implies southern evangelicals proclaimed a restricted message of personal salvation, one that was too individualized to serve a proper social function and instead offered soldiers an "otherworldly triumph" in the face of military defeat. Yet such an interpretation ignores the social possibilities offered in the Christian message during the war. The message of salvation, fused with the hope of Confederate triumph, related repentance to victory and thereby explained defeat as divine possibility with present implications. This fusion of beliefs, proclaimed in the RMP, illustrated its important social function during the Civil War. The social impact of the message within the RMP also went beyond the Civil War itself. The religion of the Lost Cause was more than just a civil religion. At the very heart of this postwar message was a manly Christianity. Proclaimed by men like J. William Jones—aptly designated by one historian as the evangelist of the Lost Cause—this version of Christianity sacralized the South's defeat, elevated her lost sons to martyrdom, and, above all else, confirmed the rightness of the cause.[51]

Given the RMP's large voice and passionate admonitions, what did soldiers actually comprehend of their message? Diaries and letters provide some indications to the extent the fighting men identified with the message they heard, but they can never adequately portray the extent men believed the worldview proclaimed by the editors. James McPherson's book, *What They Fought For, 1861–1865*, indicates that a number of soldiers adopted the heritage of 1776 to explain their actions. In the hundreds of letters and diaries he surveyed, over two-thirds claimed some form of patriotic motive for their conduct. Others, according to McPherson, discerned a Divine roll for the Confederacy. The new nation would, one soldier wrote, "become a nation among the nations of the earth, designed, in the hands of God, to fulfill a glorious destiny." There is also a smattering of evidence within the religious military press that some soldiers over zealously identified with the worldview proclaimed by the editors. Several articles appeared warning soldiers that death on the battlefield did not guarantee entrance into heaven. It seems as if in their efforts to Christianize the cause and pay tribute to the "martyred" heroes, editors fused the sacred and secular in the minds of some soldiers in an undesired way. Seeking to counteract such beliefs, one writer reminded readers, "It is not the blood of man but *'the blood of Jesus Christ that cleanseth from all sin.'* " Perhaps all editors knew the difference between a Christian martyr and a noble patriot, but obviously not all soldiers made the same distinction.[52]

The extent to which soldiers adopted the RMP's message is not completely clear, but the persistence of the editors cannot be disputed. Copies of the last issue published still exist for five of the religious military papers: *The Soldier's Visitor* (February 1865), *Messenger* (March 16, 1865), *The Soldier's Paper* (April 1, 1865), *Herald* (April 13, 1865), and the *Mississippi Messenger* (May 11, 1865). Not surprisingly, within these issues one finds evangelistic messages, calls for repentance, and summaries of military and political news. In addition, each continues to express hope in God's final deliverance. The editor for the *Herald* saw "no cause for discouragement" in the evacuation of Richmond. After summarizing news, the *protem* editor for the *Soldier's Paper* wrote, "We find much encouragement in the belief that the sincere prayers of many thousands of our countrymen are ascending to the God of battles in our behalf. Let the soldiers pray also . . . [and] doing their duty nobly and faithfully, he will reward them with victory, and bless our wasted, torn and bleeding country with peace." Asking, "Shall We Succeed?," an article in *The Soldier's Visitor* pointed out the distinctions between North and South in government, social, and spiritual life. After acknowledging ever so briefly that his rationale might be fallacious, the writer concluded, "He has his own methods and his own time to work out his grand designs. Let us trust him in the midnight of reverses, as well as under the sunlight of victories. Let us 'hope in God,' and 'we shall yet praise him.'" One column later, a writer noted, "We cannot but believe that, for the present, God is giving our enemies to strong delusion, as one step in the recompense he purposes to mete out to them." In the final issue of the *Messenger*, several articles focused on sins found in the army and called for repentance. And an essay entitled "Bible Warriors" found parallels in the experiences of Israel and called the nation to prayer. Only the last paper in print, the *Mississippi Messenger*, varied from its normal stand of unvanquished hope. The final issue appeared a little more than a month *after* Lee's surrender at Appomattox. On the front page, Norris printed an evangelistic message. The text, Isaiah 12:2, stated, "I will trust, and not be afraid." The paper also printed a selection of resolutions from various divisions promising to fight on. Only the editorial by Norris deviated from the usual message. For the first time, Norris acknowledged the possibility of defeat. Nevertheless, he recognized the benefits of "wholesome reading [that] purifies and elevates the man." In his final admonition, Norris called upon the soldiers who had "displayed physical courage in the highest degree" to show now their "moral courage in the purest type." Perhaps this present generation had, in some way, failed. Despite this failure, Norris still held hope for the South. Once again, this hope lay in the future. Like the losses of Vicksburg, Atlanta, and Richmond, this final defeat would prove to be a temporary setback. Norris knew the cause was right and that ultimately God would prove faithful. As Norris noted, "if the sun of the Confederacy should set for a season it will go down in glory, and as *we believe*, will rise again with renewed strength and splendor."[53]

Notes

1. [John Leyland], "Our Paper," *The Soldier's Visitor*, August 1863, 2.

2. Two of the better works that address the role of religion in the Civil War are Drew Gilpin Faust, *The Creation of Confederate Nationalism* (Baton Rouge, 1988); and Harry S. Stout, *The Life and Death of the Confederate Jeremiad*, James A. Gray Lectures, Duke Divinity School, October 1992. While use of the term *evangelical* often raises as many questions as it answers, for the purposes of this paper it refers to the four largest denominations in the South: Methodist, Baptist, Presbyterian, and Episcopal. Although the Episcopal church did not publish its own paper for the soldiers, it was represented on the governing board of the Evangelical Tract Society. At the time of the Civil War, all four of these denominations placed great emphasis on the conversion experience. See Henry Smith Stroupe, *The Religious Press in the South Atlantic States, 1802–1865* (Durham, NC, 1956), for examples of religious papers that circulated some of their number to the troops. Biographical information on the papers comes from Stroupe, *The Religious Press*, 34–35, 42–43, 102–103; *Mississippi Messenger*, September 15, 1864.

3. Gardiner H. Shattuck Jr., *A Shield and Hiding Place: The Religious Life of the Civil War Armies* (Macon, GA, 1987), 44. Reid Mitchell notes that predictions by soldiers of an imminent end to the war continued throughout the war; *Civil War Soldiers: Their Expectations and Their Experiences* (New York, 1989), 184–185. On expectations the

war would be short-lived, see James McPherson, *Battle Cry of Freedom: The Civil War Era* (New York, 1988), 317; Allan Nevins, *The War For The Union: The Improvised War, 1861–1862* (New York, 1959), 94–98. On regular religious weeklies circulated among the armies, see Stroupe, *Religious Press*, 63, 91. "The Evangelical Tract Society—Its History, And What It Has Accomplished," *Messenger*, March 16, 1865, 2.

4. By late March of 1865, the *Army and Navy Herald* doubled its size from four to eight pages; March 23, 1865. *The Soldier's Friend* promised to increase publication numbers to meet demand.

5. "Gen. Robert E. Lee," *Messenger*, June 15, 1863, 2, 4; A sample giving list includes General Joseph R. Anderson, $50; Col. John M. Patton, $50; the 8th Virginia Regiment, $182; Officers of the 24th Alabama regiment, $40; a "Georgia soldier," $20; W. G. Hill, 28th Alabama, $20; and Private John Houston, $10, *Messenger*, February 1, 1864, 3; General Cooke's gift, *Messenger* 2 January 1865, 3; See also *Army and Navy Herald*, March 16, 1865, 3. Initially *The Soldier's Paper* collected money from civilians only. As the costs of production and distribution rose, it began to solicit financial aid from the army. See "To Our Patrons and Friends in the Army," *The Soldier's Paper*, February 15, 1865; *The Soldier's Paper*, April 1, 1865, 3; March 16, 1865, 3; "Interests of the Soldiers," *The Soldier's Friend*, January 10, 1863, 2. Only one, *The Soldier's Visitor*, failed to solicit money from its readers. On advertising see "Report," *Herald*, March 23, 1865, 2. "Twenty-five cents per line, or $1 per square of ten lines, each insertion. "Rates of Advertising," *Herald*, February 9, 1865, 2. The largest single listing of contributions is in the *Messenger*, February 1, 1864, 3. Of 162 contributions, 30 came from men in the military, 66 from women, and the rest from men in civilian life. The pattern of civilian giving outnumbering military giving holds true throughout the war as does the consistently high percentage of women contributors. The December 15, 1864, *Messenger* even lists four "Colored Contributions." On *The Soldier's Friend* soliciting money from other churches, see Stroupe, *The Religious Press*, 34. On the rise of inflation and shortages of goods, see McPherson, *Battle Cry of Freedom*, 337–342. The amount of money received remained fairly consistent until near the very end of the war when giving dropped off dramatically. For example, the Evangelical Tract Society collected between $2,500 and $3,500 monthly for publication of the *Messenger*, not enough to keep up with inflation. By March 1865 money received decreased to $553. Advertisements appeared in only two papers, the *Messenger* and *The Soldier's Paper*. For increased subscription rates, see "New Rates," *The Soldier's Paper*, May 2, 1863, 1. On rate increases, see "Rates of Advertising." *The Herald*, April 6, 1865, 1; "Notice," *The Soldier's Paper*, June 1, 1864, 1. For an example of a nonmonetary gift, see "Report," *The Herald*, March 23, 1865, 1.

6. "The Evangelical Tract Society," *Army and Navy Messenger for the Trans-Mississippi Department*, September 15, 1864, 1; and "Our Operations in the Trans-Mississippi Department," *Messenger*, December 15, 1864, 2. For production disruptions caused by the war, see "Our Paper," *Messenger*, December 15, 1864, 1; and *Messenger*, February 8, 1865, 2. On the failure of the postal system, see "Papers Not Received." *The Soldier's Visitor*, January 1865, 3; February 1865, 3; Robert J. Harp, "Directions How to Obtain the Army and Navy Herald," *Herald*, April 6, 1865, 2.

7. Some of the largest urban papers produced larger issues, but not many. The *Richmond Christian Advocate*, 4,000; *Confederate Baptist* (Columbia, SC), 4,000; *Christian Index* (Washington, GA) 3,000; *North Carolina Christian Advocate* (Raleigh), 5,000; Stroupe, *The Religious Press*, 65, 72, 59, 93. Two children's papers, *Children's Friend* (Richmond), 10,000 and *Child's Index* (Macon, GA), 12,000, produced print runs the size of the RMP. The only adult paper to reach a similar number was Alexander Campbell's *Millennial Harbinger* (Bethany, VA), which at 8,000 copies rivaled

the size of the RMP. Stroupe, *The Religious Press,* 33–34, 55–56, 88. For distribution size of the RMP, see Stroupe, *The Religious Press,* 42–43, 102–103; *The Soldier's Friend,* January 10, 1863, 2; *The Soldier's Paper,* August 1, 1863, 2. Publishing details do not exist for either the *Herald* or the *Mississippi Messenger,* though both were printed semi-monthly. This is in addition to the large volume of tracts, hymnals, and pocket Bibles printed and distributed by these agencies. Many of the papers printed the distribution efforts of their agents in the field.

8. Philip Slaughter, "Personalities and Parties and Sections," *Messenger,* June 15, 1863, 2 (first quotation); "The Want of Our Soldiers," *Messenger,* January 2, 1865, 2 (second quotation); Adolphus Spalding Worrell, "Salutatory," *The Soldier's Friend,* January 10, 1863, 3 (third quotation, italics his); W. B. Norris, *Mississippi Messenger,* September 15, 1864, 2 (fourth quotation). There even appears to be a degree of harmony among Protestants and Catholics. The RMP almost never attacked the Catholic church and the *Messenger* lists the service times of the Catholic church in its church directory. *Messenger,* "Petersburg Church Directory," December 15, 1864, 3.

9. *Colporteur* is a French word that denotes a peddler of religious literature.

10. W. B. Wellons, "The Confederate Army As A Field for Religious Labor." *Messenger,* December 15, 1864, 1 (first quotation, italics his). The two most often cited sources for the Confederate revivals are William W. Bennett, *A Narrative of the Great Revival Which Prevailed in the Southern Armies during the late Civil War between the States of the Federal Union* (Philadelphia, 1877); and J. William Jones, *Christ in the Camp; or, Religion in Lee's Army* (Richmond, 1887). Jones estimates 150,000 soldiers converted during the war. For modern estimates on numbers converted, see Shattuck, *A Shield and Hiding Place,* 96, 99; and Gorrell Clinton Prim Jr., "Born Again in the Trenches: Revivalism in the Confederate Army," Ph.D. dissertation, Florida State University, 1982, 55, 102–103, 198–200.

11. Bennett, *A Narrative of The Great Revival,* describes the gradual increase of religion in the army during the first year, 115. For summaries of revivals that occurred at different times and in different settings, see "Revivals in our Army of the West." and William Norris, "Religious Intelligence from the Army," *Messenger,* June 15, 1863, 1, 3. See also "To Chaplains," *Mississippi Messenger,* September 15, 1864, 2 (first quotation); Numbers reported by George W. Primrose, "Editors Messenger," *Mississippi Messenger,* March 16, 1865, 1; "Chaplains meeting," *Messenger,* March 16, 1865, 1; and S. M. Cherry, "The Revival in the Army of Tennessee," *The Soldier's Paper,* June 11, 1864, 2. For other examples, see "Revivals in Our Army of the West," *The Messenger,* June 15, 1863, 1. One writer tells of more than "5,000 persons converted to God." *Mississippi Messenger,* September 19, 1864, 1. Almost every issue listed several reports on the revivals. Other examples include *Mississippi Messenger,* "Army Intelligence," September 15, 1864, 1; "Army Intelligence," and "Gen. Parsons' Command," September 29, 1864, 1; "A Brief Account of the Great Revival in Johnson's Army," October 13, 1864, 1; in *The Soldier's Visitor,* see "Religion in the Army," August 1863, 2; "Camp Meeting," and "Religious Interest in the Army," September 1863, 4; "Religion in the Trans-Mississippi Army," March 1864, 28; in the *Herald* see "Religion in the Army," March 16, 1865, 4. If there is a consistent pattern to the revivals, I have not been able to locate it. Drew Gilpin Faust, "Christian Soldiers: The Meaning of Revivalism in the Confederate Army," *Journal of Southern History* 53 (February 1987): 72, suggests that the greatest revivals came after defeats. The reports of revivals in the RMP do not appear to substantiate this claim. Although there were several large revivals after disasterous losses, they also report significant conversions during winter camps, after victories, and while on the march.

12. "Army Revival As Argument For Our Success." *The Soldier's Visitor,* September

1863, 4 (first quotation); on the idea of God blessing a remnant, see "Shall We Succeed?," *The Soldier's Visitor*, February 1865, 26 (second quotation), and "God Our Trust
and Strength," *The Soldier's Paper*, August 1, 1863, 2; "A Prayer." *The Soldier's Visitor*,
January 1864, 19; "Army Intelligence," *Mississippi Messenger*, September 15, 1864, 1 (third
and fourth quotation); see also "The Work of Grace in the Army," *The Soldier's Paper*,
August 15, 1863, 2.

13. A number of articles noted that proof of conversion ultimately rested in
changed behavior. See, for example, "The Fruits of the Spirit the Only Infallible Test
of Conversion," *Messenger*, June 15, 1863, 2; "Influence of Religion," *Herald*, November
1, 1863, 4 (first quotation). On southern notions of feminine Christianity, see Timothy
A. Long, "Divine Confederacy: Southern Evangelicals and the Civil War," master's
thesis, University of North Carolina, 1990, 4–6, 22. For descriptions of southern women
as noble, virtuous, pure, and gentle in the RMP, see "Lay Me At Thy Feet, Mother,"
Messenger, December 15, 1864, 3; *Mississippi Messenger*, September 29, 1864, 1; "The
Influence of Women," *The Soldier's Paper*, August 1, 1863, 3. On the almost 2:1 ratio of
women to men, see, Donald G. Mathews, *Religion in the Old South* (Chicago, 1977),
47–48.

14. "Piety in the Army," *Messenger*, June 15, 1863, 2 (first quotation); Bishop Atkinson, "The Different Standards Of Morals Which Men, The Masters of Opinions,
Have Made For Women And for Themselves—The Law Of Honor," *Messenger*, July
15, 1863, 4 (second quotation). For another criticism of southern honor, see Philip
Slaughter, "The Law of Honor," *Messenger*, September 1, 1863, 4. "Religion and Fighting," *The Soldier's Visitor*, September 1863, 4 (third quotation). See also *Messenger*, March
3, 1865, 1; W. C. Rives, "Correspondence of the Messenger," *Messenger*, June 15, 1863,
3; "Letter From Gen. J. E. B. Stuart in Relation to the Biography of Randolph Fairfax,"
Messenger, February 1, 1864, 2. See Faust, "Christian Soldiers," 75–76 for an explanation
of Confederate beliefs about the effects of religion on a soldiers "efficiency and discipline." On a Christian soldier's ability to face death, see *The Soldier's Paper*, September
1, 1863, 1; "The Dying Soldier," *The Soldier's Paper*, September 1, 1863, 1; "For the
Soldier's Paper," *The Soldier's Paper*, August 15, 1863, 3.

15. Adolphus Spalding Worrell, "The People of the Confederate States," *The Soldier's Friend*, July 9, 1863, 1 (first quotation); Rev. Stiles, "Fruits of the Revival in the
Army," *The Soldier's Visitor*, September 1863, 3 (second quotation, italics his); C. C.
Gillespie, "The Confederate Motto, No Compromise," *Mississippi Messenger*, March 16,
1865, 2 (third quotation). For claims of the army's Christianizing influence on civilians,
see "The Confederate Army as a Field for Religious Labor," *Messenger*, December 15,
1864, 1, and *Mississippi Messenger*, February 16, 1865, 1.

16. "The Blood of Atonement," *Messenger*, July 15, 1863, 2; You Are in Danger,"
Mississippi Messenger, February 16, 1865, 1; George Kramer, "Eternal Punishment," *The
Soldier's Paper*, June 18, 1863, 3. See also "Simplicity of Faith," *The Soldier's Visitor*,
October 1863, 7; "Repent Ye," *Mississippi Messenger*, February 16, 1865, 1. On Christian
unity, see, for example, "Not Denominational," *Messenger*, December 15, 1864, 2. There
were some previous examples of denominations joining together for revival meetings in
the antebellum South, though in many cases denominational relationships were marked
with acrimony. For examples of unity and the emphasis of revival preaching, see Anne
C. Loveland, *Southern Evangelicals and the Social Order, 1800–1860* (Baton Rouge, 1980),
71. While agreeing with Loveland that the "way" evangelistic sermons were presented
was important, I am hesitant to say they were lacking in doctrine. Pastors could easily
omit theological jargon from their sermons and suggest practical reasons for accepting
the gospel and yet these sermons still presented the fundamental doctrines of the faith.

17. For examples, see "My Dear Son," "The Sick Soldier in the Hospital," and "Think of the Consequence," *The Soldier's Friend,* January 10, 1863, 1; or "A Letter to a Soldier," *The Soldier's Paper,* August 1, 1863, 3. For sample letters, see Samuel T. Preston, *The Soldier's Paper,* November 1, 1863, 1; and "A Word To Neutral Persons," *The Soldier's Paper,* June 1, 1864, 1. Examples of deathbed conversions include Michael Runy, "A Most Touching Story," *Messenger,* January 1, 1864, 4; Philip Slaughter, "An Original Tract for the Hospital," *Messenger,* June 15, 1863, 1; "Be Ye Also Ready," *The Soldier's Visitor,* December 1863, 15; L. B. M., "Life and Death Scenes," *The Soldier's Paper,* November 1, 1863, 3. For examples of parables, see "The Heavy Burden," *The Soldier's Visitor,* August 1863, 1; see also "The Lost Sheep," *The Soldier's Visitor,* February 1864, 26; and "Man's Gracious Recovery to the Favor of his Offended God," *Mississippi Messenger,* October 13, 1864, 1.

18. [W. B. Wellons,] "A Sad Incident," *Messenger,* December 15, 1864, 4; see also "The Private and the Corporal," *The Soldier's Visitor,* January 1865, 20. On Civil War heroes, see "Memorial to Lieutenant Colonel Thornton." *The Soldier's Visitor,* February 1864, 23; and "Polk," *Mississippi Messenger,* September 15, 1864, 2; "Walking With God." *Messenger,* January 2, 1865, 2; Philip Slaughter, "A Sketch of the Life of Randolph Fairfax," *Messenger,* January 1, 1864, 2–3; January 15, 1864. 1–3; February 1, 1864, 1–2. Announcement of the printing of a tract containing Fairfax's story in response to numerous requests is found in "The Memoir of Randolph Fairfax," *Messenger,* January 15, 1864, 2. See also "Sketch of Capt. Dabney Carr Harrison," *Messenger,* July 15, 1863, 2. On Washington and Napoleon, see "Walking With God," *Messenger,* January 2, 1865, 2; "Napoleon on the Divinity of Christ," *Mississippi Messenger,* September 15, 1864, 1; and "Napoleon's Argument for the Divinity of Christ," *Mississippi Messenger,* January 5, 1865, 1; "Sir Henry Havelock," *The Soldier's Visitor,* November 1863, 11.

19. See, for example, "Who Is He That Would Forbid Us," *Messenger,* March 16, 1865, 4; "Jesus Is With Me," *Messenger,* March 3, 1865, 3; "What Must I Do?," *Mississippi Messenger,* March 2, 1865, 1 (first quotation); "The Gospel Effects of Religion," *Messenger,* March 16, 1865, 4 (second quotation); "A Happy Soldier," *The Soldier's Visitor,* November 1863, 12 (third quotation). See also "Happy Jack," *The Soldier's Visitor,* October 1863, 9; "Death of a Christian Soldier," *Herald,* March 16, 1865, 4, tells of a Christian wounded and left to die in the heat of battle. Despite his discomfort and fast approaching death, *"he was happy."* (italics original). For descriptions of soldiers who "died happy," see Bennett, *Great Revival,* 161, 183, 226.

20. On the popular antebellum understanding of Providence, see Lewis O. Saum, *The Popular Mood of Pre-Civil War American* (Westport, CT, 1980), 3–26. Saum notes two distinct views on Providence in antebellum America. Individuals primarily spoke of Providence in immediate or past terms. They acknowledged thanks to God for what He had done or was currently doing. Public statements more often used Providence for future orientation, to speak of a manifest destiny for the nation. This dichotomy is clear in the RMP. When speaking of a national destiny, editors claimed providential blessing for the future. When addressing the soldiers on a more personal level, they asked them to consider how God has protected and provided up to that point in time. See also Loveland, *Southern Evangelicals,* 128. "The Wounded, Or, A Time To Think," *The Soldier's Visitor,* August 1863, 1 (italics in original, first quotation). See also Philip Slaughter, "An Original Tract For The Hospital," *Messenger,* June 15, 1863, 1; "A Kind Word To The Sick," *Messenger,* July 15, 1863, 2; "Brother Soldiers," *Messenger,* December 15, 1864, 1 (second quotation).

21. "A Voice of Warning," *The Soldier's Visitor,* August 1863, 1; William Norris, "A Word of Encouragement," *Mississippi Messenger,* March 16, 1865, 1 (first quotation);

M. F. C., "The Time is Short," *Herald,* April 6, 1865, 4 (second quotation). For other examples, see also "Believe and Be Saved," *Messenger,* March 3, 1865, 1; "Be Ye Ready," *The Soldier's Visitor,* December 1863, 15; "When Is the Time to Die," *The Soldier's Visitor,* February 1865, 27; "Time Is Short," *Messenger,* January 2, 1865, 3; *Messenger,* February 8, 1865, 2 (third quotation).

22. Quoted from the *N.C. Advocate,* "Death of a Christian Soldier," *Herald,* March 16, 1865, 4 (first quotation, italics in original). Reid Mitchell discusses the various reactions of soldiers to death in *Civil War Soldiers,* 62–64.

23. •Reformed soteriology long dominated American religion beginning with the Puritans. For descriptions of the process of conversion, see Charles Lloyd Cohen, *God's Caress: The Psychology of Puritan Religious Experience* (New York, 1986), 75–110; and Patricia Caldwell, *The Puritan Conversion Narrative: The Beginnings of American Expression* (New York, 1983). The nature and acceptance of Reformed soteriology in the South begs further study. Methodists with their Arminian presentation made great inroads into the religious landscape of the South. Still, it is likely many Baptists and almost all Presbyterians would have articulated—or claimed to articulate—a traditional Reformed soteriology. Anne Loveland finds evidence for some shift toward Arminianism in traditional Reformed groups in the antebellum era. Whether the war, with the powerful awareness of death it brought, furthered this shift remains to be seen. One would expect to find the traditionally Reformed line held to within theological journals. If a change occurred, it would likely be in the sermons of preachers and chaplains. Loveland, *Southern Evangelicals,* 70, 71. L. T. A., "Religious Intelligence From the Army," *Messenger,* June 15, 1863, 3 (first quotation); "Go Among Them," *The Messenger,* January 2, 1865, 2 (second quotation).

24. The contextualization of the message of the gospel to specific settings is not new. The pattern for it is found within the Bible itself. The Scriptures, and especially the gospels, portray the offer of salvation as intended for those in need and distress. The all too common emphasis on the "otherworldly" elements in evangelicalism hides the "worldly" implications so prominent in the message. One needs to look no further than records of church discipline to see the concern evangelical churches had with life on earth. "Preaching to Ourselves," *Mississippi Messenger,* March 2, 1865, 1. See Faust "Christian Soldiers," for an analysis of the psychological factors relating war to the conversion experience.

25. For a summary of chaplains' efforts to overcome feminine stereotypes of Christianity, see Long, "Divine Confederacy," 5, 17–18; "Revivals," *Mississippi Messenger* 27 October 1864, 1. Conversations with Michael Van Horn provided clarification of thoughts concerning the significance of immersion in an all-male environment. The differences between sprinkling and immersion as forms of baptismal practice and the symbolic meaning associated with these rituals begs further study. The mode of baptism was a hotly contested subject in the nineteenth century. For an example of the debate, see two sermons by Methodist Numa Reid in which he explains and refutes the Baptist doctrine of baptism in James W. Reid and Frank L. Reid, *Sermons and Speeches of Rev. Numa F. Reid, D.D. Late of the North Carolina Conference* (New York, 1874), 240–286. The idea of baptism as identification with Christ's death, burial, and resurrection is based on Romans 6:3–4. Reid argues against this "Baptist" interpretation of Romans on pp. 261–263. For a brief summary of various controversies over the rite of baptism in America, see Daniel G. Reid, Robert D. Linder, Bruce L. Shelley, and Harry S. Stout, eds. *Dictionary of Christianity in America* (Downers Grove, IL, 1990), s.v. "Baptism" by Stanley J. Grenz; Daniel G. Reid, et al, eds. *Dictionary of Christianity in America,* s.v. "Sacraments and Ordinances," by E. Brookes Holifield. J[ohn] William

Jones, *Christ in the Camp: or, Religion in Lee's Army,* 2nd ed. (Akron, OH 1904), 255 (first quotation), 246 (second quotation); Bennett, *A Narrative of The Great Revival,* 104 (third quotation).

26. The most recent documentation of Baptist gains in the aftermath of the Civil War can be found in Roger Finke and Rodney Stark, *The Churching of America, 1776–1990: Winners and Losers in Our Religious Economy* (New Brunswick, NJ, 1992), 145–149. The first historian to suggest that the converted veterans played an important role in the spread of religion in the years after the Civil War was one of the war's participants, Jones, *Christ in the Camp,* 462–463. More recently Harry Stout has noted, "It is not coincidental that great revivals in the post-war South were led by Confederate veterans serving as lay pastors, elders, deacons, and colporters"; "The Confederate Jeremiad in Defeat," *The Life and Death of the Confederate Jeremiad,* 18. The importance of these Christian veterans in shaping the postwar South has been noted by Charles Wilson, who has called J. William Jones the "Evangelist of the Lost Cause" and devotes a whole chapter to him in *Baptized in Blood, The Religion of the Lost Cause, 1865–1920* (Athens, 1980), 119–138.

27. Philip Slaughter, "Personalities and Parties and Sections," *Messenger,* June 15, 1863, 2 (first quotation). These ubiquitous terms were used throughout the war by both the secular and Christian press. For a few examples, see "Our Soldiers Fight like Christian Heroes, not like Demons," *Herald,* November 1, 1863, 4; "Stirring Words," *Herald,* February 9, 1865. 2; "Shall not the Judge of all the Earth Do Right?," *The Soldier's Friend,* June 18, 1863, 2.

28. For a summary of the doctrine of the spirituality of the church, see James Oscar Farmer Jr., *The Metaphysical Confederacy: James Henley Thornwell and the Synthesis of Southern Values* (Macon, 1986), 188–189, 256–260 (quotation, 188). On the role of evangelicals in temperance reform in the South, see Ian R. Tyrrell, "Drink and Temperance in the Antebellum South: An Overview and Interpretation," *Journal of Southern History* 48 (November 1982): 485–510; W. J. Rorabaugh, "The Sons of Temperance in Antebellum Jasper County," *Georgia Historical Quarterly* 64 (Fall 1980): 263–279. For an example of an antebellum southern public fast-day sermon that reveals the seeds of the arguments that were to dominate in the Civil War and further questions the dominance of the "spirituality of the church," see Methodist Whitefoord Smith, "God, The Refuge of His People. A Sermon Delivered before the General Assembly, South Carolina, on Friday, December 6, 1850, Being a Day of Fasting, Humiliation and Prayer" (Columbia, SC, 1850). Harry S. Stout finds a much more open identification of covenant status with the Confederacy in the fast-day sermons he examines; see Stout. *The Life and Death of the Confederate Jeremiad.*

29. A. S. Worrell, "Keeping the Issue Distinct," *The Soldier's Friend,* January 10, 1863, 2 (first quotation); "God Our Trust and Strength," *The Soldier's Paper,* August 1, 1863, 2 (second quotation); "Declaration of Independence," *The Soldier's Visitor,* December 1863, 16 (third quotation); "The Times," *Messenger,* January 1, 1864, 1 (fourth quotation). For the appropriation of the Revolutionary heritage late in the war, see "Take Courage." *Herald,* February 9, 1865, 2. The author notes the "faith" of the revolutionary leaders.

30. C. C. Gillespie, "The Confederate Motto, No Compromise," *Mississippi Messenger,* March 16, 1865, 2 (first quotation); "The Confederate Army As A Field For Religious Labors," *Messenger,* December 15, 1864, 1 (second quotation); W. B. Wellons, "Our Paper," *Messenger,* December 15, 1864, 1 (third quotation); William Norris, "Massachusetts, And A War For Religion," *Mississippi Messenger,* September 29, 1864, 2 (fourth quotation); "Rev. C. C. Gillespie at Camp Chase," *Mississippi Messenger,* March

2, 1865, 1 (fifth quotation). The most unusual expression is found in a series of articles by the Rev. L. Pierce. Pierce taking Psalms 33:12 as his text, "Blessed is the nation whose God is the Lord," proceeded to attack the Confederate government because it was not a Christian government. It only expressed Christian sympathies. Until that changed, problems would continue. Pierce was unique in attacking the government. "To the Officers and Soldiers of the Confederate Army," *Herald,* March 23, 1865, 2; March 30, 2865, 2; April 6, 1865, 2.

31. *The Soldier's Friend,* January 10, 1863, 1. "Massachusetts, and a War for Region," *Mississippi Messenger,* September 29, 1864, 2 (first quotation); "Shall not the Judge of all the Earth Do Right?," *The Soldier's Friend,* June 18, 1863, 2 (second quotation).

32. "War From the Pulpit," *Mississippi Messenger,* March 30, 1865, 1 (first quotation); "The Church and the War in the North," *The Soldier's Paper,* August 1, 1863, 2 (second quotation); "The Contrast," *Mississippi Messenger,* January 5, 1865, 1 (third quotation, italics in original); "The Contrast," *Mississippi Messenger,* January 5, 1865, 1 (fourth quotation); "Massachusetts, and a War for Religion," *Mississippi Messenger,* September 29, 1864, 2 (fifth quotation); "Shall We Succeed?," *The Soldier's Visitor,* February 1865, 26 (sixth quotation). See also "Shall Not the Judge of all the Earth Do Right?," *The Soldier's Friend,* June 18, 1863, 2. Of course, most of their assessment is distorted. Huge revivals also swept through Union armies and the southern church was equally guilty in functioning as a war propaganda tool.

33. Whiteford Smith, "Re-Construction: A Short Sermon For the People," *The Soldier's Paper,* March 15, 1864, 1 (first quotation); The story of the tower of Babel (plains of Shinar), which Smith refers to, is found in Genesis 11:1–8. "Divine Providence," *Mississippi Messenger,* February 16, 1865, 1 (second quotation). See also "The Confederacy," *Mississippi Messenger,* March 2, 1865, 2.

34. "Address of the Second and Third Corps of the Army of Northern Virginia," *Messenger,* April 15, 1864, 2 (first quotation); "Our Martyrs," *The Soldier's Paper,* June 1, 1864, 2 (second quotation).

35. "The Messenger," *Mississippi Messenger,* September 15, 1864, 2 (first quotation). See also A. S. Worrell, "Salutatory," *The Soldier's Friend,* January 10, 1863, 3. Harry Stout defines "rhetorical world" as the paradigm or symbol system operating in the world of public discourse. It "represents the master assumptions that speakers and their audiences cannot prove or disprove, but which both accept because, intellectually, they conform to the community's passionately held assumptions of self, society, and the cosmos and, socially, because they make the system work." Of course, not everyone in the Confederacy adopted the religious language of the clergy, but as Faust, *Confederate Nationalism,* has shown, it was the dominant form of discourse in creating the new national identity; Harry Stout, "Rhetoric and Reality in the Early Republic: The Case of the Federalist Clergy," in *Religion & American Politics: From the Colonial Period to the 1980s,* ed. Mark A. Noll (New York, 1990), 63–64; "The Contrast," *Mississippi Messenger,* January 5, 1865, 1 (second quotation).

36. Reid Mitchell talks about the soldiers' horror over the treatment of the dead even by their own side and especially in hospitals; *Civil War Soldiers,* 62–63, 143. The poem "Lay Me at My Mother's Feet," *Messenger,* December 15, 1864, 3, reflects the soldier's desire for burial at home. "The Memory of the Dead," *Messenger,* January 1, 1864, 4; "Beyond the River," *Messenger,* March 2, 1865, 1; "The Soldier Who Died Today," *Messenger,* February 2, 1865, 4; "Our Departed Heroes," *The Soldier's Paper,* August 1, 1863, 4. See also *The Soldier's Paper,* September 1, 1863, 4; November 1, 1863, 4; March 15, 1864, 4; April 1, 1865, 3.

37. For a listing of Confederate hospitals, see "Principal Hospitals in the Confederate States," *Confederate States Medical and Surgical Journal* 1 (September 1864): 152; 1 (October 1864): 176. Examples of the "Soldier's Guide," *Messenger,* January 1, 1864, 4; *The Soldier's Paper,* June 1, 1864, 3; and April 1, 1865, 4. "The Wounded Soldier," *The Soldier's Friend,* January 10, 1863, 3 (first quotation); For an estimate of illiteracy in the Confederate Army, see James M. McPherson, *What They Fought For 1861–1865* (Baton Rouge, 1994), 14. Calls to educate the wounded were not unique to the RMP; see *The Soldier's Visitor* announcement of free education at the University of Virginia and Mercer College, February 1865, 27. Examples of calls for soldier schools as well as announcements of ones recently started include, "An Important Suggestion," *The Soldier's Friend,* January 10, 1863, 3; "To the People of the Confederate States," *The Soldier's Friend,* July 9, 1863, 1; *Herald,* April 6, 1865, 2; and "Soldier's Schools," *The Soldier's Visitor,* January 1865, 21. *Herald,* March 16, 1865, 2, announced a new "soldiers school" at the Asylum for the Blind. On the role of chaplains in the Civil War, see Long, "Divine Confederacy," 24–56.

38. "The Enemy's Loss in the Mississippi Campaign," *Messenger,* July 15, 1863, 3; Discrepancies like this are common in the summaries provided by the RMP. "News Summary," *Herald,* November 1, 1863, 2; "News Summary," *Herald,* March 30, 1865, 3. *The Soldier's Friend* declared total killed, wounded, and missing at Murfreesboro for the Confederate army to be 5,000 to 7,000; for the Union troops, 10,000 to 15,000. Compare these numbers with those provided in E. B. Long in *The Civil War Day By Day, An Almanac* (New York, 1971), 307, 654–655. See also "Telegraphic Dispatches," *Mississippi Messenger,* October 27, 1864, 1. For other examples, see *The Soldier's Paper,* March 15, 1864, 3; *The Soldier's Paper,* June 1, 1864, 3; *Mississippi Messenger,* March 16, 1865, 2.

39. William B. Norris, "The Critical Hour," *Mississippi Messenger,* March 16, 1865, 2.

40. The story of Gideon's battle is found in Judges 7. "The People Are Too Many For Me," *The Soldier's Visitor,* January 1865, 23 (reprinted from the *Baptist Banner,* first quotation); see also "Bible Warriors," *Messenger,* March 16, 1865, 4 (first quotation, italics in original); "Rebellion," *Messenger,* June 15, 1863, 2 (second quotation); "God's Merciful Protection of Petersburg," *Messenger,* December 15, 1864, 2 (third quotation); "Forty Fourth Psalm," "A Prayer Against The Enemy," *Messenger,* January 15, 1864, 3; "A Soldier's Morning Prayer," *The Soldier's Visitor,* August 1863, 2; "Power of Prayer," *The Soldier's Visitor,* December 1863, 16; "Our Soldiers' Fight like Christian Heroes, not like Demons," *Herald,* November 1, 1863, 4.

41. William Norris, *Mississippi Messenger,* October 27, 1864, 2 (first quotation); "Cheering Signs," *The Soldier's Paper,* August 15, 1863, 2 (second quotation); for descriptions of losses as temporary, see "The News," *The Soldier's Friend,* July 9, 1863, 3; William Norris, *Mississippi Messenger,* February 16, 1865, 1 (third quotation); "Evacuation of Richmond," *Herald,* April 13, 1865, 2 (fourth quotation).

42. A. S. Worrell, "For What Shall We Pray?," *The Soldier's Friend,* July 23, 1863, 1 (first quotation, italics in original); Worrell, "A Fatal Error Exposed," *The Soldier's Friend,* July 30, 1863, 2 (second quotation; italics in original).

43. "Lessons from Reverses," *The Soldier's Visitor,* August 1863, 2 (first quotation); Philip Slaughter, "An Original Tract for the Hospital," *Messenger,* June 15, 1863, 1 (second quotation); "The Book of Job," *Messenger,* July 15, 1863, 1 (third quotation); "Shall We Succeed?," *The Soldier's Visitor,* February 1865, 26 (fourth quotation); "The Confederacy," *Mississippi Messenger,* March 2, 1865, 2 (fifth quotation); "Our Victories and Reverses," *Messenger,* January 2, 1865, 2. See also Robertson, *Messenger,* June 15, 1863, 2;

B. B. Ross, "To the People of the Confederate States," *The Soldier's Paper*, November 1, 1863, 1; W. A. P., "Sketches and Incidents," *Herald*, March 16, 1865, 2.

44. "The Soldier's Pocket Bible," *Herald*, November 1, 1863, 1 (first quotation); "Twenty-Eight Chapter of Deuteronomy," *Messenger*, January 1, 1864, 3 (second quotation). See also Mitchell, *Civil War Soldiers*, 186–187.

45. "The War and the Church," *The Soldier's Visitor*, November 1863, 12 (first quotation). Throughout the war, numerous passing references were made regarding the influence of women on men. See, for example, *Mississippi Messenger*, September 29, 1864, 1; "Keeping The Heart," *Messenger*, February 8, 1865, 1. On the churches early concern for the moral well-being of soldiers, see Long, "Divine Confederacy," 16–18; Faust, "Christian Soldiers," 68–70; Shattuck, *A Shield and Hiding Place*, 46, 48, 96–98. Articles attacking sin include "The Soldier's Deception," *The Soldier's Friend*, May 2, 1863, 1; "The Power of Habit," *The Soldier's Friend*, May 2, 1863, 2. "An Appeal for Our Country," *Messenger*, July 15, 1863, 3; "The Confederate Army as a Field For Religious Labor," *Messenger*, December 15, 1864, 1; "Our Worst Enemy," *Messenger*, March 3, 1865, 2. On the dangers of alcohol, see "Doaksville, Choctaw Nation," *Mississippi Messenger*, February 2, 1865, 1; "Intemperance in the Army," *The Soldier's Visitor*, January 1865, 21. For sins of gambling, see "Ruinous Consequences of Gambling," *Herald*, November 1, 1863, 4. On the sin of Sabbath breaking, see "A Voice From the Grave of Jackson. His Testimony Against Sunday Mails," *Messenger*, June 15, 1863, 3: "Gen. Jackson And The Sabbath," *Messenger*, July 15, 1863, 1; "Do Not Rob God—Give God his Day," *Messenger*, June 15, 1863, 2; "Sunday in Camp," *The Soldier's Friend*, June 18, 1863, 1. Articles against swearing include "Profane Officers," *The Soldier's Paper*, June 1, 1864, 2; "The Influences of Woman," *The Soldier's Paper*, August 1, 1863, 3; "To Our Soldiers," *The Soldier's Paper*, June 1, 1864, 4; "Profanity in the Federal Army," *The Soldier's Visitor*, November 1863, 12: See Faust "Christian Soldiers," 79–80 on the evangelical concern with swearing.

46. E. M. M. "Revivals in the Trans-Miss. Department," *Mississippi Messenger*, October 17, 1864, 1 (first quotation); "The War and the Church," *The Soldier's Visitor*, November 1863, 12 (second quotation); "Chaplain's Meeting," *Messenger*, February 8, 1865, 1; "A Contrast," *Soldier's Visitor*, August 1863, 4; "Profanity in the Federal Army," *Soldier's Visitor*, November 1863, 12. See also Bennett, *Great Revival*, 176, 212, for further testimony to the decrease of sin in the camp.

47. For an analysis of public concern over the sin of extortion, see Faust, *Confederate Nationalism*, 41–57. Faust lists extortion as one of two preeminent sins that consumed southerners. The other was slavery. In the RMP, only one article charged slavery with being a national sin while attacks on extortion increased as the war continued. See also Mitchell, *Civil War Soldiers*, 164–166. "The Yankee Trade," *The Soldier's Friend*, July 9, 1863, 4; "The Love of Money Stronger than the Love of Country," *The Soldier's Friend*, July 23, 1863, 1; "Our National Sins," *Messenger*, February 8, 1865, 2. "The Army Praying for the Church," *The Soldier's Visitor*, September 1863, 5 (first quotation); "The Great Victory," and "Encouraged Indications," *The Soldier's Visitor*, October 1863, 8 (second quotation); See also "Missionary Ridge, November 22d, 1863," *Messenger*, January 1, 1864, 3; "Our Army," *The Soldier's Visitor*, March 1864, 30 (third quotation); "Doaksville, Choctaw Nation," *Mississippi Messenger*, February 2, 1865, 1. Charges of a select few contaminating the whole include, "The Yankee Trade," *The Soldier's Friend*, July 9, 1863, 4; B. H. Hill, "Eloquent Extract," *Herald*, April 6, 1865, 8. On occasion there were allusions to other problems at home, such as fault finding with military and civil leaders, and irreverent social life among

the ladies. "Dress and Diseases," *Messenger,* January 1, 1864, 3. Bennett, *Great Revival,* 41–42, also argued that extortion was the most prominent and greatest evil in the Confederacy.

48. R. F. Bunting, "The Successes and Reverse of the War," *Herald,* February 23, 1865, 2–3 (italics his). For a similar analysis of the war, see "Our Victories and Reverses," *Messenger,* January 2, 1865, 2. Despite the best efforts of the RMP, despair did occur in the army. As evidenced by desertion rates, despair radically increased near the end of the war. Editors counteracted despair in several ways. They frequently printed articles noting plentiful southern harvests. They also drew parallels between the Confederate situation and other rebellions in history. Some articles reminded soldiers it was their Christian duty to be cheerful; a proper understanding of Providence brings encouragement. Finally, civilians were charged with being the source of despair. Desertion was a result of soldiers going home to comfort discouraged families. If they would be strong at home, the army would be strong. *Mississippi Messenger,* February 16, 1865, 1; "Be Cheerful," *Messenger,* March 16, 1865, 2–3; "Agricultural Resources of the South," *Mississippi Messenger,* October 27, 1864, 2; *Mississippi Messenger,* February 16, 1865, 1; "The Right Spirit," *Messenger,* March 3, 1865, 2; "A Talk With the Soldiers," *Messenger,* January 2, 1865, 1; "The Brave Home," *Mississippi Messenger,* March 30, 1865, 1; "Stonewall Jackson's Last Camping Ground—His Message to the Women of the Confederacy," *Messenger,* June 15, 1863, 1.

49. Philip Slaughter, "The Old And The New Year," *Messenger,* January 1, 1864, 2 (first quotation); see also "The Messenger," *Mississippi Messenger,* September 15, 1864, 2; "Peace," *Messenger,* February 8, 1865, 1 (second quotation); "Something for the Soldiers," *Mississippi Messenger,* February 2, 1865, 1 (third quotation). See also *Mississippi Messenger,* September 29, 1864, 1. There are very few suggestions that the people might not sufficiently repent before God. Rather, "When He sees that it is best, we shall be delivered." "A Talk With Soldiers," *Messenger,* January 2, 1865, 1. For the suggestion people might not repent, see "Prayerfulness," *Messenger,* March 16, 1865, 1.

50. E. M. M., "Revivals in the Trans-Miss Department," *Mississippi Messenger,* October 27, 1864, 1 (first quotation); "The Work of Grace in the Army," *The Soldier's Paper,* August 15, 1863, 2 (second quotation). Saum, *Popular Mood,* 13–15, argues that the belief in Providence did not preclude human activity. For another essay that argues religion "helped prop morale rather than undermine it," see Timothy A. Long, "Victory: North Carolina Baptists Fight and Write the Civil War," presented at the 1993 Spring East Regional Meeting of the American Society of Church History, College of William & Mary, Williamsburg, Virginia.

51. See Shattuck, *A Shield,* 95–109. Shattuck uses the term "otherworldly triumphs" on page 102. A number of historians see guilt over slavery as undermining Confederate morale and hence contributing to defeat. See, for example, Kenneth Stampp, "The Southern Road to Appomattox," in Stampp, *The Imperiled Union: Essays on the Background of the Civil War* (New York, 1980); Charles G. Sellers Jr., "The Travail of Slavery," in *The Southerner as American,* ed. Charles G. Sellers Jr. (Chapel Hill, 1960); and Richard Beringer, Herman Hattaway, Archer Jones, and William N. Still Jr., *Why the South Lost the Civil War* (Athens, GA, 1987), 336–367. Commentary on slavery was virtually nonexistent in the RMP. Only one article suggested one of the South's primary sins was abuse of the institution. Near the end of the war, several articles reported on the proposal to arm slaves. Beyond that, discussion of slavery did not appear. Charles R. Wilson applies the phrase "evangelist of the Lost Cause" to Jones in *Baptized in Blood,* 119.

52. McPherson, *What They Fought For,* 9–25, 12 (first quotation). See also Mitchell, *Civil War Soldiers,* 186. "Patriotism Not Piety," *Messenger,* April 1, 1864, 1 (second quotation, italics in original).

53. "Evacuation of Richmond," *Herald,* April 13, 1865, 2 (first quotation); "Summary of News," *The Soldier's Paper,* April 1, 1865, 3 (second quotation); "Shall We Succeed?," and "Our Enemy's Evil Deeds," *The Soldier's Visitor,* February 1865, 2 (third quotation); "Profane Swearing," "To Young Men," "Bible Warriors," *Messenger,* March 16, 1865, 1, 3 (fourth quotation); William Norris, *Mississippi Messenger,* May 11, 1865, 2 (fifth quotation, italics his).

7

"Yankee Faith" and Southern Redemption

White Southern Baptist Ministers, 1850–1890

PAUL HARVEY

The southern ministry before the Civil War largely reaffirmed the view that "pure religion" involved defining and enforcing the proper behavior of individuals in their God-given social duties, not questioning the roles themselves. Ministers called people to their duties, exhorted the unconverted to repent, and condemned slaveowners who failed to evangelize their property. They also offered elaborate justifications of the rights of white Americans to own as property people of African descent. The axiom that politics had no place in the pulpit muffled the larger voice of southern divines. They shied away from participation in political controversies over the tariff or state constitutional controversies. Their main contribution to public issues was to develop and endlessly reiterate versions of the proslavery argument. They were leaders in the "sanctification of slavery," as Mitchell Snay has explained. The defense of chattel slavery in a liberal democracy, they came to realize, necessitated an insistence in the Divine approval of "our way of life." That slaveowners often made up the most respectable, stable, and financially generous members of southern Baptist congregations hardly encouraged brave souls who might engage in any searching questioning. Black ministers seized on the prophetic possibilities rejected by the established white clerics, but they often did so "on the sly," as ex-slave Anderson Edwards remembered of his days as a slave preacher in Texas.[1]

After the war, during days of fundamental struggle to define the future of their society, white southern Baptist ministers provided their parishioners with a compelling narrative of their recent history, and rarely hesitated to advise their congregations about the stakes of political contests. Although they excoriated northern missionaries who mixed "politics" and "religion," white southern ministers actively entangled the two. The word *Redemption*, meaning "washed in the blood," graphically symbolized the often bloody mixing of religion and politics in the postbellum South. In this sense, these ministers articulated a social vision that extended far beyond their carefully limited public voice before the Civil War.[2]

During Reconstruction and into the 1880s, southern Baptist ministers proclaimed a white southern cultural identity founded on a particular brand of democratic evangelicalism, christened "Baptist democracy." Baptist ministers joined other clerics in suggesting how the sacrifice of brave Confederate soldiers cleansed the South of its sin, and how the cultural determination of whites after the war prepared the way for the return of a righteous order. Once preached in the idiomatic language of the white evangelical South, this narrative soon hardened into an orthodoxy that dominated southern evangelical historical interpretation for a century to come.

One hundred years later, the descendants of these white ministers would preach, with the same fervor as their Reconstruction-era ancestors, of the threat to the regional soul posed by the second Reconstruction. There were more dissenters the second time around. Martin Luther King Jr.'s clarion call to the Christian conscience convicted a growing number of southern believers, who understood that the narrative of southern history handed down to them was not sacred writ. Yet in most white southern Baptist pulpits in the 1950s and 1960s, preachers resisted outside agitators as much as they had during the first Reconstruction. In the 1960s they lost their battle, owing in part to the major shift in the nation's own civil religious impulses in favor of pluralism. In the 1860s and 1870s, though, white elites and their ministerial allies succeeded in making their story of the oppressed but heroic white South the normative narrative of Reconstruction.[3]

The religious culture of Baptists in the colonial and Revolutionary-era South developed within the context of eighteenth-century revivalism. Southern Baptists cultivated a democratic evangelicalism with an emphasis on communal emotionalism and a conscious self-denial of worldly goods, together with a significant bent toward acquiring the same in the form of newly opening western lands. The evangelicals defined as sin personal actions that, for the gentry, were key signifiers in a system of honor—gambling, horse racing, fashionable dressing, and dueling. Southern plain folk found in their brand of evangelicalism the elements of a common consciousness. The great camp meetings of the early nineteenth century extended and solidified the hold of evangelicalism on a people intent on settling new territories and breaking ground in frontier regions.[4]

In the antebellum era, southern Baptists acquired the trappings of a self-conscious establishment. By the Civil War, prominent ministers and congregations could claim a respectability far removed from their humble beginnings in the colonial era. In the older southeastern states, particularly Virginia and North Carolina, leaders of state conventions took the lead in welcoming the "benevolent empire" to the South. They erected colleges for ministerial education, edited religious newspapers, organized mission societies, and built impressive churches in southern towns and cities. Baptists boasted of the conversion of many of the respectable folk in their society, a claim that recent historians have documented as largely accurate.[5]

The march from the popular enthusiasms of the eighteenth century to the denominational respectability of the nineteenth came at some cost. Concurrently with southeastern Baptists forming a self-conscious establishment, Baptists in the hill country and in the southwestern states created alternative theologies, schools, and publications. "Antimission Baptists" rejected the notion that church people should advance the causes of the benevolent empire. They focused instead on their local communities and congregations, clinging to a rigidly defined Calvinist orthodoxy that preached the uselessness of "means" to bring men to salvation. More important, their extreme localism arose from the divisions that rent the ostensibly united white South into social classes based on wealth, geography, and access to market-based staple crop production economies. In scattered pockets throughout the South, yeoman farmers, most of whom were not slaveowners, flocked to preachers and congregations that condemned denominational and political elites in the same breath.[6]

The Landmark movement offered the strongest ideological alternative to the denominational establishment. It summoned Baptists back to their original "landmarks," especially congregational independence and "closed communion" (refusal to serve communion to non-Baptists). The Landmarkers challenged the authority of central denominational organizations, substituting instead the "pure" local church as the authoritative voice. James R. Graves, the northern-born ideologist for Landmarkism, waged unceasing polemical battles against Methodists and against established figures within the Southern Baptist Convention. His views obtained wide influence in the Old Southwest through the *Tennessee Baptist and Reflector*, edited by Graves and circulated widely through the Mississippi Valley. Later, Graves became an outspoken proponent of slavery and secession. His southern-born Landmarkist colleague J. M. Pendleton did not share Graves's secession fervor. Other Kentuckians as well worried that sectional controversies would impair the preaching of the gospel. The divisions that rent Kentucky's churches during the Civil War gave them good reason for this fear.[7]

In the late eighteenth century, a brief moment of opportunity for a biracial religious order seemed to present itself. Whites and blacks in backcountry congregations worshipped together. They called each other by the respectful evangelical titles "brother" and "sister" and wept to each other's exhortations. It quickly became evident that whites would make the necessary moral accommodations to ensure the growth of their evangelical institutions.[8] White Baptists who had questioned slavery in late-eighteenth-century Virginia came to defend it as a divinely sanctioned social order. In South Carolina, where few whites challenged the peculiar institution even during the Revolutionary era,

Baptists in the early nineteenth century fleshed out a Christian proslavery apologetic. Richard Furman, a well-known cleric in the state, argued in one early tract that God would use the means of slavery to bring the Christian message to heathen Africans and to teach superior peoples to care for the inferiors entrusted to them, just as God watched over humans and husbands provided for wives and children. By the 1830s, such a view reigned as a virtually unchallenged orthodoxy among white southern evangelicals, whether they were elite divines or folk exhorters.[9]

Southern Baptists never accepted African Americans as equals in their churches. They lacked the will, the fortitude, the theology, and the intellectual tools even to contemplate doing so. Despite the occasional southern antislavery divine (such as David Barrow), and despite the number of church members who used the terms "brother" and "sister" to refer to black believers, white southern Christians were determined to keep the realms of the spiritual and the temporal strictly separate. Freedom from the bondage of sin would never equal freedom from human bondage. Virginians had articulated that principle in the 1660s and 1670s, when candidates for baptism petitioned for freedom based on their Christian baptism. In the decades following the American Revolution, before the flourishing of a full-fledged proslavery orthodoxy, Virginians and Carolinians reaffirmed that conversion and baptism remained separate issues from enslavement. Individual slaves might be manumitted, but this was a highly personal decision that would not affect the existence of the institution as a whole.[10]

Slavery fractured nearly every American denomination and split Baptist benevolent societies along sectional lines. Mainline northern Baptists, predominantly antislavery and antiabolitionist, tried unsuccessfully to mediate the conflict between abolitionists and proslavery southern Baptists. The division worsened in the early 1840s, when northerners contested the appointment of slaveholders as home missionaries. In 1844, southerners demanded a policy statement from the directors of the American Baptist Home Mission Society. The northerners replied, "One thing is certain: we can never be a party to any arrangement which would imply approbation of slavery." Deeply affronted by this statement, and impressed with their duty to evangelize more actively in their own region, white southern Baptists convened in 1845 in Augusta, Georgia, and organized the Southern Baptist Convention (SBC).[11]

Southern evangelicals in the antebellum era expressed far less optimism than their northern counterparts about the future of a "Christian America." Evangelicals in the North fused spiritual piety with a Calvinist concern for the commonweal. Later in the nineteenth century, liberal theological elites moved away from evangelicalism into modernist theology and social gospel concerns. Northern conservatives refined their Calvinist cosmologies and invented intellectual fundamentalism. Southern Christians, faced with the overwhelming fact of racial slavery, were less enthusiastic about millennial visions of an American society cleansed of sin. Southern evangelicalism was oriented to the private, to reforming individual behavior rather than assuming a role as a critic of the social order. The evangelical emphasis later became the primary domain of popular revivalists such as Dwight Moody. They appealed to suspicious conservative southern evangelicals, showing that widespread spiritual awakenings did not necessarily spur political radicalism, as they sometimes had in the First and Second Great Awakenings of the mid-eighteenth and early nineteenth century.[12]

The Civil War and Reconstruction revolutionized southern religious life and reshaped the relationship of the ministry to public life. In the controversies of the winter of 1860–1861, Baptist ministers played an active part in deciding the future of their section. Some fervently supported secession. Others feared it as a rash and unwarranted move. Alabaman Basil Manly Sr., a prominent planter, minister, and college president, took a prominent role in these discussions. In 1862, he informed his congregation that taking the oath of allegiance to the Lincoln government in order to save property or life was tantamount to "malign[ing] Christianity, to save property or life." The genteel Virginian and ministerial educator John A. Broadus, by contrast, privately opposed secession, but in early 1861 he decided that "it would be worse than idle to *speak* against it now." If secession was the course chosen, he would then "resolve to do my duty as a citizen here." Public affairs lay beyond the range of ministerial authority, he believed. As the Apostle Paul advised, allegiance to the governing authorities was required of Christians.[13]

Clerics in the Deep South also divided over the wisdom of seceding. In South Carolina, James P. Boyce, a wealthy Whig and founder of the Southern Baptist Theological Seminary in Greenville, opposed secession and mourned its coming. Boyce invested much of his wealth in worthless Confederate bonds and lost a good deal of his estate when the Union army marched through the state. Basil Manly Jr., son of the fiery Alabama secessionist, resigned himself to the inevitability of war because of the rash actions of the "Charlestonians." "The whole is in the hands of God," he concluded. "It may be a cup of wrath for our sins in which he has mingled those elements of confusion and misery— but he knows how to use it, and when to desist."[14] Basil Jr. kept his doubts private, and soon became a devoted Confederate.

Methodist and Baptist clerics preached to the commonfolk who would make up the bulk of the southern armies. This fact was not lost on southern political leaders. As a result, ministers could accept a greater sense of public responsibility. They could now find a voice beyond the simple repetition of the standard proslavery orthodoxy. They could sanctify the new nation.

Religious organizations such as the SBC flooded Confederate camps with pious pamphlets. Ministers throughout the region worried, as did Charles Manly, that "it will be sad, if our young men, the strength of our communities, come back to us, at the close of the war, companions in vice and having learned to do without religion."[15] A tract entitled *A Mother's Parting Words to Her Soldier Boy*, written by Virginia Baptist minister and newspaper editor Jeremiah B. Jeter, was probably the single most popular piece of religious literature in the Confederate army, with over 250,000 copies distributed.

Baptists made up about two-thirds of the colportage force in the army.

By 1864, Baptists had published about one hundred different tracts of some 50 million pages for the Confederate army. They sold and distributed Bibles, hymnals, and pieces of religious ephemera. Soon after the war, Virginia Baptists pronounced that "the history of the world, we presume, reports no instance of an army so thoroughly under the influence of the gospel as was our noble Southern army." Wartime service had roused young men from spiritual slumber and stamped them with "a marked development of the Christian character," they suggested. "Far from home and friends, toiling on the march, or languishing in the hospital, their eyes have been turned to him, whose love, shed abroad in the heart, is 'strength in the time of weakness.' "[16]

Chaplaincy in the Confederate army was a formative experience for a generation of evangelical ministers. Many ministers later mythologized themselves (or were memorialized as) "fighting chaplains" who shot as straight as they preached. They all singled out wartime service as a central moment in their spiritual journey. The best-known example of the Baptist fighting chaplain was Isaac Taylor Tichenor, later president of what would become Auburn University. He preached to his Alabama regiment, impressed his comrades with his sharpshooting, and rallied his men at the Battle of Shiloh in 1862. Confederate soldier Edwin Hansford Rennolds, a native of Tennessee who resisted conversion as a teenager, saw the vagaries of fate in his constant contact with death in the army. "I began to consider how uncertain were all things unearthly," he recalled, "and there came a longing for something sure and certain." After the war, talks with his wife persuaded him that he was a convert. Despite his poverty and lack of education, he preached successfully for fifty years, proud that he could carry the gospel to the poor and humble of his state. The obituary of a Tennessee-born minister who died in 1911 recalled how he "often spoke with pride of the service he rendered his country as a soldier and made special request that he be put away at last in his gray uniform, a soldier of the Southern army and a soldier of the cross." The Alabama cleric J. J. D. Renfroe, who delivered sermons from written-out manuscripts to his beloved Alabama regiment, was another who identified the war as a turning point in his own life, giving him seriousness of purpose. It also impressed such men with a sense of mission: sacralizing the Confederate cause in the minds of future generations of white southerners.[17]

In public, southern Baptists rarely wavered in their certainty that God was on the side of the Confederacy. As Basil Manly Sr. explained to his son after the secession discussion, "I think we are right, and I do not shrink from the responsibility of all that I have done." Delegates to Southern Baptist Convention meetings reaffirmed their belief that the war was "just and necessary." State conventions acknowledged the "divine hand in the guidance and protection of our beloved country." They believed, as did Virginia Baptists, that the course pursued by the North was "alike subversive of the teachings of Christianity and the genius of constitutional liberty and order." They felt the "sweet assurance that our cause is a righteous one."[18] Throughout the conflict, ministers warned of the punishments awaiting the region for its transgressions, especially for failure to evangelize slaves with sufficient vigor. But few doubted that ultimate victory would come to the South. Confederate setbacks simply meant, as an Alabaman put it, that the "people of God are not exempt from calamities." As late as the fall of 1864, Baptists in Texas rejected "lukewarmness or despondency" and found inspiration for "redoubled energies for the deliverance of our country from Yankee thralldom and oppression which we most solemnly regard as a direful curse—even worse than death itself."[19]

In private there were doubts. In July 1863, as he entertained thoughts of the eventual collapse of the Confederacy, Basil Manly Jr. anguished that surely it could not "be God's will to expose us to the treacherous & fiendish malice & band of robbers & murderers." In South Carolina late in the war, attempting to maintain the recently opened Southern Baptist Theological Seminary in Greenville, Manly wondered what hope "in maintain[ing] our independence" would remain if Charleston fell. He felt "a gloom & great darkness" envelop him in envisioning the future. As the war fortunes of the South declined after Gettysburg, men such as Manly wondered what God was trying to teach Confederate Christians. They had been faithful; they had sacrificed their sons for a holy endeavor; their armies were replete with stirring examples of young men devoted to a cause that they embraced with evangelical fervor. Perhaps, they surmised, it was the faithlessness of church members at home that had caused the disaster. With the reelection of Lincoln in 1864 and Sherman's march through Georgia, it appeared God had a different lesson to teach than had been presumed previously by the Confederacy's spiritual leaders.[20]

Gloom and great darkness afflicted white southern Christians when Union forces commandeered church buildings for use as hospitals or meeting points, or placed churches in conquered areas under the care of northern missionary agencies. In February 1862, as a service began on a Sunday in the Central Baptist Church in Nashville, news came of Fort Donelson's surrender, "whereupon the congregation dispersed in the wildest confusion." The pastor fled south, and the care of the congregation fell to a northern missionary who never gained the support of the members. Andrew Johnson, the Unionist governor of the state, ordered the jailing of R. B. C. Howell, the most senior southern Baptist minister in Nashville, for Howell's refusals to take the required loyalty oath to the Union. Howell remained in jail for two months, while his church congregation scattered. The black congregation of the church, which met in an independent mission, doubled in size, as fleeing ex-slaves moved into Nashville. The Reverend Howell's struggles garnered him significant respect. Formerly reviled by Landmarkists because of his very public feuding with James R. Graves, Howell elicited sympathy for his stay in jail and refusal to take the loyalty oath. He became a political martyr.[21]

The final defeat of the southern forces proved difficult to accept, even for ministers who professed belief in God's foreordaining of events. In early 1865, many ministers still insisted that southern defeat would come only if "we fail to Trust, honor and implore the aid of Jesus," as a Virginian put it.[22] By then, however, easy theological formulas no longer satisfied the hunger for explanation of the reversal of Confederate fortunes and the sufferings of the home folk. As a Baptist minister from Richmond later explained, white southerners in this period learned that "their plans did not fit the divine purpose." Defeat compelled profound questionings among the faithful. When William Wingate, a minister and educator in North Carolina, heard the news of the South's calamities in the spring of 1865, he "rose in rebellion against God," as a friend of his later remembered. Wingate "loved our beautiful Southern country and could not bear to think that it had been conquered and lay at the mercy of our enemies."[23]

In the immediate postwar years, the lesson of defeat remained a theological mystery. Those such as Richard Furman in South Carolina, who had opposed secession while defending slavery, advised Baptists to "reverently acknowledge the hand of God in the great events which have transpired and calmly to acquiesce in the orderings of Providence." Few of his brethren followed this advice, even in his home district of Charleston. While one minister in South Carolina, speaking of the war's conclusion, granted that "God *has brought it about*," he also disputed the necessity of loyalty to the reconstructed governments, a notion that was "such daring and insulting blasphemy, that thousands here feel like abandoning a religion which gave birth to such atrocities."[24] Lansing Burrows, born in Pennsylvania but destined to serve his career as a Southern Baptist Convention worker, witnessed the devastation of Richmond in 1865. He vividly remembered his shock at seeing black soldiers parading in the streets. Though he tried to accept defeat as "God's will," he still remained an "earnest rebel." A decade later, he came to understand the good purposes that the war served: "Many wrongs were perpetrated, but many rights have been established." Burrows's interpretation of the war as an instrument of God to heal the sectional split and unite white Americans in a sense of global mission later grew to be a standard orthodoxy of white Americans North and South. But his defiance in remaining an "earnest rebel" more accurately characterized white ministerial sentiment in the immediate postwar years.[25]

Prospects for the reconstruction of southern Baptist churches after the war appeared bleak. At official gatherings of white Baptists in many states, messengers heard of the "vast regions" that enjoyed "no preaching at all." Without renewed efforts at religious work, a North Carolinian warned, "darkness will prevail in many sections of the State."[26] Ministers and denominational leaders feared for the future of religious life in their region. The sheer physical destruction necessitated more attention to temporal than to spiritual matters. As a correspondent wrote to a southern Baptist educator in 1866, the brethren were "generally very much obsessed with temporal concerns and so considerably indifferent to any religious enterprise. The churches are cold—almost frozen, and the impenitent recklessly pursuing wickedness." Charles Manly succinctly expressed it: "the crops are destroyed and the people have little religion."[27]

Evangelicals resurrected their critique of the code of honor (still important in shaping gendered norms of behavior) in their search for explanations for defeat. Returning to a familiar jeremiad from prewar years, religious moralists blamed the "pride, ingratitude, folly, and wickedness" of southern people for the condition of the region. The male self-assertion required by the norms of honor always had clashed with evangelical notions of humility and self-loathing; now honor had come to be a cause for defeat. Intending to humble a "proud vain-glorious vaunting people," God allowed southerners to walk into their own destruction. It was, one minister intoned, "surely a most impressive lesson, if we had ears to hear, respecting the utter impotency of man, and our certain ruin without help from God."[28]

The physical and emotional devastation of the South during the war might have compelled whites to question the sacralization of their own cause, just as the American defeat in Vietnam forced soul-searching among American churchgoers in the 1960s and 1970s. Instead, the Confederate experience ultimately reinforced white southern evangelicals in their view that a sanctified, purified South would rise from the ashes to serve as God's "last and only hope" in a secularizing nation. Many southern Christians felt that the war was the cleansing and chastening experience that the region had long needed.[29]

Despite the destruction of church buildings and the demoralization of their believers, white southern Baptists rebuilt their churches and revitalized their denomination. By the 1906 religious census, they claimed about 54 percent of white churchgoers in the South, the majority of them in congregations affiliated with the Southern Baptist Convention. The convention itself, barely functioning in the late 1860s, remained relatively impoverished but was remarkably successful in expanding its influence throughout the region. Southerners may have been divided by class and regional differences, but evangelicals closed ranks around the defense of white supremacy and evangelical Protestantism as the bulwarks of a stable social order.

Early in Reconstruction, white Christians returned to a theme they had rejected during the war: ministers should refrain from comment on public affairs except when obvious and uncontroversial moral issues were involved. The lesson "so hard to be learned and to be felt," Baptists in Charleston suggested, was that "we are pilgrims and strangers upon earth" who "doubtless needed these chastenings of his hand." When political confidence and religious faith were shaken, many Baptists retreated to a private evangelicalism, shorn of the confident public pronouncements of Civil War sermons. In considering whether to take the loyalty oath, for example, Charles Manly decided to eschew politics and devote his "thoughts and energies to the service of that Kingdom that cannot be shaken." He took up Sunday School work, hoping to coax more people "out of lecture halls and into churches."[30]

Charles Manly and others who took solace in a domesticated evangelicalism were soon brought back to the public sphere by Radical Reconstruction. Even as southern evangelicals pondered the theological implications of defeat, they remained unrepentant about the sanctity of their system. A northern Baptist in 1865 described the response of his southern colleagues to the end of the war this way: "They submit to the new order of things as a necessity, from which there is no escape, but claim that they have been conscientious in treason and beneficent in slaveholding."[31] Charles Manly, as a university professor and president, spoke for a white South united in defense of its "sacred heritage" of social conservatism and white supremacy. In 1862, he swore that he would have "lived too long" when he beheld the "horrors accompanying U.S. supremacy."

The prospect of civil rights for black Americans was especially disquieting to him, for he feared it would lead to plunder and miscegenation. After the war, while acknowledging that the region deserved "chastisement," he felt that "to undergo subjugation and extermination at the hand of the Yankees is too much." Even as late as 1904, he had not "learned to rejoice in our defeat" but only "honestly and faithfully" accepted the outcome "as authorized by an almighty Providence, whose ways are often past finding out."[32]

For white southern Baptists, "redemption" signified individual salvation as well as the deliverance of society from the disorder imported by outside agitators. Submission to the North in politics, they believed, would inevitably be followed by the "loss of freedom of conscience." As John A. Broadus explained, "Under Yankee rule, we may not expect to worship God but according to Yankee faith."[33]

White Baptists viewed political and religious reconstruction as the same process in different institutional settings. Just as carpetbaggers had "stolen" the reins of government, so northern missionary organizations would seize control of the institutions and customs of southern religious life. Attending northern Baptist meetings after the war, John A. Broadus, the preeminent southern Baptist educator of the late nineteenth century, found himself "prayed at" and "cursed." Broadus's experiences left him with little hope for any postwar reunion of Baptist forces. "Unless we acknowledge ourselves to have been criminals," he wrote to his fellow southerners, "and ask forgiveness and absolution from these men, and admit their superiority, wisdom and integrity, they refuse to recognize us as equals and fellow-laborers in the Kingdom of Christ."[34] Since the "whole drift and spirit" of northern meetings suggested the obsession of northern religious organizations to "maintain the perfect religious and social equality of the races," then white southern Baptists could not cooperate with them "without endorsing their reconstruction, both political and ecclesiastical."[35]

Proposals for intersectional denominational cooperation or reunion drew attention and debate but always met rejection from leaders of the SBC. Controversies over Reconstruction politics destroyed any chances of religious reunion. If northerners meant to continue "thrusting their missionaries and agents into our fields, . . . tacitly regarding our churches and ministers as inferior or unworthy," a southern minister explained in 1867, then the South could never consent to reunion. "We mean to maintain our dignity and our self-respect," he advised his northern counterparts. Even into the 1880s, observers noted the "frequent appeals to sectional feeling" at SBC meetings, where "issues long ago buried" were "dug up . . . to strengthen those appeals."[36]

The term "political preacher," always used pejoratively, designated those who worked in black education or supported Republican candidates or ideological stands. Men who might once have represented the epitome of evangelical zeal now fell into public disgrace because of their support for the rights of the freed people. In Virginia, for example, a well-known minister who accepted an appointment from the northern Baptist home missionary agency soon found that "his churches and the community had denounced and deserted him." He had become a pariah because he was a "political-religionist."[37] As a South Carolina Baptist Redeemer explained, "political preachers and political religionists have done more to ruin the country than any other one element." Dissent in this matter was unacceptable. Churches expressing sympathy for the Union or for Republicans found themselves booted out of Baptist associations and other religious organizations. The much-vaunted "Baptist democracy" proved to be a Tocquevillean tyranny of the majority.[38]

Though fond of complaining about political preachers, southern Baptists preached the political ideology of white supremacy from the pulpit. Ministers who organized resistance to Reconstruction measures rarely found themselves labeled as "dabblers" in politics. Most southern Christians did not even recognize such activity as political matters but as extensions of a cosmic struggle between order and disorder. They were defending God's divinely sanctioned social and racial hierarchy. "Everything held sacred and dear by the white race was at stake," an Alabaman commented of a fiery Redemptionist speech delivered by a Baptist minister in 1868. The issue, as speaker Jabez Lamar Monroe Curry (then a minister and later the head of the conservative Southern Education Board) made clear, was "patriotism and religion—the feeling of life against death—of liberty against the worst form of enslavement."[39] The editors of state denominational newspapers, particularly the Georgia-based *Christian Index and Southwestern Baptist*, used their public forums for organizing Redemptionist sentiment. Federal troops actually shut down the *Christian Index* for its advocacy of disloyalty as a moral and religious duty of the white South. A South Carolinian who condemned black ministers for delivering "political harangues" that "engender[ed] strife and bitter hatred" advised his own ministerial troops to be "vigilant and active" in their state electoral contests. "I consider that minister recreant to his duty he owes to his country," he wrote in 1868, "who does not feel and *manifest* an interest in political affairs in the current crisis." He advised white Christians to set aside "personal considerations . . . in the united efforts to save our state," and to put in office those who represented "the white man's interest in the State and out of it."[40]

These views, more candidly expressed than most, demonstrated that white Baptist views on preserving "pure religion" in the region ultimately hinged on preserving the racial hierarchy. This language was instrumental in justifying the continued existence of sectional organizations such as the SBC. An Alabama Baptist felt northern offers of reunion of Baptist forces would "complete our own degradation by making our former servants, wrested from us by force, not only the political equals of ourselves, but the superiors of those who were formerly our legislators and executive officers." Meeting as equals with black Christians in religious work would mean submission to the northern subversion of the proper social order in religion and politics. "As Seward found a higher law than the Federal Constitution, in politics," another Alabama minister reasoned, northern fanatics insisted on "a higher law than the inspired Constitution [the Bible] in religion." He interpreted contemporary events as part of God's plan for allowing the "twin sisters" of "liberalism and fanaticism" to run their ruinous course, and for southern piety to emerge cleansed and strengthened. "Who can tell," he exulted, "what the Almighty may have in reserve for his people in the Southern lands."[41]

The antebellum rhetoric of cultural separatism undergirded these emerging views of religious republicanism. It was the political language by which white southerners interpreted and fought the centralization and extension of governmental powers during Reconstruction. White southern Baptists perceived their churches as religious forms of the republican ideal of localized, independent, self-governing institutions. A delegate to a state Baptist meeting in 1887 illuminated these ideological affinities between Redemption politics and white Protestantism in the post-Reconstruction South. By that time conservative Democrats were again in power and the remaining social and civil rights of African Americans in the South were soon to be stripped away in the Jim Crow legislatures of the 1890s and 1900s. In this Baptist layman's account, Democratic party politics were linked to the Baptist polity in ways which defined orthodox southern religious thinking:

> As a Democrat I love all Democrats. All Baptists are Democrats. . . . It is *THE* political faith of the great majority of the members of the church. . . . A Baptist is a Democrat because his church government is democratic and because it has about it none of the paraphernalia or trappings of monarchies and despotisms. . . . All power not DELEGATED remains in the individual churches. He believes in no strong centralized powers.

When threats to this cherished religious republicanism appeared in the form of northern missionaries, the outside agitators of the 1860s, few hesitated to apply the appropriate religiopolitical language. Yankee oppressors looked equally undesirable even when outfitted in clerical garb. Regional religious spokesmen assured their constituents that southern white Protestantism stood "distinctively and powerfully" on the side of a "sound and healthy conservatism in doctrine."[42]

Postbellum Baptists retained antebellum notions of the separate culture of the South, which had provided the ideological underpinning for secession and nation building. As a prominent North Carolinian expressed it in 1899, "we are a different people, a different blood, a different climate, a different character, different customs, and we have largely a different work to do in this world." This gulf separating the two peoples made "organic union" of religious organizations impossible. By 1880, in fact, few from either section still argued for a "reunion." They settled for a divorce that might grow more amicable over the years but would remain permanent.[43]

The survival of the Southern Baptist Convention as a sectional institution—one that represented the church of the white South—was certain by the 1880s. The difficult days of the Civil War and Reconstruction had given its organizers a renewed sense of their purpose. Their next task was to provide permanent footing for institutions that would ensure the future growth of their organization, particularly the rebuilding of the Home Mission Board of the SBC.

After breaking from northern Baptists in 1845, the SBC carried on independent missionary work much like that of other religious agencies in the "benevolent empire." Convention workers distributed Bibles, preached to blacks and Indians, opened churches in newly settled areas, and evangelized fervently for their sect's doctrines. Funding disputes and theological controversies limited the effectiveness of this work. During the Civil War, the home missionary agency assisted in distributing religious literature to the soldiers and produced a Confederate hymn book, as well as a children's Sunday school magazine. After the war, the agency struggled for survival. Paid sporadically and always uncertain of the receptiveness of local believers to outsiders, southern Baptist home missionaries carried on difficult work in unpromising circumstances.[44]

In 1882, the Home Mission Board moved from its previously obscure location (Marion, Alabama) to Atlanta, a city soon to be known as the center of the New South movement. Isaac Taylor Tichenor, the "fighting chaplain" of Shiloh, undertook the work of resurrecting the board in the 1880s. He began with little yearly income and only forty missionaries, few of whom worked west of the Mississippi. Tichenor successfully reorganized home missions work for the SBC, assigning district canvassers who markedly increased the income of the agency. In 1892, he boasted that "there was not a missionary to the white people of the South who did not bear a commission from either the Home Mission Board of the Southern Baptist Convention, or one of our State Boards in alliance with it. Its territories had been reclaimed." In 1880, the board listed 35 missionaries and 435 converts, and operated with a yearly income of about $20,000. In 1902, 671 missionaries worked under the board's auspices or evangelized locally in cooperation with the agency. By 1915, 1,409 laborers reaped a harvest of 44,000 new church members and 167 church congregations.[45]

From the 1890s forward, southern and northern Baptists worked out various "territorial agreements," largely benefiting the southern Home Mission Board. The Fortress Monroe agreement of 1894, for example, increased the southern board's stature in relation to the more established and well-known American Baptist Home Mission Society. Except for supporting their colleges for African Americans, northern Baptists in the early twentieth century ceded southern work to the southern denominations, while the SBC gradually expanded its work westward. The Home Mission Board missionaries sunk the roots that would in a short time grow into a network of churches throughout the South. The establishment of the Home Mission Board and solidifying of other agencies of the convention gave SBC leaders the victory they had sought during Reconstruction: maintenance of a separate religious culture that would be a cornerstone of white supremacy and theological conservatism in the region.[46]

In the 1890s, the romantic liaisons between northern officers and southern belles in the works of popular novelists and the nationalist fervor surrounding the Spanish-American War exemplified the growing racial consensus of North and South. Both professional and amateur historians acknowledged Reconstruction to be the "tragic era," as Claude Bowers's bitterly partisan but widely accepted popular history of the period termed it. White Americans North and

South agreed on the superiority of "Anglo-Saxon manhood" and collectively worried for the future of an America with a large "backward" class of southern Negroes and cities full of dangerous and strange immigrants. Despite the heroism of some longstanding missionaries in the South and the efforts of some northern journalists to call attention to southern outrages (such as the lynchings and peonage system), and despite the attacks launched on the southern oligarchy by the Populists, the questions raised by Reconstruction were considered settled by white northerners: southerners knew best how to take care of "their Negroes."[47]

Southern Baptists were instrumental in the mythologizing of the "horrors" of the Civil War and Reconstruction. This boilerplate rhetoric quickly became part of the folklore, and soon the official history, of the era. Before Republicans took control of the House of Representatives in the 1866 elections, prominent Virginia Baptists portrayed white southerners as victims of northern marauders, setting the tone for the exaggerated attention given to the supposed depredations of the carpetbaggers. Northern Christians had

> waged against us a lawless war, which, instead of being regulated by the rules of warfare, . . . has been conducted in a spirit of savage, or rather, draconian cruelty and devastation. Not satisfied with the unbridled spoilations, robberies and thefts, which we have suffered; or with the midnight screams of naked females escaping from their burning houses; or with our incarcerated ministers, separated from the people of their charge, and doomed to lose their health and strength in filthy prisons; not satisfied that we have accepted the issues of the war, and declared our allegiance to the existing government, or with the impoverished and ruined condition to which we have been reduced . . . not satisfied with all this their unsatiated and insatiable malice (what else can we call it) is still ever pouring upon us its bitter and dirty streams of vituperation and abuse.[48]

With this imagined disaster at hand, white Baptists foresaw a cultural and political war to defend white supremacy. If violence was necessary to this end, they were prepared to defend it. In North Carolina, one of the original Baptist churches created in the eighteenth century questioned the action of a "vigilant committee" in the county that had executed a black man suspected of radical political activity. "But under the excitement of the times," the church noted, "we forgive all who were concerned." Other church leaders felt no need even for this backhanded apology. E. T. Winkler, pastor of prominent churches in South Carolina and Alabama, explained to northern Baptists in 1872 why groups such as the Ku Klux Klan were justifiable: "In a state of society where there is no law, and where men must form temporary organizations for the redress of intolerable grievances and the maintenance of social order, justice itself is perverted by attacks on these organizations." The Force Act of 1871, which took action against groups that blocked the exercise of civil rights (such as the Klan), seemed to Winkler an example of the "oppression" to which the white South had been subjected. Winkler offered no such justifications for "temporary organizations" (such as Union Leagues) that defended the embattled rights of the freed people.[49]

In the 1890s, white southern Baptists disseminated the popular view of Reconstruction as a tragic era when the good white men of the South fell under the evil rule of scheming carpetbaggers and ignorant freedmen. They spread the notion that the white South would take care of the Negro best without northern interference, a key implication of the conservative interpretation of Reconstruction. Southern Baptist Convention messengers in 1891 enthusiastically endorsed the standard canards of the tragic era interpretation. White southern Christians, one speaker insisted, played the part of the innocents who "refused to enter a contest with politicians." The end of "Negro domination" meant the beginning of a government sanctioned by God to restore sanity to the South. Biracial government in religion would have led, he suggested, to the same "corruption" and "degradation" as was the case when Radical rule fastened its hold on the South. Resistance to northern religious radicalism provided a heroic example for the fight against northern political radicals. Southern self-determination had been at stake, and white people in the region had responded gallantly.

This account of history, already standard in academia and popular perceptions by 1890, failed to mention (among other excisions) the corruption of the Redeemer governments, the murderous guerrilla groups that terrorized freedmen attempting to exercise their civil rights, and the tightening stranglehold placed on southern lives by the policies of Democratic governments. It reinforced the process of selective recall and the misremembering of the Civil War and Reconstruction. White southern Baptists instead immortalized those who engaged in a political struggle to maintain white supremacy, whether in politics or religion. They remembered when "designing political demagoguery laid its polluted, scourging hand" on the region and led it "away from truth, happiness and prosperity." And they thanked God for having been redeemed "by the blood of the Lamb." They might have added another note of thanks for their "redemption" from "political-religionism"—that of the blood of the Ku Klux Klan.[50]

Notes

1. See Donald Mathews, *Religion in the Old South* (Chicago, 1977); Anne C. Loveland, *Southern Evangelicals and the Social Order, 1800–1860* (Baton Rouge, 1980); Eugene D. Genovese, *The Slaveholders' Dilemma: Freedom and Progress in Southern Conservative Thought, 1820–1860* (Columbia, SC, 1992); and Mitchell Snay, *Gospel of Disunion: Religion and Separatism in the Antebellum South* (Cambridge, 1993). Anderson Edwards, quoted in Eugene Genovese, *Roll, Jordan, Roll: The World the Slaves Made* (New York, 1974), 263. Discussions with Professors Charles Reagan Wilson, Andrew Manis, and David Chappell in an NEH seminar on southern religion at the Center for the Study of Southern Culture, University of Mississippi, clarified many of the ideas in this essay.

2. The best overview of the political process of Redemption is Michael Perman, *The Road to Redemption: Southern Politics, 1869–1879* (Chapel Hill, NC, 1984).

3. My argument is obviously indebted to the work of Charles Reagan Wilson, *Baptized in Blood: The Religion of the Lost Cause, 1865–1920* (Athens, GA, 1980); and to Andrew Manis, *Southern Civil Religions in Conflict: Black and White Baptists and Civil*

Rights, 1947–1957 (Athens, GA, 1987). A very similar argument, focused especially on the state of Virginia and documented carefully from ministerial records, may be found in Beth Barton Schweiger, "The Transformation of Southern Religion: Clergy and Congregations in Virginia, 1830–1895," Ph.D. dissertation, University of Virginia, 1994.

4. See Rhys Isaac, *The Transformation of Virginia, 1740–1790* (Chapel Hill, NC, 1982). For an argument that suggests that the culture of honor and the culture of evangelicalism were not mutually exclusive, but could reinforce one another, see Ed Crowther, "Holy Honor: Sacred and Secular in the Old South," *Journal of Southern History* 58 (November 1992): 619–636. But see also Frederick Bode, "The Formation of Evangelical Communities in Middle Georgia: Twiggs County, 1830–1861," *Journal of Southern History* 60 (November 1994): 711–748, which suggests that honor and evangelicalism could exist only in uneasy tension; and Christopher Waldrep, "The Making of a Border State Society: James McGready, the Great Revival, and the Prosecution of Profanity in Kentucky," *American Historical Review* 99 (June 1994): 767–784, which shows how evangelicals in that state attempted to use popular courts, the grand juries, to enforce an evangelical language and suppress swearing. The way in which evangelicalism was transformed into support for a paternal slave order began in the late eighteenth century, according to Alan Gallay, "Planters, Slaves, and the Great Awakening," in *Masters and Slaves in the House of the Lord: Race and Religion in the American South, 1740–1870*, ed. John Boles (Lexington, KY, 1988), 19–36.

5. See Robert Baker, *The Southern Baptist Convention and Its People, 1607–1972* (Nashville, 1974), and Randy Sparks, *On Jordan's Stormy Banks: Evangelicalism in Mississippi, 1763–1877* (Athens, GA, 1994). A parallel process of "respectability" through church architecture among Georgia's Methodists is documented in Chris Owen, "By Design: The Social Meaning of Methodist Church Architecture in Nineteenth-Century Georgia," *Georgia Historical Quarterly* 75 (Summer 1991): 221–253.

6. For discussion of the Antimission Baptists, see Bertram Wyatt-Brown, "The Antimission Movement in the Jacksonian South: A Study in Regional Folk Culture," *Journal of Southern History* 36 (November 1970): 501–529; and Cecil Lambert, *The Rise of the Antimission Baptists: Sources and Leaders, 1800–1840* (New York, 1980). See also Nathan Hatch, *The Democratization of American Christianity* (New Haven, 1989), for a vivid discussion of the antiestablishment apostles of democratic Christianity who peopled America's religious frontier in the antebellum era; and see chapter 4 of Robert Abzug, *Crumbling Cosmos: Reform and the American Religious Imagination* (New York, 1994). For a parallel process in politics, see Daniel Dupre, "Barbecues and Pledges: Electioneering and the Rise of Democratic Politics in Antebellum Alabama," *Journal of Southern History* 60 (August 1994): 479–512, which shows how the enthusiastic political campaigns in this age of democratization paralleled the democratization of evangelicalism.

7. For a discussion of Landmarkism, see James Tull, *A History of Southern Baptist Landmarkism in the Light of Historical Baptist Ecclesiology* (New York, 1980). An attempt to place Baptist Landmarkism within the interdenominational tradition of Protestant primitivism may be found in Richard T. Hughes and C. Leonard Allen, *Illusions of Innocence: Protestant Primitivism in America, 1630–1875* (Chicago, 1988). The best overall interpretation of Landmarkism is Marty Beall, "James Robinson Graves and the Rhetoric of Demagogy: Primitivism and Democracy in Old Landmarkism," Ph.D. dissertation, Vanderbilt University, 1990.

8. This brief "moment" and its rapid eclipsing are documented and provocatively analyzed in John Boles, "Evangelical Protestantism in the Old South: From Religious Dissent to Cultural Dominance," in *Religion in the South*, ed. Charles Reagan Wilson

(Jackson, MS, 1985), 13–34; John Boles, *The Great Revival, 1787–1805: The Origins of the Southern Evangelical Mind* (Lexington, KY, 1972); Mechal Sobel, *Trabelin' On: The Slave Journey to an Afro-Baptist Faith* (Westport, CT, 1978), and Sobel, *The World They Made Together: Black and White Values in Eighteenth-Century Virginia* (Princeton, 1987).

9. See Jewell Spangler, "Salvation Was Not Liberty: Baptists and Slavery in Revolutionary Virginia," *American Baptist Quarterly* 13 (September 1994): 221–236, for a quantitative look at this phenomenon in the context of local churches; and Margaret Washington-Creel, *"A Peculiar People": Slave Religion and Community-Culture Among the Gullahs* (New York, 1988), for a brilliant analysis of Richard Furman and the proslavery apologetic in South Carolina. An equally provocative analysis may be found in Larry E. Tise, *Pro-Slavery: A History of the Defense of Slavery in America, 1701–1840* (Athens, GA, 1987). Snay discusses the "sanctification of slavery" in *Gospel of Disunion*, 78–109.

10. For a powerful empirical documentation of this point, see Spangler, "Salvation Was Not Liberty."

11. The quotation comes from Robert Baker, ed., *A Baptist Source Book, With Particular Reference to Southern Baptists* (Nashville, 1966), 106–108. For the role of slavery in denominational splits, see Clarence C. Goen, *Broken Churches, Broken Nation: Denominational Schisms and the Coming of the American Civil War* (Macon, GA, 1985); David Bailey, *Shadow on the Church: Southwestern Evangelical Religion and the Issue of Slavery, 1783–1860* (Ithaca, NY, 1985); Donald Mathews, *Slavery and Methodism: A Chapter in American Morality* (Princeton, 1965); and Snay, *Gospel of Disunion*. This summary of Baptist background comes primarily from Baker, *The Southern Baptist Convention and Its People*, 15–57; W. W. Barnes, "Baptists," in *Encyclopedia of Southern Baptists*, eds. Clifton Allen et al. (Nashville, 1958), 1: 135–141; and Robert G. Torbet, *A History of the Baptists* (Valley Forge, PA, 1963).

12. This discussion of the relationship between evangelicalism and public life in the nineteenth century is based most directly on Donald Mathews, "The Second Great Awakening as an Organizing Process, 1780–1830: An Hypothesis," *American Quarterly* 21 (Spring 1969): 23–43; Hatch, *Democratization of American Christianity*; Ronald Walters, *The Anti-Slavery Appeal: American Abolitionism Before 1830* (Baltimore, 1976); Samuel Hill, *The South and the North in American Religion* (Athens, GA, 1980); Ernest R. Sandeen, *The Roots of Fundamentalism: British and American Millenarianism, 1800–1930* (Chicago, 1970); George M. Marsden, *Fundamentalism and American Culture: The Shaping of Twentieth-Century Evangelicalism* (New York, 1980); Timothy Weber, *Living in the Shadow of the Second Coming: American Premillennialism, 1875–1925* (New York, 1979); and Beth Barton Schweiger, "Religious Life in the New South: Baptist and Methodist Ministers in Virginia, 1865–1910," paper presented at the Southern Historical Association, New Orleans, November 1990, copy in author's possession. For fuller explanations of the literature of Christian sentimental Victorianism, particularly including autobiographies, memoirs, doggerel, and gospel hymns, see Colleen McDannell, *The Christian Home in Victorian America* (Bloomington, IN, 1986); and Sandra S. Sizer, *Gospel Hymns and Social Religion: The Rhetoric of Nineteenth-Century Revivalism* (Philadelphia, 1985). The best analysis of concepts of afterlife in revival preaching may be found in Jon Butler, *"Softly and Tenderly Jesus is Calling": Heaven and Hell in American Revivalism* (New York, 1991).

13. Diary of Basil Manly, entry for February 9, 1861, in Manly Family Papers, reel 6, Southern Baptist Historical Library and Archives, Nashville, TN (hereafter SBHLA); Basil Manly Sr. to children, May 21, 1862, in Basil Manly Sr., Papers, reel 1, folder 134; J. A. Broadus to Miss Cornelia Taliefferro, January 22, 1861, in *Life and Letters of John A. Broadus*, ed. Archibald T. Robertson (Philadelphia, 1901), 181.

14. Basil Manly Jr. to parents, March 1, 1861, in Manly Family Papers, SBHLA.

15. Charles Manly to Basil Manly Sr., Manly Family Papers, reel 1, folder 142, SBHLA.

16. See Sidney Romero, *Religion in the Rebel Ranks* (Lanham, MD, 1983), 94–95, 163, for statistics on Baptist publishing and colportage efforts for the Confederate army. Quotation from *Religious Herald*, April 4, 1867, and Southern Baptist Convention *Proceedings*, 1863, 68–70. Drew Gilpin Faust, "Christian Soldiers: The Meaning of Revivalism in the Confederate Army," *Journal of Southern History* 53 (February 1987): 63–90, provides the single best source for interpreting the meaning of evangelical Protestantism in the Confederate army. See also Gardiner H. Shattuck, *A Shield and a Hiding Place: Religion in the Civil War Armies* (Macon, GA, 1987). Drew Faust, *The Creation of Confederate Nationalism: Ideology and Identity in the Civil War South* (Baton Rouge, 1988), examines the way the ministry both supported and ultimately undermined the Confederate cause. For a fine primary source for this subject, and for looking at the development of the religious symbolism of the Lost Cause, see John William Jones, *Christ in the Camp; or, Religion in Lee's Army* (Richmond, 1887).

17. J. S. Dill, *Isaac Taylor Tichenor, The Home Mission Statesman* (Nashville, 1908); Edwin Hansford Rennolds, "Autobiography," 52–54, typed manuscript in E. H. Rennolds Sr. Papers, SBHLA; W. H. Ryals, "Death of Rev. Asa Cox," undated newspaper clipping (ca. July 1911), typewritten manuscript and copy of original clipping in Asa Cox Papers, SBHLA; J. J. D. Renfroe, "Manuscript Sermons," microfilm copies consulted at SHBLA.

18. Basil Manly Sr. to Basil Manly Jr., February 10, 1861, in Manly Family Papers, reel 1, folder 125, SBHLA; Southern Baptist Convention *Proceedings*, 1863, 54; North Carolina Baptist State Convention *Minutes*, 1861, 22; Baptist General Association of Virginia *Minutes*, 1861, 15–16.

19. "Report on Religious Instruction of Colored People," Alabama Baptist State Convention *Minutes*, 1863, Appendix; Texas Baptist State Convention *Minutes*, 1862, 6, and 1863, 6; Basil Manly Sr., "The Purpose of Calamities," sermon preached in Montgomery on February 28, 1862, newspaper clipping in Manly Family Papers, reel 5, folder 758a, SBHLA.

20. Basil Manly Jr. to parents, July 13, 1863, in Manly Family Papers, reel 5, SBHLA.

21. Minutes of the Central Baptist Church, Nashville, TN, February 16, 1862; July 10, 1864, SBHLA; Lynn May, *The First Baptist Church of Nashville, Tennessee, 1820–1970* (Nashville, 1970), 100–105; May, " 'They Can Never Both Prosper Together': Black and White Baptists in Antebellum Nashville, Tennessee," *Tennessee Historical Quarterly* 38 (1979): 296–307; T. S., "Letter from Nashville," *Christian Watchman and Reflector*, May 6, 1875.

22. Richard Andrew Fox, handwritten sermon delivered early 1865, in Richard Andrew Fox Papers, folder for 1865, Virginia Historical Society, Richmond, VA.

23. William Hatcher, *Along the Trail of Friendly Years* (New York, 1910), 112; L. R. Mills, "My Recollections of Dr. Wingate," in Lansing Burrows Papers, box 10, folder 232, SBHLA.

24. Charleston Baptist Association *Minutes*, 1865, 8; E. A. C. "The Signs of the Times," *South Carolina Baptist*, April 20, 1866; *South Carolina Baptist*, June 29, 1866.

25. Lansing Burrows, "The Fall of Richmond," copy of handwritten speech delivered in Louisville, 1875, in Lansing Burrows Papers, box 9, folder 196, SBHLA.

26. *Biblical Recorder*, November 4, 1868.

27. G. F. Williams to John A. Broadus, February 10, 1866, in John A. Broadus letter file, Boyce Library, Southern Baptist Theological Seminary, Louisville, KY; Charles Manly to Basil Manly Jr., September 25, 1866, in Manly Family Papers, reel 2, folder 179, SBHLA.

28. *Biblical Recorder*, November 17, 1869, August 9, 1871.

29. See chap. 1 of Bill Leonard, *God's Last and Only Hope: The Fragmentation of the Southern Baptist Convention* (Grand Rapids, MI, 1990), for an acute and succinct summary of the major themes of SBC history in the late nineteenth century.

30. *Religious Herald*, May 2, 1868; Charles Manly to Basil Manly Sr., September 28, 1868 and October 30, 1868, in Manly Family Papers, reel 2, folder 208, SBHLA.

31. *Christian Watchman and Reflector*, June 29, 1865.

32. Charles Manly to parents, March 27, 1862, Manly Family Papers, reel 1, folder 149, SBHLA; Charles Manly to Basil Manly Jr., July 15, 1867, in Manly Family Papers, reel 2, SBHLA; Charles Manly, untitled speech delivered at Confederate Memorial Exercises, Lexington, VA, June 4, 1904, in Manly Family Papers, feel 4, folder 735, SBHLA;

33. *Biblical Recorder*, January 5, 1867; *Christian Index*, February 23, 1865.

34. *Religious Herald*, October 19, 1865.

35. *Religious Herald*, June 3, 1869.

36. *Christian Watchman and Reflector*, July 18, 1867; "Why Not Dissolve the Convention," *Religious Herald*, April 4, 1885.

37. *Christian Watchman and Reflector*, July 2, 1866.

38. Greenville Baptist Association *Minutes*, 1867, 7.

39. *Religious Herald*, March 5, 1868 (J. J. D. Renfroe).

40. Daniel Hollis, *A History of the First Baptist Church, Jacksonville, Alabama, 1836–1986* (Jacksonville, AL, 1987); B. F. Riley, *A Memorial History of the Baptists of Alabama: Being An Account of the Struggles and Achievements of the Denomination from 1808 to 1923* (Philadelphia, 1923), 175; *South Carolina Baptist*, July 19, 1867; July 10, 1868; April 10, 1868 (W. B. Carson).

41. *Christian Index and Southwestern Baptist*, August 4, 1870 (George Brewer); W. Wilkes, "Religious Schism and Defection," *Alabama Baptist*, January 5, 1875.

42. *Biblical Recorder*, December 7, 1887; "Why Not Dissolve the Convention," *Religious Herald*, April 4, 1885.

43. *Biblical Recorder*, July 12, 1899.

44. See Baker, *The Southern Baptist Convention and Its People*; and Ronald Tonks, "History of the Home Mission Board of the Southern Baptist Convention, 1845–1882," doctoral dissertation, Southern Baptist Theological Seminary, 1968.

45. Home Mission Board Minutes, March 12, 1883, in Home Mission Board Papers, reel 1, SBHLA; Southern Baptist Convention *Annual*, 1892, Appendix A; Clifton Allen et al., eds. *Encyclopedia of Southern Baptists* (Nashville, 1958), 1: 646.

46. For a general description of the rebuilding and future work of the Home Mission Board of the Southern Baptist Convention, see Allen et al. eds., *Encyclopedia of Southern Baptists*, 1: 635–640.

47. The "reunion" of North and South in popular culture, especially in the popular novels of the era, is compellingly explored in Nina Silber, *The Romance of Reunion: Northerners and the South, 1865–1900* (Chapel Hill, NC, 1993). The activities of the northern Baptist missionaries Joanna Moore and Mary Burdette, and the alliance of white northern Baptist women with black southern Baptist women, are detailed in Evelyn Brooks-Higginbotham, *Righteous Discontent: The Women's Movement in the Black Baptist Church, 1880–1920* (Cambridge, MA, 1993), 88–119. The popular view of Recon-

struction as the tragic era was most vividly, and crudely, exemplified by Claude Bowers, *The Tragic Era: The Revolution After Lincoln* (New York, 1929).

48. *Religious Herald*, September, 9, 1866.

49. Minutes of the Sandy Run Baptist Church, December 1869, quoted in Wade W. Bridger, *From the Wilderness to the Hilltop: A History of the Sandy Run Baptist Church* (Gastonia, NC, 1973); E. T. Winkler, quoted in *Christian Watchman and Reflector*, January 4, 1872.

50. Southern Baptist Convention *Annual*, 1891.

8

Stonewall Jackson and the Providence of God

DANIEL W. STOWELL

When General Thomas J. "Stonewall" Jackson died on May 10, 1863, all white southerners were stunned. Religious southerners were especially disturbed, however, because Jackson embodied the Christian attributes they considered vital to the success of the Confederacy. A Presbyterian deacon and Sunday school superintendent, Jackson had encouraged revivals among his troops and had often inquired about the spiritual state of his men. He prayed fervently before and during battles and ascribed all successes to God's providential assistance. For a people committed to the belief that an omnipotent God controlled the destiny of men and of nations, Jackson's death was a spiritual crisis.[1]

Midway through the Civil War and nearly eight weeks before the disasters at Gettysburg and Vicksburg, Jackson's death forced white southern evangelicals for the first time to consider whether God would ultimately grant them victory. What did Jackson's life—and death—mean, they pondered. The ways in which southern Christians answered this question revealed much about the southern religious interpretation of the Civil War that began to take shape. Two years later, when faced with the larger crisis of the death of the Confederacy, religious southerners revived and extended the understandings of God's providence that they had developed in the aftermath of Jackson's death. Furthermore, Jackson's death and the mourning that followed formed an important cultural ritual that later helped southerners individually and collectively grapple with the end of the Confederate States of America. Jackson became the first of a pantheon of heroes that would later be enshrined in southern hearts through the Lost Cause movement. His death at the zenith of the Confederacy's bid for independence began a process of individual religious reflection and corporate cultural ritual that would continue for decades. What white religious southerners told themselves about God, the Confederacy, and its leaders would shape southern culture into the twentieth century.

On the evening of May 2, 1863, Stonewall Jackson, a few of his officers, and several couriers rode beyond Confederate lines to reconnoiter the federal forces along the Plank Road near Chancellorsville, Virginia. Jackson was planning a night attack in the moonlight to capitalize on the successes of the past few hours, when Jackson's men had overrun the surprised right flank of the Army of the Potomac. As Jackson's party rode back toward its own lines over the unfamiliar terrain, men of the 18th North Carolina Regiment mistook the horsemen for federal cavalry and opened fire. Several members of the party were shot from their horses. One of the officers shouted to the pickets that they were firing on their own men. Believing this announcement to be a Yankee trick, the North Carolinians fired again. In this volley, three bullets struck Jackson, one in the right hand and two more in the left arm.

Jackson's horse, Little Sorrel, bolted into the woods, carrying its wounded rider crashing into the branches. Jackson managed to rein in the horse and return to the road. Two of his officers carefully removed him from his saddle, and Jackson muttered, "My own men." In the midst of a federal artillery bombardment, Jackson's men with difficulty carried him half a mile to the rear, where they met Dr. Hunter McGuire and an ambulance. McGuire transported the wounded general to a field hospital and a few hours later amputated Jackson's left arm just below the shoulder. After the amputation, Jackson slept for several hours and appeared to be recovering well by the next morning.

Despite the success of Jackson's bold flanking maneuver against superior Union forces, General Robert E. Lee was deeply troubled when Captain R. E. Wilbourn, Jackson's signal officer, told him that Jackson had been wounded by his own soldiers: "Any victory is dearly bought which deprives us of the services of General Jackson, even for a short time." Lee sent a short note to Jackson congratulating him on his victory and assuring him that "for the good of the country," he would have chosen to be disabled in Jackson's stead.[2]

On May 4, Jackson was moved to the home of Thomas Coleman Chandler at Guiney's Station, ten miles south of Fredericksburg. There he showed signs of recovering from the amputation, but two days later he developed pneumonia. Jackson's wife Mary Anna and their infant daughter Julia, not yet six months old, arrived the next day. He assured his wife that he was "perfectly resigned" to accept God's will. Jackson had seen his daughter only once, some two weeks earlier before federal troops marched toward Chancellorsville. He saw her only once more on Saturday, May 9. By the next morning, Jackson's doctors had little hope for his survival. Anna told him he must prepare for the worst, and asked him if he wanted God to have His will with him. "I prefer it," he replied. "Yes, I prefer it." A few hours later, Jackson told those at his bedside, "I always wanted to die on Sunday." And that Sunday afternoon at 3:15, his wish was fulfilled.[3]

The Confederacy grieved as it had for no other loss. Sara Pryor wrote in her published reminiscences: "On May 10 the General died, and we were all plunged into the deepest grief. By every man, woman, and child in the Confederacy this good man and great general was mourned as never man was mourned before." Louise Fellowes of Canton, Mississippi, wrote in a letter to Jackson's widow, Mary Anna Jackson, "The death of your beloved was felt keenly by every daughter of the South; we can form some idea of your agony when we, who never saw his face, loved him so much."[4]

The residents of Winchester, Virginia, were particularly saddened by Jackson's death. He had driven the federal troops from the town on May 25, 1862, and they hoped he would return again to force the Union army out of Winchester. Riding into town in mid-June 1863, Henry Kyd Douglas, a member of Jackson's staff, noted that the inhabitants' joy at being again liberated was "clouded" by Jackson's death: "every citizen of the town mourned as for a great personal bereavement." A few days later, Winchester resident Fanny Graham wrote to Mary Anna Jackson: "The state of suspense in which we were kept was agonizing. The reports in the Yankee papers were so unreliable, that we would not believe it for a moment. It was really touching to see the people wandering about (each one looking as though their dearest friend had been taken) eagerly asking each other if they believed the terrible news. Thus we were hoping & fearing." When the "overwhelming truth" ended the agonizing suspense, "no words can express our grief."[5]

Although the Army of Northern Virginia won perhaps its greatest victory in the battle of Chancellorsville, Jackson's death turned this triumph into a defeat for many southerners. In their estimation, his loss was equally as devastating as the 12,000 other Confederate casualties sustained in the battle— perhaps more so. One veteran, after noting Confederate and Union losses in the battle, added, "but we lost Jackson, who was a whole corps in himself." Georgian Kate Peddy wrote to her husband Dr. George Peddy, a surgeon with the army at Vicksburg, "We have just heard of the death of Stonewall Jackson. I am so sorry, for he was worth ten thousand men to our cause." For Confederate soldier Fred Fleet, "the victory of our brave troops gained at Chancellorsville was no victory with so severe a loss." Kate Stone, a young woman of the planter elite in Louisiana, believed that "in the death of Stonewall Jackson we have lost more than many battles. We have lost the conqueror on a dozen fields, the greatest general on our side."[6]

Throughout the remainder of the war, southerners speculated about how defeats might have been victories had Jackson been present. Even the war itself might have unfolded differently if Jackson had lived. A member of the Stonewall Brigade, Jackson's old command, reflected years later: "I believed at the time, and believe now, and always shall believe, that if we had had Jackson with us at the battle of Gettysburg he would have flanked the enemy off those heights with his corps." Confederate cavalryman John N. Opie declared in his memoirs, "Had he survived, there would have been no Gettysburg, and, consequently, no Appomattox."[7]

Looking back after the war, many southerners believed that Jackson's death marked the beginning of the Confederacy's downfall. Sara Pryor insisted that "from the moment of his death the tide of fortune seemed to turn. Henceforth there would be only disaster and defeat." Opie believed that "his death was the harbinger of the downfall of the Confederacy. When he fell, the Almighty proclaimed the indestructibility of the American Union." John H. Worsham, a veteran of Jackson's old division, concluded simply that "the army never recovered from the loss of Jackson."[8]

Southern Christians also felt the shock of losing a great military leader, but their reasons for mourning were deeper and more distressing. Jackson's death was not simply another of war's misfortunes; it was a message from God. In a sermon on June 13, 1861, the first Confederate fast day of the war, the pastor of the First Presbyterian Church in Charleston had insisted that the bloodless fall of Fort Sumter was "a signal display of the powerful providence of God." The Rev. Thomas Smyth declared to his congregation, "Extraordinary providences are instructive warnings, of great importance in God's government of the world, and to be very solemnly considered." Smyth assured his hearers that the South could confidently view this victory as "an earnest of God's continued presence, providence and power, with her counsellors, her armies, and her people." Southern ministers like Smyth intended to use these memorable events as evidence that providence favored the Confederacy, but such an argument also had a negative side. As southern successes clearly demonstrated God's favor, so reverses became chastisements for southern shortcomings. Each major and minor incident of the war became an important moral lesson for religious southerners. Certainly the death of Stonewall Jackson, the Christian Warrior, was another of Smyth's extraordinary providences. This time, however, the meaning was different.[9]

What was God's message for the South in this calamity? As Jackson's friend and biographer, the Rev. Robert Lewis Dabney, later remembered, "Men were everywhere speculating with solemn anxiety upon the meaning of his death." The Rev. James B. Ramsey pointed out to his congregation in Lynchburg, Virginia, that even the way Jackson died seemed curiously providential: "The very time and circumstances of his death were all such as to awaken peculiar and melancholy interest, and so force attention to his example, as if God intended not a single element should be wanting to perfect the influence of that example." He was unquestionably a Christian general, devoted to prayer and the religious welfare of his men; certainly God had not taken him because of his iniquity. He was at the height of his success; his troops had performed brilliantly in what became known as Lee's masterpiece, the battle of Chancellorsville. He was shot down by his own men, not by those of his enemy. He did not die immediately, but lingered for a week and died on a Sunday.[10]

Kate Cumming, a Confederate nurse in Chattanooga, noted in her journal that when she first heard of Jackson's death, she was speechless. Her thoughts turned to a passage of Scripture in the book of Romans: "How unsearchable are His judgments, and His ways are past finding out. For who hath known the mind of the Lord." Cumming wrote, "Dark and mysterious indeed, are his ways. Who dare attempt to fathom them, when such men as Jackson are cut down in the zenith of their glory, and at the very hour of their country's need?" Like many other southerners, Cumming was perplexed by the way Jackson died: "The honor of taking this great man's life was not reserved for the foe, but for his own men, as if it were a sacrifice they offered to the Lord. . . ."[11]

On Monday, May 11, Jackson's body was taken to Richmond, where it was embalmed and placed in a metal casket. The Confederate Congress had recently adopted a new design for the flag of the Confederacy, and President Jefferson Davis sent the first one produced to Mrs. Jackson to be placed upon the coffin. On Tuesday, the body was escorted through the streets of Richmond by a procession of military and political leaders including President Davis and Vice President Alexander Stephens. The procession ended at the Capitol, where the body lay in state and thousands of people viewed their hero for the last time. On Wednesday, the casket was moved to the Executive Mansion and from there to the train depot. Escorted by friends, family members, and the governor of Virginia, Jackson's remains were transported to Lexington, Virginia, and laid in his old Lecture Room at the Virginia Military Institute.[12]

On the morning of May 15, Jackson's body was borne on an artillery caisson to the Presbyterian church where Jackson had been a deacon and the superintendent of a black Sunday school. Jackson's friend, the Rev. Ramsey, offered a prayer, and his pastor, the Rev. William S. White, delivered the funeral address. White began by reading from the fifteenth chapter of I Corinthians: "O death, where is thy sting? O grave, where is thy victory. . . . But thanks be to God, which giveth us the victory through our Lord Jesus Christ." The coffin was covered with flowers and the grave too was "heaped with flowers." "Sincerer mourning was never manifested for any one, I do think," Jackson's sister-in-law later wrote in her journal.[13]

The mourning and funeral for Jackson became the first cultural ritual of the Lost Cause movement, and Jackson became the first great southern hero and martyr. In Lost Cause mythology, he remained for decades after the war second only to Robert E. Lee among Confederate heroes. In May 1863, only Jackson—not the cause—was lost, but the later patterns of the Lost Cause movement began to form here. As Charles Reagan Wilson has noted, "religion was at the heart" of the Lost Cause, and Jackson's image as a zealous Christian as well as a skillful warrior made him the ideal hero for southerners who wanted to assert the righteousness of their cause after 1865.[14]

Annie G. Baker, using a blank Sabbath school ledger book for a diary, wrote on May 17: "This day week our hero Jackson died, strange that of all he should have been called away, just when his presence seemed to be so necessary to his country." Baker considered it "a great comfort that we are all 'immortal till our work is done,' and his I suppose was accomplished, but it seems very sad. The sun does not shine as brightly as it did, and this terrible war seems to be claiming all the bravest and the best for its victims." On the same day, Eliza Rhea Fain, a devout East Tennessee Presbyterian, also reflected on Jackson's death: "This evening week our great our noble our lamented Jackson was taken from us. For him we mourn, but may his death teach us an instructive lesson that God will be honored and if we in any way rob him of the honor and glory due to him alone he will bring us to see the evil of our way." Saddened and chastised, Fain was still confident of southern success and demanded retribution; Jackson's "ashes will mingle with his native soil, but his blood crieth for vengeance on the oppressor."[15]

Christians across the South struggled with the meaning of the sad event. The leading ministers of the Presbyterian church were meeting in their General Assembly when the grievous news came. A committee led by Benjamin Morgan Palmer prepared a minute on Jackson's death: "We shall not attempt here the interpretation of the mysterious providence which has taken away from the country, at such a juncture, so strong an arm. It is enough that He has done it who does all things well; we will 'be still and know that He is God.'" The ministers went on to encourage Confederates to take heart and trust in God: "But in the depth of our own sadness, we would speak a word of cheer to our bereaved countrymen; that in the disappointment of many of our most reasonable calculations, no less than in unexpectedly blessing us when all seemed dark and forbidding, God seems to us only the more to have charged Himself with the care and protection of this struggling Republic; and in this new chastening we recognize the token of Him whose way it is to humble those whom it is His purpose to exalt and to bless." The minute was unanimously adopted when the assembled ministers rose silently to their feet.[16]

The editors of the *Christian Observer* in Richmond urged their readers to say as Jackson did after being told he was dying, "It is all right." Yet, they admitted, "Are we not sorely tempted to feel as if it were *not right?* as if God were dealing hardly with us amid the wrongs inflicted upon us by our enemies? We confess that we cannot now see that 'it is all right'—that we are in darkness respecting this event." Christians in the South, however, must "not presume, in our short-sighted wisdom, to sit in judgment upon the works of the Almighty."[17]

Many southern evangelicals insisted that southern sins had provoked God into taking Jackson's life. The chief transgression they identified was that of idolizing Jackson himself. Margaret Junkin Preston, the sister of Jackson's first wife, declared, "The people made an idol of him, and God has rebuked them." Fain agreed: "Have the people of the South not been guilty of idolatry in regard to our good Generals?" she wondered. "Have we not often felt and said if Stonewall is there all will be right? The arm of flesh was omnipotent in our eye. Behold what our Father hath done." William Pegram wrote to his sister, "I have no doubt . . . that 'all things are for the best.' Some of our troops made too much of an Idol of him and lost sight of God's mercies." Episcopal clergyman Alfred A. Watson of North Carolina insisted that God had permitted Jackson's death because southerners had "trusted too much in *him* and too little in *God.*" The Baptist *Christian Index* in Georgia was one of very few publications to suggest that perhaps Jackson himself bore some of the responsibility. He might have "grown presumptuous because his head had been so often covered in the day of battle," yet this explanation was only one of several possibilities suggested by the Georgia Baptist editor. Jackson may have become "too much an idol with the army and the people of the Confederate States. We were trusting too much to the invincibility of Stonewall Jackson and too little to the arm of Almighty God."[18]

Testimony that Jackson was idolized by Confederate soldiers and civilians is plentiful. Early in 1863, journalist P. W. Alexander described Jackson as "the idol of the people" and "the object of greater enthusiasm than any other military chieftain of our day." On the day Jackson died but unaware of his death, Mrs. Henry Grafton Dulany of Upperville, Virginia, reflected in her diary: "Could he know—perhaps he does know—how beloved he is by every Southern man, woman and child, he would feel richly repaid for all he may have to suffer." Fanny B. Graham in Winchester, Virginia, wrote to her friend Mary Anna Jackson six weeks after his death, "I can but feel how utterly inadequate language is to express all that I feel, but you know my darling how we loved your noble Husband, how we *idolized* him, how we, of the Valley, felt as if he was our peculiar property, *our Deliverer*, & you can have some idea of how every heart bleeds at his loss." The memorial song, "Stonewall's Requiem," declared him to be "The Martyr of our country's cause, / Our Idoliz'd Stonewall." Soldiers also idolized the general. As one member of the Stonewall Brigade later recalled: "The news of the wounding of General Jackson filled the army with the most profound and undisguised grief. His men loved him devotedly, and he was the idol of the whole army." Many "stout-hearted veterans . . . wept like children when told that their idolized General was no more." As James Dabney McCabe wrote in his wartime biography of Jackson, the news of his death meant "that the idol of the South was no more."[19]

Paradoxically, as southern Christians denounced Jackson idolatry, they hoped and prayed for "another Jackson." In their grief, religious southerners prayed that God would bless other generals as He had Jackson. General Lee lamented to his wife, "I know not how to replace him; but God's will be done! I trust He will raise up someone in his place." Mary Jones in Georgia wrote to her son, "The death of our pious, brave, and noble General Stonewall Jackson is a great blow to our cause! May God raise up friends and helpers to our bleeding country!" Fred Fleet, a soldier in the Twenty-Sixth Virginia Regiment, wrote to his father two days after Jackson died, "May God raise up another Jackson in his place."[20]

Not only did southern evangelicals want another Jackson, they also wanted all southerners to emulate his example. Episcopalian Francis H. Smith, superintendent of the Virginia Military Institute where Jackson had been a professor, proclaimed that "God has, by a mysterious providence, presented to the young soldier such a model of a Christian soldier in the life and death of Lieutenant General T. J. Jackson, which has scarcely a parallel in the annals of Christian heroism." Jackson's life and death were designed by God to teach young men that "true greatness rests upon a trustful submission to the will of God, as he is revealed to us in his Son Jesus Christ." Mary Jones wrote to her son, Colonel Charles C. Jones Jr., "The example of our noble Jackson . . . is worthy of imitation by our officers of every grade. He dared to honor the law of his God at all times and in all places and circumstances." A Herndon, Virginia, resident sent Mary Anna Jackson a prayer in the form of a poem, which expressed the hope that southern soldiers would "closely imitate the Christian virtues of their sainted leader." Robert Lewis Dabney, in his biography of Jackson, reported that "all agreed" that "the imitation of Jackson's example by his countrymen would make his people invincible, and their final triumph absolutely certain, and that this was the practical lesson set forth by God in his life and death."[21]

Ironically, even many of his northern enemies praised Jackson's skill, energy, and sincerity, although they were employed in support of a wrong cause. Novelist and poet Herman Melville captured the ambivalence of secular northerners in his poem "Stonewall Jackson":

> The Man who fiercest charged in fight
> > Whose sword and prayer were long—
> > > Stonewall!
> > Even him who stoutly stood for Wrong,
> How can we praise? Yet coming days
> > Shall not forget him with this song.

> Dead is the Man whose Cause is dead,
> > Vainly he died and set his seal—
> > > Stonewall!
> > Earnest in error, as we feel;
> True to the thing he deemed was due,
> > True as John Brown or steel.

> Relentlessly he routed us;
> > But we relent, for he is low—
> > > Stonewall!
> > Justly his fame we outlaw; so
> We drop a tear on the bold Virginian's bier,
> > Because no wreath we owe.

Methodist layman and General O. O. Howard, whose troops Jackson's men had surprised and routed at Chancellorsville, expressed the attitude of northern Christians. Shortly after Jackson's death, Howard wrote that he wished God would give the North "more men and more leaders than we now have, who possess the virtues of that man." In an article on the battle of Chancellorsville written decades after the war, Howard admitted that "even his enemies praise him; but, providentially for us, it was the last battle that he waged against the American Union." Henry Ward Beecher announced Jackson's death in his newspaper, *The Independent*, by declaring, "A brave and honest foe has fallen!"[22]

The most systematic efforts to grapple with the theological implications of Jackson's death were in the form of memorial sermons by southern ministers. Three such sermons from the summer of 1863 have survived, all by Presbyterian ministers. In these sermons, the ministers reiterated the questions with which many southerners struggled when they learned of Jackson's death. Each minister also offered his thoughts on the meaning of Jackson's life and death. Each man condemned southern sins and insisted that Jackson's death was God's chastisement for those sins. Yet God still favored the southland. In these memorial sermons, the southern clergymen also sharpened a theological understanding of the war which southern Christians amplified after Appomattox. In 1863, southern sins caused southern reverses; by 1865, the workings of Providence took a new and mysterious turn. The response, however, of clergy and laity was markedly the same. In each event—the gunfire on the Plank Road and the stacking of arms at Appomattox—southern Christians tried to discern God's larger plan, but ultimately they rested on the assurance that God would not and did not abandon them.

The Rev. Ramsey, Jackson's friend and pastor of the First Presbyterian Church in Lynchburg, delivered a memorial sermon on May 24. Ramsey spoke for the entire Confederacy when he asked, "God has taken him, and why? . . . Why this terrible blow? Why raise up just the instrument we needed, and then remove him when we seemed to need him as much if not more than ever?" Like others who reflected on this question, Ramsey insisted that "if this nation had an idol it was Jackson. . . . God has thus taught us that we must depend directly upon him." "If we will not honor God," Ramsey continued, "he will not honor us." Nothing could better teach this lesson than the loss of Jackson. If Jackson's death accomplished that task, "it will be a blessing fully equal to his life; if it fails to do it, it would seem that nothing else can, we can look only to be a cast off people." Ramsey reminded his congregation that although "his loss seems irreparable" to both the church and the country in "this hour of our peril," God could raise up others in Jackson's place. Instead of questioning God's decision to take Jackson from them, southerners should be thankful and hopeful that the Confederacy was blessed with such a "perfect Christian Hero." Who could believe that "God would have given us such a man, and answered in every step his prayers for two eventful years, and blessed him as our defender, if he had not designs of mercy for us, and was not preparing for us a glorious deliverance, and us for it?" Jackson was great, Ramsey maintained, because "he honored God with all his heart and life," and his success stemmed from his dependence upon God. If southerners followed his example, God would certainly secure their independence. "Let the watchword then of our whole country" be, Ramsey concluded, " 'Forward and remember Jackson,' only adding, 'In the name of Jackson's God.' "[23]

The Rev. Dabney, Presbyterian minister, Confederate chaplain, and Jackson's chief of staff for a time, also delivered a discourse on Jackson's life soon after the general's death. Searching for God's purposes, Dabney asked rhetorically, "Can the solution be, that having tried us, and found us unworthy of such a deliverer, he [God] has hid his favorite in the grave, in the brightness of his hopes, and before his blooming honours received any blight from disaster, from the calamities which our sins are about to bring upon us?" Dabney answered with a resounding "Nay." Instead, he suggested, "may it not be, that God, after enabling him to render all the service which was essential to our deliverance, and showing us in him, the brightest example of the glory of Christianity, has bid him enter into the joy of his Lord, at this juncture, in order to warn us against our incipient idolatry. . . ." Dabney exhorted his audience that "while man is mortal, the cause is immortal. Away then, with unmanly discouragements, God lives, though our hero is dead."[24]

Presbyterian minister George William White also delivered a sermon "On the Death of Genl Stonewall Jackson" to one of the churches he pastored on the fourth Sunday in May and to the other on the first Sunday in June of 1863. White began with the text of II Samuel 3:38: "Know ye not that there is a prince and a great man fallen this day in Israel?" Across the Confederacy, White declared, "every heart has been afflicted." White told his congregation that "such an event as this is not without lessons of deep and solemn instruction. We cannot close our eyes to its teachings. It is indeed a deep mystery— one that we never, perhaps, in this life shall fully comprehend." That Jackson— "apparently so essential to the welfare of our country and so important to the prosperity of the church"—should be taken seemed "strange indeed." However, southern Christians, by reflecting upon Jackson's life and death, might "discover some glimpse of God's design and profit by so severe a lesson." What was the source of Jackson's greatness? White asked rhetorically. His greatness lay in "an inflexible will guided by the principles of religion." Jackson had both a "fixed purpose to do his duty in dependence upon God" and "a holy regard for God's glory." He feared that "our country would be guilty of the great sin of rendering that praise to man which was due to God." White quoted a letter written by Jackson in July 1862 after his successes in the Shenandoah Valley. Jackson wrote, "If people would but give all the glory to God and regard his creatures as but unworthy instruments, my heart would rejoice." This attitude made Jackson great, and although White knew that "men of the world" would not accept this analysis, he defied them to explain Jackson's success "on any other ground." After recounting Jackson's attributes and his successes, White concluded simply, "He honored God and God honored him."[25]

From Jackson's life, White turned to his death and the practical question, "What does this sad providence mean?" "That God hath done it," he continued, "none of us will doubt, who hold this book to be his word." The first great lesson to learn from all afflictions was "humble submission to the will of God." "However dark and mysterious the dispensation may be, however crushing and irreparable to human sight it may appear, yet if we can be still and know that it is God . . . then may we patiently wait his own solution of it, assured that he has purposes of wisdom in it which we shall yet be made to praise." Perhaps Jackson's death is "the harbinger of peace." Like Moses at the edge of the promised land, Jackson may have been called to heaven just as God's people were to enter the promised land.[26] Perhaps, but White saw instead in "this dark dispensation" a "solemn judgment." He believed it was "a stern reproof for our idolatrous regard for man." The result that Jackson feared most "has come to pass": "we have honored and gloried man and forgotten God." God removed Jackson and will "force us to see that it is not this hand or that, but by his own mighty power that we are to be delivered." White assured his listeners, however, that this judgment did not shake his confidence in the ultimate success of the Confederacy. "I do not see in it an evidence that God has forsaken us. His heaviest afflictions are often but fatherly chastisements." God "means not to forsake us, but he means to bring us to a more humble reliance upon his power and goodness." When Confederates acknowledge God in all their affairs, "then would we discern the light of a bright morning breaking through darkness." Unfortunately, however, White did not see such a spirit among southerners: "Do we not even hear murmurings against this very providence? Instead of being humbled are not the hearts of men filled with stubborn rebellion and a wicked questioning of God's ways." The South was filled with all manner of evil: "extortion, drunkenness, profanity, Sabbath breaking, dishonesty." White called on the southern people to recognize that "God is dealing with you for your sins" and to "put away sin, learn righteousness, and thus secure the independence and peace of your country." Then will "the sainted Jackson" look down upon "his ransomed country with a holy joy."[27]

Ramsey's and Dabney's sermons were printed and circulated in pamphlet form among soldiers and civilians. These sermons and the wartime biographies of Jackson were read and discussed by southern evangelicals as they pondered the meaning of Jackson's death. Jedediah Hotchkiss, Jackson's topographer, recalled attending a fast-day sermon in August 1863 in the Army of Northern Virginia's encampment. After the sermon by the Rev. B. T. Lacy, Hotchkiss and other staff officers discussed Dabney's memorial sermon on Jackson from which one of them read excerpts.[28]

While Ramsey, Dabney, and White offered their answers to the question "Why?" others were not as certain of the providential meaning of the hero's death. For the religious citizens of the Confederacy, Jackson was "the chosen standard bearer of liberty" and "the anointed of God to bring in deliverance for his oppressed Church and Country." Some feared that God had "taken the good man away from the evil to come"; because of their sins, southerners were unworthy of such a deliverer. Many, however, agreed with these ministers and told themselves that God intended to emphasize Jackson's Christian and military virtues by taking him in the zenith of his career and to teach the South to trust in no man, but in God alone. In February 1864, Chaplain John Paris expressed the hope, the resignation, and the renewed commitment that characterized most religious southerners' reaction to Jackson's life and death: "His very appearance seemed to be the presage of victory. He seemed like one sent by God. But God has seen proper in His providence to take him away, and whatsoever He doeth is right. Let us then bow to the hand that afflicts in such dispensations as this, take courage, and press onward." Armed with the assurances that God was chastising them for their sins (including the sin of idolizing Jackson) and that they would soon regain divine favor, Confederate Christians faced the next two years of civil warfare.[29]

Southerners endured repeated chastisements between May 1863 and April 1865—Gettysburg, Vicksburg, Chattanooga, Atlanta, Petersburg, and Appomattox. Even before the war ended, some ministers were developing a framework within which they could accommodate both the assurance of God's continued favor and the military defeat of the Confederacy. In April 1864, Baptist clergyman Thomas S. Dunaway warned a Virginia congregation against believing "an idea which I have heard some advance, when they say if our cause is just and right it will succeed in any event; and if it fail it is conclusive that our cause is a bad one, and God is displeased with our institutions." Dunaway insisted that "an accurate acquaintance with the ways of Providence as manifested in the scriptures, will disabuse our minds of this error." Failure did not imply God's final judgment. Rather, it might simply be part of his own "wise purposes" to "withhold success from his most faithful servants even in his own cause."[30]

The death of Leonidas Polk, Episcopalian bishop and Confederate general, again gave Confederate Christians cause to ponder God's purposes in the war. Polk was killed atop Pine Mountain, Georgia, on June 14, 1864 by federal artillery. Polk and Generals Joseph E. Johnston and William J. Hardee had ridden to the top of the hill to observe the position of General William Tecumseh Sherman's army in its advance through north Georgia toward Atlanta. As Polk approached the summit for a final look, a federal cannon shot hit him in the chest, killing him immediately. General Johnston declared in his announcement of Polk's death to the army: "The Christian, patriot, soldier, has neither lived nor died in vain. His example is before you; his mantle rests with you." Polk's funeral was held in Augusta, Georgia, where he was buried until the war ended. Bishop Stephen Elliott, who succeeded Polk as the Senior Bishop of the Protestant Episcopal Church in the Confederate States of America, declared that Polk died in the defense of a "holy cause" after having wielded his sword in "the battles of Religion and the Church" against the "hordes of lawless men" who filled the northern armies.[31]

When she learned of General Polk's death, Confederate nurse Kate Cumming wrote in her diary, "Another of our brightest and best has left us; a star has gone from earth to shine in the 'bright galaxy around God's throne.' When we see such taken from our midst, at a time when we have so much need of them, we think 'how unsearchable are the ways of the Lord!' " Cumming heard Dr. Charles T. Quintard preach a sermon on the subject, in which he declared that "these things are sent to remind us that we are not of this world, and that God makes it one of weariness; so we may lift our thoughts aloft and think of what is holy."[32]

Two years after Stonewall Jackson's death, southern evangelicals faced a far greater disaster: the death of their hopes for political independence. Defeat crushed the people of the South, and deeply perplexed religious Confederates.[33] They had been "taught in every Southern paper, and in almost every Southern pulpit, that the justice of the Southern cause must ensure its success." Now they faced overwhelming defeat. Anna Safford wrote in her diary, "When the news of Lee's surrender reached us, we could not believe it. It seemed such a tragic, thoroughly unbelieved-in termination—so dreadful—that we thought it incredible." "The South lies prostrate," seventeen-year-old Emma LeConte confided to her diary in Columbia, South Carolina, "there is no help. . . . Who could have believed who has watched this four years' struggle that it could have ended like this! They say *right* always triumphs, but what cause could have been more just than ours? Have we suffered all—have our brave men fought so desperately and died so nobly for *this*?" A month later, when remnants of the southern army had returned to Columbia, LeConte still found it hard to believe the Confederacy was no more: "The army is disbanded now— oh! Merciful God!—the hot tears rush into my eyes and I cannot write."[34]

Eliza Fain, who in 1863 castigated herself and other southerners for idolizing Jackson, wrote in her diary that the surrender of Lee's army "does not for one moment shake my confidence in my God as to the position which the South shall occupy amongst the nations of the earth when this struggle shall cease. She is not, I do feel, to be given up." Six days later, Fain was still certain of "our final triumph," but that success had been subtly transformed from a military into a moral victory: "Whether it is to be independence or not I cannot know but I do believe the honor and character of the South will be maintained before the nations of the earth. I feel God has not caused us to hope upon his holy words that all these hopes may perish. I feel he has not caused the ministry almost to a unit in all the different branches of his church to stand as they have done for the South, that all these precious hopes which they have been enabled to inspire in the hearts of their church members and soldiers are to perish." She concluded, "I feel it is of God and cannot die or fall." Fain and many other devout southerners initially had difficulty reconciling the failure of the Confederacy and the faithfulness of God. Since they could not change God's character, they redefined what success meant for God's people and dismissed the destruction of their hopes for political independence as a hard lesson in the mysterious workings of providence.[35]

The Rev. Moses Drury Hoge, Presbyterian pastor in Richmond, wrote to a close friend in May 1865: "The idolized expectation of a separate nationality, of a social life and literature and civilization of our own, together with a gospel guarded against the contamination of New England infidelity, all this has perished, and I feel like a shipwrecked mariner thrown up like a seaweed on a desert shore." He continued, "God's dark providence enwraps me like a pall; I cannot comprehend, but I will not charge him foolishly; I cannot explain, but I will not murmur. . . . I await the development of his providence, and I am thankful that I can implicitly believe that the end will show that all has been ordered in wisdom and love." Hoge, like other southerners, drew comfort from the Old Testament account of Job's righteous suffering. Like Job, he concluded, "Though he slay me, yet will I trust him." In September, he was still uncertain of God's purposes in the war: "I have not been very well since the surrender. . . . These inscrutable providences are like the half lines written in the palaces of the Cæsars—what is to come after will explain and complete their meaning."[36]

The Rappahannock Baptist Association gathered just six weeks after Lee's surrender to survey the remnants of their group of churches and begin anew. They were certain that "the sore trials through which we have passed and the darkness which now overshadows us are a part of the workings of Providence." Reflecting the common Confederate understanding of the war, they declared, "our severe chastisements . . . are ordained of God, as instruments to work for us a far more exceeding and eternal glory."[37] Like these Virginia Baptists, most religious southerners believed Hebrews 12:6–7 explained God's dealings with them: "For whom the Lord loveth he chasteneth, and scourgeth every son whom he receiveth. If ye endure chastening, God dealeth with you as with sons; for what son is he whom the father chasteneth not?" God loved the South even though he allowed them to be defeated. He had greater things planned for the South that southerners could not then comprehend, according to the scriptural promise, "all things work together for good to them that love God." They had to cling to faith when they lacked understanding.[38] The firm belief that the defeat of the Confederacy did not signal God's disapproval shaped white religious southerners' responses to life in the New South.

The primary duty of southern ministers and editors in 1865 and 1866 was to convince themselves and their congregations that God had not deserted the South. To accomplish this task, they assured their churches that the southern cause had been righteous, that their afflictions were God's chastisement rather than his judgment, and that God would eventually vindicate the South in some unknown way. The righteousness of the southern cause, the justice of God, and Confederate defeat could and would be reconciled.[39]

Near the end of 1865, a writer in the Baptist *Religious Herald* reflected on the providential meaning of Confederate defeat. Because Confederates were certain of the righteousness and the eventual triumph of their cause, "the blow that overthrew the Confederacy, shook their faith in the righteous providence of God." Something was obviously awry; "either the Confederate cause was wrong, or Providence does not always favor the right side." The author quickly revealed where the problem lay. "Believing that the Confederate cause was righteous, we need not have our confidence in Divine Providence shaken by its failure." Clearly, right did not invariably triumph over might. "That truth and righteousness will finally triumph, we have no doubt; but it is one of the mysteries of Providence, that in this world, and for a season, they are permitted to be obscured and perverted." In conclusion, "there is nothing in the issues of our late unhappy and ruinous war to change our views as to the rectitude of the Southern struggle for independence." The author examined the southern quest, and found it, on the whole, virtuous. It was their view of God's providence, not their purposes in the war, that Confederate Christians needed to reevaluate.[40]

The General Assembly of the Presbyterian Church in the Confederate States of America, meeting in Augusta, Georgia, in December 1865, assured southern Presbyterians that God had not forsaken them, just as they had done in May 1863 after Jackson's death. "Our national sins have aroused God's wrath, and caused Him to visit us with sore national calamities and bereavements." They must "cordially acquiesce in the dispensations of his inscrutable Providence," with the firm hope that God would pity his people and deliver them. Georgia Baptist S. G. Hillyer wrote to the *Christian Index*, "let us not falter in our faith, in this time of public and private calamity. Let us accept the chastenings of the Lord with all humility. They are the dealings of a father's hand. His love in the method of its manifestation, may be incomprehensible. But he is too wise to err, and too good to be unkind."[41]

Henry Holcomb Tucker, the editor of the *Christian Index*, admitted that "when the Southern Confederacy fell, thousands of hearts were crushed." To those men and women, the editor offered Christian consolation: "Whether you see the good that is to come of what has happened or not, is immaterial. God will be certain to subserve some grand purpose of mercy by it. The present result is not of man's doings. God is the author of his own providences." While many believed that "Providence had sent upon them an overwhelming calamity," they must not challenge God's will or lose faith in his plans: "The hand of the Lord is then in this thing. It is God who has done it. Will his saints complain? Do they doubt his wisdom? Do they question his goodness?" Instead of questioning God's decision in the conclusion of the war, southern Christians must accommodate themselves to their changed circumstances. If they refused to do so, they were "fighting against his providence, and disobeying the evident inclinations of his will." Tucker insisted that "the facts before us are the materials God has given us with which to operate, and to glorify him." In conclusion, Tucker wrote, "we may console ourselves with this even in what seems to us to be the darkest providences, that 'all things work together for good to them that love God'; so therefore comfort one another with these words."[42]

Although convinced that right did not always triumph, some southern Christians confidently expected future earthly, as well as heavenly, vindication. Presbyterian minister Benjamin Morgan Palmer, driven from New Orleans to Columbia, South Carolina, by the war, believed God would ultimately vindicate the southern cause. Even after Lee's surrender, Palmer encouraged his congregation with the hope of future deliverance. Emma LeConte wrote in her journal on April 23, 1865: "Dr. Palmer this morning preached a fine and encouraging sermon. He says we must not despair yet, but even if we should be overthrown—not conquered—the next generation would see the South *free* and independent." Brigadier General William Nelson Pendleton, later an Episcopal rector, wrote to his daughter about the subject in June 1865. Echoing pronouncements against idolizing Jackson, Pendleton suggested that God had allowed Confederate defeat because southerners had idolized their region. In the future, however, he expected God to allow them to achieve their independence. In his 1867 *Defence of Virginia, [And Through Her, of the South]*, Robert Lewis Dabney insisted that southern sins had led to the chastisement of Appomattox, just as earlier sins had led to the chastisement of Jackson's death. "A righteous God, for our sins toward Him, has permitted us to be overthrown by our enemies and His," Dabney concluded. Although southerners were "oppressed," they "suffer silently, disdaining to complain, and only raising to the chastening heavens, the cry, 'How long, O Lord?' "[43]

Shortly before his death in 1872, the Rev. William S. White, the minister who had been Jackson's pastor in Lexington and who had preached his funeral sermon, wrote his memoirs. Exemplifying the attitude of many southern Christians, White wrote with a mixture of hope and resignation: "Though persecuted, we will not be forsaken; though cast down, we will not be destroyed. God's purposes are hidden from mortal sight, but I rest calmly in the belief that these purposes will move steadily on to wise and beneficent results. . . . Forced back into a position from which we sought to escape, the mortified victims of a power we have hated, I bow reverently to God." [44]

In the aftermath of the war, Jackson's death took on new meaning as a crucial episode in the developing religious myth of the Lost Cause. In this myth, Jackson came to embody southern religious values, and his life and death were used to instruct the young and encourage the old. Only by emulating the virtues of Stonewall Jackson, Lost Cause advocates insisted, could the South retain its cultural identity and righteousness in the face of defeat. Some southerners explicitly connected Jackson's death with the defeat of the Confederacy through their choice of a date for Confederate Memorial Day. Many Deep South states recognized April 26, the date of General Joseph E. Johnston's surrender, but towns in North and South Carolina and some areas of Virginia chose May 10, the date of Jackson's death, as their Confederate Memorial Day.[45]

For southern Christians, neither the death of Stonewall Jackson nor the collapse of the Confederacy were indications of God's stern hand of judgment. Instead, these tribulations were signs of the Father's hand of chastening. This distinction was central to the Confederate understanding of the war and to the formation of the Lost Cause. The mysterious providence of God had a greater purpose for the South, which was beyond the pale of human understanding at the time. In both events, God was scolding white southerners for their sinfulness but not abandoning them. Religious southerners reenacted and extended their response to Stonewall Jackson's death in 1863 to comprehend defeat in 1865. These episodes illustrated the power of evangelical Christianity to support the Confederacy at war and to console the South in ruin.

Notes

1. Much has been written about the role of religion in supporting Confederate soldiers and civilians. See James W. Silver, *Confederate Morale and Church Propaganda* (Tuscaloosa, AL, 1957); Willard E. Wight, "The Churches and the Confederate Cause," *Civil War History* 6 (1960): 361–373; Sidney J. Romero, *Religion in the Rebel Ranks* (Lanham, MD, 1983); Richard E. Beringer et al., *Why the South Lost the Civil War* (Athens, GA, 1986); Gardiner H. Shattuck Jr., *A Shield and Hiding Place: The Religious Life of Civil War Armies* (Macon, GA, 1987); Drew Gilpin Faust, *The Creation of Confederate Nationalism: Ideology and Identity in the Civil War South* (Baton Rouge, 1988); and W. Harrison Daniel, *Southern Protestantism in the Confederacy* (Bedford, VA, 1989).

Charles Royster's fascinating study of the Civil War examines briefly the reaction among southerners to Jackson's death, but Royster's interpretation focuses on Sherman and Jackson as men who epitomized "the waging of successful war by drastic measures justified with claims to righteousness." This article explores the reaction to Jackson's death among religious southerners as a defining episode in later religious understandings of southern defeat and in the formation of the Lost Cause. Charles Royster, *The Destructive War: William Tecumseh Sherman, Stonewall Jackson, and the Americans* (New York, 1991; reprint, New York, 1993), xi.

The author wishes to thank Kurt Berends, John Fain, Robert K. Krick, and Bertram Wyatt-Brown for their assistance in the preparation of this article.

2. R. E. Wilbourn to John Esten Cooke, December 12, 1863, John Esten Cooke Scrapbook, #5295-E, John Esten Cooke Library, Alderman Library, University of Virginia, Charlottesville, VA; R. E. Lee to Thomas J. Jackson, May 4, 1863, in *The Wartime Papers of R. E. Lee*, ed. Clifford Dowdey (Boston, 1961), 452–453.

3. This account of Jackson's wounding and death is based on Hunter McGuire, "Death of Stonewall Jackson," in *The Confederate Soldier in the Civil War*, ed. John S.

Blay (Princeton, NJ, 1959), 158–160; Mary Anna Jackson, *Memoirs of Stonewall Jackson* (Louisville, KY, 1895), 427–464; Charles Royster, *The Destructive War*, 193–231; Byron Farwell, *Stonewall: A Biography of General Thomas J. Jackson* (New York, 1992), 506–530; Ernest B. Furgurson, *Chancellorsville, 1863: The Souls of the Brave* (New York, 1992), 212–215, 307–309, 324–329; and Robert K. Krick, "The Smoothbore Volley That Doomed the Confederacy," in *Chancellorsville: The Battle and Its Aftermath*, ed. Gary W. Gallagher (Chapel Hill, 1996), 107–142.

4. Sara Pryor, *Reminiscences of Peace and War* (New York, 1905), 243; Louise Fellowes to Mrs. Stonewall Jackson, August 14, 1863, Thomas J. Jackson Papers, Virginia Military Institute Archives, Lexington, VA. Northern Christians faced a similar crisis in the assassination of Abraham Lincoln shortly after Lee's surrender. Christians in the North reacted to Lincoln's death on Good Friday, 1865, in much the same way that Confederate Christians had responded to Jackson's death. Some ministers believed that this act of providence was inscrutable, but would ultimately produce some larger blessing. Some saw this mysterious providence as a chastisement by God for idolizing Lincoln or for other sins. Others thought that Lincoln's death would make his influence greater. These similarities emphasize the common evangelical outlook that Christians in the North and the South shared. The contexts of the two deaths, however, were very different. Lincoln's death came at the end of the conflict with a Union victory. Within two months after Jackson's death, Confederates faced Vicksburg and Gettysburg; within two months after Lincoln's death, all Confederate armies had surrendered and the Union was restored. Therefore, the theological implications of Jackson's death became central to southern Christians' understanding of the war itself. In contrast, Lincoln's death was of secondary importance within northern evangelicals' interpretation of the meaning of the conflict. David B. Chesebrough, *"No Sorrow Like Our Sorrow": Northern Protestant Ministers and the Assassination of Lincoln* (Kent, OH, 1994), 66–78; Thomas Reed Turner, *Beware the People Weeping: Public Opinion and the Assassination of Abraham Lincoln* (Baton Rouge, 1982), 77–89; Reid Mitchell, *Civil War Soldiers: Their Expectations and Their Experiences* (New York, 1988), 199–200.

5. Henry Kyd Douglas, *I Rode with Stonewall* (Chapel Hill, 1940), 243; Fanny B. Graham to M. A. Jackson, June 20, 1863, Mary Anna Jackson Papers, Humanities Research Center, University of Texas at Austin.

6. John O. Casler, *Four Years in the Stonewall Brigade* (Girard, KS, 1906), 153; Kate Peddy to George W. Peddy, May 12, 1863, in *Saddlebag and Spinning Wheel, being the Civil War Letters of George W. Peddy, M.D., and his wife Kate Featherston Peddy*, ed. George Peddy Cuttino (Macon, GA, 1981); Fred Fleet to Dr. Benjamin Fleet, May 12, 1863, in *Green Mount: A Virginia Plantation Family During the Civil War: Being the Journal of Benjamin Robert Fleet and Letters of His Family*, eds. Betsy Fleet and John D. P. Fuller (Lexington, KY, 1962), 229; John Q. Anderson, ed., *Brokenburn: The Journal of Kate Stone, 1861–1868* (Baton Rouge, 1972), 211. See also Marion Hill Fitzpatrick to Amanda Fitzpatrick, May 16, 1863, in Henry Mansel Hammock, comp., *Letters to Amanda, 1862–1865* (Culloden, GA, 1976).

7. Casler, *Four Years in the Stonewall Brigade*, 153–154; John N. Opie, *A Rebel Cavalryman with Lee, Stuart, and Jackson* (Chicago, 1899; reprint, Dayton, OH, 1972), 144.

8. Pryor, *Reminiscences of Peace and War*, 243; Opie, *A Rebel Cavalryman with Lee, Stuart, and Jackson*, 144; James I. Robertson Jr., ed., *One of Jackson's Foot Cavalry* (Jackson, TN, 1964), 102.

9. Thomas Smyth, *The Battle of Fort Sumter: Its Mystery and Miracle: God's Mastery and Mercy* (Columbia, SC, 1861), 9, 10, 23; Ronald Glenn Lee, "Exploded Graces:

Providence and the Confederate Israel in Evangelical Southern Sermons, 1861–1865," M.A. thesis, Rice University, 1990, 138–139. See also Robert Lewis Dabney, "Publick Calamities Caused by Publick Sins: A Sermon," May 12, 1862, Robert Lewis Dabney Papers, Union Theological Seminary, Richmond, VA.

10. Robert Lewis Dabney, *The Life and Campaigns of Lieut.-Gen. Thomas J. Jackson* (New York, 1866), 727–728; James B. Ramsey, *True Eminence Founded on Holiness: A Discourse Occasioned by the Death of Lieut. Gen. T. J. Jackson* (Lynchburg, VA, 1863), 19. Dabney's biography was originally published in two volumes in 1864 and 1866 in London by J. Nisbet & Co. A Confederate version was to be published in 1865 in North Carolina, but the work was never finished.

11. Richard Barksdale Harwell, ed., *Kate: The Journal of a Confederate Nurse* (Baton Rouge, 1959), 103. The passage Cumming quoted was Romans 11:33–34. Cumming likened Jackson's death at the hands of his own men to the biblical story of Jephtha's sacrificing his daughter. See Judges 11:30–40.

12. *Biblical Recorder* (Richmond, VA), May 20, 1863.

13. "Funeral of Lieut. General T. J. Jackson," *Lexington* (VA) *Gazette*, May 20, 1863; Jackson, *Memoirs of Stonewall Jackson*, 463–464; Elizabeth Preston Allan, *The Life and Letters of Margaret Junkin Preston* (New York, 1903), 166.

14. Thomas L. Connelly, *The Marble Man: Robert E. Lee and His Image in American Society* (New York, 1977), 25; Gaines M. Foster, *Ghosts of the Confederacy: Defeat, the Lost Cause, and the Emergence of the New South* (New York, 1987), 59; Charles Reagan Wilson, *Baptized in Blood: The Religion of the Lost Cause, 1865–1920* (Athens, GA, 1980), 1. For an examination of how funerals reflect changing southern culture, see Charles Reagan Wilson, "The Death of Southern Heroes: Historic Funerals of the South," *Southern Cultures* 1 (Fall 1994): 3–22.

15. Entry for May 17, 1863, Annie G. Baker Diary, 1863–1866, Presbyterian Church (U.S.A.) Department of History, Montreat, NC; entry for May 17, 1863, Eliza Rhea Anderson Fain Diaries, John N. Fain Collection, McClung Historical Collection, Knox County Public Library System, Knoxville, TN.

16. General Assembly of the Presbyterian Church in the Confederate States of America, *Minutes*, 1863 (Columbia, SC, 1863), 153. Presbyterians were not alone in their grief; all southern evangelicals felt a profound sense of loss. Delegates to the Southern Baptist Convention were assembled in Augusta, Georgia, when they learned of Jackson's death. Dr. J. L. Reynolds, the vice president of the convention, stated that "our hearts have been pained this morning by the announcement of the death of that great favorite of the people, and what is more, the friend of God, General Jackson." He asked another minister to lead in prayer "in reference to this sad event." Southern Baptist Convention, *Proceedings of the Ninth Biennial Session*, 1863 (Macon, GA, 1863), 17.

17. *Christian Observer* (Richmond, VA), May 21, 1863.

18. Allan, *Life and Letters of Margaret Junkin Preston*, 165; entry for May 17 1863, Eliza Rhea Anderson Fain Diaries; William Pegram to sister, May 11, 1863, Pegram-Johnson-McIntosh Papers, Virginia Historical Society, Richmond, VA; Alfred A. Watson, *Sermon Delivered Before the Annual Council of the Diocese of North Carolina* (Raleigh, NC, 1863), 23; *Christian Index* (Macon, GA), May 18, 1863.

19. P. W. Alexander, "Confederate Chieftains," *Southern Literary Messenger* 35 (January 1863), 37; Marietta Minnigerode Andrews, ed., *Scraps of Paper* (New York, 1929), 75; Fanny B. Graham to M. A. Jackson, June 20, 1863, Mary Anna Jackson Papers (emphasis in the original); M. Deeves, *Stonewall's Requiem*, in Paul Glass, comp., *Singing Soldiers, The Spirit of the Sixties: A History of the Civil War in Song* (New York, 1968; reprint, New York, 1975), 203–205; Casler, *Four Years in the Stonewall Brigade*,

155; James Dabney McCabe, *The Life of Thomas J. Jackson, by an Ex-Cadet*, 2nd ed. (Richmond, VA, 1864), 191.

20. R. E. Lee to Mrs. Lee, May 11, 1863, in Robert E. Lee, *Recollections and Letters of General Robert E. Lee* (Garden City, NJ, 1924), 94; Mrs. Mary Jones to Col. Charles C. Jones Jr., May 19, 1863, in *The Children of Pride: A True Story of Georgia and the Civil War*, ed. Robert Manson Myers (New Haven, CT, 1972), 1063; Fred Fleet to Dr. Benjamin Fleet, May 12, 1863, in Fleet and Fuller, eds., *Green Mount*, 229. See also *Christian Observer*, May 14, 1863.

21. Francis H. Smith, *Discourse on the Life and Character of Lt. Gen. Thos. J. Jackson* (Richmond, VA, 1863), 7; Mrs. Mary Jones to Col. Charles C. Jones Jr., September 18, 1863, in Myers, ed., *The Children of Pride*, 1100; E. W. W., "In Memoriam," May 15, 1863, Thomas J. Jackson Papers, Virginia Military Institute Archives; Dabney, *The Life and Campaigns of Lieut.-Gen. Thomas J. Jackson*, 728. See also *Christian Observer*, May 28, 1863.

22. Herman Melville, *Battle-Pieces and Aspects of the War* (Gainesville, FL, 1960), 79–80; Oliver Otis Howard to Roland B. Howard, May 16, 1863, Howard Papers, Bowdoin College, Brunswick, ME, quoted in Royster, *The Destructive War*, 213; Oliver O. Howard, "The Eleventh Corps at Chancellorsville," in *Battles and Leaders of the Civil War*, eds. Robert Underwood Johnson and Clarence Clough Buel (New York, 1884–1888), 3: 202; *The Independent*, New York, May 14, 1863.

23. Ramsey, *True Eminence Founded on Holiness*, 9, 14, 18–19, 21.

24. Robert Lewis Dabney, *True Courage: A Discourse Commemorative of Lieut. General Thomas J. Jackson* (Richmond, VA, 1863), 22–23.

25. George William White, "On the Death of Genl Stonewall Jackson," sermon delivered in May and June 1863, George William White Collection, Presbyterian Church (U.S.A.) Department of History, Montreat, NC, 1–2, 7, 11–13, 18.

26. John Randolph Tucker, the attorney general of Virginia, used the same imagery in his lecture to the Young Men's Christian Association of Richmond on May 21, 1863: "this Moses of our host, from Pisgah's top, looking to and hoping for the independence of his nation, but doomed, without reaching and enjoying it, to die in 'The Wilderness;' resigned his mighty soul to heaven; met its solemn decree, with the trustful words, 'It is all right;' and left the glorious heritage of his name to the Christian Church and to his weeping country!" John Randolph Tucker, *The Southern Church Justified in its Support of the South in the Present War: A Lecture Delivered Before the Young Men's Christian Association of Richmond* (Richmond, VA, 1863), 33.

27. White, "On the Death of Genl Stonewall Jackson," 18–23.

28. Archie P. McDonald, ed., *Make Me a Map of the Valley: The Civil War Journal of Stonewall Jackson's Topographer* (Dallas, TX, 1973), 169.

29. A Virginia [John Esten Cooke], *The Life of Stonewall Jackson* (Richmond, VA, 1863), 1; Dabney, *The Life and Campaigns of Lieut.-Gen. Thomas J. Jackson*, 727; John Paris, *A Sermon Preached Before Brig.-Gen. Hoke's Brigade, at Kinston, N.C., on the 28th of February, 1864, By Rev. John Paris, Chaplain Fifty-Fourth Regiment N.C. Troops, Upon the Death of Twenty-Two Men, Who had been Executed in the Presence of the Brigade for the Crime of Desertion* (Greensborough, NC, 1864), 14.

30. Thomas S. Dunaway, *A Sermon Delivered by Elder Thomas S. Dunaway, of Lancaster County Virginia, before Coan Baptist Church, in Connection with a Day of National Fasting, Humiliation and Prayer, April 1864* (Richmond, VA, 1864), 18. Dunaway's sermon should not be interpreted as defeatist. Although he insisted that "the cruel war now waged against us, in the Providence of God, is a punishment for our sins," Dunaway was confident that if southerners would repent, God would forgive

them and uphold their independence. In contrast, the authors of *Why the South Lost the Civil War* insist that as the war began to turn against the South, evangelical Christianity undermined southerners' will to fight in what was obviously a cause forsaken by God. Richard E. Beringer et al., *Why the South Lost the Civil War*, 336–367, 427.

31. Joseph H. Parks, *General Leonidas Polk, C.S.A.: The Fighting Bishop* (Baton Rouge, 1962), 382–383; *The War of the Rebellion: A Compilation of the Official Records of the Union and Confederate Armies*, series 1, 38, pt. 4, 776; Stephen Elliott, *Funeral Services at the Burial of the Right Rev. Leonidas Polk, D.D.* (Columbia, SC, 1864), 12, 17.

32. Harwell, *Kate*, 205–206.

33. For the postwar efforts of white southerners to come to terms with defeat, see Daniel W. Stowell, *Rebuilding Zion: The Religious Reconstruction of the South, 1863–1877* (New York, 1998), 33–48; Charles Reagan Wilson, *Baptized in Blood*; Gaines M. Foster, *Ghosts of the Confederacy*; and Thomas L. Connelly and Barbara L. Bellows, *God and General Longstreet: The Lost Cause and the Southern Mind* (Baton Rouge, 1982).

34. "The Scepticism Engendered by the War," *Christian Index*, January 13, 1866; Anna C. Safford diary, Safford Family Papers, Presbyterian Church (U.S.A.) Department of History, Montreat, NC; Earl Schenck Miers, ed., *When the World Ended: The Diary of Emma LeConte* (Lincoln, NE, 1987), 90, 99.

35. Entries for April 13 and 19, 1865, Eliza Rhea Anderson Fain Diaries.

36. Peyton Harrison Hoge, *Moses Drury Hoge: Life and Letters* (Richmond, VA, 1899), 235–237. Confederate Vice President Alexander H. Stephens, imprisoned in the North, also drew comfort from the biblical account of Job's struggle to understand why God was allowing such affliction to befall him. In late June he wrote in his prison journal, "My before-breakfast reading was from Job—a favorite book with me. I have read Job oftener than any other book in the Bible, except perhaps St. John." Myrta Lockett Avary, ed., *Recollections of Alexander H. Stephens* (New York, 1910), 262.

37. Rappahannock Baptist Association, Mss. Minutes, 1865, Virginia Baptist Historical Society, Richmond, VA, quoted in W. Harrison Daniel, "Southern Protestantism—1861 and After," *Civil War History* 5 (September 1959): 276–282.

38. See "Religious Literature for the South," *Christian Index*, January 13, 1866.

39. Rufus B. Spain, *At Ease in Zion: A Social History of Southern Baptists, 1865–1900* (Nashville, TN, 1967).

40. "The Scepticism Engendered by the War," *Christian Index*, January 13, 1866.

41. "Narrative of the State of Religion," General Assembly of the Presbyterian Church in the United States, *Minutes*, 1865, 380–381; S. G. Hillyer, "To the Baptists of Georgia," *Christian Index*, November 9, 1865.

42. "All Things Work Together for Good to Them that Love God," *Christian Index*, January 13, 1866. In November 1865, the *Christian Index* reported revivals among Georgia's country churches and concluded, "We should feel grateful for this evidence that the Divine favor is still graciously left to us." "Revivals in Georgia," *Christian Index*, November 9, 1865.

43. Miers, ed., *When the World Ended*, 95; William Nelson Pendleton to daughter, June 12, 1865, in *Memoirs of William Nelson Pendleton*, ed. Susan Pendleton Lee (Philadelphia, 1893), 415; Robert Lewis Dabney, *A Defence of Virginia, [And Through Her, of the South]* (New York, 1867), 356. See also Charles Reagan Wilson, *Baptized in Blood*, 73–74. For the personal turmoil that overwhelmed Dabney with Confederate defeat, see Charles Reagan Wilson, "Robert Lewis Dabney: Religion and the Southern Holocaust," *Virginia Magazine of History and Biography* 89 (January 1981): 79–89. Gardiner H. Shattuck Jr. rightly draws attention to a group of conservatives in the New South, of whom Dabney was one of the most prominent, who "utterly refused to compromise their

antebellum principles." They, unlike fellow evangelicals such as J. William Jones and Atticus Haygood, were never able to embrace the New South creed and sectional reconciliation. Shattuck concludes that: "Defeat in the war, after all, triggered much soul-searching among religious southern whites." Most southerners, however, seem to have embraced parts of both schools of thought. Few brooded as long or as deeply about Confederate defeat as did Dabney. Most considered defeat to be divine chastisement, and they moved on to reconstruct the South politically, socially, economically, and religiously. They did not thereby reject the righteousness of either slavery or secession. Gardiner H. Shattuck Jr., " 'Appomattox as a Day of Blessing': Religious Interpretations of Confederate Defeat in the New South Era," *Journal of Confederate History* 7 (1991): 3.

44. H. M. White, ed., *Rev. William S. White, D. D., and His Times: An Autobiography* (Richmond, VA, 1891), 198.

45. Charles Reagan Wilson, *Baptized in Blood*, 37–57; Gaines M. Foster, *Ghosts of the Confederacy*, 42. See also "The Last Hours of Stonewall Jackson," *Christian Advocate*, February 27, 1886; J. William Jones, "Reminiscences of Stonewall Jackson," *Confederate Veteran* 1 (April 1893): 108–110; J. William Jones, "Worked His Way Through: How a Poor Orphan Boy Becomes One of the Immortals," *Confederate Veteran* 9 (December 1901): 535–537.

9

Lincoln's Sermon on the Mount

The Second Inaugural

RONALD C. WHITE, JR.

S ince Abraham Lincoln's death more words have been wasted on the question of his religion than any other aspect of his life." So wrote Richard N. Current in 1945.[1] Current delivered this verdict as the study of Abraham Lincoln was finally assuming its place in the professional discipline of history, and judging by the scholarship over the past fifty years, his criticism might hold today.[2] But such a judgment about what others have said about Lincoln's religion should not distract attention from what Lincoln actually said about religion and the ways religious values and images informed his ideas about the character of the Union.[3]

Lincoln's religion, in fact, laid a foundation for his political thinking. The culmination of Lincoln's religion was his attempt to discern the meaning of the Civil War. Even though there is widespread evidence that in his presidential years Lincoln was embracing a faith that would sustain him in times of stress and grief, the bulk of his reflection about the meaning of God and faith evolved in the context of the political questions and issues of the Civil War. Sometimes this reflection was done in private, as in his "Meditation on the Divine Will," written in the summer of 1862 after a crushing Union military defeat. Most often it was worked out in public addresses and comments. What strikes the modern reader is not that Lincoln was sure he knew the will of what he called a "living God," but rather that he was continually wrestling, often out loud and in public, with the meaning and manner of a God whom he became increasingly certain acted in history.[4]

Lincoln's Second Inaugural Address, which he regarded as his best speech, was in several ways the prism through which he refracted his understanding of the involvement of God in history. In the Second Inaugural, Lincoln's mature biblical and theological insights show through as they illuminate his message to a nation approaching the end of its most grievous internal struggle. It is fascinating but futile to speculate on the trajectory of Lincoln's thoughts about religion and politics after the Civil War. Already in 1864 Lincoln was looking forward to peace and reconstruction. His speech spoke to those concerns. As the final major address of the martyred president, his Second Inaugural became for many contemporaries Lincoln's last will and testament to the American nation. It provided a framework for Andrew Johnson's policy of reconciliation after the war and the Radical Republicans' insistence that binding the nation's wounds meant justice for the freedmen had to be done. The religious cast in Lincoln's address gave it a power and authority after the war that few public papers have commanded.

Any analysis of Lincoln's public religion must include the question: Was he using religious words simply for public consumption? William H. Herndon, Lincoln's law partner in Springfield, first charged that Lincoln's public religion was the offering of an astute politician. Herndon argued that Lincoln's use of religious ideas and language was calculated to strike a responsive chord. This thesis has been suggested and augmented by others down through the years. In modern dress, the argument would be that Lincoln used religious language in the same way that many used it in the Christianized culture of his era. As a literate speaker, Lincoln drew on biblical images and language as a source of the metaphors that populated his addresses. Yes, he valued the Bible as a literary source of great wisdom, so the argument goes, but so have many other astute politicians, then and now.

Herndon's charge may be more on the mark about contemporary political leaders. We look back at Lincoln with ears that have come to anticipate as routine "God bless America" as an expected benediction in the addresses of presidents and political candidates. Lincoln, on the other hand, was much less assured about God blessing America. He was continually striving to discern exactly how God was dealing, in both judgment and redemption, with the United States.

The temptation at this point is to move directly to the text. To do so, however, would be to miss the context. To prepare ourselves to *hear* the Second Inaugural in fresh ways, we need to use historical imagination and place ourselves with those who were coming to Washington on March 4, 1865.

Context

Washington had never seen so many people. All through the week, delegations arrived from every part of the country. Hotels were full and overflowing. Firehouses offered extra sleeping spaces.

On the eve of Lincoln's Second Inauguration, the sixteenth president had every reason to be encouraged. Despite his mood of resignation in August 1864 that he would be defeated for reelection, Lincoln had won by more than 400,000 votes over his Democratic opponent, General George McClellan. The

election 1864

electoral vote total was more convincing—221 for Lincoln and only 21 for Mc-Clellan.

As the day of the Second Inaugural drew near, news from the battlefront was promising. On February 1, Sherman led 60,000 troops out of Savannah to South Carolina, the seedbed of secession. In Washington, on February 22, Lincoln ordered a night illumination of the Capitol. Crowds in song celebrated victories in Columbia, Charleston, and Wilmington. Grant had Lee so contained near Richmond that the Confederacy had no possibility of sending troops to stop the advance of Sherman. Everything pointed toward victory. How would Lincoln address this auspicious moment?

On Friday evening, March 3, a dense fog descended over the city. The Senate had been meeting all day and now determined to continue its session into the evening. The session did not conclude until seven o'clock in the morning. Government officials were weary from four long years of war. The agony of numerous battles was taking its toll. Many citizens were filled more with anger than hope as spring approached in 1865.

Rumors flew about the capital that desperate Confederates, now realizing that defeat was imminent, would attempt to abduct or assassinate the president. Edwin M. Stanton, secretary of war, took extraordinary precautions. He ordered guards stationed at all entrances to the city. Sharpshooters were posted on the buildings ringing the inaugural ceremonies. Plainclothes detectives roamed the capital, keeping track of all suspicious persons.

On March 4, amid an incessant rain, a crowd numbering between 30,000 and 40,000 began arriving for the ceremonies. For the first time in thirty-two years, a president would be inaugurated for a second term. The rain stopped at 9:30, but started again an hour later. Ten inches of mud covered the unpaved streets. Because of the rain and mud, thought had been given to constructing bridges across important streets but the idea was abandoned. Noah Brooks, correspondent for the *Sacramento Bee*, wrote that women were "bedraggled and drenched," their "crinoline smashed, skirts bedaubed, and velvet, laces and such dry goods streaked with mud from end to end."[5]

At twelve noon, President Abraham Lincoln traveled by carriage up Pennsylvania Avenue to the Capitol. Lincoln saw what no president before him had seen: the new iron dome of the Capitol towering above the crowd. Armed Liberty, the nineteen-foot bronze statue that had been placed on the dome in December, looked down upon an inaugural ceremony, seemingly blessing the moment with her outstretched arms.

As Lincoln took his place on the inaugural platform that extended out from the East Front of the Capitol, the immense crowd grew hushed. Behind Lincoln sat a bevy of government officials. In front of him, in the crowd, he recognized Frederick Douglass, the notable African-American leader whom he admired. Up behind the right buttress stood the actor John Wilkes Booth, whom Lincoln had seen perform at Ford's Theater the previous November. Other dignitaries and well-known Washington figures crowded the scene.

When Lincoln was introduced, cheers went up and flags waved. Journalist

Brooks reported that "a roar of applause shook the air." After taking the presidential oath to begin a second term, the fifty-six-year-old Lincoln stepped to the podium to deliver his Second Inaugural Address. Noted Washington camera artist Alexander Gardner was poised to record for posterity the only occasion in which Lincoln was photographed delivering a speech. The president held a half sheet of foolscap on which his address was printed in two columns.[6] As Lincoln began his address, the sun broke through the overcast skies, flooding "the spectacle with glory and with light."[7]

We pause to inspect the historical setting for two reasons. First, the context for the Second Inaugural usually has been overlooked or forgotten when evaluating the address. This is in marked contrast to the Gettysburg Address, where the battlefield setting and soldiers' cemetery have been central to any reckoning of Lincoln's words. Second, the scene suggests a quite different kind of address than what Lincoln delivered. Only when we place ourselves within the setting can we appreciate the surprising content of Lincoln's words. When we remember that many newspapers were unimpressed or were critical of the president's remarks, we are more able to consider how much his remarks were in direct contrast to the expectations of his assembled audience.

Most people came to the inaugural events expecting that the bugle sounds of marching soldiers would be accompanied by the trumpet sounds of an inaugural address. Surely Lincoln would meet these expectations with victorious words over a soon to be vanquished foe. The inaugural seemed the moment for vindication, for the Union and for the president. This day was surely the occasion for the celebration of recent military victories by Grant and Sherman. Many expected harsh punishment to follow on the conclusion of the war. If this speech was the occasion to look to the future, now was the opportunity for Lincoln to lay out the public policy that he would be undertaking at the conclusion of the war.

At the end of a long and bitter civil war, all of these expectations were present that blustery morning of March 4. Lincoln did not satisfy the assembled masses with his speech. His Second Inaugural Address caught most of his hearers by surprise by offering a benediction more than a renewed call to arms. The speech's brevity alone diminished its immediate effect on a loyal Protestant people raised on soaring sermons that gained conviction as they rose in tempo and reference to Scripture. The crowd wanted more than the few words Lincoln gave them, and no doubt their unfulfilled expectations muted their ability to understand what Lincoln said that day.

Text

The Second Inaugural Address consists of seven hundred one words in twenty-five sentences arranged in four paragraphs. It is the second shortest inaugural address in United States history.[8] By way of contrast, the First Inaugural Address was 3,700 words. The shortness of the speech thus gives extra weight to each word in it. In his remarkably brief Second Inaugural, Lincoln mentions

God fourteen times and he refers to prayer three times. Lincoln quotes or paraphrases passages from the Bible four times. Counting up the references to God, however, does not begin to explain the meaning of Lincoln's words.

Lincoln commences the Second Inaugural Address in a diminished key, almost as if he wants to lower expectations and reduce the tensions surrounding the inaugural events. He begins:

> Fellow Countrymen:
>
> At this second appearing to take the oath of the presidential office, there is less occasion for an extended address than there was at the first. Then a statement, somewhat in detail, of a course to be pursued, seemed fitting and proper. Now, at the expiration of four years, during which public declarations have been constantly called forth on every point and phase of the great contest which still absorbs the attention, and engrosses the energies of the nation, little that is new could be presented. The progress of our arms, upon which all else chiefly depends, is as well known to the public as to myself, and it is, I trust, reasonably satisfactory and encouraging to all. With high hope for the future, no prediction in regard to it is ventured.

The speech opens in an impersonal style, summarizing events as if Lincoln were more a chronicler than a president. He uses the pronouns *I* and *myself* in the first paragraph, but uses no more personal pronouns in the entire speech. Rather, Lincoln directs the focus of his remarks away from himself by speaking in a passive voice. Avoiding the active voice sets up a paradigm that Lincoln follows throughout the address. And as rhetorician Lois J. Einhorn argues, that syntax and rhetoric "implied" that Lincoln was "a passive President who is being acted upon rather than being an active participant in the events of the past four years."[9] Also significant is that the first paragraph contains the only mention of the course of battle and is neither predictive nor self-congratulatory.

The second paragraph, which makes the transition into the main body of the speech, begins the shift in tone and content that will give this address its singular and memorable meaning.

> On the occasion corresponding to this four years ago, all thoughts were anxiously directed to an impending civil-war. All dreaded it—all sought to avert it. While the inaugural address was being delivered from this place, devoted altogether to saving the Union without war, insurgent agents were in the city seeking to destroy it without war—seeking to dissolve the Union, and divide effects, by negotiation. Both parties deprecated war, but one of them would make war rather than let the nation survive; and the other would accept war rather than let it perish. And the war came.

This paragraph is a marked divergence from the approach of the First Inaugural. In that address Lincoln said to those who would secede: "In your hands, my dissatisfied fellow countrymen, and not in mine, is the momentous issue of civil war." To be sure, in the last paragraph Lincoln invokes "the mystic chords of memory" and "the better angels of our nature" to reach out in the hope that reconciliation could yet be realized. But Lincoln still assigned blame to leaders in the South for starting the Union down the road to disunion.[10]

This second paragraph is dominated by inclusive language: "All dreaded it . . . all sought to avert it . . . both parties deprecated war." Now, after four years of terrible war, Lincoln does not assign blame. He signals that already, before the war has drawn to a close, the time has come to think about peace and reconciliation. Again, by what Lincoln does not say we become expectant of what he will say.

"And the war came." The second paragraph concludes with an astounding sentence. In this brief, understated sentence, Lincoln acknowledges that the war came in spite of the best intentions of the leaders of the land. And when the war came, it took its own course. Great generals might believe they were managing war, but human agency alone did not decide the outcome or even the character of the war. As Lincoln looked back from the perspective of four long years, he saw that all along the war had a life of its own.

This sentence is both a transition and a foreshadowing. "The war came" lifts the conflict beyond mere human instrumentality. It suggests that no mortal being, not even the commander-in-chief, can control the fortunes of war. Lincoln wants the audience to understand that this war cannot be understood simply as the fulfillment of human plans. How, then should one grasp the purpose of the war? We are now at the body of the address.

The third paragraph begins:

> One eighth of the whole population were colored slaves, not distributed generally over the Union, but localized in the Southern part of it. These slaves constituted a peculiar and powerful interest. All knew that this interest was, somehow, the cause of the war. To strengthen, perpetuate, and extend this interest was the object for which the insurgents would rend the Union, even by war, while the government claimed no right to do more than to restrict the territorial enlargement of it.

Lincoln states that slavery is the cause of the war. "Somehow." The "somehow" is the key that holds the four sentences in equilibrium. The "somehow" qualifies the assertion that "all knew" that slavery was the cause of the war. What does he mean? Lincoln is intimating that the North, even when it spoke of defending the Union, knew that slavery was the key moral issue underneath its political rhetoric. He is suggesting that the South, even when it spoke of the right to be independent, knew that slavery was foundational to its way of life. Lincoln is at his most argumentative—though quite mild in tone—when repeating his often-heard contention that, regarding slavery, "the government claimed no right to do more than to restrict the territorial enlargement of it."

> Neither party expected for the war, the magnitude, or the duration, which it has already attained. Neither anticipated that the cause of the conflict might cease with, or even before, the conflict itself should cease. Each side looked for an easier triumph, and a result less fundamental and astounding.

Lincoln structures this paragraph so that it builds in a crescendo of anticipation. "Neither party expected. . . . Neither anticipated. . . . Each looked for an easier triumph." Lincoln's use of parallel structures conveys his underlying message that both sides have shared values and attitudes.

In the third paragraph, we enter the heart of Lincoln's theological thinking about the Civil War. Central to the Puritan dilemma was how to sort out and combine divine and human initiative. Eleven months before the Second Inaugural, on April 4, 1864, Lincoln had pondered the dilemma of historical causation in a letter to Albert G. Hodges, editor of the Frankfort, Kentucky, *Commonwealth*. Lincoln wrote: "At the end of three years struggle the national condition is not what either party, or any man devised, or expected."[11] Not quite one year later, Lincoln picks up this same theme. He is here laying a foundation for a fundamental assertion. Lincoln's public religion usually addressed questions about both the nature of humanity and the nature of God. He begins this discussion by laying the groundwork for his understanding of the finitude of human judgment. In a masterful rhetorical passage, Lincoln points up the irony that both sides failed to understand adequately both the cause and the result of the civil strife.

The story of war is usually written by the victors. Many in the audience might have expected Lincoln to offer assurances that God was on the side of the Union. Instead, after a series of parallelisms that are characteristic of his speaking style, Lincoln asks rather than answers. No sentence is framed grammatically as a question, but it is clear that Lincoln, as President, is asking where God is in the public realm.

> Both read the same Bible, and pray to the same God; and each invokes His aid against the other.

With these words Lincoln appears to be offering approval. But there is more here than affirmation. Two and a half years earlier, at a time of "bitterest anguish" after the Union army's defeat at the second battle of Bull Run, Lincoln wrote out for himself a "Meditation on the Divine Will." In this private musing, in one of the darkest moments of the war, Lincoln strained to see the light of God's purposes. In the second sentence of the "Meditation," Lincoln notes, "In great contests each party claims to act in accordance with the will of God." Lincoln, conscious of the jingoism on both sides, wryly observes, "Both may be, and one must be wrong. God can not be for, and against the same thing at the same time."[12] The Second Inaugural makes this general observation more concrete by invoking the image of soldiers reading the same Bible and praying to the same God.

> It may seem strange that any men should dare to ask a just God's assistance in wringing their bread from the sweat of other men's faces; but let us judge not that we be not judged.

The crescendo builds to an irony. Implicit in this address, as in many of Lincoln's public discourses, is a profound doctrine of human nature. Lincoln, after years in his dual career as lawyer and politician, offers an assessment of human nature that is aware of both pretension and possibility.

Early in the Second Inaugural, the focus is on pretension. Lincoln points out how "strange" it is that "any men," should ask "a just God" to be on their side. As Lincoln's religious life and insight matures in the presidency, he maintains a lover's quarrel with the religious traditions that intersected his life. Whether Separate Baptist or Old School Presbyterianism, Lincoln was acutely aware that religion, precisely because of its appeal to the absolute, is capable of the most maniacal pretension by clothing limited causes with ultimate sanction.

Lincoln poses this irony by invoking the first of several biblical passages to be used in the address. Rhetorician Michael Leff observes that this is the critical turning point in the speech seen as an artistic whole. Until now Lincoln has "remained strictly within the confines of secular events." From this point forward "virtually every sentence quotes, paraphrases, or alludes to a passage in scripture." In this case, Lincoln appropriates a favorite biblical allusion—Genesis 3:19, in which God orders Adam and Eve out of the garden of Eden—to build his case for the renunciation of slavery. This biblical figure of speech raises the ante about who is man and woman and who is God. Its translation in antebellum America was that white persons were saying to black persons: you work and I will eat. However pretentious this attitude is, it becomes more so when appeal or defense is made in the name of a "just God."

Most of the scholarship about Lincoln's religion has focused on inheritance. In attempting to understand Lincoln, authors have sifted competing heritages. How to assess the influence of Lincoln's father's Separate Baptist tradition? What about the youthful Abe's readings of Voltaire, Paine, and Volney in his New Salem years? Not as much attention has been paid to the Old School Presbyterian preaching that Lincoln heard in Springfield and Washington.

Political scientist J. David Greenstone focuses not on inheritance but on adoption. Greenstone, in *The Lincoln Persuasion*, argues that Lincoln, the prairie lawyer, adopted as his own ideas and behaviors from both eighteenth-century New England Puritans and nineteenth-century Whigs. Both adopted cultures believed strongly in communities rooted in moral development. Both Puritans and Whigs had little patience with self-indulgent individualism.[13]

Greenstone's larger interest is the bipolarity in American liberalism between what he calls "humanist liberalism" and "reform liberalism." The former, and dominant tradition, can be defined as "the satisfaction of self-determined preferences." The result is what Hartz calls "atomistic social freedom" with its devotion to negative liberty and the absence of constraints.[14]

"Reform liberalism" is a dissenting tradition in American politics. Rooted in New England Puritanism, reform liberalism believes that "individuals have an obligation—not just the option—to cultivate and develop their physical, intellectual, aesthetic, and moral faculties" and to encourage others to do so. In a more organic understanding of reality, "the role of community is to set standards of mastery and excellence."[15]

Lincoln grows into the dissenting tradition of reform liberalism in his political pilgrimage. Greenstone argues that "Lincoln's position drew upon a tradition of religious thought and a conception of sainthood and citizenship that occupied a central place in New England culture." The Puritans' goals were "not merely to found a new sect but to redeem the religious life of an entire society." <u>Lincoln thus combines the Puritan concept of visible saints with the Republican call for citizen virtue.</u>[16]

In this brief essay, it is not possible to speak about the extended evolution of Lincoln's views on slavery. On the one hand, Lincoln's position on slavery reflected a broadly humanitarian position. Unlike the abolitionists, his humanitarianism was political rather than personal. He believed, as espoused at Gettysburg and in the Second Inaugural, in <u>"rededicating the American regime to the moral, material, and intellectual self-improvement of every citizen."</u> On the other hand, Lincoln's views on slavery finally partook of that reform liberalism wherein "reformers must first work to convert political institutions to the rightness of their cause and then seek, over time, to help particular individuals." In the Second Inaugural, Lincoln appeals to political institutions as well as to individuals.[17]

Lincoln's moral language, however, is not the moral judgment of either the abolitionists or the Radical Republicans. Some in these groups, long impatient with Lincoln's slowness to make the abolition of slavery the central issue of the war, were coming round to the president after he issued the Emancipation Proclamation. As Lincoln lifted up this figure of speech from Genesis against the arrogance of slavery, one can imagine many in the crowd that day saying "yes" or "that's right!"

The searing light of Lincoln's moral judgment, however, is refracted through a justice that is evenhanded: "Let us judge not that we be not judged." Lincoln, whose religion has often been depicted as Old Testament in character, here uses a teaching from the New Testament. Jesus, in the Sermon on the Mount, offers an explicit contrast to an older, legal understanding of human relationships. Surely Lincoln knew this passage from memory. As was common in his use of Scripture, however, he makes two subtle but significant changes. He adds "let us" at the beginning of the injunction, making it at the same time less personal but more inclusive. The addition of "we," in the place of the "ye" of the King James Version used in his day, is also inclusive.

The trajectory of this remark is toward the North. Lincoln's struggle with the abolitionists was often with the moral pretentiousness of their rhetoric. Likewise, his struggle with the churches was with their attitude of self-righteousness, which invariably led to a judgmental spirit. This biblical quotation, occurring in the middle of the paragraph, is central in setting the tone of the address.

> The prayers of both could not be answered, that of neither has been answered fully.

Lincoln mentions prayer three times in this address. His religious language, although speculative in terms of asking questions about divine intention, is also rooted in religious practice. His own faith pilgrimage to a more personal God is accompanied by a greater practice of prayer. We must understand that Lincoln is not now belittling either prayer or the soldiers who pray. Rather, in this transitional sentence, he is connecting <u>human devotion, with its ten-</u>

dency toward pretentiousness, to what will become the central teaching in this address: the purposes of God.

God's Purposes in History

"The Almighty has His own purposes."

In attempting to understand Lincoln's religion, both biographers and historians have depicted him as atheist, agnostic, deist, fatalist, spiritualist, and Christian. The search for Lincoln's religious views has been complicated by conflicting testimony. A weakness of many of the preachers' books on Lincoln is that they have uncritically accepted reminiscences that were uttered years if not decades after Lincoln's death.

Modern biographers, when they have treated Lincoln's religion, have focused on fatalism as the key category to understand Lincoln. Stephen Oates describes the young Lincoln in 1833 as "a religious fatalist like his mother." Fatalism is a belief in "the Doctrine of Necessity," wherein the human mind is "impelled" to act by some power in the universe. In 1846, Lincoln discovered in a newspaper the poem "Mortality." This prose, with its invocation of eternal and unchanging rhythms of life, borrowing themes from Job and Ecclesiastes, spoke to Lincoln because it touched in him chords of "deepening sadness and human fatalism." However valid the analysis of Lincoln's early years, Oates continues to speak of Lincoln's belief in fatalism right up into the presidency.[18]

The death of Abraham and Mary Todd's son Willie, in 1862, seems to be a critical moment in Lincoln's faith journey. William J. Wolff and Elton Trueblood, in their developmental schemes, believe this episode spurred Lincoln's transition to a more personal God. Oates understands the same events within the circumference of fatalism. He admits that "After Willie's death, he talked more frequently about God than he had before." Whereas it seems clear that Willie's death is a turning point in Lincoln's understanding of God, Oates will only say: "Yet his fatalism was more intense and more deeply felt."[19]

David Herbert Donald, in the Preface to his biography, *Lincoln*, connects Lincoln's fatalism with his own thesis of "Lincoln's reluctance to take the initiative and make bold plans." Donald argues that Lincoln, from his earliest days, "had a sense that his destiny was controlled by some larger force, some Higher Power." The theme of fatalism lies more dormant in Donald's biography. In coming to the Second Inaugural, Donald struggles to understand the God language that is at the center of the address. Rather than accepting the language and analyzing the theological content, Donald argues "He might have put his argument in terms of the doctrine of necessity, in which he had long believed, but that was not a dogma accepted by most Americans." In a gesture of blaming the audience, Donald observes, "Addressing a devout, Bible-reading public, Lincoln knew he would be understood when he invoked the familiar doctrine of exact retribution, the belief that the punishment for a violation of God's law would equal the offense itself."[20]

A more penetrating analysis of the changes in Lincoln's thinking is suggested by Kenneth M. Stampp. He observes that "Southern secession and the resulting Civil War seemed to produce a significant change of emphasis in Lincoln's ideas about historical causation." What was the change? He contrasts Lincoln's new emphasis on the will of God with the "environmental determinism" that governed Lincoln's thinking in the 1850s.[21]

The magnitude and fury of the Civil War seems to be the catalyst for this change. "As the war progressed, his [Lincoln's] conviction of a divine purpose increased." However, Stampp contends that "until the summer of 1863 Lincoln's reflections on the will of God as a force in history had not affected his determination to wage the war solely to preserve the Union." As the war took on a life of its own—"And the war came"—Lincoln was forced to "perceive the war as a conflict not only to defeat the southern Confederacy but also to purge the land of slavery." Stampp ties in Lincoln's changing understanding of the purpose of the war with his fresh desire to try to understand the will of God as a force in the political and social affairs of persons and nations.[22]

Were Lincoln's words tailored to the audience? Or did they grow out of his own search for a deeper understanding of cause and effect?

> "Woe unto the world because of offences! for it must needs be that offences come; but woe to that man by whom the offence cometh!" If we shall suppose that American Slavery is one of those offences which, in the providence of God, must needs come, but which, having continued through His appointed time, He now wills to remove, and that He gives to both North and South, this terrible war, as the woe due to those by whom the offence came, shall we discern therein any departure from those divine attributes which the believers in a Living God always ascribe to Him?

This jeremiad stands out from all that goes before or follows after. Lincoln is appealing here to a moral universe, but there is much more. Lincoln, like a Puritan preacher, calls forth thundering judgment on the world. The world is focused here as "both North and South." Lincoln is quite specific about the source of that judgment: slavery.

Religious communities often lament the sins of society, but they do not always name those sins when they are endemic to the social fabric. In South Africa, in the early 1980s, a word went forth from some church leaders: apartheid is a heresy. In a land proud of its roots in the Dutch Reformed church, an appeal to the faith of the fathers was part of the prevailing culture. As apartheid grew in the land, government leaders, most of them members of the Dutch Reformed church, were content to treat apartheid as a political or social matter. The declaration "apartheid is a heresy" became a turning point in beginning to treat racial injustice as a theological and moral issue.

Notice the way Lincoln moves from the passive to the active voice as he speaks about slavery and God. Earlier we pondered "And the war came." Now we hear that American slavery "must needs come." However, it comes not on its own terms. Slavery comes not by benign neglect. American slavery, so awful and hideous, is to be understood in the larger context of "the providence of God."

Having stated the problem—American slavery—what will be the answer? The solution is a God who acts in history. In this paragraph, Lincoln invokes not the creator God of Jefferson but the redeeming God of Calvin and the Puritans. Sacvan Bercovitch, in *The American Jeremiad*, points out that the jeremiad always combined social criticism and reaffirmation. Thus, in this jeremiad, we hear about both judgment on the nation and reaffirmation of the attributes of God.[23]

For several years now, Lincoln had been grappling with the reality that behind all the struggles and anguish of war an Almighty God was at work. This idea was expressed poignantly in a reply to Mrs. Eliza P. Gurney, who had profoundly impressed Lincoln with what amounted to the presentation of a sermon she preached to him during a visit of the Society of Friends in September 1862. Lincoln tells Mrs. Gurney, "If I had had my way, this war would never have commenced; If I had been allowed my way this war would have ended before this, but we find it still continues." He offers an affirmation to her: "we must believe that He permits it [the war] for some wise purpose of his own, mysterious and unknown to us; and though with our limited understandings we may not be able to comprehend it, yet we cannot but believe, that he who made the world still governs it."[24]

In September 1864, Lincoln continued the correspondence with Mrs. Gurney. This time, Lincoln's letter foreshadows some of the language of the Second Inaugural by six months. "The purposes of the Almighty are perfect, and must prevail, though we erring mortals may fail to accurately perceive them in advance. We hoped for a happy termination of this terrible war long before this; but God knows best, and has ruled otherwise." Lincoln again strains to understand, from the standpoint of divine purpose, what good can come from a terrible war. "Meanwhile we must work earnestly in the best light He gives us, trusting that so working still conduces to the great ends He ordains. Surely He intends some great good to follow this mighty convulsion, which no mortal could make, and no mortal could stay."[25]

In the Second Inaugural, Lincoln points beyond himself to the actor in history he calls "a Living God."

> Fondly do we hope—fervently do we pray—that this mighty scourge of war may speedily pass away. Yet, if God wills that it continue, until all the wealth piled by the bond-man's two hundred and fifty years of unrequited toil shall be sunk, and until every drop of blood drawn with the lash, shall be paid by another drawn with the sword, as was said three thousand years ago, so still it must be said "the judgments of the Lord, are true and righteous altogether."

For the third time in this short address, Lincoln invokes the practice of prayer. These are not words for a consumer public. They are spoken by a man of sorrows who prayed often that the scourge of war would pass away. It is at this point that one would like to switch on an audio or video recording. In what spirit or tone were these words uttered? Were they said defiantly, to both North and South, to emphasize the retribution due an arrogant and self-righteous people? Were they said in anguish as he had come to understand the terrible price of a war whose cost would continue for generations after an armistice that he knew was near? One can imagine that they were said slowly and sorrowfully.

Lincoln's confidence in the judgments of the Lord is keyed from the nineteenth Psalm. Several of the president's friends reported that in his White House years Lincoln carried with him a popular version of the Bible that consisted of the New Testament plus the Psalms. Lincoln learned as a child to commit favorite poems and passages of literature to memory. It was his habit, as it was for many in his generation, to memorize passages of Scripture. He did this with entire Psalms.

Although the Psalm may seem to be uttered by Lincoln as a word of terrible judgment, if we pay attention to the entire Psalm, as Lincoln undoubtedly did, we can be helped to understand the tone or spirit in which he concludes this central paragraph. The Psalmist is actually expressing his confidence in a great and good God. The Psalm begins: "The heavens are telling the glory of God, and the firmament showeth His handiwork." Not denying that the Second Inaugural sounds at its center like a jeremiad, full attention to the Psalm underlines the confidence, if not serenity, with which the Psalmist, and Lincoln, speaks. Some have argued that Lincoln's words about God's role in history are spoken with resignation. The contention here is that the final words in this paragraph, "the judgments of the Lord are true and righteous altogether," were spoken with resolution not resignation. At the end of the paragraph Lincoln does not intend to be adversarial but actually quite the opposite. He concludes with serenity and hope.

The final paragraph, although greatly appreciated, has not been well understood.

> With malice toward none; with charity for all; with firmness in the right, as God gives us to see the right, let us strive on to finish the work we are in; to bind up the nation's wounds; to care for him who shall have borne the battle, and for his widow, and his orphan—to do all which may achieve and cherish a just, and a lasting peace, among ourselves, and with all nations.

Most interpreters, whenever they choose to focus on the Second Inaugural, invariably will quote all or part of the final paragraph. Curiously, most analysis fails to connect the final paragraph with what went before. Richard N. Current even argues that there is "no material connection" between the last paragraph and the previous content of the address.[26]

In Lincoln's penchant for parallelisms, he begins this final paragraph by juxtaposing three quite different human attitudes. "Malice" is not simply evil, it is directed evil. Malice is the intent to harm other people. As the war moved toward its inevitable climax, Lincoln found himself being asked with more and more frequency: how would he treat those in the South? He begins to answer the question: "With malice toward none."

The opposite of malice is love. Lincoln used the word *charity* because that is the way the King James version translated all three of the Greek words for love. In the passing of thirteen decades, charity has lost its earlier thrust. Today charity sounds paternalistic. Love, for Lincoln, was the basic meaning of his religious experience.

Lincoln's religious experience did not include official membership in a congregation. Lincoln repeated often his explanation of why he did not join any church. For Lincoln, theology must be translated into ethics. His complaint was that churches were either caught up in emotionalism or bogged down in complicated theological formulae. He said he was ready to join any church that would "inscribe over its altar as it sole qualification for membership the Savior's condensed statement of the substance of both the law and the Gospel, Thou shalt love the Lord thy God with all thy heart, and with all they soul, and with all thy mind, and thy neighbor as thyself."[27] Love is the sum of faith.

As Lincoln moves from the broad brush strokes of evil and love toward the particularity of soldiers, widows, and orphans, it is easy to skip over "with firmness in the right, as God gives us to see the right." This line is an echo from Lincoln's Cooper Union address of February 27, 1860. In that address, Lincoln concluded with the words: "Let us have faith that right makes might, and in that faith, let us, to the end, dare to do our duty as we understand it."[28]

At Cooper Union, Lincoln spoke boldly that the nation's leaders must not be "frightened . . . by menaces of destruction to the Government nor of dungeons to ourselves."[29] At the end of the war, the open hands of "charity for all" is spoken within the same breath as the backbone to persevere with "firmness in the right." There is one critical difference, however, in the ending of the two speeches. The angle of vision is different. At Cooper Union, the concluding angle of vision is "as we understand it." In the final paragraph of the Second Inaugural, Lincoln's angle of vision has changed: "As God gives us to see the right."

The address ends with a coda of healing: "to bind up . . . to care for . . . to do all which may achieve and cherish a just, and a lasting peace." The tumultuous images of drops of blood and swords are now balanced by portraits of widows and orphans.

A biblical "therefore" is implied at the beginning of this last paragraph. Why should we bind and care when the mood of the country is much more one of triumph and vengeance? In this final paragraph, Lincoln's ethics follow from his theology. Caring is not a legal duty that can be imposed. It is the responsiveness of a people fully cognizant that they live and move and have their being in God's good providence. The religious faith that Lincoln is invoking is not individualistic but communitarian. The "lasting peace" is at the essence of Lincoln's vision beyond the Civil War. But it will be achieved only in a very concrete and particular way as people "bind up the nation's wounds" by caring for those individuals most hurt and maimed by the conflict.

With the address completed, the applause began. Lincoln bowed to the crowd. He placed his right hand on an open page of the Bible and repeated after Chief Justice Salmon P. Chase the oath of office. Lincoln ended with an emphatic "So help me God."![30]

Response

American newspapers gave the address a quite mixed reception. Their responses, to be sure, reflected their respective positions on the political spectrum. Nevertheless, the reactions of newspapers corresponded to the variegating attitudes of Lincoln's contemporaries.

The *New York Times* was disappointed. "He makes no boasts of what he has done, or promises of what he will do. He does not reexpound the principles of the war; does not redeclare the worth of the Union; does not reproclaim that absolute submission to the Constitution is the only peace." The *New York World* was even more dissatisfied. "It is with a blush of shame and wounded pride, as American citizens, that we lay before our readers to-day the inaugural addresses of President Lincoln and Vice-President Johnson." The *Chicago Times* offered the opinion: "We did not conceive it possible that even Mr. Lincoln could produce a paper so slip shod, so loose-jointed, so puerile, not alone in literary construction, but in its ideas, its sentiments, its grasp. . . . By the side of it, mediocrity is superb."[31]

The *Philadelphia Inquirer* had quite a different opinion. "The address is characteristic of Mr. Lincoln. It exhibits afresh the kindness of his heart, and the large charity which has ever marked his actions toward those who are his personal enemies as well as enemies of his country." The *Jersey City Times* commented, "It will stand forever as an announcement, grand in its simplicity, and unflexible in its resolve, of the faith of the American people in the stability of their free government and the justice and invincibility of their cause. It will make thousands say, who have not hitherto said, 'God bless Abraham Lincoln.' "[32]

Known and unknown individuals who attended the inaugural recorded their responses as well. Unknown to Lincoln, young Charles Francis Adams was in the crowd that day. Counting two presidents in his lineage, the twenty-nine-year-old Adams asked his father in a letter on March 7, "What do you think of the inaugural?" He then offered his own estimation. "That rail-splitting lawyer is one of the wonders of the day. Once at Gettysburg and now again on a greater occasion he has shown a capacity for rising to the demands of the hour." Adams concluded, "This inaugural strikes me in its grand simplicity and directness as being for all time the historical keynote of this war."[33]

Lincoln did notice Frederick Douglass in the crowd. It was the first time African Americans were present in any numbers at an inauguration. As Douglass gauged the responses of those around him, he observed, "I saw in the faces of many about me expressions of widely different emotions." Douglass decided to go to the inauguration reception that evening at the White House. He found himself barred at the door by two policemen who informed him that their "directions were to admit no one of color." When Lincoln heard that Douglass was at the door, he sent for him. "Here comes my friend Douglass." Taking him by the arm, the president said, "I am glad to see you. I saw you in the crowd today, listening to my inaugural address; how did you like it?" Douglass replied, "Mr. Lincoln, that was a sacred effort."[34]

A most important commentator was the president himself. Although in our time the Gettysburg Address has received preeminence, Lincoln considered the Second Inaugural his best effort. "It will stand the test of time," he told friends at the inaugural reception. A few days later, writing to New York Republican leader Thurlow Weed, he commented: "I expect the latter (Second Inaugural Address) to wear as well—perhaps better than anything I have produced." Lincoln then adds a fascinating caveat that reveals much about his own perception: "but I believe it is not immediately popular."

Why this disjuncture between Lincoln's self-perception and the perception of others? Lincoln answered the question. "Men are not flattered by being shown that there has been a difference of purpose between the Almighty and them." The issue is finally one of purpose. "To deny it, however, in this case, is to deny that there is a God governing the world."[35]

Lincoln's comments to Weed are his own exegesis of the text. His words underscore that the central theme of the address was "The Almighty has his own purposes." Lincoln's beliefs have unquestionably moved far beyond any doctrine of necessity or environmental determinism. In the Second Inaugural Address, Lincoln "abandoned his secular view of history and resigned himself to serving as an instrument in the hands of God."[36]

In conclusion, in the Second Inaugural we have the finest presentation of the relationship between religion and the Civil War. An inaugural address is one of the highest public occasions in American public life, but Frederick Douglass was on the mark when he observed, "The address sounded more like a sermon than a state paper."[37]

To enter into a familiar text in a fresh way demands an openness for surprise. The audience that day expected to hear words of vindication. Many in the crowd and across the nation were not able to hear reconciliation. As Lincoln spoke publicly, there was a brooding, almost private quality to his remarks. The faithful were prepared to hear, "God is on our side," and did not understand Lincoln's invoking a God whose ways were not always known but were always just.

As the war drew to a close, Lincoln offered the Second Inaugural as the prism through which he strained to see the light of God in the darkest hour of the nation's history. The refractions from this prism pointed backward in judgment and forward in hope. The Second Inaugural illuminates Lincoln's understanding of the various ways God is at work in history.

Notes

1. James G. Randall, *Lincoln the President* (New York, 1945), 4: 372–373. Randall was the first academic historian to create a career around Lincoln studies. He died in 1953, leaving the final volume half finished. Richard N. Current, who had been a graduate student under Randall, was selected to complete the final volume. The last chapter was entitled "God's Man."

2. The major Lincoln biographers of the past half-century have treated Lincoln's

religious views quite sparingly. Benjamin P. Thomas (1952), Stephen B. Oates (1977), and David Herbert Donald (1995) utilized the best Lincoln research in their biographies, but had little to say about religion. The subject heading "Religion" is not listed in the index of any of their three biographies. And Lincoln's Second Inaugural, which is filled with religious metaphor and meanings, is the subject of one page in Thomas and three pages in Oates and Donald.

3. In the last half-century, academic historians have not wasted many words on Lincoln's religion. Preachers and theologians continued to write about Lincoln, but their words hardly seem noticed by the guild of Lincoln scholars. There has been an understandable reaction against an earlier generation of preachers turned historians. Those writers set out to utilize every piece of reminiscence to prove that Lincoln was a religious person imbued with Protestant Christian values. Their studies did not situate Lincoln within the broader contours of religion and the Civil War. The best books about Lincoln's religion include William J. Wolf, *The Almost Chosen People: A Study of the Religion of Abraham Lincoln* (New York, 1959); and Elton Trueblood, *Abraham Lincoln: Theologian of American Anguish* (New York, 1973), a fine study that has not been noticed in the scholarly community. Wayne C. Temple, a student of Randall, completed a lifelong study in 1995, *Abraham Lincoln: From Skeptic to Prophet* (Mahomet, IL, 1995).

4. Glen E. Thurow, *Abraham Lincoln and American Public Religion* (Albany, NY, 1976), xii, argues cogently for the primary character of Lincoln's public religion.

5. Noah Brooks, *Washington in Lincoln's Time* (New York, 1896), 235.

6. There is only one account of the manuscript of the Second Inaugural before March 4. Francis B. Carpenter, who spent six months at the White House, tells of sitting in the president's office on the evening of February 22. "Mr. Lincoln came in . . . holding in his hand a roll of manuscripts. 'Lots of wisdom in that document, I suspect,' said he; 'it is what will be called my 'second inaugural,' containing about six hundred words. I will put it in my drawer until I want it." Francis B. Carpenter, *The Inner Life of Abraham Lincoln* (New York, 1874), 234. Carpenter became famous for his historical painting *First Reading of the Emancipation Proclamation*.

The draft of the address was set in type, and the galley proof was clipped and pasted in an order to indicate pauses for emphasis and breathing. Lincoln gave the original draft to John Hay, one of his secretaries, on April 10, 1865. For a copy of the original draft and the galley proof arrangement, see the commemorative booklet prepared for the reenactment of the Second Inaugural in 1965. *Upon the Occasion of the One Hundredth Anniversary of the Second Inauguration of Abraham Lincoln, 1865–1965* (Washington, DC, 1965), 8–12.

7. Brooks, *Washington in Lincoln's Time*, 238–239.

8. George Washington's Second Inaugural Address in 1793 was two paragraphs.

9. Lois J. Einhorn, *Abraham Lincoln the Orator: Penetrating the Legend* (Westport, CT, 1992), 87.

10. Abraham Lincoln, "First Inaugural Address," March 4, 1861, in Roy P. Basler, ed., *The Collected Works of Abraham Lincoln* (New Brunswick, NJ, 1953–1955), 4: 271.

11. Abraham Lincoln to Albert G. Hodges, April 4, 1864, in Basler, ed., *Works*, 7: 281–282.

12. Abraham Lincoln, "Meditation on the Divine Will" [September 2, 1862?], in Basler, ed., *Works*, 403. The bracketed date is given to the Meditation by Lincoln's secretaries and biographers, John M. Hay and John G. Nicolay.

13. J. David Greenstone, *The Lincoln Persuasion: Remaking American Liberalism* (Princeton, NJ, 1993), 264. Greenstone died in 1990. He had been working on the book

for twelve years, but it was unfinished. Unfortunately, the book does not include intended chapters on Lydia Maria Child and Frederick Douglass.

14. Ibid., 53–55. Louis Hartz, *The Liberal Tradition in America* (New York, 1955), 62.

15. Greenstone, *Lincoln Persuasion*, 59.

16. Ibid, 265–266.

17. Ibid., 244, 257.

18. Stephen Oates, *With Malice Toward None: A Life of Abraham Lincoln* (New York, 1977), 29, 70–71.

19. Ibid., 292–293.

20. David Herbert Donald, *Lincoln* (New York, 1995), 15, 566–567.

21. Kenneth M. Stampp, "Lincoln's History," in *"We Cannot Escape History,"* ed. James M. McPherson (Urbana, IL, 1995), 28.

22. Ibid., 29.

23. See Sacvan Bercovitch, *The American Jeremiad* (Madison, WI, 1978).

24. Abraham Lincoln to Eliza P. Gurney, October 26, 1862, in Basler, ed., *Works*, 5: 478. There is some debate about the date of the letter. Donald suggests the letter was written in September 1862.

25. Abraham Lincoln to Eliza P. Gurney, September 4, 1864, in Basler, ed., *Works*, 7: 535–536.

26. Oates, *With Malice Toward None*, quotes the entire last paragraph (411) and Donald, *Lincoln*, quotes all but seventeen of the seventy-five words in the paragraph (567–568).

27. There are a number of versions of this story. William J. Wolf, *The Religion of Abraham Lincoln* (New York, 1963), 74–75, quotes Henry C. Deeming, *Eulogy upon Abraham Lincoln before the General Assembly of Connecticut* (1865), 42.

28. Abraham Lincoln, "Address at Cooper Institute," February 27, 1860, in Basler, ed., *Works*, 3: 550. William Lee Miller, "Lincoln's Second Inaugural: The Zenith of Statecraft," *The Center Magazine*, July/August 1980, 60.

29. Abraham Lincoln, "Address at Cooper Institute," 550.

30. Oates, *With Malice Toward None*, 411; Donald, *Lincoln*, 568.

31. A selection from eleven contemporary newspaper accounts is included the commemorative program *Upon the Occasion of the One Hundredth Anniversary of the Second Inauguration of Abraham Lincoln*, 22–23.

32. Ibid., 22–24.

33. Charles Francis Adams Jr. to his father, March 7, 1865, in *A Cycle of Adams Letters, 1861–1865*, ed. Worthington Chauncey Ford (New York, 1920), 2: 257.

34. Frederick Douglass, *Life and Times of Frederick Douglass* (Hartford, CT, 1882), 404, 405–407. Douglass explains that the rebuff at the door was not at anyone's direction but simply continued the usual custom of barring African Americans.

35. Abraham Lincoln to Thurlow Weed, March 15, 1865, in Basler, ed., *Works*, 8: 356.

36. Stampp, "Lincoln's History," 29.

37. Douglass, *Life and Times*, 403.

III

PEOPLE

10

Days of Judgment, Days of Wrath

The Civil War and the Religious Imagination of Women Writers

ELIZABETH FOX-GENOVESE

Just as war tests the spirit of combatants, so does it test the imagination of civilians, especially women, who live intimately with its terrors and deprivations. For them, as much as for combatants themselves, war notoriously shatters the assumptions and practices of everyday life, thrusting those who experience its fury into a maelstrom for which their previous lives have not prepared them. The magnitude and rapidity of the changes promote the sense of a world turned upside down. Monumental disruptions of the unremarkable flow of everyday life lend even the most ordinary events an aura of significance. Suddenly, that which always had been taken for granted is called into question. Habits become challenges, and instinctive attitudes and beliefs fall open to scrutiny and doubt.

Accordingly, we should not find surprising the many attempts by American women to make sense of civil war through the prism of religion. For both sides, the waging of the war and the endurance of its pain were informed by religious conviction. From the start, northern abolitionists had announced their cause as a crusade, and even as secular purposes gained ground among the Republicans, the sense of the religious justification for antislavery persisted. Southerners, for their part, knew that their defense of slavery derived from biblical teaching, and they took second place to none in their conviction that the defense of their section's independence derived from religious imperatives. Even as the tide of war turned against the South, southern ministers preached fast-day sermons enjoining their countrywomen and men to understand that

God was testing and chastising them, not for holding slaves but for failing to realize their responsibilities as Christian slaveholders.

If the sense of religious purpose sustained and inspired many of the men who participated in the war, how much more did it sustain and inspire the women who, perforce, found themselves relegated to the margins of action, waiting and praying for the return of loved ones and, increasingly among southern women, for the safety of themselves and their households. Under any circumstances, war prompts diarists and letter writers in unaccustomed numbers to take up their pens with more frequency than is normally their wont. At the beginning of June 1860, Catherine Ann Devereux Edmonston, in Halifax County, North Carolina, began her war diary, noting that although she had previously commenced diaries, she had always left off, "perhaps from weariness, perhaps from an absolute dearth of events."[1] Now, events would not be lacking, for "in these troublous times a lack of incident can be no excuse for dullness."[2]

During the ensuing years, dullness never plagued Catherine Edmonston, who, like countless other women, white and black, southern and northern, kept daily company with a surfeit of uncommon events, large and small. Disruptive events cascaded with special abundance upon white southern women, confronting them with the constant fear, too frequently realized, that they would lose the men they held most dear and with the threat of invasion, forced evacuation, loss of income, and the devastation of their homes. These blows also fell upon black slave women, but with a difference: They had less to lose and, ultimately, much to gain from Yankee military success. So, even when they shared the disruptions, discomforts, and dangers of everyday life, many more blacks than whites could acknowledge a harbored secret conviction that today's travail might "granny" tomorrow's freedom. Northern women were spared the immediate physical danger that overshadowed the lives of southern women, but they too lived with constant fear for the safety of loved ones, as well as large and small disruptions and material deprivations.

For all American women, the immediacy of the war lay in the accumulation of events that provided such unaccustomed stuffing for the pages of diaries and letters, even as they chipped away at the customary routine. By accretion, or in one fell swoop, events might plummet women completely beyond the bounds of the customary routine, offering new opportunities and imposing unaccustomed obligations. Thus did women, frequently with much gnashing of teeth, find themselves thrust into roles that had but recently fallen to servants or to men. In this respect, war simultaneously extended and blurred the boundaries of what it meant to be a woman. And notwithstanding the radically different experiences of women of different classes, races, and regions, the results of expansion and blurring had remarkably much in common. Whether an elite southern woman found herself nursing in hospitals, managing a plantation, organizing and overseeing her family's emigration, or teaching school, she had something in common with the northern middle-class white woman who went to Washington to nurse, became a clerk in the federal government, went South to teach freed people, or simply participated in relief

associations.[3] In each case, the woman was drawing upon the skills and expectations with which she had been reared, but she was now trying to do
something for which nothing in her upbringing had prepared her. She was
called upon to mobilize her most fundamental resources to move beyond the
responsibilities for which those resources had been intended to prepare her.

For many women throughout the severed Union, religion constituted the
bedrock of the resources upon which they drew. Reared in the tenets of the
Judeo-Christian tradition, primarily one or another Protestant denomination,
American women had long been wont to turn to religion to anchor and inspire
their sense of personal integrity and worth. In this respect, their expectations
for themselves as individuals had, with rare exceptions, been closely tied to
their culture and to their community's traditional view of the woman's proper
place in society. Thus, during the decades before the war, women's writing,
whether in diaries, letters, or fiction, had invariably expressed one or another
aspect of the tension between women's sense of themselves as individuals and
as women—in that term's socially prescribed sense. But for most, a worthy
sense of self meant precisely some reconciliation or accommodation between
the two—that is, between personal yearning and socially acceptable role. Contemporary scholars, who have noted that tension, are, more often than not,
tempted to emphasize the tension rather than the reconciliation on the grounds
that prescriptions of womanhood normally embodied external constraints imposed upon the woman's true "self" by a world that sought to restrict women
to a carefully circumscribed sphere. Consequently, they have been led to embrace every indication of women's striving for independence as a sign of their
healthy quest for personal liberation from oppression.

This tendency to view nineteenth-century women as having suffered, in
greater or lesser measure, the oppressive weight of a "patriarchal" society has
further tempted scholars to emphasize the similarities that transcended the
differences among women as members of specific communities and regions, or
even classes and races. And even those who acknowledge the differences among
women's social and personal situations continue to homogenize their imaginative experiences and expressions. Thus, scholars who focus on women's literary expression rarely grant much weight to regional difference in literate
women's deepest sense of themselves.[4] Yet the published writings of northern
and southern women—and frequently their unpublished diaries and letters as
well—suggest that however much women drew upon a common tradition, they
were likely to interpret it differently.

Here, I shall explore aspects of the female literary tradition that matured
during the antebellum period and drew countless nonliterary women into the
web of literary women's imaginative recreation of women's experience and aspirations. By the opening of the Civil War, women's writing had established
an uncontested, if not always prestigious, place in American letters. Women
in large numbers wrote novels and poetry, which other women, in much larger
numbers, faithfully and enthusiastically read.[5] The heart of this tradition lay
in the sentimental or domestic fiction through which women brought the world
of households and homes into public consciousness as the stage for the devel-

opment and realization of the female self. This was a world in which, as Jane Tompkins and others have argued, women presided over the routines of every-day life and wove together the threads of people's destinies, notably their own. It was also, as Rachel Blau DuPlesis and others have complained, a world in which women were destined to find the realization of their hopes and dreams in marriage and domesticity—in subordination of their independence to the imperatives of others, especially men.[6] Yet the forms of domesticity and women's response to them differed according to region, as well as according to class and race.

Before turning to the divisions, let us consider the commonalties that united women of different regions. Whether northern or southern, literate women drew upon a common Western culture and, especially, a common commitment to Protestant Christianity, which, in many instances, structured and enlivened their sense of individual purpose and worth. The unity of their commitment becomes all the more impressive when we take account of non-literate women, including black slave women, for whom Protestant Christianity vastly outweighed the secular texts of Western culture as a source of meaning. Thus we may safely assume that of those women who learned to read, most began with the Bible or rapidly graduated to it and that even those who did not learn to read absorbed significant portions of the Bible through preaching and hearing others read it. And among women who could not only read but write, especially those who kept journals or wrote for publication, the Bible and Christian teachings enjoyed a privileged place in their attempts to bring order and meaning to their own lives.[7]

The Christian precepts dear to northern and southern ministers empha-sized women's responsibility to find meaning in the station ascribed to their sex and in their obligations to other, especially their own families. They also emphasized the faith, hope, charity, and reverence for Christian duty that ar-guably applied to men as well as women. Thus women who attended closely to their minister's preaching and read their Bible regularly imbued a dual mes-sage that simultaneously engaged them as women and as sinful mortals who hoped for salvation. No doubt, the two messages intertwined in most cases so that the path to salvation lay through the meeting of one's specific womanly duties. Many women nonetheless understood the difference between them—namely, that if womanly duties frequently entailed subordination to men, Christian duties required subordination to God. Women writers from all regions of the country deployed these themes in their fiction, implicitly or explicitly offering adherence to the Christian teaching as the essence of a woman's personal vocation. Thus northern and southern women alike fre-quently took *Pilgrim's Progress* as a template for the female quest, as, after the war, Louisa May Alcott so successfully did in *Little Women*.

Protestant women, independent of denomination, grew up within a web of biblical teachings about women's special nature and responsibilities. And if they were well schooled in Eve's sin and its consequences, they were no less well schooled in the myriad ways in which a woman could be virtuous. Today, some are quick to dismiss the book of Proverbs' celebration of the good wife as yet more evidence of the ways in which religion consigned women to an inferior domestic role. But for women who lived in a world in which women's domestic responsibilities frequently determined the health and prosperity of families, the good wife often figured as an ideal worthy of emulation—and difficult to attain. Some women may have privately resented biblical injunctions that wives obey their husbands and maintain silence in church, but, clearly, most accepted both as proper indicators of a social order that delineated the boundaries and privacy of women's religious experience. Nor does it appear that most Protestant women believed that such injunctions curtailed either their faith or their Christian action in the world or, indeed, in church affairs.

More commonly, women worried about the magnitude of the responsibilities that fell especially to them, notably the responsibility to rear children to meet their own responsibilities in life, and, especially in the South, they attempted to apply that rule to the supervision of servants. In both instances, the Bible reminded them that they were accountable for the maintenance of a delicate balance between firm discipline and enlightened love. As many a woman complained to her journal, under the press of daily events and multiple pregnancies, neither came easily. Furthermore, especially in the North, women increasingly felt a responsibility to bring the adult men of their family to church attendance and membership.[8] Indeed, throughout the nineteenth century, women's church membership exceeded that of men, although more dramatically and with considerably different significance in the North. Tellingly, the North rapidly emerged as the cradle not merely of the middle class but also of women's church-related reform activities. More important, the growing individualism of northern culture fostered a new preoccupation with women's distinct religious authority and even with their personal and religious freedom. Southern culture, in contrast, remained more skeptical about the claims of individualism and certainly less willing to apply its own understanding of individualism to women. And it remained much less willing to confine religion to the exclusive, or even preeminent, custody of women within the domestic sphere. Thus, even the Christian faith that united American women also divided them, and the divisions worked their way into women's fiction, which often engaged theological as well as devotional questions.

In the North, the tightening bonds between women and religion, like the complementary loosening of the bonds between religion and men, has led Ann Douglas to discern a progressive "feminization" of religion throughout the antebellum period.[9] Douglas especially focuses on the evidence from northeastern women's writings, and she convincingly argues that their feminine interpretation of American culture was infinitely more influential than those who emphasize women's victimization acknowledge. Nineteenth-century women writers, Douglas insists, effectively conquered the literary terrain, triumphing over the difficult visions of a Hawthorne or a Melville and trivializing religion even as they trivialized literature. Focusing on the Northeast, Douglas does not question the growing hold of individualism upon American culture and literary imagination. Nor does she criticize some women's ambition to participate in it as individuals in their own right. She assumes that the great moral and existential dramas of the nineteenth century consisted in the struggles of the individual consciousness against the fetters of suffocating, middle-class convention and is prepared to admire women who joined in the revolt against it. Most women did not. Rather, they attempted to contain gut-wrenching tragedies within their own sphere of sentimental domesticity. Women, she charges, set themselves up as the implacable opponents of the most searing human dramas, reducing irreconcilable conflicts to moral platitudes fit for the ears of children.

Douglas does not consider the possibility that the reductive sentimentalism she deplores was an integral part of the northeastern individualism she admires. Yet Harriet Beecher Stowe's *Uncle Tom's Cabin*, which she takes as the premier example of feminized religion and emasculated tragedy, unmistakably defended the theological principles and religious attitudes that informed northeastern antislavery thought.[10] Daughter of the influential minister Lyman Beecher, Stowe was an integral part of the northeastern cultural and literary elite that, at an accelerating pace throughout the first half of the nineteenth century, was ensconcing the individual conscience as the principal site of moral discrimination and judgment. Thus, the abolitionists increasingly argued that if it could be shown that the Bible failed to condemn slavery, it would stand revealed as the Devil's own Book. Bible or no Bible, slavery was a sin. As a result, and for whatever complex reasons, they embraced the position that individual freedom was a greater moral good than revealed religion and thus, by implication, that individual freedom was the standard against which any religion must be judged.

Implicitly in *Uncle Tom's Cabin* and explicitly in *The Key to Uncle Tom's Cabin* Stowe drew upon New England New Divinity theology to condemn slavery as unchristian. In *The Key to Uncle Tom's Cabin*, she described it as "absolute despotism, of the most unmitigated form." For, she argued, the "worst kind of despotism has been said to be that which extends alike over body and soul, binds the liberty of the conscience, and deprives a man all right of choice in respect to the manner in which he shall learn the will of God, and worship him."[11] Even at the time, it was clear to some that Stowe's arguments against slavery might be extended to women as a number of early defenders of women's rights did.[12] But those who drew that connection did not normally repudiate what was becoming accepted as women's special religious responsibilities. So, as a rule, women's opposition to slavery and even to their own condition leaned heavily on the feminization of religion rather than mounting a repudiation of it.

Northeastern women's willingness to reap the benefits of moral superiority to which the separation of spheres apparently entitled them consigned them to an ambiguous position with respect to their own freedom. For the very American culture that celebrated the value of individual freedom consistently asked women to forswear it for themselves. Many, like Stowe herself and assuredly her sister Catharine, were willing to trade an illusory freedom for the power that should accrue to them as the custodians of religion and conscience.

Stowe drew heavily on a revised and allegedly humanized version of Calvinist belief in moral perfectibility, and identified home—woman's domain—as the "site of perfect love on earth." By emphasizing the separate and complementary nature of men's and women's roles, she claimed the necessity of women's experience and sentiment on the intellectual development of her region's theology.[13]

In contrast to Stowe, Elizabeth Cady Stanton, also drawing upon northeastern Protestantism and especially provoked by women's subordinate position in the antislavery movement, took a more jaundiced view of the moral authority that women could draw from the prevailing sexual division of labor.[14] Stanton insisted that man, having restricted woman to a subordinate position in church and state, and having deprived her of education, had transformed her into a morally "irresponsible being," whom he refused even to hold accountable for crimes committed in the presence of her husband. By assigning a different code of morals to woman than to himself, man, in Stanton's view, had usurped to himself "the prerogative of Jehovah," claiming the right to assign her to a specific sphere of action, when that right "belongs to her and to God." Thus, had man degraded women, by mobilizing every means at his disposal "to destroy her confidence in her own powers, to lessen her self-respect, and to make her willing to lead a dependent and abject life."[15]

The true radicalism of Stanton's Declaration of Sentiments lay in her insistence that autonomous individualism constituted the essence of freedom, which she defined as the antithesis of slavery. The denial of individualism, by endowing women with the psychology of slaves, thus reduced them to the demeaning and degrading status of slaves and colored their entire relation to the world. In her speech to the Seneca Falls Convention, she disingenuously insisted that she had no intention of transforming men's and women's roles, yet her passionate denunciations of women's deprivation of freedom betrayed a lurking perfectionist temptation radically to refashion both.

At Seneca Falls, Stanton neither mentioned nor protested biblical teachings about women's subordination, prudently avoiding any attack on religion, which she believed supported her cause. She reserved her attack for the men who had assumed the position of God and closed church leadership to women. This strategy severed revealed religion from existing religious institutions, opening the possibility that women might claim an unmediated personal knowledge of religious truth. In this spirit, she emphasized the importance of each individual's living worthily and acknowledging individual accountability to God. Woman, she insisted, must "live *first* for God," in full knowledge that her spirit was "fitted for as a high a sphere as man's." Only when woman refrained from making "imperfect man an object of reverence and awe," would she learn that she must depend only upon God and that her true happiness lay in the accomplishment of her duty as an individual. "Thus will she learn the lesson of individual responsibility for time and eternity."[16]

Stanton's emphasis on the individual soul's direct relation to God bore the strong imprint of the abolitionists with whom she and many other advocates of women's rights had worked. Like them, she held that the dictates of individual conscience took precedence over the teaching of ministers or even the Bible. Thus did she join them in the radical claim that Christian freedom included the right—some said the obligation—of the individual Christian to define the meaning of freedom.[17] Her postbellum writings, notably "Solitude of the Self" and *The Woman's Bible*, revealed the full implications of her position. In them, she openly challenged prevailing religious authority in the name of women's emancipation and self-determination. Women's freedom required a liberation from the artificialities of law and custom that, by freeing women, would transform society.[18] In *The Woman's Bible*, Stanton offered a series of harsh commentaries on the Old Testament, including a reproach to Moses for not having been "more merciful in his judgments of all witches, necromancers and soothsayers," since they, "possessing the same power and manifesting many of the same wonders that he did, should not have been so severely punished for their delusions."[19]

She nonetheless reserved her real fire for the New Testament, which she judged even less friendly to women. Rejecting the Christian claim that the New Testament brought "promises of new dignity and of larger liberties for women," she announced that women's inferior position is actually "more clearly and emphatically set forth by the Apostles than by the Prophets and the Patriarchs."[20] She especially deplored the position of Mary, whom she described as having belonged to the Jewish aristocracy. With this distinguished ancestry, Mary should have been granted a husband of her own rank rather than a humble craftsman. But then Stanton could not understand why Mary had to be human at all. "If a Heavenly Father was necessary, why not a Heavenly Mother? If an earthly Mother was admirable, why not an earthly Father?" Above all, she objected to the idea that Mary's motherhood of Jesus honored women as a sex. In her view, "a wise and virtuous son is more indebted to his mother than she is to him, and is honored only by reflecting her superior characteristics." These and similar complaints amply prepare Stanton's reader for her concluding observation that "Biblical mysteries and inconsistencies are a great strain on the credulity of the ordinary mind."[21] But as so many Christian southern women were wont to counter, what of Christianity remains?

The logical outcome of Stanton's radical religious individualism may be found in contemporary feminist theology.[22] In time and place, however, most northern women were less likely to share her attitudes toward women's relation to religion than Stowe's, and the war did not significantly change their views, although in many instances it strengthened their conviction that the moral guidance of society fell to their auspices. If anything, the war enhanced their moral fervor, since they, like many men, were quick to justify wartime suffering by the righteousness of the Union cause. Julia Ward Howe's vision of the northern army's "trampling out the vineyards where the grapes of wrath are stored" and loosening the "fateful lightning of His terrible swift sword" had been primarily intended to strengthen northern will in the crucible of battle, but its spirit lingered as a moral justification for the sacrifices so many had endured. As the dust settled and federal unity was restored, it nonetheless became clear that the true source of northern fervor lay more with mammon than with God.[23]

If anything, the aftermath of the Civil War widened the divide between religion and the affairs of the world and reinforced the sense that religion was a private matter best left to women's keeping. In the event, Stowe herself moved toward Episcopalianism, following the conversion of her sister Catharine and several of her daughters.[24] Many other women, who remained in evangelical churches, embraced their special responsibility for religion but increasingly refused to agree that religious values should be relegated to the domestic sphere. Rather, they drew from religion a compelling justification for their own growing intervention in the affairs of the world. In the measure that the outcome of the war had strengthened their conviction of the righteousness of their faith, they believed themselves obligated to bring its moral standards to bear upon what they perceived as an increasingly dangerous and Godless world.

Northern women's sense of moral responsibility to reform the world, as embodied in the Woman's Christian Temperance Union and countless smaller organizations, coexisted with a growing interest in their own individualism.[25] And if most did not embrace Elizabeth Cady Stanton's radical views about women's freedom, many did express a growing interest in women's independent cultivation of their talents and minds. The hold of individualism upon American women's literary imaginations emerges most clearly from women writers' continuing preoccupation with their own version of a female *bildungsroman*—novels that explored young women's coming of age and entrance into womanhood. Louisa May Alcott's *Little Women*, which may well stand as the classic exemplar of the genre, clearly reveals the underlying tensions.[26] The novel especially chronicles the coming of age of Jo March, Alcott's main heroine and thinly disguised alter ego. Jo, an avid reader, who passionately aspires to become an author herself, ranks as a classic tomboy. In full rebellion against the conventions of society in general and womanhood in particular, Jo struggles for physical and mental self-assertion. Significantly, however, Alcott casts Jo's story as a modern version of *Pilgrim's Progress*, thereby linking Jo's acceptance of her own womanhood to her progress toward mature religious faith. In this progress, Jo's most daunting obstacle proves her own temper, which, with the patient and loving help of her mother and the example of her sister's death, she ultimately masters. Fortuitously, her successful domination of her own anger coincides with her realization of her ambition to become an author.

It is hard to put down *Little Women* without a suspicion that Alcott saw a fundamental contradiction between womanhood and the independence of authorship. For Jo, as for herself, she resolved the contradiction in the being of the woman author, who successfully channels her unwomanly ambition into the paths of righteousness—novels fit for the eyes and ears of children. But Alcott's understanding of the tensions that lurk beneath the calm surface of domestic life surfaced in the mystery stories that she published under a pseudonym.[27] She was far from alone among women writers in recognizing the dangers that threatened to shatter the placid surface of blissful domesticity and even to shatter the composure of acceptable women's identities. But she, like others, remained unwilling or unable to represent the demons as decisively crippling her heroines. In this, feminist critics are correct: nineteenth-century American literature severely limited the ambitions that women could attribute to themselves or even fictional characters. If evil surfaced in their pages, it normally adhered to characters who could be killed off or ultimately conquered by the religion of domesticity.

Thus in essential respects, the Civil War did not dramatically transform the religious attitudes and experience of northern women, although it did reinforce and accelerate existing tendencies, not least, northern culture's tendency to feminize religion and some northern women's intensified determination to claim individualism for themselves.[28] What the war did transform—or better, destroy—was the social world in which those attitudes and experiences were rooted—namely, the rural New England villages from which Stowe's devout and orderly Miss Ophelia sprang.[29] In *Uncle Tom's Cabin*, Stowe lovingly introduces the details of Miss Ophelia's home as if that mere description would evoke the values she embodies. Miss Ophelia's world is, Stowe reminds us, one which "whoever has traveled in the New England States" will recognize. There, in some "cool village," the traveler will have seen "the large farmhouse, with its clean-swept grassy yard, shaded by the dense and massive foliage of the sugar maple." And the traveler will recall

> the air of order and stillness, of perpetuity and unchanging repose, that seemed to breathe over the whole place. Nothing lost, or out of order; not a picket loose in the fence, not a particle of litter in the turfy yard, with its clumps of lilac bushes growing up under the windows. Within, he will remember wide, clean rooms, where nothing ever seems to be doing or going to be done, where everything is once and forever rigidly in place, and where all household arrangements move with the punctual exactness of the old clock in the corner. In the family 'keeping-room,' as it is termed, he will remember the staid, respectable old book-case, with its glass doors, where Rollin's History, Milton's Paradise Lost, Bunyan's Pilgrim's Progress, and Scott's Family Bible, stand side by side in decorous order, with multitudes of other books, equally solemn and respectable.

This is a house, Stowe pointedly notes, without servants. There is only "the lady in the snowy cap, with the spectacles, who sits sewing every afternoon among her daughters, as if nothing ever had been done, or were to be done,—she and her girls, in some long-forgotten part of the day, *did up the work*, and for the rest of the time . . . it is *'done up'* " (244–245).[30]

For Stowe and many other women, the values of this world were simultaneously timeless and regulated by the clock, which subjected nature to human discipline. The domination of the clock confirms the interdependence of her womanly religion with the emerging world of industrial capitalism. But her rhetoric suggests a stasis—suggests a permanence or a suspension in time—that history would mock. The cruel irony for Stowe and her compatriots would be that the war they had thought would preserve this fragile balance shattered it. For in destroying the cause of the slaveholding South, New Englanders, as Lewis Simpson has brilliantly argued, destroyed their own cause as well.[31] The consequences were not immediately apparent to northern women, who carried their sense of religious justification and stewardship into the postbellum world. Yet the long arm of industrialization reached ever deeper into the interstices of households, as Stowe herself acknowledged in describing Miss Asphyxia of her postbellum novel *Oldtown Folks* as "a working machine, forever wound up to high-pressure working point." This industry's being Miss Asphyxia's nature, "she trod down and crushed whatever stood in the way of her work, with as little compunction as if she had been a steam-engine or powerloom."[32] Recognizing that the world increasingly defied their perfectionist dreams of reformation, many, at least among the literate elite, would turn to the principles of secular individualism, which already lurked in their religion, to defend their actions on their own and others' behalf.

The more heavily the events of the war weighed on northern women, the more they appeared to justify the morality of the northern cause and hence the righteousness of northern women's faith. Those same events did not treat southern women so kindly. The succession of defeats, combined with the constant presence of death, loss, and deprivation, tried the faith of many.[33] Before the war, many southern women saw their religious responsibilities as a vocation or a "calling." Even when religious faith did not come easily, they saw the struggle for faith as a central part of their life and a meaningful story about their own aspirations. It helped them to define who they were in the world. And even as religion taught them to be meek and self-sacrificing, it gave them a higher standard by which they could judge others.

In southern as in northern women's antebellum writings, religion intertwines closely with female identities, which it is frequently taken to ground, and both religion and female identity intertwine closely with the defense of southern society.[34] Just as Stowe invoked religion to justify her attack on slavery, so did southern women invoke religion to defend it. Like Stowe, southern women argued that they were not defending their region in the narrow sense, but defending the true meaning and nature of American history and society.[35] Caroline Lee Hentz, who answered Stowe directly in her novel *The Planter's Northern Bride*, drew upon southern proslavery theology to attack the notion that freedom derived from social and political institutions. Freedom, she insisted, derives only from God, "who has not made all men equal, though men wiser than God would have it so."[36] Hentz and her compatriots had scant patience with northern women's view that women enjoyed a special claim on morality and religion. In morality, there was only one sphere—God's—and the earthly attempts to approximate it fell to the direction of men.[37] Thus, in the measure that they favored reform—and many did on their own terms—southern women sought not to transform or perfect the world, but to restore it to conformity with God's design.[38]

Under these conditions, it is easy to understand that many southern women experienced their region's succession of military defeats as ominous. And as deaths and war-weariness mounted, more than one felt her soul sorely tried. Knowing the proslavery argument to have been grounded in the Bible, and believing it to reflect God's purpose, many took the military defeat of their cause as a sign of God's displeasure.[39] They feared He was turning His face away from them and theirs. In October 1865, Gertrude Thomas wrote bitterly in her journal that the surrender of the southern army and the abolition of slavery had reduced her "from a state of affluence to comparative poverty." Only she knew the real bitterness of her heart; only she knew the real effect the abolition of slavery had had upon her. For not until that abolition had she known "how intimately my faith in revelations and my faith in the institution of slavery had been woven together—true I had seen the evil of the latter but if the *Bible* was right then slavery *must be*—Slavery was done away with and my faith in God's Holy Book was terribly shaken. For a time I doubted God. The truth of revelations, all—everything—"[40]

Many other slaveholding women experienced a crisis of faith at some point during the later years of the war or following the ultimate defeat. Elizabeth Kilcrease, a Georgian like Gertrude Thomas, quoted one of her friends in a letter to another, "I have lost my religion since the Yankees set my negroes free." That experience, Kilcrease added, was probably more typical than many suspected.[41] Yet, like Gertrude Thomas who became active in the Woman's Christian Temperance Union, most of the women who felt that defeat had shattered their faith rapidly regained both their faith and their loyalty to their region. The Protestant tradition in which they had been reared had always taught them that faith could never be taken for granted—that it always had to be struggled for. The seemingly endless days of the war might at any given moment provoke doubt and despair. It would have been extraordinary if they had not. Before the war, the death of a family member or friend did the same, and the deaths of infants and children were common in the antebellum South. They were hard, sometimes bitterly hard, to bear, but one prayed they were sanctified. The difference this time lay in the possibility that God had judged southern society as a whole and found it wanting.

Southern women, like southern men, feared that they, as a people, might have merited God's harsh judgment. Their preachers had long warned of that possibility, calling upon them to bring southern slave society up to the standards of the Abrahmic model. And even when things looked bleakest, most persisted in the conviction that His judgment was a call to do better, not a final condemnation. On Christmas Day 1864, Catherine Edmonston sadly noted in her diary that the prospects for a "merry" Christmas seemed to recede into a distant future. How, she asked, could they be "merry with our best & dearest gone, exposed to Yankee bullets, to danger & to sudden death! We sit quiet spectators of this gigantic game of War, a game where all we hold dear is at stake, when the next turn of the wheel may behold us houseless exiles, wanderers on the face of the Earth!" Facing disaster, she prayed, "Grant us Faith, good Lord, faith in they merciful Providence, and humble resignation of ourselves into Thy hands, & an earnest conviction that whatever befall us, Thou has ordained it & that therefore it is right." And, she concluded, "Thou wilt not leave us comfortless. Increase our Faith."[42]

As southern women survived the unthinkable defeat and began to put their lives back together, they manifestly continued in or resumed their faith in religion and their confidence in their society.[43] The crises of the war loom large to historians because they loomed large to participants, for whom each day assumed unaccustomed significance. The more difficult issue for historians concerns the long-term consequences of the wartime travail. Even after emancipation, the South remained more rural and more household-based—in a word, less industrialized—than the North, which was itself developing at an accelerating rate. But, as the Republicans had expected it to do, the abolition of slavery opened the South to the influences of industrial capitalism and individualism. And postbellum poverty forced women to take up responsibilities and occupations that most would not have pursued before the war. In sum, however haltingly, the South began to move toward a modernization that, in the North, had been characterized by a separation of spheres and the feminization of religion.

The growth of the Woman's Christian Temperance Union, numerous women's clubs, and women's steady entry into teaching, among other developments, suggest that, following the abolition of slavery, the South did pursue that course. But if it did, it becomes difficult to argue that the Civil War decisively undercut women's religious conviction. For as women pursued new opportunities, they almost invariably did so under the mantle of religion, which, they claimed, justified their movement into the world.[44] Thus, the real change that the war may have effected in southern women's religion may have less to do with a loss of faith than with a new understanding of their relation to it.

Augusta Jane Evans, perhaps better than anyone else, traced the progress of women's faith through the late antebellum period, the war, and its aftermath. Her antebellum novel, *Beulah*, offers an extraordinary and rare exploration of a young woman's crisis of faith. The novel ends with Beulah Benton's recovery of faith and acceptance of her socially ordained role as wife—that is, with her repudiation of the claims of female independence. But in *Macaria*, written during the dark years of the war's end, Evans's heroine, Irene Huntington, doubly denied by paternal decree and her lover's death in the war from marriage to the man she loves, embraces the values of single-blessedness and devotes herself to binding the wounds that the war has inflicted upon her countrymen. Two years after Appomattox, Evans published *St. Elmo*, the most popular of all her novels and the final chapter in her trilogy. *St. Elmo* carried the themes of southern nationalism, social conservatism, and young women's coming of age that had characterized the earlier novels into the period of Reconstruction.[45]

St. Elmo, the novel's sardonic hero, so strikingly resembles the Lucifer of Milton's *Paradise Lost* that the reader is entitled to speculate that Evans explicitly aspired to retell the story for her own age. It is as if in the character of St. Elmo she sought to capture the essential flaw of male individualism in her day. St. Elmo's failings are but an exaggerated version of the commonplace failings of ordinary men. What they do on a small scale he does on a grand scale. But in having him end as a minister, she does not condemn him to feminization. Rather, she seems to be suggesting that the ministry is the proper forum for the expression of legitimate male power and authority.

Without slighting the singular importance of St. Elmo as a character, the true center of the novel lies in Edna Earl and, through her, in Evans's reconsideration of female independence following the war. In many respects, *St. Elmo* can be read as a rewriting of *Beulah*, from the vantage point of Evans's own new status as a successful author. On the surface, Edna is as much an exaggeration in her way as St. Elmo is in his. Too good and too beautiful to be true, she charms all who encounter her with her modesty and winning ways. During the course of the novel, three different and eminently desirable men, in addition to St. Elmo, propose marriage to her. Her learning surpasses that of most of the men of her acquaintance; her gifts as a writer win her a vast and devoted readership. Altogether, she embodies the essence of womanly virtue and warmth.

Edna is, nonetheless, supremely ambitious and, in her own way, as proud and willful as St. Elmo is in his. At the same time, Evans represents her, within the bounds of decorum and convention, as intensely vulnerable to the passionate love that St. Elmo arouses in her. Although as a child in St. Elmo's mother's house, Edna regarded him with dread, no sooner than he tells her of his past and declares his love for her does she acknowledge to herself that he is the king of her heart. Throughout the second half of the novel, her love persists unabated, although she steadfastly refuses to admit it to him and shuns all opportunities to see him, presumably for fear that she might weaken in her resolve. Long after St. Elmo has reformed his ways and, in innumerable acts of extraordinary generosity, undertaken to improve the lives of those around him, long after those whom he has harmed have wholeheartedly forgiven him, Edna remains intransigent. Love him she may, marry him she will not. Only the knowledge of his ordination leads her to relent.

It is tempting to read Edna's intransigence as evidence of postbellum southern women's determination to subject men to the claims of the domestic sphere. This reading would confirm that southern women were indeed espousing the view that women embodied distinct domestic values that could not compromise with the corruption of the masculine world and would reinforce the notion, dear to Stowe and her countrywomen, that women were the custodians of morality. But that reading, in my judgment, misses Evans's intent. More than once in the novel, Evans reminds us that Edna 's favorite chapter in the Bible was the fourteenth chapter of the book of John. The chapter abounds in passages that might have especially touched Edna, notably the constant insistence upon the importance of faith and the certainty of salvation for the faithful. Twice in the chapter, Jesus repeats the command, "Let not your heart be troubled." And, in verse 6, He says to Thomas "I am the way, the truth, and the life: no man cometh unto the Father, but by me." Throughout John, the question of judgment recurs frequently, and elsewhere, although not in the fourteenth chapter, Jesus explicitly tells the disciples, "Judge not, that ye be not judged."

Judgment runs like a thread through *St. Elmo*. At one point, St. Elmo's mother, who is pleading his case with Edna, asks Edna by what right she judges St. Elmo. Edna responds, "I believe that every man who kills another in a duel deserves the curse of Cain, and should be shunned as a murderer" (413). She adds that her conscience tells her that any man who seduces and betrays a woman deserves no less. Her belief. Her conscience. Have individualism and pride taken hold of her faith, leading her to set herself up as judge of the hearts and motives of others? Is she substituting herself for Jesus as the way? Toward the end of the novel, Evans gently suggests that her saintly heroine may have leaned too far in that direction. One Sunday when she is attending church, her eye is caught by a child's Sabbath-school picture of Jesus delivering the Sermon on the Mount. The inscription beneath the picture read, "Judge not, that ye not be judged. For with what judgment ye judge, ye shall be judged; and with what measure ye mete, it shall be measured to you again" (437). Twice during the day's sermon, the minister repeats the phrase, reminding his listeners that it was Jesus' "awful admonition" (439). Even then, Edna does not relent, although she lingers in the church to have one last view of St. Elmo's face. Evans describes Edna's face, as her eyes met St. Elmo's, as "calm" and "holy," "like those of an angel" (440). And she concludes the chapter with a bit of verse:

'Ah! well for us all some sweet hope lies
Deeply buried from human eyes;
And in the hereafter, angels may
Roll the stone from its grave away.' (440)

On the face of it, Evans appears to be endorsing Edna's intransigence. Certainly she refrains from punishing her with the doubts and anxieties that plagued Beulah. Yet more than once the novel suggests that to usurp, as Edna does, God's right of judgment is indeed to succumb to the sin of pride. The problem is all the more difficult, since Edna so steadfastly resists the pride of authorship and literary success to which she might easily have yielded. Withal, it is difficult to ignore the implicit suggestion that for all her saintliness, Edna Earl is in danger of setting her conscience up as co-equal to God's judgment. At one point, Edna asks her respected editor, Mr. Manning, if he does "not regard the writers of each age as the custodians of its taste as well as its morals" (320). He unhesitatingly replies, "Certainly not; they simply reflect and do not mold public taste" (320). Readers, he elaborates, expect authors "to help them kill time, not improve it" (321). The exchange betrays Edna's ambition to serve as custodian of the morals of her age. It no less clearly raises the possibility that, in thinking to shape the morals of others, she is merely reflecting their most cherished values. Thus, to follow the syllogism to its conclusion, in aspiring to judge and shape morality she is inadvertently reflecting the status quo.

Clearly, Evans does not intend to repudiate Edna's accomplishments as an author, not least because she demonstrably identifies them with her own. If anything, she implicitly likens Edna's influence to that of a minister in its ability to bring inspiration and dedication to ordinary women's lives. Throughout the novel it is never in doubt that Edna's writing contributes decisively to her readers' lives. Her writings, which Evans enthusiastically defends, embody a unique combination of masculine learning and feminine understanding, thus demonstrating the possibility of unity in American literary culture. Yet in her own life, Edna risks confusing the authority of authorship with a moral authority to which she cannot lay claim. And Evans, in exposing Edna's ambitions in the moral sphere, seems to be gently criticizing the prevailing sensibility that would reduce morality to an exclusively female concern.

In the end, the marriage of Edna and St. Elmo—the union of her authorship and his ministry in the service of humanity—resolves the contradictions that Evans has so cautiously exposed. Together, the humbling of Edna's moral pride and St. Elmo's recovery of his moral conscience promise a convergence of religious and secular culture. In their union is realized the promise of a faith that informs both male and female spheres whether in life or in letters. Significantly, the realization of the promise required the union of two individuals in the service of a truth that transcends both. In this sense, both Edna and St. Elmo had to sacrifice individual pride—to acknowledge that no single mortal can be sure of knowing the way.

Evans specialized in transforming young women's lives into parables or allegories for the state of southern culture as a whole, and *St. Elmo* is no exception. It would be hard to doubt that the novel indeed embodies her recognition that the postbellum South was embarking on the social and religious path laid out by the North. Notwithstanding the obvious temptations for a woman of her intelligence and ambition, Evans repudiates the separation of morality and power that the northern model of the feminization of religion embodied. We do not know how many southern women shared her views, nor even if many others perceived the danger. As George Rable has convincingly argued, the vast majority of southern women settled back into traditional gender roles.[46] And we may be sure that those who above all sought to pick up the pieces of their lives continued to understand those lives within the contours of Protestant Christianity. What remains less clear is whether they returned to the faith of their fathers and mothers or turned to the feminized and individualistic faith of their recent foes.

It is almost irresistible to view Evans's trilogy of *Beulah*, *Macaria*, and *St. Elmo* as an extended, if fictionally disguised, autobiography. Her letters from these years to her friend, Rachel Lyons, explore many of the issues she deploys in her novels, notably the appropriate place of religion, writing, and marriage in a woman's life.[47] There is a striking similarity between Evans's preoccupations in *St. Elmo* and those of Alcott in *Little Women*, which is widely recognized as largely autobiographical. Published only a year apart, both novels reflect on the education and responsibility of the woman writer. Evans and Alcott especially share a concern to delineate the respective and appropriate places of faith and ambition in the life of the young female author. Above all, both understand the woman writer's work as a vocation that must not repudiate women's special moral responsibilities. But where Alcott has her heroine marry a superficially unprepossessing, slightly older, absent-minded professor, Evans endows hers with the handsome, vibrant heir to a substantial fortune, whom she domesticates by having him embrace the ministry in atonement for his youthful sins.

The contrast between the two heroes suggests that whereas Alcott banished the dark, Gothic outpourings of her imagination to the thrillers she published under an alias, Evans ensconced brooding, Gothic danger at the heart of her most popular work. Not only does St. Elmo himself manifest all of the signature attributes of the tormented Gothic male, but the novel abounds with Gothic tropes. St. Elmo's room, which resembles a sinister cross between a lion's lair and an oriental palace, features exotic artifacts, dark corners, and mysterious lighting. And on a table at its center, in the manner of an altar, sits a locked box. His stern prohibition that the box, under no circumstances, be opened further suggests that, like some urn in a Gothic tale, it might contain a dangerous mysterious substance, or perhaps evidence of some irreparable crime. The contrast to the luminous openness of the tidy March cottage, with its pervasive evidence of a beneficent female dominion could not be stronger. The March girls grow up at the heart of the comforting, sustaining domesticity so beloved of northeastern women writers.

Alcott's and Evans's different strategies with respect to setting and decor bring us back to their understanding of women's relation to religion. Victor Sage has argued that "horror," or Gothic fiction, introduces theological issues in a way that nineteenth-century readers could readily grasp and that a form of "theological uncertainty" accounted for the novels' effect upon readers.[48] Few novels are more devoid of Gothic elements than *Little Women*, which features a reassuring domestic transparency. The novel, notwithstanding its indisputable merit, has completed the process that Douglas reproached the antebellum domestic sentimentalists for initiating: it has drained religion of all danger and theological conflict. Alcott turned to Bunyan not for the anxiety and discipline of his stern Christian orthodoxy but in order to transform the arduous and perilous drama of salvation into general thoughts on the formation of female character. Each of the little women faces a specific temptation, which takes the form of a weakness of character that proper training and earnest practice will overcome. The novel's precepts are unmistakably intended to apply to all young women's coming of age, and they assume that Christianity itself has become a matter of admirable and appropriate behavior in the world. Thus does Bunyan's "slough of despond," with its evocation of damnation or loss of faith, become a mere figure of speech to evoke depression or anxiety. The fear of maternal disapproval has replaced the terrors of Hell as the custodian of individual conscience.

Notes

1. Beth Gilbert Crabtree and James W. Patton, eds., *Journal of a Secesh Lady: The Diary of Catherine Ann Devereux Edmonston, 1860–1866* (Raleigh, NC, 1979). On war-

time diary keeping and letter writing, see Elizabeth Fox-Genovese, "Diaries, Letters, and Memoirs," in *Encyclopedia of the Confederacy*, ed. Richard Current (New York, 1993), 2: 470–478.

2. Crabtree and Patton, eds., *Journal of a Secesh Lady*, 1.

3. See, especially, Drew Gilpin Faust, *Mothers of Invention: Women of the Slaveholding South During the American Civil War* (Chapel Hill, NC, 1996); George Rable, *Civil Wars: Women and the Crisis of Southern Nationalism* (Urbana, IL, 1989); Mary Elizabeth Massey, *Bonnet Brigades: American Women and The Civil War* (New York, 1966).

4. For example, Anne Goodwyn Jones, whose pioneering book, *Tomorrow Is Another Day: The Woman Writer in the South, 1859–1936* (Baton Rouge, 1981), drew renewed attention to southern women writers, tends to read them through the prism of modern (northern) feminist assumptions. See also Joyce Warren, *The American Narcissus: Individualism and Women in Nineteenth-Century American Fiction* (New Brunswick, NJ, 1989; orig. ed., 1984), who explores the representation of women and the possibilities for female individualism in male fiction without regard to regional variation. Even Nina Baym's impressive and learned *American Women Writers and the Work of History, 1790–1860* (New Brunswick, NJ, 1995), which includes many southern women writers whom most critics ignore, does not take regional variations in women's experience as of noteworthy significance.

5. On the establishment of that tradition, see Cathy Davidson, *Revolution and the Word: The Rise of the Novel in America* (New York, 1986). See also Mary Kelley, *Private Woman, Public Stage: Literary Domesticity in Nineteenth-Century America* (New York, 1984); Susan Coultrap-McQuin, *Doing Literary Business: American Women Writers in the Nineteenth Century* (Chapel Hill, 1990); Jane Tompkins, *Sensational Designs: The Cultural Work of American Fiction, 1790–1860* (New York, 1989); and Alexander Cowie, *American Novel* (New York, 1948).

6. Tompkins, *Sentimental Designs*; Rachel Blau DuPlessis, *Writing Beyond the Ending: Narrative Strategies of Twentieth-Century Women Writers* (Bloomington, IN, 1985).

7. On literate southern women, see Elizabeth Fox-Genovese, *Within the Plantation Household: Black and White Women in the Old South* (Chapel Hill, 1988), and my "Religion in the Lives of Slaveholding Women of the Antebellum South," in *That Gentle Strength: Historical Perspectives on Women in Christianity*, eds. Lynda L. Coon, Katherine J. Haldane, & Elisabeth W. Sommer (Charlottesville, VA, 1990), 207–229. See also Jean E. Friedman, *The Enclosed Garden: Women and Community in the Evangelical South 1830–1900* (Chapel Hill, 1985); Donald G. Mathews, *Religion in the Old South* (Chicago, 1977).

8. Mary Ryan, *Cradle of the Middle Class: The Family in Oneida County, New York, 1790–1865* (New York, 1981), and her "A Women's Awakening: Evangelical Religion and the Families of Utica, New York, 1800–1840," *American Quarterly* 30 (1978): 602–623.

9. Ann Douglas, *The Feminization of American Culture* (New York, 1977). Cf. Tompkins, *Sentimental Designs*, who emphasizes the positive contributions of women's domestic fiction. See also Laura Wexler, "Tender Violence: Literary Eavesdropping, Domestic Fiction, and Educational Reform," in *The Culture of Sentiment: Race, Gender, and Sentimentality in 19th-Century America*, ed. Shirley Samuels (New York, 1992), 9–38.

10. For a full development of this argument, see Jamie Stanesa, "Slavery and the Politics of Domestic Identities: Ideology, Theology, and Region in American Women

Writers, 1850–1860," Ph.D. dissertation, Emory University, 1993. See also Joan D. Hedrick, *Harriet Beecher Stowe: A Life* (New York, 1994).

11. Harriet Beecher Stowe, *The Key to Uncle Tom's Cabin: Presenting the Original Facts and Documents upon Which the Story is Founded. Together with Corroborative Statements Verifying the Truth of the Work* (Boston, 1853). Ellen Carol DuBois, *Feminism and Suffrage: The Emergence of an Independent Women's Movement in America 1848–1869* (Ithaca, NY, 1978), 32, insists that women's dissatisfaction with their position was as much cause as effect of their participation in the antislavery movement.

12. Blanche Glassman Hersh, *The Slavery of Sex: Feminist-Abolitionists in America* (Urbana, IL, 1978). See also Jean Fagan Yellin, *Women and Sisters: Antislavery Feminists in American Culture* (New Haven, 1990).

13. Stanesa, "Slavery and the Politics of Domestic Identities"; Kathryn Kish Sklar, *Catharine Beecher: A Study in American Domesticity* (New Haven, 1973); Jeanne Boydston, Mary Kelley, and Anne Margolis, *The Beecher Sisters on Women's Rights and Woman's Sphere* (Chapel Hill, 1988).

14. Elizabeth Cady Stanton, *Eighty Years and More: Reminiscences 1815–1897* (New York, 1971; orig. ed., 1898), 81.

15. Stanton, "Declaration of Sentiments," in *The Concise History of Woman Suffrage: Selections from the Classic Works of Stanton, Anthony, Gage, and Harper*, eds. Mari Jo and Paul Buhle (Urbana, IL, 1978), 95.

16. Elizabeth Cady Stanton and Susan B. Anthony, *Correspondence, Writings, Speeches*, ed. Ellen Carol DuBois (New York, 1981), 33.

17. Lewis Perry, *Radical Abolitionism: Anarchy and the Government of God in Antislavery Thought* (Ithaca, NY, 1973). See also Ronald G. Walters, *The Antislavery Appeal: American Abolitionism after 1830* (Baltimore, 1976).

18. *Concise History of Woman Suffrage*, 311. Elizabeth Cady Stanton and the Revising Committee, *The Woman's Bible*, Pts. I & II (Seattle, 1974; orig. ed. 1898).

19. Elizabeth Cady Stanton, *The Woman's Bible*, Part I, 134.

20. Stanton, *Woman's Bible*, Part II, 113.

21. Stanton, *Woman's Bible*, Part II, 113.

22. See my discussion of these issues in "At Cross Purposes: Feminism and the Christian Faith," *Regeneration Quarterly* 1 (Fall 1995): 6–11.

23. On the general trend toward individualism and, indeed, secularism, see James Turner, *Without God, Without Creed: The Origins of Unbelief in America* (Baltimore, 1985).

24. Hedrick, *Harriet Beecher Stowe*, 302–304, 340–342.

25. Ruth Bordin, *Women and Temperance: The Quest for Power and Liberty, 1873–1900* (Philadelphia, 1981). See also Rosemary Radford Ruether and Rosemary Skinner Keller, eds., *Women and Religion in America: A Documentary History*, Vol. 1, *The Nineteenth Century* (New York, 1981); Amanda Porterfield, *Feminine Spirituality in America: From Sarah Edwards to Martha Graham* (Philadelphia, 1980); Lois A. Boyd and R. Douglas Brackenridge, *Presbyterian Women in America: Two Centuries of a Quest for Status* (Westport, CT, 1983).

26. Louisa May Alcott, *Little Women* (New York, 1983; orig. ed., 1868). See also Ednah D. Cheney, *Louisa May Alcott: Her Life, Letters, and Journals* (Boston, 1889); Elaine Showalter, "Editor's Introduction," to *Alternative Alcott* (New Brunswick, NJ, 1988).

27. Madeleine Stern, ed., *Behind a Mask: The Unknown Thrillers of Louisa May Alcott* (New York, 1975). See also Ann Douglas, "Mysteries of Louisa May Alcott," in *Critical Essays on Louisa May Alcott*, ed. Madeleine Stern (Boston, 1984), 231–239.

28. For the origins of some of these attitudes during the war, see Elizabeth D. Leonard, *Yankee Women: Gender Battles During the Civil War* (New York, 1994).

29. On the special tendency of the postbellum North to underscore and heighten the boundaries between male and female spheres, see Carroll Smith-Rosenberg, *Disorderly Conduct: Visions of Gender in Victorian America* (New York, 1985). On the growing exclusion of literary women from an increasingly all-male world of letters, see Hedrick, *Harriet Beecher Stowe*; and Carolyn L. Karcher, *The First Woman in the Republic: A Cultural Biography of Lydia Maria Child* (Durham, NC, 1994).

30. Harriet Beecher Stowe, *Uncle Tom's Cabin; or, Life Among the Lowly*, ed. Ann Douglas (New York, 1981; orig. ed., 1852), 244, 244–245.

31. Lewis Simpson, *Mind and the American Civil War: A Meditation on Lost Causes* (Baton Rouge, 1989).

32. Harriet Beecher Stowe, *Oldtown Folks* (Boston, 1896; orig. ed., 1869), 1, 121.

33. Elizabeth Fox-Genovese, "Contested Meanings: Women and the Problem of Freedom in the Mid-Nineteenth-Century United States," in *Historical Change and Human Rights: The Oxford Amnesty Lectures 1994*, ed. Olwen Hufton (New York, 1995), 179–216; Mary Margaret Johnston-Miller, "Heirs to Paternalism: Elite White Women and Emancipation in Alabama and Georgia," Ph.D. dissertation, Emory University, 1994; Drew Gilpin Faust, "Altars of Sacrifice: Confederate Women and the Narratives of War," in her *Southern Stories: Slaveholders in Peace and War* (Columbia, MO, 1992).

34. Elizabeth Fox-Genovese, "To Be Worthy of God's Favor: Southern Women's Defense and Critique of Slavery," *32nd Annual Fortenbaugh Memorial Lecture* (Gettysburg College, 1993); Fox-Genovese, *Within the Plantation Household*; Fox-Genovese, "Religion in the Lives of Slaveholding Women," 207–229.

35. Elizabeth Fox-Genovese, "Stewards of Their Culture: Southern Women Novelists as Social Critics," in *Stepping Out of the Shadows: Alabama Women, 1819–1990*, ed. Mary Martha Thomas (Tuscaloosa, 1995), 11–27; Elizabeth Moss, *Domestic Novelists in the Old South: Defenders of Southern Culture* (Baton Rouge, 1992); and Stanesa, "Slavery and the Politics of Domestic Identity," passim.

36. Caroline Lee Hentz, *The Planter's Northern Bride*, ed. Rhoda Coleman Ellison (Chapel Hill, 1970; orig. ed., 1854), 305.

37. For an extended discussion of Hentz's views, see Stanesa, "Slavery and the Politics of Domestic Identities."

38. Fox-Genovese, "To Be Worthy of God's Favor."

39. On the relation between proslavery and religion, see Elizabeth Fox-Genovese and Eugene D. Genovese, "The Divine Sanction of Social Order: The Religious Foundations of the Southern Slaveholders' World View," *Journal of the American Academy of Religion* 55 (June 1987): 210–223; and our "The Religious Ideals of Southern Slave Society," *Georgia Historical Quarterly* 70 (1986): 1–16. On responses during the war, see Drew Gilpin Faust, *The Creation of Confederate Nationalism: Ideology and Identity in the Civil War* (Baton Rouge, 1988). On responses following defeat, see Charles Reagan Wilson, *Baptized in Blood: The Religion of the Lost Cause, 1865–1920* (Athens, GA, 1980); and Gaines M. Foster, *Ghosts of the Confederacy: Defeat, the Lost Cause, and the Emergence of the New South 1865 to 1913* (New York, 1987).

40. Ella Gertrude Clanton Thomas Diary, 8 October 1865, Perkins Library, Duke University. There is also an abbreviated published version of the Thomas diary, *The Secret Eye: The Journal of Ella Gertrude Clanton Thomas, 1848–1889*, ed. Virginia Ingraham Burr (Chapel Hill, 1990).

41. Elizabeth Kilcrease to Clara Barrow, November 30, 1865, Barrow Family Papers, University of Georgia.

42. Crabtree and Patton, eds., *Journal of a Secesh Lady*, December 25, 1864, 648.

43. On southern women's attempts to make sense of defeat and to shape their region's understanding of its own history, see Sarah Gardner, " 'Blood and Irony': Southern Women's Narratives of the Civil War, 1865–1915," Ph.D. dissertation, Emory University, 1996.

44. See, for example, Elizabeth York Enstam, "They Called It 'Motherhood': Dallas Women and Public Life, 1895–1918," in *Hidden Histories of Women in the New South*, eds. Virginia Bernhard, Betty Brandon, Elizabeth Fox-Genovese, Theda Purdue, and Elizabeth H. Turner (Columbia, MO, 1994), 71–95; Glenda Elizabeth Gilmore, " 'A Melting Time': Black Women, White Women, and the WCTU in North Carolina, 1880–1990," ibid., 153–172. See also Anne Firor Scott, *The Southern Lady from Pedestal to Politics, 1830–1930* (Chicago, 1970).

45. Augusta Jane Evans, *Beulah*, ed. Elizabeth Fox-Genovese (Baton Rouge, 1992; orig. ed., 1859). Augusta Jane Evans, *Macaria, Or, Altars of Sacrifice*, ed. Drew Gilpin Faust (Baton Rouge, 1992; orig. ed., 1864); Augusta J. Evans-Wilson, *St. Elmo* (New York, n.d.; orig. ed., 1867). On Evans's life, see William Fidler, *Augusta Evans Wilson: A Biography* (University, AL, 1951). See also Drew Faust's introduction to *Macaria* and my introduction to *Beulah*.

46. Rable, *Civil Wars*; Faust, *Mothers of Invention*.

47. The original letters are in the possession of William Fidler of Tuscaloosa, Alabama, to whom I am deeply indebted for having shared copies of them, as well as his own extensive knowledge of Evans's life and career, with me.

48. Victor Sage, *Horror Fiction in the Protestant Tradition* (London, 1988), xvi–xvii.

11

"Without Pilot or Compass"

Elite Women and Religion in the Civil War South

DREW GILPIN FAUST

One of the most notable and distinctive features of the Old South, we have long been told, was its overwhelmingly Protestant and, in particular, evangelical character. From Virginia to Texas, from soon after the Revolution to the Civil War, a shared religious orientation united the vast majority of blacks and whites, rich and poor, women and men into a single culture of belief and behavior. At a time when immigration, economic development, and expansion were introducing diversity and conflict into northern life and religion, the South clung both to traditional social forms and common religious orientation. As sectional strife and Civil War approached, the political and cultural spokesmen for the white South celebrated the region's freedom from the dangerous and divisive "isms" of feminism, atheism, and abolitionism. Its religious unity and strength, secessionists argued, would prove as important as the strongest battalions in establishing southern independence.[1]

Yet neither God nor the Confederacy's bravest legions would ultimately deliver the anticipated triumph. Four years of civil war would reveal more than just the South's economic and military weakness in comparison to the more populous and industrialized North. Social conflict and emerging class divisions among whites undermined unity on both home and battlefront, while on plantations across the South slaves waged their own war against their masters and the larger system of human bondage.[2] The Civil War would demonstrate underlying fissures in the South's religious harmony and uniformity as well. The region's much vaunted evangelical unity would prove to be in part at least a rhetorical formulation—a prescription as much as a description—a generali-

zation that obscured significant divisions among those whose religious understandings had important differences as well as commonalities.[3]

It was over two decades ago that Eugene D. Genovese's *Roll, Jordan, Roll*
offered a compelling example of both the extent and the limits of this shared
southern evangelical culture. African-American southerners at once embraced
Protestantism and reshaped it to fit their own needs, joining the liberationist
message of Moses to the less worldly promises of New Testament salvation.
The discourse and vocabulary of evangelical religion, moreover, became the
language of social negotiation between white and black, as notions of duty,
obligation, mastery, and subordination were enshrined in the ideology of paternalism. And just as differing black and white perspectives on Christian belief
lay beneath a shared evangelical outlook, so contrasting understandings of
power were masked by the social operations of paternalism. Slaves played at
"puttin' on ol' Massa" while, often oblivious to their manipulations and even
their scorn, Massa himself offered a simultaneous and complementary performance of the role of benevolent patriarch. Social actors, we are reminded, may
participate with apparent harmony in shared behaviors and yet retain quite
different and even opposing interpretations of the meaning of their activities.[4]

The inherent social conflict of slavery made the appearance of overt divisions and differences between black and white religion all but inevitable. Yet
other groups of believers held particularistic positions as well, embracing religious perspectives that reflected their locations and identities within this world
as much as any hopes or expectations for a world to come. And just as Civil
War brought a "moment of truth"—to borrow Genovese's apt phrase—to mas-
ter-slave interaction and to the evangelically based doctrines of paternalism, so
too its social dislocations forced other groups to explore their social and spiritual identities, to look anew at their lives and experiences within the context
of meaning that religious belief had always provided.

The women of the South's master class were a group for whom religion
would provide an important instrument of support, of self-examination and—
in time—of self-transformation during the crisis of civil war. Situated within
the privileged hierarchy of the Old South, women of slaveowning families
would only with the demands and sacrifices of war begin to see their identities
and interests as distinct from those of their men. This evolution toward an
altered, more particularistic, newly gendered consciousness would be limited,
for these women would cling above all to the class and racial privilege that
defined their position as ladies. But the shift would encompass new attitudes
about the nature of religious practice and the place of God in these women's
lives.[5]

From the outbreak of conflict, Confederate women, like their husbands, brothers, and sons, found both justification and consolation in religion. Charlestonians, Emma Holmes reported the day of the firing on Fort Sumter, were
neither anxious nor terrified, but "calm and grave," for they were "so impressed
with the justice of our cause that they place entire confidence in the God of
Battles." Government officials and church leaders alike nurtured belief in the

divine purpose of the Confederate experiment. Ministers preached patriotism; politicians vaunted their religious purposes and invoked the will of God as the highest legitimation for southern unity. Political nationalism and religious mission came to seem all but inseparable.[6]

But this convergence of religion with politics in the wartime South would have significant implications for privileged white women, for it provided them a new justification and a new language with which to scrutinize public affairs. Religion, long regarded as a central component of the female sphere, opened an avenue into the male world of politics and public action.

At the outset, however, religion most immediately provided women, like Emma Holmes, with confidence and equanimity as they faced the prospect of war. "It matters not," Kate Carney of Tennessee reassured herself early in 1861, "how weak our cause, if but God and justice is on our side, we will at last triumph." Early Confederate successes reinforced this belief in divine Providence. Nancy Emerson of Virginia, for example, explained southern victories and her own optimism in the language of biblical prophecy. "This judgement from God has fallen upon the North because of their delusion from him. . . . We shall achieve our independence, & if guided aright, shall fulfill a high destiny, & be far more prosperous than ever before. Never for one moment since the struggle commenced has my mind wavered as to the final result."[7]

But mounting losses, personal as well as national, gradually forced a revision of war's typology to accompany eroding confidence. Death and battlefield defeat soon made it clear that Confederates had perhaps been chosen not simply for God's favor but, like Job, for the suffering that tests and ultimately strengthens and purifies faith. As Sarah Estes struggled to remember, " 'The Lord loveth whom he chasteneth.' "[8]

As the unimaginable horrors of war began to reveal themselves, women turned to religion to make sense of their anguish and to find the courage to endure. "Oh that a righteous God may subdue the wicked spirits of man & cause them to cease this cruel war," wrote Anne Darden of North Carolina in summer 1861. "But he seeth best to afflict us more deeply. I say thy will be done, my Savior & we will trust thee though thou slay us, for we know there is help in no other power but thine to quell to raging storm." Suffering, Christianity promised, was not useless, was not without meaning. Rightly managed, it could prove the avenue to deeper faith and ultimate salvation. Wartime theology emphasized that chastisement demanded reformation; the Confederates had to repent of their sins to end the trial of war. But God's punishment, expressed in interim defeats or failures, did not mean that ultimate success was impossible. Instead, setbacks had to be seen as warnings, urging southerners to transform themselves and their world to find God's favor.[9]

By casting the hardship of war into a narrative of punishment, reformation, and deliverance, clergy offered southerners a basis for strength and confidence even amid disaster. Such a rendering of their experience made religion a fundamental source of consolation for Confederate women. "If we did not have a Bible," wrote Lizzie Ozburn of Georgia, "what would we do—tis more comfort to me than anything else now." "If it was not for religion that keep[s] me up," declared a young New Orleans mother, "I would kill myself." After three successive Confederate reverses in the West, Alice Ready of South Carolina banished her distress by designating the setbacks as "a punishment God has sent upon us for our boastfulness." Some defeats, she assured herself, were to be expected: "it would be an unparalleled war were [we] to meet with none and so far am I from being discouraged, that my *faith* has only grown stronger—I feel that we must and will succeed finally with the help of God."[10]

Yet the God of this narrative of punishment and deliverance was sterner, more judgmental than the God who had heretofore served as the center of these women's belief. He was more the God of Job than of Jesus, his promised help ultimate not proximate. And in the meantime, women's own actions—of pious devotion and reformation—necessarily took on increased importance. Just as many of these women found themselves confronting unprecedented responsibilities on the homefront in the absence of husbands departed for war, so they faced new religious expectations as well. Women's daily lives would be profoundly shaped by both these sets of demands—those of their newly female-headed households and those of an apparently angry God. Women's relationships to masters both terrestrial and divine were in considerable flux.

God would not find reason to stay his wrath in a revitalization of traditional institutional religion on the Confederate home front. Many churches closed their doors or sharply reduced the number of their services because of the departure of clergymen to the front. Countless southerners shared the experience of eleven-year-old Belle Strickland of Mississippi, who recorded in her diary in January 1865, "We went to church today but there was none." Sometimes several denominations were compelled to ignore their differences and meet together in order to share a single available minister. But even when services were held, worshipers were often deterred by lack of transportation because horses, mules, and carriages had been impressed for war. Sarah Estes, a refugee, was unable to attend church because of her frequent movements and feared, "I will get to be almost a heathen." Numbers of church buildings were severely damaged or destroyed. During the siege of Vicksburg, one minister held services only at the insistence of two of his female parishioners, who had a difficult time finding places to sit amid the bricks, mortar, and glass that filled the damaged structure.[11]

Although revivals swept through the Confederate army from 1862 until the last months of the war, no comparable work of grace seemed to take place behind the lines. Yet charges of "coldness" or godlessness against Confederate civilians must be examined within the framework of the particular style of religious expression that characterized the southern home front. The falling off of formal worship, the scarcity of dramatic revivals comparable to those in army camps should not be seen as necessarily representing a failure of devotion or piety. Religious forms changed behind the lines, with emphasis shifting from church-centered liturgy and ritual led by ordained ministers to home-centered observances often both directed and largely attended by women. As the gender of civilian worshipers shifted, so too religious practice moved from a more public and male to a more private and female sphere.[12]

Women organized regular prayer groups in towns and villages across the South. Newly installed as heads of households, women often turned to formal group prayer for families black and white as a vehicle for strengthening their unaccustomed leadership. When the Holmes family refugeed from Charleston to the upcountry, Emma's mother inaugurated a system of morning and evening family prayer, something, her daughter noted, "we have never had before." During one of the first of many large religious meetings at her home in Winchester, Mary Lee felt awkward acting the part of minister for the several dozen assembled ladies, so even though she "conducted the services," she "confined myself to the prayer book prayers." Ready to serve as a conduit for God's words, she was not yet comfortable assuming the authority implied by uttering her own. At a military hospital in Virginia, Kate Rowland and her mother served as nurse and matron, but soon took on spiritual responsibilities as well. Not only did they read regular Sunday services to the convalescents, they offered a rite of Christian burial for patients who failed to respond to their therapeutic ministrations. "We have had no Chaplain all winter," Kate explained, "so we had to make up the deficiency as far as possible ourselves."[13]

As army evangelists acknowledged, women had formed the foundation of the prewar church; it was largely men who, at the outset of war, remained unconverted and unobservant, appealing targets for revivalists. Women, at home, already believers, provided no such field for the harvest. Female wartime piety did not, therefore, focus on conversion, but instead on practice and even leadership, as civilian religion became in a sense domesticated—located and performed increasingly within the family and the home.

And at least some of the celebrated religious enthusiasm within Confederate army camps had its origin behind the lines, among women fearing the loss of their husbands, not just in this world but for all time. As women searched their own souls for shortcomings that might be contributing to God's displeasure, they urged their husbands to do the same. The organized churches exploited the power of this female message, institutionalizing it in the most popular of the many religious tracts supplied to soldiers during the war. By the end of 1862, interdenominational tract societies had distributed more than 150,000 copies of *A Mother's Parting Words* throughout the Confederate army, reminding soldiers that "of all men," they had "the greatest need for piety," and assuring them too that despite the female preponderance in prewar church membership, "Piety will not make you effeminate or cowardly."[14]

Before the war, women had abided their husbands' lack of godly commitment. But the dangers of battle made disbelief intolerable. The death of an unconverted husband would mean eternal separation, the impossibility of a blessed reunion in the great hereafter. "Do you feel," Julia Davidson of Atlanta demanded of her husband, "that you have made peace *with God*? tell me Johnny dear what are your *prospects* for *eternity*." Rachel Craighead felt sufficiently strongly about religious questions to risk an all-out confrontation with her husband by insisting that he attend religious services. He was furious at her presumption in trying "to rule," but she felt empowered in her assertiveness by the higher purpose that inspired her, even though his fury made her "miserable." In the prevailing narrative of divine chastisement and deliverance, piety was an important prerequisite for victory, and women felt encouraged to exercise considerable spiritual authority in its pursuit.[15]

Yet as months of war stretched into years, deliverance began to seem increasingly remote and the pain of individual bereavements nearly unbearable. The ever-mounting death toll worked its terrible effects on women's sensibilities. By the middle years of the war, almost no family remained exempt. On a round of visits to friends on a September day in 1863, Catherine Edmondston of North Carolina directly confronted the meaning of the bloody summer of Gettysburg and Vicksburg. Calling at eight houses, she found each one in mourning for a husband, a brother, or a son.[16]

In the early years of war, deaths were marked with elaborate ceremony. When Charleston's slain were returned from First Manassas on July 26, 1861, business was suspended throughout the city, and three companies of cavalry escorted the bodies from the railroad depot to City Hall. There the dead heroes lay in state until more than a thousand soldiers accompanied them to St. Paul's Church and at last to Magnolia Cemetery. A little more than a year later, Constance Cary described her distress at a very different burial scene in Richmond: "six or seven coffins dropped into one yawning pit, and hurriedly covered in, all that a grateful country could render in return for precious lives." At a military hospital in Oxford, Mississippi, a nurse remembered that soldiers had been interred "in bunches, just like dead chickens," with no ceremony to mark their passage to eternity.[17]

This altered behavior expressed significant shifts in attitude. "People do not mourn their dead as they used to," Kate Stone observed in April 1864. "Everyone seems to live only in the present—just from day to day—otherwise I fancy many would go crazy." Not just mourning but death itself had taken on a new meaning. "Death does not seem half so terrible as it did long ago," Stone acknowledged. "War has hardened us," confirmed young Nannie Haskins of Tennessee in the summer of 1864. Numbness offered protection, a defense against unfathomable losses and pain. Kate Foster recognized the origins of her own emotional transformation in her brother's death. After his departure, "My heart became flint. I am almost afraid to love too dearly anyone now." But such denial represented another kind of loss as well, an abandonment of feeling, a deadening of sensibility that was fearful in itself. "Bury me not in war times," Mary Lee remarked, "no one feels anything now."[18]

Christian doctrines of resignation seemingly supported this psychological process of numbing and denial, but, however sanctified, submission to God's will remained a severe trial for those struggling to accept the pain of bereavement. Part of the difficulty lay in coming to terms with a new understanding of God and his attributes. The deity ruling over the Confederate South was showing himself not to be a benevolent, all-loving, and forgiving father. Rather, this was the severe, vengeful, wrathful God of the Old Testament, a divinity willing to let many a cherished sparrow fall for his own larger and inscrutable purposes. This was a God willing to demand rather than committed to relieve the suffering of his subjects. This was a God very distant from the daily needs and desires of his worshipers.

Women struggled to adapt to this changed relationship with the Supreme Being, invoking religious doctrines and texts almost as incantations in their effort to transcend suffering and grief, to wean themselves from the cares of this world. "*Il faut se resigner a la volonte de Dieu et accepter les croix qu'il nous envoie. . . . Il faut me soumettre et prier et esperer,*" wrote A. Grima of New Orleans as she worried about her son at the front.[19]

But resignation and denial had their limits; accepting this new understanding of God was difficult. Susan Caldwell of Virginia complained repeatedly of her inability to "gain power over my own rebellious heart to say God's Will be done. Oh! how hard to be submissive." Even with the supports of religion, Caldwell believed, "I cannot stand a great deal more." She longed to be a pious Christian, to live for Heaven, to be certain she would reach there and find rest. "But I find it hard. My heart is so *rebellious.*" An anonymous woman described her questioning in a poem for an Atlanta newspaper:

> I cannot weep, I dare not pray;
>   Sad and rebellious thought
> Has swayed my lonely soul today,
>   And night no calm has brought.

But after expressing her distress, the poet abandoned her challenge, impugning its very legitimacy in the face of God's omnipotence.

> Systems of worlds roll vast and grand,
>   Each round its central sun,
> And I dare doubt their maker's Hand
>   Can wisely govern *one?*

> Humbled and awed, to earth I sink,
>   How weak I seem, how vain
> When even this earth is but a link
>   In great creation's chain.

This writer resolved doubt in female self-abasement, a belittling of the self, of the "I" that dares to question. Yet significantly, God's legitimacy here derived not from his benevolence, but his power; the evidence she cited for his wisdom was his strength, and her own worship was expressed as arising not from love, but humility, awe, vanity, and weakness.[20]

Some women at least resisted subordination and the humble acceptance of defeat and slaughter. Alice Ready, contemplating the almost unmentionable possibility of ultimate Confederate failure, confessed, "I would not [wish to] rebel against His decree, but my faith has never been so weak as tonight." Eroding confidence in the Confederacy would begin to undermine religious certainty. Some women "plainly indicated," Mary Gay reported, "that if our cause failed they would lose all faith in a prayer-answering God." For Gay, a brother's death proved the test of her faith, but one that she failed. "I did not believe it was God's will that my brother should die, and I could not say to that Holy Being, 'Thy will be done.' "[21]

Significantly, some women no longer able passively to bear war's suffering were propelled to action in pursuit of their own interests in this world. As Ida Wilkom wrote in a letter to the Confederate secretary of war demanding the release of her husband from the army, "I have tried everything," she explained, "to submit to the will of God in tranquil resignation; but I find, a human being can suffer only according to human strength."[22]

Political petitioning emerged directly from the traditions and habits and even the language of divine prayer. Yet, as a Virginia woman readily admitted, writing public officials represented a new departure for most Confederate females. "I am unused to sue any one save my Maker." The thousands of letters from women that poured into state and Confederate offices often opened with apologies for this intrusion into the public sphere and demonstrated as well a more comfortable familiarity with a sacred realm of action and expression. As a North Carolina woman explained to Jefferson Davis in a request for her husband's military discharge, "I know not how to ask the favor that I have Attempted. Yet I have been taught to ask in faith believe and I would receive and I now ask of you as Earthly Father one favor that is in your power to grant." As Henrietta McDonald explained to the Confederate president, she appealed to him for help just "as I would the God of heaven for the salvation of my soul."[23]

The governments of heaven and earth seemed of a piece. Elizabeth Collier of Hillsborough, North Carolina, understood their relationship clearly: "the ultimate person on whom all depend is God," she wrote, ". . . but it is also true that . . . women learn the necessity of dependence on Him by the necessary resting of their nature on men." Dependence and subordination were enjoined by both theology and politics, yet by the late years of the war, the protection that was their guaranteed accompaniment had seemingly disappeared and dependence had proven dangerous. Neither God nor Jefferson Davis was attending to women's desperate needs; women, now alone, struggled to take care of themselves, paying a high price for their new and enforced autonomy. Increasingly, suffering began to produce not resignation but anger—directed against both God and the state.[24]

Confederate surrender posed an all but insurmountable challenge to Confederate women's faith, to the system of belief that had explained their world and had justified the costly sacrifices demanded of them for four long years. Suffused with rage and betrayal, some women even for a time explicitly rejected God. "I know not how to bear it," Grace Elmore reflected in May 1865. "I cannot be resigned. Hard thoughts against my God arise; questions of his justice, of his mercy . . . and refuse to be silenced." Women struggled to reconcile reality with the Christian narratives of suffering and redemption that had consoled them for so long, but could find little reason or understanding. "Day and night in every moment of quiet," Elmore explained, "I am trying to work out the meaning of this horrible fact." Mary Lee confessed herself "utterly bewildered." She was, she wrote, "like a ship at sea without pilot or compass." The hierarchies of belief and social order within which they had located their souls and identities had been overthrown. Neither God nor Jefferson Davis remained to pilot their vessel; neither Christianity nor Confederate nationalism seemed any longer available to serve as guiding compass.[25]

Most of these women ultimately regained some measure of faith—in both religion and the patriarchal society they worked hard to restore to the defeated South in the years after Appomattox. But their belief, their understanding of God, their relationship to Him and to the men who stood as His deputies on earth were significantly changed. Neither religion nor society would be as it has been before the war. Women of the South's master class had come face to face with the unfamiliar and even frightening aspects of the "lords of creation"—both divine and terrestrial—upon whom they had depended. War had dealt a significant blow to the logic of Christian—and, by implication, female—submission. At the same time, the warborn merging of religion and politics had brought to the South a justification for women's relevance within a more public realm. Antebellum northern reform had been erected on just such a configuration of belief and action. But southern women had not shared the spiritual and social empowerment experienced by so many of their northern sisters during the prewar years. For southern women, necessity, not choice, would prove to be the source of change. The realities of life in the Confederacy would impress upon white southern women the dangers of passive dependence upon God or man. Husbands, brothers, and sons had failed to protect and support them during the war and had brought the South to defeat; God had proved distant and even indifferent to their sufferings and hardships. Not so much out of any confidence in their own abilities as from a profound distrust of their men and a changed understanding of God, Confederate women would assume a new independence in the postwar world. Women themselves would feel compelled to serve as both pilot and compass.[26]

Notes

1. Donald G. Mathews, *Religion in the Old South* (Chicago, 1977); Drew Gilpin Faust, *The Creation of Confederate Nationalism: Ideology and Identity in the Civil War South* (Baton Rouge, 1988); Mitchell Snay, *Gospel of Disunion: Religion and Separatism in the Antebellum South* (New York, 1993).

2. On class divisions within the Confederacy, see, for example, Paul Escott, "The Moral Economy of the Crowd in Confederate North Carolina," *Maryland Historian* 13 (Spring 1982): 1–18; on slaves, see Armstead Robinson, "Day of Jubilo: Civil War and the Demise of Slavery in the Mississippi Valley, 1861–1865," Ph.D. dissertation, University of Rochester, 1976; see also Ira Berlin, Barbara J. Fields, Thavolia Glymph, Joseph P. Reidy, and Leslie Rowland, eds., *Freedom: A Documentary History of Emancipation, 1861–1867: Series I, Vol. I: The Destruction of Slavery* (New York, 1985).

3. On the multiple and often conflicting uses of evangelicalism, see Faust, *Creation of Confederate Nationalism*.

4. Eugene D. Genovese, *Roll, Jordan, Roll: The World the Slaves Made* (New York, 1974). Anthony Wallace first made me think about the significance of intersecting be-

haviors that did not necessarily imply common belief. See his work on mazeways, in particular. Anthony F. C. Wallace, *Culture and Personality* (New York, 1970) and *Religion: An Anthropological View* (New York, 1966).

5. On privileged white women in the Old South and the Civil War, see in general, Anne Firor Scott, *The Southern Lady: From Pedestal to Politics* (Chicago, 1970); Elizabeth Fox-Genovese, *Within the Plantation Household: Black and White Women of the Old South* (Chapel Hill, 1988); Catherine Clinton, *The Plantation Mistress: Woman's World in the Old South* (New York, 1982); Jean E. Friedman, *The Enclosed Garden: Women and Community in the Evangelical South, 1830–1900* (Chapel Hill, 1985); George C. Rable, *Civil Wars: Women and the Crisis of Southern Nationalism* (Urbana, 1989); Francis Butler Simkins and James Welch Patton, *The Women of the Confederacy* (Richmond, 1936).

6. Emma Holmes, *Diary of Miss Emma Holmes, 1861–1866*, ed. John Marszalek (Baton Rouge, 1979), 25–26. Stephen Elliott, *Ezra's Dilemna [sic]. A Sermon* (Savannah, 1863); Faust, *Creation*, 26–28; James Silver, *Confederate Morale and Church Propaganda* (Tuscaloosa, 1957); Richard Beringer, Herman Hattaway, Archer Jones, and William N. Still Jr., *Why the South Lost the Civil War* (Athens, GA, 1986) 82–107.

7. Kate Carney Diary, February 28, 1861, Southern Historical Collection, University of North Carolina, Chapel Hill; Nancy Emerson Diary, July 4, 1862, University of Virginia.

8. Sarah Estes Diary, November 14, 1862, Tennessee State Library, Nashville.

9. Annie Darden Diary, July 20, 1861, North Carolina Department of Archives and History, Raleigh.

10. Lizzie Ozburn to Jimmie Ozburn, October 21, 1861, Katherine Elizabeth Ozburn Papers, Georgia Department of Archives, Atlanta; Anais to My Dear Husband, April 19, 1863, Warren Ogden Papers, Tulane University; Alice Ready Diary, February 11, 1862, Southern Historical Collection, University of North Carolina.

11. Belle Strickland Diary, January 21, 1865, Mississippi Department of Archives and History, Jackson; Sarah Estes Diary, August 17, 1862; Emma Balfour Diary, June 2, 1863, Mississippi Department of Archives and History, Jackson.

12. See Drew Gilpin Faust, "Christian Soldiers: The Meaning of Revivalism in the Confederate Army," in Faust, *Southern Stories: Slaveholders in Peace and War* (Columbia, 1992), 88–109. On "coldness," see *Biblical Recorder*, June 17, 1863.

13. Emma Holmes, *Diary*, 170; Mary Greenhow Lee Diary, May 16, 1862, Winchester-Frederick County Historical Society, Handley Library, Winchester, VA; Kate Rowland Diary, March 3, 1862, Museum of the Confederacy, Richmond, VA. On women performing ministerial roles, see also Faust, "Race, Gender and Confederate Nationalism: William D. Washington's *Burial of Latane*," in Faust, *Southern Stories*, 148–159.

14. Mrs. Frances Blake Brockenbrough, *A Mother's Parting Words to her Soldier Boy* (Petersburg, VA, 1862), 4. On the phenomenal success of this tract, see *Religious Herald*, October 23, 1862.

15. Julia Davidson to John Davidson, September 19, 1862, Davidson Family Papers, Atlanta History Center; Rachel Craighead Diary, September 14, 1862, Tennessee State Library, Nashville.

16. Catherine Edmondston, *Journal of a Secesh Lady: The Diary of Catherine Ann Devereux Edmondston, 1860–1866*, eds. Beth Crabtree and James W. Patton (Raleigh, 1979), 461.

17. See description of Charleston in Holmes, *Diary*, 69–70, and a similar description of New Orleans in Clara Solomon Diary, July 16, 1861, Louisiana State University; Constance Cary Harrison, *Recollections Grave and Gay* (New York, 1911), 188; Mrs.

Calvin Brown, "Lafayette County, 1860–1865: A Narrative," Mississippi Department of Archives and History, Jackson.

18. Kate Stone, *Brokenburn: The Journal of Kate Stone, 1861–1868*, ed. John Q. Anderson (Baton Rouge, 1955), 277, 258; Nannie Haskins Diary, July 14, 1864, Tennessee State Library, Nashville; Kate Foster Diary, November 15, 1863, Duke University; Mary Greenhow Lee Diary, July 24, 1863.

19. A. Grima to Alfred Grima, October 30, 1863, Grima Family Papers, Historic New Orleans Collection. "It is necessary to resign oneself to the will of God and accept the crosses he sends us. . . . It is necessary for me to submit and pray and hope." French translation by the author.

20. Susan Caldwell to Lycurgus Caldwell, October 9, 1864, November 15, 1865, *'My Heart Is So Rebellious': The Caldwell Letters, 1861–1865*, ed. J. Michael Welton (Warrenton, VA, 1991), 241, 255; M. E. B., "Lights and Shadows of a Solitary Woman's Thoughts," clipping in M. L. Lawton Scrapbook, 25, Atlanta History Center.

21. Alice Ready Diary, March 24, 1862; Mary Ann Harris Gay, *Life in Dixie During the War* (Atlanta, 1892), 195.

22. Ida Wilkom to Secretary of War, February 7, 1862, Letters Received, Confederate Secretary of War (hereafter, LRCSW), RG 109, M437, 11167, reel 27, National Archives.

23. Annie Craig to Secretary of War, September 17, 1861, LRCSW, 5689, reel 10; M. V. Caho to Jefferson Davis, January 28, 1864, LRCSW, C177, reel 123; Henrietta McDonald to Jefferson Davis, September 15, 1861, LRCSW, 5668, reel 10.

24. Elizabeth Collier Diary, July 3, 1862, Southern Historical Collection, University of North Carolina.

25. Grace Elmore Diary, May 10, 1865, South Caroliniana Library, University of South Carolina, Columbia; Mary Greenhow Lee Diary, April 15, 1865, Handley Library. On women's reactions to defeat, see also Richard M. Weaver, *The Southern Tradition at Bay: A History of Postbellum Thought* (New Rochelle, 1968), 270–273; and Rable, *Civil Wars*, 223–225.

26. For examples of women losing and then regaining at least some measure of faith, see Cornelia Peake McDonald, *A Woman's Civil War*, ed Minrose C. Gwin (Madison, 1992); and Ella Gertrude Clanton Thomas, *The Secret Eye: The Journal of Ella Gertrude Clanton Thomas*, ed. Virginia Ingraham Burr (Chapel Hill, 1990).

12

Catholic Religion, Irish Ethnicity, and the Civil War

RANDALL M. MILLER

In 1988, while looking for relics on the Antietam battlefield, a collector happened on an extraordinary discovery. Unearthing a brass hook, ammunition, and buttons at one site, he dug deeper. He found a tooth. The collector and his fellow workers reported the findings to the landowner and then to the National Park Service. Archeologists returned to the spot and eventually uncovered the bones of four Union soldiers, who had been hastily buried and forgotten on September 17, 1862, the bloodiest day of the Civil War. After six years of analysis of the physical remnants and surrounding artifacts, and a thorough combing of historical records, a team of archeologists and anthropologists determined that all of the men had been members of the 63rd New York Infantry, part of the famous Irish Brigade that had covered itself in glory with its gallant charge at Bloody Lane that fateful day in 1862. As one of the men was a private likely in his forties, which was older than most soldiers, his identity could be narrowed down to a choice of three— James Gallagher, a stonecutter from Kilkenny, Ireland; Martin McMahon, a laborer from County Clare, Ireland; or James McGarigan, an Irish American. That Irishman had died with a rosary looped around his neck, after three bullets smashed his breastbone while the brigade approached the crest of Bloody Lane. His remains and those of his wholly anonymous comrades have since been reburied, after a Catholic Mass, at the National Cemetery at Antietam.[1]

This short tale says everything about the problem of writing the history of the Irish Catholics, or any immigrant group, in the Civil War. Although roughly 145,000 Irish Catholics served in the Union army, their experience has been largely forgotten. Ella Lonn's thick volumes on the foreign-born in the Union and Confederate armies and William Burton's more recent treatment of the Union's ethnic regiments are the notable exceptions, but even they devote most of their attention to the officers and slight the common soldiers. The faith of the immigrants gets shorter shrift. Indeed, save for filiopietistic ethnic texts offered to Catholic schoolchildren early in this century and a few albums of Civil War esoterica, the Catholic experience has been left off the pages of the enormous literature on the war. Even modern scholarly books on the Irish, Catholics, or immigrants generally skim over the war, as if the central event in American history has no place in ethnic or religious history and culture. The stories of the immigrant, ethnic, and Catholic soldiers lie buried, waiting excavation by scholars.[2]

This essay promises only a preliminary dig into one level of the story—namely, the interplay between the way the American Catholic church used the war to demonstrate its Americanism and the way Irish Catholics used their own service in the war to define themselves as an American ethnic group. Too much basic spade work needs to be done to write a full account of all ways the war affected, and was affected by, all manner of Catholics in arms. This essay looks only at the northern side and within that context, the Irish Catholic story. Lacking so much of the basic information on any Catholic group in either section, it would be presumptuous to try to do more. Like the archeologists and anthropologists working the Antietam find, we are struggling just to know the names. Excavating enough sources to reconstruct the religious and ethnic history of the soldiers and their communities will take time, and, much like writing the history of lost civilizations from a few scattered potshards, it likely will take much imagination and many wrong turns. For now, getting to know the Irish Catholics in the Union army will serve to invite fuller studies of Irish Catholics at home and in southern settings and circumstances and then of other Catholics, too. (The same aforementioned caveats hold true for studying Jews, Lutherans, Reformed Protestants, or members of any religious group outside those British-American mainline denominations whose particular histories too often stand for all.)

As the largest, most visible Catholic group, the Irish Catholics increasingly defined "American" Catholicism by mid-century, even as they fought Germans and others for control of immigrant parishes. To outsiders looking in, the Irish were the church. To insiders, too, the Irish seemed to hold sway, by force of numbers and by savvy church politics. The Irish supplied the majority of the priests and religious to the American "mission" field and controlled much of its ecclesiastical structure by 1860. In urban America, Irish bishops preached a militant Catholicism that combatted nativism and anti-Catholicism at every turn and insisted on Catholic education for its children, free of the Protestant influences prevailing in the public schools. The Irish bishops, more than clergymen from any other ethnic background, urged construction of an array of educational, charitable, and fraternal institutions to insulate Catholics from the hostile host culture and to inculcate Catholic piety. They believed only a strong Catholic church could ease immigrants into American society and command respect. Their policies reflected their self-consciousness about Catholics' place in America.[3]

It is often said that the Civil War was a forge of nationalism. It was also a test of religious and ethnic loyalties. How the intensely Irish nationalist Irish Catholics responded to the war as soldiers can suggest how the crucible of war melted down those outside the mainstream culture and how national, religious, and ethnic identities intersected, or diverged. The Irish Catholics bear examination on their own count. Only blacks were more self-conscious about, or had more invested in, the relationship between wartime military service and their acceptance in the nation. If the Irish Catholic case was less urgent and fundamental, it was, for them and for Catholics thereafter, no less important.

The discovery of the Irishmen's remains at Antietam not only serves as metaphor for the historiographical neglect of Irish and Catholic involvement in the war but also points to the pivotal role that September day at Antietam played in Irish Catholic thinking about the war. The Irish Catholics' bravery at Bloody Lane answered the questions about the willingness of the Irish to fight, silencing Know-Nothingism on that score for a generation. The slaughter that day, when the Irish Brigade suffered 60 percent casualties, also led Irish Catholics to reassess their place in the war and the nation. The character of the Irish Catholic soldier was changing as well by summer 1862. Many of the first Irish Catholic soldiers, drawn from Irish Americans and Irish immigrants already settled in America before the war, had largely spent their earlier enthusiasm and gone home, or were counted among the thousands of Irish Catholic casualties left behind. A new group of Irish Catholic soldiers, many of them recent arrivals who joined to get bounties and pay rather than promote Irish and American nationalism, had begun to replace the first ones. The anonymity of the soldiers unearthed a century and a quarter later conceals real differences among Irish Catholics. Finally, and significantly, the evidence of Catholic faith left by the almost-named soldier (Gallagher, McMahon, or McGarigan), his rosary around his neck, suggests how much the war tested faith. Likely, the brigade chaplain had time only for a general absolution for those dying on the field. The soldier with the rosary died alone. All that and the lack of a Christian burial, until over a century later, speak volumes on the hurried and even gerry-rigged religious practices in war. Catholics, especially Catholic soldiers, during the war would themselves rethink obligations to church and country.

The Catholic side of the war experience is in some ways easier to reconstruct in its basic form than the ethnic one. The clergy and Catholic establishment made their positions known. Bishops issued pastorals and delivered addresses; the Catholic press cranked out editorials; and the chaplain priests and nursing sisters in the fields wrote letters home. The church took a stand in the war—to allow Catholics to follow their section. It thus continued the American Catholic policy of avoiding political involvement while holding Catholics to their faith and securing Catholic institutions. In short, the church tolerated disunity in political matters so that it could concentrate on achieving ethnic unity in religious ones. Southern Catholics largely supported the Confederate cause, and northern Catholics the Union one, though with many misgivings as the war continued. Still, the war promised northern Catholics the opportunity for a show of American patriotism that would at once counter nativism and anti-Catholicism and focus Catholics of different backgrounds on a common cause.[4]

Church leaders understood that judgments about Catholics generally would be based on observations of Catholic soldiers particularly. The Catholic church therefore sought to ensure that the soldiers fought bravely, acted responsibly, and honored their Catholic faith. That interest, and the church's mission to meet the religious needs and obligations of Catholics, demanded a regular clerical presence in the ranks. Only priests could administer the sacraments that formed the core of Catholic worship and practice. Only they could keep Catholics truly Catholic and morally upright—or so the thinking went.[5]

The religious character of the war heightened the urgency of getting priests to the camps. As James Moorhead has shown so well, many Protestant churchmen and organizations viewed the armies as fertile grounds for evangelization. Contrasting the demoralizing effects of army life in previous wars with the military vigor and resolve of religious soldiers in ages past, northern clergymen made their case for assuming a large role in building morale and regulating discipline. Specifically, they sought the appointment of chaplains and the distribution of Bibles and religious tracts. Their arguments rapidly evolved into policy as the Protestant clergy and publishing houses blanketed the armies with their influence and the Protestant-based U.S. Sanitary Commission and the Christian Commission gained control of organized relief. Already wary of Protestant efforts before the war to "steal souls" among ill and dying Catholic immigrants in city hospitals and Catholic children in public schools, the northern Catholic hierarchy realized it must supply chaplains for Catholic soldiers.[6]

The priests' presence in the field and the Catholic sisters' work in the hospitals did much to sustain Catholic identity and interest among soldiers. According to Father Joseph O'Hagan, S. J., chaplain of General Daniel Sickles's Excelsior Brigade, in the Army of the Potomac, the Catholic religious presence made "comparatively decent fellows" out of convicts and the "scum of New York society" who had come to the army "reeking with vice and spreading a moral malaria" only to be "settled down" by church and military discipline and priestly attention. The successes priests such as O'Hagan reported in soldiers saved from sinful ways and blessed by sacraments encouraged Catholic leaders to hope that those whose faith was made steadfast in war might reinvigorate the church in peace. Ennobled by his patriotic service, the Christian (Catholic) soldier would stand as the Christian (Catholic) sentinel of freedom and faith for generations after the war.[7]

During the war, the selection of chaplains rested largely with the churches. Nothing in government regulations specifically excluded or encouraged Catholic participation. Indeed, the federal government spelled out few qualifications for chaplains, save that they be "a regularly ordained minister of some Christian denomination," a requirement the government revised after Jewish protest to read of "any religious denomination." The government further required that a chaplain must have the endorsement of some "authorized ecclesiastical body." The president designated the chaplain for each regiment at specified army posts and general hospitals, but volunteer companies chose their own chaplains, who upon approval by the state governor received an appointment from the War Department. Chaplains held no rank with command, though by the end of the war they did receive the pay and allowances of captains of cavalry. Congress and the War Department left definitions of the chaplain's responsibilities to the churches and the soldiers. Lacking official authority in command or duty, and even uniforms for much of the time, chaplains derived their authority from whatever respect their ordained office and behavior the soldiers might grant them.[8]

If official policy opened the door to Catholic participation in the army, circumstance and practice often closed it. Understaffed in peacetime, the church was hard-pressed to reassign priests from parish or other duties to chaplaincies in wartime. Only forty priests, often called "Holy Joes" by the soldiers, served with northern armies during the war, for a Catholic population numbering over 200,000 men in uniform (of whom roughly 145,000 were Irish). Further eroding the Catholic chaplains' influence was the fact that many of them served for a short time. Bishops held on to their priests whenever possible, as did heads of seminaries and religious orders, all struggling to minister to ethnically diverse and swelling immigrant populations. Administering the diocese at home superseded "missionary" work among men far away. Bishops even recalled chaplains from service whenever parish needs demanded it. Such was the case of the young Irish-born priest Fr. John Ireland (later archbishop of St. Paul, Minnesota), whose tenure with the 5th Regiment Minnesota Volunteers lasted less than a year because his bishop wanted him to return to Minnesota. As Ireland explained it in 1863, his replacement in Minnesota had fallen ill and was "totally unable to attend to the spiritual wants of a large congregation," and further, the number of Catholics in the Minnesota regiment was "comparatively so reduced [by casualties], as not to warrant any more of the continual attendance of a [Catholic] clergyman."[9]

A more pressing concern was the reluctance, and often the outright refusal, of Protestant officers to accept Catholic priests as chaplains—a subject of sometimes bitter complaint by Catholics who felt forsaken by their church and cheated by their government. In regiments where Catholics were in the minority, priests were not called. To be sure, a few Protestant officers with Catholics in their units recognized the injustice and invited priests to visit the camps, but such appeals were rare, and even when successful, meant only irregular visitation by a priest. More typical was the practice of Protestant officers evangelizing among the troops. Catholics chafed at the Protestant prodding of such men as "the one wing devil" General O. O. Howard, who wanted to convert their armies into Protestant crusaders. The shortage of priests was mitigated somewhat by long encampments that allowed a few priests to circulate among the different regiments and also by the strategic juxtaposing of regiments with priests next to those without. But the priests could not be everywhere. Catholic chaplains served almost exclusively in Catholic regiments.

Such practice promised to make soldiers in Catholic regiments more Catholic but Catholics in Protestant regiments less so, though in the latter case it sometimes hardened Catholic identity as a persecuted minority.[10]

The scarcity and character of chaplains in some ways worked against the ecclesiastical interest of the church. Those priests most eager and able to go off to war were often young. Youthful zeal did not compensate fully for their lack of pastoral experience and a tentative grasp of church teaching. Ethnic differences between soldiers and chaplains also hurt. Supplying an English-speaking priest to a German regiment for all practical purposes left the Germans without pastoral guidance. Finding a German speaker sometimes compounded the problem of relying on youthful priests. German soldiers stationed near Washington first looked to a German Sister of Charity to interpret for them and finally got a young German-speaking Jesuit to visit them and hear their confessions.[11] For a church trying to impose a strict regimen of religious worship, eliminate ethnic idiosyncrasies, reduce lay autonomy, and unify the church, the shortage of priests and reliance on younger clergy posed problems.

So, too, did the exigencies of setting up sacred space in army camps. By mid-century "bricks-and-mortar" bishops in northern cities were laboring mightily through ambitious construction programs to embody the power and majesty of the church in cathedrals and other church buildings. That message was conspicuously absent in the camps, where priests celebrated Mass on makeshift altars in open-air settings. Also, with armies on the move, ecclesiastical oversight lapsed as bishops rarely visited the priests in the field. The energetic Archbishop John Purcell of Cincinnati, who visited the camps several times to administer the sacraments, preach, and meet with his priests, was the noteworthy exception. When Union forces were stationed close to towns or cities, it was possible for soldiers to attend services at the local church and for the chaplains to meet with their ecclesiastical superiors. Such occasions might even blur sectional divisions, as, for example, when Union forces occupied Nashville in spring 1862, the Union Catholic chaplain sang Mass in the cathedral and the vicar-general, who was the chaplain of the Irish regiment raised among Confederates in Nashville, preached. Whatever the salutary effects of such reminders of Catholic universalism, bishops saw little of the chaplains and Catholics in the ranks, who, after all, spent most of their war years away from cities. The chaplains in the field were left to themselves to make do with whatever the military and circumstance might provide.[12]

Father William Corby, who served three years with the "Irish Brigade" in the Army of the Potomac, described the chaplain's duties. During the winter he spent his time "in much the same way as parish priests do, except in this— we had no old women to bother us, or pew rent to collect." The Catholic chaplain "celebrated Mass, heard confessions, preached on Sundays and holydays," and during the week performed "many minor duties." He also was "called on at times to administer the pledge to a few who had been indulging too freely, to settle little difficulties, and encourage harmony and good-will; to instruct such as needed private lessons on special points of religion, and everywhere to elevate the standard of religion, morality, and true patriotism." In addition, priests enlivened camp life with concerts and humor. On a more somber level, they counseled men sentenced to death by court-martial and walked with them to the gallows. Most important, the priests tried to visit hospitals and to follow the men in battle, to provide comfort and, if death approached, to hear confession and administer the last rites. On the eve of battles, even lapsed Catholics crowded into makeshift confessionals to make their peace with God. As one priest reported from Kentucky in 1862, the night before a battle he sat for eight hours hearing confessions. More than anything else, soldiers wanted the assurance that a priest would be at hand to do that much. The fate of their souls depended on it.[13]

The principal duty of Catholic chaplains was to hold worship services and administer the sacraments. Whenever and wherever possible, priests tried to arrange for Sunday Mass. The constant movement of the armies interrupted such efforts, and Sunday inspections and drills, poor weather, and diversions added to the difficulties. Many soldiers preferred to play more than pray. Paydays on Sundays further drew soldiers' attention away from matters of heaven and toward those of mammon. As one priest lamented, payday meant drinking and "a picture of hell I had never seen." Whatever their faith, the men of the 116th Pennsylvania, which counted many Irish in its ranks, for example, played "mumble meg" and thought of "greenbacks and suttlers wares instead of preaching" on the Sundays they got paid. Simple exhaustion after long hours on fatigue or picket duty kept others asleep in their tents on Sunday mornings. Like their Protestant counterparts, priests learned to adapt to the rhythms of military life, celebrating the Mass "on the fly" and at makeshift altars.[14]

In his reverent recollections of the New York "Irish Brigade," Captain D. P. Conyngham told of the midnight Mass on Christmas 1861, with the priests officiating on an altar of "hewn logs, sheltered on each side and overhead by boughs of trees, supported by poles." In his *Memoirs of Chaplain Life*, Fr. William Corby recalled fondly the little altar made of "four crotched sticks" driven into the ground and split lumber stretched across, which Corby dressed with linens and lighted with two candles for celebration of his first Mass in the army. Corby almost reveled in the rusticity, which made him feel a kinship with earlier missionaries among the Indians. He later acquired a circus tent to serve as his chapel and an altar made of boards laid over cracker boxes. The men knelt in the mud inside and outside the tent to listen to prayers. All seemed one with God, Nature, and one another.[15]

Catholic soldiers who hewed the logs and laid the boards for the altars also must have felt a sense of ownership over the chapels they were building in the wilderness. The American church's longstanding struggle to curb lay initiative and claim title to the churches the laity had built still smoldered in the 1850s but was dampened in the camps. Establishing a sacred space in the field joined Catholic soldiers and their priest in a common enterprise that made ecclesiastical insistence on lay subordination to clerical authority temporarily irrelevant. With no aura of a church authority stretching back to the ancients, no statues or icons for veneration, and no pageantry to inspire awe, the priests relied on the familiar rituals and their simple blessings and sermons during worship.

We do not know much of what the priests preached in public or what words of instruction or discipline they meted out in private sessions with soldiers. The Catholic revival (also known as parish mission) movement just entering eastern cities through the Redemptorist and other orders of priests did not reach the Union army, and so many pastoral duties beckoned that there was little time to prepare sermons or deliver them. What soldiers and priests both recalled about the chaplains' activities was the saying of Mass, the administration of last rites to dying soldiers, the comforting of men in pain. As the Protestant experience showed, organized revivals might reap a rich harvest during war, but the Catholic church had other priorities for the allocation of its scarce human resources. Priests and nuns recorded many instances of conversions or restored faith, especially among soldiers who had faced battle, but such acts were individual rather than the result of a coordinated revival effort.[16]

The hurrying about reduced priests to few words that would have to carry much weight. The moment when words really counted, when men really listened, occurred just before battle. The most noteworthy instance was the general absolution given to soldiers before a fight, a blessing and short speech that spoke volumes on the nature of Catholic preaching during the war. The message was both succinct and salient.

The most widely reported and oft-recalled general absolution was given by Fr. William Corby of the Irish Brigade on the second day of Gettysburg. Corby stood on a large rock in front of the Irish Brigade, "saying that each one could receive the benefit of the absolution by making a sincere Act of Contrition and firmly embracing the first opportunity of confessing his sins." He then urged the men to "do their duty . . . reminding them of the high and sacred nature of their trust as soldiers and the noble object for which they fought," and added that the church would condemn those who deserted the Union in its moment of decision. Catholic and non-Catholic alike bowed their heads, and even the battle-hardened and cynical General Winfield Scott Hancock removed his hat and "bowed in reverential devotion." Corby intended the general absolution for all, irrespective of religion or region, about to fight. Most memorable about the absolution was the silence that ruled the Second Corps in worship, as Catholic and Protestant united in prayer. The thunder of guns broke the silence but not the bond that Corby's few words had forged, words of God's mercy and of patriotic duty.[17]

To win a place in the soldiers' confidence, and a good mention in their accounts of wartime service, chaplains had to prove themselves. They also had to find ways to reach the men in arms. In their unofficial duties as much as in their religious ones, chaplains earned the trust of the soldiers and strengthened religious identity. Chaplain priests carried soldiers' letters and money to loved ones back home and brought back news, gifts, and various articles of clothing and toilet for the men, thereby establishing an important link between home and field. Soldiers about to die sometimes entrusted the disposition of their effects and last letter to family to the chaplain. Priests, as did nuns serving in hospitals, wrote letters for soldiers who could not write, read letters and papers for those who could not read, nursed wounds and lifted spirits, and in countless other ways eased the burdens and boredom of the soldier's life. Few priests stayed long enough with any regiment to cultivate the kind of mutual respect and affection that a successful parish priest established with his flock, but the loneliness of camp life, the intensity of war, and the imminence of death often worked to forge powerful, even intimate bonds between priests and men. Such relationships became the stuff of legend after the war, when the incompetence or intemperance of some priests was forgotten and only the selflessness of the others recalled and revered.[18]

Character then counted much in winning soldiers' trust and affection. The priest must be attentive, sensitive, and energetic, and, of course, devout and able to meet soldiers' spiritual needs. He also must be brave. Captain Conyngham thought it important to remember that his Catholic chaplain "never left the field" and even risked capture "sooner than neglect the spiritual or temporal welfare of our brave sufferers." Another soldier wrote admiringly about the priest who accompanied the men to battle and faulted their Protestant commander for wasting his regiment in a futile assault across a river.[19]

Both sides of the contemporary record illustrate the importance placed on courage. Just as the Catholic priest reported home in accounts intended both for private consolation and general Catholic edification that the individual Catholic soldier died game—a noble warrior whose last thoughts were of faith, family, and flag as life left him—stories about the priests themselves invariably remarked on their bravery. Embattled courage of the Victorian kind, in which the dying soldier had a face and the real horrors of mass slaughter had no place, was the stuff of Catholic accounts.

Such accounts emphasized quiet rather than sabre-rattling courage. Heroic priests did not become soldiers, hardened to suffering and bellicose. As Reid Mitchell has argued for Protestant chaplains, so, too, for Catholic ones—frightened men valued a chaplain for his sensitivity as much as for his bravery. A chaplain who would become more like the soldiers would sacrifice his pastoral authority. Families back home wanted their men to return as they had left, honor-bound and brave but also kind and generous. The chaplains could help keep them so. It was partly for that reason that Archbishop John Hughes of New York recalled Father Thomas H. Mooney from duty with the 69th New York in 1862 after learning that the militant Mooney had baptized with holy water one of the big guns mounted at Fort Corcoran and had strongly urged the men to flail the enemy. Fr. Mooney acted too much like a warrior for Archbishop Hughes, who worried that the war would make Catholics killers and change their nature.[20]

Aware of the "fighting Irish" Catholic stereotype rattling around in the Anglo-American Protestant popular imagination, the American church hierarchy sought to emphasize sacrifice and heroism, even to ennoble death, rather than acknowledge the ferocity of its men in arms. The Irish "nationalist" press was more ambivalent, taking pride in the Celtic tradition of almost wild courage and aggressiveness in the face of any enemy, while still insisting that the Irish fought for conviction rather than the love of fighting itself. As the numerous anti-Irish cartoons and lampoons showed, the distinction was easy to overlook. Thus, the church emphasized the softer side of manliness as well as the hard facts of battle.[21]

A courageous and caring priest might become the very soul of a Catholic regiment. Such was the case of Father Peter Paul Cooney, who served almost four years with the heavily Irish 35th Indiana Volunteers (the longest tenure of any Catholic chaplain with any regiment). The soldiers admired him not only for his bravery in tending the wounded while cannon balls shot past him but also for his trustworthiness in handling their personal and financial matters and for his comforting letters of condolence to fallen soldiers' relatives reassuring them that their loved ones had died nobly and with the priest's final blessing. Cooney's steadfast service made him the regiment's most stable element, and his own letters reveal he was a man of common sense as well as conviction and courage. The officers intrigued among themselves for command; the non-Irish in the regiment complained that the officers favored the Irish; the casualties mounted; but through it all Cooney commanded the affection and loyalty of the men. His example no doubt helps to explain why several Protestants converted to Catholicism. Only once did Cooney interfere in the jockeying of various officers for personal advantage and rank; in 1864 he assailed the former commander, Colonel Bernard F. Mullen, for trying to extract a percentage of the bounties paid to the men in the regiment. In a regiment rent by so much internal strife and external danger, the chaplain as much as anyone saved the regiment from self-destruction.[22]

When priests were not available, the church struggled to sustain Catholic faith, instruct in Catholic doctrine, or provide a Catholic vocabulary for spiritual and social discourse. In the hospitals, and in desperate moments on the battlefields, various sisterhoods took up the burden. The Sisters of Mercy and Sisters of Charity especially provided such succor. The opposition of many lay people back home and some church authorities to women in nursing notwithstanding, Catholic nuns marched to the fields to comfort all who had fallen, regardless of religious or regional loyalty. Of necessity, they also assumed pastoral roles. For many a dying Catholic soldier, the prayers of a woman clutching a rosary served in lieu of the last rites. Some non-Catholics even tried to cheat the devil with deathbed conversions, with nuns performing the baptism. When the necessary priests were not at hand to administer the other sacraments, the image of the Holy Mother Mary loomed large with the soldiers, who may have carried it over into the postwar Marian adoration movement among Catholics. The immediate religious consequence of the nuns' work, however, was the momentary enlargement of the ministry, a further dispersal of religious authority among Catholics in crisis.[23]

Catholic soldiers had scant reading materials to instruct them and fortify their faith. Individual Catholic soldiers relied on prayer books brought or sent from home, and lay organizations such as the Society of St. Vincent de Paul collected Catholic reading matter from booksellers, publishers, and newspapers to distribute among the soldiers in camps and hospitals. Bishops and religious orders also tried to supply their priests who were off to the war with literature. The most ambitious program to provide Catholic soldiers with spiritual reading came about in late 1861, when Archbishop Hughes recommended the Superior Council of New York publish and distribute gratis to soldiers and their families back home its *Manual of the Christian Soldier*. The *Manual* became the most widely disseminated single Catholic publication among soldiers. A "compact little '*vade mecum*,'" it consisted of prayers, devotional exercises, meditations, instructions, and short explications of church teaching. But outside of New York, such efforts were not well organized, leading the editor of the *Catholic Herald* to suggest, only half in jest, that officers provide Irish nationalist papers to get Catholic ideas into the "hands of every soldier."[24]

The *Manual*, and other Catholic reading materials, caught the essence of the emerging Catholic emphasis on devotional piety, premised on a dark view of the world as a sinful place ripe for God's wrath, and on the obligation of the Catholic to confront his or her sinful nature. The devotional revolution underway in nineteenth-century Catholicism described a culture of sin and a need for clerical authority, which through the Mass and the sacraments provided access to the supernatural. For the individual Catholic, self-discipline and prayer were demanded. This style of religion came to dominate Catholic life by the end of the century, but it is not possible to know how influential it was among the Catholic soldiers, or even the chaplain priests and sisters. Still, insomuch as Catholic devotional literature reached soldiers at all, its message about the corrupt world and its call for personal moral discipline spoke to immediate realities and prescribed a course of behavior that seemingly assured God's favor. Only the authority of priests was lacking to give the message full force. Much responsibility for discipline and piety thus was left to the soldier.[25]

A smattering of Catholic ecclesiastical papers or Catholic newspapers also circulated in the camps to remind Catholic soldiers of religious identities and obligations. Those Catholics who could, and did, read such papers might glean a textbook Catholicism from them, for in addition to home matters and exhortations to patriotism and sacrifice, they served the usual fare of calls for religious devotion and obedience. The ethnic-based Catholic periodicals such as the Irish Boston *Pilot*, the most widely circulated Irish Catholic publication, and the German *Wahrheitsfreund* and *Katholische Kirchenzeitung* also filled their columns with reminders to honor the ethnic group by acts of courage.[26]

The suppression of such papers as James A. McMaster's rabidly anti-Lincoln New York *Freeman's Journal* and the inundation of the camps with Protestant tracts limited the Catholic influence and range of thought that might have been extended through the written word. The most constant complaint about Catholic literature in the army was the lack of it. Typical was the following complaint from several Catholic soldiers published in 1862: "They say that they want chaplains, and that they have them not. They say that they want books and Catholic reading, and that nothing is offered them except trash from Protestant sources, offensive at once to their faith, their reason, and their good taste." Catholic prelates and publicists wrung their hands in despair, and the chorus of lamentations became louder.[27]

The shortage of publications cut Catholic soldiers off from their homes as well as from their faith. Local and religious newspapers served as vital links between soldiers and homefolk, following the exploits of the community's men at war and rallying support for them. Reading such fare could remind soldiers they were not forgotten while away from home. Yet such literature might just as well undermine the soldiers' commitment to the cause or alienate them from the homefront if it criticized the war and pressured the soldiers to return home.

After body counts began to pile up during the 1862 campaigns, the ethnic and Catholic press grew critical of the Republican conduct of the war and the high casualty rates for Irish and German Catholics. Meanwhile, private correspondence brought the growing civilian doubts about war service to the soldiers. Letters from home decried the absence of the men and catalogued all the troubles of being left alone to find work and fend off a cruel world.

Soldiers had to explain why they stayed away. When Margaret Welsh complained about the hard times the family suffered with a husband and father away fighting for a "foreign" power, to calm her and, no doubt, to assuage his own guilt, Peter Welsh of the 28th Massachusetts regiment wrote several long letters justifying his and their sacrifice in the interests of religion, Irish liberation, and the Union. Margaret Welsh remained unconvinced, and Peter tried to enlist her father in his defense by writing him on the duty of Irish Catholics to serve. Welsh was unusual in the eloquence and extent of his insistence that family obligation and patriotic duty were joined. Others doubted it, as the rising incidence of desertion attested. Lacking constant reinforcement from family, community, and church, both soldiers and family members had to wonder what place Catholics had in the fight.[28]

Soldiers ambivalent about their loyalties might have been comforted by the assurances of priests that the church and its charitable institutions stood ready to assist any Catholic family in need. One of the most important contributions the church made to the war—and one of the least studied aspects of any connection between a church and support for soldiers—was the relief it provided for the families of soldiers away to fight. The Society of St. Vincent de Paul and parish-based aid societies set up relief depots to distribute aid to the needy and comforted soldiers' families.[29]

How much such efforts convinced Catholic soldiers to stay with their regiments we will never know. But the rapid erosion of support for the war (see below) and rising desertion rates suggest that the vital connection between church and country that American Catholic leaders urged was never very strong among the folk. The slight Catholic church presence in the ranks made the connection seem unduly abstract during the war. The realities of war, and the nature of ethnic and Catholic loyalties, led the soldiers, and their families, elsewhere.

The net result of the limited Catholic presence, particularly the shortage of priests, was a redefinition of working Catholicism—at least for a time. For some, it meant a loss of faith. Effective religious authority devolved downward for many Catholics in uniform, as soldiers and chaplains fashioned a simpler Catholic worship and dispersed the religious duties of prayer and catechism and even baptism among priests, nuns, and lay leaders. The Catholicism understood by soldiers also differed in some ways from that presented by church authorities. Many soldiers took to wearing the rosary or other religious objects as talismans, which bespoke a more mystical and less rigorous priest-centered Catholicism than the church demanded. The long-term effects of such democratic and "superstitious" tendencies on the character of Catholicism or individual Catholic communities remain unclear. Too many soldiers died before they could bring their experiences and understandings home, and the church there already was mobilized to resist such lay impulses whenever they surfaced anyway.[30]

As historian Kerby Miller has shown so well, the Irish in America had varied origins and interests. The earlier, more middle-class Protestant Irish arrivals had little in common with the largely Catholic famine immigrants who swelled the docksides, boweries, and back alleys of urban America during the 1840s and 1850s. By 1860, the Irish Catholics in America were congealing into a separate ethnic group, self-conscious of its identity and suspicious of outsiders. Although many famine immigrants were lax in their religious affairs, by 1860 the vast majority of Irish in America had come into the church, and many felt the first tremblings of the devotional revolution of Catholic piety that would soon sweep over Irish Catholicism. Further binding them together was their hatred of all things British. And to be anti-British was to be Catholic. For the Irish, Catholic identity acquired an ethnic meaning independent of religious duties. Thrust from old Erin by famine and British injustice, the Irish immigrants of the 1840s and 1850s never abandoned their homeland in thinking about family and faith and the mutual obligations thereof. Irish nationalism already had crossed class lines to become the single most powerful glue in Irish ethnic identity before the Civil War brought Irish Catholic ethnic identity into focus.[31]

Irish Catholics saw the war as a way to advance Irish nationalism by linking it with the defense of the American republic. As a result, the war accelerated the Irish Catholic takeover of Irish identity in America by focusing the nation on Irish Catholic interests and actions and by engaging so many Irish Catholics in the war effort. If the religious Catholicism of the Irish sometimes lapsed while they were in the army, their ethnic Catholicism did not. A sense of common purpose as representatives of their emerging ethnic group grew as wartime service became a test of loyalty to the memory of Irish ancestors, the needs of Irish liberation, and the demands of the Catholic church.

In the North, the immediate Irish Catholic response to the bombardment of Fort Sumter and Lincoln's call for volunteers was one of unity and Union. Casting aside for the moment their opposition to the Republican party and the memories of nativist attacks, Irish speakers and Catholic leaders rallied to the American banner. Orators linked Irish and American nationalism in arguing the need to fight oppression and pretenders on both sides of the Atlantic.

Part of this display was coerced, as patriotic "American" mobs silenced one-time southern sympathizers and demanded public demonstrations of immigrants' loyalty to the republic. In Philadelphia, for example, pro-Union mobs visited the offices of several religious papers suspected of southern leanings, demanding that the editors show the American flag to proclaim their loyalties. The mob singled out the Catholic church's official organ, the *Catholic Herald*, which under John Duffy's editorship had spewed forth much anti-Republican and anti-black venom before the war, and the chastened Duffy complied by flying the American flag and, for a time, by toning down his criticisms of the Lincoln administration. The mobs need not have tried so hard in 1861. The Irish Catholic rush to the colors was genuine when the war broke out. Several northern bishops led by Archbishops Hughes of New York and Purcell of Cincinnati delivered patriotic addresses, blessed the flags of Union regiments, and prominently displayed American flags from their cathedrals and residences after Fort Sumter.[32]

The prelates knew that any hint of Irish Catholic disloyalty would feed nativism, and only Irish Catholic service in the war would silence the nativists. As the most despised Catholic group in the American mind, the Irish stood out in worries about Catholic loyalty and intentions. On the Irish Catholics, then, rode the fate of Catholics in America. Although the vast majority of Irish Catholic soldiers served in non-Irish regiments, most judgments about the loyalty and character of the Irish Catholic soldier came from observations of Irish regiments. Consequently, the recruitment and performance of those regiments became a matter of public interest and ethnic focus.

The recruitment of Irish regiments followed a varied course. In the first flush of war enthusiasm, the personality and politics of the would-be captain counted most in getting Irishmen to join his regiment. Irish Catholic political chieftains wanting to raise regiments from their followers appealed to ethnic pride. In their speeches and recruiting posters from 1861 and 1862 they invoked the heroes of Irish history to remind Irish Americans of their ethnic obligation to honor the old sod by their willingness to shed blood on American soil. More than anything else, the politicians traded on Irish nationalism to garner enlistments, promising that the fight to save the Union would be the first step in a general move against tyranny everywhere. Because the British seemingly supported the Confederacy, a blow against the South would strike at England also.[33]

Many Irish-American sachems had ties to the Fenian Brotherhood, a radical Irish nationalist group. Despite the Catholic church's disapproval of the Fenians as a secret society, Fenianism had a strong hold on Irish Catholics. Yankee Catholics winced at the connections Irish recruiters made to Irish nationalism, rightly fearing that a too vocal Irish nationalism would leave the American public to equate all Catholics with the Irish. The Irish recruiters cared not one whit for the sensibilities of the "lace-curtain" native-born American Catholics. Instead, they played to their local audiences in the saloons, hiring halls, fraternal meetings, and other places Irish men gathered. Exploiting Fenianism shamelessly, some even said that military training and experience in the American contest would prepare Irish "patriots" for an assault on British Canada after the Civil War. They thus linked Unionism with Fenianism in ways that made it seem almost anti-Irish not to join an Irish regiment. Part of the motivation to enlist came from Irishmen's desire to get pay when unemployment loomed during the uncertain times, but "patriotism" also counted. As James Rorty explained to his father in 1861, after escaping from Confederate hands, he reenlisted in the 69th New York to renew his moral and physical health through military service and to follow Irish nationalist leader Thomas Francis Meagher, the regiment's colonel, fight for both Ireland and the Union.[34]

Many of the Fenians who invaded British Canada after the Civil War had served in Irish companies during the war. The recruiters' Fenian appeals had proved highly effective where Irish ethnic organizations already were in place, where Irish nationalism informed local politics, and where Irish leaders had the credibility and speaking ability to command respect. In New York City, for example, there was such a rush to enlist that Michael Corcoran had to turn away several thousand volunteers for his Irish Brigade for want of places and arms in 1861.[35]

Historian William Burton rightly observes that the manner and extent to which Irish-American recruiters used Irish nationalism hinged on their own political ambitions. Leaders whose political vision did not extend beyond the local machine or political club draped themselves in the green flag of Irish nationalism and stepped to the beat of Irish folk culture. Irish-American politicians who looked to winning statewide office wore both the green and the red, white, and blue and avoided too close an association with the extremist Irish nationalists. Whatever the case, some brand of Irish nationalism infused all the Irish regiments in 1861 and 1862.[36]

Several Irish regiments traced their roots to antebellum volunteer militia companies or regiments. The most famous Irish regiment, the New York 69th Infantry Regiment, soul of the "Irish Brigade" in the Army of the Potomac, in 1861 had been brought into Union service almost en masse from the 69th New York State Militia. Indeed, the war saved the 69th's rabidly Irish nationalist commander, Michael Corcoran, from court-martial for refusing an order to parade his regiment in honor of the visiting Prince of Wales in 1860. That incident had pointed out both the capital an Irish nationalist might gain from command of an Irish unit and the strains that might be put on military authority if the commander put ethnic interest first. In the immediate crisis of 1861, however, past indiscretions were forgiven, if not forgotten, as the Union clamored for ready-made military units to defend the nation's capital. Military policy in 1861 encouraged the formation of volunteer companies and relied on local political chieftains such as Corcoran to assume the burden of drumming up enlistments in exchange for the rewards of prestige, power, and patronage.[37]

Posters and newspaper advertisements calling for Irish recruits traded on ethnic pride. Stump-speakers trumpeted the military and moral superiority of their group, and the posters echoed the theme. From pulpits, too, the Irish heard drum-and-bugle paeans to heroes past and duties present. Irish recruiters invariably depicted the Irish as fighters by nature. To shrink in the face of a recruiting appeal was to call into question one's Irish identity. The Irish recruiters thus seized a stereotype and made it their own, for now the pugnacious Irish brawler of caricature could become the sturdy defender of Union. The war would settle the question of patriotism and manhood.[38]

It helped that the Irish Catholics produced real heroes. The valor of the 69th New York at Bull Run and the capture of Colonel Corcoran in 1861 supplied the first heroics. In the baptism of fire the Irish proved themselves men. After Corcoran became a national hero during his imprisonment for refusing to give his parole, he and the "Gallant Sixty-ninth" became a rallying cry for Irish recruiters, and Catholic children sang of their bravery in song for years thereafter. The northern press, desperate for a hero, elevated the Irish Catholic colonel and his men to a pedestal previously reserved for native sons. Archbishop John Hughes sealed the bargain by getting Corcoran promoted to general, after convincing Lincoln that Irish Catholic support for the war required recognition of their own men as patriots. The nation found other heroes soon enough, and the draft riots in 1863 and desertions by Irish soldiers sullied the Irish Catholic reputation among non-Catholics, but Irish Catholics never forgot their beloved Irish Brigade. In postwar histories and remembrances it seemed as if the brigade had been in the thick of the fight in every battle and every Irish Catholic soldier had been wherever the Irish Brigade fought. In memory at least, they were of one blood.[39]

Making a case for Irish-American patriotism and bravery was by implication making a case against those who had traduced Irish character. Acknowledging the supposedly congenital Irish fighting spirit spurred eager Irish lads to sign up for the big fight, but it also loaded on them the burden of being braver than the brahmin reformers and old-stock Americans who had shot nativist barbs at the Irish before the war. Enlistment further required that their fighting be disciplined rather than random, purposeful rather than wild, lest the old image of the besotted bogside brawler come back to haunt them all the more when the war ended. To keep the record straight, Irish Catholic leaders celebrated every triumph and refuted every calumny. And they honored their dead as national and Irish patriots. The myth of Irish-American courage as an ethnic trait was born in the Civil War.[40]

By 1862, however, ethnic recruiting began to change markedly. Irish Catholics were no different from other Americans in rethinking their commitment to a war that seemed to be going nowhere. The Boston *Pilot*, known as the "Irishman's Bible" for its vast influence among Irish Catholic readers, took the lead in questioning the Irish obligation to fight. Its editor Patrick Donahue asked why Irishmen had to face Irishmen, as happened at Bull Run when the "gallant Sixty-ninth" fought Irish longshoremen in the Louisiana Zouaves and at the Stone Wall on Marye's Heights at Fredericksburg in December 1862 when the Irish Brigade met Confederate Irishmen. While it marked up every instance of Irish bravery, the *Pilot* speculated that Republicans wanted to kill off the Irish. Smelling a nativist conspiracy in the high casualty rates of Irish troops, Donahue opined that the Republicans were exploiting Irish courage to make the Irish battering rams while native-born American soldiers who were held back reaped the glory. Other Irish Catholic papers, such as the *Irish-American*, that had been early supporters of the war chimed in with similar doubts about Republican motives and the slaughter of Irishmen. Continued discrimination against the Irish at home also rankled. In 1863, the Philadelphia *Catholic Herald* asked why the "glorious Irishman" should go off to war when his countrymen were abused and barred from numerous occupations on the home front. These resentments reached a wider audience on the popular stage with such blackface minstrel songs as "The Bonny Green Flag" that went: "They say that the Irish need not apply,/ But when soldiers they want, in the front Pat is seen."[41]

If new volunteer enlistments measure support for the war, it declined among Irish Catholics as their perception of the conflict as a Republican party enterprise grew. Loyalty to the Union was conditional for Irish Catholics. As Democrats, they distrusted Republican motives on sectional issues; as immigrants and the children of immigrants and as Catholics, they distrusted the Protestant, reformist, and almost nativist character of the Republicans; and as working-class day laborers, miners, and factory hands, they distrusted the close association of Republican leaders with business and industrial capital. The Republicans were remaking the war in ways that seemed to undermine the Irish Catholics' political, cultural, and economic interests. The Union of 1863 was no longer the Union of 1861. Now Republican industrial and financial policies at the national and local level threatened to wrest final control of the workplace from mechanics, miners, and shopkeepers, many of whom were Irish. The Republicans' emancipation and conscription policies of 1862 and 1863 left Irish Americans, who were the chief competitors of African Americans for jobs and housing in northeastern cities, feeling further betrayed. Irish Catholic volunteer enlistments dropped dramatically in late 1862 and never recovered as class and race were joined in the Irish Catholic backlash against Republicans and blacks.[42]

The turning point for many Irish had come in September 1862, first at Bloody Lane, Antietam, and then with Lincoln's preliminary emancipation proclamation, issued after the Union victory at Antietam that the Irish thought their blood had won. Following the battle, several Republican publicists sullied the good name and effort of the Irish by suggesting that the Irish Brigade's commander—Thomas Francis Meagher, a true Irish nationalist hero who had earned the name "Meagher of the Sword" fighting in the 1848 Irish uprising—had fallen from his horse drunk during the battle. The Irish Catholic press countered the calumnies by publishing accounts of the Brigade's valiant assault, but the Irish resented and remembered the slur.[43]

The second round of Irish soldiers that entered the Union army was much less receptive to appeals to Irish pride and the unity of Irish and American nationalism. Instead, recruiting posters from 1862 on set information on bounty money and pay in the largest type and reduced the patriotic lines to small type. In late 1861, by contrast, on fences and walls throughout Boston's Irish wards, recruiting posters headlined "The Glorious 9th! Irishmen to the Rescue" of the beleaguered Union, and further linked memories of the "indominitable valor and bravery" of Irish ancestors with the more recent evidence of "Irish bravery and valor" having "to a great extent, thus far, impeded the march" of southern "Vandals" and the "contemptible and Despotic" southern aristocracy. The posters noted that the Irish flag went hand-in-hand with the Stars and Stripes into battle and also promised that the regiment would have "a chaplain of the old faith." A $100 bounty and $188 first pay thus were only two of several inducements offered to volunteers in 1861. By 1863, the message was simpler: avoid the draft and collect the bounty. So said the poster used by Mulligan's Brigade from Illinois, which less than two years earlier had filled its ranks with appeals to Irish nationalism and Catholic pride.[44]

By 1863, some of the Irish ethnic regiments ceased to exist, having been folded into other regiments when they were no longer able to keep up minimum troop levels. Others remained "Irish" but lacked a unified sense of ethnic purpose. The new men coming into formerly Irish units were not Irish or were recent immigrants, with no ties to the local Irish community from which the regiment originally had been raised.

The new men often joined out of desperation for work. In the face of the almost universal condemnation of the northern war effort by the press in Ireland and numerous letters from America urging them not to leave their native soil, the Irish came anyway, to hire on as substitutes and to collect the bounties. Destitution at home drove them to America's ordeal by fire. Consular records for 1862 through 1864 reveal legions of poor Irishmen begging passage to America in return for enlisting in the Union army. The armies bid for such labor.[45]

Bounties rather than Irish nationalism or Catholic duty called these Irishmen to arms, and remittances home by the Union soldiers kept alive their ties to home in Ireland. As Thomas McManus wrote to his relatives, enclosing over half the $700 bounty he had received for enlisting the first day he arrived in America, he had not been forced to join the army, but "the bounty was very tempting." Nevertheless, as Kerby Miller points out, the net effect of such migration was the further impoverishment of old Ireland, for the war in America "left rural Ireland with thousands of 'starving and bereaved widows and widowed mothers' of husbands and sons who had perished on southern battlefields, often before they had been able to remit home the rewards of their sacrifice." Those Irish Catholic soldiers would get neither monuments nor mention in the Catholic and ethnic memoirs of the war. They would lie buried in the potter's field of historical memory.[46]

No matter why they came, new arrivals in America could not easily escape the nets cast by state recruiters or agents eager to fill quotas. Some were even kidnapped. Many poor Irishmen in America joined the army after 1862 for the practical reason that survival counted more than honor. Because most of them entered non-Irish regiments, they were effectively lost to direct Irish and Catholic influence during the war.[47]

Newcomers in ostensibly Irish regiments did not find circumstances there congenial, either. They were outsiders, more rural and poorer than the men of 1861 and 1862 who were still in the regiments and formed its character. They also were outsiders in that their Catholicism was more a birthright than a developed faith. The devotional revolution had not yet reached them; indeed, many were for all practical purposes unchurched, following folk religious practices and having few encounters with the institutional church. Theirs was not the more disciplined Catholicism of the Irish-American Catholics and those Irish immigrants who had been in America during the 1850s. In attitudes, beliefs, and community ties, the newcomers were different men.[48]

In the end, it is not possible to know how much ethnic and religious pride moved Irish Catholics, or anyone, to enlist. That Irish Catholic political and religious leaders dwelt on themes of Irish nationalism and moral obligation suggests that such a message had effect, otherwise why persist in the message. Recollections of wartime service, not surprisingly, put patriotism at the head of the list as to why the veteran authors had gone to war, but no clear definition of what patriotism meant during the war emerges from their accounts.

In his recent reassessment of why the Union soldiers, generally, fought, James McPherson has discovered a much higher level of patriotic feeling and antislavery sympathy than earlier writers such as Bell Wiley calculated. McPherson, like others probing motivations, rightly bases his argument on readings of soldiers' diaries and letters rather than their reminiscences, but he confuses why soldiers might have joined the army with why they fought. Ideals might propel enlistment, but soldiers generally fight in battle to survive and to protect their immediate fellow soldiers. Irish Catholics probably were no different.[49]

Assessing the Irish Catholic common soldier's commitment is difficult, for few diaries and bundles of letters exist to plumb his mind and soul. The postwar accounts are often self-serving and colored by the public's bloody shirt memory of the war and the Catholics' desire to cast themselves in the best light. Few such accounts survive anyway to chart the Irish Catholic soldiers' beliefs with confidence. Patriotism, adventure, peer pressure, and the promise of pay all figured in Catholic soldiers' expressed reasons for joining the Union army, but no pattern emerges. Still, the theme of countering anti-Irish, anti-Catholic prejudices surfaces enough in soldiers' accounts to suggest it mattered. That such men were all Irish Americans who had volunteered in 1861 or 1862 no doubt also says much.

Whatever their reasons for joining, Irish Catholics bristled at any hint of their disloyalty or any ethnic slurs. The Irish demanded respect from the non-Irish with whom they served and usually got it as fellow soldiers. When they did not settle disputes with their fists or other informal means, which most soldiers preferred to the intervention of officers in their affairs, they sometimes sought official redress. One Irish officer in an ethnically mixed Indiana regiment angrily reported a drunken soldier who had bleated out that he had not voted for the Irishman and "wouldn't vote for any damned Irish son of a bitch" because, for one, a "damned Irishman always gets his ass up in about two days after he is promoted."[50]

In 1863, amid renewed charges that the Irish were untrustworthy and undisciplined and fearing that his Irish commander was about to retire, Patrick

Casey of the 23rd Illinois entreated his colonel to stay and hoped that the Irish in the regiment "won't be forgotten altogether [and] that some Good Father will come amongst us to help and console us in the time of danger." Casey resented the native-born Protestants for whom "Black abolishism . . . [was] potent," because they did not give the Irish Catholics their due. Without the Irish Catholics, he insisted, the war would "last fifty years to come." Although he expected that the Irish Catholics would "get no thanks" for their bravery when peace came and that as soon as they tired of helping blacks the nativists would return to "burning of Convents and Churches as they have done before," he still wanted the Irish Catholics to fight because they could claim "all the credit" for victory. Likewise, in 1863, R. F. Farrell complained that "brave men deserving [of promotion] are ignored unless they belong to Masonry or some other 'charitable' brotherhood" and that an "Irishman, particularly a Catholic has a . . . hard road to travel when not in an Irish regt." Himself "Irish at heart," Farrell feared "that the darkest hour of our [Irish] trouble has not arrived." In the case of men such as Casey and Farrell, continued ethnic prejudice during the war reinforced Irish Catholic identity and refired Irish nationalism.[51]

The appeal to Irish nationalism and to Irish Catholic duty that moved Casey, and others, to fight had limits. The image of the Irish Catholic warrior defending Irish, American, and Catholic interest was a masculine ideal. It had no female counterpart.[52] The call to arms also meant the Irish Catholic man might have to choose between honor and family. The vital link between defense of one's country and defense of one's family that formed so much of native northerners' and southerners' definitions of nationalism was not yet forged for immigrants and their children. Recruiting posters included assurances that the state would care for needy families left behind and provide relief to any veteran and his family who suffered from the war, thus acknowledging the clash of interests—but only in small print. The posters played to masculine courage, not obligations to home.

Irish Catholic soldiers felt the tug of loyalties. When the claims of Union and even of Irish nationalism impinged on the family, Irish Catholics were hard-pressed to justify continued sacrifices for abstract ideals in the face of real need. In 1861, when the 69th New York Infantry made its triumphant departure from New York City, with its regimental flag of an Irish harp with the stars and stripes unfurled, Irish women lined the streets and crowded from windows and housetops along the way to cheer their men. By 1863, the cheering had stopped. It was time to come home.[53]

For any number of reasons ranging from camaraderie to conviction, and the need for paychecks and the bounties paid for reenlisting, many of the first Irish Catholic volunteers stayed with the Union army. One reason was ethnic duty. In 1862, for example, the Irish nationalist priest, Denis Dunne of St. Patrick's Church in Chicago, stung by doubts about Irish Catholic loyalty, helped form the 90th Illinois Volunteers to silence the critics and called on Irish immigrants who hid behind "the blood-stained felon flag of Great Britain to escape their duty" to join their countrymen in the ranks. The old theme of ethnic obligation also resurfaced in soldiers' accounts. The ardently Catholic and Irish William White of the 69th Pennsylvania Regiment, for example, wrote his parents that "if I cannot get home in an honorable way I don't want to go home until my time is up, so you need not trouble the habeus corpus act." Recall, too, Peter Welsh's long letters to his wife Margaret, pleading the case of Irish and American nationalism to explain his continued military service while she labored to keep the family fed and together. While Peter rhapsodized on his masculine duty, Margaret complained that he affronted her by writing on patriotic stationery and by citing St. Paul and Archbishop Hughes on the moral obligation to fight for a just cause. Her view of duty had no room for his lofty ideals. Welsh stayed with his beloved Irish Brigade and died from a wound suffered while carrying the green flag at Spotsylvania Court House in 1864. Others followed conscience and went home.[54]

By 1863, for many Irish, bounty money and pay provided the only justifiable cause to be in uniform. They waited on paydays as the moment when their service would benefit those left behind. As one officer of the heavily Irish 155th New York Infantry observed on payday, the men greeted the paymaster with their "usual joyous welcome" and among them many "a poor fellow exalted in the thought of how much good his $26 would do his Bridget, his Mary or his Biddy at home." However generous the remittances, mercenary motivations could no longer sustain early ideals of the Irish Catholic warrior embodying the whole identity and interest of the Irish and Catholic community.[55]

By 1863, the conflict between interest and loyalty needed a catharsis. The redefinition of the war in 1862–1863 created a sense of betrayal that fueled the Irish Catholics' doubts about the need to serve. War losses further cut into patriotism. When added to the straitened circumstances of many Irish families, amid inflation and job competition, the anger over Republican policies and the anxiety over family needs made for a highly combustible psychology among Irish Catholics, as indeed among many working-class Americans whatever their ethnic stripe. The Conscription Act of 1863 ignited the mix.

The act required all able-bodied men between the ages of twenty and forty-five to enroll for possible conscription, but it allowed draftees to hire a substitute or avoid their obligation by paying a $300 commutation fee. It discriminated against the working class and hit poor immigrant neighborhoods hard. Already deeply suspicious of Republican intentions from earlier state militia drafts, which in 1862 had led to violent resistance in several places, Irish Catholics knew they were vulnerable. In saloons, fire company halls, and other places where they congregated, staying home to fight an oppressive government quickly replaced marching off to war as the test of Irish-American manhood. They pointedly ignored the advice of Archbishop Hughes that they accept the draft as good citizens and consider it a way of hastening the war's successful end. Irish men would decide for themselves for whom and where to fight. They even would decide if their priest would serve. In 1864, for example, the parishioners of St. Patrick's in Detroit raised money to furnish a substitute for their priest, Father J. A. Hennesy, who had been drafted. Hennesy praised the soldiers who chose to fight but opposed the "impious means" the government used to force men into the army.[56]

Class and racial identities reinforced ethnic ones. The impact of the draft on the working classes seemed to confirm what the Democratic party long had told the urban masses about the Republicans. That the draft came in the wake of emancipation—indeed, as the manpower policy to make emancipation possible—made more credible to Irish thinking the belief that the Republicans were plotting to ship freed slaves north to "steal the work and the bread of the honest Irish."[57]

The tensions exploded in New York City. With its large black and Irish populations already jostling for places in day work and on the docks, with incidents of Irish working-class violence against black strikebreakers as recent as 1862, and with a Democratic political machine fanning any racial and class fears that might hurt Republican interests, New York was primed for violence. The effort to implement the draft in mid-July 1863 detonated it. For four days, mobs of men and women, made up mostly of Irish, and after the first day almost wholly of unskilled workers, vented their wrath. After sacking the draft office and attacking Republican newspapers and businesses on the first day, the rioters turned on blacks with a special fury, burning an orphanage for black children and the homes of many blacks and committing unspeakable acts of torture on their black victims.[58]

The violence was purposeful, not random, as the rioters struck at their enemies, real and imagined. It was also an assertion of "community," in which the mobs sorted out who belonged and insisted on their own view of a proper social order. A Catholic priest calmed one group of rioters who then allowed him to administer the last rites to a young Irish girl they had killed for protesting the violence. The rioters respected authorities who respected them, for the priest appealed to them as Irish Catholics to think of the Irish Catholic girl's soul. Another priest convinced a gang to leave a provost marshal's house by proposing that the city purchase draft exemptions for the poor, further showing the purposefulness of the crowd activity and the ability of individual priests to check the violence by taking the Irish side. The rioters, however, refused to bend to any other authority, not even Irish policemen, and the church's condemnation of the violence did not check its advance into black neighborhoods. Instead, 20,000 troops, including contingents from the Irish Brigade, came from Gettysburg to put down the rioting with cannon and gunfire. Over one hundred people (most of them Irish) died during the rampages.[59]

Irish Catholic violence against the draft also occurred in Chicago's Third Ward ("the Patch"); in Newark, New Jersey; in the Vermont marble quarries; in the Pennsylvania anthracite coal region; and elsewhere. The outbreaks represented more than Irish opposition to the draft; they invariably involved older disputes over control of the workplace and reform, each with its particular local ethnic animosities and personalities to stir the brew. But it was the mayhem in New York City that flashed across the northern wires and fixed the image of the Irish hooligan in the public mind.[60]

All that had been gained by Irish Catholic service in the war lay mortally wounded in the smoking ruins of New York City, the role of the Irish Brigade fresh from its Gettysburg heroics in restoring law and order notwithstanding. The Irish Catholic place in the Union no longer seemed so secure as Irish and Catholic discovered how brittle was the nation's appreciation of their sacrifices. Now they would have to prove their loyalty anew.

Irish Catholics did not entrust rehabilitation of their image to others. Before the war was over, members of the group moved to secure posterity's regard for Irish Catholic patriotism and valor. After the war, in reminiscences and then in monuments, the Irish Catholics continued to immortalize their heroes. Captain D. P. Conyngham's memoir of the Irish Brigade, published in 1867, began the parade of Irish Catholic officers who reminded the nation that Irish arms won Union victory. They said nothing of draft riots or soldiers who fought for bounties or pay, and the desperate Irish arrivals of 1863 and 1864 had no place in the image of the loyal Catholic the memoirs and histories projected. For them, the first soldiers who answered Lincoln's call and stayed the course embodied the "real" Irish Catholic.

As a result, it became an article of faith in the Catholic church that Catholics helped to build the nation. The Civil War provided Irish Catholic heroes to make the case. As early as the 1840s, Irish Catholic apologists had tried to graft Irish and Catholic symbols onto the American standard. By the late nineteenth century, remembering the Catholic, especially the Irish Catholic, role in the Civil War had emerged as an important new element in the church's effort to demonstrate its Americanism. That effort gained special urgency when the surge of southern and eastern European Catholic immigrants reawakened anti-Catholicism and nativism and because the Irish-dominated American church needed to assert its authority over an increasingly contentious and ethnically diverse Catholic population. As the Civil War became recognized as the defining moment for American identity, Irish Catholics wanted to make sure their contributions to preserving the Union would be recalled and revered.[61]

The memory of the war also promised a lesson in moral discipline and patriotic duty for Catholic children and new immigrants. Within the church a battle raged between Americanizers and those who wanted a more diverse Catholicism, but the church's public pose was unflinching in its insistence that Catholics were, and must be, good citizens. American symbols decorated Catholic schools, and American pageants such as Thanksgiving Day celebrations became part of the Catholic curriculum as well. With such display Catholics showed their true colors while they simultaneously claimed their own place in American history.

The mix of ethnic pride with patriotism that became the stock in trade of Tammany Hall orations was regular fare across Irish Catholic America. Typical was the July 4th flag-raising at the Our Lady of Mercy parish school in Philadelphia, in 1894, where after a short street parade the participants marched into the school, which was festooned in flags and banners, to salute the American flag run up the pole by a descendant of the Catholic Commodore Barry of Revolutionary War fame. All who gathered sang the "Star Spangled Banner" and the "Battle Hymn of the Republic" and then listened to a reading of the Declaration of Independence. Several orators then expounded on patriotism in a way, reported the archdiocesan newspaper, "that was enough to make not only Catholics but all Americans proud." The ceremony concluded with a public address recounting the battles fought to win American liberty, from Bunker Hill to Gettysburg. It was understood by all that as comrades-in-arms Catholics were Americans.[62]

Catholic policy sometimes worked against such reverent recollection. Catholics largely stayed away from the national Union veterans' organizations, including the powerful Grand Army of the Republic (GAR), which the church regarded as a quasi-Masonic secret society. Thus, Catholic veterans were left out of the principal organized national efforts to memorialize the war. Catholics joined their own regimental veterans associations, but such organizations remained parochial rather than national in vision.[63]

In a further example of the late nineteenth-century "ghettoization" of Catholic culture, Catholics formed their own historical and literary societies to collect the records and tell the stories of their contributions to building the nation. Even older societies joined in. The official history of Philadelphia's Friendly Sons of St. Patrick society, published in 1892, for example, brimmed with patriotism and the deeds of Irish Catholic soldiers; the achievements of the Irish Brigade alone required an entire section of the book to recite. But the Catholics were talking to themselves. The "mainstream" histories of the war, written largely from a New England Protestant perspective, passed over the Irish Catholics. So, too, the many regimental histories and memoirs, written largely by former officers, focused on command and battle and neglected the common soldier. Some Catholics read conspiracy into the omissions. A Catholic newspaper thus complained in 1899, "Recent school histories of the Civil War have been written with the manifest purpose of minimizing, if not ignoring the magnificent services of the Irish troops."[64]

The Catholic response to the nation's slight was to project a strong, masculine Catholic image. Amid the feminization of American religion, Catholics, like Protestants, at century's end began to give their literature and symbols a more manly pose. The Civil War soldier thus had religious, ethnic, and political uses. A series of articles written for national publications and campaigns to erect monuments celebrated the heroism of Irish Catholic men in battle. The nuns later would get their due in articles and books, and eventually a monument in Washington, D.C., honoring their selflessness as "angels on the battlefield," but it was the men who would fix the Irish Catholic place in the war and national memory.[65]

No one was more significant in shaping the Irish Catholic response than the Irish-born General St. Clair Mulholland, who had served with the 116th Pennsylvania, part of the famous Irish Brigade, and who had received the Medal of Honor in 1895 for his bravery more than three decades earlier at Chancellorsville. Despite his ties to the Republican party, Mulholland enjoyed excellent relations with Irish Catholic veterans. While he prepared for the twenty-fifth reunion of veterans of Gettysburg in 1888, he found his calling as the "historian" first of his regiment and then of his people. Gathering information for a history of the 116th, he reestablished contact with former soldiers. In his scrapbooks, he pasted letters from the men, wartime and postwar patriotic memorabilia, and any published account of his many speeches on Irish Catholic valor. He took to the newspapers to defend the Irish from charges of desertion during the Civil War and recited casualty lists of Irish and German soldiers to rebut any hint of disloyalty or lack of courage. In 1888, Mulholland played the lead role in the placement of a monument to the 116th at Gettysburg, which the archbishop of Philadelphia consecrated in a ceremony that let no one forget what Irish Catholics had done to save the Union.[66]

The most important and enduring symbol Mulholland contributed to the memory of Catholic patriotism and courage was the statue of an Irish priest. In making the case for Catholics as Americans, Catholic writers placed priests alongside soldiers in recalling Catholic participation in the wars for independence and the Union and joined their Protestant counterparts in describing the Union army as a "Christian army" reminiscent of the Crusades.[67] D. J. Murphy, for example, took the occasion of the U.S. Senate's acceptance of the statue of Charles Carroll, a Catholic Founding Father, to remind Americans how much Catholics had contributed in blood to the nation's liberty. After bows to Catholic generals in the Civil War, Murphy focused on the piety, patriotism, and bravery of the priests, who seemingly formed the marrow of the Catholic soldier's identity. Catholic veterans writing to Mulholland likewise recalled the war as an ennobling experience because the priests had given them courage. From such material, Mulholland gave numerous speeches across the North, wrote his regimental history, and lobbied for a monument to the Catholic priest.[68]

For Catholics at least, no event during the Civil War bound together Catholic and Protestant so fully or united Catholics more with the nation than the moment when the soldiers of all faiths knelt before Fr. William Corby on the dawn of the second day of Gettysburg. Corby's general absolution symbolized the union of American Catholic faith and American patriotism and the strength that came from standing together before God. In poems, sculpture, and painting, Catholics relived the moment well into the next century, making Corby a national hero. As part of the general trend late in the nineteenth century in which particular veterans' groups staked off a share of the hallowed ground at Gettysburg, Irish Catholic veterans and clergymen, led by Mulholland, pushed hard to erect a statue of Corby on the spot where he delivered his absolution. The effort succeeded, after several starts, with the unveiling of the bronze Corby statue, its hand upraised in blessing of all who would walk before it, in October 1910. With that statue, Catholics entered American sacred space and memory.[69]

Ironically, the Corby statue and all that it symbolized about the Irish Catholic effort to become one with the nation in memory obscured the Irish Catholic experience in fact during the war. The meaning of Catholicism for soldiers was never so priest-centered as memory would have it. On the contrary, the lay initiative and simple worship that the war briefly encouraged were at odds with the church's continuing emphasis on clerical authority and religious uniformity. So, too, the official Catholic memory of the war hardly fit with the Irish Catholics' intense Irish nationalism and conditional American one, and it denied the poverty and desperation as factors causing them to fight. The memory of the war propounded by Mulholland and other "professional" Irish Catholics at the end of the century no doubt contributed to the growing acceptance of middle-class Irish Catholics in Protestant America, but it did so at the cost of forgetting the many Irish for the few. Like the bronze Corby on its pedestal, drawing the eye upward, the historical memory embodied in the statue ignores those at the bottom of Irish-American society—the unchurched or ignorant, the shirkers, the deserters, the rioters, the desperate men from Ireland who joined to get bounties, or the women who wanted their men home. It does not lead us to the anonymous men who died at Antietam or to those for whom Catholic and Irish interests did not always converge. What it meant to be Irish and Catholic amid and because of the war is thus only partly revealed in bronze, books, or even in bones.

Notes

For reading and commenting on an earlier version of this essay, I thank Paula Benkart, John Boles, Frank Gerrity, Marion Roydhouse, Eric Schneider, and Steve Wright. For sharing photocopies of documents and his immense store of information about the Irish, I especially thank the late Dennis Clark. I also profited from comments by Joseph Casino, Anne Rose, and Charles Reagan Wilson on the general direction of my work and from criticisms and suggestions about religion, ethnicity, and war by Kathleen Conzen, Maureen Harp, and participants in the University of Chicago Social History Workshop.

1. Among the several newspaper accounts of this discovery, see, for example, the useful summaries: "Unmarked Graves Give a Glimpse into a Civil War Soldier's Life," *New York Times*, September 16, 1994; and "A Soldier's Story—from 1862," *Philadelphia Inquirer*, September 25, 1994.

2. For the Union experience, see Ella Lonn, *Foreigners in the Union Army and Navy* (Baton Rouge, 1951); and William L. Burton, *Melting Pot Soldiers: The Union's Ethnic Regiments* (Ames, 1988). Of all the ethnic regiments, the Irish Brigade regiments have received the most attention. For a recent collection of useful essays that reflect the character of that enthusiastic literature, see Philip T. Tucker, ed., *The History of the Irish Brigade: A Collection of Historical Essays* (Fredericksburg, VA, 1995). On the Irish generally, see also the still useful summary in Carl Wittke, *The Irish in America* (Baton Rouge, 1956), chap. 13. The standard general account of Catholics in the Civil War remains Benjamin J. Blied's *Catholics and the Civil War* (Milwaukee, 1945). The literature on religion and the war is enormous, but virtually all such literature either ignores Catholics and other "minority" religions altogether or gives them short shrift. For an excellent recent summary and analysis of religion in the North during the war, though with only a brief mention of Catholics, see Phillip Shaw Paludan, *"A People's Contest": The Union and the Civil War* (New York, 1988), chap. 14.

3. On the character of American Catholicism, see especially John Tracy Ellis, *American Catholicism*, 2nd ed. (Chicago, 1969); James Hennesey, *American Catholics: A*

History of the Roman Catholic Community in the United States (New York, 1981); and Jay P. Dolan, *The American Catholic Experience: A History from Colonial Times to the Present* (Garden City, 1985).

4. See Blied, *Catholics and the Civil War*, 36–50 and 70–82; Hennesey, *American Catholics*, 148–157; Ellis, *American Catholicism*, 94–100; New York *Irish-American*, March 8, 1862. Regarding the war as a way to bring Catholics together, Archbishop John Hughes of New York privately opposed the creation of exclusively Irish or German ethnic regiments, even though he publicly blessed them, because he feared such regiments would divide Catholics and retard assimilation into the church and the state. See Hughes to William Henry Seward, September 12, 1861, in John Hassard, *The Life of the Most. Rev. John Hughes, D. D., First Archbishop of New York, with Extracts from His Private Correspondence* (New York, 1866), 443–444.

5. The most quoted and noted advocate of Catholic patriotic and military duty was Archbishop John Hughes of New York, who spelled out his position in a series of public letters and pastorals. See, for example, Lawrence Kehoe, ed., *The Complete Works of the Most. Rev. John Hughes, D. D. Archbishop of New York*, 2 vols. (New York, 1866), 2: 157, 513–520; Hassard, *Life of the Most Rev. John Hughes*, 438–439; and Richard Shaw, *Dagger John: The Unquiet Life and Times of Archbishop John Hughes of New York* (New York, 1977), 342–360. For an example of a bellicose sermon calling Irish Catholics to arms, see the April 1861 sermon of Father Creedon of Auburn, New York, in *Anecdotes, Poetry, and Incidents of the War: North and South, 1860–1865*, ed. Frank Moore (New York, 1866), 460–461.

6. On the war as a Christian enterprise, see especially James Moorhead, *American Apocalypse: Yankee Protestants and the Civil War, 1860–1869* (New Haven, 1978); and Gardiner H. Shattuck Jr., *A Shield and Hiding Place: The Religious Life of the Civil War Armies* (Macon, 1987), 13–33.

7. "Father Joseph O'Hagan," *Woodstock Letters* 8 (1879): 173–183; Boston *Pilot*, May 30, 1863; New York *Irish-American*, February 1, 1862.

8. On the authority and duties of chaplains in the Union armies, see Shattuck, *A Shield and Hiding Place*, 51–72; Bell Irvin Wiley, *The Life of Billy Yank: The Common Soldier of the Union* (Garden City, 1971), 263–268; and James I. Robertson Jr., *Soldiers Blue and Gray* (Columbia, 1988), 172–189.

9. For a listing of Catholic chaplains and their assignments, see D. Aidan Germain, comp., *Catholic Military and Naval Chaplains, 1776–1917* (Washington, 1929). For good thumbnail sketches of the most prominent Catholic chaplains, see Lonn, *Foreigners in the Union Army and Navy*, 308–320. For Ireland's wartime account, see James P. Shannon, ed., "Archbishop Ireland's Experiences as a Civil War Chaplain," *Catholic Historical Review* 39 (1953–54): 298–305; and Ireland's April 3, 1863 letter of resignation, in Germain, comp., *Catholic Military and Naval Chaplains*, 71.

10. William White to "Dear Parents," November 8, 1861, and April 23, June 21, July 13, and October 5, 1862, box 1, William G. White Papers, Archives of the Archdiocese of Philadelphia; Thomas Halpin to "Friend Cole," " July 11, 1862, printed in New York *Irish-American*, July 26, 1862; Betty Perkins, "The Work of the Catholic Sisters in the Civil War," M.A. thesis, University of Dayton, 1969, 91; and Thomas Halvey to Fr. Patrick Reilly, November 24, 1861, Patrick Reilly Papers, Archives of the Archdiocese of Philadelphia.

11. George Barton, *Angels of the Battlefield: A History of the Labors of the Catholic Sisterhoods in the Late Civil War*, 2nd ed. (Philadelphia, 1898), 96–97.

12. Blied, *Catholics and the Civil War*, 111–112; Peter Paul Cooney to "My Dear Brother," March 30, 1862, in "The War Letters of Father Peter Paul Cooney of the

Congregation of Holy Cross," ed., Thomas McAvoy, *Records of the American Catholic Historical Society* 44 (1933): 61. Priests from nearby towns might be persuaded to visit encamped regiments, but they rarely stayed long because parish duties came first. Thus, for example, Fr. Thomas Anwander of St. Peter's Church in Cumberland, Maryland, responded to Colonel James A. Mulligan's request to visit the 23rd Illinois Regiment by saying he might be able to come on a Tuesday, say Mass in the morning and stay for the day hearing confessions, and then say Mass again early on Wednesday before leaving that same morning on the train—provided he could get approval from his provincial to spend that much time away from his church. See Anwander to Mulligan, March 25, 1863, box 2, James A. Mulligan Collection, Chicago Historical Society.

13. W[illiam] Corby, *Memoirs of Chaplain Life* (Notre Dame, 1894), 27–28; W. Springer Menge and J. August Shimrak, eds., *The Civil War Notebook of Daniel Chisholm: A Chronicle of Daily Life in the Union Army 1864–1865* (New York, 1989), 54–55; and Peter Paul Cooney to My Dear Brother, October 2, 1862, in McAvoy, ed., "The War Letters of Father Peter Paul Cooney," 68–69. For a soldier's contemporary view of the priests' influence, see "Gallowglass" [Capt. James Turner] letter describing the Irish Brigade encampment near Yorktown, published in the New York *Irish-American*, May 17, 1862.

14. Reverend Father Tissot, "A Year with the Army of the Potomac," (United States Catholic Historical Society) *Historical Records and Studies* 3 (1908): Part 1, 46; Menge and Shimrak, eds., *The Civil War Notebook of Daniel Chisholm*, 12 and 31; William L. Lucey, ed., "The Diary of Joseph B. O'Hagan, S. J., Chaplain of the Excelsior Brigade," *Civil War History* 6 (1960): 405–406, 407–408; Edward P. Smith, *Incidents Among Shot and Shell* (New York, 1866), 432. One Protestant Irishman in the 116th Pennsylvania thought that the Catholics in the Irish Brigade were less zealous and faithful in their weekly worship than were Methodists: see Kevin E. O'Brien, ed., *My Life in the Irish Brigade: The Civil War Memoirs of Private William McCarter, 116th Pennsylvania Infantry* (Campbell, CA, 1996), 49.

15. D[avid] P. Conyngham, *The Irish Brigade and Its Campaigns: With Some Account of the Corcoran Legion, and Sketches of the Principal Officers* (New York, 1867), 82; Corby, *Memoirs of Chaplain Life*, 37–38, 42–43; "War Letters of Father Peter Paul Cooney," 57.

16. On Catholic revivalism, see Jay P. Dolan, *Catholic Revivalism: The American Experience, 1830–1900* (Notre Dame, 1978); on revivals in the Union army, see Shattuck, *A Shield and Hiding Place*, 79–93. On the renewed faith of a lapsed Catholic (after the loss of 90 of his comrades in battle), see, for example, John H. Dowling (4th Delaware Volunteers) to Fr. Patrick Reilly, June 22, 1864 (typescript), Reilly Papers. On piety among wounded soldiers, see, for example, Mother Mary Gonzaga, "Notes in Saterlee Hospital, West Philadelphia, Penna. from 1862 until Its Close in 1865" [a diary/memoir, 1862–1865], 4–5, 8, Archives of the Archdiocese of Philadelphia.

17. For the Corby story, see especially St. Clair A. Mulholland's version (quoted herein), first delivered in his address, "The Last Muster," at the September 11, 1889 reunion of the 116th Regiment Pennsylvania Volunteers, copy in St. Clair A. Mulholland Scrapbook, Civil War Library & Museum, Philadelphia; reprinted with minor changes in capitalization and wording in Mulholland, *The Story of the 116th Regiment Pennsylvania Volunteers in the War of the Rebellion: The Record of a Gallant Command* (Philadelphia, 1903), 407–408; and in William Corby to John Bachelder, January 4, 1879, in Tucker, ed., *History of the Irish Brigade*, 208–209; and Corby, *Memoirs of Chaplain Life*, 181–185.

18. See, for example, Peter Welsh to Margaret Welsh, January 23, 1863, and April 14, 1864, in Lawrence F. Kohl and Margaret C. Richard, eds., *Irish Green and Union*

Blue: The Civil War Letters of Peter Welsh, Color Sergeant 28th Regiment Massachusetts Volunteers (New York, 1986), 59 and 150; New York *Irish-American*, July 20, 1861; Corby, *Memoirs of Chaplain Life*, 57, 71–73, 237–239, and passim; Thomas Halvey to Fr. Patrick Reilly, March 30, April 19, December 1, 1861, Reilly Papers; and Patrick O'Neill to Fr. Reilly, June 12, 1863, ibid. For the accounts of money deposits left with the church, to be sent to family members in America and Ireland, see, for example, Deposit Ledger No. 5, Cathedral of Sts. Peter and Paul, Archives of the Archdiocese of Philadelphia.

19. Conyngham, *The Irish Brigade*, 226; William White to [parent], n.d. [1862], box 1, White Papers. For a good example of the adulation of a priest's reputed battlefield bravery, see Maria Lydig Daly's July 28, 1861, diary entry relating Fr. Bernard O'Reilly's heroic conduct at Bull Run, when the chaplain, "seeing the ensign [who carried the green flag of the 69th New York] fall, held the standard himself . . . and showed the greatest coolness and courage." Harold E. Hammond, ed., *Diary of a Union Lady 1861–1865* (New York, 1962), 40–41. See also New York *Irish-American*, August 2, and December 21, 1861.

We can never know how many priests shrank back when the guns sounded, neglected their duties, drank too much, and otherwise embarrassed their office, thus losing the soldiers' respect. The Catholic church and press remained too defensive about the church's reputation and too self-conscious about any criticism that might diminish Catholics' claims to full "citizenship" in the republic to air any such feelings in the open. But the Catholic soldiers' diaries and letters that survive also say nothing. Perhaps there was no such criticism to render. Or perhaps soldiers as well felt the need not to "give scandal" on such matters, even to loved ones. We do not know.

20. Reid Mitchell, *Civil War Soldiers: Their Expectations and Their Experiences* (New York, 1988), 70–71. On the Mooney incident, see Frank Moore, ed., *The Rebellion Record: A Diary of American Events, with Documents, Narrative, Illustrative Incidents, Poetry, Etc.* 12 vols. (New York, 1861–1868), II, Part 3: 42–43.

21. On the press, see below. For the image of the Irish, see Dale T. Knobel, *Paddy and the Republic: Ethnicity and Nationality in Antebellum America* (Middletown, 1986), especially chap. 6. Knobel notes how the Civil War, with its emphasis on race, helped transmute American nationality into one of "blood" and to lift the Irish by means of their color. By the end of the century, with social applications of Darwinian theory in hand, native-born Protestant Americans included the middle-class, assimilated Catholic Irish in the core group of the American "race" in defining nationality. Knobel rightly argues that the war helped to reduce anti-Catholic feeling, but it did not uniformly reduce anti-Irish feeling. That process took longer. On the decline of nativism because of and after the war, see also John Higham, *Strangers in the Land: Patterns of American Nativism, 1860–1925*, 2nd ed. (New Brunswick, 1988), 12–14, 26, 28–31.

22. McAvoy, ed., "The War Letters of Father Peter Paul Cooney," passim.

23. Barton, *Angels of the Battlefield*, 95; Sister Angela Heath, "Memoir," in "Annals of the Civil War, 1861–1865" (photocopy), 95–98, Archives of the Sisters of St. Joseph, Philadelphia; "Convent Annals," in Kathleen Healy, ed., *Sisters of Mercy: Spirituality in America 1843–1900* (New York and Mahway, 1992), 78–81. The best overall treatment of Catholic nuns as nurses is Sister Mary Denis Maher, *To Bind Up the Wounds: Catholic Sister Nurses in the U.S. Civil War* (New York and Westport, 1989), especially chap. 5. Ellen Ryan Jolly, *Nuns of the Battlefield* (Providence, 1927), is uncritical but has many first-hand accounts.

24. Daniel T. McGolgan, *A Century of Charity: The First Hundred Years of the Society of St. Vincent De Paul in the United States*, 2 vols. (Milwaukee, 1951), 1: 240–242; *The Manual of the Christian Soldier* (New York, 1861). John H. Greene (of the Cincinnati

Catholic Telegraph) to James Mulligan, June 5, 1863, box 2, Mulligan Collection. For one soldier's use of his prayer book, see William White to "Dear Parents," July 13, 1862, box 1, White Papers, in which White asked his parents to send his "little Irish prayer book," which he had forgotten, while assuring them that he kept his other prayer book in his pocket.

25. On the Catholic ethos of mid-nineteenth-century America, see Dolan, *American Catholic Experience*, chap. 8; on the devotional revolution's Irish character, see Emmet Larkin, "The Devotional Revolution in Ireland, 1850–1875," *American Historical Review* 77 (1972): 625–652.

26. On the Catholic press during the war generally, see the sampling in Blied, *Catholics and the Civil War*, chap. 5. My comments are based on a reading of various Catholic and Irish papers for the war years.

27. Ellis, *American Catholicism*, 94–95; New York *Freeman's Journal*, October 4, 1862; and letter of Thomas Halpin to "Friend Cole," from Chicago, July 11, 1862, printed in New York *Irish-American*, July 26, 1862.

28. See Peter Welsh to Margaret Welsh letters, February 3, 15, and 22, 1863 and August 2, 1863, and Peter Welsh to Patrick Prendergast, June 1, 1863, in Kohl and Richard, eds., *Irish Green and Union Blue*, 64–67, 71–72, 73–75, 115, and 100–104, respectively.

29. See, for example, New York *Irish-American*, October 4, November 15, December 13, 1862, October 10, and November 14, 1863. On relief, see Edward K. Spann, "Union Green: The Irish Community and the Civil War," in *The New York Irish*, eds. Ronald H. Bayor and Timothy J. Meagher (Baltimore, 1996), esp. 196–198, 201–202.

30. It is highly unlikely that nuns or laymen actually administered any other sacraments besides baptism. The accounts suggest the nuns and laymen were present for analogies: hearing about sins/Penance; praying with the dying/Extreme Unction; dispensing pre-consecrated wafers/Eucharist. On the wearing of religious medals, scapulars, and other objects, see, for example, the observations of Mother Mary Gonzaga, "Notes in Saterlee Hospital," 8–9, in which she related the story of one soldier who escaped death when a bullet hit his scapular and noted that many soldiers "attributed their preservation to one or the other" of such religious objects. Even Protestants asked for Catholic medals as talismans.

We also know very little how wartime experiences with Catholicism, or any religion, played out within the families, communities, and parishes soldiers reentered after the war. The records are largely silent on such private matters.

31. Kerby A. Miller, *Emigrants and Exiles: Ireland and the Irish Exodus to North America* (New York, 1985). For a good distillation, discussing the variegated character of Irish-American nationalism and the Catholic church in the United States, see Miller, "Class, Culture, and Immigrant Group Identity in the United States: The Case of Irish-American Ethnicity," in Virginia Yans-McLaughlin, ed., *Immigration Reconsidered: History, Sociology, and Politics* (New York, 1990), 96–129.

32. Moore, ed., *Rebellion Record*, 1: 83–119; Burton, *Melting Pot Soldiers*, 35–36; Joseph George Jr., "Philadelphia's *Catholic Herald*: The Civil War Years," *Pennsylvania Magazine of History and Biography* (hereafter, *PMHB*) 103 (1979): 196–221 (202–203 on the mob attack); Mrs. J. Blakeslee Frost, *The Rebellion in the United States; or, the War of 1861*, 2 vols. (Hartford, 1862–1864), 1: 144; Hennesey, *American Catholics*, 148–151.

33. Michael Cavanaugh, *Memoirs of Gen. Thomas Francis Meagher, Comprising the Leading Events of His Career Chronologically Arranged* (Worcester, 1892), 369–371; William P. Fox, comp., *New York Monuments Commission for the Battlefields of Gettysburg and Chattanooga . . .* , 3 vols. (Albany, 1900), 3: 487.

34. Albon P. Man Jr., "The Irish in New York in the Early 1860s," *Irish Historical Studies* 7 (September 1950): 103–105; Comte de Paris, *History of the Civil War in America*, trans. by Louis F. Tasistro, 4 vols. (Philadelphia, 1876–1878), 1: 177–178; William D'Arcy, *The Fenian Movement in the United States, 1858–1886* (Washington, 1947), 11, 37; Thomas N. Brown, *Irish-American Nationalism, 1850–1890* (Philadelphia, 1966), 1–57 (on concerns about radical Irish nationalism inciting anti-Catholicism and nativism); Miller, *Emigrants and Exiles*, 342–343; James Rorty to "My dear father," November 15, 1861, James Rorty Pension File, National Archives, photocopy courtesy of Maureen A. Harp. The literature on the Fenians is vast. For a good case study of the Fenians operating at the local level, showing all the personal rivalries and factionalism that beset the movement, see Dennis Clark, "Militants of the 1860's: The Philadelphia Fenians," *PMHB* 95 (1971): 98–108. The Fenian Papers in the Archives of the American Catholic Historical Society of Philadelphia, St. Charles Seminary, Overbook, Philadelphia, brim with letters, circulars, and reports on Fenian appeals, associations, and activity during and after the war.

35. Hassard, *Life of the Most Rev. John Hughes*, 482; Lonn, *Foreigners in the Union Army and Navy*, 119; James Rorty to "My dear father, November 15, 1861, James Rorty Pension File.

36. Burton, *Melting Pot Soldiers*, 9–14, 22–23, 118–122, 135–140, and passim.

37. Lonn, *Foreigners in the Union Army and Navy*, 118–121; Burton, *Melting Pot Soldiers*, 42–44, 57–58.

38. See the recruitment poster collections at the Chicago Historical Society and the Massachusetts Historical Society. See also Colonel James A. Mulligan's (23rd Illinois) recruitment lectures delivered in churches, orphanages, and public halls, in which Mulligan typically fused Irish nationalism, Catholicism, and service in the Union army and depicted the Irish Union soldier as fearless and happy: Moore, ed., *Rebellion Record*, 3: 439–442. For an example of florid recruiting oratory, see ibid., 1: 391. For examples of the fusion of Irish nationalism, Catholicism, and patriotism, see James Rorty to "My dear father," November 15, 1861, James Rorty Pension File; and S. A. Walker to James Mulligan, January 28, 1863, box 2, Mulligan Collection.

39. On the use of Corcoran and the "gallant 69th" for recruiting, see, for example, Philadelphia *Evening Bulletin*, August 22, 1862. On Hughes and Corcoran, see Hassard, *Life of the Most Rev. John Hughes*, 443. For a vivid description of one leg of Corcoran's triumphant whistle-stop eastern tour following his release from prison, see James Moore, *History of the Cooper Shop Refreshment Saloon* (Philadelphia, 1866), 60–84, which also points to the importance of linking the local Irish population simultaneously to Irish nationalism and the Union cause through public ritual; and for New York, see Hammond, ed., *Diary of a Union Lady*, pp. 166–67. Corcoran's death in December 1863, after falling off a horse, briefly revived his fame nationally: *New York Times*, December 25, 1863. Through his fictional hero Private Miles O'Reilly, Charles Graham Halpine recited the same trinity of purpose: see *The Life and Adventures, Songs, Services, and Speeches of Private Miles O'Reilly* (New York, 1864), 159. For Corcoran's own self-promotion, see Michael Corcoran, *The Captivity of General Corcoran* (Philadelphia, 1862).

40. New York *Irish-American*, October 4, 1862; and Thomas Francis Meagher, *The Last Days of the 69th in Virginia* (New York, [1862]), one of the most bellicose statements of Irish pride and prowess, repeating all the old canards of British and Protestant perfidy, which was published by the New York *Irish-American* in pamphlet form to drum up recruits and support for the reorganized Irish Brigade, after Meagher had assumed command.

41. Boston *Pilot*, April 27, 1861, May 4, 1861, August 24, 1861, August 9, 1862, October 4 and 11, 1862, March 28, 1863; New York *Irish-American*, July 26, 1862, and December 14, 1862 (letter of William Nagle describing being "slaughtered like sheep" because the generals were indifferent to Irish lives); Philadelphia *Catholic Herald*, February 21, 1863; New York *Metropolitan Record*, 14 February 1863; Eric Lott, *Love and Theft: Blackface Minstrelsy and the American Working Class* (New York, 1993), 237. It should be noted that the *Pilot*'s Donahue privately put military capability ahead of ethnic pride when urging the appointment of officers for Irish regiments. See his letter to Massachusetts governor John Andrew, September 13, 1862, excerpted in Barry Lee Spink, "Colonel Richard Byrnes, Irish Brigade Leader," in Tucker, ed., *History of the Irish Brigade*, 131.

42. James Mulligan "Diary," October 29, 1862, and January 3, 1863. (antiblack statements following the Emancipation Proclamation), in Mulligan Collection; Peter Welsh (letter fragment, ca. February 1863), in Kohl and Richard, eds., *Irish Green and Union Blue*, 62; William White to [parents], n.d. [1862], box 1, White Papers; Man, "Irish in New York in the Early 1860s," 105–106; Craig L. Kautz, "Fodder for Cannon: Immigrant Perceptions of the Civil War," Ph.D. dissertation, University of Nebraska, 1976, p. 70, on Irish mobs in Indianapolis opposing emancipation (I want to thank Frederick Luebke for this reference).

43. Stephen W. Sears, *Landscape Turned Red: The Battle of Antietam* (New Haven and New York, 1983), 242–243; J. Cutler Andrews, *The North Reports the Civil War* (Pittsburgh, 1955), 284; Burton, *Melting Pot Soldiers*, 123–126; William White to [parents], n.d. [1862], box 1, White Papers; and Robert G. Athearn, *Thomas Francis Meagher: An Irish Revolutionary in America* (Boulder, 1949), 115–117, for an accurate account of Meagher and the Brigade at Antietam.

44. See recruitment poster collections at the Chicago Historical Society and the Massachusetts Historical Society. The promise of bounties and good pay had formed part of the the recruiters' appeal from the beginning of the war, but they had been secondary to ones of patriotism.

45. Lonn, *Foreigners in the Union Army and Navy*, 410–413. The Irish press and many Irish patriots, abetted by Confederate propaganda in Ireland, discouraged emigration to fight for the Union, which they regarded as corrupt, incompetent, and nativist. See Joseph M. Hernon Jr., "Irish Religious Opinion on the American Civil War," *Catholic Historical Review* 49 (1963–1964): 508–523.

46. Miller, *Emigrants and Exiles*, 359–361 (MacManus quotation on 360). Some Irish immigrants were coerced, and even kidnapped, by overeager agents; Lonn, *Foreigners in the Union Army and Navy*, 449, 452, 473, 475–477.

47. To cite one example: One poor Irishman was "anctious to return" to James Mulligan's 23rd Illinois Regiment, even though the doctors considered him unfit for duty, because his wife was "about to be confined, his three children are very sick with Scarlet fever and one will probably dy." S. B. Nevel to Mulligan, March 28, 1863, box 2, Mulligan Collection. Some newcomers were Irish Confederates, who joined the Union army after being captured and then recruited by the promise of release and pay and the services of a Catholic priest. See U.S. War Department, *The War of the Rebellion: A Compilation of the Official Records of the Union and Confederate Armies*, 70 vols. (Washington, 1880–1901) [hereafter, *O. R.*], series 3, 3: 766; and Fr. Peter Cooney to "My Dear Brother," September 7, 1863, in McAvoy, ed., "The War Letters of Father Peter Paul Cooney," 220. The extent to which the draft succeeded as a prod to encourage immigrants and laborers to volunteer to escape conscription is much debated in the literature. The arguments are summarized in James W. Geary, *We Need Men: The Union Draft*

in the Civil War (DeKalb, 1991), 88–101. From my view, the draft worked unevenly to bring Irish Catholics in as a threat, but recruiters in heavily Irish areas expected to do well drawing on recent immigrants. See, for example, *O. R.*, series 3, 4: 631, for the boast (August 20, 1864) by the mayor of Springfield, Massachusetts, that he could get 300 immigrant recruits in a month.

48. On the religious state of the Irish of this generation, see Miller, *Emigrants and Exiles*, 325–344, 356–361; and Jay P. Dolan, *The Immigrant Church: New York's Irish and German Catholics, 1815–1865* (Notre Dame, 1983 ed.), 54–58.

49. James McPherson, *What They Fought For, 1861–1865* (Baton Rouge, 1994). Even though McPherson's sample grossly underrepresents immigrant soldiers (immigrant accounts make up only 2 percent of his sample, while the Irish and the Germans made up 11 percent and 12 percent of the Union army, respectively), he still aligns immigrants with native-born Union soldiers in holding high ideals about democracy and the meaning of Union (pp. 31–32, 36–37). The other studies of soldiers' attitudes largely ignore the foreign-born in their sampling.

50. Headquarters, Army of the Potomac, General Orders, 38, February 1, 1862, Records of the Adjutant General, War Department, National Archives. Such feelings even led Irish soldiers to desert en masse from a unit where they were a minority to join another with an Irish majority. For one such instance, see George A. Bruce, *The Twentieth Regiment of Massachusetts Volunteer Infantry* (New York, 1906), 7. For an excellent discussion of the internal dynamics of regimental life in a veteran regiment of farmers, laborers, mechanics, immigrants, and others, with observations on the ways religion and ethnicity intruded into camp life, see Warren Wilkinson, *Mother, May You Never See the Sights I Have Seen: The Fifty-Seventh Massachusetts Veteran Volunteers in the Army of the Potomac, 1864–1865* (New York, 1990).

51. P. Casey to James Mulligan, March 23, 1863, box 2, Mulligan Collection; Capt. R. F. Farrell to James Mulligan, February 8, 1863, box 2, ibid. See also M. W. Toole to Mulligan, February 10, 1863, box 2, ibid. That Casey's and Farrell's fears were partly justified is revealed in the private comments of several soldiers, even ones who served with Irish Catholics (perhaps because they served with Irish Catholics). See, for example, Daniel Faust to "My Dear Sister," November 2, 1864, Harrisburg (PA) Civil War Round Table Collection, U. S. Army Military History Institute, Carlisle, who wrote that when the Civil War ended, the next war would be against Catholics, who were "almost" like slaveholders in being antithetical to American values. Complaints by Irish soldiers, and other immigrants, that they lost out getting commissions, promotions, and pay were rife. The best study testing actual practice is Kevin J. Weddle, "Ethnic Discrimination in Minnesota Volunteer Regiments during the Civil War," *Civil War History* 35 (1989): 239–259, who finds that the foreign-born did suffer from such discrimination.

52. There were rare exceptions. The most famous was Bridget Divers, known as "Irish Biddy," who followed her husband and won notice for her courage in taking fallen men off the field, rallying the troops under fire, and at Fair Oaks urging the 7th Massachusetts on by shouting "Arrah! go in boys, and bate the bloody spalpeens, and revinge me husband [who had been wounded], and God be wid ye." See Frank Moore, *Women of the War: Their Heroism and Self-Sacrifice* (Hartford, 1866), 533–535.

53. On the 69th's original grand procession, from its armory on Prince Street, down Broadway, to the North River, see Moore, ed., *Rebellion Record*, I, Part 2, 142–143.

54. *Chicago Tribune*, August 10, 1862; William White to "Dear Parents," August 19, 1862 box 1, White Papers; for Welsh, see note 28 above; James Rorty to "My dear

father," November 15, 1861, James Rorty Pension File. For a contrasting view, wherein an Irish Catholic chaplain who recruited for the army privately advised his brother on how to avoid the draft, see Fr. Peter Paul Cooney to "My Dear Brother," September 7, 1863, in McAvoy, ed., "The War Letters of Father Peter Paul Cooney," 220–221. The worries of paying rent and doctor's bills, feeding children, and protecting home while her husband was away in the army and the government was providing no dependency allowances is graphically expressed in a wartime poem written by an Irishwoman, "Mary O'Connor, The Volunteer's Wife," reprinted in Gerda Lerner, ed., *The Female Experience: An American Documentary* (Indianapolis, 1977), 171–172. See also the poem on Irish dead by Kate Boylan in the New York *Irish-American*, May 2, 1863.

55. John Winterbotham to "My Dear Family," February 22/23, 1864, John Winterbotham Collection, Chicago Historical Society. On the importance of pay, see, for example, the New York *Irish-American*, February 1, 1862, which reported that in the first pay three New York Irish regiments had received in almost five months, the Irish soldiers had remitted roughly $20,000 to their families.

56. The draft and its social consequences are ably described and analyzed in Adrian Cook, *The Armies of the Streets: The New York City Draft Riots of 1863* (Lexington, 1974); and Iver Bernstein, *The New York City Draft Riots: Their Significance for American Society and Politics in the Age of the Civil War* (New York, 1990). Bernstein particularly recognizes the male and kinship ties among the Irish and the role of "manhood" among the Irish working class (e.g., 118–123). On the Irish and the 1862 riots, see Joseph Hernon Jr., *Celts, Catholics, and Copperheads: Ireland Views the American Civil War* (Columbus, 1968), 11–12, 38. On the Detroit incident, see Eugene C. Murdock, *One Million Men: The Civil War Draft in the North* (Madison, 1971), 215–216.

57. Quoted in Cook, *Armies of the Streets*, 205.

58. For a graphic rendering of the riots, with much attention to the shift from their initial anti-Republicanism, antidraft phase to their antiblack one, see Bernstein, *New York City Draft Riots*, 17–42.

59. New York *Herald*, July 15, 16, 1863; New York *Tribune*, July 16, 1863; Cook, *Armies of the Streets*, 119, 121 (on Catholic priests interventions), and 195–196; Hammond, ed., *Diary of a Union Lady*, 251. On Hughes and the church's response, see Albon Man Jr., "The Church and the New York Draft Riots of 1863," *Records of the American Catholic Historical Society* 62 (1951): 33–50; Hennesey, *American Catholics*, 150–151.

60. Murdock, *One Million Men*, 52–53, 57, 58, 86–88; Peter Levine, "Draft Evasion in the North During the Civil War, 1863–1865" *Journal of American History* 67 (1981): 816–834; Wayne Broehl, *The Molly Maguires* (Cambridge, 1964), 83–90; and especially the insightful discussion in Grace Palladino, *Another Civil War: Labor, Capital, and the State in the Anthracite Regions of Pennsylvania, 1840–68* (Urbana and Chicago, 1990), 3–14, 95–117, and passim. At least one Irish soldier lamented that the riots would set the Irish back in the public's estimation: "God help the Irish. They are to[o] easily led into such snares which gives their enemys an oppertunity to malighn and abuse them." See Peter Welsh to Margaret Welsh, August 2, 1863, in Kohl and Richard, ed., *Irish Green and Union Blue*, 115. The Irish Catholic immigrants' and working-class's resentments toward their Protestant "overlords" did not end with the war. The New York riots in 1870 and 1871 between Irish Catholics and Irish Protestants, for example, showed that the combination of ethnic, religious, and class distrust remained highly explosive. See Michael Gordon, *The Orange Riots: Irish Political Violence in New York City, 1870–1871* (Ithaca, 1993).

61. Thomas D'Arcy McGee, *A History of Irish Settlers in North America* (Boston, 1852); and Michael J. O'Brien, *A Hidden Phase of American History: Ireland's Part in*

America's Struggle for Liberty (New York, 1918). For an example of the Catholic argument that the bravery of Catholic soldiers undid nativism and affirmed Catholics' patriotism to all observers, see the overly optimistic reminiscence of Fr. August J. Thebaud, *Forty Years in the United States of America, 1839–1885* (New York, 1904), 256–257, 297. On Irish-American Catholic upward mobility, adaptations, self-perceptions, and identities generally, see especially Miller, *Emigrants and Exiles*, 493–555.

62. Philadelphia *Catholic Times*, July 7, 1894.

63. Stuart McConnell, *Glorious Contentment: The Grand Army of the Republic, 1865–1900* (Chapel Hill, 1992), 69–71, 81, 131–132; and George J. Lankevich, "The Grand Army of the Republic in New York State, 1865–1898," Ph.D. dissertation, Columbia University, 1967, 125–26. On church opposition to secret societies, see Dolan, *The American Catholic Experience*, 312–313.

64. John H. Campbell, *History of the Friendly Sons of St. Patrick and of the Hibernian Society for the Relief of Emigrants from Ireland to Philadelphia* (Philadelphia, 1892); Philadelphia *Catholic Standard and Times*, September 16, 1899. The complaints flared anew during the fiftieth anniversary of the war: see, for example, Thomas S. Lonergan to *New York Sun* [1911], clipping sewn into personal copy of Martin I. J. Griffin's *The American Catholic Historical Researches for 1911*, vol. 28 (Philadelphia, 1911), 310–311, Martin I. J. Griffin Papers, Saint Joseph's University Archives. On the formation of Catholic historical societies, see John Paul Cadden, *The Historiography of the American Catholic Tradition* (Washington, 1944), chap. 3.

65. Dolan, *American Catholic Experience*, 232, 257–258; Dorothy Dohen, *Nationalism and American Catholicism* (New York, 1967). An interesting early example of Civil War Irish Catholic hagiography, celebrating the selfless devotion of Irish Catholic soldiers and the manliness of their priests, is Capt. David P. Conyngham's unpublished manuscript, "Heroism of the Cross; or Nuns and Priests of the Battlefield," n.d., Conyngham Papers, University of Notre Dame.

66. On Mulholland's activities, see the many clippings and memorabilia in the Mulholland Scrapbooks. No scholarly biography of Mulholland exists. Philadelphia *Evening Bulletin*, March 7 and 11, 1898; Philadelphia *Public Ledger*, May 30, 1902; *Zanesville* (Ohio) *Daily Courier* [1902], clipping in Mulholland Scrapbooks.

67. Mulholland waxed glorious about the piety of his regiment, the 116th Pennsylvania, and the Union army generally. He averred that "Seldom was an obscene word or an oath heard in camp. Meetings for prayers were of almost daily occurrence, and the groups of men sitting on the ground or gathered on the hill side listening to the gospel were strong reminders of the mounds of Galilee when the people sat upon the ground to hear the Saviour teach. Ofttimes in the Regiment the dawn witnessed the smoke of incense ascend to heaven and the templed trees where serious groups knelt on the green sod and listened to the murmur of the Mass. In the evening Lieutenant Colonel Dale or Captain Samuel Taggart would hold a meeting for prayers where the larger number of the men would gather in reverence and devotion, while others would kneel around the Chaplain's tent to count their beads and repeat the rosary." Mulholland, *The Story of the 116th Regiment*, 194–195.

68. D. J. Murphy, "Catholics in American History," Washington, D.C., *The New Century*, February 7, 1903. Veterans painted word pictures of noble death for the devout Catholic. J. C. Delancy from Harrisburg, Pennsylvania, for example, carried with him the memory of the Irish Catholic soldier who had made "the sign of the cross on his brave forehead as he was falling into the arms of his aid[e] when the cruel ball tore out his glorious eyes." Delancy to St. Clair Mulholland, April 8, 1902, Mulholland Scrapbooks.

69. Philadelphia *Catholic Standard and Times*, June 28, 1902. Mulholland's appeals won enthusiastic endorsements but much less financial aid, thus prolonging his effort; see *The American Catholic Historical Researches for 1911*, vol. 28 (Philadelphia, 1911), 56. For an excellent discussion of the historical sanctification of Corby in sculpture, painting, and verse, and on the Catholics' reception to Corby's memoirs and Mulholland's efforts on behalf of Corby, see Lawrence F. Kohl's introduction and appendices in Kohl, ed., *Memoirs of Chaplain Life: Three Years with the Irish Brigade of the Army of the Potomac* (New York, 1992), ix–xxv, 393–404.

13

Christian Soldiers?

Perfecting the Confederacy

REID MITCHELL

And standing here this day I charge the historian of these times
that he shall not fail to tell to future ages that the Southern soldier
was a Christian warrior, and that he was brave, he was irresistible,
because his faith was in God and in the justice of his cause.

—REV. H. MELVILLE JACKSON, D.D., 1887

The Rev. H. Melville Jackson got his wish.
The figure of the Confederate soldier as Christian soldier has had
a powerful hold on our imagination. It remains a crucial part of the
myth of the superiority of the Confederate soldier, itself one of the most enduring components of Lost Cause mythology. While historians of the Civil
War might disagree with the relationship between Confederate Christianity
and Confederate irresistibility, some arguing that the impact of religion on
military service has been exaggerated, the Confederate Christian soldier himself
endures as an article of faith.

He endures in the popular mind. He also lurks in the historical literature.
In *The Life of Billy Yank*, Bell Irvin Wiley, still the preeminent scholar of Civil
War soldiers, contended that Confederate soldiers were more religious than
Union ones. On this point, later historians seem to be content to echo Wiley.
For example, Gerald F. Linderman, discussing the importance of religious faith
in both armies, nonetheless describes religion as "pervasive in the Confederate
armies" and "less conspicuous" in the Union. In a recent book review, Gardiner
H. Shattuck Jr. accepts that "southern soldiers were generally more pious than
their northern counterparts."[1]

Since Wiley's interpretation has proved so influential, it is well to consider why he believed rebels more religious than Yankees. In his *Life of Johnny Reb* and his *Life of Billy Yank*, Wiley usually based his arguments on the letters and diaries left behind by Civil War soldiers. But when he compared the piety of the soldiers, he did not cite this type of evidence. Indeed, Union letters and diaries are as much characterized by religious concerns as Confederates ones.[2]

Instead, departing from his usual type of evidence, Wiley argued the superior religiosity of Confederate soldiers from the large-scale revivals that spread through the Confederate armies during the war. And since the 1870s, the Confederate revivals have been key to the assertion that Confederate soldiers were more Christian than Union ones. In "Christian Soldiers: The Meaning of Revivalism in the Confederate Army," Drew Gilpin Faust follows Wiley in suggesting that revivalism—and thus perhaps religion—played a greater role in the Confederate army than in the Union. Wiley thought that Confederate defeat best explains the relative strength of Confederate revivalism, while Faust proposes that the "more profound stresses on southern soldiers" explain the difference. Clearly, the two positions complement one another, as well as my argument in *Civil War Soldiers* that, in an evangelical society with a premillennial theology, Confederates turned to individual soul-searching in response to wartime crisis.[3]

The revivals in the Confederate army did occur. It seems likely that the missionaries may have exaggerated the number of soldiers converted, but the revivals themselves are well documented, not simply by the accounts of chaplains and ministers but also in the letters and diaries of the soldiers themselves. As another essay in this volume shows, they were also the subject of widespread newspaper coverage, at least in Richmond, designed to rebuke flagging citizen morale. The story of the revivals and the legend of the Christian Confederate soldier, nonetheless, were also carefully crafted Lost Cause artifacts that should be approached with suspicion. Furthermore, despite postwar claims, extensive revivals hardly prove that the Confederate army was more religious than the Union army. It is time that Bell Wiley's argument be reconsidered; it is time that the religion of the common soldier be addressed from some perspective other than the altar calls of the Confederate revivals. Confederate chaplains and southern ministers have held the high ground long enough.

While discussions of the army revivals are frequent in Lost Cause literature, two texts are key to the creation and dissemination of the myth: William W. Bennett, *A Narrative of the Great Revival Which Prevailed in the Southern Armies During the Late Civil War Between the States of the Federal Union*, which appeared in 1876, and J. William Jones, D. D., *Christ in the Camp: or, Religion in the Confederate Army*, which first appeared in 1887. While both books often numb the reader with their series of seemingly interchangeable conversions, revivals, and "good deaths," *Christ in the Camp* is by far the better fashioned work. Jones, a secretary of the Southern Historical Society and the author of numerous books on the war, was a principal creator of the Lost Cause in all of its aspects, not merely the religious; for example, in *Christ in the Camp* as elsewhere, he helped southerners envision the war as principally a Virginian affair.[4]

Bennett and Jones, as well as other Lost Cause spokesmen, explicitly asserted that the Confederate army was the most Christian army in the history of the world—and so the Union army, like every other one, had to be less Christian. Indeed, the Union army wasn't even in the running for the title "Most Christian Ever"—the comparisons were generally made with Cromwell's army. Jones wrote, "no army in all history—not even Cromwell's 'Roundheads'—had in it as much of real, evangelical religion and devout piety as the Army of Northern Virginia." In 1893, another writer claimed, "There has never been, even in the army of Cromwell or Gustavus Adolphus, a stronger religious feeling than there was in the army under Joseph E. Johnston." According to Confederate general Dabney H. Maury, "There has never been in any army of modern times a soldiery so sober, so continent, so religious or so reliant, as was to be found in the armies of the Southern Confederacy." Thus, the Confederacy was perfected: how could the most Christian army support a less than Christian cause?[5]

Jones in particular reveled in the Christianity of the Confederacy. Its soldiers were Christian, its ranking officers were Christian, its proclamations and prayers were Christian, its mothers and wives were Christian. Stonewall Jackson alone provided Jones enough grace to redeem the entire Confederacy. Let Jefferson Davis and Alexander Stephens conduct the defense of the Confederacy on constitutional lines; Jones saw that *character* offered the greater chance for victory. Once the bravery and Christianity of the Confederates were established, ideology became irrelevant. The blood shed in battle wiped clean any taint of proslavery and rebellion. The South had thrown up a generation of Christian heroes. Lee superseded Davis. Jackson meant more than Calhoun. Even the North might accept this valuation of the Confederate cause—as, indeed, in the end it did. A band of Christian soldiers had gone to war under Christian leaders; this became the meaning of the Confederacy.

Nonetheless, the revivals, the principal evidence for the argument that Confederates were the most Christian soldiers ever, created immediate problems for that argument. The emphasis of revivalism is conversion, which suggests that the war might have helped Christianize southern men, but also suggests that they had to be Christianized. Counting the number of conversions would seem to mean counting the number previously unconverted. In part, some missionaries pointed to those saved in the revivals who had been Christian before but had suffered from backsliding. In this regard, the army revivals differed little from civilian revivals in the South, which also often attracted more backsliders than unbelievers. Nonetheless, if those whom the revivals had reached had all been backsliders, the missionaries would have less to brag about than they wanted. *Christ in the Camp* leaves little doubt that the ethos of the South was Christian, that the unconverted were often merely unchurched, and that for others salvation meant giving psychological assent to truths already intellectually acknowledged. Others agreed. For example, Albert Porter, a devout Mississippi soldier who spent his leisure time reading evangelical sermons, noticed that at Methodist experience meetings most of those who testified had been brought up in the Christian faith for years before they underwent conversion. (Once, while in the hospital, Porter bought a New Testament. Someone stole it—either a desperate but confused Christian or somebody who knew where testaments could be sold.)[6]

Still, in order to trumpet news of the revivals, Jones seemingly had to acknowledge their necessity. What had happened to this most Christian army? It had become demoralized. The revivals had been necessary first to stop the spread of impiety and indifference and then to turn them back. But another problem immediately arises. What demoralized the Confederate Christians? While Jones was committed to the centrality of the revivals to the soldiers' Christianity, he also argued strenuously that warfare and military service in themselves are not inimical to Christianity—indeed, that the best Christians make the best soldiers.

Christ in the Camp was not simply about the Lost Cause. For Jones, the image of Christianity was as much at stake as the image of the Confederate soldier. Indeed, Jones wrote with the assurance that his audience accepted the admirable heroism of that soldier and needed to be persuaded of his religious faith so that faith itself appeared heroic. Jones used the Confederate soldier to glorify Christianity as much as he used Christianity to glorify the soldier.

The postwar literature on the Confederate Christian soldier appeared as part of the late-nineteenth-century concern with manhood and "the strenuous life." In his preface to the 1904 edition, Jones claimed that *Christ in the Camp* "may prove use[ful] in showing our young people the power of religion to promote real manhood." In the original preface, he insisted that any history of the Army of Northern Virginia must be a religious history because it was religion that made it valiant. The Rev. H. Melville Jackson shared Jones's worry about the relationship between manhood and Christianity. In 1887, he said, "There is many a fool who thinks it a fit thing for women and children, but somehow detrimental to manliness and incongruous with the most exalted types of character, as they are manifested in the stirring action of life." Besides portraying Christian soldiers, Jones used *Christ in the Camp* to show virile chaplains—chaplains who took risks and endured hardships side by side with the soldiers, chaplains who were *men*.

So, if Christianity and soldiering went hand in hand, why did the Confederate soldier fall out of grace? Why did an army of heroes require heroic chaplains?

Jones identified two sets of culprits. The first was citizens back home who, puffed up by the easy victory at First Manassas, turned from praying for their soldiers to speculation and profiteering. Their example demoralized the soldiers. The second was the Confederate officers, who led the way in drunkenness, profanity, and gambling. Their example infected the rank-and-file. Pointing the finger at civilians and officers, Jones seems to suggest that the Confederate elite, more likely to be officers and to have the wherewithal to speculate, let the soldiers down.

Thus, the events of 1862—the early defeats which necessitated hard campaigning and hard prayer, the successes of Lee's army that summer, but the ultimate defeat at Antietam—proved a religious blessing to the South, whatever their military consequences. According to Jones, it was after the Sharpsburg campaign that revivalism truly caught hold of the Confederate army, never to let go.

In his *Narrative of the Great Revival,* William W. Bennett also blamed the immorality of the camp for a laxness in religion in the early months of the war. Young men away from the influences of home easily fell prey to temptation. He identified intemperance as the principal vice of the army, speculation and extortion as the leading sins of the Confederacy at large. Indeed, it was "this cursed lust for gain" that "finally broke the spirit of the people and the army."[7]

Once the revivals began, Bennett and Jones agreed, Christianity spread rapidly through the Confederate army. While Bennett stressed the on-going nature of the revival, which began as soon as southern men were gathered in camps, and Jones offered a narrative line in which the Sharpsburg campaign brought men to the sense of their dependency on the Lord, both present the war as worship services marked by conversions and interrupted by battles that were inevitably accompanied by triumphant deaths.

Claiming more extensive Christianity for the Confederate army became one way of claiming moral superiority for the Confederacy itself, just as the faith of Lee and Jackson was used to justify the Lost Cause. This southern strategy of making sweeping religious claims was not limited to discussions of the Confederate army. During the late nineteenth century, southern churches became accustomed to equally grandiose bragging. Samuel S. Hill Jr. writes, "As far as denominational issues are concerned, we can only be impressed by the self-consciousness and immodesty of the southern bodies." He continues, "From Reconstruction forward, ecclesiastics compared the religious situation of the South with that prevailing elsewhere—itself a revealing disposition and always to the South's advantage. From many quarters came assessments of the superior purity of regional Methodism, Presbyterianism, or Baptist life, with the implication or even the assertion that their brand was the hope of the world." When one encounters these grandiose southern claims, one is reminded of the arguments of proslavery ideologues. The Christian has been long taught that he shall be hated by the world; the South has long been willing to accept hatred as proof of its Christianity.[8]

The Christian Confederate stood near the center of Lost Cause ideology. Proponents of the cause argued that ultimately God would vindicate the South. In 1877, former Confederate general D. H. Maury hoped that "Providence, who works in a misterious [sic] way, may manifest how surely the right will triumph in the end." Maury said, "the principles we fought to uphold are essential to civil liberty in its highest perfection, and the time seems near at hand when all the world will know it." Presumably, Maury referred to the approaching end of Reconstruction.[9]

As 1865 became more remote, however, most Lost Cause spokesmen concentrated on the vindication shown by God's love for the southern people. He had rewarded their devotion to the right, not with material prosperity or national independence but with spiritual gifts. "While the Southern people bow in submission to the will of God in the defeat of their effort for an independent and separate government," the Rev. James H. M'Neilly wrote in 1913, "we should find compensation in the evidences of God's favor to us in the mighty spiritual uplift beginning with religious lives in the army." In 1909, H. D. C. Maclachlan proclaimed that "the spirit of the Old South—all that was best and truest purged from the dross of it—has survived the dark days of defeat and is still moving from victory to victory." The military and political defeat of the Confederacy was nothing compared to its religious victory.[10]

The characterization of Confederate soldiers as more religious than Union ones, whether made by William W. Bennett, J. William Jones, or Bell Irvin Wiley, would have surprised Yankees of the 1860s. The superior morality of the North over the South was already a commonplace among northern beliefs. It also would strike many historians of American religion or of nineteenth-century northern culture as implausible. The mid-century North was imbued with evangelical values; of necessity, the army it produced shared them. Indeed, the more intensely evangelical a northerner was, the more likely he was to end up in the Union army, at least in the first rushes to save the Union in 1860 and 1861. Southerners may have denounced prewar reform, including abolition, as godless, but the reform movements had their intellectual roots in a post-millennial evangelical theology and their geographic concentration in revivalistic areas such as New York's "burned-over district." The Union soldiers who sang "The Battle Hymn of the Republic" would not have been pleased—nor convinced—to hear that their southern opponents were more religious than they.[11]

Indeed, many northerners were as convinced of the impiety of the South as southerners were of northern atheism. For example, once down south, the Union soldier Frederick Pettit concluded that the South was fundamentally unchristian. His principal piece of evidence came from observation: he had decided that in the slaveholding regions, southerners did not respect the Sabbath. "I believe there are people here who do not know what the Sabbath is. The whole south is in this ignorant, heathenish condition." So there was divine purpose in the killing and destruction that the war occasioned. "It appears to me there is no other means of reaching the root of all this [slavery] but through war and bloodshed." Slavery kept Christianity from the South; slavery destroyed, the South might be converted. "What a wide field will soon be opened for Christian labor," he exclaimed. The tasks he saw were many and burdensome: "The masses of poor whites will needed [*sic*] to be educated and christianized. The Negroes must be colonized sooner or later."[12]

Furthermore, while the Union army may not have witnessed any revivals as extensive as those of the Army of Tennessee and the Army of Northern Virginia, revivalism was hardly unknown at the company and regimental level. Any historian who reads the letters and diaries of Union soldiers is aware of this fact. For example, the 21st Maine had revivals in October 1862—the same period in which the revivals in Lee's army began. The First New York Light Battery had a revival the winter of 1864, the 93rd Pennsylvania in February 1865. Prayer meetings, sermons, and small-scale revivals characterized the Union army as much as they did the Confederate.[13]

Religious observances could be difficult in an active army. In November 1864, George C. Lawson, an English-born soldier in Sherman's army, located a room in a house in which to hold a prayer meeting. He cleaned the room, arranged benches for the congregation, and built a fire to keep worshippers warm. When he, the chaplain, and two hundred soldiers returned to hold the meeting, they found the entire house in flames: "the 20th Corps was burning & destroying the R Road, and burnt all the buildings close to it." Resignedly, the men went to a grove and held the meeting there.[14]

Phillip Paludan discusses the religious dimensions of the war for the Union in *"A People's Contest."* Religious activity seems to have been at least as strong in the Union army as in the Confederate. "Claims of conversion were large and unconfirmable," he observes. "One hundred thousand, two hundred thousand saved souls, depending on the source." The conversions in the Union army were aided by the activities of chaplains, volunteers, and the soldiers themselves; for example, Paludan points out that soldiers in the Army of the Potomac built sixty-nine churches in their camps the winter of 1863–1864—the same winter during which the Army of Northern Virginia conducted its now better-known revival. The principal difference between Union and Confederate revivals may have been that Confederate revivals had better postwar publicists.[15]

"O for a revival of religion in this army"—George Lawson wrote this sentiment in spring 1865. He told his wife, "I sometimes think that if the work of the Lord was once to commence in the army, that the chance would be great for a glorious revival. [I]t is not oft the case, that a minister can get a congregation of men, numbered by the thousands, and men generally of good intellect, and the flower of the North." But the very same letter revealed that he and others in the army were holding religious meetings. Lawson also reassured his wife that "We have thousands of Catholicks in the army, but those do not pretend to come to our meetings, so we have men of protestant proclivities."[16]

Those "thousands of Catholicks" in the Union army, many of them German and Irish immigrants, also obscured the Christianity of the Union soldier. Somehow, Catholics don't get counted when historians compare the two armies. And in the nineteenth century, to be blunt, Americans often said "Christian" when they meant "Protestant." After the New York City draft riots, when for many native-born Americans the Irish clinched a reputation for disloyalty, one Union soldier concluded that when the war against slavery was won and the rebellion put down, the next war to be fought would be against the Roman Catholic population. Catholics, like slaveholders, were opponents of American values; in fact, he argued "they are the next thing to Slavery."[17]

The standard of the Christian soldier by which the Confederates usually were measured was Protestant—Cromwell, Havelock, Gustavus Adolphus, and Lee and Jackson themselves. Bell Wiley and others, myself included, wrote the social history of the Civil War soldiers from literary sources in which Catholic immigrants are rarely heard. Furthermore, Wiley, by using revivalism as his principal index of Christianity when comparing the Union and Confederate armies, assured that Catholics, who did "not pretend to come to our meetings" would be ignored. If conversion experiences and river baptisms are the principal index of Christianity, the nonrevivalist Catholics, as well as more liturgical Lutherans and other Protestant denominations, will not register as Christian. But, of course, Catholics are Christian and Catholics can be as religious as Protestants, and should not disappear from the record because of nineteenth-century American Protestant standards. It seems likely, for example, that most of the estimated 145,000 Irish-Americans who served in the Union army were Christian.

Certainly the tenth of the Union army that was black was largely Christian. Black soldiers practiced an African-American Christianity that had its origins in the same eighteenth-century evangelical movement as white southern Protestantism. Thomas Wentworth Higginson, commander of the First South Carolina Volunteers, used the same standard of comparison employed by those who praised Confederates; speaking of the black soldiers, he wrote "It used to seem to me that never, since Cromwell's time, had there been soldiers in whom the religious element held such a place."[18]

Despite the fervor of Christianity in the United States Colored Troops, like Catholics they seem to be left unconsidered in most discussions of religion among the soldiers. Partly, this is because the comparison between Union and Confederate soldiers is almost always a comparison between white and northern Union soldiers and white and southern Confederate soldiers; Wiley explicitly wrote about "Billy Yank." But earlier, when the figure of the Christian Confederate soldier was created, white Americans, either northern or southern, generally refused to take black religion seriously. Many Union soldiers dismissed African-American religion as nonsense. One Connecticut soldier called black prayer meetings "howlings." Even Higginson, despite his respect for black Christianity, did not entirely approve of its emotional nature; the New Englander confessed that he could not "encourage" their "extremes of religious enthusiasm . . . honestly."[19]

The men who created the myth of the Christian Confederate soldier do not seem to have regarded either the African-American Christians or the immigrant Christians in the Union army as challenging their assertion that the Confederate army was more Christian. Bennett made explicit the presumption that the immigrants were morally inferior. He boasted that "The armies of the South were homogeneous. There were but a few thousand foreigners at any time in the Confederate ranks." This contributed to the gallantry of the Confederate army. "There was but little of the beastliness and brutality displayed which marked the foreign mercenaries in the opposing armies. Our forces were strictly native American." And the black soldier, like the immigrant, was part of the alien "scum" and "hirelings" with whom white southerners contrasted their own virtuous soldiery. (Ironically, southern revivalism, to which the Confederates pointed with such pride, had and has a strong African-American component.)[20]

But men like Bennett were constructing a consoling myth for the white South. Southerners claimed that Confederates were more Christian than Yankees. And the pain of defeat and occupation made them believe they knew the real character of their enemies. Why or when northerners—who ended the war enjoying what they considered superior morality along with material victory, the besetting American sin—dropped their claim to Christianity I do not know. But it had more to do with postwar changes in northern society than with the sentiments of the men in the Union army. Perhaps at some time religion became viewed as something quaint and therefore probably southern.

Ordinarily in studies of American culture, particularly antebellum religion, there is a tendency to use the values of the evangelical North as a yardstick to judge the South. In fact, I suspect that it's this wrongheaded acceptance of New England religion as the American norm that leads to certain misreadings of southern Protestantism. (I don't need, for example, to read any explanations of why southern Christianity wasn't postmillennial; I need to be told how Yankees could get it so wrong.) Surely this question of religion in the armies is one of the very few in which southern expressions of religion have been used as the yardstick to measure northern piety.

There was never good reason for historians to ignore the presence of non-Protestant Christians—or of non-Christian men of religion—in the Union army. Nor was there ever good reason for them to accept Confederate judgments on the piety of Union soldiers. Even Bennett admitted, "To what extent the religious element prevailed among the soldiers of the North, they can best tell who labored among them in word and doctrine." We don't have to take our marching orders from the Rev. H. Melville Jackson.[21]

What did the Confederate revivals mean to those soldiers who participated? For that matter, what went on in the army revivals? I would like to suggest—*suggest*—that the revivals, while a response to the suffering caused by the war, may not have tied southern faith in salvation to the Confederate cause as much as some postwar spokesmen assumed.

For that matter, what was preached in the Confederate revivals? Much of Confederate culture, as Drew Gilpin Faust has shown, was manufactured by the Confederate elite. Were the revivals part of a strategy of nation-making? What we know of Confederate religion comes from the published sermons of eminent, self-consciously Confederate ministers who spoke for the cause. As David B. Chesebrough points out in *God Ordained This War*, we don't have the words of less-educated, country ministers; yet they were the chaplains preaching the verities of the old faith to men living and dying in anguish.[22]

In his introduction to *Christ in the Camp*, John Cowper Granbery, a former Methodist chaplain, said that what was preached in the army revivals was "Jesus Christ and Him crucified." "The sermons in the camp would have suited any congregation in city or country," Granbery said, "and with even less change might have been preached to the Union armies." According to Granbery, the rectitude of the Confederate cause was always assumed but rarely dwelt on. "Eternal things, the claims of God, the worth of the soul, the wages of sin which is death, and the gift of God which is eternal life through Jesus Christ our Lord—these were the matter of preaching." Granbery insisted that "the man of God lifted up, not the Bars and Stars, but the cross."[23]

But Granbery wrote after the war as did most of those who describe revival doctrine. Hugh Roy Scott, an Episcopalian clergyman, testified that during the revivals he preached "a plain practical sermon, in which the great doctrines of justification by faith, evangelical repentance, and the new birth were set forth in the simplest language." Jones himself wrote that during the revivals ministers did "not discuss 'the Relation of Science to Religion,' or the slavery question or the causes which led to the war, or the war itself." "When the preacher stood up before these congregations of veterans, his very soul was stirred within him and he 'determined to know nothing among them save Jesus Christ and Him crucified.' "[24]

The tracts the colporteurs distributed to the soldiers were also far more evangelical than nationalistic. Reading them often gives no clue that a war was under way. This is true even of those whose titles suggest a direct connection to the war, such as *Blood Upon the Door Posts; Or, Means of Safety in the Time of Danger, Joy in Sorrow; or, Comfort for the Bereaved, The Gospel of Peace, The Christian Officer*. Others discuss the war, but primarily in terms of the salvation of the individual soldiers. *Pitching the Tent toward Sodom* is a call for prayer in the army; *Jesus, the Soldier's Friend* summons the soldier to conversion; *The Soldier's Great Want* is Jesus.[25]

The revival sermons were not always as free from politics as the postwar accounts claimed. In August 1863, John Cowper Granbery was just one of several chaplains conducting services in Pickett's Division of the Army of Northern Virginia. After the failed assault at Gettysburg on July 3, 1863, and the casualties suffered that day, Pickett's Division turned eagerly to religious consolations. Granbery's letters to his wife give an idea what he and others taught. On August 21, preaching to Armistead's Brigade, Granbery took for his text Hebrews 11:6—"But without faith, it is impossible to please him: for he that cometh to God must believe that he is, and that he is a rewarder of them that diligently seek him." Granbery proclaimed to his congregation that, even in the wake of defeat, "The independence of our country may be won by this potent principle." The sin of pride had caused the Union to break up; pride caused the war; pride caused the war to continue. "Covetousness, a boastful, haughty, vindictive spirit, and self-confidence are mentioned by the President and Gen. Lee as prominent sins of our people." If Confederates turned from their sins and back to God, He would reward them not only with salvation but with military victory and peace.[26]

Granbery's motivations were not tidy. Did his sermon put religion to the service of nationalism, or patriotism to the service of religion? In either case, it contained something more than Jesus Christ and Him crucified. On the one hand, William W. Bennett, who of course identified Confederate nationalism with Christianity, suggested that "the patriotic fervor which prevailed among the Southern soldiers superinduced a state of mind highly favorable to the work of religion." As he saw it, "the feelings of true patriotism lie next to the higher sentiments of religion in the heart, and the man that cheerfully bears the yoke for the sake of his oppressed country will not stubbornly refuse to bear the yoke of Christ." On the other hand, James H. M'Neilly argued that the army revivals "did more than anything else to support and encourage the devotion of our people to their cause amid sufferings and sacrifice."[27]

Nonetheless, some revivalists refused to honor a consistently pro-Confederate line. During the same August 1863 revivals, Granbery identified a "Bro. McCarthy" who preached a different kind of sermon to the soldiers, one that attracted "much unfavorable comment." McCarthy "ridiculed . . . *paper* acknowledgments of God, such as in the constitution, proclamations by the Prest., and reports of victories by Lee and Jackson." He criticized officers for failing to attend worship, and "said Gen. Lee did go to church when *Gen. Pendleton preached.*" Beyond this, McCarthy spoke to other immediate concerns of the soldiers, and took a political line: "denounced extortioners, and proposed to the soldiers to seize and divide their gains after the war; thought that the price of fighting ought to rise with the price of food, and the soldiers should hold primary meetings to insist on this, & c."[28]

The South needed more Bro. McCarthys. The soldiers in the congregations were more likely to be subjected to Granbery's pro-Confederate thought than to any mild radicalism. Nonetheless, what they responded to was more likely "old-time religion" than official Confederate doctrine.

The letters home and the diaries kept in camp mention "Jesus Christ and Him crucified" far more often than they do God's special plan for the Confederacy. One example among many is Kenneth Rayner Jones, returning to the army after a furlough, who happily noted in his diary: "I found the Spirit of the Lord had visited my camp and a great many souls had turned to Christ, and a great many more were seeking mercy at his feet."[29]

Whatever the ministers and chaplains preached, the soldiers—those men unchurched but coming from a church culture—heard God's plan of salvation. Either they had ears only for that which they needed to hear or the ministers told the truth when they testified that they concerned themselves more with harvesting souls than with shoring up the Confederacy. Southern folk culture, subcategory white—we should scorn words like "hillbilly" or "redneck"—has been remarkably resilient, and less easily seduced by the elite than some historians think. The revivals themselves, a fervent outpouring of plain-folk culture, could only be claimed in part by the Confederacy.

There seems to have been little doctrine that was peculiarly Confederate in the Confederate army revivals. Some of the appeal of the revivals lay in the way they recreated the old-time religion practiced back at home before the war. Bennett recognized that one draw the revivals had for the soldiers was that "the gospel preached to them in the camp was not a new sound to them, nor were the words of prayer a strange language." Instead, among these men who missed their families, "It was homelike to meet for the worship of God."[30]

Most southern soldiers wanted answers out of God about death, suffering, and hardship more than about southern independence or Confederate defeat. Like much else of Confederate culture, Confederate religion did not sink deeply into the souls of these southerners. They turned to their God not for confirmation of a holy cause but for that which they and those like them had always sought: blessed assurance. The final victory was never supposed to be here on earth anyway.[31]

Notes

I'd like to thank Nan Woodruff and Gary Gallagher for inviting me to present an earlier version of this paper at Penn State University, and the Stanley Brothers for helping me think things through.

1. Bell Irvin Wiley, *The Life of Billy Yank: The Common Soldier of the Union* (New York and Indianapolis, 1952); Gerald F. Linderman, *Embattled Courage: The Experience of Combat in the American Civil War* (New York, 1987), 102; Gardiner H. Shattuck Jr., review of *The Confederacy's Fighting Chaplain, Journal of Southern History* 60 (February 1994): 149–150.

2. This is my conclusion, at least, after the research I conducted to write *Civil War Soldiers* (New York, 1988).

3. Drew Gilpin Faust, "Christian Soldiers: The Meaning of Revivalism in the Confederate Army," *Journal of Southern History* 53 (February 1987): 67–68. Mitchell, *Civil War Soldiers*, 173–174.

4. William W. Bennett, *A Narrative of the Great Revival Which Prevailed in the Southern Armies During the Late Civil War Between the States of the Federal Union* (Harrisonburg, VA, 1989, reprint of 1876 edition). J. William Jones, D. D., *Christ in the Camp: or, Religion in the Confederate Army* (Harrisonburg, VA, 1986; reprint of 1904 edition).

5. Jones, *Christ in the Camp*, 20. S. A. C. [S. A. Cunningham], "Religion in the Southern Army," *Confederate Veteran* 1, no. 1 (January, 1893): 15. General Dabney H. Maury, "The Defence of Mobile in 1865," *Southern Historical Society Papers* 3, no. 1 (January 1877): 2–3.

6. Albert Quincy Porter Diary, February 24, March 12, April 18, 21, 22, 1864, Library of Congress.

7. Bennett, *Narrative of the Great Revival*, 31–45, quotation on 42.

8. Samuel S. Hill Jr., *Religion and the Solid South* (Nashville, 1972), 42–43.

9. Maury, "Defence of Mobile," 2–3.

10. Rev. James H. M'Neilly, "Religion in the Confederate Armies," *Confederate Veteran* 21, no. 5 (May 1913): 230–231. Rev. H. D. C. Maclachlan, "The Religious Aspect of Patriotism," *Confederate Veteran* 25, no. 6 (June 1917): 261–264.

11. For a recent discussion of the centrality of evangelicalism to northern culture, see Daniel Walker Howe, "The Evangelical Movement and Political Culture in the North during the Second Party System," *Journal of American History* 77 (March 1991).: 1216–1239. Reid Mitchell, *The Vacant Chair: the Northern Soldier Leaves Home* (New York, 1993) is my lengthiest discussion of the northern soldier.

12. William Gilfillan Gavin, *Infantryman Pettit: The Civil War Letters of Corporal Frederick Pettit* (New York, 1991), 106.

13. Frank Fogg to parents, October 8, 1862, Civil War Miscellany Papers, U.S. Army Military History Institute, Carlisle, PA; Elbert Corbin Diary, February 14, 1864,

Civil War Miscellany Papers, U.S. Army Military History Institute; Daniel Faust to mother, February 17, 1865, Harrisburg Civil War Round Table Collection, U.S. Army Military History Institute. See also George H. Allen Diary, October 19, 1862, University of Texas; Kilian Van Rensselaer to mother, December 13, 1864, Erving-King Papers, New-York Historical Society; Horace Snow to parents, August 3, 1862, Snow Family Papers, Duke University.

14. George C. Lawson Diary, November 13, 1864, in Robert Shaw Collection, Atlanta Historical Society.

15. Phillip Paludan, *"A People's Contest": The Union and the Civil War, 1861–1865* (New York, 1988), 339–374.

16. George C. Lawson to wife, undated [April 1865?], George C. Lawson Papers, in the Robert Shaw Collection, University of Georgia.

17. Daniel Faust to "My Dear Sister," November 2, 1864, Harrisburg Civil War Round Table Collection, U.S. Army Military History Institute.

18. Thomas Wentworth Higginson, *Army Life in a Black Regiment* (originally published 1869; reprint, New York, 1984), 240.

19. Mitchell, *Civil War Soldiers*, 120. Higginson, *Army Life*, 241.

20. Bennett, *Narrative of the Great Revival*, 23.

21. Ibid., iii.

22. Drew Gilpin Faust, *The Creation of Confederate Nationalism: Ideology and Identity in the Civil War South* (Baton Rouge, 1988), particularly 7–21, 22–34. David B. Chesebrough, *God Ordained This War: Sermons on the Sectional Crisis, 1830–1865* (Columbia, 1991), 13.

23. Jones, *Christ in the Camp*, 14–15. Note: While *Christ in the Camp* gives this name as "Granberry," the Granbery papers at the University of Virginia show that the minister himself preferred this spelling.

24. Ibid., 244–245, 287.

25. *Blood Upon the Door Posts: Or, Means of Safety in the Time of Danger*, Evangelical Tract Society, Petersburg VA, no. 72; *Joy in Sorrow; or, Comfort for the Bereaved*, Evangelical Tract Society, Petersburg, VA, no. 70; *The Gospel of Peace*, Evangelical Tract Society, Petersburg, VA, no. 220; *The Christian Officer*, South Carolina Tract Society, Charleston, no. 43; T. D. W., *Pitching the Tent toward Sodom*, Evangelical Tract Society, Petersburg, VA, no. 216; *Jesus, the Soldier's Friend. By a Young Lady of Virginia* (Petersburg, VA, 1862); *The Soldier's Great Want*, Evangelical Tract Society, Petersburg, VA, no. 250.

26. John Cowper Granbery to Ella, August 22, 1863, John Cowper Granbery Papers, acc #4942, Alderman Library, University of Virginia.

27. Bennett, *Narrative of the Great Revival*, 17–18. M'Neilly, "Religion in the Confederate Armies," 230–231.

28. John Cowper Granbery to Ella, August 27, 1863, John Cowper Granbery Papers.

29. Diary, March 13, 1864, Kenneth Rayner Jones Papers, Southern Historical Collection, University of North Carolina.

30. Bennett, *Narrative of the Great Revival*, 20.

31. The hymn "Blessed Assurance" was written a few years after the Civil War, but the centrality of "assurance" to southern folk religion is well known. See Dickson D. Bruce Jr., *And They All Sang Hallelujah: Plain Folk Camp Meeting Religion, 1800–1845* (Knoxville, 1974), 67–68, 96–97.

IV

PLACES

Civil War, Religion, and Communications

The Case of Richmond

HARRY S. STOUT AND CHRISTOPHER GRASSO

I t was inevitable that the juggernaught of the New Social History would eventually catch up with that last bastion of political and military history, the Civil War. After a century of domination by political and military historians, professional and antiquarian, the war is at last recognized for the "total" event that it was: a social convulsion affecting civilian populations as much as armies, women and children as much as men, slaves as well as free blacks, laborers as well as soldiers. To the 50,000 books and articles already written on the Civil War, entirely new histories are appearing that tell the other stories, the stories of noncombatants at war.

A second development in the 1970s and 1980s also has given shape to the kind of Civil War histories that are now being written. The turn of the French *Annales* school from social and economic structure toward the history of *mentalites*, the widespread interest in the cultural anthropology of Clifford Geertz, and interpretive strategies borrowed from literary criticism have all informed what has been called the New Cultural History: the study of texts and discourse, cultural patterns and symbolic meanings, ideology and hegemony.[1] In place of quantitative studies, cultural historians are exploring texts for shared patterns of meaning. What did the Civil War mean to its ordinary participants? What did they believe so strongly that they would venture all? These preoccupations have centered on the categories of popular "ideology," "nationalism," and, in the case of the South, "guilt" and "demoralization."[2]

Lying on the periphery of this social and cultural recovery of the Civil War is religion. This has been particularly true in the case of the Confederate South, where recent studies have explored the ways in which religion both helped shape Confederate ideology and contributed to or thwarted a demoralizing guilt over slavery that explained "Why the South Lost the Civil War."[3]

If these studies are laudable for bringing religion into the historians' dialogue, they are not without their shortcomings. As long as religion is on the periphery it will never be appreciated for the dynamic and changing force that it was. While ideologies "evolve," "transform," and "react" to the changing events of war, religion in these studies seems to remain an unchanged "evangelical" presence, formed in the antebellum period, surviving in the postbellum period, and static in between. In fact, combatant and noncombatant southerners alike were very much caught up with religion; it not only shaped their public and private discourse but did so in dramatically different ways between 1861 and 1865. The concern of this essay is to bring religion—too often merely a prop in a military or political drama—onto center stage and see it as the dynamic process it was.

In exploring religion's role in the Confederacy, we follow the methodological lessons learned from social and cultural history. From cultural history, we will not be surprised to find evidence for the appearance of broad-based consensus, cultural integration, and a continuity of values, as well as evidence of incompatible differences, bitter partisan conflicts, and dramatic change. The challenge lies not in choosing one pole or another—conflict or consensus, continuity or change—but in showing the relationship between religious sensibility and wartime ideology as it unfolds within historical experience. From social history, we realize that big questions often require local answers. The same sort of community studies that proved so successful in generating a synthetic social portrait of colonial New England need also to be applied to the Civil War and, more particularly in our case, to the South. The number of local case studies of Civil War communities that focus on culture, communications, and texts is regrettably small.[4] In this essay, we propose a religious and cultural portrait of white Richmond society at war.

The reasons for choosing Confederate Richmond as a model test case for community studies in the Civil War are obvious. As the legislative, military, and propaganda headquarters of the Confederacy, it combined more official and public functions than any other city, North or South. Besides its strategic importance came an even larger symbolic importance that led to almost unrivaled blood baths in the North and the South. The battle cry "On to Richmond" served as a federal motto, while the Confederate campaign to protect Richmond bordered on an obsession, sometimes at considerable strategic expense. In short, Richmond is both local study and microcosm of a nation at war. We examine it, not because it is a "typical" community (which it most assuredly was not), but because it was *one* community in war and, for much of the time *at* war with a near and immensely powerful neighboring nation.[5]

To the local case of Richmond we bring the following big questions: Why did the people of Richmond fight on so tenaciously in a city where all were combatants of one sort or another? Were they impelled by a common motivation and "nationalism," or were there competing motivations (and nationalisms) impelling different people to act for different reasons? Where in this mix of motivations was religion and how important was it? Did the religious ingredients in the mix of Confederate nationalism change over time? To all of these questions, we allow religion the central stage. At the same time, however, we do not ignore such other—and competing—cultural strains as republicanism, white supremacy, southern "honor," the "culture of violence," or "cavalier" pride.[6] It is only when religion is studied in relation to these reinforcing or countervailing themes that its relative importance can be gauged. Nor do we limit religion to churches and sermons. Of all media of public communications, printed and oral, we ask: What of religion can be found in these sources? To recover the full range of cultural impulses circulating in Richmond's public discourse, we have canvased virtually all of the surviving religious and secular newspapers printed in Richmond (of which there were eight major publications), together with printed and manuscript sermons and official proclamations. From all of these disparate sources, a fascinating picture emerges of a community at war. Richmond virtually reinvents itself in the religious categories of the "jeremiad" in the early phases of the war, divides over these categories in the face of defeats in 1863 and 1864, and finally reasserts religion in a new, more spiritualized vein in its final death throes as the capital city of the Confederate States of America.

A Social Portrait of Richmond on the Eve of War

In 1860, Richmond was a medium-size southern city with a northern tilt. It was the third-largest city in the Confederacy, but only the twenty-fifth largest in the nation.[7] Its population of 38,000 included 23,635 whites and 14,275 blacks, of whom nearly 12,000 were slaves.[8] The city's economic base was industry, and business interests centered around milling, iron, tobacco, and railroads. Railroad connections had been completed by the 1850s, and the economy had entered its greatest rate of growth in business, industry, and construction. The Gallego flour mill was exporting flour to Latin America as early as the 1840s, and the Tredegar Iron Works was the largest foundry in the South. By 1860, there were fifty tobacco factories with an annual gross income of nearly $5 million. In 1860, business was booming and that meant business with the North. With many northerners living in the city, attitudes toward secession were cautious or opposed. Unlike Charleston or New Orleans, Richmond had much to lose from a northern invasion, and very little to gain.

Although slaves were not as numerous in Richmond as farther south, the city represented the country's second largest slave mart, exceeded only by New Orleans. In fact, the number of Richmond property owners who owned slaves decreased from nearly universal ownership in 1840 to one-third of the 1860 property owners. At the same time, the number of corporations owning slaves increased steadily over two decades of industrial growth.[9] Few community leaders doubted the rightness of the South's "peculiar institution." Over the years a solid alliance had been forged between slave masters and clergy, upholding slavery on both economic and moral grounds. If there was "guilt" over slavery in Richmond, it did not appear in public speech or print.[10]

Though no public schools would exist in Richmond until after the war, private schools abounded. In all, there were over sixty private schools operating in the city by 1860, offering secondary education to boys and girls.[11] The indirect effect was to create a city of high literacy rates among whites that belied the South's reputation for ignorance and illiteracy. Richmond also boasted several institutions of higher learning including the Virginia Baptist Seminary (now the University of Richmond) founded in 1832, the medical school of Hampden-Sydney College, and the Richmond Female Institute.

Education and literacy produced a reading public in Richmond. Newspapers, magazines, and lending libraries flourished. In all, Richmond boasted four secular newspapers and six religious weeklies to a white reading public of under 20,000 white adults. As the war unfolded, newspapers realized a new and vitally important function. Where "news" was once a casual and distant affair before the outbreak of the Civil War, it became urgent and indispensable thereafter. Secular newspapers created a "public" as powerful in its own right as the public of churches, schools, and political parties.[12] Secular and religious leaders, no less than ordinary men and women, participated in the common world of print and depended on it to shape their understanding and interpretation of the war's events. Together, the secular and religious press represent the best index to what was said and done publicly in Richmond.

If newspapers were important, they did not supplant speech, especially when battles loomed and word-of-mouth raced to keep up. The most important center of corporate and civic speech remained the churches. Throughout the war, news circulated most completely on Sundays within and between the city's churches. Messengers routinely appeared to the military officers in the congregation; rumors spread quickly. Constance Cary fled to Richmond from Alexandria and couldn't get over Sundays in Richmond. The time when people came out of church was as important as when they went in, for then the most current news gathered from a hundred mouths reading a hundred sources would be proclaimed and compared. "It is a curious fact," Cary noted, "that most of our exciting news spread over Richmond on Sunday."[13]

By 1860, Richmond boasted thirty-three churches from every major denomination and styled itself "the City of Churches."[14] Included among them were Methodist (6), Episcopalian (5), Presbyterian (4), Roman Catholic (3), Society of Friends (1), Unitarian (1), and Jewish synagogues (3). The center of the city was ringed by the major denominations, each with great structures proudly proclaiming their heritage. St. Paul's Episcopal, St. Peter's Cathedral, Beth Shalom Synagogue, and First Presbyterian encompassed the leading statesmen, merchants, and intellectuals of the community. It is not possible to determine the percentage of Richmond inhabitants who were church members, though regional figures suggest membership rates less than the North. With thirty-three churches and a population of nearly 40,000 whites, each church would have to serve over 1,000 members. Clearly, many inhabitants of Richmond, as throughout the antebellum South, remained "unchurched," though equally clearly the unchurched were found primarily in the laboring classes.[15]

Most important elites were attached to one of the Protestant denominations, particularly the Presbyterian, Methodist, and Episcopalian churches.

Within Richmond's religious community, Presbyterians dominated the intellectual and theological scene from their pulpits and from their presses. More than any other denomination, their communications network was nationwide. Richmond's Moses Hoge, prominent pastor of the Presbyterian church, was a frequent correspondent with Princeton's Charles Hodge. Both were part of a national network held together by print and institutional ties, most particularly Presbyterian religious newspapers and Princeton Seminary.

In contrast to the "fire-eaters" to the south, Richmond's citizens were not eager for secession. As late as April 4, Virginia's Convention voted 2 to 1 against secession, with Richmond's delegate voting with the majority. In 1860, Robert Lewis Dabney, young Presbyterian pastor destined to be Stonewall Jackson's chief of staff and a preeminent champion of Confederate nationalism, was anything but that.[16] In a letter to Hoge written in 1860, Dabney styled himself a "Washington-Madison politician" who feared disunion and the "terrific" consequences of a war setting all adrift in "a sea which has no chart."[17]

With Lincoln's election, talk of slavery and the territories dominated both the religious and secular press. The nation was in crisis, and President James Buchanan declared a day of national fasting and humiliation for January 4, 1861. Richmond's Hoge and T. V. Moore—the two most powerful Presbyterian clerics in Richmond—complied, though in the traditional "spiritualized" form of the South. In a letter to Dabney, Hoge insisted that "Moore and myself do not mean to introduce anything political into our sermons, but wish to direct the minds of the people from man to God. . . . I think of taking for my text: 'Give us help from trouble: for vain is the help of man.' " But the boundaries between politics and piety were hurriedly being redrawn as sectional tension escalated. In a letter to Princeton Seminary's venerable Charles Hodge, dated January 23, 1861, Dabney observed that the "dividing line between secular and sacred journals was virtually removed." At that point, he still hoped for reconciliation between North and South, though storm clouds were clearly visible on the horizon. It was not at all surprising, Dabney continued, that the most religious southerners were the first to enlist. Religion and its rightness would be at the center of this conflict. Dabney thanked Hodge for defending the South against abolitionists in the pages of the *Princeton Review*, and went on to defend slavery. In religious terms slavery was not the product of the white man's sins but of God's providential opening up of a way to bring salvation to the Africans. In reply, Hodge insisted that no "sane man" wanted war and preferred a "peaceable separation" to war. At the same time, he feared that "forcible separation is inevitably war."[18]

The move to war in Richmond unraveled with blinding speed—so fast that it would transform almost overnight erstwhile southern American citizens into revolutionary soldiers and southern sectionalists into Confederate nationalists. Following news of the surrender of Fort Sumter on April 13 and Lincoln's call for 75,000 troops, opinions reversed and, on April 17, Virginia seceded. The scene following news of secession was bedazzling. Streets were "brilliantly illuminated" by torches and bonfires, signaling with "triumphal acclaim" the birthday of a new nation. J. B. Jones described universal enthusiasm: "Ladies everywhere seem embued with the spirit of patriotism." Former president John Tyler delivered a stirring oration invoking "benign providence" to bless the Confederacy's "holy effort" all in the spirit of the "Revolution of 1776."[19]

The first church services in the new nation took place on Sunday, April 21. Sermons implored divine guidance even as rumors of invading federal warships brought thousands to the heights in expectations more curious than scared. On April 22, Robert E. Lee arrived in command of the army together with Vice President Alexander Stephens. Their goal was to seek Richmond out as the possible capital of the new nation. On May 20, the Confederate Congress voted to move the national government to Richmond, which Richmond citizens proudly accepted.

Richmond at War: Confederate Jeremiads and the Birth of a Nation

From the first days of the Confederacy to the last, cannons sounded in Richmond's hearing. The population would increase threefold to over 100,000. An army was raised and an ideology articulated. At any given time, 10,000 to 15,000 soldiers were stationed in Richmond for training or were passing through on battle maneuvers. John Moncure Daniel, editor of the *Richmond Examiner* and destined to be Davis's greatest critic, initially urged action and praised the new president. The even larger Richmond *Dispatch*, with a subscription of 18,000 and a reading audience probably double that, supported the new administration. In the heat of passion, with the spectacle of mass armies forming in their very midst, the transition was easy to make.

The secular press and magistrates were not the only ones to celebrate secession and, if necessary, war. The clergy and religious press were equally enthusiastic and unwaveringly certain about the morality of their course. Contrary to earlier southern traditions, this generation of ministers would preach the politics of secession from the pulpit and confirm it in print. From the very first stages of secession and war, ministers throughout the South had responded to Davis's calls and had articulated a powerful vision of the Confederacy as a chosen nation fighting a righteous crusade. Recalling Hoge's reservations about preaching politics in Buchanan's fast, the transformation is nothing short of revolutionary. With secession, these previously patriotic American men of God put aside their past and reinvented themselves as divine spokesmen for a new Christian nation. People in their congregations seemed to respond to the new religious patriotism. Government war clerk Jones observed in his diary: "I have always differed with preachers in politics and war, except the Southern preachers who are now in arms against the invader."[20]

Without the clergy's active endorsement of secession and war, there could not have been a Confederate nation. Christianity represented the most powerful cultural system in the Old South. For men, women, and children, Christianity offered the only terms out of which a national identity could be constructed and a violent war pursued. Without Christian legitimation, there could be no sense of rightness. Independence was painful to contemplate and wrenching to execute, and only the highest ideals could justify it. Those ideals were religious. Whether in undergirding proslavery ideology, Confederate nationalism, or eventually the Lost Cause, religion and the Bible had to be invoked.

In ways that scholars have only begun to appreciate, the religion of the fast day contributed a novel and formative influence upon the Confederacy. Confederate fast-day sermons would imitate earlier northern jeremiads and insist that southerners were a single people, bound together in a unique Christian nation favored by God; they argued that victory and national glory would be achieved only if the people lived up to God's high expectations and turned away from sin. As fast-day rituals proclaimed a relationship between church and state that was unlike anything the antebellum South had known, the jeremiads built Confederate nationalism upon a foundation of corporate Christianity that was as new to the South as the Confederacy itself. How the clergy came to this great reversal over the spirituality of the church and refusal to "preach politics" is one of the untold stories of Confederate ideology.

Historians, to be sure, have written frequently of Confederate fast days and summarized the jeremiads preached on those occasions. But they have not sufficiently appreciated the novelty and power of those events in the evolving life of the Confederacy.[21] Located in the sense of legitimacy and the yearning for a Confederate identity was a simple idea: a covenanted nation. For this idea to be realized in the life of the Confederacy, it required a ritual action—a civil sacrament that conferred legitimacy and sacred pretense to the evolving nation. That civil sacrament came to be the public fast. In town after town throughout the upper and lower South, the ritual of a public fast and the incantation of the jeremiad created a Confederate identity grounded in fundamentally religious values.

If historians have missed the innovative cultural and ideological significance of the public fast day in white southern society during the Civil War, one reason is that fast days per se did not originate in the Confederacy, and so would not appear to be novel. Denominational fasts were common throughout the colonial and Old South, as were church-wide fasts in dissenting congregations and liturgical fasts in the Anglican calendar. But with the exception of a spate of fast and thanksgiving observations surrounding the 1850 Compromise, all of these were narrowly religious and deliberately separated out from politics. They were spiritual events confined to the spiritual space and time of the churches.[22] With rare exceptions, fast sermons delivered on these occasions were not published, nor did they constitute a central genre of public discourse. Denominations or congregations ordained them, and communities of faith observed them privately.

References to "religious nationalism" or "civil religion" in the antebellum South are misleading to the extent they imply a clerically based theocratic

sensibility similar to what prevailed in the North. There was no ongoing southern tradition of what the nineteenth-century historian W. D. Love termed
"civil" or "public fasts"—fast days called by civil authority and observed by the
political community meeting outside its religious confines.[23] By the 1850s, most
northern and midwestern states proclaimed a day of national thanksgiving.
Richmond's leaders demurred, citing, among other authorities, Thomas Jefferson, who during his presidency refused to proclaim a national day of thanksgiving on grounds of the separation of church and state. Only a handful of
printed fast sermons survive from antebellum southern presses, and references
to public fasts are relatively scarce in public records. In times of crisis, the fast
was not the resort of instinctive choice in the way it was for the North. In the
South's greatest confrontation before secession, the nullification controversy,
South Carolina's Governor Robert Y. Hayne proclaimed a day of fasting for
January 1833, only to discover that nobody heeded his proclamation. Most
churches failed to honor the fast, and hardly any newspaper in South Carolina
reported it.[24] Richmond was very much a part of this tradition, boasting no
fast-day sermons from its presses. As late as 1856, Virginia's governor Henry
A. Wise refused to proclaim a day of thanksgiving, observing that "the Governor of Virginia is not authorized by her laws to call upon the people to bow
to any authority in Heaven or on earth besides their own authority." With
northern abolitionists in mind, he then closed the case with the observation
that "[t]his theatrical national claptrap of Thanksgiving has aided other causes
in setting thousands of pulpits to preaching '*Christian politics*' instead of humbly
letting the carnal kingdom alone and preaching singly Christ crucified."[25] In
the southern pulpit, the doctrine of the church's "spirituality"—the strict separation of church and state—reigned, so that even slavery could be addressed
only in terms of the duties masters owed their slaves, not as a political and
economic institution.[26]

Viewed in this tradition, the ascendance of the public fast in the Confederacy, and in Richmond in particular, is truly remarkable. Through all of
American history to 1860, public fasts were quintessentially northern and "Puritan." Yet when secession came to war, the Confederacy would employ the
public fast *more* frequently than the North. In all, Abraham Lincoln would
proclaim three national fasts throughout the war while, in the same period,
Jefferson Davis would proclaim ten.[27] In addition, there were multiple state
and local fasts in the Confederacy, as well as fasts in the army.

For the Confederacy to adopt the public fast day as its own national ritual
of self-affirmation, a profound revolution had to have taken place in a remarkably compressed period of time. Where the Puritans had taken two generations to invent a rhetoric of nationhood and war around the ritual convention of the fast and thanksgiving day, the Confederacy would achieve it in a
year, and it would grow thereafter until the very last battles were lost. The
public fast enlisted Christianity for ritual and ideological service to the Confederacy, even though churches for decades had reflexively affirmed the apolitical spirituality of the church. With a rhetorical sleight of hand, ministers
would continue to celebrate the historic spirituality of the southern pulpit,

while at the same time ringing the charges of tyranny against the North and preaching political liberty for the South with a ferocity—and frequency—unmatched in the North.

How did the reversal work? The expropriation and redirection of the jeremiad actually began before the war, when news of Lincoln's election reached South Carolina. The rhetorical transformation is nicely illustrated by the preaching of James Henley Thornwell, a distinguished theologian and famed defender of the spirituality of the church. In response to the Presbyterian synod of South Carolina's declaration of a state-wide fast for the nation on November 21, 1860, Thornwell preached a politically charged sermon on Isaiah 37:1: "When King Hezekiah heard it, he rent his clothes." Thornwell confessed at the outset of his sermon: "I have never introduced secular politics into the instruction of the pulpit." But with Lincoln headed for the White House, Thornwell was prepared to preach for the first time to what he called "an organized political community," signaling a revolutionary departure from form. In antebellum southern orthodoxy, magistrates addressed political communities and ministers addressed churches, and never did the twain meet. For years, ministers had explained that prophets only spoke politically in the Old Testament because Israel was unique, a theocracy in which God reigned through His Word and prophets. But even before formal independence, it must have appeared to Thornwell that maybe the South was also unique and sacred. With that tantalizing maybe, he took the fateful plunge into political preaching, invoking the language of the Hebrew prophets for the political community as if it were a church. His sermon was not on the morality of slavery and the relations of masters and slaves (long acceptable in antebellum preaching), but on the politics of slavery and the rights of sovereign states. There was not yet a new nation to proclaim a public fast, but Thornwell's summons to a rising Christian republic would echo in Richmond's pulpits and throughout the Confederacy in the blood bath to come.[28]

The Jeremiad at War

The successful creation of a Confederate jeremiad involved much more than simply borrowing preconceived theological categories or rhetorical formulas pulled from the Old Testament or the tradition of political preaching in Puritan New England. The task of interpreting God's involvement with the Confederate cause and defining the role of the Christian churches in the Confederate nation was a creative struggle with a history of its own.

The clergy's new burden of political preaching was made immensely easier by the new Confederate Constitution, adopted on February 8 and ratified March 11, 1861. Unlike its federal counterpart, it explicitly declared its Christian identity, "invoking the favor and guidance of Almighty God." This meant that the South was now in a position more analogous to ancient Israel's theocratic constitution than to the North's republican constitution that failed to invoke— or even mention—God.[29]

The national motto, *Deo Vindice* ("God will avenge"), added additional weight to the South's claim to be a uniquely Christian nation. Now was the time, President Davis proclaimed, to consecrate the new nation and "to recognize our dependence upon God . . . [and] supplicate his merciful protection." The times were ominous, for war had begun. Both in tone and substance, Davis made it clear that this was no exercise in "mere" rhetoric, or "Confederate propaganda." The words were serious business because they played with the fire of divinity. To be glib or insincere would be worse than infidelity. And President Davis was anything but glib or infidel. If preachers could now politicize from the pulpit, magistrates could preach from the podium. In terms reminiscent of the pulpit, Davis, who would soon convert to the Episcopal church, implored the people to call on God "to guide and direct our policy in the paths of right, duty, justice and mercy; to unite our hearts and our efforts for the defense of our dearest rights; to strengthen our weakness, crown our arms with success, and enable us to secure a speedy, just, and honorable peace."[30]

Davis proclaimed the first national fast for June 13, 1861, and Richmond's preachers, like clergymen throughout the Confederacy, rallied to make the religious grounds of political union explicit. O. S. Barten's fast-day sermon for June 13, 1861, preached at Warrenton, Virginia's, St. James Church and published in Richmond, contrasted the U.S. Constitution to the Confederate Constitution, and noted that while the federal document failed even to acknowledge a higher power, the new Confederacy promoted a close relation between religion and government. For Barten and many other Virginia ministers, the South's constitutional invocation of God might not automatically elevate the nation to a unique status among peoples, as it seemed to for other southern preachers. But it did mean that they could preach politics in a way that was impossible before. For them, the Confederacy was a liberating event. The biblical grounding and constitutional circumstances of the Confederacy's founding pointed to a glorious future and announced the birth of a unique Christian nation. Great nations, Barten argued, display a distinctive character: Judea exemplified divine unity; Rome, political power; England, constitutional liberty; the United States, human rights. The Confederate States could become the greatest of all as the embodiment of the Christian rights and liberties derived from God and confirmed in Jesus Christ. The North had some Christians, and was once part of a divine commission that issued in independence. But it was now run by infidels and fanatics under a godless government; the South had Christian men in a Christian government over a Christian people. Therefore, Barten concluded, as the South struggled to *become* a truly Christian confederacy, even then God's "purposes are bound up with us as a nation!"[31]

God's purposes seemed to be gloriously revealed to Richmond and the rest of the South with the victory at First Manassas a few days after Barten spoke. Preaching a thanksgiving sermon on July 21, 1861, to commemorate the victory, William C. Butler declared in Richmond's St. John's Episcopal Church that the opportunity to constitute a truly Christian nation amounted to a special calling for the South. The Confederacy did not receive its divine commission from heaven when men ratified the Confederate Constitution, however; God had to ratify it, and He did so by bestowing the remarkable victory at Manassas. That astounding success proved that the South fought for principles that were fundamental to God's "Divine government."

> God has given us of the South to-day a fresh and golden opportunity—and so a most solemn command—to realize that form of government in which the just, constitutional rights of each and all are guaranteed to each and all. ... He has placed us in the front rank of the most marked epochs of the world's history. He has placed in our hands a commission which we can faithfully execute only by holy, individual self-consecration to all of God's plans.

To appreciate the novelty and power of these words, we must hear them as Butler's Richmond audience undoubtedly heard them in the flush of stunning victory. And we must hear them in a southern setting deeply religious, but previously alien to national fasts and thanksgivings. Whether they could articulate it or not, southern audiences were experiencing a new ritual of social order. Through words like Butler's, repeated in similar settings throughout the Confederacy, a nation was being born. Perhaps in South Carolina, clerics like James Henley Thornwell had glimpsed the new birth months earlier, even before the old nation had been dissolved. But in Richmond, where many had resisted secession and had been wary of war, the sheer fact of the victory validated all the hopes for the emergence of a righteous Christian nation in the South. Now they had a "history"—however brief—of their own, as a newly constituted, divinely ratified, and victorious covenant nation. Preachers could now freely adopt the language of the Hebrew prophets for their own without it being the "political preaching" they had condemned for so many years. It would be God speaking. If the language they used sounded remarkably like the Puritans of old, that fact was never announced. Confederate clergymen spoke as if theirs were the first truly legitimate, God-honoring political fast and thanksgiving days spoken in America since the Revolution.

From this point on in Confederate history, nearly three-quarters of all printed sermons would be public fast or thanksgiving sermons or similar political and war-related sermons preached on other days. Once a rarity in southern print, these sermons became a staple religious product of the Confederate press. Religious publications as a whole, excluding periodicals, would amount to over 40 percent of the unofficial imprints appearing in the Confederacy.[32]

Of course, printed sermons represented only a small fraction of the total fast and thanksgiving sermons preached in the Confederacy—and Richmond—during the Civil War. But they remain a useful index to what was heard publicly throughout the Confederacy in churches and synagogues of all faiths and denominations. When we realize that most of the hearers of sermons delivered in churches were female, moreover, we see a powerful source of women's involvement in the war and their growing sense of political involvement in the struggle. *Their* morality and *their* covenant keeping, no less than the men's, would hold the key to success or failure in the conflict. In *Mothers of Invention*, Drew Faust demonstrates how religion "opened an avenue into the male world of politics and public action." Certainly, the new politicized fast and thanksgiving sermons, recorded in print and repeated to female-centered congregations throughout the land, accelerated the transformation that Faust describes.[33]

While all Confederate magistrates and clergymen agreed on the religious rightness of the South's cause, they varied in characterizing the war as a "just war" or a "holy crusade."[34] In contrast to more virulent communities to the South, most Richmond preachers, writers, and public speakers invoked the ancient "just war" tradition to provide moral arguments for the South's defensive war against northern aggression: war against the North was simply an extension of the individual right of self-defense against a murderous attack. In Charleston and Savannah, where the coals of controversy burned brighter, some thought more aggressively about a religious crusade, justifying an offensive war of conquest by adopting Israel's national covenant for their own and proclaiming a holy war against northern infidels.[35] Clearly there was room for varieties of emphasis (and vituperation) within a larger common theme. Sussex County pastor I. R. Finley's 1863 fast sermon, printed in Richmond by the Soldier's Tract Association, discussed the South's privileged status, not by drawing parallels to Israel as Butler had done but by putting Israel and the Confederacy into the larger context of providential history, in which an individual, a family, or a people stepped forward in every age to be the primary instruments of God. He argued that the southern Confederacy was the most likely candidate to be the next leading actor on the world stage, following the likes of Noah and his family, Abraham and his descendants, Moses and Aaron; Nebuchadnezzar, Cyrus, Napoleon, and Washington; Luther, Calvin, and Wesley. The Confederacy had but a brief history, Finley explained. Hardly a world shaker, it was still unrecognized by foreign nations. But the South had received a special commission from God, not just to create a model Christian government but also to Christianize the blacks. Perhaps when the South achieved her freedom, that commission would vault the Confederacy to the forefront of God's Christian forces as an example of self-denial and vigorous action.[36]

The 1861 Constitution may have created the Confederate States of America as a corporate entity under God's moral law, and First Manassas may have signaled God's favor, but Richmond clergymen argued that official pronouncements and acknowledgments of God's grace from the pulpit had to be answered by united righteous action if nationhood was to have any lasting reality. In the effort to mold a sense of unity and compel moral action, preachers of the Confederate jeremiad faced obstacles that the second- and third-generation New England Puritans, who developed the jeremiad as an American idiom, did not have to face.[37] Logically and rhetorically, the nation must precede the jeremiad; that is, a people's sense of being joined in a single corporate body under the eyes of God must precede the preacher's castigation of public sins and calls for repentance. The jeremiad's ritual denunciation, as Sacvan Bercovitch has shown, can then, in turn, reinforce both nationalism and a people's presumption of "chosenness."[38] But some ministers acknowledged that the Confederacy did not begin the war as a unified people, as a nation in anything more than name. States' rights ideology and regional differences overrode identification with "the South." Finley's definition of the Confederate errand as a mission to black slaves could not have been the nation's definitive, unifying moral calling, especially in border states where the idea of slavery as a necessary evil (rather than a positive good) still lingered. Richmond Presbyterian T. V. Moore addressed the diverse interests and cultures of the South's border, gulf, and western states, a diversity that even the common institution of slavery was unable to unite: "What our young republic needed was a feeling of oneness, a broad, deep, national unity, binding together the separate sovereignties of the Confederacy."[39]

Neither could Confederate clergymen easily evoke that feeling of oneness by appealing to a sacred founding in the past, a shared origin in a golden age of piety and virtue against which the present could be castigated for declension and from which it could draw inspiration.[40] In fact, one of the most striking differences between the Confederate jeremiad and its Puritan predecessor was its peculiar avoidance of the span of sacred history, its lack of a strong eschatological dimension. The evolution of the Confederacy came so rapidly and the war was so immediate that circumstances left no opportunity for historic celebration or millennial glory.

In severing their connection with the North, the Confederacy severed, or at least severely attenuated, their rhetorical connections to a preexistent nation. Much of the rhetoric of civil religion, after all, originated in the North. If the South had a civil religion before the war, it existed independent of the fast, and tended instead to draw its genius from civic observances that highlighted southern participation in the Revolution and the patriotism of the planter aristocracy, personified by Patrick Henry, George Washington, and, above all, Thomas Jefferson. Its citizens prided themselves on many aspects of American republicanism and celebrated the ideals of civic virtue, together with religious liberties ensuing from the separation of church and state and freedom of religion. But the jeremiad was not part of their tradition, nor was it the vehicle through which a civil religion was ritualized.[41] In this sense, their sacred history—their covenant with God—came through adoption into the northern colonies. Jamestown was no Plymouth Rock or Puritan City on a Hill; as Richmond's Bishop William Meade explained, Jamestown was founded upon religious principles as strict as New England, but its religious character had quickly declined. Furthermore, Meade admitted, the Revolutionary era was no pious golden age; although it called forth noble virtues, it was also rife with immorality, infidelity, and corruption.[42] Neither was there any sustained attempt to attach typological significance to the Revolution. Certainly the Revolutionary forefathers and the "Spirit of 1776" are mentioned in Richmond fast-day oratory.[43] But the references were always martial and genealogical, not typological. As an event in sacred history, the Revolution stood out in Confederate oratory as an uncaused cause, an event whose precursors went unnamed.

If there was no unbroken past of fast-day covenanting for the South to draw upon in Richmond print and oratory, neither was there much of a post-millennial future to muse over in abstract reckoning. Historian James Moorhead's *American Apocalypse* documents how thoroughly suffused northern rhetoric was with millennial urgency.[44] The same cannot be heard in the Confederate jeremiad. While it is technically accurate to speak of a "proslavery millennialism" in southern theological discourse, that concept and terminology seldom appeared in fast sermons, whether printed in Richmond or elsewhere in the South.[45] To the extent that millennial themes can be located at all in Confederate jeremiads, they appeared only toward the end of the war, in terms less optimistic and postmillennial than apocalyptic and foreboding.

Placed without friends in a war of unimagined ferocity on their near borders, Confederate Richmond had no sacred time but the present. There was no rehearsing of ancient covenants nor speculations on Christ's Second Coming, as Puritans were wont to do two centuries earlier. The overriding theme of fast sermons was the ultimate reality of national righteousness. Confederate jeremiads could not repeat this fact too often. Their readers and listeners did not need to know anything more than this. With God's imprimatur, surrender was unthinkable, for deliverance lay just beyond the most recent trial. Since ultimate deliverance was certain in a truly sacred cause, ministers assured listeners, then deprivations and defeats could be interpreted as providential punishment for the sake of correction rather than an indictment of southern guilt.

The logic of the Confederate jeremiads and thanksgiving celebrations as they unfolded through the war defined each victory as God's work, a gracious favor just short of the miraculous that signified a triumph of divine justice. A defeat, however, was never a sign that the cause was not righteous, that slavery or secession or the actions taken by the Confederate government might be unjust or sinful after all. Battlefield defeats were God's punishments for the sins of the southern people—women as well as men. Card playing, profanity, usury, and drinking were clearly male sins. But covetousness, pride, excessive attachment to worldly apparel, gossip and "loose talking" were clearly directed to the females. This inevitably created even greater strains on women's guilt; not only couldn't they lead troops to victory on the battlefield, or run plantations with an iron fist, they couldn't even please the Lord through virtuous living.[46] Their failure to embody spirituality determined that the Confederate people would have to suffer greatly before being awarded their ultimate victory.

Through repetition and nearly universal exposure, the Confederate jeremiad shaped male and female responses to the war from the highest to the lowest levels of white southern society.[47] Churches, magistrates, generals, religious newspapers, and even the secular press through the early campaigns all developed the themes of the jeremiad along separate but parallel tracks. Government officials and military leaders from Jefferson Davis to Robert E. Lee and Stonewall Jackson invariably invoked the terms of the jeremiad in their battlefield reports and public proclamations.[48] Ecclesiastical reports invoked battlefield successes to proclaim the divine truth of the jeremiad's message. The Presbyterian Synod of Virginia's annual report in 1862, for example, identified the public fast as the cause of victory at Manassas:

At first God did not seem to smile on our defensive operations. . . . Then God put it into the heart of [President] Davis to call for a day of fasting, humiliation, and prayer. . . . The united supplication of the whole people went up before the God of battles and was graciously accepted through the intercession of our great High Priest. . . . We were wonderfully delivered out of the hands of our enemies.[49]

The themes of the jeremiad dominated local, unpublished oratory as well as printed sermons and official pronouncements. Not surprisingly, few unpublished sermons survive from the midst of war. But one remarkably complete selection survives from Richmond's Jeremiah Bell Jeeter, pastor of the Third Baptist Church, co-founder of the Southern Baptist Convention, teacher at Richmond College, and "reluctant" slave owner. Throughout the war, Jeeter preached weekly in Richmond. At the front of his sermon booklet, he wrote: "This volume of notes was prepared during the war. Many sermons I prepared during that trying period with the roar of battle in my ears."[50] In the spring and summer of 1862, Richmond was under siege. McClellan's army was massed on its border. Richmond's citizen militia was willing but ill-prepared to fight. But then in July, word reached the city of a federal reversal. Lee had attacked on the Virginia peninsula and pushed McClellan's powerful army back from Richmond. Jeeter promptly penned a thanksgiving sermon "on the occasion of the national victories," insisting that God was on the side of the Confederacy. At first, "it was a dark day for the Confederacy." But then the Confederacy knelt in national humiliation and God smiled upon His people. Apart from some naval defeats, there was victory on almost every front. "The siege of Richmond has been raised"; the enemy was on the defensive. What meaning should be taken from this? Victories "are not to be ascribed to the number or skill of our troops—nor to the superiority of our generals—but to the divine hand."[51]

The Religious Press

Considered as a rhetorical form, the jeremiad was as amenable to print as to speech. If literacy rates were no higher in nineteenth-century Richmond than they were in colonial New England, where the jeremiad was first voiced, printing rates were much higher, transforming the form and, in some ways, making it more powerful than its Puritan predecessor. The story of the rise of the penny press in the 1830s and the development of competing dailies in every antebellum American city is well known.[52] Less familiar but equally important was the mass religious press. Protestants had always been pioneers in the utilization of mass media, and Richmond Protestants were no exception.[53] Religious weeklies representing the major denominations had been published in the city since the early 1840s. Their function was to report both religious and secular news. In most issues, biblical studies were accompanied by a magazine-like summary of the week's political (and, after 1861, military) events. Like the secular press, commercial advertisements were a mainstay of every religious publication. Richmond religious titles included the *Central Presbyterian*, *The*

Commission; or Southern Baptist Missionary Magazine, The Religious Herald, the *Richmond Christian Advocate, The Southern Churchman,* and *The Southern Friend: a Religious, Literary, and Agricultural Journal.* Like the secular press, circulation levels were high and destined to grow far higher with the onset of hostilities. Literate Richmond inhabitants read secular and religious newspapers regularly, supplemented with "outside" reading from the New York penny press and northern denominational papers whenever they could be smuggled into the city.[54]

In one important respect besides subject matter, religious newspapers differed from the secular penny press: their editors were not professionals. Unlike the secular press edited by men who viewed journalism as their profession, religious newspapers were edited and published, for the most part, by ministers who saw the newspaper as an extension of the pulpit and the Sunday school. They were not caught up in the journalistic penchant for the exposé and political in-fighting, nor were they willing to attack the secular press or competing denominational publishers. The religious press had no political affiliations and used its doctrine of "spirituality" to avoid—for the most part—partisan comment in its pages. This distinction between the secular and religious presses would become enormously important by 1862 and 1863 as Confederate defeats mounted and as secular newspapers divided along party lines.

When viewed collectively, it is surprising how little religious newspapers varied from one to the next. Together they reinforced the rhetoric of the jeremiad and beat the drum for a righteous war. The circulation of the South's denominational newspapers and religious tracts underwent a phenomenal expansion during the war, making the growth of Richmond's secular press seem modest by comparison. The Baptists acted first, and their Virginia Sunday School and Publication Board would publish over 30 million pages. The Soldier's Tract Association of the Methodist Church was established in 1862 and published 40,000 copies of two semimonthly papers (one entitled *The Soldier's Paper*) and various missionary publications. The Evangelical Tract Society, based in Petersburg, published more than 100 tracts and the *Army and Navy Messenger.* In 1864, the *Central Presbyterian* claimed that Richmond alone was sending out 10,000 copies of religious journals each week to the Confederate soldiers, and that religious newspapers had a total circulation of 90,000 per month in the armies.[55]

The religious press interpreted the weekly news within an explicitly Christian frame of reference. As an advertisement for the Episcopal *Southern Churchman* explained, "It surveys the world not with the eye of the politician, or the merchant, but condenses, arranges, and reports the events of the day, as connected with the religion of Christ. It is emphatically the poor man's friend. It inspires the child with a taste for reading, gives to the young enlarged views of the Christian effort, presents to the active Christians the calls of duty, and develops the benevolent feelings of the heart."[56] The *Churchman,* like other religious weeklies, was true to its word. An examination of their contents reveals materials suited for all ages, including children. In many ways, the secular press, with its emphasis on politics, was a male medium. The religious press, on the other hand, appealed equally to men, women, and children, to pious soldiers and politically apathetic civilians. In this sense, it brought the war's ideals and mission to the widest audience of all.

At the beginning of the war, the secular press endorsed religion and the religious press preached politics. A clerical writer for the *Central Presbyterian* explained that while party politics was best left to others, "there are times when none can be silent."[57] The Methodist *Richmond Christian Advocate* championed the Confederacy's moral patriotism and insisted that it was grounded in "evangelical and vital religion." Unlike the secular press, the religious weeklies explained the doctrinal underpinnings of the Confederacy. In an early editorial, the *Advocate* pointed out the distinction between federal covenants and the covenant of grace, and the necessity to incorporate the entire "political community" into the national fast. Non-Christians, or those "who make no pretensions to experimental religion," who participated in the sacrament of communion would be blasphemers, but they *should* participate in the ritual of the national fast.[58]

In addition to national fasts, denominational newspapers announced fasts for their own denominations. On May 30, 1861, the Baptist *Religious Herald* noted a day of fasting recommended by the Southern Baptist Convention "on account of our national troubles." It went on to assure that "effectual fervent prayer may cause the storm to pass away."[59] The religious weeklies could at times be far bolder than the Richmond fast sermons in their characterization of the conflict as a holy war against the "monster heresy" of abolitionism, their defense of slavery as the central institution of Christian civilization, and their identification of the Confederacy as God's Covenant People, the most Christian nation on earth.[60]

Civil religion was not the only religion propagated in the religious press. Religious periodicals echoed ministers' contentions that the rhetoric of the jeremiad did not interfere with Sunday salvation preaching. Many if not most of the narratives, dialogues, essays, and anecdotes printed in the denominational weeklies for southern families and Confederate soldiers focused on moral uplift or conversionist exhortation. Most of the tracts distributed to soldiers and families, too, aimed at personal moral reformation and the salvation of souls. The war, of course, remained the great unspoken given behind selected biblical and devotional themes, whether in regular Sunday preaching, religious tracts, or the denominational weeklies. Frequent topics in both Richmond's religious print and its unpublished oratory, such as "suffering" and the need to remain faithful, "Death a sorrowful event," and "The Call of Sinners as Soldiers of Christ" all reflected the reality of siege and war around the city.[61] The churches were unrelenting in their efforts to bring sinners, military and civilian alike, to their knees before the cross. The secular *Richmond Examiner* even worried that "the colporteurs who circulated on the eve of expected battles little pamphlets headed, 'Are You Ready to Die,' and 'Sinner, You are Soon to be Departed' " were deflating morale and "doing more harm than good."[62]

The Secular Press, 1860–1862

Commentary in the secular press suggests that religion was not the monolithic influence indicated by the religious press and official proclamations.[63] In time, significant fissures would appear in the secular press, as some papers would go so far as to call the fast (though never spirituality) into question. In the first year of war, no paper, however critical of military or political strategy, failed to promote fast and thanksgiving days or to urge all citizens to honor and promote the rituals. As the war dragged on, though, each newspaper, either implicitly through a shift in assumptions, tone, and emphasis, or explicitly, through direct disavowal, challenged the jeremiad's version of the religious grounding of Confederate ideology, thus revealing a community at war with itself as well as with the North.

In 1861, Richmond represented, in J. Cutler Andrews's words, "the hub of the Confederate news enterprise."[64] The city boasted four major daily newspapers: *The Richmond Daily Whig*, *The Daily Richmond Enquirer*, *The Richmond Examiner*, and *The Richmond Daily Dispatch*. In July 1863, it added another, when the *Alexandria Sentinel* began publishing from Richmond.[65] Richmond's total newspaper circulation in 1860 was 84,000, but the reach and influence of Richmond papers expanded greatly during the war.[66] Forty newspapers throughout the South suspended publication in the first year, and only twenty-two remained by 1865.[67] The *Dispatch*'s prewar circulation of 8,000, however, grew to 30,000 before the war's end (equal to that of its rivals combined).[68] To a news-hungry society, secular papers grew in frequency as well as circulation. The "extra" became a staple of journalism in the Civil War, North and South. Often these extras were extracts from newspapers in enemy territory.[69]

Although the secular dailies in Richmond had devoted most of their prewar newsprint to political news, commercial notices, and miscellaneous trivia, religious matters were sometimes considered newsworthy, especially to the editors of the Richmond *Dispatch*.[70] The *Dispatch* and the *Enquirer* had regularly printed advance notices of special religious lectures, summaries of local religious meetings, and synopses or even sometimes the minutes of regional church conferences.[71] The papers also had devoted some attention to local prayer meetings and revivals.[72]

With the onset of war, the daily secular press, with its frequent afternoon "extras," was especially important for "current" news of battles, troop deployments, and proclamations. As "professionals," moreover, its editors did not hesitate to criticize military and governmental policy directly. Edited by James A. Cowardin and John D. Hammersley, the *Dispatch* was considered less polemical than many other southern newspapers.[73] One historian wrote that it was designed to give news rather than opinions, but it actually filled at least as much editorial space as the other dailies by 1861.[74] The *Enquirer* has been characterized as appealing to the more genteel members of the community with editorials that were supposedly more restrained, balanced, and literary; one of its editors was Capt. O. Jennings Wise, son of a former Virginia governor.[75]

The *Dispatch* supported President Buchanan's fast day on January 6, 1860, noting that it was common practice for all nations since the time of the ancient Jews, and it would be honored by all but infidels.[76] The next day, it described services held by Baptists, Methodists, Presbyterians, and Episcopalians in Richmond, and took three long paragraphs to summarize Moses Hoge's sermon. "Catholics, as well as Protestants, observed the day with great devotion, and the same may be said of our Jewish population." The *Dispatch* closed the account by reprinting the prayer that J. M. Michelbacher delivered in Richmond's German Hebrew synagogue.[77] The paper hailed the Confederacy's first fast-day proclamation for June 13, 1861, as an outgrowth of the sentiments of the people, and for the November 15, 1861, fast the paper spent nearly two columns reporting the activities at St. John's and summarizing other local sermons.[78]

To this point, the *Dispatch*'s tone had been similar to the sermons themselves, urging repentance and humility. But as ministers began to decry post-Manassas declension, the paper tried to stir the spirits of its readers to combat post-Manassas lethargy. The editors became loathe to print bad news that would dampen morale. They condemned greedy speculators and hoarders, but increasingly responded to reverses on the battlefield with a shrug at God's mysterious ways, rather than blaming the sins of the South. The *Dispatch* joined its thanks for the imposition of providence to increasingly extravagant praise for Lee and Jackson.[79]

Like the *Dispatch*, the *Enquirer* supported Buchanan's fast day in 1860. But it also printed Governor John Letcher's letter declining calls from clergymen to proclaim an additional day of prayer in Virginia. It reminded its readers that the custom in Virginia was to avoid any interference in religious duties, and it repeated Letcher's contention that civil magistrates should have nothing to say about religious matters—that rites of thanksgiving or humiliation were the province of ecclesiastical organizations.[80] The paper, unlike the *Dispatch*, had little to say about the national fast day itself beyond a story about a minister silenced by his congregation because he drew a parallel between the sectional crisis and I Kings 12:16–24 ("Ye shall not go up, nor fight against your brethren").[81] The first Confederate fast day prompted the *Enquirer* to call upon ministers to support the "just and holy cause" of Constitutional liberty and the principles of 1776; the fasts to follow merited little more than short comments and reminders.[82]

While the *Dispatch* used fast days to remind its readers that all was in God's hands, and to console them that the North would eventually be punished for its sins, the *Enquirer* saw such days as opportunities to seek God's blessing upon the cause and instill confidence in the populace. If interdenominational efforts within Richmond were merely "hurly-burlies of pious contradictions," as the paper would later lament, the mission to the army drew the *Enquirer's* praise. War threatened to turn soldiers into savages, the editors warned, and relying on a chivalrous Cavalier spirit or instinct would not do. The "natures and dispositions of man" needed to be "cultivated in the same degree as the mind." While the press was in charge of cultivating the mind and southern

women cultivated the heart, the churches were supposed to be cultivating conscience, and that was just what the army chaplains and missionaries were doing:
"They have succeeded in making the army of Virginia respectful acknowledgers
of the Divine Director, if not devout and pious disciples of the Redeemer."[83]
So while devoting less attention to fasts on the home front than the *Dispatch*,
the paper did publish Gen. Lee's orders calling for strict observance by the
troops.[84]

In 1861, the Richmond *Examiner*'s treatment of fast days was more extensive than the *Enquirer*'s and nearly indistinguishable from the *Dispatch*'s. But
unlike the religious press, the *Examiner* did group clergymen with women and
children as it defined war as an enterprise for adult males.[85] The war would
be won by "the full exertion of our manhood," an editorial declared in February
1862, and again, five days later, "if the inhabitants of the South have any real
manhood, these reverses will inspire them with determination." The *Examiner*
stressed manly honor rather than pious humility. "No reverses can destroy the
Southern Confederacy if its people have the amount of moral courage common
to the stronger races of mankind."[86] "The South fights . . . for honor, character,
standing, and reputation. She must not only wipe off the stigma of effeminacy
with which Abolition has branded her, but she must prove that she possesses
that high-toned chivalry, that enduring and indomitable courage that is peculiar to a privileged caste."[87]

Like the *Enquirer*, the *Examiner* turned to shorter notices of fasts and
gave less attention to the Confederacy's civil religion after the fall of 1861. In
March 1862, the *Examiner* complained that Richmond's Unitarian minister,
Alden Bosserman, had refused to preach a fast sermon for the Confederacy
on the appointed day.[88] By late 1862, however, the *Examiner* began to offer
editorial interpretations of events and an approach to the problem of morale
that almost seem designed to contradict the calls for piety and humiliation
coming from the pulpits and the president. In a "Lay Sermon" printed in early
1862, the paper mentioned Providence, but dwelt on the lessons of "natural
philosophy." The "philosopher" learns that the world is like a great mart of
commerce, where Fortune exposes various commodities, some good and some
bad.[89] In a sign of what was to come, the *Examiner* began to complain that
after a defeat, too many people imagine that "the only course left is to grovel
in the dust and beg, like whipped curs, for mercy."[90] Seven months later, as
yet another fast approached and ministers were trying to read the will of God
in the signs of the times, the paper declared that "War is a game of chance;
and in all games of chance there are unaccountable runs of good and bad
luck."[91]

Defeat and Discord, 1862–1863

The newspapers' shift of emphasis and attitude cannot be understood apart
from the experience of wartime Richmond itself. With Richmond threatened
in the spring of 1862, war news crowded out any fast-day reports. As the center
of Confederate communications, Richmond both received and transmitted in-

formation in advance of most other locales. Historian William Kimball observes that "a special demand was placed on those who elected to live in the nerve-center of the Confederacy. Every blow struck at any point vibrated there; every rumor of ill luck or distress occurring in any part of the country was listened to and felt there."[92] Richmond trembled as federals were poised on the peninsula, hoping to take the city by water. At the same time, Norfolk fell and the *Merrimack* was scuttled. Battles at Seven Pines and Seven Hills took place within hearing distance from Richmond. As McClellan pushed his campaign up the peninsula, Richmond inhabitants not only read about it in the papers but could also spy his forces from church spires. This time the siege would be lifted, but not without horrific costs experienced first-hand by Richmond's inhabitants. Battles fought in the wilderness spewed their wounded and prisoners into Richmond.

Fredericksburg and Chancellorsville would be the last great Virginia victories. In Richmond itself, currency inflated at a staggering rate as speculators profited and ordinary men and women watched savings dwindle and disappear. Kimball observes that "by the end of 1862 there were obviously two distinct classes of people in wartime Richmond . . . the haves and the have nots."[93] These class tensions exacerbated tensions raised by military defeats and would only grow worse.[94] Just as the Davis administration could no longer speak for the people at large, or even the state and local governments, so neither magistrates nor ministers could any longer claim to speak for the poor in all their interests.[95] As scarcity fell unevenly on the population, many laborers sank into a depression that gave up on the Confederacy.

Economic tensions further strained Richmond society. On May 23, an exasperated and wildly anti-Semitic Jones exclaimed: "Oh the extortioners! General Winder has issued an order fixing the maximum price of certain articles of marketing, which has only the effect of keeping a great many things out of market. The farmers have to pay the merchants and Jews their extortionate prices. . . . It does more harm than good."[96] Wages did not keep up with inflation, while the salaries of city officers had been increased by a total of more than 200 percent.

The winter of 1863 was bitterly cold with dwindling supplies. Social life shifted to the young ladies, who, if wealthy enough, continued with "elegant receptions" even as the poor grew poorer. In April, 1,000 women and children, led by the painter's wife Mary Jackson, marched for food. On April 2, a crowd of angry men, women, and children massed in the Capitol Square, saying they were hungry. Soon the crowd grew from hundreds to thousands. By midmorning, a "mob" marched down Ninth Street, crossing Main Street looking for "something to eat." By the time they reached the shops on Cary Street the mob had grown large and angry. According to Jones, "They impressed all the carts and drays in the street, which were speedily laden with meal, flour, shoes etc."[97] The mayor appeared and called out troops, who read the Riot Act and threatened to fire into the crowd. Only the appearance of President Davis prevented carnage.

In this sea of contention and fear, the unanimity forged in the creation of the Confederate republic would not last, and, by extension, the jeremiad could no longer forge a consensus among Richmond's population. In August 1863, the *Examiner* reported the fast observance and added that while *some* of the churches were well attended, the streets were filled with men, women, and children strolling about in their best attire.[98]

Civil religion and faith in the efficacy of the fast diminished even as personal religiosity was expanding on the battlefield and the president's mansion. Jones observed that, after January 1862, Davis was "rarely seen in the streets now." In place of the streets, Davis was seen most often at St. Paul's, leading Jones to conclude: "I am rather inclined to credit the rumor that he intends to join the church. All his messages and proclamations indicate that he is looking for a mightier power than England for assistance."[99] In fact, Davis did convert, and the conversion was a sincere search "for a mightier power." Like many of his generals, and his counterpart Abraham Lincoln to the north, religion became increasingly significant to Davis as the battles raged on. In all these cases, conversion was preparation for death; it meant no surrender.

Although the ministry did invent a rhetoric of nationhood around the ritual conventions of the fast and the thanksgiving day, they could not fix its meanings nor shape a cohesive and consensual Confederate ideology that automatically absorbed alternative visions.[100] At the beginning of the war, southern pulpits and the secular press were engaged in a common enterprise: banging the drum for the war effort. But the strains on the Confederate government in the midst of total war and the social stresses upon a rapidly transforming capital city could not smooth over ideological differences among various factions for long. Not everyone embraced the new political function for the church and religious role for the state, especially in the middle years of defeat and disappointment. Vicious political battles over Confederate policy, public discontent over the moral decline of wartime Richmond, economic profiteering, hoarding, and the social breakdown dramatized by the Richmond bread riot—all blatantly contradicted the spiritual and national consensus called for on fast days.

The jeremiad's prescription for future success in the face of defeat—public humiliation, moral reformation, and corporate exaltation of God over the works of men—began to clash with the secular press's efforts to boost morale and praise heroic generals through a Cavalier ethic of war and masculine nobility. In place of consensus, conflicting strains between the secular and religious press, and even within the secular press itself, emerged. The new and immensely popular magazine *Southern Illustrated News*, published in Richmond and intended to displace the northern *Harper's* magazine, made virtually no reference to religion, instead highlighting (and canonizing) its generals. The political and religious positions articulated by the most influential Richmond dailies—the *Dispatch*, the *Enquirer*, the *Daily Whig*, and the *Examiner*—reveal alternative and contending voices in the ideological construction of the Confederacy.

Class and ethnic tensions were not the only tensions to rend Richmond society. Political attacks on Davis increased, and so did conflict between the Confederate and state authorities in Richmond. Political partisans confronted each other anew as they coalesced into pro- and anti-Davis factions. The hybrid nationalism built so effectively on the unity of sacred and political oratory in the secular and religious press at the dawn of the Confederacy faced increasing strains in the face of mounting defeats. In fact, the secular press was not one press but many, and in its mid-war divisions we see the multiple and contending themes that distraught Richmondites confronted amid the din of nearby battles.

Criticisms of Davis focused both on his strategy and initiative and on his appeals to heaven. Increasingly, Davis's newfound religiosity became portrayed as a feminizing agency weakening his manhood. Already in February 1862, following the loss of Fort Donelson, the *Whig* openly questioned whether "more energetic men might not have effected far more important results."[101] In 1862, Jones observed that "Our army has fallen back to within four miles of Richmond. Much anxiety is felt for the fate of the city." Faced with this danger, and mindful of Davis's recent baptism and private confirmation at St. Paul's, the secular press began having questions about policies founded on piety and fasting. But the first explicit complaint about Davis's fast days came on May 19, 1862, when the Richmond *Examiner* argued that "Piety is estimable, but energy, common sense, impartial justice, courage and industry are also qualities very useful to rulers and to nations."[102] Davis's proclamations were signs not of religious faith but of unmanly weakness: "When we find the President standing in a corner telling his beads, and relying on a miracle to save the country, instead of mounting his horse and putting forth every power of the government to defeat the enemy, the effect is depressing in the extreme."[103]

Among all Richmond newspapers, the *Examiner* provides the best example of the "secular patriotism" that some preachers became increasingly concerned about as the war dragged on. For its editor John Moncure Daniel, perpetually in a paper war and wounded in a duel with the Confederacy's treasurer, violence was an end in itself, and the celebration of violence constituted the core of what he termed "patriotism." "Patriotism is the most unrelenting, self-sacrificing, honorable and elevated of all human sentiments. It is love of one's natal or adopted soil."[104] In this Spartan celebration of violence as a validation of manliness, the male citizen became a fighting animal, and the only real test of his patriotism was through war.[105] "Nothing could be more beautiful than the enthusiastic devotion to country which is manifesting itself on every hand."[106] In May 1863, the paper rejoiced at "the spectacle of a nation in which the martial virtues were happily conjoined with pure patriotism and political intelligence."[107] Challenging its readers after defeat in July, the *Examiner* argued that the South had still not shown "that tenacity of purpose, that indomitable obstinacy of patriotism."[108]

On May 19, 1862, the *Richmond Examiner* published the most scathing complaint to appear in print against President Davis's repeated calls for national fast days in the Confederacy:

> Never has any one year seen so many of these affairs. It is hoped that this latest is the last. The country has had quite enough of them. . . . [t]hough it is well that a government should pay proper respect to the religious ceremony, that has been done and overdone by the Confederacy. In truth, these devotional proclamations of Mr. Davis have lost all good effect from their repetition, are regarded by the people as either cant or evidence of mental weakness and have become the topic of unpleasant reflection with intelligent men.[109]

The editorial was more than another of the *Examiner's* attacks upon the Davis administration. It was an expression of grave misgivings about the state of the Confederacy's civil religion and about the effect of its central ritual, the fast day, upon southern morale. The editorial signaled the first explicit break between Richmond's pulpits and secular press over the religious meaning of the Civil War. As internal strains, mounting casualties, and battlefield defeats tore apart the superficial unity shaped by the flush of early success, the secular presses of Richmond, the news hub of the South, increasingly avoided what the *Examiner* would call the pulpit's "sanctimonious terminology" when discussing the deeper meanings of the war. Newspaper pundits would attack even the Confederacy's ritual bows to God as another failed policy of an ostentatiously religious Davis administration.

Throughout the war, the *Enquirer* sought to avoid controversy and "scolded" other papers for being too critical of the administration and hurting morale. The *Examiner* expressed its disagreement with Davis policy in August 1861 and, along with the *Whig*, took on a consistently anti-Davis stance by the early weeks of 1862.[110] The severity of its criticism escalated in July 1863 with the defeats at Gettysburg and Vicksburg; it was after that point, too, that the *Enquirer* and the *Sentinel* became more vocal defenders of Davis, while the *Dispatch* tried to maintain its "benign neutrality."[111] Jones observed in his diary: "Again the *Enquirer*, edited by Mitchel, the Irishman, is urging the President to seize arbitrary power; but the *Examiner* combats the project defiantly."[112]

In this increasingly contentious atmosphere, religious themes did not altogether disappear in the secular papers. Religious meetings and revivals were occasionaly noted. Even more telling than religious announcements were the religious aspects of each paper's editorial opinions. The *Dispatch's* repeated diatribes against "Puritanism" rooted this paper in old Virginia Anglicanism and a genteel latitudinarianism. The *Dispatch's* central interpretation of the crisis and the war, consistent from 1860 to 1865, was a less pious David against an anti-Christian Goliath than it was a struggle between Puritans and Cavaliers. In this more ethnically based cultural construction, modern Yankees were the direct descendants of Cromwellian Puritans, and although the North was a polyglot nation (compared to the supposedly homogeneous Anglo-Saxon South), the Puritans were the dominant element. This interpretation fit both the editorial policy and the broader philosophical stance of the editors. By concentrating on a deeply ingrained (albeit imaginary) southern ethnic lineage, the "nonpartisan" *Dispatch* could avoid focusing on particular policies that might alienate some of its readers. The Puritan versus Cavalier interpretation also gave the editors a rationale for their repeated declarations that the war was inevitable. Even when a Confederate senator from Louisiana disavowed the "Cavalier" label, saying that he no more wished to be associated with the violent and licentious Cavaliers of 1649 than with the Puritans, the *Dispatch* held its ground.[113]

The *Dispatch's* editorial policy can be summed up by a statement they made in an apology to an offended Episcopalian: the newspaper extended courtesy to all denominations, and certainly had not intended to make an exception for a Christian church "which challenges our reverence and respect, alike by its age and its conservatism, by the combined simplicity and grandeur of its religious worship, and its unobtrusive piety and zeal."[114] The *Dispatch* defended religious toleration as a sacred principle and blasted "Yankee historians" who traced the idea back to the Puritans.[115] The editors seemed to make a point of welcoming Catholics and Jews into the southern tent by publishing commentaries by a rabbi or a bishop who supported the Confederate cause.[116] They also explained that Irish Catholics were being duped into fighting for the North, and they defended the Jews when they were singled out as extortionists later in the war.[117] The *Dispatch*, however, had no tolerance for Mormonism and Spiritualism, which were considered less as religious phenomena than as expressions of a deeply rooted, Puritan-derived fanaticism that had taken a religious form.[118]

Echoing antebellum arguments, the *Dispatch* charged that abolitionism was a species of fanaticism too, an idolatry of the black slave that had grown up in Puritanism even as the specific theological tenets from Cromwell's day had died away.[119] It was a fanaticism that had hurt the effort to convert the slaves by breeding the slaveowner's distrust of slave missions.[120] Abolitionist agitation, the paper had also cautioned before the war, had tainted others with a style of preaching and prayer that dangerously mixed religion and politics. New England prayers were "an exhortation to the by-standers instead of [a] supplication to the Almighty." The *Dispatch* even frowned upon "the practice of opening all sorts of secular gatherings with public prayer" as having "more the appearance than the reality of religious worship."[121] On the other hand, "the pulpit is the proper place for preaching Christ and Him crucified" and not for other kinds of orations.[122] "The blending of politics and religion is a distinctive characteristic of Puritanism."[123] In 1860, the editors had discouraged the attempt of one or two southern preachers to "return [the] fire of spiritual musketry" at Henry Ward Beecher and his ilk: "in general the Southern pulpit keeps on the old fashioned way of preaching the Gospel, and leaving political matters to political men. The Founder of the Christian Religion declared that His Kingdom was not of this world."[124]

Puritan self-righteousness, the *Dispatch* also contended, was at the root of the absurd notion of Manifest Destiny.[125] The North's national self-conceit had convinced many before the war, even in the South, that the millennium was at hand, an opinion the paper continued to discourage throughout the war.[126] If the cant about being a chosen people had deluded the masses in the North, the "political and commercial leaders" there knew that the cause of Union was the pursuit of the Almighty Dollar.[127]

Compared to the *Dispatch*'s unwavering support of church leaders and continuing praise for the religious sentiments of Richmond's people, the *Enquirer's* portrayal was more mixed. It encouraged the clergy to give its seal of approval to the cause, but also pointed out that church leaders had been slow to recognize the justice of the South's position, implying that the people had known better than their religious leaders. Later in the war, it printed a sarcastic—even mocking—report on how a fast day was observed in Richmond, while highly praising the efforts of the Colportage Society to spread religion through the army.[128]

Unlike the *Dispatch* and *Enquirer*, the *Daily Whig* did not hesitate to criticize Davis both for his conduct of the war and for his work in Richmond. With particular disdain, the *Whig* attacked the *Sentinel* for supporting Davis "in the affair of Colonel Myers."[129] Following the defeat at Gettysburg, the *Whig* continued to invoke religion, but the main themes of arousal were drawn from secular history. When news of the true disaster at Gettysburg reached Richmond, the *Whig* turned to antiquity, not Israel:

> The glory of Athens and the strength of Sparta were acquired by making every man a soldier, and considering non-combatants as drones in the national hive. . . . No nobler principle, no dearer homes, no fairer land were ever fought for, bled for, died for than hang upon the issue of this conflict. Natal rights and native land, hereditary titles to property, the immunities of free citizenship, the sanctities of the hearthstone, the appealing voice of innocent and helpless womanhood—all that can touch the heart or nerve the arm, cry trumpet tongued to all brave and true men to fight this fight out to victory or death.[130]

Critical of Davis and Spartan in its martial orientation, the *Whig* did not adopt the language of the jeremiad, although it continued to cease operations on days of fasting so that its employees could observe the occasion. In its March 27, 1863, editorial, the paper supported the fast and went on to observe "the religious portion of the community and the Pharisees too will attend the various places of public worship. We trust that the congregations will be large." When, in August, Davis called for another fast, the *Whig* eagerly complied. Rejecting the notion that God rained defeat on them for their cause, the *Whig* instead singled out sins, not the sins of pride or profanity or Sabbath breaking—the stock-in-trade general sins applicable to all peoples at all times—but the sins of materialism and hoarding, particularly acute in Richmond: "No man or woman in the Confederacy who is familiar with the doctrines or commandments of the inspired Word can be greatly surprised at the present state of affairs. Have not the people everywhere devoted themselves to the worship of Mammon? Have they not all practiced extortion?"[131]

On August 6, 1863, after the humiliations of Gettysburg and Vicksburg, the *Examiner* bitterly declared that "There is neither Christianity nor religion of any kind in this war. We prosecute it in self-defense, for the preservation of our liberty, our homes and our Negroes." This statement grew as much out of frustration with Davis's policies as from philosophical commitment. Although the *Examiner* argued that Christianity was at the core of southern society, the paper had no patience with religion being mixed up with politics, public occasions, or national policy. In terms reminiscent of antebellum religious orthodoxy, the editor complained about Davis's May 1862 fast, noting that "Religion is the sentiment of individuals, not a matter of military order or formal injunction."[132] Daniel and Pollard criticized Davis's government for "what might be called the white-cravat policy; the practice, in a deadly struggle with the devil's own brood, of the Christian precept of doing good for evil, of turning another cheek when smitten."[133] Politicians, in their public and political capacities, should stay away from religion, and clergymen should avoid politics. "That in times of high excitement the clergy should share the feelings of the community, is natural; and it may be difficult to prevent all confusion of earthly and heavenly considerations in pious discourse; yet the nature of our Government, widely adverse to the union of the secular and the sacred arm, forbids it."[134] After the defeats in the summer of 1863, the *Examiner* gave very clear advice to the clergy:

> [I]t is rather their duty to soften the passions aroused in the contests of the world, and withdraw our thoughts from their fevered excitement, than to stimulate them by passionate discourse. . . . Let [the Southern clergy] inculcate virtue, stimulate patriotism, and expound Christianity, but let them argue from universals, and trust the good sense of their hearers to make the application to particulars. Let them, in their clerical capacity, confine themselves to the holy province whose separation from temporal interests is alike conducive to sound religion and good government.[135]

For the *Examiner*, separation of church and state also meant a separation of religion and politics. Where advocates of the jeremiad were not able to see the contradictions between their Confederate jeremiad and the antebellum tradition of the spirituality of the church, Daniel saw it all too clearly. In words that made explicit the reversal most ministers and magistrates glossed over, Daniel wrote:

> Fast days and Thanksgiving days strike the Southern ear with a puritanical sound, always disagreeable, and, now, pre-eminently hateful. They smack of Latter Day sanctity; savor of the nasal twang and recall disagreeable reminiscences of Praise-God-Barebones, the Pilgrim Fathers, and their Yankee descendants. . . . It is well that the Confederacy should display a trust in Divine aid, ingrained, as it undoubtedly is, in the hopes, the thoughts, and the progress of the people, as well as approved by the universal practice of the world. Still, it is to be regretted that the phraseology we use should be unfortunately associated with all that is repugnant to our taste and our feelings. . . . This revolution should secure us social as well as political independence. We should get rid of Yankee manners as well as of Puritan laws; and one of the most obnoxious is the vice of political preaching. Let the Southern clergy, then, be

assured that they will win more lasting respect, and exert more legitimate influence, in abstaining from a custom discordant to our manners.

The *Examiner* actually differed from the *Dispatch* and the *Enquirer* in degree rather than in kind: it was simply more rigid in its insistence upon the separation of religion and politics than its competitors were. The *Examiner* was not irreligious, and even "anti-clerical" is perhaps too strong a term. In this sense, we are not dealing with an irrevocable divide between secular and religious press. For all of his fulmination against churches and fasts, Daniel never attacked the religious press as antithetical to Confederate goals, nor did he criticize denominational statements in support of the Confederacy. Indeed, for a Christian republic, these were all good pure traditions. His criticisms were reserved for political sermons, and in particular fast-day sermons uttered in the ashes of defeat. These, he correctly recognized, departed from the customs of the Old South and more closely resembled the hated Puritans; they promoted a supernatural fatalism that placed the chief burden on God rather than Confederate guns. In words reeking with bitter irony, Daniel observed that the North—the originator of fasts—had itself outgrown them, while the South foolishly picked them up: "They [the North], by the way, do not seem now to rely on fasts and humiliation. They have recently indulged in thanksgiving for victory, but their panacea for defeat seems to be fresh levies of men, more ironclads and additional fifteen-inch guns."[136]

The North and South had social movements going in opposite directions, the *Examiner* claimed: the North was rapidly becoming more radical, the South more conservative, more attached to its institutions.[137] The South's unique social organization made it special: "we are the only religious and conservative people in Christendom. . . . It is nothing but our social institutions and our domestic slavery that distinguishes us from the rest of the nations of Europe." Because of slavery, the South escaped "the moral and political evils that afflict other countries." Christian morality was natural to a slave society and impracticable in a free land "where all men are equals, [and therefore] all must be competitors."[138]

Other secular papers in Richmond shared in ideals of manliness and the Revolution, but not at the expense of the fast. A complicated picture emerged in which all secular papers invoked the Revolution and gallantry, but divided over religion—or, more specifically, the civil religion of the fast day. Often the religious press would reprint military news from the secular daily papers. In the waning moments of the Confederacy, the secular press borrowed from the religious. Alongside its proclamation and endorsement of the fast, the *Whig* reprinted a two-column essay on "A Definition of Fasting" reprinted from the *Southern Churchman*. Again religious and secular press were finding common cause in the face of almost certain defeat.

The Religious Press, 1862–1864

On July 27, 1863, a disheartened Jones contextualized the setting for another fast-day proclamation:

Nothing but disasters to chronicle now. Natchez and Yazoo City, all gone the way of Vicksburg, involving a heavy loss of boats, guns, and ordnance stores; besides the enemy have got some twenty locomotives in Mississippi. Lee has retreated as far as Culpepper Court House. The President publishes another proclamation, fixing a day for the people to unite in prayer. The weather is bad.[139]

On July 29, a beleaguered Jones raised the ultimate question: "Still raining! The great fear is that the crops will be ruined, and famine, which we have long been verging upon, will be complete. Is providence upon us for our sins, or upon our cause?"[140]

The answer, as it emerged from virtually every pulpit and religious publication in Richmond, was that the Confederacy's cause was just, and God's punishment was purification for sin. If fast-day preaching was losing "its good effect through repetition" among many observers in the government and secular press, a flood of religious print continued to drape the carnage with spiritual significance. Denominational newspapers trumpeted the "Christian heroism" of generals like Stonewall Jackson and Robert E. Lee, spread the news of religious revivals in the army camps, and reported stories of Christian nurture and sanctified suffering in the hospitals. Church societies directed thousands of conversionist pamphlets and tracts toward every southern town and Confederate army tent. In Richmond, colporteurs worked feverishly with the armies and in the greatly expanded hospitals to urge the soldiers on to revival. A revitalized southern spirituality, concentrated on individual salvation, along with the logic of the Confederate jeremiad, which sanctified the entire South, would shape the perceptions of white southerners long after the fall of Richmond and the surrender at Appomattox.

The religious press did not remain silent when journalists or politicians deviated from the rhetoric of the jeremiad or suggested that the Confederacy was engaged in something other than a pious crusade. The *Central Presbyterian* complained when Governor Letcher exempted workers from the daily secular press and not the religious press from military duty, claiming that religious publications were far more important to the soldiers. The paper denounced the governor even more bitterly when he exempted theatrical performers from duty as well. The New Richmond Theater, in fact, became something of a symbol of the widening gulf between the attitudes expressed in religious and secular print. The *Enquirer* mocked a religious assembly held in the theater as a meeting of two worlds, and pointed out that the stage usually drew bigger audiences than Richmond's pulpits. As the *Examiner* criticized fast days, it praised performances in the theater as the high point of wartime Richmond's cultural life. Even before the *Central Presbyterian's* bitter attack upon the governor's preference for theater people over religious printers, John Lansing Burrows, pastor of Richmond's First Baptist Church, published a sermon denouncing the New Richmond Theater and the moral decadence and debauchery it represented.[141]

To clergymen and religious publishers who recognized the power of the press to mold opinion, however, a more immediate danger as the war continued was the shifting tone they detected in the secular press generally and the increasingly harsh criticism of the Davis administration in the opposition papers. They defended the government and Davis's calls for fast days, and started to see the rise of a more secular nationalism promoted in some newspapers as one of the sins crippling the South. Patriotism without piety was the "defective patriotism" that Leroy Lee decried in a fast-day sermon reprinted as a soldier's tract by the Methodist Episcopal church in Richmond.[142] In another soldier's tract, a Virginia chaplain wondered why this patriotism seemed more motivating than the cause of Christ.[143]

Discussions in the secular press that shifted from "Providence" to "fate" or "chance" were denounced as creeping atheism. The *Central Presbyterian* was especially perturbed when the *Dispatch* characterized Stonewall Jackson as "a fatalist." Southern pulpits and religious publications also expressed outrage over the signs of defeatism they detected in some Confederate newspapers. In March 1863, on the eve of a public fast, the *Central Presbyterian* complained: "One or two of our newspapers have at times not obscurely hinted their approbation of the maxim Napoleon is *reported* to have sanctioned that God was always on the side of the strongest regiments and the heaviest artillery. The remark . . . is an atheism our Christian nation will disdain to take upon its lips."[144] Following the March fast, the *Richmond Christian Advocate* added its own complaint against those "who have written in bitter terms of denunciation against various chief men—especially against the President." Such criticism was traitorous: "Every man who contributes to depress the public heart helps the enemy."

Alongside the religious press's support of war came a significant shift in focus that hinted at a coming spiritualization of the fast. After the war's second year, the pulpit and religious press increasingly addressed the public heart rather than the public mind. Reasoned arguments could articulate issues that could generate debate and conflict, but they could not sustain courage in the face of the carnage witnessed in this war. Nor could they cross the divide from public, civil religion to private, experiential, "saving faith." Sentiments of the heart would take over and push the drum beat harder. Justifications for the cause shifted from a legalistic list of "principles" (which, after all, changed as the war progressed) to an assessment of the "sentiments" motivating each side. This shift in rhetorical strategy can be seen in two sermons preached and published by D. S. Doggett, pastor of Richmond's Broad Street Methodist Church, and later bishop. The first, delivered in September 1862, reasoned from a list of "facts" revealing that God was interested in the struggle and defining the war as a defense of "the rights asserted by our forefathers, in the immortal Declaration of Independence; the rights of self-government, self-protection, and of conscience." Doggett's second sermon, preached in the spring of 1864 and published by the Soldier's Tract Association in Richmond, argued that the war received its moral character by the passions and fundamental convictions of either side. It was a war of truth and justice against lust and prejudice; a war of Bible believers against heretics and infidels.[145] If rationalizations became tangled and confused as the war progressed, a Christian's heart could still be in the right place. If God's designs for the South seemed less clear in 1864 than in 1862, putting trust in Him was an even greater act of faith.

Clearly, the varied opinions of the secular newspapers do not express a wholehearted consent to the pulpit vision of the war, the jeremiad's logic of Christian legitimation, or the new role of the clergy in the civil religion hastily constructed by the fast and thanksgiving day rituals and endorsed by the religious press. Instead, they reflect a conflicted pattern of vacillating agreement and disagreement, though all within a common embrace of the war. For Richmond readers, the conflict had to have been intensely personal. They were, after all, reading both the secular dailies and the religious weeklies. What lessons did they take? All ideologies struggle to contain conflicting strains and all worldviews succeed in part through their capacity to absorb differences and contradictions. What Richmond's male inhabitants took from their world of print and speech must have been the sense that they had to be both Christian and Spartan, both converted and manly, both loving and violent. And it is in this tension that Confederate ideology in Richmond derived its tensile strength and upheld its citizens to the last days of defeat and beyond.

A Reinvented Faith, 1864–1865

The blasts against the Confederacy from rival newspapers, the poor, and the disaffected were real, but not unending in duration. Citing class tensions, political factionalism, mounting losses, and religious guilt over slavery, some writers have argued that Confederate failure was virtually inevitable. Yet just as it is easy to exaggerate the consensus of the war based on initial proclamations made in the euphoria of secession and independence, so is it easy to err at the other extreme by positing irreconcilable divisions that were deeper than the Confederacy itself, thus dooming it to failure.

By late 1863, it was clear that fasts would cause neither victories nor defeats. Blasts against fast days receded and the secular press enjoined universal observation. The South was beaten by superior forces rather than excessive piety or the lack thereof. The *Examiner* backed off its diatribes, swallowing its disdain for the Confederacy's politicized religion and apparently hoping for a miracle. The religious press continued its endorsement of the fast and its expectations of divine deliverance. But this was no simple return to the monolithic civil religion that bound sacred and secular together in the creation of the Confederacy. Religion was invoked, to be sure, but less the hard-headed civil religion of "Christian Sparta" than the heart-centered conversionist religion of evangelicalism. In the ashes of the last days of the Confederacy, a "modern" southern evangelicalism would be born.

In the last days of the Confederacy, religious expression was shaped less by borrowed formulas than by the experience of the passing days—the carnage of the battlefields, the hardships of the camps, the suffering in the hospitals, the overloaded prisoner-of-war camps, the social and moral transformation of central places like Richmond. The fast-day Confederate jeremiad weighed every public action in the balance of sin and redemption and powerfully invested shared ordeals with sacred significance. But it was the power of *every*day southern spirituality—the army camp revivals, the hospital-bed evangelism, the daily devotions of the pious on the home front—that was able to transform scenes of brutal slaughter into occasions of personal salvation. The religious basis of Confederate ideology for white southerners was the jeremiad's vision of a truly Christian nation joined to a spiritual rhetoric grounded in the common experience of individual sacrifice and regeneration.

Of all the true believers in the Confederacy, none believed more deeply than the magistrates and ministers entrusted with the delivery of the divine message. Far from being propagandists, they really believed God was on their side and they would win. Neither "stubberness" nor a retreat from reality can alone account for the Davis administration's dogged pursuit of the war. Faith, they firmly believed, would win out. Throughout 1863 and 1864, fast-day sermons and the religious press promised victory and deliverance as the reward of faith. The men who fought and bled on the battlefields, rather than the civilians starving in Richmond, seemed to be the most receptive audience for the message. The religious press spread the news of army camp revivals during the winters of 1862–1863 and 1863–1864—the "rainbow" of revival over the storm of war, as the *Central Presbyterian* put it. Alongside the religious press, denominational tracts and broadsides inundated the army, leading many pastors to characterize army revivals as "silent revivals" because so many soldiers "read their way to heaven."[146] Religious newspapers published letters from chaplains, reports from A. E. Dickinson on the progress of the mission to the soldiers, articles and addresses emphasizing both the Confederacy's holy crusade and the importance of individual repentance, reformation, and conversion. By mixing poems, stories, dialogues, letters, speeches, and news reports, by alternating public pronouncements with personal exhortations, the religious press managed to join the logic of the jeremiad to the spirituality of the southern church, just as it combined the aggressive evangelizing of revivalism with the function of the secular press—spreading the news.

The Confederate army revivals were not only a religious event but a journalistic event as well. As defeats mounted, stories of revivals in the army became more conspicuous in both the religious and the secular press. Headlines like "Revival in Hood's corps," or "Christ in the Camp" increasingly overwhelmed military news dominated by headlines like "Vicksburg fallen," "Longstreet beat," "Savannah evacuated," or "Federals land at Fort Fisher." By 1864, most secular and religious papers included a regular column on "Religion in the Army" featuring news of revivals, letters from soldiers, or reports from chaplains, all attesting to "a mighty work of the Spirit going on now in the camps."[147] Through stories of revivals in print, churches, soldiers, and the press were all drawn together in a mutually reinforcing process. In an ongoing circle, churches and soldiers read of revivals, more soldiers converted, and newspapers printed more stories.

How do we understand this journalistic obsession? Clearly there is an extrareligious significance to these revival events, one that represented a "victory" of sorts in a world otherwise dominated by defeats. With southerners deprived of victory on the battlefield and vibrant faith in the church, news of army revivals filled spiritual and cultural needs that could not be met anywhere else. The news served two purposes. First, it confirmed that the South was a godly nation where it counted most—in the army. And second, it served to inspire revival at home among a people spiritually dying. In four years of war, a great reversal had taken place. Where once churches sought to civilize and Christianize the armies, the armies now sought to Christianize an utterly defeated, embittered home front. A Confederate chaplain expressed this reversal perfectly in 1865: "When the war began the church was praying for the army. But a great change has taken place. Many in the church have lost the spirit of prayer and the army is now praying for the church."[148]

By March 1865, with Lee desperately maneuvering to avoid Grant's army and Sherman slashing through the Carolinas, it was clear to any neutral observer that the war was lost. If ever there was a time for defeatism, it was then. On March 3, a beleaguered, but still believing President Davis proclaimed another fast-day observance for March 10. Outside of Richmond, Grant was massing one of the largest armies in modern history, ready at any moment to break through the Confederate lines. Inside the city, besieged Richmonders had nowhere to turn but to their God. Such was the severity of the situation that the lead time between proclamation and observance shrank to a week. For the last Confederate fast day, on March 3, 1865, the *Dispatch* again urged the ministers to blast away at sin: "This is no time to be nice."[149]

Despite inclement weather, worshipers poured into the churches. The *Central Presbyterian* observed: "It is the common impression that no occasion of the kind has been so generally observed in Richmond as the last. The universal suspension of worldly business, and the worship in the sanctuaries indicated the solemnity resting upon the mind of the community." In reporting on Baptist services held in Richmond that day, the *Religious Herald* singled out the theme of deliverance:

> Those of our people who have grown despondent under the reverses of the times, should not think that, because disasters have befallen us, God is unfriendly to our cause. We must remember the terrible character of this war. Our enemy have all the material advantages. We are shut out from the world. . . . Notwithstanding these things, we have borne the bloody strife, and yet remain unsubdued. Surely God has been the friend of the South and purposes our ultimate independence.[150]

On March 23, with Grant's noose tightening around Richmond and Petersburg, the *Richmond Christian Advocate* did not waver in prosecuting the sacred cause of the Confederacy. The paper had by then shrunk to half its regular size and often missed press runs as workers were impressed for military service. But the spirit remained unchanged. On its front page it printed a stirring "Hymn to the National Flag," followed by an enjoinder to "Maintain the Spirit of the Fast Day." After attacking the "folly and wickedness" of those who "abandon hope and courage under adversity," the paper went on to urge its readers to "trust in God and take Courage. We shall assuredly conquer in the end."

On Sunday, April 2, with guns sounding in the distance, all Richmond turned out to hear God's Word. Richmond's chronicler Cooper DeLeon recalled that:

> The churches were crowded with plainly-dressed women—most of them in mourning—passed into their pews with pale, sad faces, on which grief and anxiety had both set their handwriting. There were few men, and most of these came in noisily upon crutches, or pale and worn with fever. It was no holiday gathering of perfumed and bedizened godliness, that Sunday in Richmond.[151]

By then, even Sundays were observed as a fast and the jeremiad sounded throughout Richmond's churches. But it would be the last toll. That day word arrived from Lee to evacuate the city. A shaken Jefferson Davis left the church and, soon after, the city. The following night, Richmond burned. Six days later, Lee surrendered the Army of Northern Virginia at Appomattox Court House. To all intents and purposes, the Confederacy was dead, and with no national fasts to sustain it, the Confederate jeremiad should not have survived the Civil War. Yet this is not what happened. Both the Confederacy and the jeremiad would be resurrected in a new, spiritualized form that promised providential meaning in the ruins of defeat.

Conclusion: Toward the Religion of the Lost Cause

Ideologies, like religions, derive their strength from their capacity to command assent despite opposite and competing tendencies. When functioning as cultural systems, they may not stand for and express all the conflicting, impassioned themes *within* a society, and yet they may still mark off the values and ideas that collectively separate this "people" from that "people." Such was the case with Confederate ideology in Richmond. If most historians now reject the guilt thesis for why the South lost the Civil War, and point instead to an ongoing patriotism and biblically upheld self-righteousness, the sources of that ideology and their change over time have been less clear.

Christianity was necessary but not sufficient to inform and motivate a people for four years of almost uninterrupted war. Such a view does not ignore the enduring facts of paternalism and slavery, but presumes them; it does not deprive the Civil War of its economic and racial struggles, its long tradition of sectionalism, and its culture of violence; it does not minimize the political debates and pressures exacerbated by a constantly expanding empire; it does not deny—indeed, it alone explains—the upsurge of evangelical and reformist zeal that triumphed in the New South; nor does it rob the military struggle of its importance. It merely explains how, in one particular place at one particular point in time, religion enabled the inhabitants of a city to rebel, fight, and suffer enormous deprivations and defeat. Contained within Richmond's world of churches and newspapers was a powerful fuel for civil and military rebellion and sacrifice that would kindle and sustain them through sacrifices few, if any, other communities were required to endure.

Inevitably, Richmond's ideology was neither static nor monolithic. The highly combustible blend of religious and secular energies shifted in emphasis as events transformed life in the capital city. The dominant fact of the earlier years had been the intensification of ideological passions first ignited by the states' rights debates, the response to abolition, and the doctrine of self-defense. Religion was a crucial, but supporting theme, providing the biblical basis for slavery, blessing political leaders, and urging righteous unity. When the fast was instituted as a nationwide ritual, Christianity proclaimed itself at the spiritual center of the Confederacy. Religion's centrality, then, was chiefly as a civil religion, informing and reinforcing the overnight creation of the Confederate republic as an explicitly "Christian state."

But the Confederate spirit was changing as the original élan slowly filtered through the ordinary activities of Richmond life. Professional journalists, led by John Moncure Daniel, increasingly criticized the government; women suffered deprivations; citizens encountered price fixing and hoarding. The initial outburst of religious patriotism, in which most of Richmond's citizens shared to some degree, could not be sustained, nor could the agreement on essentials that had brought together quite disparate groups. Passions cooled in the winter interim between battles, even as shortages heated up home-front animosities. Cultural, social, and gender differences became exacerbated. Religion came to be reviled by some critics as a false crutch, even as it became increasingly embraced by the Confederate leadership and politicized by Richmond's clergy.

In the years 1863 and 1864, the central themes of Confederate nationalism became immensely more complicated, and they cannot be understood by the same simple matrix that brought the Richmond faithful into the war. By 1865, with many state capitals already under federal rule, Richmond's citizens faced the end. Meanings again shifted. Religion reasserted itself, though not in the same pattern that began the war. A single characteristic of this later religion predominates. Despite defeats, doubts, and fears for the future, revivals flourished both as facts in army camps and as civilian news in the secular and religious press. Even as temporal defeats loomed large, hope appeared in the army.

The Confederacy would live on after the war in what Charles Reagan Wilson has described as the "Religion of the Lost Cause." Far from being guilt-ridden over slavery and ashamed of their weaker God, the former Confederates retained a separate identity; indeed, it was a southern civil *religion*: "Religion was at the heart of this dream, and the history of the attitude known as the Lost Cause was the story of the use of the past as the basis for a Southern religious-moral identity, an identity as a chosen people. The Lost Cause was therefore the story of the linking of two profound human forces, religion and history."[152]

If Wilson has shown *what* happened in the New South, he did not make it clear *how* it happened. The origins of the religion of the Lost Cause lie in the particular historylessness of the Confederacy seen in their jeremiads. Whereas the North, as part of the ongoing Puritan covenant, could not extract a unique history from the Civil War, the South, whose sacred history began in 1861 and ended in 1865, could. White southerners would hallow and preserve the memory of the Christian Confederacy and claim that identity in defeat by spiritualizing the jeremiad.

In a curious, but quite logical process, postbellum white southerners would simultaneously reject and affirm the jeremiad by breaking it down into its two constituent parts: its rhetoric of triumph and its rhetoric of chosenness. Positively, they would retain that aspect of the jeremiad that promised chosen peoplehood and nobility of spiritual purpose. By returning to the antebellum doctrine of the spirituality of the church, and once again refusing to "preach politics," they could affirm a spiritual destiny for themselves that had nothing to do with temporal events or contingencies, and that was continuous with their prior experience in the Old South. Just as the early church was a peculiar people of God in bondage to Rome, so they too were a chosen people, a spiritual temple, preserved and protected for the sake of their fidelity. Negatively, they would reject that aspect of the jeremiad that was triumphalist and that they themselves had sounded so loudly right down to the last day of the Confederacy. Defeat could not mean that God had abandoned them. They knew themselves to be Christian *and* they knew themselves to be unconditionally defeated as a political nation. Their conclusion from this was that the triumphalism was wrong, not the South. God could and did choose losers as well as winners for his chosen people.

Evangelical Christianity and its generator, the religious revival, also thrived in the postbellum South. Like the return to spirituality, evangelical revivalism after the war would not be a simple replication of evangelicalism in the Old South. As popular as evangelicalism was before the war, it was not the cultural system in the Old South that it would become in the New.[153] Antebellum evangelicalism was always in some sense countercultural—a "dissenter" faith of primarily Baptists and Methodists that did not embrace the upper reaches of the establishment. The revivals themselves, moreover, were in no sense place-specific. Adherents self-consciously participated in a vast, transatlantic evangelical empire that subordinated time and place to the universal summons of the gospel. Postwar evangelicalism, on the other hand, would be as all-inclusive in terms of its class appeal as the camp revivals that touched generals and privates alike. Faith would be nurtured in denominations that were formally or informally separate from the North and the larger evangelical world. And revivals would be conducted within regional settings that self-consciously identified evangelical faith with the religion of the Lost Cause.[154]

Surrender had ended revivals in the Confederate army, but it did not end revivals in the South. It is not coincidental that great revivals in the postwar South were led by Confederate veterans who had served as lay pastors, elders, deacons, and colporteurs. Preachers like Robert Dabney, revivalists like James B. Gambrell, president of the Southern Baptist Convention, or J. William Jones, revivalist and chronicler of the army revivals, all served combat posts in the war.[155] If soldiers could not win on the battlefield, they could win their people to Christ and snatch some victory from the torments of defeat. The triumph of evangelicalism as a cultural system in the South came only after the Civil War, when "born-again religion" came to mean something more than a response to the simple gospel message. In the postbellum white South, it meant the Confederate army as well as the southern pulpit; pride and manliness as well as humility and submission; true womanhood as well as female self-sufficiency. It meant planters and the poor; Richmond and rural Georgia; Episcopalian as well as Baptist. Evangelicalism and the religion of the Lost Cause would coexist in a symbiotic union. Revivals and sentimentalized history would be even more successful than fast days and jeremiads in providing an ongoing and persistent sense of southern identity for the white South.

Public religion in the postbellum South recombined elements that had defined Confederate religion during the Civil War: the spirituality of the southern church; evangelicalism, which the camp revivals had lifted to a new, inclusive prominence; and the Confederate jeremiad, which gave the white South its self-proclaimed sacred identity. In the final analysis, then, the Civil War in Richmond must be judged a religious as well as a military and political event, and a religious event that constituted nothing less than the watershed in white southern religious history.

Notes

1. For recent social histories of the Civil War, see, e.g., Maris Vinovskis, ed., *Toward a Social History of the American Civil War* (Cambridge, 1990); Catherine Clinton and Nina Silber, eds., *Divided Houses: Gender and the Civil War* (New York, 1992); George Rable, *Civil Wars: Women and the Crisis of Southern Nationalism* (Urbana, 1989); and, most recently, Drew Gilpin Faust, *Mothers of Invention: Women of the Slaveholding South in the American Civil War* (Chapel Hill, 1996). On cultural history, see Lynn Hunt, "Introduction: History, Culture and Text," in *The New Cultural History*, ed. Lynn Hunt (Berkeley, 1989), 1–22.

2. Some outstanding studies of religion in the Old South have appeared in which the authors effectively recreate the world the slaveholders made. See especially Donald G. Mathews, *Religion in the Old South* (Chicago, 1977); Eugene D. Genovese, *The World the Slaveholders Made: Two Essays in Interpretation* (orig. pub. 1969; reprinted Middletown, CT, 1988); Elizabeth Fox-Genovese and Eugene D. Genovese, "The Divine Sanction of Social Order: Religious Foundations of the Southern Slaveholders' World View," *Journal of the American Academy of Religion* 55 (1987): 211–233; Drew Gilpin Faust, "Evangelicalism and the Meaning of the Proslavery Argument: The Reverend Thornton Stringfellow of Virginia," *Virginia Magazine of History and Biography* 85 (1977): 3–17; Larry E. Tise, *Proslavery: A History of the Defense of Slavery in America, 1701–1840* (Athens, GA, 1987); James Oscar Farmer Jr., *The Metaphysical Confederacy: James Henry Thornwell and the Synthesis of Southern Values* (Macon, GA, 1986); Mitchell Snay, *Gospel of Disunion: Religion and Separatism in the Antebellum South* (New York, 1993).

On denominational splits, the best overview is C. C. Goen, *Broken Churches, Broken Nation: Denominational Schisms and the Coming of the Civil War* (Macon, GA, 1985). On institutional histories of denominations in the Confederacy, see especially W. Harrison Daniel, *Southern Protestantism in the Confederacy* (Bedford, VA, 1989); Benjamin

J. Blied, *Catholics and the Civil War* (Milwaukee, 1945); Joseph B. Cheshire, *The Church in the Confederate States: A History of the Protestant Episcopal Church in the Confederate States* (New York, 1912); Edgar J. Pennington, "The Church in the Confederate States," *Historical Magazine of the Protestant Episcopal Church* 17 (1948): 308–448; and Willard Eugene Wight, "Churches in the Confederacy," Ph.D. dissertation, Emory University, 1949. On Civil War preaching in the Confederacy, see especially James W. Silver, *Confederate Morale and Church Propaganda* (Tuscaloosa, 1957); Charles Stewart, "Civil War Preaching," in *Preaching in American History*, ed. Dewitte Holland (Nashville, 1969), 184–205; or David B. Chesebrough, *God Ordained This War: Sermons on the Sectional Crisis, 1830–1865* (Columbia, SC, 1991). On chaplains in the Confederacy, see Gardiner H. Shattuck Jr., *A Shield and Hiding Place: The Religious Life of the Civil War Armies* (Macon, GA, 1987); Sidney J. Romero, *The Rebel Chaplain; Religion in the Rebel Ranks* (Lanham, MD, 1983); Charles F. Pitts, *Chaplains in Gray: The Confederate Chaplain's Story* (Nashville, 1957); Herman Norton, *Rebel Religion: The Story of the Confederate Chaplains* (St. Louis, 1961); Arthur L. Walker, "Three Alabama Baptist Chaplains, 1861–1865," *Alabama Review* 16 (1963): 174–184; or Philip Thomas Tucker, *The Confederacy's Fighting Chaplain: Father John B. Bannon* (Tuscaloosa, 1992).

One pioneering study of the Civil War that begins to recapture Christianity's centrality to the Confederacy is Drew Faust's *The Creation of Confederate Nationalism: Ideology and Identity in the Civil War South* (Baton Rouge, 1988). See also Allen C. Guelzo, *The Crisis of the American Republic: A History of the Civil War and Reconstruction* (New York, 1995); and Richard Rankin, *Ambivalent Churchmen and Evangelical Churchwomen: The Religion of the Episcopal Elite in North Carolina, 1800–1860* (Columbia, SC, 1993).

3. Richard E. Beringer, Herman Hattaway, Archer Jones, and William N. Still Jr., *Why the South Lost the Civil War* (Athens, GA, 1986). For earlier statements focusing on "will" or "morale" or the "guilt" of slavery, see especially Bell Irvin Wiley, *The Road to Appomattox* (Memphis, 1956); Charles H. Wesley, *The Collapse of the Confederacy* (Washington, DC, 1937); Kenneth M. Stampp, "The Southern Road to Appomattox," in *The Imperiled Union: Essays on the Background of the Civil War*, ed. Kenneth Stampp (New York, 1980); Clement Eaton, "The Loss of the Will to Fight," in his *A History of the Southern Confederacy* (New York, 1954); Carl N. Degler, *Place Over Time: The Continuity of Southern Distinctiveness* (Baton Rouge, 1977); and Charles Grier Sellers Jr., "The Travail of Slavery," in *The Southerner as American* (Chapel Hill, 1960). On absence of guilt generally in the Confederacy, see Gaines M. Foster, "Guilt Over Slavery: A Historiographical Analysis," *Journal of Southern History* 56 (1990): 665–694; and Eugene D. Genovese, *The Slaveholders' Dilemma: Freedom and Progress in Southern Conservative Thought, 1820–1860* (Columbia, SC, 1991).

4. One prominent exception is Orville Vernon Burton's *In My Father's House Are Many Mansions: Family and Community in Edgefield, South Carolina* (Chapel Hill, 1985).

5. Yet for all of this self-evident importance, Richmond has been largely ignored in the New Social History. In a recent survey of the historical literature on Virginia and the Confederacy that applies most directly to Richmond, Gary W. Gallaher observes:

Unbelievably, no one has undertaken a broad scholarly study of the [Virginia] commonwealth behind the lines. Did Virginians suffer from more or less internal division than other Confederate states? . . . Was nationalism more fully developed in Virginia because of the presence of Richmond? Did the fact that the South's best army won more victories on Virginia's soil than any other Confederate army won anywhere else promote nationalist feelings. Answers to these and other questions relating to the Confederacy's most important state remain uncertain.

Gary W. Gallagher, "Home Front and Battlefield: Some Recent Literature Relating to Virginia and the Confederacy," *Virginia Magazine of History and Biography* 98 (1990): 135–168, quoted at 153. Two comprehensive surveys of Richmond in war are Emory Thomas, *The Confederate State of Richmond: A Biography of the Capital* (Austin, 1971); and Ernest B. Furgurson, *Ashes of Glory: Richmond at War* (New York, 1996).

6. William Robert Taylor, *Cavalier and Yankee: The Old South and American National Character* (New York, 1961); George M. Fredrickson, *White Supremacy: A Comparative Study in American and South African History* (New York, 1981); Bertram Wyatt-Brown, *Southern Honor: Ethics and Behavior in the Old South* (New York, 1982); John McCardell, *The Idea of a Southern Nation* (New York, 1979); and Dickson D. Bruce, *Violence and Culture in the Antebellum South* (Austin, 1979).

7. Thomas, *Confederate State of Richmond*, 21; and Michael B. Chesson, *Richmond After the War, 1865–1890* (Richmond, 1981), 4.

8. Richard C. Wade, *Slavery in the Cities: The South 1820–1860* (New York, 1964), 327.

9. Chesson, *Richmond After the War*, 9–10; 15.

10. On the alliance of slaveholders and clergy on the morality of slavery, see Mathews, *Religion in the Old South*; Faust, *Mothers of Invention*; Tise, *Proslavery*; Snay, *Gospel of Disunion*; Genovese, *The World the Slaveholders Made*; and Anne C. Loveland, *Southern Evangelicals and the Social Order, 1800–1860* (Baton Rouge, 1980).

11. The boys received a classical curriculum outfitting them for the University of Virginia or other colleges to the north. Girls learned art, music, languages, and social etiquette.

12. Michael Schudson, *Discovering the News: A Social History of American Newspapers* (New York, 1978); Jurgen Habermas, *The Structural Transformation of the Public Sphere: An Inquiry into a Category of Bourgeois Society* (Cambridge, MA, 1989).

13. In Katherine M. Jones, ed., *Heroines of Dixie: Confederate Women Tell Their Story of the War* (Indianapolis, 1955), 81.

14. Chesson, *Richmond After the War*, 17; Thomas, *Confederate State of Richmond*, 35.

15. On the unchurched majority in the antebellum South, see Christine Leigh Heyrman, *Southern Cross: The Beginnings of the Bible Belt* (New York, 1997).

16. Charles Reagan Wilson, "Robert Lewis Dabney: Religion and the Southern Holocaust," *Virginia Magazine of History and Biography* 89 (1981): 79–89.

17. Robert Dabney to William Hoge, December 5, 1860, mss. archives, Union Theological Seminary, Richmond.

18. Robert Dabney to Charles Hodge, January 23, 1861, mss. archives, Union Theological Seminary, Richmond.

19. J. B. Jones, *A Rebel War Clerk's Diary* (Philadelphia, 1866), 19, 22–23. See also Thomas, *Confederate State of Richmond*, 6.

20. Jones, *A Rebel War Clerk*, 42.

21. In *Confederate Morale*, 64–65, James W. Silver points to the ubiquity of fast sermons, but by limiting his concept of religion to a form of "propaganda," Silver misses the ritual power of the fast day to shape a people's view of itself in a war. More recently, Faust has summarized the fast-day jeremiad in *Confederate Nationalism*, 26–27, in terms that recognize its inclusive significance as "a recurrent occasion for clerical solemnization

of this marriage of sacred and secular." But the sheer novelty of the public fast in a southern culture inhospitable to a pulpit "marriage of the sacred and the secular" is not noticed. In *Proslavery* (p. 197), Tise recognizes that public fast and thanksgiving sermons "were printed and distributed widely only in connection with important national events and in the midst of crises throughout the eighteenth and much of the nineteenth centuries." He fails to note, however, that these printed fast and thanksgiving sermons were almost exclusively of northern origin. Snay, in *Gospel of Disunion*, 160, also assumes the South shared fully in the North's fast tradition. In W. D. Love's calendar of printed fast and thanksgiving sermons, only 7 of 622 titles originated in the South. See W. D. Love, *The Fast and Thanksgiving Days of New England* (Boston, 1895).

22. On pre-Civil War Thanksgiving and fasts (observed chiefly in South Carolina), see Robert Bonner, "Americans Apart: Nationality in the Slaveholding South," Ph.D. disseration, Yale University, 1997.

23. Love, *Fast and Thanksgiving Days*, 85, distinguishes "public" or "civil" fasts from church fasts, noting that the first such fast appointed by an order from the governor as the civil magistrate was in Plymouth on July 16, 1623. In time, Love adds, "the transfer of authority [for proclaiming fasts] from the church to the state was gradual. During the colonial period no embarrassment could arise, for the state was the church acting in a civil capacity" (223). But this transformation never took place in the South.

24. Snay, *Gospel of Disunion*, 42. South Carolina was here, as in so many other ways, exceptional. For an analysis of South Carolina occasional sermons, see Bonner, "Americans Apart." For some rare examples of antebellum southern fast and thanksgiving sermons in South Carolina, see Arthur Buuist, *A Sermon Delivered in the First Presbyterian Church on Thursday November 7 1822 Being the Day of Thanksgiving* (Charleston, 1823); or C. E. Gadsen, *A Sermon Preached at St. Philip's Church on the Fast Day May 14, 1841* (Charleston, 1841).

25. Gov. Wise is quoted in W. M. E. R., "The Thanksgiving Day Contention," *Virginia Cavalcade* 1 (1951): 9–11. In contrast, northern publishers printed over forty fast and thanksgiving sermons following the Fugitive Slave Act in 1850–1851.

26. The term "spirituality" was appropriated by southern Presbyterians, but spoke for the larger southern tradition of the strict separation of church and state. The doctrine is most closely identified with James Henley Thornwell, who observed:

> The Church of Jesus Christ is a spiritual body. . . . Its ends are holiness and life, to the manifestation of riches and glory of Divine grace, and not simply morality, decency and good order, which may to some extent be secured without faith in the Redeemer, or the transforming efficacy of the Holy Spirit. The laws of the church are the authoritative injunctions of Christ, and not the covenants, however benevolent their origin and aim, which men have instituted of their own will; and the ground of obligation which the Church, as such, inculcates is the authority of God speaking in His Word, and not pledges of honor which create, measure and define the peculiar duties of all voluntary associations.

Thornwell spoke these words in 1848 and would live to reverse them in the crisis of secession. Before the Civil War, virtually all southern Protestants agreed that the doctrine of spirituality of the church precluded the sort of "federal covenant" on which public fasts rested and through which "political sermons" were preached. Thornwell is here quoted from John H. Leith, "Spirituality of the Church," in *Encyclopedia of Religion in the South*, ed. Samuel S. Hill (Macon, GA, 1984), 731. See also Farmer, *Metaphysical*

Confederacy, 256–260. On how slavery was treated in antebellum preaching, see Snay, *Gospel of Disunion*.

27. In *Confederate Morale*, 64–65, Silver lists the following Confederate fasts: June 13, 1861; November 15, 1861; May 16, 1862; September 18, 1862; March 27, 1863; August 21, 1863; April 8, 1864; November 16, 1864; March 10, 1865. In addition, Basil Manly lists February 28, 1862, "Day of Pub. humiliation, fasting and prayer, appointed by the President of the Confederate States." See W. Stanley Hoole, ed., "The Diary of Dr. Basil Manly, 1858–1867, *Alabama Review* 4 (1951): 227. Abraham Lincoln proclaimed fasts for September 1861, April 30, 1863, and August 1864. In addition, Lincoln proclaimed four thanksgiving days and Davis two. We have recovered the texts of Davis's proclamations from the Confederate newspapers. Lincoln's proclamations are reprinted in H. S. J. Sickel, *Thanksgiving; Its Source, Philosophy and History* (Philadelphia, 1940).

28. See Farmer, *Metaphysical Confederacy*, 261–263.

29. Nineteenth-century churchmen were acutely aware of the absence of God in the federal Constitution and the implications of this for Christian nationhood. See Harry S. Stout, "Rhetoric and Reality in the American Revolution: The Case of the Federalist Clergy," in *Religion and Politics: From the Colonial Period to the 1980s*, ed. Mark A. Noll (New York, 1990), 62–76. Southern interpretations of the significance and meaning of the Constitution in the context of new nation-forming are described in E. Merton Coulter, *The Confederate States of America 1861–1865* (Baton Rouge, 1950); and Emory M. Thomas, *The Confederate Nation, 1861–1865* (New York, 1979).

30. Davis's proclamation was reprinted in virtually every Confederate newspaper.

31. O. S. Barten, *A Sermon Preached in St. James Church, Warrenton, Virginia, on Fast Day, June 13, 1861* (Richmond, 1861).

32. Data calculated from Marjorie Lyle Crandall, *Confederate Imprints: A Check List Based Principally on the Collection of the Boston Athenaeum* (Boston, 1955); and Richard Harwell, *More Confederate Imprints* (Richmond, 1957). Crandall and Harwell list 1,146 religious titles in 2,828 unofficial publications (these figures exclude periodicals, newspapers, and sheet music).

33. See Faust, *Mothers of Invention*, 179–195.

34. On the just war–holy war distinction, see Melvin Endy, "Just War, Holy War, and the Millennium," *William and Mary Quarterly* 42, 3rd ser. (1985): 3–25.

35. For examples, see Faust, *Creation of Confederate Nationalism*, chap. 2.

36. I. R. Finley, *The Lord Reigneth: A Sermon Preached in Lloyd's Church, Sussex County, Virginia, Sunday August 16, 1863* (Richmond, 1863).

37. On the generational sequence in Puritan jeremiads, see Harry S. Stout, *New England Soul: Preaching and Religious Culture in Colonial New England* (New York, 1986), 5.

38. Sacvan Bercovitch, *American Jeremiad* (Madison, WI, 1978).

39. T. V. Moore, *God Our Refuge and Strength in this War: A Discourse before the Congregations of the First and Second Presbyterian Churches on the Day of Humiliation, Fasting, and Prayer Appointed by President Davis, Friday, Nov. 15, 1861* (Richmond, 1861), 11.

40. Perry Miller, "Book I: Declension," in *The New England Mind: From Colony to Province* (Cambridge, MA, 1953), 19–130.

41. For a good overview, see Richard Beale Davis, *Intellectual Life of Jefferson's Virginia, 1790–1830* (Chapel Hill, 1964), 131–142.

42. William Meade, *Sermon Preached by Bishop Meade at the Opening of the Convention of the Protestant Episcopal Church of Virginia, in the City of Richmond* (Richmond, 1861), 11.

43. See, for example, D. S. Doggett, *A Discourse Delivered in the Broad Street Methodist Church* (Richmond, 1862), 13; Meade, *Sermon Preached by Bishop Meade at the Opening of the Convention of the Protestant Episcopal Church of Virginia*, 11–121; T. V. Moore, *God Our Refuge and Strength in this War* (Richmond, 1861), 14–18; J. J. D. Renfroe, *The Battle is God's* (Richmond, 1863), 11, 20; P. Slaughter, *Coercion and Conciliation* (Richmond, 186–), 3.

44. James Moorhead, *American Apocalypse: Yankee Protestants and the Civil War 1860–1869* (New Haven, 1978).

45. In "Proslavery Millennialism: Social Eschatology in Antebellum Southern Calvinism," *American Quarterly* 31 (1979): 46–62, Jack P. Maddex Jr. describes the prominent place of millennial speculation in southern Presbyterian thought, but virtually all of his sources either predate the Civil War or consider the topic in the abstract. In the crucible of war and the rhetoric of the jeremiad, prolonged millennial speculations exceeding a paragraph in length simply do not appear in any significant numbers.

46. On women's "profound sense of their own incapacities," see Faust, *Mothers of Invention*, 56.

47. O. S. Barten explained that God recognized the body politic as a "moral person" rewarded and punished in this world because it would have no existence in the afterlife. This logic was independent of any special covenant or presumption of the Confederacy as the New Israel. "Nations are but aggregates of individuals who compose them, and what God requires of one in his individual capacity, he demands of the whole in their associated character" (*A Sermon Preached in St. James Church*, [Richmond, 1861], 8–9). The Baptist preacher Thomas Dunaway of Lancaster County, Virginia, supported the same point by quoting the canon of international law (*A Sermon Delivered by Elder Thomas Dunaway . . . April, 1864* [Richmond, 1864], 8). William Norwood, preaching in Richmond's St. John's Church, distinguished more carefully between the aggregate sins of individuals, which brought judgments down upon the whole people, and the people of the Confederacy "acting in the national transactions" of their government, which had done nothing to call down God's curse (*God and Our Country* [Richmond, 1863], 7).

48. On Lee, see, e.g., *The War of the Rebellion: A Compilation of the Official Records of the Union and Confederate Armies* (Washington, DC, 1887), 141, 550; and *Official Records of the Union and Confederate Armies*, 60: 1150.

49. Presbyterian Synod of Virginia, *Annual Report 1862* (Richmond, 1862).

50. Jeremiah Bell Jeeter's sermon notes are preserved at the Virginia Baptist Historical Society in Richmond. Special thanks to the society and its director, Fred Anderson, for access to these notebooks. All quotations are taken from the microfilm collection at the Baptist Historical Society.

51. J. B. Jeeter, "Notes and Sermons," Virginia Baptist Historical Society.

52. In between colonial New England and the Civil War stood a printing and a journalistic revolution, made possible by steam presses, cheaper paper, and improved transportation. Cities everywhere produced competing dailies, which increasingly came to stand as the official information transmitter of the community. See Schudson, *Discovering the News*; and Richard D. Brown, *Knowledge is Power: The Diffusion of Information in Early America, 1700–1865* (New York, 1989).

53. On the development of the nineteenth-century religious press, see David Paul Nord, "Systematic Benevolence: Religious Publishing and the Marketplace in Early Nineteenth-Century America," in *Communication and Change in American Religious History*, ed. Leonard I. Sweet (Grand Rapids, 1993), 239–269.

54. A Reading Room on 11th Street kept on file all the city papers and all available

papers from every state, city, and town in the South. See William J. Kimball, *Starve or Fall: Richmond and Its People 1861–1865* (Ann Arbor, MI, 1976), 74.

55. *The Central Presbyterian*, June 2, 1864, and June 30, 1864.

56. *Southern Churchman*, April 25, 1862. Religious presses such as the Methodist *Southern Churchman* or the *Southern Presbyterian* printed on their mastheads, "a Religious Family Newspaper." Virtually all religious weeklies registered a family focus with sections particularly directed at women and young readers. They also assumed that they were the only source of news. A writer for the *Central Presbyterian*, November 24, 1860, responded to criticisms that the paper included too much secular news with the observation that "many of our subscribers read no other paper. [Our] chief purpose, in this day, is to furnish instructive and useful reading, to discuss religious and ecclesiastical topics, to arouse and develop the Christian zeal and efforts of the church, and to help forward the cause of truth and righteousness." A female writer to the same paper in 1862, however, informed the editors that her family had other sources of news: "We read the latest news through the week, the Bible and our own 'Southern Presbyterian' on the Sabbath" (*Central Presbyterian*, Dec. 18, 1862). Most religious papers other than the *Episcopalian* included, like the secular press, advertisements for everything from women's colleges to cocaine treatments for baldness.

57. *Central Presbyterian*, December 15, 1860; *Richmond Christian Advocate*, November 14, 1861, and February 20, 1862.

58. *Richmond Christian Advocate*, March 26, 1863.

59. *Religious Herald*, May 30, 1861.

60. *Religious Herald*, March 9, 1865.

61. Phrases are from Jeeter, "Notes and Sermons," and *Religious Herald* March 9, 1865.

62. Silver, *Confederate Morale*, 94.

63. From newspaper circulation rates, it is clear that most newspaper-reading Richmond inhabitants subscribed to both a religious and a secular paper. It is, therefore, as important to examine the secular press as the denominational papers in reconstructing religious meanings in Richmond. The secular papers contained some but not much religious material in their columns, and taken by themselves would give a very different picture of the power and pervasiveness of religion in Richmond public discourse and Confederate ideology than that which appears in the religious press. Interestingly, Beringer et al., *Why the South Lost the Civil War*, derive much of their evidence for religion's supposed abandonment of the Confederacy from the secular press.

64. J. Cutler Andrews, "The Confederate Press and Public Morale," *Journal of Southern History* 32 (November 1966): 447.

65. Other notable newspapers and periodicals include *The Southern Literary Messenger*, *The Magnolia Weekly*, *The Record of News, History and Literature* (first publication June 18, 1863), and a humorous magazine, the *Southern Punch* (first publication Aug. 29, 1863). *The Southern Illustrated News* (fall 1862) became the most popular periodical in the wartime South.

66. Thomas, *The Confederate State of Richmond*, 30.

67. Andrews, "The Confederate Press," 464, n. 78.

68. Andrews, "The Confederate Press," 463, n. 77.

69. For one account of this borrowing, see Jones, *A Rebel War Clerk's Diary*, 161.

70. Extracts from other papers occasionally appeared with editorial comment, but often the point of the news item, in the context of the editorial opinion established by the *Dispatch*, was clear enough. Small items about Catholics passing the collection plate to fund papal militarism, developments within Mormonism, or bizarre acts by spiri-

tualists, for example, did not require editorial disapproval to make their point. At other times, the paper would make its obvious opinion more explicit, as when it took an extra dig at Puritans within a discussion of the merry rites of Christmas.

71. On May 15, 1860, for example, the paper devoted a paragraph to the YMCA's annual meeting in New Orleans, but much more space right above it was filled with the results of local horse races.

72. When a "Daily Union Prayer meeting" in the spring of 1860 started to draw significant numbers, coverage in the *Dispatch* grew from a short notice to a five-paragraph description of what went on; when attendance dwindled, so did coverage. Parish revivals usually merited a short formulaic announcement: "A religious revival has commenced in Sydney Methodist Church, and much interest in regard to it is manifested in this community"; *Dispatch*, March 31, 1860. The *Dispatch* even noted the success of a Roman Catholic parish mission conducted by the Redemptionist Brothers who, with 2,000 communicants, doubled the number from their last visit to Richmond (November 13, 1860).

73. The *Dispatch* only advocated secession after what historian Emory Thomas, in *The Confederate State of Richmond*, described as a tortuous editorial monologue from summer 1860 to January 1861.

74. See Harrison A. Trexler, "The Davis Administration and the Richmond Press, 1861–1865," *Journal of Southern History* 16 (May 1950): 190.

75. Trexler, "Davis Administration," 178.

76. *Dispatch*, January 4, 1861.

77. *Dispatch*, January 5, 1861; see also January 7, 1861.

78. *Dispatch*, January 12, 1861; November 16, 1861; November 20, 1861.

79. *Dispatch*, September 17 and 18, 1862.

80. *Enquirer*, December 18, 1860.

81. *Enquirer*, January 14, 1861.

82. For the fast day of March 27, 1863, for example, the paper ran an editorial about taxation and reprinted what it called a mocking and facetious story from the *New York Tribune* that criticized President Davis's calls for fasts. Preoccupied with discussions about the new Confederate tax laws, the *Enquirer* carried little beyond Davis's proclamations until April 11, 1864. In that issue appeared a sardonic description of the fast-day assembly in the Richmond Theater. "Catholic, Protestant, and Jew [were] mixed up together in a great hurly-burly of pious contradictions." Gentlemen and ladies who had never been in such an ungodly place scrambled for the best seats in the luxurious surroundings. The local ministers, the *Enquirer* noted, had never been able to draw such a crowd—a fact that "does not speak very much in favor of the church, in competition with the theater as a point of attraction."

83. *Enquirer*, June 4, 1864. This is the only mention of the Puritan-Cavalier theme we came across in the *Enquirer*.

84. *Enquirer*, August 18, 1863.

85. *Examiner*, March 29, 1860.

86. *Examiner*, February 14, 19, 20, 1862.

87. *Examiner*, July 16, 1861.

88. See George H. Gibson, "The Unitarian-Universalist Church of Richmond," *Virginia Magazine of History and Biography* 74 (1966): 321–335.

89. *Examiner*, February 17, 1862.

90. *Examiner*, February 18, 1862.

91. *Examiner*, September 5, 1862.

92. Kimball, *Starve or Fall*, 144.

93. Ibid., 131.

94. On increasing class tensions that would continue into the New South, see, e.g., Paul D. Escott, "The Failure of Confederate Nationalism: The Old South's Class System in the Crucible of War," in *The Old South in the Crucible of War*, eds. Harry P. Owens and James J. Cooke (Jackson, MI, 1983), 15–28; Lawrence N. Powell and Michael S. Wayne, "Self-Interest and the Decline of Confederate Nationalism," in ibid., 29–45; or Stanley Lebergott, "Why the South Lost: Commercial Purpose in the Confederacy, 1861–1865," *Journal of American History* 70 (1983–84): 58–74.

95. This does not mean, however, that political news sheets critical of Davis were also critical of the rich. *Examiner*, for example, ridiculed the "rioters" in the bread riots and suggested they be shot on the spot. In this sense, the poor had no vehicle to express their grievances other than oral demonstration and desertion.

96. Jones, *Rebel War Clerk's Diary*, 128. On widespread anti-Semitism, see Chesson, *Richmond After the War*, 52.

97. Jones *Rebel War Clerk's Diary*, 285.

98. *Examiner*, August 24, 1863.

99. Jones, *Rebel War Clerk's Diary*, 104.

100. In this sense, we diverge from notions of a monolithic jeremiad and speak instead of reconciling strains that are ultimately unreconcilable, but that do not automatically issue in social conflict.

101. *Daily Whig*, February 26, 1862.

102. *Examiner*, May 19, 1862.

103. *Examiner*, May 19, 1862, quoted in Thomas, *Confederate State of Richmond*, 184.

104. *Examiner*, May 5, 1865.

105. *Examiner*, April 12, 1865.

106. *Examiner*, April 26, 1861.

107. *Examiner*, March 4, 1863.

108. *Examiner*, July 21, 1863.

109. *Examiner*, May 19, 1862.

110. Trexler, "Davis Administration," 185; Cutler, "The Confederate Press," 455. Emory Thomas considered it "almost irrational" in its opposition to the Davis administration, *Confederate State of Richmond*, 17. Pollard wrote histories of the war as it progressed, and Daniel's writings were collected in *The Richmond Examiner During the War; or, The Writings of John Moncure Daniel* (New York, 1868). The city's fourth major daily at the time of secession, *The Richmond Daily Whig*, under Robert Ridgeway, supported the Constitutional Union ticket and said secession was illegal. Ridgeway was forced to resign in 1861, even though the paper was more in line with popular sentiment by then, and a former editor named Moseley came out of retirement to replace him.

111. Thomas, *Confederate State of Richmond*, 142.

112. Jones, *Rebel War Clerk's Diary*, 300.

113. *Dispatch*, March 14, 1860, September 11, 1861, November 15, 1861, December 25, 1861, May 28, 1862, October 4, 1862, December 12, 1862, February 7, 1863, March 23, 1863, May 1, 1863, July 29, 1863, September 14, 1863, December 25, 1863, July 13, 1864.

114. *Dispatch*, April 10, 1861.

115. *Dispatch*, February 23, 1863. Puritan fathers like Shepard and Cotton Mather, the paper argued, not only inherited the intolerance of their age but were intolerant on principle, with Roger Williams as the lone exception. See also *Dispatch*, January 16, 1863, on Grant's purported expulsion of Jews from his department as "all in keeping

with the professed religious toleration of the puritans"; and October 4, 1864, on Puritan intolerance and fanaticism at the root of the Know-Nothing party.

116. *Dispatch*, December 31, 1860; January 1, 1861; March 7, 1861.

117. *Dispatch*, May 19, 1861.

118. *Dispatch*, May 2, 1861, January 18, 1862.

119. *Dispatch*, May 29, 1862, October 27, 1862.

120. *Dispatch*, January 7, 1860.

121. *Dispatch*, May 17, 1860. The paper also criticized the northern press's habit of "puffing and publishing prayers" as "not in the best possible taste, nor exactly in accordance with the common idea of religious reverence."

122. *Dispatch*, May 25, 1860.

123. *Dispatch*, July 29, 1864.

124. *Dispatch*, November 16, 1860.

125. *Dispatch*, September 28, 1860, July 3, 1862.

126. *Dispatch*, December 12, 1862, August 10, 1863, January 28, 1864. The *Dispatch* discouraged a preoccupation with biblical prophecies on July 18, 1861.

127. *Dispatch*, November 4, 1862. See also August 10, 1863.

128. *Enquirer*, July 13, 1863, April 11, 1864, June 4, 1864.

129. *Whig*, August 20, 1863.

130. *Whig*, July 10, 1863.

131. *Whig*, August 21, 1863.

132. *Examiner*, May 19, 1862.

133. *Examiner*, August 6, 1863.

134. *Examiner*, August 24, 1863.

135. Ibid.

136. *Examiner*, August 24, 1863.

137. *Examiner*, July 2, 1861. This theme is amplified in James M. McPherson, "Antebellum Southern Exceptionalism: A New Look at an Old Question," *Civil War History* 29 (1983): 230–244.

138. *Examiner*, July 17, 1861.

139. Jones, *Rebel War Clerk's Diary*, 388–389.

140. Jones, *Rebel War Clerk's Diary*, 390.

141. John Lansing Burrows, *The New Richmond Theater. A Discourse Delivered on Sunday, Feb. 8, 1863, in the First Baptist Church, Richmond, Virginia* (Richmond, 1863).

142. Leroy M. Lee, *Our Country—Our Dangers—Our Duty. A Discourse preached in Centenary Church, Lynchburg, Virginia, on the National Fast Day, August 21, 1863* (Richmond, 1863), 13, 21.

143. P. Slaughter, *Coercion and Conciliation. A Sermon Preached in Camp, at Centerville, Virginia, by the Rev. P. Slaughter, Chaplain of the 19th Regiment Virginia Volunteers, Condensed, by Request, into a Tract for the Times* (Richmond, 186–), 7.

144. *Central Presbyterian*, March 19, 1863.

145. D. S. Doggett, *A Discourse Delivered in the Broad Street Methodist Church, Richmond, Virginia, Thursday, September 18, 1862* (Richmond, 1862); Doggett, *The War and Its Close. A Discourse Delivered in Centenary Church, Richmond, Virginia, Friday April 8th, 1864* (Richmond, 1864).

146. *Central Presbyterian*, June 2, 1864. On the "silent revival" brought about by print rather than preaching, see Beth Barton Schweiger, "The Transformation of Southern Religion: Clergy and Congregations in Virginia, 1830–1895," Ph.D. dissertation, University of Virginia, 1994, 228.

147. *Central Presbyterian*, June 11, 1863. From Gettysburg and the surrender of

Vicksburg on, virtually every issue of every newspaper made at least one reference to revivals in the army.

148. Quoted in Herman Norton, "Revivalism in the Confederate Armies," *Civil War History* 6 (1960): 422.

149. *Dispatch*, March 10, 1865.

150. *Central Presbyterian*, March 16, 1865; *Religious Herald*, March 9, 1865.

151. Quoted in A. A. Hoehling and Mary Hoehling, *The Day Richmond Died* (Lanham, MD, 1981), 108.

152. Wilson, *Baptized in Blood*, 1.

153. See Heyrman, *Southern Cross*.

154. Wilson, *Baptized in Blood*, 8.

155. On James Gambrell, see Eugene C. Routh, *The Life of Dr. J. B. Gambrell* (Oklahoma City, 1929). On J. William Jones, see Wilson, *Baptized in Blood*, chap. 6; and on Robert Dabney, see Wilson, "Robert Lewis Dabney," 179–189.

15

Religion and the Results of the Civil War

SAMUEL S. HILL

In 1843, in western New York State, the Wesleyan Methodist Connection of America called itself into being. The provocation was its founding members' disagreements with the Methodist Episcopal church to which they had belonged. One issue was the power and authority of the episcopacy; the new body proceeded at once to designate its leader as president, not bishop.

The more dramatic incentive for their departure was abolitionism. Not that the large parent body sanctioned slavery; rather the M. E. Church was pursuing a gradual, noninterventionist strategy toward freeing the people and dismantling the institution. The Methodists who formed the Connection were caught up in the radical policy of immediate abolition, without regard to what practical disruptions might ensue.

A report of schismatic church behavior in antebellum America hardly startles us (especially in upstate New York).[1] The question for highlighting now and treating later is: What was the impact of the Civil War on this come-outer band of radical Methodists? Accordingly, the hypothesis of this paper is that the war led to a great many more, and more complex, changes than abolition and emancipation. Indeed, it wrought changes as dramatic as the churches' agendas, their sense of their missions; when that happens, the changes are basic, perhaps radical. In this one, apparently easy-to-read setting, what impact did the Civil War make? Or, turning the issue another way, we ask: was such a religious group's forthright behavior before the war matched by comparable behavior after it?

The North Carolina Friends, or Quakers—stalwart abolitionists in the antebellum South—had seen their ranks, never very large, diminished by the migration of many to the free states of Ohio and Indiana. But their company maintained a notable presence in Guilford, Alamance, and Randolph Counties. Having chosen to stay at home and having witnessed a kind of pyhrric victory, they now had to make out their lives in Reconstructioned and Redeemered neighborhoods where segregation bore unmistakable continuities with slavery.

The hypothesis just mentioned, *mutatis mutandis*, applies here too: did the war lead to changes in spirit and policy that bespoke an impact they hardly would have anticipated? A fair number switched to the Methodist denomination. Is there any possibility that radical changes in the southern society of which they were a part took some new shapes in the thinking of these brave abolitionists? That is, this observation needs to be added to the standard explanation that the evangelical fervor was too exciting and popular for the Quietists to resist.

Long before Ken Burns's public television series on the Civil War, the American populace knew something about that conflict and its ravages—perhaps even that it was the only war fought on the soil of the American republic in the past 184 years. What consequences that war had for the religious life of the American people of both sections is less well known, even to students of later nineteenth-century history.

The first part of this essay launches this exploration by recollecting some familiar and quite significant consequences of the war, from indirect to direct ones. The second part seeks to place developments of this period in the setting of American religious history. We will do so by reflecting on such questions as these: (1) What issues in Americans' religious or spiritual life had been settled, laid to rest before the 1860s? (2) What had religious people and organizations been dealing with that persisted, that overlapped the war years? (3) What new issues and problems appeared in the last third of the century, for which previous experience had left them unprepared?

The third part sharpens the focus by examining the two abolitionist denominations referred to at the beginning of this essay. Looking at them—one northern, the other southern—we wrestle with what became of church communities that owed their *raison d'être*, to greater or large degree, to the cause of abolishing slavery, once abolition had occurred. When a major animus was removed, when success had been achieved, how did they respond?

Consequences of the War

We open by noting some indirect consequences of the war. An intriguing one that falls under the political/spiritual category rather than the religious/spiritual category has to do with Robin Winks's interpretation of the timing of the Canadian Federation in 1867. Reflecting on the strife recently befallen their still-young neighbor to the south, Canadians came to terms with some of the disadvantages of the United States confederation, less a united whole than a congeries of states. Partly inspired by our history to reconsider their own national destiny, the provinces, so severely elongated and diverse, set to work to accomplish their first federating.[2]

Back on this side of the border, a spirit or sentiment utterly unintended by the war's provocateurs, and hardly predictable by anyone, arose in the 1880s and 1890s. This quality was one dimension of what George Fredrickson has called "the inner Civil War."[3] "Inner" locates its terrain—*within* the human psyche, spirit, mentality; its traits were passion, courage, resolution to endure, action. It realized its embodiment in the strenuous life, with Theodore Roosevelt as legendary exemplar. The age's master explorer was, of course, William James, who mapped out the working category, "The Moral Equivalent of War." But the principal spokesman was Oliver Wendell Holmes Jr., who provided the keynote: "Life is a profound and passionate thing." The particular event-setting for such a claim—Memorial Day addresses in 1884 and 1895—is arresting. Nearby Harvard Stadium was as vital a locus as Holmes's podium. Football—also lacrosse, hockey, and baseball—was coming into its own as intercollegiate athletics strode onto the American popular scene.

Action, ardor, the strenuous life, resolution to endure, courage—Fredrickson views these spiritual developments as a "nonideological interpretation of the Civil War" and contends that the Civil War had channeled this element into the stream of American sensibility. One source of it was the residual vitality that had generated abolitionism in the early life of major figures of the time—Holmes, Moncure Conway, Mrs. Josephine Shaw Lowell, and Charles F. Adams Jr. Now new outlets had to be found for uplift, citizenship, and humanitarian activism of various sorts. "The Inner Civil War" took no prisoners as it energized a maturing, bumptious society during a vibrant era.[4] A great deal was happening, after all; modern psychology was born, American imperialism expanded, the athletic field became a shrine, and utopian social visions grew apace. Almost, but not exactly a direct legacy of the war, nor precisely religious, was this transference of militancy to the inner life; but real and spiritual it was, just the same. To my knowledge, no comparable strenuosity of spirit emerged in the South. But the question deserves pursuit, perhaps by probing the élan of the New South promoters.

Drawing closer to direct and religious/spiritual consequences of the war, we come upon the religion of the Lost Cause—a phenomenon of the South, of course, a concept and historical reality placed in the public domain by the work of Charles Reagan Wilson.[5] The war was over, the short-lived Confederacy had given way to the restored national government, and life took on some normal hues in a kaleidoscope of vexing conditions and limitations. But in the southern heart, mind, and spirit, the past was not dead, nor the region-become-section blotted out. Moreover, there were veterans about, and cemeteries filled with the fallen; from 1866 on, they were brightened with flowers on one or another Memorial Day. There continues to be power in the interpretation that the Civil War and its aftermath gave birth to the South.

These stirrings in the southern soul attained transcendent status.[6] The cause was lost at one level, but it was grand and triumphant deeper down. Politically, the determination that the old way of life be perpetuated issued in segregation replacing slavery, with the Democratic party becoming the only game in town and a new bourgeoisie fulfilling the old vision of a social hierarchy. Dynamically, the identity of a people and their social arrangements, which both had been and never had been, were recast.

This historical creativity resulted in some kind of religion—"civil religion" will have to do. It manifested itself in classic religious categories—creed, code, cult, and community (formulated by Joachim Wach). *Creed*: There were beliefs and convictions about truth, what is real, good, and lasting. *Code*: There was a pattern of conduct exhibited by men and women of the Old South and the heroes and heroines of the war years that bore repetition in postwar society as people of strong convictions practiced honor, good manners, neighborliness, simple virtues, and a hold on memory, memory seen as a moral question, not merely a heritage.

Cult: Meaning both personal and public reverence for the everlasting South and its heritage, this took concrete form as monuments and statues, also as seasonal celebrations, with flags and uniforms serving as symbols. *Community*: This category bulked as significant as the other religious dimensions. Southerners were one people; they knew who they were, in large part because they knew where they had come from. Even the former slaves, now segregated free people, had a place. Their participation in the social order was as vital and distinguishing to regional identity as any single aspect.

Curiously, from the outside at any rate, native African Americans appeared to be more at home than immigrating Euro-Americans who were Caucasoid. Perhaps the latter would have found, or established, a welcome had larger numbers actually moved in and settled. But such kinds of people, even when middle class and Protestant, had not been part of the pre–Civil War South, thus could not figure prominently after the war. Those immigrants who did come and stay had either to accommodate to a specialized role or to assimilate as rapidly and fully as possible.

Wilson and the others who have traced the lineaments of the mythic South—the society's civil religion—have helpfully highlighted the public displays of that phenomenon. Here I only hope to add a little phenomenology of religion analysis to strengthen awareness of its implications.

If space is permitted, we ought to draw parallels between the South's civil religion and the quasi-religious character of the Grand Army of the Republic (G.A.R.) from 1865 to 1900. Anyone who makes that comparison draws on the presentation in Stuart McConnell's work, *Glorious Contentment: The Grand Army of the Republic, 1865–1900*. One infers that the G.A.R. perceived a transcendent dimension *in its own organized life*. But it does not seem to have assumed the task of symbolizing regional, or national, societal culture, as the Lost Cause did in the South. Cult (a semblance of worship) was there to the point of an altar in the post rooms; so was the code of personal honor, character, and manliness. Publicly, morality played out in various relief activities for members and other Americans. But the impact of the G.A.R. was more limited than the celebration of the Lost Cause as a spiritual force, which occurred in the nation's only truly mythic, history-defined region.[7]

The direct consequences of the Civil War on America's spiritual and religious life now claim our attention. We note at once that the South received more of this impact than the eastern and midwestern states. Two facts of the South's experience go far toward accounting for this. First, the war was fought on southern soil. The physical destruction and comprehensive social disruption of even the most ordinary activities and relationships were, in a word, vast. Second, the freed men and women were residents of the South. They were catapulted into an independence that nothing in their experience—or that of their white neighbors, masters, and owners—had equipped them. Life as they had known it had ended. The brunt of physical and material ravages fell on the white southerners, for obvious reasons. Yet they were in a better position to make adjustments. Ironically, the black population lost a framework for carrying out life. But saying that hardly exhausts the conditions or, in particular, tells how the people met them. There are many stories of phenomenal courage and resourcefulness. No dimension of African-American society reveals those qualities as clearly as the people's religious/spiritual life.

It is a truism that southern black people participated in few public activities and agencies during the long season of slavery. Further, limitations on such participation had increased, imposed on them whether they were leaders or followers by a justifiably extra-cautious white society. Not in business, not in government, only a little in voluntary societies had enslaved or free black people learned much about forming or guiding social institutions.[8] They knew the most by far about church life, although their knowledge was less organizational than theological.[9] With respect to creating organizations, they learned to form their own because whatever they had, they had formed for themselves. This included their churches for the most part, although, as we will soon see, they received some assistance from northern black churches, which sent ministers and teachers.

Southern black people continued their Christian devotion, now with an added incentive: the celebration of their freedom and the ventilating of their gratitude. Had emancipation occurred three or four decades earlier, the religious factor would have been less significant, it is important to note. The number of Christians in the slave sector grew rapidly in the late slavery period, and faith achieved a formative power in the slaves' lives. It is worth noting that in the 1790s, the number of black Methodists was 12,000, of black Baptists was 13,000—and of course small numbers belonged to other bodies, Catholic, Friends, and Presbyterian, for example. At the end of the antebellum period, the aggregate membership figures stood at 400,000. The 1900 ratio of church members to the total black population is stunning: 2.7 million members out of a total of 8.3 million black people—and there were many more unaffiliated believers.[10] These churches were overwhelmingly the products of freed men and women's faith capacity for a kind of in-service training—that is, learning to organize by organizing. Unaffiliated believers made up a sizable portion of the black population, undoubtedly. Secularism had not invaded the African-American community to any notable degree.[11]

Church meetings cropped up everywhere, in existing all-black congregations, of course. The dramatic new condition is captured in William Montgomery's matter-of-fact explanation: "thousands of blacks began organizing their own autonomous congregations." He continues, "The months that followed emancipation marked the beginning of an exciting new era for the black church, a time during which it began to mature and to take on new forms and functions."[12]

The supposition that biracial churches had disappeared would be nearly 100 percent accurate. Now freed people could preach, sing, shout, pray, and fellowship in their own company. The elements of their service had acquired a distinct African-American character. For the first time in decades, no one else would be in the building or under the arbor, either to take orders from or be wary of. Fellowship was just as important as worship style. The people needed each other for laughing, talking, sharing, and planning—for caring for one another during a cataclysmic period. They relished being "under their own vine and fig tree," a phrase borrowed from Micah 4 in their beloved Old Testament.

Black Baptists and Methodists did not just get together, however; they built something together—church buildings and church organizations. Fine and refined by Euro-American standards these hardly were, but these were theirs and they were constructed to last. From the first, the disposition was to join with other black Christians of like order. I believe most stories have yet to be told of how a congregation knew about an emerging "denomination" so as to be able to affiliate with it or precisely why a group would link up with one Methodist body rather than another. The idea of sheer local independence seems to have had few takers.[13] Join Methodist and Baptist bodies they did, along the lines that distinguished the two institutional systems.

We have many testimonies from the immediate postwar South to indicate the place was teeming with Yankees. And for good reason. Among these Yankees were teachers, social workers, and ministers from the two "African Methodist" bodies that had originated in 1816 and 1821, respectively, in the Philadelphia and New York areas. (Their roots traced back to the 1790s.) Actually, some of them came to the war-torn communities before the war had ended. The older AME body trailed only a little behind, initially and most specifically in North Carolina.[14] But after April 1865, the missionary ranks swelled and northern Methodists were making colleagues of brothers and sisters in the region. Some of the advance guard, by the way, had been born in the South, a few into slavery. Both of these northern groups were more attractive to the freed men and women than the Methodist Episcopal church, which was also reaching out, although the latter did meet with some success, being both well financed and well organized. The final act in the Methodist drama was the formation of an indigenous body, the Colored Methodist Episcopal church (CME), in 1870. These Christians had been members of the Methodist Episcopal Church, South, and believed they had been deeded the property of their churches. But that was an erroneous impression, partly fostered by a regional, white-led denomination that judged it wisest to retain control over its black membership. Anyway, comparatively amicably, the CME was born.[15]

The two mostly northern bodies assisted in bringing about much that self-supporting southern churches would have had difficulty doing on their own. They helped construct church buildings, formulate Sunday school programs, educate ministers, and train lay people in basic skills (also trades and farming), and alerted them to mission causes at home and abroad. "Modernization" in this pertinent form was arriving in southern black churches.[16]

Baptist organizational advance, if anything more effective than the Methodist, occurred more gradually and largely from a native base. A northern agency, the American Baptist Home Mission Society, dispatched personnel to work with southern Negroes as early as 1862, but the work was not strong for long after the war's end.[17] The launching pad for vigorous growth of black Baptist efforts and membership in the postbellum South was the antebellum South. Then and there, white Baptist numbers had swelled phenomenally and Baptist features came to represent Christianity for a great many people. The slaves, too, had found Baptist theology, polity, and worship to their liking. Both because they responded and because the white Baptists were active in offering them churchmanship, slaves had flocked to the Baptist services and beliefs. Emancipation then gave them the opportunity to continue being what many of them were, this time on their own terms and claiming their own destiny.

The National Baptist Convention was organized in 1895, the culmination of a thirty-year movement toward black Baptist cooperative self-government. It stood, in James M. Washington's words, as "the seeming end of a painful quest." Efforts toward its ultimate realization were numerous, if a bit sporadic, in the East and Midwest as well as the South. Thus, the Atlanta conference of 1895 did indeed coordinate concerns and recognize institutional developments that had been in progress for a long time. Now black Baptists would sponsor their own missionary societies, Sunday school programs, publishing enterprises, and schools and colleges.[18] Here, too, "modernization" had come, in ways and patterns pertinent to that black population and their institutions at the time.

All things considered, the formation of independent black congregations and denominations—meaning black religious self-determination—proved to be the most profound religious change brought on by the Civil War. But there were other direct points of impact, too. For example, the devastation of religious institutions and properties in the white South, so well known, needs brief mention here.

The destruction of southern church buildings was severe and general. Historian W. Harrison Daniel has described the lengths to which federal forces sometimes went to establish their superiority and show their contempt for the rebellious society, often "to a degree far exceeding military necessity." They wrought "desecration and damage of property." "Church buildings, equipment, records, and parsonages were often attacked and destroyed." Desecration extended even to playing "lewd songs on the church organs," dancing in the buildings, and stealing silver communion services.[19]

Church finances were profoundly disrupted by the destruction. Inflation ate up the value of the limited funds there were. The costs of rebuilding and restoring seemed astronomical to these decimated congregations. Ministers' salaries were often either reduced or not paid at all. Denominational newspapers, such a vital part of church leaders' lives, were issued irregularly and in smaller size owing to a shortage and the high cost of materials.

Colleges and seminaries, always requiring so much funding, suffered drastically. Some schools simply closed, never to reopen. Others, their endowments invested in Confederate securities, lost a large percentage of their assets and hobbled on prosthetics for decades. Similarly, missionary activities underwent drastic curtailment.

In summarizing these effects of the Civil War on religious communities, we note a predictable but less obvious effect—namely, the impact of these impoverished conditions on the spirit of the people and their churches. "The social instability of a people at war, the absence of clergymen, the scattered nature of many congregations, the destruction wrought by the invaders, and a preoccupation with matters of war had a debilitating influence upon the church," as Daniel has summarized the devastation.[20]

A final, direct impact of the war on the churches concerns the role of women. Scarcely a sentence in this essay has failed to pertain to women and men as members of churches. But hardly a word has been directed to their participation and the changes in their roles.

We begin to overcome this silence by means of a graphic paragraph from Marjorie Spruill Wheeler's, *The New Women of the New South*:

> During the Civil War, southern women were called upon to perform many tasks normally fulfilled by men, including meeting the needs of soldiers through soldiers' aid societies, managing plantations, mills, and stores in the absence of men, and in many instances 'refugeeing' whole families—finding food and clothing for them where there was little to be found.
>
> After the War, southern women rebuilt or aided husbands in building plantations, and often taught school or took in sewing to generate badly needed income. Many women had to support themselves or their families alone. Of the million men who served in the Confederate Army, at least one-fourth died in battle or of disease, and many more were incapacitated and unable to support their families.[21]

By the 1880s and 1890s, so much was new for southern women of the white middle classes, notably new occupational options, new public school systems with new normal schools for training teachers, new southern colleges for women, and a new leisure that permitted volunteer work. Another item on that list was women's clubs, which as they cleared their own paths helped lead to suffrage activities. Among the areas that these clubs gradually enlarged were church missionary societies, the Woman's Christian Temperance Union, and a variety of social service reform agencies, many based in church life. Their achievements in these regards are impressive. Some women went as missionaries to China, India, and Africa, whether single or with their husbands. Most women made their mark in churches at home, where, in order to create and keep viable societies, they frequently took on the pastor, the all-male ruling board, and even other women.[22]

Many years were to pass before white southern women sat around the table for meetings of deacons, elders, the session, the council, or the vestry, even more before they presided or celebrated at The Table after heralding from the pulpit. But the late decades of the nineteenth century witnessed some breakthroughs. Led by Methodists, southern church women became a conspicuous presence, not simply mainstays or workers behind the scenes. They served in church buildings and agencies, with correspondence and contributions dispatched to Atlanta, Richmond, or Nashville and even as far away as the Chinese provinces. Beyond all this, they were on the streets, by the docks, in the prisons, in the black neighborhoods, and gradually at court houses and state capitals.[23]

The northern story of women's changing roles is better known to us, partly because it was more nationally productive. We take nothing away from women in the eastern, midwestern, and western states, but they struggled against weaker obstacles. Their colleagues had tackled these tasks earlier, and it still was not easy. There they were, laying it on the line in behalf of prohibition, suffrage, and myriad Social Gospel causes. They were also fomenting the Holiness movement and founding new denominations. We ought to raise a toast to such women as Phoebe Palmer, Mary Baker Eddy, and Ellen Gould White. (But I doubt if they would have approved of the toasting ritual or enjoyed each other's company.)

Black church women drew up some of the same agenda as their white counterparts. Some items, like suffrage, were hardly within their purview. They attained more leadership positions within congregations, positions difficult to deny them in view of their major, if not always official leadership for decades. From W. E. B. Du Bois to Evelyn Brooks Higginbotham, members of the American black community have insisted that we understand this fact of history. The range of these black women's involvements and accomplishments is staggering. Feeding and clothing the poor, starting and supporting schools, carrying on overseas mission work, combating racism, expanding civil rights such as voting and gaining employment—these efforts belong high on a list that is even longer. Black women in churches throughout the South, of course, and north to New Jersey and New York and out to the Midwest, were raising themselves by dint of their own dedication and lifting others in the process.[24]

American Religious History as the Setting

What were the results of the Civil War on the religious life of citizens in both regions? How do developments in this era fit the flow of American religious history? What vital concerns and issues of the pre-Civil War decades—and perhaps back even to the colonial period—had been dealt with, largely been settled, laid to rest, or were no longer pertinent? What issues and concerns had been confronted but still persisted? What were the new issues for which the churches lacked sufficient precedent to resolve? Finally, what links these daunting challenges to the war—what are the cause-effect relations or antecedent-subsequent factors?

The impetus for social reform is an appropriate place to begin. Nearly sixty years ago, Richard Niebuhr, in *The Kingdom of God in America*, termed the nineteenth century the "Kingdom of Christ."[25] This was the season following early America's quasi-theocracy, when the vision of a Christian civilization held but now had to be worked on. No longer were magistrates the "nursing fathers," no longer were church and state commissioned partners in realizing that vision. The new, problem-strewn *modus operandi* was voluntarism. Traces of the old expectations endured, of course, but now society had to be made Christian rather than merely fulfilling the goal that legally and structurally was meant to guarantee its occurrence. American society was less often in line with the divine mandates for a godly nation. Deprivations and disorders were everywhere. God's new American people were confronting chaos much as ancient Israel had known (and helped create).

But Americans knew better than to fail, and so they sought more authenticity. Reform movements emerged at an incredible pace and included Sunday schools, prison ministries, hospitals and clinics, and eleemosynary institutions, as well as attempts to ameliorate labor conditions, cleanse politics of corruption, provide special care for females, encourage temperance, and peacefully resolve conflicts. Of great concern to many was the condition of the slaves in the American states (the southern states only after the 1830s). But that expression of concern for the slaves knew no regional or sectional boundaries. Southerners worked to prevent abuse, to live up to "contract" with human chattel, and to provide literacy and religious instruction. Northern citizens (and some southern) laid ties for the Underground Railroad, offered protection for fleeing slaves, and cast votes for abolition, even sought to set up schools and health care for African-American people nearby and, especially, miles to the south.

Residents of both regions sought to save the trans-Appalachian civilization from such hostile forces as skepticism, foreign religious domination, and chaos. America fought to combat incursions into the Protestant destiny of the "nation with the soul of a church" and to do so at all points of the compass, on issues great and small, local and national.

Did the Civil War and the conditions surrounding it alter that devotion to social reform? No, except in detail and even then, not drastically. Americans remained "do-gooders," builders of a benevolent way of living, fixers of things gone wrong in an increasingly heterogeneous and complex society. They witnessed human misery and injustice, as well as threats to traditional ways of personal and cultural living, and worked to deal with them. The Protestants were in the forefront, naturally, though now they were joined by numerous Catholic "charities" and some Jewish social services.

The Social Gospel movement, which attracts our initial notice, was decidedly a Protestant vision and mission. More precisely, it was largely a spirit and agenda prevailing in the traditional Anglo-northern denominations—Methodist, Congregational, Presbyterian, Baptist, and Episcopal. The people of these churches knew either first-hand or through a progressive leadership that people were often shockingly destitute. In exploding urban populations, under novel workplace and conditions, and among people who had neither knowledge nor know-how for this strange new world—not all of them foreign-born, either—people with gnawing needs cried out. It was clear that the God of the Bible cared about human bodies as well as souls, about people in their context as well as within themselves or in the family framework.[26]

The churches thus were constrained to revise their theologies—but not so much, really, since among these Christian legions, revival and renewal had burst forth in the decade before the war, nor were they brand-new then. Things had changed—really worsened—but the impetus for dealing with human tragedy and need simply carried over. In any event, theologies did shift somewhat. The line of thinking moved from the individual outward to society. This was consistent with the church's practice of a spiritual life that incorporated forgiveness received and salvation known, and was expressed in dedicated actions. In its revised interpretation, society took on an ontological life of its own: society would be redeemed by redeemed persons.

Among Methodists, the perspectives in both northern and southern white bodies responded to these new societal conditions. In the South, the "type of piety that prevailed" only intensified the evangelical patterns, guiding them to mind the churches' own business, in heart and soul. Accordingly, southern Methodists accused their northern coreligionists of becoming a political body. The Methodist Episcopal church assumed responsibility for renovating the moral life of society and civilizing this Protestant-oriented nation. It embarked on a quest for a Christian America.[27] But admirable as were the efforts begun at Cape May in 1876 to reunite white Methodists, diverging positions rendered that quest impossible.

A two-party system within the Protestant community was emerging but had not yet developed into separate, ranked categories. That change was to take shape in the postwar period, in the more sectarian spirit of a newly emerging evangelical party of Protestants. The latter's disposition was to divide life into "private" and "public," and to domesticate the spiritual life in the private. Hitherto, *evangelical* had been a little-used term—in truth, nearly redundant. In the prewar decades, the distinction had to do with the supernaturalists, the Protestant denominations, versus the proto-naturalists, the deists, and the later Unitarians and the Universalists.[28]

Later-century developments required such classification, however. New social conditions overwhelmed both the private and the public, demanding a response—one "checked out," the other "caved in," so to speak. The private life hewed to a strictly supernaturalistic agenda, the public life took its cues from the industrial, demographic, and intellectual stage onto which America was stepping.

What did the Civil War have to do with this division? I, for one, am not entirely sure. Nor do I know of research undertaken that would move past the *post hoc ergo propter hoc* level of understanding. But some new American thinking was appearing, and one can scarcely avoid the suspicion that the war—its corrosive power, its carnage, and its calamitous effects—contributed to that thinking. Those who undertake research in this period with an eye toward religious/spiritual issues are encouraged to learn what the war's consequences were.

One major continuity between the Civil War and the social-reform philosophies of the generation that followed does suggest itself rather forcefully. Simply, it is the exposure to destruction. Southern people saw it materially, and experienced it emotionally, with a depth still bearing consequences a century and a third later. Convulsion reigned. Citizens of the northern states lost family members to war—some 360,000 of them (58 percent of the war's casualties)—not to mention the thousands who came home maimed in body or spirit. The war represented a horrendous national loss and was such a distressful waste. Church people could not escape a response to destruction of this magnitude. Some—the new evangelical party—divined the need for human redemption, one convert at a time. Nothing short of the supernaturalization of humankind, flowing from each soul to a society regarded more as atomized than as collectivized, could call down God's forgiving and healing and prevent a recurrence of such destruction.

Others—the Social Gospel–inclined interpreters—heeded a call to redeem existing structures and infrastructures. Theirs was the direct approach; in so envisioning, they could draw upon America's Puritan heritage to the crusade for a "Christian America." In any event, the convulsive destruction wrought by the war demanded a policy of some description. The two philosophies were worthy responses, both insistent and dedicated. America's religious life had generated social reform long before the Civil War, and it continued to do so after the war with a fervor somewhat redirected but still passionate.

A second set of concerns and issues involves spiritual revitalization. The student of American religious/spiritual history could almost build the case that that history congeals around renewal and revival, both locally and nationally. We have always been "awash in a sea of faith," in Jon Butler's choice description.[29] In this precise respect, too, the Civil War changed nothing except perhaps to intensify the heritage. The Second Awakening of the early century was followed by the Charles G. Finney–led and –inspired "early modern" revivals of the second quarter of the century. Finney stirred up sinners inside and outside churches from Boston to Detroit and Cincinnati, and he left a permanent imprint on Oberlin College. Moreover, even though he was a spiritual ancestor of the postwar private party in American Protestantism, he was dedicated to abolition and temperance, among other social-reform causes. Following Finney, the urban revivals of the 1850s continued the American church's propensity for revitalization as a biorhythm.[30]

The postwar years ran true to form. The nation's religious rhythms kept pulsating. "Spasmodic" and "episodic" are descriptions that fit, but they must not be taken to mean artificial and superficial. In a free society where the evangelical heart beats so strong, these periodic renewals are de rigueur and are often healthy. Dwight L. Moody, from Massachusetts and joining those who relocated to an urban context and westward (Chicago in his case), spearheaded the postwar revivals. Actually, he did so by way of Tennessee battlefields. There he tightened his conviction that personal conversion is the desperate need and the solution to the nation's problems.

Contemporaries looking back at earlier century revitalizations, while caught up in the latest tide of renewal themselves, might aver that nothing had changed. But of course it had. These were saddened and chastened Americans, yet also optimistic and ebullient ones, who acknowledged the need for personal righteousness and a more godly society. "We survived Armageddon," one can almost hear them saying. "Never again will we be party to such hostility and cataclysm." "Spiritual forces must be allowed to prevail." Besides, the Lord had brought the Apocalypse on them to teach them about His ways and will.[31]

Some spiritual energy went into new movements of the Spirit that issued in new Christian denominations. Thus, the state of denominations is the third topic in this section on post–Civil War trends and movements in American religious history. Here, too, little had changed but much was changing. The creation of new denominations was an old American habit. In the first decade of the republic, various groups typically called "Republican" and "Christian" seized the opportunity to follow the political lead with religious formation. But a flurry of new bodies appeared between 1825 and 1860: the Latter-Days Saints, the Adventists, the Methodist Protestants, the Wesleyan Methodist Connection, the Free Methodists, the Southern Methodist Church, the Primitive Baptists, and, of course, the sectional deployments of Presbyterians, Methodists, and Baptists. The national contest over slavery, states' rights, abolition, and tariffs contributed to the rise of several denominations in both inventories. Perhaps the most arresting is the strictly northern Wesleyan Methodist group, mentioned earlier and the subject of treatment in the third part of this essay.

The incentives giving birth to the new bodies were multiple, divided among issues of polity, theology, and regional cultural interests. The nation's soil was fecund with innovation. Liberty was at issue. "New presbyters" were no more acceptable than "old priests." But equally strong was a yearning to hold on to a national culture, only recently developed, that was beginning to mature with its own mores, values, and structures. Revisionist theology also provided impetus for the new bodies. However, the Mormons, the most innovative of the lot, knew their "innovation" to be that only phenomenally; substantively this was the Gospel restored. And the Adventists were only recognizing, not really predicting, what the eternal God had been planning all along.

If anything, the generation after the war witnessed a greater number of new formations. The observer is struck first by the contraction of incentives. In that phase, the impetus was not polity or local cultural conservatism, but theology. The war finally over, it was time for normalcy; for rebuilding family, community, and spiritual life; for attending to moral issues pressing on a national society as new as always. Not least, in the North, the challenge of growing industrial, urban conditions demanded attention. The labor force was enlarging, and both it and its situation were undergoing major changes. Life in the cities and towns, most notably, was nearly unbearable.

These last were the layers of life that called forth creative responses in theology. Church polity concerns receded. Public polity matters were more than enough to fill the society's plate. Cultural conservatism remained, its expressions confined to the South, as we are about to see. Theology was the principal driving force in the new religious movements of the post–Civil War period. In addressing this theme—the rise of new denominations—we arrive at a somewhat distinctive field of answers to our prompting questions: What has been settled? What has been laid to rest, but persists? What is new, a daunting challenge, requiring fresh thinking and acting?

Holiness and Pentecostal movements dominated. Both insisted on the possibility and necessity of a distinct work of grace wrought by the Holy Spirit after conversion. All traditional evangelical Protestants believed in the conversion event, whether a single experience or a change that occurred over a brief period of time. The cultivation of the moral and spiritual was both a gift tendered and a self-discipline to be exacted. The new movements predicated more. Holiness currents had been in evidence from the 1840s, gaining momentum through the 1850s and 1860s—in the North, that is—but then evolving into a formidable force during the rest of the century. Holiness is about moral enduement, a heightened sanctification en route to the "higher Christian life," toward the goal of complete righteousness or "sinless perfection." We need to be clear that Holiness people were clear that such progress is God's gift in a distinct work of grace, not a human achievement that one induces by effort.

Pentecostalism, historically, is an outgrowth of the Holiness movement. What sets it apart is a different, "distinct work of grace," the action of the Spirit evidentially in the gift of tongues. What Holiness and Pentecostalism have in common is the important matter here; the link is the "something more" by contrast with church as usual. Now deep faith is more than conversion; it is openness to a definitive experience that calls, then equips, Christians to soar to a higher plane.

Christian movements deserve the respect of treatment as creative (and in some sense legitimate) expressions, without being accounted for as reactionist. But none, not even gnostic instances, transcends cultural conditions. In these cases, when looking around them, church people saw both the worldliness of the churches and the spiritual poverty of a society facing daunting conditions. Their eyes turned upward, whence came new revelations of the Almighty's power and plan. We need also to confirm general opinion that social class contributed to the new emergences. It did; these were the "disinherited," those left out of churches caught up in upward social mobility and modern organizational development.

Christian Science is better known to students of general American history, owing partly to its social location in the middle and upper classes. The 1870s are also the date of its origins. One can hardly imagine two Christian expressions more different than Christian Science, on the one hand, and Holiness and Pentecostal denominations on the other. But they share the deep level of conviction that God is very near, His power so manifest and accessible. What others regarded as supernatural or miraculous seemed to Mary Baker Eddy and her followers just the way a loving, all-powerful God is and how naturally He incorporates divine power into human frailty to overcome it. Heaven and earth are effectively one to Christian Science thought; the former readily claims its unity with the latter when people see and trust. Classic cosmic dualism is dealt heavy blows by these disparate movements, ontic in one case, epistemic in the other.

Along these lines, new denominational formation characterized American religious life in the postwar period, but in continuation of an old national pattern. Would all this have occurred without the Civil War? Who can say? What this interpreter will contend is that the war assisted the modernization cause toward a greater rationalization of life. Countering that current occasioned their birth, but embracing aspects of modernity proved to be equally attractive to them.

The final feature of our examination of the American religious history issue is the South's response to the impact of the war. That response is singular in American history, religious and otherwise, and is seen quite clearly in its religious life. A region became a culture, constructively and defensively, creatively and reactively, although it was denied the luxury of being oblivious to participation in a wider world.

Starting with the most empirical, we note the denominational scene. The large white bodies maintained their great size and cultural dominance. In fact, both strengthened in the late century. Presbyterians were third in numbers, but they had great power in leadership throughout the society, owing to their high educational and financial rank. Baptists were everywhere, with as impressive urban churches as rural and with seemingly undifferentiated representation in shop, factory, farm, and the professions. Their expansion is one of the dazzling stories in southern institutional and cultural history. (Research is waiting to be undertaken on the subject of this growth and the relative uniformity of styles and programs this body attained in congregations ranging from the Carolinas' coastal plain to the Ozarks to Texas and back to the gulf coastal regions.)

Methodists slipped from first rank to second by century's end, the Baptists having coopted the recruiting techniques that the Methodists had invented and exploited. But there were still nearly a million and a half members in the Methodist Episcopal Church, South, in 1906. They, too, were everywhere, dominating county populations less fully than they once had, but everywhere. District superintendents oversaw small and large, urban and rural, wealthy and strapped congregations. Methodists, too, crossed the social-educational-financial spectrum, thus were not left out of any significant sector or enterprise in the society.

But two other factors combined with size and strength to make the denominations such a power. First, they were organizing mission boards and treasuries; support for missionaries captivated the churches and enlarged members' worlds. Women led the way, of course. Publication of church materials, for Sunday schools in particular, became an enormous industry. Among Baptists and Presbyterians, already smitten with a proud denominational identity, these printed materials from headquarters went far toward solidifying their respective identities. The perpetuation of the Southern Baptist Convention and the (southern) Presbyterian church in the United States was heavily reinforced in this period.

Thus, the second factor is the persistence of regional identity. Methodists were meeting with their northern brothers and sisters to explore some form of reunion from the 1870s, sporadically, until that reunion was accomplished in 1939. Always, division inflicted something of a bad conscience on a people with a strong connectionalist sense. But they lived with "comma South" as their last name for a long time.

The Baptist phase of the story is straightforward: no reunion, no interest in reunion. The reason is simple. The Southern Baptists became a culture, a whole way of life, something akin to "incipient nationality," an old sociological coinage for describing the early Mormons in Utah and comparable voluntary societies. The remarkable institutional drive and prowess of that body are rendered possible by its cultural cohesiveness, strength, and pride.

Presbyterians, north and south, did create a national church in 1983 after decades of thrusts in that direction. Theological differences formed one obstacle to such action. But southern regional identity rooted in the antebellum period was foundational; following the war a generation of influential thinkers helped perpetuate a pride, rectitude, and identity that was indistinguishably regional and religious. Presbyterians were overrepresented in the ranks of the architects of "the South" and the Lost Cause. Thornwell, Jackson, Palmer, and Dabney were forces to be reckoned with.[32]

Many interpreters of southern history have penetrated the subject of the mythic South to tell us that "the South" is a function of the Civil War and its aftermath more than it is of the antebellum period. "The Confederacy became immortal" is the way Robert Penn Warren expressed it. David Potter's dicta dramatize the greater power of the Civil War "to produce a southern nationalism"—in the "cult of the Lost Cause," that is—than "southern nationalism did to produce the war." The white churches were in lockstep with that creativity: part and parcel; brains and supporters; themselves myth makers, those who supplied the transcendent philosophy and benefited from its effectiveness.

To amplify the postwar South's distinctive place in American religious history, we highlight its insularity. From Reconstructionism until the 1950s, the southern churches turned inward and to their regional culture with moral and civic superiority. They were the legions defending against a world prostituting itself; better, they were uniquely equipped with the spiritual resources and dedication to wage the war. The Civil War placed the southern churches on a course of their own making; obviously that distanced them from the rest of American religious history for an astonishingly long stretch.

The Case of Two Abolitionist Denominations

We return to the two abolitionist bodies that received a glimpse in the beginning of this essay: the Wesleyan Methodist Connection of America and the Yearly Meeting of the North Carolina Friends. The Wesleyan Methodists withdrew from the Methodist Episcopal church in western New York State, principally because of the former's insistence on a policy of immediatism, rather than noninterventionism or gradualism, in abolishing slavery. They formed the new denomination in 1843.

The southern Friends did not adopt an antislavery position in any given year. Theirs was a policy shared by the Quaker people everywhere in antebellum America, from the colonial period, back to the pacifism and equality theology of George Fox and the founding generation in mid-seventeenth-century England. The arresting news is, then: (1) that some northern Christians belonging to a tradition that had long manifested opposition to slavery heeded the call to take an implacable stand against the institution; and (2) that a small band of southern Christians kept on seeing and being on the subject of human equality and peaceable living, which could only mean a firm insistence on abolition.

Our main concern here is with what became of two abolition-driven companies of Christians after the Thirteenth Amendment had been ratified in 1865 and its implications were apparent. One item of special note helps prepare us for that complex of developments: the two groups interacted. The first encounter was by means of the printed page. In the late 1840s, Edward Smith, a Wesleyan Methodist minister in Pittsburgh, gave an antislavery address, the transcription of which came into the hands of a Pennsylvania Quaker, one Dr. Stanton. He had the sermon printed, then saw to its circulation among North Carolina Friends.

More significant was personal interaction. In 1847, Adam Crooks, an Ohio Wesleyan Methodist minister, carried his fervent message south to Guilford County. He made the journey at the behest of a contingent from the recently formed Methodist Episcopal Church, South, who objected to the regional body's position permitting slaveholding by members. At least two colleagues joined him in founding churches and preaching their message in central North Carolina and southern Virginia. All three had encounters with southern laws. One enforcement was especially harsh. Crooks and Jesse McBride were arrested "for inciting insurrection by distributing antislavery literature." (The charges were mostly false.) McBride received twenty lashes and imprisonment. Crooks, more fortunate, was set free after the trial.[33]

These episodes are notable for disclosing the passion and courage of the northerners for venturing so far and putting themselves at risk in hostile territory. Even more, they acquaint us with the meeting of Wesleyans and Friends. One of the attorneys defending Crooks and McBride in Forsyth County was the prominent Quaker George C. Mendenhall (a member of the state's General Assembly, incidentally). Mendenhall later "warned Crooks not to attend a public gathering . . . [in a nearby community] because of the danger of riot." We know additionally that Crooks was a visitor in the home of George's brother, Richard.[34] Despite distance and danger, the zealots from far away had intercourse with the radicals in a heartland of slaves and a hotbed of support for slavery. In making inquiry into the results of the Civil War, we learn what happened to the passion and courage expended earlier on bringing down slavery. In both cases, denominational dynamics changed along lines no one could have been expected to foresee.

The Wesleyan Methodist Connection from its inception throbbed with the "witness of the spirit," a quality that is endemic to the tradition from Wesley's evangelical revival in eighteenth-century Britain. While the term *holiness* gained currency only in the 1860s and following, many Methodists were embodying it long before. These Wesleyan Connection devout were, on any reckoning, early American Holiness Christians. That conviction emboldened them to take such a courageous stand in favor of immediate abolition, including those high-risk missions to the South.[35] But the war ended and the Thirteenth Amendment became the law of the land; slaves became the "freedmen." That perilous conditions persisted for the African-American people of the South does not seem to have been a matter of vital concern to the Wesleyans. They did not lose their moral passion; far from it, as we are about to see. But the cause that had fueled their initiation was gone. And few of the people liberated were in areas of Wesleyan strength. Not quite "out of sight, out of mind," perhaps, their distance from the freed people affected their self-understanding and their mission in the postwar period.

This near-Midwest denomination did spread its reaches for ministry to the South. Not surprisingly, it did so from the tiny base and slight experience we have noted for the years 1847–1851. In 1879, the still-young North Carolina Wesleyan Mission became an annual conference—meaning there were enough churches and members for cooperative activities to be undertaken. Two of its major leaders were ministers sent by the Indiana Conference in 1871 to revive the work begun two decades earlier. Actually, the two selected were both North Carolina–born and a part of the exodus that occurred when the Wesleyans came under fire for their abolitionist stand. The planting of this denomination among southern white people was largely restricted to the Old North State.

Their black neighbors were hardly "out of sight" and not so easy to place "out of mind." But the Wesleyan Methodists sponsored little evangelistic or mission work among them. The Wesleyan Methodist historian Roy S. Nicholson has captured the real shift that had taken place since the prewar days, this time, of course, in the minds of an indigenous membership: "The attitude of the Wesleyans in the South was that the Negro could and would rehabilitate himself faster if he were allowed to work in congregations with his own race, rather than if he were too closely associated with the whites." Although evidence is scarce, the likelihood that there were racially mixed congregations is remote. Indeed, just how many black Wesleyan congregations existed is difficult to ascertain. One suspects few or none. A remotely relevant datum derives from a later time in southern Ohio, where southern blacks had removed in the nineteenth century. There the Conference's first meeting, in 1894, comprised blacks almost exclusively. Much later, in 1957, this southern Ohio Conference merged with Negro Wesleyan churches from west Tennessee.[36]

Clearly, the southern Wesleyan Methodists of the postwar period were both in and of the South. So far as we know, they did not strain to accommodate; they simply practiced regional racial values along with everyone else.

The abolitionist animus had been excised. The Civil War had wrought its effects.

The extent of the Wesleyans' blend into the cultural landscape—that is, their inability to establish a distinctive identity—is revealed in the report that, in 1902, New York State leaders sent several church representatives to "bury the corpse." Historian Nicholson agonized to explain: "It was truly a struggle for the work to retain its identity." External challenges contributed, including poverty and the growing liquor traffic—the Wesleyans were ardent teetotalers and prohibitionists. He points also to a major internal factor, "a lack of proper indoctrination with the essential principles of the church."[37] A community once sharply clear on its reason for existence had abandoned the pace-setting one and seems not to have found others. Also, there was to be little Holiness sustenance available in the surrounding culture until the years before and after the turn of the century.

A final note on the Wesleyan Methodists. In their homeland, from the Rochester area west to Indianapolis, they took on a solid identity; they were part of the Holiness movement seeking to purify and strengthen the evangelical community. In the North, more notably, the ethical coals glowed. In line with their long-time commitment to "entire sanctification," they sought the "higher life." Somewhat curiously, their new leading cause was opposition to tobacco. This took form in the main as a proposed test of membership. Such a test was never officially approved, but tobacco use continued as a moral hallmark of Wesleyan reputation. More significantly, the 18th General Conference meeting in 1911 approved a revised category of membership called "associate members." While more stringent than any usual form of half-way membership, it was also more than a "probationary relation" for those considering becoming members.[38]

The success of the abolitionist cause, then, made its mark on Wesleyan Methodist moral vitality. Much of the change came as a lateral transference from one mandate to others. Mostly, however, this company became part of the larger Holiness wave among evangelicals generally. It was not again to launch so forthright and controversial a crusade against a public evil. The Civil War had forced a difference.

The story of the North Carolina Friends is more complex and more socially significant. The commitment to peace and equality theology held fast after the war. Needless to say, Friends vary in their exact beliefs and in the consistency of their behavior. In the northern states, for example, nearly all the Friends meetings were segregated. But their lives were undergoing drastic alterations. This was true in the face of a remarkable steadfastness in the antebellum years, a quality best demonstrated by the fact that the North Carolina Yearly Meeting was the only one that did not split among Gurneyite, Wilburite, and Hicksite factions. It resisted a temptation to join the Wilburites because of its solidarity in opposition to one monstrous enemy, slavery.

Anyone working with the history of this association of Quakers in the late nineteenth century is indebted to the research of Damon D. Hickey. He goes to the heart of the matter in saying that Quakerism "could not remain as it was."[39] The social and cultural reasons for this condition are numerous and known to us rather generally. Here we have occasion to investigate what those external forces did to the internal life of the North Carolina Meeting.

The larger internal context is "the end of Quaker religious isolation." Their avenues of contact with Quakers in the Middle Atlantic territory increased sharply. In particular, the Baltimore Association took it upon itself to assist in restoring war-wracked properties and structures. Its members set up a model farm, engaged in teacher training, built schools, and sought to address the plight of the freedmen.[40] The prevailing tone of these efforts was part of America's "search for order," toward "progress" by the route of centralization and efficiency.

From sundry sources resulted a major diminution of "their role as prophetic social critics." Their outward posture reflected major inward modifications. They moved away from silence in the weekly meetings and toward a policy of paid clergy, wider involvements in a national Quaker denomination and in ecumenical dealings, permitting intermarriage and reducing disownments, and social and business activity in secular society. Perhaps the most telling alteration, summed up by Hickey, is that "strong testimonies [were] . . . muted or abandoned," referring to classic Quaker patterns of dress and speech, gender equality, and the practice of peace.[41]

As for the black people whose enslavement they had opposed with such tenacity, in the postwar years these southern Friends did not admit them to membership in their congregations, nor did they find a way to avoid segregation in the schools they operated. For the greater part, they simply turned away from public pronouncements or activities aimed at nipping segregation in the bud or rendering it illegal. They did take stands in behalf of the education of African Americans and they spoke out against lynching. Also, peace was still on their minds. They sent delegates to international conferences and, much later, they informed Congress of their opposition to American entry into World War I. Much evidence supports the view that they made their peace with a society rebuilding, seeking to expunge memories of the recent past and to stoke the burgeoning industrialism of the piedmont section. Indeed, several principal entrepreneurs in textiles were prominent Quakers. Small as their numbers were, they were active in business—they provided it with major leadership.[42]

A venerable religious factor, revivalism, played a part in Quaker transformation. One wonders how these central Carolinians resisted its excitement and allure as long as they did. This manner of conducting Protestant services was all around them, engulfing the population. But they were classical Quakers whose services were quiet meetings. In addition, so long as they were preoccupied with the abolitionist cause, their identity was intact. But here, as with the Wesleyan Methodists, the Civil War had a heavy impact. Their animating soul had been tempered by war and national policy. By the 1870s, revivalism as technique and mode had appeal for them.

Hickey concludes that revivalism led to the enlargement of their own meetings and drew them to other denominations. Their ranks swelled from

2,000 members in 1860 to 5,000 in 1881, despite some emigration to Indiana. Let us recall that a version of evangelical Protestantism had earlier invaded the American Friends movement. It came through the Gurneyite movement that dated to the 1820s in the career of J. J. Gurney, in England, and from 1837 to 1840 stemming from his influential visit here. So Quaker ears had heard something about delineating between justification and sanctification (among other issues).[43] But revivalism was a real intensification of that earlier awareness and it caught on in the North Carolina meetings. We must note that it effectively denied the ancient Friends' doctrine of the Inner Light. Now one must have faith given to him, as distinct from his cultivating the spiritual life imparted at birth. Acceding to this position required no minor doctrinal adjustment.

Repeating, we judge that Quakerism "could not remain as it was." At any rate it did not. The war and its results transformed its nature and its teaching to a degree hardly predictable in the Friends' heroic era during slavery.

We have seen even in this brief essay that the Civil War had a sizable impact on the nation's religious life. We began with such fundamentally important changes as the rise of black churches, the material destruction of the war, and the trend toward "modernization" in church organization. We moved into noting how, against a backdrop of the religious history of the nation, either new matters of concern or dedication arose, or old patterns took new forms. We glanced at reform movements, organization and growth, and new denominations. Finally, we explored how two abolitionist bodies—one northern the other southern—were transformed by the success of their prewar efforts into organisms responding to somewhat different outer and inner causes.

In many respects, Robert Penn Warren wrote this essay in 1980 in *The Legacy of the Civil War,* or at the least, much of this is a footnote to that work. Among the historians of America's religious life, no one has painted so beautifully, with so broad a brush, as Jon Butler. He and I concur that powerful changes were wrought in the nineteenth century's last four decades. But we both insist that all of those changes were, in some sense, continuous with traditions and sentiments long present. A prime Butler conclusion serves as well as my own: "In short, as Americans moved into even more modern times, they did not move beyond now familiar processes of religious evolution."[44]

Notes

1. Whitney R. Cross, *The Burned-Over District: The Social and Intellectual History of Enthusiastic Religion in Western New York, 1800–1850* (Ithaca, NY, 1950).

2. Robin W. Winks, *Canada and the United States: The Civil War Years* (Baltimore, 1960), 376.

3. George M. Fredrickson, *The Inner Civil War: Northern Intellectuals and the Crisis of the Union* (New York, 1965).

4. Ibid., 217–238.

5. Charles Reagan Wilson, *Baptized in Blood: The Religion of the Lost Cause, 1865–1920* (Athens, GA, 1980).

6. Ibid., pp. 12–15.

7. Stuart C. McConnell, *Glorious Contentment: The Grand Army of the Republic, 1865–1900* (Chapel Hill, 1992), 89–93.

8. C. Eric Lincoln and Lawrence H. Mamiya, *The Black Church in the African-American Experience* (Durham, NC, 1990), chap. 7.

9. William H. Montgomery, *Under Their Own Vine and Fig Tree: The African-American Church in the South, 1865–1900* (Baton Rouge, 1992), chap. 3.

10. Sydney E. Ahlstrom, *A Religious History of the American People* (New Haven, 1972), chap. 42.

11. Montgomery, *Under Their Own Vine*, 116–117.

12. Ibid., 42.

13. The issue of sheer local independence is one I mean to raise here rather than address extensively, much less resolve. I doubt if many black church members objected to cooperative, associative or connectionalist linkages. Strident insistence on holding out for purity was neither a part of the heritage nor a pressing concern for a people newly granted the opportunity to create their own institutions and culture. Fellowship with others, whether formally sealed or not, was surely a compelling option.

14. Montgomery, *Under Their Own Vine*, 64–65.

15. Will B. Gravely, "The Social, Political and Religious Significance of the Formation of the Colored Methodist Episcopal Church (1870)," *Methodist History* 18 (October 1979): 3–25.

16. At root an economic concept and movement, modernization results when less developed societies become more developed. It is associated with enlarging population, the growth of cities, changing family structures, and increased importance of education and the mass media. In the setting of this discussion, it bespeaks greater participation by people in the groups and the society to which they belong and a heightening of their organized ("rationalized") life.

17. Montgomery, *Under Their Own Vine*, 58.

18. James M. Washington, *Frustrated Fellowship: The Black Baptist Quest for Social Power* (Macon, GA, 1986), chap. 7.

19. W. Harrison Daniel, "The Effects of the Civil War on Southern Protestantism," *Maryland Historical Magazine* 69 (1974): 47–48.

20. Ibid., 59.

21. Marjorie Spruill Wheeler, *New Women of the New South: The Leaders of the Woman Suffrage Movements in the Southern States* (New York, 1993), 9.

22. John Patrick McDowell, *The Social Gospel in the South: The Women's Home Mission Movement in the Methodist Episcopal Church, South, 1886–1907* (Baton Rouge, 1982), 132, 134, 137.

23. Ibid., 57–58, 84–118.

24. Evelyn Brooks Higginbotham, *Righteous Discontent: The Women's Movement in the Black Baptist Church, 1880–1920* (Cambridge, MA, 1993), chap. 6.

25. H. Richard Niebuhr, *The Kingdom of God in America,* (New York, 1937).

26. Social Christianity, or the Social Gospel, was and is a perspective on Christian responsibility. Christians are to devote themselves to the earthly realization of the Kingdom of God, with respect to values such as justice, peace, and compassion. This emphasis arose in response to the new conditions of growing urbanization and industrialization. The underlying Christian teaching was the "brotherhood of man," all people irrespective, under the "fatherhood of God." This goal is to be reached through Christians and churches working through organized rescue and reform efforts, both secular and sacred.

27. Donald Gene Jones, "The Moral, Social, and Political Ideas of the Methodist Episcopal Church from the Closing Years of the Civil War through Reconstruction, 1864–1876," Ph.D. dissertation, University of Michigan, 1969, 259.

28. Martin E. Marty, *Righteous Empire* (New York, 1970), chap. 17.

29. Jon Butler, *Awash in a Sea of Faith: Christianizing the American People* (Cambridge, MA, 1990).

30. Garth M. Rosell and Richard A. G. Dupuis, eds., *The Memoirs of Charles G. Finney: The Complete Restored Text* (Grand Rapids, MI, 1989).

31. On this point, see, for example, James H. Moorhead, *American Apocalypse: Yankee Protestants and the Civil War, 1860–1869* (New Haven, 1978).

32. Richard T. Hughes and C. Leonard Allen, *Illusions of Innocence* (Chicago, 1988), 188–204.

33. Damon Douglas Hickey, "Let Not Thy Left Hand Know: The Unification of George C. Mendenhall," *The Southern Friend* 3 (1981): 17.

34. Ibid.

35. Ira F. McLeister and Roy S. Nicholson, *Conscience and Commitment: History of the Wesleyan Methodist Church of America* (Marion, IN, 1976), 612–637.

36. Ibid., 630.

37. Roy S. Nicholson, *Wesleyan Methodism in the South* (Syracuse, 1933), 127.

38. McLeister and Nicholson, *Conscience and Commitment*, 134–135.

39. Damon Douglas Hickey, "The Quakers in the New South," Ph.D. dissertation, University of South Carolina, 1989, 21–23.

40. Ibid., 59.

41. Ibid., 2.

42. Ibid., 135, 181–182.

43. Ibid., 58–61.

44. Butler, *Awash in a Sea of Faith*, 292.

V
COMPARISONS

16

Religion and the American Civil War in Comparative Perspective

CHARLES REAGAN WILSON

Some three decades ago, historian David Potter wrote an article chiding historians for their failure to look at the American Civil War in comparative perspective. It was part of a broader pattern of parochialism, he observed, whereby historians in this country wrote about liberty without reference to the French Revolution and about antebellum reform without considering the ferment in Britain to end the slave trade and to aid industrial workers. Decades later, comparative history has made much progress, becoming part of a historiographical movement to look beyond American exceptionalism and place the national story in broader contexts. But comparative understanding of the war is still limited, with few sustained efforts to explore aspects of the issue; certainly no comprehensive effort has appeared. This essay makes no claim to comprehensiveness, but attempts simply to examine a few case studies and to suggest issues that are important to understanding religion's role in a comparative understanding of civil wars.[1]

Potter asked the question whether the American Civil War had "historical significance for anyone except Americans." He concluded in his comparative study that the Civil War was significant in world history for two reasons: "first, it turned the tide which had been running against nationalism for forty years, or ever since Waterloo; and second, it forged a bond between nationalism and liberalism at a time when it appeared that the two might draw apart and move in opposite directions." Potter did not consider religion at all as a factor in the war, but this essay's intention is to explore religious issues in the English Civil War of the mid-seventeenth century, the Spanish Civil War of the 1930s, and the American Civil War. These examples were chosen after a wide survey of civil conflicts in Europe, Latin America, and Asia, which suggested these instances were among the most significant ones where religion played a part in civil war. The following accounts will describe the progression of events to capture something of the processes at work.[2]

The English Civil War seems an appropriate conflict to start with because of the seemingly clear and well-known religious aspects to it. The conflict began in 1642, with Royalist armies and Parliamentary forces fighting, went through several stages, and finally ended with the Restoration of the 1660s. It included such dramatic events as the purging of Parliament, abolition of the House of Lords, and execution of a monarch, Charles I. Enduring popular stereotypes picture romantic Cavaliers on one side and militant, righteous Puritans on the other. Historians who have long referred to the Civil War as the Puritan Revolution express the centrality of religion to the conflict. Historians in the Whig tradition identify constitutional issues as closely if sometimes obscurely tied to Puritan rebellion and to religious toleration as well. More recently, historians have explored the role of social class, developments in county communities, and political and social radicalism. Scholars have analyzed not only the causes of civil wars but also events during the latter phases of the conflicts.[3]

The end result of these historiographical trends has been a reaffirmation of the centrality of religion in the coming of the English Civil War and as a dynamic force as events progressed. A recent student of the conflict, Anthony Fletcher, notes that "there is a real sense in which the English civil war was a war of religion," and B. Reay concludes that religion "stimulated and fired revolution." John Morrill argues that "it was the force of religion that drove minorities to fight and forced majorities to make reluctant choices." Religion was so central that he characterizes the English Civil War as "not the first European revolution" but "the last of the Wars of Religion."[4]

Long-term causes of the Civil War included a decline in the respect of the monarchy, a seeming crisis in the status of the aristocracy, the accompanying rise of the gentry, and an inability of the Anglican church to accommodate Puritan concerns. In terms of the latter, part of the problem was William Laud, whom Charles I selected in 1633 as Archbishop of Canterbury. Laud was no theologian, but he disliked Calvinist predestinarianism and some Puritans convinced themselves that he was a papist in Anglican robes. Charles himself insisted that England needed an orderly Anglican religion to go with an orderly English society. Laud and Charles did not hide their lack of sympathy for Puritans, who had been trying to reform the church since Elizabethan times. Oliver Cromwell was typical of many Puritans in seeing the Church of England as still too ritualistic, hierarchical, and Arminian. Puritans desired far-reaching change in church government—to remove, for example, the bishops as a structural step toward fundamental reform—and they allied with those seeking to undermine the political status quo in order to diminish the authority of the monarch.[5]

The English Civil War was perhaps most fundamentally a constitutional crisis, concerned with the authority of monarch and Parliament. King Charles and Archbishop Laud had ruled England without Parliament for eleven years before 1640. Charles then needed Parliament's assistance in handling a worsening Scottish rebellion, but Parliament would assist only if fundamental changes in the governing system were made.

The Long Parliament that Charles I summoned met in late 1640, dominated religiously by moderates. Out of the frustrating search for compromise all sides drifted into civil war and the rise of a more militant political religion. In this constitutional crisis over the relative authority of monarch and Parliament, reformist religious groups of various stripes appeared. Historians now sometimes use the term "Parliamentary religion" to refer in the Civil War era to what otherwise might be termed "Puritanism." Three factions constituted Parliamentary religion, all abiding in sometimes uneasy cooperation. Presbyterians were Calvinists, but they were more moderate and conservative than other factions. They essentially advocated a national church, with a Calvinist-inspired institution replacing Anglicanism. Independents, or Congregationalists, were the center faction in the 1640s, advocates of a reformed church that would be a loose federation of local congregations retaining considerable autonomy. It would have great influence in the army, the real source of power during the Civil War. Radical sectarians were the third religious group opposing the Royalists. Some of them were Levellers, whose prime motive was democracy but who remained firmly rooted in radical religious rhetoric and inspiration. Millenarians had a vision of a dictatorship of the saints coinciding with apocalyptic events, based in the teachings of the prophetic Scriptures.[6]

In the course of the 1640s, events moved politics and religion to more extreme positions. The Second Civil War began in 1648, after news that Charles had struck an agreement with Scottish representatives for their support in exchange for his support of Presbyterianism. The Parliamentary army at this point rose up against the Royalists and their seeming new allies, the Presbyterians. The Holy Spirit now led the army's commanders to purge Parliament, judge and execute Charles I, abolish the monarchy, and abolish the House of Lords. Perhaps the millennium was indeed at hand.

The New Model Army became the embodiment of the religious reformism at the heart of the English Civil War. There were other Parliamentary armies, but the New Model Army had the crusading drive, focus, and success to earn its fame. Historians have debunked much of the legend of the purity and piety of the New Model Army, yet Ian Gentiles, the most recent historian of the army, still emphasizes its godliness. He concludes that the army was characterized by the "volume and range of religious activities" and by "spiritual and intellectual energy" that led to egalitarianism, unity, and individual discipline.[7]

The New Model Army symbolized the ideology of the Protestant Reformers in the Civil War, pressing for a reformation in society. It had a single-minded belief in itself as an instrument of God's purposes. Amid the chaos and bloodshed of the Civil War that the New Model Army spearheaded, the Army's leaders, including Oliver Cromwell, believed that it was all part of God's plan to sweep away the corrupt to make way for his new chosen people, the English, to build a New Jerusalem. As might have been predicted, radical sectarians grew in conviction and influence. The unthinkable execution of a king made millenarianism seem merely the next step in this drama; other sectarians, the Levellers, could just as easily believe that the abolition of the monarchy presaged the end of private property. Groups such as the Diggers, Ranters, Muggletonians, Fifth Monarchists, and Quakers now became emboldened by the times, part of a process in which religion was increasing its impact on what seemed now like a civil war growing into a revolution.

One also sees, though, the limits of religion's role in achieving its high expectations. Reformers aimed at a fundamental reformation of morals and manners, and the ministers' role in the conflict is revealing of religion's successes and failures in the English Civil War. Preachers delivered religious and ethical teachings through sermons, catechisms, pamphlets, and personal counseling. They wrote newsletters, delivered messages, and negotiated between Royalist and Parliamentary armies. They proclaimed the war a crusade, trumpeted victory, explained defeat, and exhorted to moral reform. The clergy was active among combat troops, and one observer, Richard Baxter, noted that the New Model soldier sang psalms on guard duty, talked of religion, and flocked to hear the ministers' sermons.[8]

Ministers were unsuccessful, though, in bringing fundamental reformation to the army, much less to society at large. Parliamentary ministers preached against idleness, immorality, recreation on the Sabbath, feasting and dancing, and celebration of festivals. They particularly tried to control the evils of swearing and drinking in the army. While many godly, upright men were in the New Model Army, no startling moral change occurred in the behavior of individual soldiers. The soldiers of the New Model Army could be pious and well disciplined, but some of them could also be violent, predatory, and disorderly. Contemporaries feared them as much as other military forces loosed among civilians. This was a frustrating failure to the visionary ministers of the 1640s who expected that the New Jerusalem, or at least the New Model Army, would achieve higher standards than before.[9]

Anglicanism represented, of course, the other side in this religious war. It was under siege in the 1640s. The episcopacy and church courts had been abolished by Parliamentary legislation by 1646. Parliamentary armies ransacked Anglican churches, destroying stained-glass windows, statuary, sacred pictures, and altar rails. In Canterbury in 1642, troops even took shots at a statue of Jesus Christ. Parliamentary laws in 1643 and 1644 ordered destruction of crosses, crucifixes, and images of the Trinity, the Virgin Mary, the angels, and the saints; legislation prohibited use of surplices, organs, and fonts. In June 1647, the festivals of Christmas and Easter were legally banned. They seemed to Puritans to be both pagan and Catholic, and that just would not do.

Anglicanism, nonetheless, was resilient. At the local level, it survived. The dramatic laws to do away with traditional English religion were often unenforced in counties. Presbyterianism was for a while to be the official religion, but there was much opposition from laypeople, who were too divided now to agree on an Anglican replacement as a state church. Anglicanism proved to be deeply rooted in the folklore and popular culture of the English. Parishioners affirmed the comfort in church rituals that reflected the seasons, regular worship that was a stabilizing force amid social turmoil, and the ultimate hope of sacramental salvation.[10]

A full view of religion's role in the English Civil War, then, needs to take into account this Anglican presence. Royalist chaplains to the troops fulfilled many of the same functions as those of the Parliamentary preachers. They prayed, preached, comforted, explained. Both sides built on an existing moral-political understanding of religion's role in what were believed to be just wars. The role of religion in the English Civil War has usually been seen only from the side of Parliamentary religion, but Anglicanism was central to the Royalist effort. It drew on the folk religion of the English, which provided a worldview embodying the importance of religion for making sense of the happenings of everyday life. It is easy to forget in the drama of war that Puritan, Anglican, and radical sectarian shared much of that folk religion.[11]

The role of radical sectarianism may have been the most significant aspect of religion's role in the English Civil War. Hundreds of independent, autonomous congregations appeared, reflecting by the 1650s the fragmentation of mainstream Parliamentary religion and the full effects of religious freedom unleashed by the Civil War. It terrified conservatives and moderates, in both Royalist and Parliamentary camps.

Radical sectarians stressed divine inspiration through the Bible or personal visions, liberty of conscience, a significant human role in salvation, the rejection of distinctions between priest and layman, and the end of the established church. Scholars stress the close ties between religious radicalism and broader social-political radicalism. The Levellers, for example, aimed for both religious liberty and political freedom. As Christopher Hill describes the feeling of the times, "Landlords, kingly power and priests will be overthrown together as Christ rises in sons and daughters: there is no distinction between economic freedom, political freedom and spiritual freedom." Millenarian expectations of dramatic transformation, united with the practical morality of the Christian golden rule, brought interconnections between religious and social expectations of reform. As historians now argue, these spiritual enthusiasms were part and parcel of class issues. In one passionate vision of the time, God appeared to a sectarian as a "mighty Leveller," who toppled individuals who "were higher than the middle sort" and raised up others who "were lower than the middle sort." These radical sectarians, though, were defeated in their political aspirations in the late 1640s, and the mysticism of the Ranters, Fifth Monarchists, and Quakers rose in the 1650s. These movements were part of the same process of protest, of what had been a civil war turned revolution.[12]

Oliver Cromwell became the central religious figure associated with the English Civil War, at first second in command of the army and, later, the Lord Protector. He supported the Regicide and saw the opportunities for a new age. But he became increasingly fearful himself of the freedom unleashed by Parliamentary triumphs in the English Civil War. He came to believe that some Englishmen and women were abusing the religious freedom they had gained. Liberty was becoming licentiousness. He became suspicious of religious radicalism. "We have an appetite to variety—to be not only making wounds but widening those already made. As if you should see one making wounds in a man's side and eager only to be groping and grovelling with his fingers in those wounds."[13]

The Restoration of the 1660s brought an end to the English Civil War. The monarchy was restored, and Anglicanism was again the English religion. But after 1660 the Church of England was no longer the established church that must include all English Protestants. The war helped secure the principle of religious toleration, so that dissent and nonconformity were thereafter accepted. A Low Church tradition was even firmly rooted now within Anglicanism itself. The godly of the English Civil War failed, though, in their self-proclaimed mission of moral and social reformation.[14]

The importance of religion to the Spanish Civil War, some three centuries after the English Civil War, is clear from one particular incident. On the night of July 19, 1936, at the beginning of the Spanish Civil War, mobs in territory controlled by the reformist Popular Front party began burning Catholic churches across Spain. Over a hundred churches were destroyed. In addition, according to historian Jose M. Sanchez, "As the sun set, trucks and busses drew up to the doors of monasteries, rectories, and convents. Priests, monks, nuns, and seminarians were forced out of their residences and into the vehicles; they were then transported into a night of terror." Some were summarily tried and executed that night, others were sent to prisons. Attacks on Catholic personnel continued for six months, until January 1937. Estimates are that seven thousand priests, monks, seminarians, and nuns were murdered, and nearly all the Catholic churches were in ruins.[15]

In response, Catholic bishops, in a pastoral letter of September 1937, asked the nation's Catholics to support the Nationalist movement of General Francisco Franco. Republican forces, in turn, appealed to their fellow citizens to support them against what they called an "unholy triumverate"—landlords, army officers, and priests—who had deprived Spaniards of political liberty and social justice. Millions of people abroad responded to these contrary appeals, which, in terms of religion, sketched extreme positions. The Catholic church was either wrong or right, manipulative or martyred. How did religion become so centrally and violently involved in civil conflict?[16]

The roots of the twentieth-century Spanish Civil War go back to the nineteenth century. In the early 1800s, an enduring conflict between liberalism and traditionalism appeared in Spanish culture. The Spanish church had already for centuries inspired nationalism, including its golden age in the Americas of the 1500s and 1600s. The church defended the institution of the monarchy against French depredations in the second decade of the nineteenth century and was rewarded with new status and authority. But secular forces were growing in Spain, symbolized by the consolidation of liberalism. Nineteenth-century Spanish liberalism included such familiar features as laissez-faire economics, constitutionalism, concern for civil liberties, and an overall rationalist outlook. Spanish liberals became profoundly convinced, though, that the Catholic church was the formidable roadblock to their modernizing reforms. Reform forces from this point allied themselves against the church. Anticlericalism became the distinguishing trait of Spanish liberals, and their anticlericalism typically was more violent than elsewhere.[17]

Liberalism was identified in Spain with the middle class, but socialists and anarchists, rooted in the working class, shared this anticlericalism. Spanish liberalism was hampered because of the country's economic stagnation, which eventually nurtured more radical philosophies. The countryside traditionally had been pastoral, but changes in landownership in the mid-nineteenth century promoted agrarianism, dominated by a small oligarchy. Most Spaniards tilled poor soil, with the best lands controlled by an agrarian elite. Meanwhile, an allied bourgeois elite haltingly introduced industrialism. The result was a rigid social stratification, with a discontented rural and urban proletariat and a miniscule middle class that proved too small to promote liberalism's reforms.[18]

The Catholic church became an institutional embodiment of the status quo. Liberals had managed in the mid-nineteenth century to push through legislation providing for expropriation and sale of church lands, but this created a Catholic church dependent on the political establishment and the economic elite. The loss of church land deprived it of its greatest source of revenue. Clergy had little financial support. Conservative governments did provide for annual stipends for clergy, who in turn sought additional funds from the wealthy. Priests had less time for the needs of the masses after this, or at least that was the perception.

Catholic leadership began taking a partisan position, with the oligarchy and government powers, and against the increasingly discontented masses who turned to socialism and anarchism. Mobs seeking scapegoats for their woes came to target priests. Spain almost went through a civil war in the 1830s, and the first violent anticlericalism appeared then. A rumor spread in Madrid that Jesuits, who had been active in the city's politics, had poisoned a well in the city, and mobs killed hundreds of priests and burned their churches. Working-class violence against priests continued intermittently through the nineteenth century. They were easy targets to find and rarely resisted. As one twentieth-century anticleric wrote, "The mob knows that Christ will not come down off the Cross to fire a machine gun."[19]

The church, by identification with the oligarchy, though, consolidated a powerful position within Spain. The Vatican's Concordat of 1851 reflected the agreement between Pope Pius IX and the Spanish government that Roman Catholicism would be recognized, in the words of the document, as "the only religion of the Spanish nation." The government allowed the church to control education in public schools, helped maintain church buildings, and set up an annual clergy salary. By the early twentieth century, though, Spaniards identified the church with traditionalism, including a rigid social stratification, although parish priests and lay Catholics did promote social reform.[20]

The proclamation of the Second Republic in 1931 brought to power a coalition of leftists, including liberals, who favored ameliorative reform, and Marxists, both of whom shared an anticlericalism. The constitution of 1931 contained dramatic religious changes: it established the principle of religious freedom, ended the state stipend for priests, shut down Catholic schools except for seminaries, prohibited priests from teaching in public schools, legalized divorce, prohibited religious burials except under certain circumstances, and banished the Jesuits and seized their property. These laws provoked a fierce antirepublicanism on the right and pushed some moderates that way, evoking more opposition sentiment than the land reforms initiated under the same constitution.[21]

The right and left struggled for political power in Spain in the early and mid-1930s. The working classes rebelled in Madrid, Barcelona, and Oviedo, and in Asturias the army needed several weeks to suppress a revolt of 30,000 workers. This rebellion portended that a peaceful solution to Spain's troubles was not likely, and when the left-wing government, the Popular Front, pardoned insurgents in 1934, right-wing violence occurred. After murders and assassinations, the army launched a coup in July of 1936. The civil war would last three years.[22]

Although religion was a long-term factor in liberal-traditionalist conflict, it was not a direct cause of the 1936 revolt that led to civil war. The right-wing Nationalist forces originally planned to continue the separation of church and state established in the early 1930s. The first Nationalist manifestos made no overt call for Catholic support and did not particularly champion Catholicism. The antirepublican intentions of the Nationalist forces, though, attracted church allies because of the church's long alienation from liberal reform forces. With the church burnings and executions from July to December 1936, Catholics generally rallied around the Nationalists. As historian Stanley G. Payne notes, "Catholic backing in terms of political support, military volunteers, financial assistance, and perhaps above all, spiritual motivation and cultural legitimization became the most important single domestic pillar of the Nationalist movement."[23] The very survival of the church and its leadership seemed in doubt, and its people rallied around the institution.

When war came, Nationalists drew on at least a decade of right-wing rhetoric questioning or outright repudiating democracy and social reform and affirming a nationalism rooted in Catholic tradition. This discourse gloried in the use of violence. Castro Albarran, for example, praised the fascist youth of Spain who would not "weep like women for what we did not know how to defend like men" and predicted a forthcoming religious-patriotic crusade. The ideology of many right-wing groups, such as the Falange, identified crusading Catholicism with defense of traditional property rights and opposed social reform. "Whatever the technically apolitical stance of the Church as an institution," writes historian Frances Lannon, "Catholic politicians and Catholic voters behind them spelt out the equation in deeds: defence of the Church equals the defence of landed property rights, whatever the social costs, which in turn equals rejection in real terms of the necessarily reforming Republic."[24]

By the end of July 1936, General Mola, organizer of the military rebellion, was speaking of "the true Catholic Spain," and in a radio speech in August he referred to "the cross that was and remains the symbol of our religion and our faith." The Catholic church responded with similar language. Bishop Olaechea of Pamplona declared on August 23 that "this is not merely a war that is being waged but a Crusade." Archbishop Pla y Deniel in September of 1936 reviewed the republican record and insisted that anticlericalism had led Catholics to "openly and officially" speak "in favor of order against anarchy, in favor of establishing a hierarchical government against dissolvent communism, in favor of the defense of Christian civilization and its bases, religion, fatherland and family, against those without God and against God, and without fatherland."[25]

Francisco Franco was not the initial leader of the military rebellion that touched off the civil war, but he soon became the key figure in the Nationalist cause. He was a devout Catholic from childhood, although his early army days could not be described as exactly pious. But marriage had renewed his Catholicism, and before the Civil War he had come to believe that Spanish nationalism and Catholicism were inextricably connected. Traditionalists had long argued that Spain had a special religious destiny, and Franco now reclaimed that heritage. His Catholicism also became the key component in Franco's sense of his own special destiny.[26]

Cardinal Isidro Goma of Toledo identified a key component of religion's ideological expectations in the Civil War. In December 1936, he wrote the Vatican that "the situation created in Spain by the war has been much more effective than a system of missions in reviving Christian faith and piety. The destruction of our churches, the profanation of objects of great devotion, and the slaughter of priests have struck a responsive note in the simple soul of the people, which expresses itself in splendid acts of piety. There is no public meeting related to the war not characterized by religious solemnity. Towns that in recent years had fallen into indifference have given proof of great fervor, not only in public acts but especially in the frequency of sacraments." Thus, the war, it was hoped, would lead to a spiritual rebirth, seen here in the intensification of the specifically Catholic importance of the celebration of the sacraments.[27]

The church had to ignore, of course, the Nationalists' own brutal treatment of Basque priests, sixteen of whom had been executed for political activities in that province, which was the only one where Catholics in significant numbers allied with the Popular Front rather than the Nationalists. After church protests, though, Franco ordered an end to clerical executions to curry favor with the bishops. In December 1936, Franco signed an agreement pledging freedom for Catholic activities, and in effect repealing the restrictions that had established the separation of church and state. Traditional church symbols and the cult of the Virgin Mary again appeared in public classrooms. The state, or at least those areas of Spain governed by the Nationalists, again recognized Santiago as the patron saint of the nation, and Corpus Cristi again was celebrated as a national holiday.[28]

In return, the Catholic hierarchy continued pressing the Vatican to allow official Catholic recognition of the Nationalists, which would give religious legitimization to the regime. On July 1, 1937, the Collective Letter of the Spanish hierarchy endorsed what it called the "civic-military movement" of General

Franco. It proclaimed that the Nationalists indeed represented the traditional Spanish national spirit and would restore Spanish culture and traditional values. The bishops thus endorsed the Nationalist cause in the Civil War, but they did not go so far as to recommend the Franco wartime regime as a specific form of government for the postwar period, reflecting an unease at its direction. Aware of Franco's ties to German Nazism and Italian Fascism, they warned, in fact, against the effects of "foreign ideology on the state that would tend to divert it from Christian doctrine and influence."[29] Nonetheless, after the Civil War, the Catholic church and General Franco entered into an alliance that became a crucial support of the authoritarian Franco regime. The church prospered from the Spanish Civil War, leading to a reborn public influence on Spanish life and a rebirth of Catholic practice in the nation. It also led to profound moral dilemmas because of the church's official support of political authoritarianism.

In examining the American Civil War, we must go back in time to the mid-nineteenth century, as we begin to think about comparisons between the English and Spanish conflicts and the American war. The sectional conflict in the United States was a political struggle for power between the northern and southern states. Constitutional issues were central, as Americans squabbled over the meaning of the Constitution agreed to in the 1780s. The flash points in the 1850s that became immediate causes of war had little overtly to do with religion, but with fears about the future of northerners and southerners under the Constitution. Social and economic issues were also directly involved in bringing political division between North and South. The North was a society well under way in modernization, while the South, despite economic participation in the broader capitalist economy, retained many more traditionalist features than the North. Above all, slavery separated North and South and came to be the crystallizing issue in the coming of war.[30]

Religion was a long-term cause of the war, though, because of its role in American society, just as Roman Catholicism was deeply if controversially a part of Spanish life as civil war later approached there. Alexis de Tocqueville had noted that religion was an institutional prop of the diverse, free society he saw in the early-nineteenth-century United States, albeit one functioning by voluntary subscription. American religion expanded enormously in the half-century before the Civil War. Roman Catholicism grew to be one of the major American faiths, and the Catholic hierarchy and troops contributed to both Union and Confederate war efforts. The same was true of Judaism, as Jewish people North and South blessed and fought for their causes, reflecting their adaptation to their separate societies.[31]

But evangelical Protestantism was the tradition that most gave a religious dimension to the sectional debate. James Dixon, an English Methodist who visited the United States in 1848, wrote that "Christianity pervades the United States in vigorous action." He did not mean "that every individual is a pious Christian, but that the spirit of the evangelical system is in sufficient power to give to religious opinion and sentiment the complete ascendant in society." In this expansive evangelical religious system within the context of a growing sectional controversy, the churches often pioneered in sectional arguments that later entered political discourse. Northern evangelicals made the antislavery movement into a righteous cause, with those calling for immediate emancipation seeing it as a matter above all of conscience. Southern evangelicals responded to this in kind, justifying slavery not in economic or social terms but as a missionary institution, the basis of a Christian civilization. Politicians eventually came to echo such language, and one can see the 1850s as a time when moralistic discourse undercut political compromise. As Richard Carwardine has recently written, evangelicalism provided "the moral meaning men and women gave to being northern and southern," and this was an essential part in the cultural self-definitions that, over a long time period, promoted northern and southern perceptions of fundamental difference from each other.[32]

Religion contributed even more directly to sectional division through institutional schisms. This development was perhaps reminiscent of the appearance of sectarian groups in the English Civil War, but the two were not comparable. Truly sectarian religious schisms did occur in North America, but they were theologically and socially based, in ways not overtly related to the sectional conflict. Despite this, the regionally based church splits sometimes did have theological dimensions, and a fuller consideration of the interplay of sectionalism and theology involved in the splitting of the Baptists, Methodists, and Presbyterians might suggest regional styles of spirituality that played a part.

The schisms that split American Protestantism in the 1830s and 1840s related to the role of slaveholders within the churches. Divisions over such issues as whether a slaveholder could be a bishop or a missionary obviously reflected already deeply held convictions separating the people of the two regions. But the aftermath of schism made it worse, with ugly fights over who would control church buildings and assets and who would have territorial rights in border areas. The church schisms unleashed angers, fears, and even violence, which further divided the nation's religious people and set the tone for eventual political division.[33]

If religion had thus paved the way for war, it was vital during wartime in dealing with the suffering that war brought and in legitimating each side's ideology. Ministers, North and South, performed similar functions. They nurtured morale and encouraged unity in the face of hardships that tested it. They celebrated fast days as somber rituals in the face of suffering. They cared for soldiers, led revivals, conducted prayer groups, performed mass baptisms. They distributed religious tracts, hymnals, and Bibles. Religious leaders were even active in the military, not only as chaplains in the ranks but also as officers, enlisted men, surgeons, and staff personnel. Behind the lines, women joined with clergy in holding rallies, preaching sacrifice for home and God, feeding the needy, teaching children of veterans, nursing, and establishing missionary societies.[34]

Religion also contributed to the ideological support of both sides in the conflict. Northerners and southerners, ironically, were motivated by similar ideologies. Republicanism had given meaning to American political life in the antebellum era, and both sides affirmed it, although with differing emphases. For the mass of southerners, the war was about freedom, the freedom of whites to control local institutions, to resist government interference, and to pursue economic opportunity. For northerners, the war was about preservation of the Union as the protection for the self-government that enabled Americans to pursue economic opportunity and self-rule. For African Americans, the war was also about freedom, but liberty with the most tangible meaning of all, symbolized by emancipation.[35]

Northerners and southerners also had a shared heritage of religious nationalism, which grew to be more important as the war progressed. Freedom, however envisioned, became a *sacred* right, part of the growing sacralization of the nation. Americans affirmed the civil, or public, religion that gave spiritual significance to the American political experiment. Rooted in the colonial Puritan idea of building a holy community, the civil religion took on its political meaning during the American Revolution, giving the American nation a special destiny under God witnessing for political democracy. This sense of mission applied the biblical archetype of the chosen people to American nationalism and implied God's judgment for failure to live up to the special providence.[36]

This outlook was especially important to evangelicalism because evangelical groups, which had begun as dissenters, could see America as the source of the religious freedom that had enabled them to thrive and put their stamp upon America. Under democracy, evangelicalism was able to pursue its own particular mission of converting the world. Even southerners, who were trying to break up the Union, had no quarrel with this sense of mission; indeed, they saw themselves embodying it better than lapsed northerners. The North now, to southerners, produced heretical groups like Mormons and Transcendentalists, who southerners derisively labeled as "isms" that were too unorthodox to fulfill America's special mission. Southerners believed they were the true bearers of America's civil religion.[37]

The American Civil War thus became a holy war, on both sides. Unionist and Confederate faithful could have equally affirmed the sentiment behind Henry Ward Beecher's words: "God hates lukewarm patriotism as much as lukewarm religion and we hate it too. We do not believe in hermaphrodite patriots." Unionists became crusaders for America's republican mission under God. Lincoln converted the Union into a near-mystical icon worthy of worship. Midway in the war, Lincoln redefined it as a struggle to end slavery, thus extending America's fundamental mission of embodying freedom and renewing religious meanings tied up with the nation. Confederates transferred their sense of civil religion from the American nation to the new southern nation, but the archetypes and language behind the sentiment remained the same. The sense of corporate mission grew, and the southern embrace of a covenanted identity under God's providence reflected a dramatic expansion of the church's sense of responsibility for public life in the Confederacy compared to the prewar period. As the war progressed, the churches summoned their people to a moral reformation. Because the war was under God's providence, and because its costs in blood were so awful, the Almighty must expect a regeneration before his people could be rewarded with victory. Millennial expectations were soon raised, reflecting the profound passions, hopes, and fears associated with the war psychology.[38]

Having briefly reviewed salient religious issues in each of these civil wars, let me highlight a few points of comparison. The English, Spanish, and American civil wars all had key constitutional aspects. The English conflict was a struggle over the relationship between Parliament and monarch, but this was tied in with a social struggle over the relationship between monarchs, aristocrats, gentry, and plain folk. Religiously, the constitutional issue was whether there would be an established church and, if so, which religious group would dominate it? The result of the war had real meaning for the entire religious context of English life, restoring Anglicanism, but also enshrining the principle of religious toleration that would enable sectarianism to thrive and even secure a Low Church tradition within the Church of England.[39]

In the Spanish Civil War, the constitutional struggle between reformers and conservatives, between the Popular Front and Nationalists, also had direct bearing on the role of religion in the state and among the masses of people. The 1876 Spanish Constitution had established near complete religious freedom, and the influence of the Catholic church among the masses had been in decline in the early twentieth century because of its alliance with the oligarchy. The Republicans in the Second Republic pushed through legislation that dramatically broke the church's remaining power and was perceived as threatening its very survival. The legal status of the Roman Catholic church within the state was in doubt. The issue was whether the church would have any significant influence on the government and the social fabric. Spain approached these problems with little tradition of political and intellectual freedom. The actions of republicans in their legislation, their failure to respond to violence against the church, and their failure to reach out to moderate elements within the church seemed ironically to backfire, leading many Spaniards to return to the church from which they had strayed, suggesting latent attachments. Under Francisco Franco's authoritarian regime, Catholicism soon achieved more influence on Spanish public life than it had enjoyed in two centuries, at the center of national life through new constitutional protections.[40]

In the American Civil War, the constitutional issue was just as central to the war, but did not have such direct meaning for the future of religion (both as a generalized force in society and in terms of specific religious groups). The American system of separation of church and state enabled religious groups to avoid many of the issues intimately tied in with the other conflicts. The security of specific denominations was not threatened (except perhaps in terms of their regional identification), nor did either side in the American Civil War endanger the fundamental American constitutional arrangement of religious freedom and voluntary religious affiliation. The war did, however, have meaning for American religion, producing societies North and South that after Appomattox turned to sectionally distinct religious denominations even more than before the war, with enrollment figures in churches rising.[41]

A second point of comparison, in addition to the limited constitutional ramifications involving religion, relates to religion's role during the war itself. The functions of religious groups and leaders in the three civil wars seem very similiar: dealing with the human traumas and dramas engendered by the wars, legitimating the ideologies of both sides in the conflicts, and promoting moral regeneration in dangerous times. I have briefly discussed the first two points, but the most important issue here, moral regeneration, deserves a few more thoughts because it was tied in with millennialism, a key factor in all three civil wars. Millennialism, of course, taught the belief in an imminent kingdom of God on earth, achieved through either a gradual thousand-year evolution (postmillennialism) or a dramatic, apocalyptic struggle (premillennialism).

In the English Civil War, millennialism took several forms. At the beginning of civil strife, a generalized form of postmillennialism was found among middle-class Puritans. It had been a part of mainstream English popular thought in the Elizabethan and early Stuart years, but it intensified in the 1640s, found in various guises among Baptists, Congregationalists, Ranters, Diggers, and Quakers. "It was indeed," wrote Bernard Capp, "the sense of exhilaration, of triumphant expectation, which was at the heart of popular millenarianism, not a sense of precise doctrinal beliefs." Euphoria, fear, skepticism, loss of hope—all of these emotions during a time of turbulent events fed millennial anticipations of the last days. The New Jerusalem of prophecy might be envisioned as an orderly moral utopia, an arcadian world of peace and prosperity, or a social revolution where the lowly would be raised and the mighty brought down.[42]

England was the leading Protestant state, and reformers insisted that their nation would have a special role in God's providence. Millennialism fed demands, therefore, for a national moral regeneration to prepare the English for their destiny. By the late 1640s, more extreme millennial sectarians, such as the Fifth Monarchists, shocked mainstream Protestant reformers by calling Presbyterianism—of all things—the Beast of Revelations. Each event of the Civil War promoted more extreme language, moving well beyond the desires of middle-class reformers. The Fifth Monarchists' millennial dreams were rooted in their poverty and lack of social position that would be threatened by extreme social change. Fifth Monarchist rhetoric tapped into feelings of betrayal, fear, and hatred. Their preachers dwelled more on the day of retribution for the persecutors of the lowly than on the peace of the millennial age, but its appeal ultimately rested on a positive vision of a land where the righteous could "comfortably enjoy the work of their own hands." Earthly paradise for the working class was thus not a place of idleness but where one could enjoy the fruits of one's toils without taxes, rent, tithes, or manorial levies. Such millennial visions were, however, to be unachieved. Although the elite complained of a "world turned upside down," in the end, the English social structure was little affected by the Civil War, and much of its institutional structure even reappeared with the Restoration. The final days had not arrived.[43]

American culture at the time of the Civil War, two centuries later, was long familiar with apocalyptic images and millennial anticipations, which fed calls for moral perfectionism. New Englander William Miller had made a popular movement out of his interpretation of biblical prophecies, for example, in the 1840s. Millennialism thrives on dramatic events, and the American Civil War fostered such thinking. Northerners came to believe the Union was God's instrument for bringing on the millennium. A year into the war saw an increase in millennialism, with mounting casualties leading ministers to speculate on the cause of such bloodletting. With their view of providential history, the clergy concluded the Almighty must have some profound end in sight. But this mighty wartime chastisement required the expurgation of sin, and slavery seemed the greatest national transgression. Lincoln's Emancipation Proclamation, of course, redefined the civil struggle as a war for freedom as well as for the Union and in the process made the northern effort into a millennial crusade, with crusaders shaped by evangelical rhetoric that came to be affirmed by nonevangelicals as well.[44]

Southern Confederates surely believed they were crusading as well. Richard Fuller, president of the Southern Baptist Convention, concluded that both religion and patriotism required southerners to counter the "savage barbarity" of northern invaders. As the war continued, and the South's position worsened, though, the result was, as in the North, a concern for the cause of God's chastisement. Ministers blamed southern greed and materialism. Religious leaders lambasted slaveholder abuses, such as failure to adequately evangelize their plantations, but did not question slavery itself. African Americans, most of whom were in the South, expressed concrete millennial hopes for the war. The Day of Jubilee seemed so dramatic an expectation that blacks developed premillennial visions, seeing their freedom as perhaps the beginning of a new kingdom brought on in an awful conflagration. Lincoln was thus a Deliverer who seemed a secular messiah—at least. "Lincoln died for we," a South Carolina slave later remembered, "Christ Died for we, and me believe him de same mans." A Union officer at a freedmen's school at the end of the war asked the students, "Children, who is Jesus Christ?" The response was clear: "Massa Linkum."[45]

While millennialism has been associated in American history with Protestantism, the dramatic events of the Spanish Civil War led to a crusading spirit among Catholics there as well, which had overtones of history's final struggle. Bishop Olaechea of Pamplona, in the rabidly Catholic province of Navarre, pronounced on August 23, 1936, for example: "This is not merely a war that is being waged but a Crusade." Archbishop Pla y Deniel, who would prove to be perhaps the best Catholic friend of General Franco, said in September 1936 that the church spoke "in favor of the defense of Christian civilization and its bases, religion, fatherland and family, against those without God and against God, and without fatherland." Cardinal Isidro Goma, impressed by Franco's apparent piety, wrote in November 1936: "This most cruel war is at bottom a war of principles, of doctrines, of one concept of life and social reality against another, of one civiilzation against another. It is war waged by the Christian and Spanish spirit against another spirit." As was clear here, the Catholic church, as well as the Nationalist movement, identified Catholicism as the specifically religious component of Spanish civilization, whose survival was at stake in this civil war.[46]

The issue of moral regeneration was connected in the Spanish Civil War to the institutional strength of religion. The most pronounced change in institutional influence in Spanish life during and after the Civil War was the increased status of the Catholic church, which resulted from the rise in religiosity associated with the Civil War. Anticlerical forces counted on anti-Catholic sentiment among the masses, but residual Catholic attachment among the middle classes and the peasantry, at least in the North, gave a key cultural basis for Franco's embrace of the church's reassertion of influence. Nationalists effectively reawakened the tie between Catholicism and national tradition. There was a sudden explosion of religious activity during the war, and the church leadership predicted it was the prelude to a true spiritual awakening.[47]

The regeneration was not so much moral, as in the United States, but rather was seen in terms of a renewal of Catholic sacramental and institutional practice. Much of the religious enthusiasm, moreover, was a carrier of political interests. Franco's regime repealed the Second Republic's laws considered anti-Catholic, restored the church's central role in public education, reinstated governmental stipends for priests, and instituted a rigorous puritanism. The church now enjoyed a new prominence in cultural life, while church attendance rose in the process. All of this had a dark underside, though. The state pursued a harsh anti-Protestantism that reawakened images of the Inquisition, which after all was also a part of the old Spanish Empire that seemed reborn now. The church's cooperation with General Franco resulted in its leadership blinking at the harsh, brutal reprisals against Republicans after the Civil War and generally keeping silent during the grim decades of Franco's rule over Spain.[48]

Finally, we should note that religion's overall role in these civil wars was to promote nationalism. A leading early student of religious nationalism, Carleton J. H. Hayes, argued that "modern nationalism, as we know it today, had its original seat in England," and the seventeenth-century Civil War was a landmark in its development. Religion operated, along with linguistic, political, and economic factors, to sharpen national consciousness in that nation well before the civil war of the seventeenth century. One might see the wars as undermining nationalism; the execution of such a symbol as Charles I, after all, and the destruction of so many institutional landmarks could, at this early point, drastically have affected the English national consciousness. "Yet both sides to the conflict," notes Hayes, "were thoroughly imbued with English patriotism. If Royal England was an 'Empire,' Puritan England was a 'Commonwealth.' And in pursuing economic nationalism and fostering overseas colonial settlement, Cromwell vied with the Stuarts."[49]

More revealing, perhaps, are the words of the Puritan John Milton during the mid-seventeenth century turmoil. He sacralized not the nation at that point but the people, suggesting an ethnic dimension: "Lords and commons of England! consider what nation it is whereof ye are, and whereof ye are the governors: a nation not slow and dull, but of a quick, ingenious, and piercing spirit; acute to invent, subtle and sinewy to discourse, not beneath the reach of any point the highest that humanity can soar to." Milton could not resist a jibe, noting that the Romans had preferred "the natural wits of Britain before the laboured studies of the French." "Now once again by all concurrence of signs . . . God is decreeing to begin some new and great period. . . . What does he then but reveal himself to his servants, and as his manner is, first to his Englishmen?" They seemed to be God's chosen people, indeed. Cromwell agreed: "The soil of Great Britain is furnished . . . with the best People in the World. . . . And in this People you have, what is still more precious, a People that are to God 'as the apple of His eye'; . . . a People under His safety and protection, a people calling upon the Name of the Lord, which the Heathen do not; a People knowing God; and a People fearing God. And you have of this no parallel; no, not in all the world!"[50]

The settlement of the English Civil War made the monarch more of a figurehead, "a kind of animated banner," observed Hayes. But this did not derail English nationalism. The war had established a firmer basis of attachment to the nation. Loyalty to a monarch was succeeded by loyalty to the law and finally by loyalty to the nation. English nationalism, in fact, would become characterized by its ability to absorb all of its past into a glorious Whig story of progress. Those who favored monarchy could ennoble Charles I, as did those in what become known as the "cult of the Royal Martyr." Cromwell, in turn, eventually became the object of admirers who praised his righteousness as giving direction to the English national destiny, although one should note that for years detractors saw him as the antichrist. In 1899, in any event, a former Liberal party prime minister gave a statue of Cromwell to the nation, and it was erected near the Palace of Westminster. Even the act of Regicide, associated above all with Cromwell, could be forgiven and seen as necessary for God's chosen people to find their place in the sun—the sun that would never set on the future Empire.[51] The religious settlement that was part of the Restoration provided the ground of religious toleration that could lead most religious groups to embrace and even sacralize the English nation.

Centuries later, another old empire seemed to come alive as a result of civil war. In July 1937, the primate of Spain, Cardinal Isidro Goma, addressed a letter to the "Bishops of the World," in which the Spanish Catholic hierarchy announced its support of the Nationalists in the Civil War. It noted that the Second Republic had violated the spirit of Spanish history through its persecution of the church. The religious appeal to Spanish history here would establish a crucial link in the church's legitimization of General Franco's regime. The Concordat of 1953, by the Vatican, recognized Catholicism as the official church of Spain, a political announcement that simply affirmed the church's role already established in Franco's traditionalist Spain.[52]

There were many reasons for the Nationalist victory over the republicans, but the Nationalists undoubtedly had succeeded partly because they reawakened the religious basis of Spanish nationality. As E. Ramon Arango writes, "the Nationalists plumbed wellsprings that were indigenously Spanish: unity, order, hierarchy, nationalism, Catholicism." Franco's Nationalist forces held a typically Spanish Festival of Victory in the Church of Santa Barbara, in Madrid, May 20, 1939, at the end of the Civil War. Franco himself led a public prayer that expressed religion's role in the new Spain that would echo the old: "Lord God, in whose hands is right and all power, lend me thy assistance to lead this people to the full glory of empire, for thy glory and that of the Church. Lord: may all men know Jesus, who is Christ the son of the Living God." Many Spaniards in the harsh years of Franco's Spain would not know the forgiving grace of Jesus, but his choice of the words "the full glory of empire," and his attachment of that phrase to another, "for thy glory and that of the Church," summoned visions of a religious nationalism rooted in the particularities of the old Spanish civilization.[53]

Francisco Franco became the embodiment of Spanish nationalism during and especially after the Civil War. He portrayed international ostracism as an insult to Spanish dignity and honor. The Caudillo was a national hero, who was said to be victimized by the "Black Legend," which pictured Spanish cruelties in the Americas, and the target of the abiding enemies of Spain. He summoned the mythic Spanish self-consciousness and asserted Catholic centrality to it. Image makers manipulated the myth of Franco as Spain's redeemer, but the Spanish people who had experienced the tumult of war embraced the security of the legend. A 1939 ode to Franco revealed the religious underpinning to his political image: "Oh portentous genius,/ illuminated by the grace of God!/ You were marvelous/ in your glorious effort against devilish Communism!"[54]

Finally, we should return to where we began, with David Potter's observations about the significance of the American Civil War in forging a link between nationalism and liberalism, at a time in the nineteenth century when the alliance seemed in jeopardy. We should add that religion, specifically evangelical Protestantism, was crucial in cementing that link through the crusading spirit of the northern ideology for Union and liberty. Both northerners and southerners, in fact, recognized the potential significance of the Civil War in fulfilling America's destiny of witnessing to the world. The evangelicals in both sections thought American democracy would influence the world, but the issue was whether it would testify for a slave civilization or a free one.

But broader than the evangelical imprint on American nationalism in the Civil War was the civil, or public, religion. Robert Bellah, of course, in the late 1960s, defined the American civil religion as a well-institutionalized expression of American faith in the transcendent importance of democracy and American nationalism. Few today would probably fully accept the idea that this religious nationalism has existed apart from churches in a fully developed structure. The Civil War does suggest, though, that Americans were investing enormous spiritual resources in the nation.

All self-conscious nations develop a sense of their peculiar self-worth, but a few have gone beyond that to develop true messianic zeal. All three nations we have examined were among those select few, and they developed features of a civil religion, tying religion to nationalism. In a study of symbolic nationalism, Wilbur Zelinsky sees "a symbiotic embrace between state and orthodox church" in "such countries as Falangist Spain, Japan (especially before 1945),

Czarist Russia, and the United Kingdom in which a single dynasty reigns over, or controls, both entities, but where the state assumes the task of propagating and executing the civil religion." In other places, such as Revolutionary France, Nazi Germany, Maoist China, Mexico, the Soviet Union, and North Korea, the government created secular faiths, with cults of Lenin and Mao and Hitler, designed to attach essentially spiritual sentiments to the nation. What may be distinctive about the United States is that throughout the nation's history a folk civil religion that saw transcendent meaning in the national experience has existed apart from both church and state. "In all other modern nation-states," Zelinsky concludes, "the state has acquired title to its civil religion and has borne the burden of cultivating and guarding the faith."[55]

The American Civil War was an outcrop of an already deep and abiding faith in the religious meaning of American nationalism. No one articulated this better than Abraham Lincoln. Oliver Cromwell was a crusader, a soldier, and a Puritan who embodied an abiding style often seen in religious contributions to civil wars. He could justify Regicide and hope for the New Jerusalem. Francisco Franco was a conventionally pious Spaniard, who drew from his nation's religious heritage, and manipulated it, in augmenting his triumph in civil war. Lincoln, the least formally religious of them all, expressed nonetheless the moral puzzles that trapped the United States in the mid-nineteenth century, as the nation lived with both a democratic ideology and the reality of slavery. Although undoubtedly a practical lawyer and politician, his words invested the Union with mystical meaning that made it worth fighting for. He preached reconciliation, accepting the Old Testament need for justice but tempering it with a New Testament grace. In his death, he was, in myth, a sacrifical martyr for the national faith. Few other leaders in civil wars have developed so many religious themes so overtly and yet with such complexity. His spirit may be the most distinctive contribution of the United States to the study of religion's role in civil war.[56]

In closing, I should add a cautionary note. We have looked at only a few case studies, widely separated in time and place. We have not examined civil wars in the contemporary period, where the issue of religion is surely intertwined with ethnicity and nationalism. From our limited survey, though, we have seen that the American Civil War was not about religion the way it was in other wars where religion's role in society itself was at stake. Moreover, we see a common pattern of religion providing legitimization to the ideologies of one or more of the contending forces. Religion, in these wars, became more important during the wars than it had been even in bringing on the civil conflicts. After the wars, religion reinforced a sense of national identity that was supposed to have made the bloodshed and suffering, and sometimes the undeniable achievements of the strife, worth it all.

Notes

1. David Potter, "The Civil War in the History of the Modern World: A Comparative View," in *The South and the Sectional Conflict*, ed. David Potter (Baton Rouge, 1968), 287–299.

2. Ibid., 290–291. See also John M. Kirk, *Between God and the Party: Religion and Politics in Revolutionary Cuba* (Tampa, 1989); R. R. Palmer, *The Age of the Democratic Revolution: A Political History of Europe and America, 1760–1800: The Struggle* (Princeton, 1964), 2: 353–362; Liah Greenfeld, *Nationalism: Five Roads to Modernity* (Cambridge, MA, 1992); and Daniel H. Levine, *Religion and Politics in Latin America: The Catholic Church in Venezuela and Colombia* (Princeton, NJ, 1981). Bruce Lincoln analyzes theoretical issues related to religion and revolutionary movements in "Notes toward a Theory of Religion and Revolution," in *Religion, Rebellion, and Revolution: An Interdisciplinary and Cross-Cultural Collection of Essays*, ed. Bruce Lincoln (New York, 1985), 266–292. Hans Magnus Enzenberger, *Civil Wars: From Los Angeles to Bosnia* (New York, 1994), deals with recent civil wars.

3. Christopher Hibbert's *Cavaliers and Roundheads: The English Civil War, 1642–1649* (New York, 1993) is a fine recent narrative describing events of the English Civil War. For historiographical issues, see R. C. Richardson, *The Debate on the English Revolution* (New York, 1977). Ann Hughes gives considerable attention to the social-cultural conflict thesis in *The Causes of the English Civil War* (New York 1991), 117–154. For the effects of the Civil War on local communities, see J. S. Morrill, *The Revolt of the Provinces: Conservatives and Radicals in the English Civil War, 1630–1650* (London, 1976). Conrad Russell, in *The Causes of the English Civil War. The Ford Lectures Delivered in the University of Oxford, 1987–1988* (Oxford, 1990), sees religion as one of three long-term causes of the Civil War.

4. Fletcher, quoted in Barbara Donagan, "Did Ministers Matter? War and Religion in England, 1642–1649," *Journal of British Studies* 33 (April 1994): 121; the B. Reay quote is in "Radicals and Religion in the English Revolution: An Introduction," in *Radical Religion in the English Revolution*, eds. J. F. McGregor and B. Reay (New York, 1984), 1. Morrill quote is in John Morrill, *The Nature of the English Revolution: Essays by John Morrill* (London and New York, 1993), 6–85.

5. Maurice Ashley, *The English Civil War* (New York, 1990, rev. ed.), 1–20; Lawrence Stone, *The Causes of the English Revolution, 1529–1642* (London, 1972).

6. Anthony Fletcher, *The Outbreak of the English Civil War* (New York, 1981), chaps. 4–6; Hughes, *Causes of the English Civil War*, 155–182. For the centrality of religion to factional divisions, see Russell, *The Causes of the English Civil War*, chap. 3.

7. Ian Gentles, *The New Model Army in England, Ireland, and Scotland, 1645–1653* (Oxford, 1992), 87, 94–95. See also Austin Woolrych, "Putney Revisited: Political Debate in the New Model Army in 1647," in *Politics and People in Revolutionary England: Essays in Honour of Ivan Roots*, eds. Colin Jones, Malyn Newitt, and Stephen Roberts (Oxford, 1986), 95–116.

8. Baxter is quoted in Maurice Goldsmith, "Levelling by Sword, Spade, and Word: Radical Egalitarianism in the English Revolution," in *Politics and People in Revolutionary England*, 65–80. See also Donagan, "Did Ministers Matter?," 124–129; and Ann Hughes, "Frustrations of the Godly," in *Revolution and Restoration: England in the 1650s*, ed. John Morrill (London, 1992), 70–90.

9. Donagan, "Did Ministers Matter?," 137–147, 154–156; Mark Kishlansky, *The Rise of the New Model Army* (Cambridge, 1979).

10. J. S. Morrill, "The Church of England, 1642–1649," in *Reactions to the English Civil War*, ed. John Morrill (New York, 1983), chap. 4; Donagan, "Did Ministers Matter?," 141–142; Reay, "Radicalism and Religion in the English Revolution," 5–8; Stephen Porter, *Destruction in the English Civil Wars* (Dover, NH, 1994), 22–23, 27, 32, 42, 66, 130–132.

11. Keith Thomas, *Religion and the Decline of Magic* (New York, 1971); Margarita Stocker, "From Faith to Faith in Reason?: Religious Thought in the Seventeenth Century," in *Into Another Mould: Change and Continuity in English Culture, 1625–1700*, eds. T. G. S. Cain and Ken Robinson (London and New York, 1992), 53–85.

12. Quotes are from Reay, "Radicalism and Religion in the English Revolution," 15, 18, 19. See also Christopher Hill, *The World Turned Upside Down: Radical Ideas during the English Revolution* (New York, 1982, originally 1972).

13. Cromwell is quoted in Morrill, *Revolution and Restoration*, 11. See also R. C. Richardson, *Images of Oliver Cromwell: Essays for and by Roger Howell Jr.* (Manchester and New York, 1993); and R. H. Parry, ed., *The English Civil War and After, 1642–1658* (Berkeley, 1970).

14. William L. Sachse, ed., *Restoration England, 1660–1689* (Cambridge, 1971); Hughes, "Frustrations of the Godly," 89–90.

15. Jose M. Sanchez, *Reform and Reaction: The Politico-Religious Background of the Spanish Civil War* (Chapel Hill, 1964), 4 (quote). For a narrative overview of the Spanish Civil War, see Hugh Thomas, *The Spanish Civil War* (New York, 1963). Gabriel Jackson, *The Spanish Republic and the Civil War, 1931–1939* (Princeton, NJ, 1965), 33–35, downplays the significance of church burnings in bringing on the Civil War. Jose M. Sanchez, *The Spanish Civil War as a Religious Tragedy* (Notre Dame, IN, 1987), focuses closely on religion's role in the conflict.

16. Sanchez, *Reform and Reaction*, 4–5 (quote). See also George Hills, *Franco: The Man and His Nation* (New York, 1967).

17. Sanchez, *Reform and Reaction*, 14–17.

18. Ibid., 17–24, 39–45.

19. Ibid., 17 (quote), 18–32.

20. Ibid., 28–29 (quote), 38–47. See also Jackson, *Spanish Republic*, 48.

21. Paul Preston, *The Coming of the Spanish Civil War: Reform, Reaction and Revolution in the Second Republic, 1931–1936* (New York, 1978); Edward Malefakis, "The Parties of the Left and the Second Republic," in *The Republic and the Civil War*, ed. Raymond Carr (London, 1971), 28; Antony Beevor, *The Spanish Civil War* (New York, 1983), 29.

22. Alfred Mendizabal, *The Martyrdom of Spain: Origins of a Civil War* (New York, 1938), especially Part III, "The Religious Problem," 149–186; Sanchez, *Reform and Reaction*, 196.

23. Stanley G. Payne, *The Franco Regime, 1936–1975* (Madison, 1987), 198 (quote); Jackson, *The Spanish Republic*, 422.

24. Frances Lannon, "The Church's Crusade against the Republic," in *Revolution and War in Spain, 1931–1939* ed. Paul Preston (London, 1984), 34–56 (quotes pp. 41, 45).

25. Payne, *The Franco Regime*, 198–199.

26. Hills, *Franco*, 300–301, 329; J. P. Fusi, *Franco: A Biography* (New York, 1987); Paul Preston, *Franco: A Biography* (New York, 1994); Payne, *The Franco Regime*, 199; Raymond Carr, *Spain 1808–1975* (Oxford, 1982), 695–704.

27. Payne, *The Franco Regime*, 199–200.

28. Ibid., 199–201.

29. Ibid., 202–203.

30. See Eric Foner, "The Causes of the American Civil War: Recent Interpretations and New Directions," *Civil War History* 20 (September 1974): 197–214; Thomas J. Pressly, *Historians Interpret Their Civil War* (Princeton, NJ, 1954); Bruce Levine, *Half Slave and Half Free: The Roots of Civil War* (New York, 1992); Raimondo Luraghi, "The Civil War and Modernization of American Society: Social Structure and Industrial

Revolution in the Old South before and during the War," *Civil War History* 18 (September 1972): 230–250.

31. Nathan O. Hatch, *The Democratization of American Christianity* (New Haven, 1989); Jon Butler, *Awash in a Sea of Faith: Christianizing the American People* (Cambridge, MA, 1990).

32. Richard Carwardine, "Evangelicals, Politics, and the Coming of the American Civil War: A Transatlantic Perspective," in *Evangelicalism: Comparative Studies of Popular Protestantism in North America, the British Isles, and Beyond, 1700–1990*, eds. Mark A. Noll, David W. Bebbington, and George A. Rawlyk (New York, 1994), 198 (Dixon quote), 211.

33. Mitchell Snay, *Gospel of Disunion: Religion and Separatism in the Antebellum South* (Cambridge, 1993); C. C. Goen, *Broken Churches, Broken Nation: Denominational Schisms and the Coming of the Civil War* (Macon, GA, 1985); Curtis D. Johnson, *Redeeming America: Evangelicals and the Road to Civil War* (Chicago, 1993); James H. Moorhead, *American Apocalypse: Yankee Protestants and the Civil War 1860–1869* (New Haven, 1978), 21.

34. Drew Gilpin Faust, "Christian Soldiers: The Meaning of Revivalism in the Confederate Army," *Journal of Southern History* 53 (February 1987): 63–90; Moorhead, *American Apocalypse*, 42–172; Phillip Shaw Paludan, *"A People's Contest": The Union and Civil War, 1861–1865* (New York, 1988), 339–374.

35. Drew Gilpin Faust, *The Creation of Confederate Nationalism* (Baton Rouge, 1988); Eric Foner, "Politics, Ideology, and the Origins of the American Civil War," in his *Politics and Ideology in the Age of the Civil War* (New York, 1980), 34–53; Michael Holt, *The Political Crisis of the 1850s* (New York, 1978); Reid Mitchell, *Civil War Soldiers* (New York, 1988), 2–15.

36. Robert N. Bellah, *The Broken Covenant: American Civil Religion in Time of Trial* (New York, 1975); John F. Wilson, *Public Religion in American Culture* (Philadelphia, 1979); Catherine L. Albanese, *Sons of the Father: The Civil Religion and the American Revolution* (Philadelphia, 1976).

37. Snay, *Gospel of Disunion*, 194–197; Carwardine, "Evangelicals, Politics, and the Coming of the Civil War," 198–218.

38. Paludan, *"A People's Contest,"* 348 (Beecher quote). See also Sidney Mead, "Abraham Lincoln's 'Last Best Hope of Earth': The American Dream of Destiny and Democracy," *Church History* 23 (March 1954): 3–16; and Faust, *Creation of Confederate Nationalism*, 22–40.

39. See David L. Smith, *Constitutional Royalism and the Search for Settlement, c. 1640–1649* (Cambridge, 1994).

40. Lannon, "The Church's Crusade against the Republic," 35–54; Hills, *The Franco Regime*, 300–303, 383–384.

41. See Laurence Moore, "The End of Religious Establishment and the Beginning of Religious Politics: Church and State in the United States," *Belief in History: Innovative Approaches to European and American Religion*, ed. Thomas Kselman (Notre Dame, 1991); and Arthur Bestor, "The Civil War as a Constitutional Crisis," *American Historical Review* 69 (January 1964): 327–352.

42. Capp, "The Fifth Monarchists and Popular Millenarianism," 165 (quote).

43. Ibid., 169, 188 (quotes); Reay, "Radicalism and Religion in the English Revolution: An Introduction," 1–20. See also Michael Walzer, *The Revolution of the Saints: A Study in the Origins of Radical Politics* (Cambridge, MA, 1965).

44. Johnson, *Redeeming America*, 184.

45. Ibid., 186, 188 (Fuller and Lincoln quotes); Carwardine, "Evangelicals, Politics, and the Coming of the Civil War," 212.

46. Payne, *The Franco Regime*, 198–200 (quotes). Timothy Mitchell, *Violence and Piety in Spanish Folklore* (Philadelphia, 1988), 191–198, argues that both sides in the Spanish Civil War "were caught in the thrall of a single closed system of sacrificial representations" that drew from traditional Spanish folk culture.

47. Payne, *The Franco Regime*, 200.

48. Ibid., 207.

49. Carleton Hayes, *Nationalism: A Religion* (New York, 1960), 39, 40.

50. Ibid., 40–41.

51. Ibid., 41.

52. Hills, *Franco*, pp. 299–305, 413–414.

53. E. Ramon Arango, *Spain: From Repression to Renewal* (Boulder, CO, 1985), 70 (first quote); Payne, *The Franco Regime*, 208 (second quote).

54. Mitchell, *Violence and Piety in Spanish Folklore*, 195.

55. Wilbur Zelinsky, *Nation into State: The Shifting Symbolic Foundations of American Nationalism* (Chapel Hill, 1988), 235.

56. William J. Wolfe, *The Religion of Abraham Lincoln* (New York, 1963).

Afterword

JAMES M. MCPHERSON

As he waited nervously to go into action at Vicksburg on May 19, 1863, a private in the 37th Mississippi "took out my Bible and read it with peculiar interest, especially 91st Psalm, and felt that I could claim the promise therein contained. Indeed I was both spiritually and physically strengthened, and believed I could go into battle without a dread as to consequences. Was determined to discharge my duty both to my God and country."[1]

The verses from Psalm 91 that strengthened this soldier were probably these:

> I will say of the Lord,
> *He is* my refuge and fortress:
> My God; in him will I trust. . . .
>
> Thou shalt not be afraid for the terror by night;
> *nor* for the arrow *that* flieth by day. . . .
>
> A thousand shall fall at thy side,
> and ten thousand at thy right hand;
> *but* it shall not come nigh thee. . . .
>
> For he shall give his angels charge over thee,
> to keep thee in all thy ways.

This soldier was scarcely unique. Thousands of his fellows in both the Confederate and Union armies carried Bibles and sought their comfort on the eve of battle. "If a man ever needed God's help it is in time of battle," wrote a private in the 24th Georgia, a sentiment echoed across the lines by a private in the 25th Massachusetts: "I felt the need of religion then if I ever did." A soldier in the 100th Pennsylvania, who carried a well-thumbed Bible while under fire nearly every day for a month in the Wilderness campaign, wrote to his sister on June 1, 1864: "I never knew the comfort there is in religion so well as during the past month. Nothing sustains me so much in danger as to know there is one who ever watches over us."[2]

Because the American Civil War was not a war of religion, historians have tended to overlook the degree to which it was a religious war. Union and Confederate soldiers alike were heirs of the Second Great Awakening. Civil War armies were, arguably, the most religious in American history. And these convictions were not confined to the armies. As the essays in this volume make clear, a heightened religious consciousness infused the home fronts as well. One of the departures in the Confederate Constitution from the 1789 U.S. model was the preamble's invocation of "the favor and guidance of Almighty God." During the war, Jefferson Davis proclaimed the religious ritual of a fast day no fewer than ten times. The Confederacy placed the motto *Deo Vindice* on its great seal. Ironically, it was while worshipping at St. Paul's Episcopal Church in Richmond (in which he had been baptized and confirmed three years earlier) that Davis received word from Robert E. Lee on April 2, 1865, to evacuate Richmond.

The U.S. government placed the motto "In God We Trust" on its coins for the first time during the Civil War. Also for the first time, Lincoln in 1863 proclaimed the last Thursday of November "as a day of Thanksgiving and Praise to our beneficent Father who dwelleth in the Heavens," thus turning a customary northern holiday into an official national holy day. In his address at Gettysburg one week before that day of thanksgiving, Lincoln added the words "under God" to his invocation of a new birth of freedom for the nation.[3] As Ronald White points out in his essay, Lincoln's extraordinary Second Inaugural refers to God fourteen times, quotes or paraphrases Bible passages four times, and mentions prayer three times in an address of 701 words, the shortest but also most profoundly meditative inaugural address in American history. Six weeks later, Lincoln was assassinated on Good Friday, a tragic irony that prompted many Easter Sunday comparisons with another Man of Sorrows who had died in the moment of his greatest triumph.

One of the themes that emerges from several essays in this volume is the masculinization of Christianity produced by the war. Although the Second Great Awakening had brought out a great increase in Protestant church membership, nearly two-thirds of these members in 1860 were women. The experience of war gathered hundreds of thousands of soldiers into the fold, not only in the Confederate army with its well-advertised revivals but in the Union army as well. "I am not the Same Man, Spiritually, that I was," wrote a corporal in the 2nd Iowa after fighting at Fort Donelson and Shiloh. "My only fear is that I am too late . . . but with Gods [sic] help I will come through." A private in the 114th Ohio assured his father: "I am trying to live a better man than I was at home. I see the necessity of living a christian here where they ar[e] droping all around you." After surviving the horrors of Cold Harbor, a soldier in the 4th Delaware became a Christian. "In that dreadful place," he wrote a week after the battle, "I resolved to forsake my evil ways and to serve god."[4]

The Christian belief in salvation of the soul and eternal life enabled many converted soldiers to face the prospect of death with greater equanimity than nonbelievers. That is why a Pennsylvania soldier was convinced that "religion is what makes brave soldiers." A private in the 33rd Mississippi agreed that "Christians make the best soldiers, as they would not fear the consequences after death as others would." The color bearer of the 86th New York had been a profane hell-raiser before he joined the army, but came to the Lord after he was twice wounded. On the eve of the final assault at Petersburg on April 2, 1865, he wrote in his diary: "Jesus owns me, O, how sweet to feel that if we fall on the field of strife, we only fall to rise to higher and more perfect bliss than this world can give. My object is to live for Heaven."[5]

These experiences produced a generation of veterans who helped modify Christian virtues from the "feminine" qualities of patience, meekness, and resignation to the energetic, virile, "masculine" and "muscular" Christianity of the late nineteenth century. It was in the postwar era that "Onward Christian Soldiers" became one of the most familiar Protestant hymns of all times. Although British in authorship and composition (Arthur Sullivan wrote the music), the hymn gained its greatest popularity in the United States where manly voices belting out the words "Marching as to war" could be heard at many a veterans' reunion.

The essays by Phillip Paludan, Bertram Wyatt-Brown, Randall Miller (on a similar phenomenon among Catholics), and especially Kurt Berends take note of the masculinization of Christianity. There can be little doubt that the war had an impact on this development, but it is a subject on which more research is needed to trace the precise nature, timing, dimensions, paradoxes, and causal relationships of the process.

The increased religiosity of the armies and of society as a whole during th war also presented a potential problem. One of God's most prominent commandments is "Thou shalt not kill." Jesus advised His followers to turn the other cheek. The message of His ministry was peace, not war. How could a true Christian take up arms to kill his fellow man? "I think it is a hard job to learn to fight, and to be a Christian at the same time," wrote an Illinois recruit in 1861. Even after two years of combat experience, the lieutenant colonel of the 57th Indiana continued to agonize about the question: "How can a soldier be a Christian? Read all Christ's teaching, and then tell me whether *one engaged in maiming and butchering men*—men made in the express image of God himself—*can be saved* under the Gospel." He had still not resolved the question when he was killed at Resaca in May 1864.[6]

As in other wars, soldiers in the Civil War resolved this dilemma by embracing the doctrine of a just war. "We look to God & trust in him to sustain us in this our just cause," wrote a Florida cavalry captain in 1863. An Alabama artillery lieutenant wrote in February of that year that "I have always believed that God was with us—if I had not my arm would long since have been palsied."[7] A Pennsylvania private, on the other hand, was sure "that God will prosper us in the movements about to be made against this cursed rebellion." A lieutenant in the 16th New York, who would be twice wounded and win the Congressional Medal of Honor, wrote in 1862 that "the cause for which we battle is one in which we can in righteousness claim the protection of heaven. Humanity is largely interested in the issuance of this monstrous rebellion hence He who is the embodiment of humanity will bestow in great abundance His blessings upon his and our cause."[8]

This theme of a just war needs additional research and elaboration for the Civil War. We know a great deal about Stonewall Jackson's blending of religiosity and bellicosity, and James Moorhead has analyzed the apocalyptic fervor of many northern Protestant clergymen. But the ways in which ordinary northerners and southerners, inside and outside the army, managed to rationalize the killing is a subject in search of a historian.

Another theme that needs further research and amplification is the role of the war in the transition from antebellum moral reform to the Social Gospel. Phillip Paludan and George Frederickson touch on this matter, and Frederickson in particular establishes a connection between the enhanced position and activism of the clergy during the war and the emergence of the Social Gospel a generation later. Yet the link between these developments remains obscure.

I suggest that the missing link may be found in the freedmen's education movement, which was itself a direct product of the war. The American Missionary Association, the Freedmen's Aid Society of the Methodist Episcopal church, the American Baptist Home Mission Society, and other northern denominations founded hundreds of schools for freed slaves during and after the war. In the 1870s, these societies focused their efforts on several dozen schools of secondary and higher education. They developed a philosophy and institutions of acculturation and social melioration for freed slaves and their children that anticipated the Social Gospel's philosophy and institutions of acculturation and social melioration for the immigrants and their children. Some of the personnel of the two movements overlapped: Washington Gladden, for example, was president of the American Missionary Association at the same time he was one of the most prominent proponents of the Social Gospel.

Both sides in the Civil War invoked God's favor and each at first was confident that God was on its side. By the time of his second inauguration, Lincoln had become convinced that the Almighty had His own purposes in this war and southerners had been forced to conclude that He did not favor Confederate victory. How southern whites coped with the shock of this discovery is an important theme in a half-dozen essays. Like Job, many southerners concluded that God was testing their faith as a preparation for reformation and deliverance; as a southern woman put it, "The Lord loveth whom he chasteneth." Just as victorious northern religion turned outward to freedmen's education and the Social Gospel, southern religion turned inward toward purification and salvation. And as Charles Reagan Wilson has shown, the Lost Cause, having been baptized in blood, would triumph in the hearts and minds of white southerners if not on the battlefield.

But surely Samuel S. Hill is right in asserting that "the most profound religious change" wrought by the war was the liberation of the "invisible" institution of the black church under slavery to become the most visible and dynamic institution of the black community in freedom. If this was the most profound change, however, it was far from the only change. Nearly a decade ago the historian Maris Vinovskis asked: "Have Social Historians Lost the Civil War?" His answer was yes, but thanks in part to his efforts they have begun to find it. Until now, the religious history of the war still seemed to be lost. With the stimulus provided by this book, however, historians should begin to find it as well. Religion was central to the meaning of the Civil War, as the generation that experienced the war tried to understand it. Religion should also be central to our efforts to recover that meaning.

Notes

1. James West Smith, diary entry of May 29, 1863, in "A Confederate Soldier's Diary: Vicksburg in 1863," *Southwest Review* 28 (1943): 296.

2. Allen Jordan to parents, June 5, 1862, in "The Thomas G. Jordan Family During the War Between States," *Georgia Historical Quarterly* 59 (1975): 135; Amos Steere to Lucy Steere, May 2, 1862, Steere Papers, Lewis Leigh Collection, U.S. Army Military History Institute, Carlisle, PA; Frederick Pettit to sister, June 1, 1864, Pettit Papers, U.S. Army Military History Institute.

3. Roy P. Basler, ed., *The Collected Works of Abraham Lincoln* (New Brunswick, 1953–1955), 6: 496–497, 7: 21.

4. A. Fisk Gore to Katie Gore, May 9, 1862, Gore Papers, Missouri Historical Society, St. Louis; Robert Bowlin to father, March 15, 1863, Bowlin Papers, in private possession; William F. Benjamin to sister, June 10, 1864, Benjamin Papers, U.S. Army Military History Institute.

5. William H. Martin to Elizabeth Martin, April 1, 1864, Martin Papers, U.S. Army Military History Institute; Mathew Andrew Dunn to wife, July 6, 1846, in "Mathew Andrew Dunn Letters," ed. Weymouth T. Jordan, *Journal of Mississippi History* 1 (1939): 119; Stephen P. Chase Diary, entry of March 31, 1864, U.S. Army Military History Institute.

6. William Martin to "Friend," undated, 1861, Civil War Collection, Missouri Historical Society; George W. Lennard to Clara Lennard, December 31, 1864, in " 'Give Yourself No Trouble About Me': The Shiloh Letters of George W. Lennard," eds. Paul Hubbard and Christine Lews, *Indiana Magazine of History* 76 (1980): 26.

7. Winston Stephens to Octavia Stephens, March 16, 1863, in " 'Rogues and Black Hearted Scamps': Civil War Letters of Winston and Octavia Stephens, 1861–1863," eds. Ellen E. Hodges and Stephen Kerber, *Florida Historical Quarterly* 57 (1978): 82; Stoughton H. Dent to wife, February 6, 1863, in Ray Mathis, ed., *In the Land of the Living: Wartime Letters by Confederates from the Chattahoochee Valley of Alabama and Georgia* (Troy, AL, 1981), 62.

8. Jacob Heffelfinger to Jennie Heffelfinger, February 27, 1862, in " 'Dear Sister Jennie' 'Dear Brother Jacob': Correspondence Between a Northern Soldier and His Sister," ed. Florence C. McLaughlin, *Western Pennsylvania Historical Magazine* 60 (1977): 127; William H. Walling to sisters, May 29, 1862, Walling Papers, in private possession.

Index